ECONOMICS FOR MANAGERS

This book will sharpen the core decision-making skills of budding managers and entrepreneurs through the concepts, logic, and principles of microeconomics used in the book with suitable examples and cases from multiple industries from across the world. By placing strong emphasis on the fundamental theories, concepts, and their application in real-life business scenarios, the book presents chapters infused with relevant case-lets, snippets, and exercises. Written in simple and engaging conversational style, this book makes complex topics easily comprehensible to the readers who have virtually no background in economics.

This book will be useful to students, researchers, and teachers from the field of economics, applied economics, and business studies. Additionally, this book would also be an invaluable companion to aspiring business managers and corporate leaders.

Satya P. Das is a courtesy faculty in the Department of Economics, University of South Florida, USA. Prior to this position, he was a visiting professor at the University of Illinois at Urbana-Champaign, USA, a professor at the Indian Statistical Institute, Delhi Centre, a professor at the Indiana University Bloomington, USA, and an assistant and associate professor at the University of Wisconsin-Milwaukee. He obtained his bachelor's degree from Utkal University, Odisha, MA degree in economics from Delhi School of Economics, and the PhD degree from the Southern Methodist University, USA. He has published numerous articles in professional journals, authored four books: a monograph on business cycles (1993), an NCERT Class XII microeconomics text (2002), Managerial Economics (2007 and 2022), and a textbook on the Economics of Terrorism (2022). He was the founding editor of the *Indian Growth and Development Review* and he has guided several doctoral theses. His hobbies include bicycling, listening to music, singing, and travelling. He currently lives in Florida, USA, with his wife, Rajashree.

J. K. Goyal is currently working as visiting faculty in Jagan Institute of Management Studies (JIMS), Sector-5, Rohini, Delhi. Earlier he was Director (2005–2018) and Professor (2018–2023) of JIMS. He started his professional career as a Lecturer in Delhi University. He graduated in Economics (Hons) from Punjab University where he stood first in the University and was awarded the Gold Medal in Economics. Dr. J.K. Goyal has done his Masters in Economics from Delhi School of Economics, University of Delhi. He received his PhD from the Faculty of Commerce and Business, Delhi University. He has over four decades of teaching experience both at the undergraduate and the postgraduate levels. He has taught subjects like Managerial Economics, Macroeconomic Management, Economic Environment of Business to MBA students and Microeconomics, Business Economics to B.Com (Hons) and BBA students. He has presented papers at various national/international seminars and has written several articles. He has guided several MPhil and PhD scholars. His hobbies include playing tennis, trekking, globe-trotting, and listening to Sufi music.

ECONOMICS FOR MANAGERS

Concepts and Implications

Satya P. Das and J. K. Goyal

Routledge
Taylor & Francis Group
LONDON AND NEW YORK

Designed cover credit: Getty Image

First published 2024
by Routledge
4 Park Square, Milton Park, Abingdon, Oxon OX14 4RN

and by Routledge
605 Third Avenue, New York, NY 10158

Routledge is an imprint of the Taylor & Francis Group, an informa business

British Library Cataloguing-in-Publication Data
A catalogue record for this book is available from the British Library

ISBN: 978-1-032-58931-2 (hbk)
ISBN: 978-1-032-58932-9 (pbk)
ISBN: 978-1-003-45219-5 (ebk)

DOI: 10.4324/9781003452195

Typeset in Times New Roman
by Deanta Global Publishing Services, Chennai, India

To
Raj and Nalini

CONTENTS

BOXES

FIGURES

TABLES

FOREWORD

I feel honoured to present to you this book titled *Economics for Managers: Concepts and Implications* by Satya P. Das and J.K. Goyal. The emergence of "Management" as a branch of social science is a rather recent development. Nevertheless, over the last three decades or so, a degree/diploma in management (both at the graduate and postgraduate levels) is by far the most sought-after degree both at the national and at international levels. A management programme essentially sharpens the decision-making skills of the aspirants. How to pick up an option out of multiple options which, *a priori*, look identical? In short, decision-making skill is the *sine qua non* of a prudent manager. The principles, concepts, and tools of Economics are of immense use in sharpening the managerial skills in any branch of specialisation—be it marketing, finance, or HR. This book has been written especially keeping in mind the students of management, many of whom join this discipline without having studied Economics at the graduate and/ or school level. However, this book is equally useful for students pursuing traditional degree programmes at the graduate level, such as BA (Hons); BCom (Hons). This book will provide the foundation of Economics through a combination of theoretical concepts, practical applications, and contemporary insights. The more theoretical, advance in detail, treatment has been put in the appendix sections of many chapters for the benefit of students.

The joint efforts of Dr Das and Dr Goyal make this book more useful because Dr Das carries with him a rich experience of teaching graduate and postgraduate students in several reputed international universities and Dr Goyal has the experience of teaching in several colleges and business schools in India. The book has been written in a manner as if the authors are sitting in front of the students and narrating a tale. This makes it equally useful for the students pursuing their degrees/diplomas in distant education mode. To drive home the relevance of an economic theory in management, the book contains boxes, activities, case studies, and numerical exercises at appropriate intervals.

This textbook will not just add great value to students but also to teachers to design their lectures effectively in business schools across the globe. I feel privileged to write the foreword of this volume. I sincerely wish that the authors write an equally useful book on macroeconomic management in the future.

Dr Pooja Jain
Director, Jagan Institute of Management Studies
Sector-5, Rohini, Delhi—110085

PREFACE

Among all the branches of social sciences (sometimes called "arts"), Economics has always been regarded as a "tough subject." Normally, students study this course only because it is a "core paper" or a required course. Have we, the teachers of Economics, ever thought why? If we introspect, we will find "the fault, dear Brutus, is not in our stars, but in ourselves" (with due apologies to William Shakespeare). When we, the authors, studied Economics in India during our undergraduate years in the early 1970s, we had books by Indian and foreign authors. The former set of books had everything "point-wise," but without much effort to build or illustrate concepts. Almost no topic will begin without giving a bunch of definitions, the most glaring of which was a collection of definitions of economics itself, essentially quotations from great economists of the past. A chapter would typically end with a list of merits and demerits of a particular theory or approach. The whole material was mostly geared towards memorisation without much room for understanding.

On the other hand, books from western authors made real efforts to build concepts. They did not "defend" their writing by overly citing what some great economist had said in the past. If one understood the grammar and sentences fully, one felt a degree of comfort and assurance that he or she has really understood something. However, we had problems with this category of books too. A simple concept that can be conveyed effectively in two lines will be sometimes explained in two paragraphs with all the caveats, exception, etc. By the end of a huge sentence or a half-page-long monotonous paragraph, one would lose track of what the author really wanted to say. But, on the whole, we liked them insofar as the understanding of concepts was concerned.

This book is written from our own teaching experiences without following any established book in the market. Definitions and taxonomy are avoided consciously. Instead, a lot of emphasis has been put on language simplicity, understanding, and economic intuition. At the same time, analytical rigour is not spared. Furthermore, we've always believed that the best and most effective way to understand concepts is through examples. We've tried our best to illustrate concepts by bringing in umpteen hypothetical and real-life examples.

Economics is a fast-developing science. New concepts, examples, and applications must substitute *some* old ones. We, the teachers, must desist clinging to the status quo, and instead, consciously and selectively *sense* which material or concept can be abandoned and which new materials be introduced.

More to the point and as a distinguishing feature, the book has four chapters—Chapters 5, 12, 13, and 15—the material of which is largely ignored in syllabi of economics for business and commerce that we've seen. Chapter 5, "Applications of Consumer Theory," includes four "applications" of consumer theory, which includes (a) consumers' surplus that measures welfare changes associated with price variations in terms of money, (b) welfare implications of cash versus kind subsidy programmes, (c) direct versus indirect tax to raise revenues, and (d) decision-making over consumption and savings. The material of Chapter 12, entitled "Decision-Making under Uncertainty," is not typically included in an introductory course in microeconomics. We deviate from this norm because uncertainty and risk are inherent in many day-to-day decision-making facing managers, households, politicians, governments, etc., and the underlying principles of choice in such situations are not hard to explain or understand. Chapter 13, "Portfolio Choice and Demand for Assets," parallels the earlier chapters on demand for goods. A student of business or commerce (even an economics student) must know some of the common financial assets offered in the market, what their characteristics are and what factors govern the demand for them. Chapter 15, "Going Global," covers international trade, foreign outsourcing, and foreign direct investment. International interdependence or globalisation has affected all of us in many ways and it is here to stay. We better learn something about the economics of it.

These are not the only differences compared to a "standard" textbook on managerial economics or microeconomics. There are many others that our fellow teachers can easily see. But despite all this, most of the material should look familiar to an instructor.

Finally, a word on our writing style is in order. We don't believe that a college textbook needs to be written in a "serious-sounding" and dry language, "as it is meant for adult students, not school children." We have consciously attempted to keep the language simple, direct, conversational, and entertaining.

It is our hope that the students and fellow teachers enjoy and benefit from this book, not just from the standpoint of scoring well or helping to score well in the exams (which is important), but also from the perspective of understanding the material so as to apply them to social and economic problems we all face.

ABBREVIATIONS

AFC	Average fixed cost
APP	Average physical product
BCCI	Board of Control for Cricket in India
BSE	Bombay Stock Exchange
CCI	Competition Commission of India
CDSL	Central Depository Services Ltd
CEO	Chief Executive Officer
CRS	Constant returns to scale
DRS	Decreasing/Diminishing returns to scale
FDI	Foreign direct investment
FII	Foreign institutional investors
FMCG	Fast-moving consumer goods
FPI	Foreign portfolio investment
GATT	General Agreement on Tariffs and Trade
GST	Goods and services tax
HEIs	Higher-education institutions
HHI	Herfindahl–Hirschman Index
ICC	Income consumption curve
IPO	Initial public offering
IR	Indian railways
IRS	Increasing returns to scale
IT	Information technology
LAC	Long-run average cost

LMC	Long-run marginal cost
MNC	Multinational Corporation
MPC	Marginal propensity to consume
MPS	Marginal propensity to save
MRP	Marginal revenue product
MRS	Marginal rate of substitution
MRTP	Monopoly and Restrictive Trade Practices
MRTS	Marginal rate of technical substitution
MU	Marginal utility
NSDL	National Securities Depository Ltd.
NSE	National Stock Exchange
OPEC	Organization of Petroleum Exporting Countries
PCC	Price consumption curve
PDS	Public distribution system
PDV	Present discounted value
PMC	Private marginal cost
PPC	Production possibility curve
SAC	Short-run average cost
SAIL	Steel Authority of India
SEBI	Securities and Exchange Board of India
SMC	Social marginal cost
SUV	Sport utility vehicle
TFP	Total factor productivity
TPDS	Targeted public distribution system
TRAI	Telecom Regulatory Authority of India
TU	Total utility
TVC	Total variable cost
TVP	Total value product
UN	United Nations
USSR	Union of Soviet Socialist Republics
VMP	Value of the marginal product
VUCA	Volatile, uncertain, complex, and ambiguous
WTO	World Trade Organization

1

INTRODUCTION

1.1 Management: A Decision-Making Skill

We appreciate your decision to pursue higher education in the field of management. Through this course, you must be looking forward to developing or sharpening your managerial skills, which may enable you to get a decent job in the corporate world, become an entrepreneur, or join your family business. We wish you success in your pursuits.

A core course in economics like this is an integral part of any management programme. Karl Marx may have been proved wrong on many accounts, but he was still right when he said: "Economics is the sub-structure, rest is superstructure." This course is taught under different titles in various business schools—like Economics for Managers, Managerial Economics, Microeconomics for Managers, Microeconomic Management, Business Economics, and Microeconomics for Business. All these titles have almost the same course content. Swami Vivekanand of India once said, "*Ekam sat vipra bahuda vadanti*" ("Truth is one, wise men call it in various ways.").

We can initiate our discussion of economics for managers or managerial economics by starting with the question, "What is management?" Those of you who have completed a course in business studies earlier may recall F.W. Taylor and his famous 14 principles of management. The oft-repeated definitions of management must be coming to your mind. We shall not go in that direction. We note simply that the *hallmark of any managerial position is decision-making.* But decision-making is not limited to managers only. In our daily lives, all of us make decisions umpteen times, often without realising it. For example, your mom sends you to the market to buy a loaf of bread. Being your mummy's obedient child (pun intended), you jump on to your bike and go to the local bread seller.

DOI: 10.4324/9781003452195-1

Picture yourself standing in front of that shop and mentally running through the list of the number of decisions you will have to make: White or brown bread? Sliced bread or whole? Full or half bread? Small or big slices? Local or branded bread? If branded, then which brand? What if four brands are available in your chosen category? Won't you compare prices? Realise the battery of decision-making that was involved because your mother asked you to buy a loaf of bread. Had your mother asked you to buy a specific brand and mentioned the size of the bread, there would have been little decision-making involved. You would merely be acting as a "support staff," assigned to perform a task without having to decide anything. The point is that decision-making involves achieving a goal, when you have two or more ways to do that. If you goof up and make a wrong decision, the responsibility falls on your shoulders. Of course, in this example, if the loaf that you picked goes to waste, the maximum loss involved is only a few bucks or rupees. The stakes are low.

Let us take an example where the stake is higher. Having cleared your qualifying degree and entrance examination, you are offered an admission in the management programme of your liking in, say, five business schools. We're sure that almost all of you have encountered this situation before finally deciding to pick "this" business school. In the Indian context, recall the parameters you must have compared: approvals and accreditations, rankings, location, accessibility, placement record, faculty, hostel facility, and in the case of private business schools, the fee to be charged. As of 2021, the total fee for a full-time, two-year, approved post-graduate programme in management in a private business school in India ranged from ₹5 to ₹25 lakh. (The unit "lakh" is equal to 100,000.) Now compare the consequences of picking a wrong business school and a bad loaf of bread.

In both instances, the loss of a "wrong" decision was borne entirely by you (or your family). However, it may not often be so in a business, unless it is a sole proprietorship. In modern times, large business organisations are owned by several individuals—the shareholders. The shareholders of a company may be in thousands or millions. They may not always be the same set of persons over time. Shares change hands when an existing shareholder sells some or all of his shares in the shares market. The buying and selling of the ownership (shares) may depend on the performance of the organisation and its manager. If you are the CEO of a company, the company's performance is reflective of the soundness of your decisions. The buck stops with you. Stakes are big and may have wide-ranging consequences. Other individuals linked to a large business organisation include employees, lenders, banks, raw material vendors, and so on. The higher the position in the management ladder you climb to (and we wish you do), the greater the stakes for your decision-making. It is, therefore, incumbent upon you to make decisions rationally and carefully. For that, you need to receive adequate and appropriate training prior to the job. This is where the role of a business school comes in. Whatever is taught to you in a business school should be directed to the single most important question: In what way does this subject or topic sharpen my managerial (read decision-making) skill? This course provides some groundwork for this endeavour. On studying this book, you will (hopefully) understand the role of economics in honing your managerial potential.

We started with understanding "management." We now move on to understand "economics." We discussed management without dwelling on (rather smartly) the task of giving a definition or a range of definitions to the word "management." We shall do the same with "economics." Let us pick the meaning of "economics" that is not just the most plausible but also the most useful for our purpose. Remember, our purpose is to acquaint you with those principles of economics which will help you in making sound decisions in your professional position.

1.2 Dispelling Myths about Economics

We begin by dispelling some common myths and fears that students normally espouse against economics as a subject.

Myth I: Economics Is a "Theory" Course, I have Joined This Business School to Gain "Practical" Knowledge

This is a very common misconception. There is a thinking among business students that theoretical and practical knowledge are different domains. Further, they (students) have acquired enough theoretical knowledge in their traditional degree programmes, and the purpose of their joining a business school is to gain practical knowledge. Dear students, theoretical knowledge does not come from Mars. Economic theories are founded on careful, systematic observations, documentation, and analysis of human behaviour. When the same behaviour is observed and is seen repeated by a large number of human beings across races and nations numerous times, it gives rise to a theoretical concept. Theory is an accumulation and a summary of practical knowledge. The problem lies in the way theoretical concepts may have been presented to you. If they are introduced in a rather dry, dull, tongue-twisting jargon—which is unnecessary—they only serve to add to your already-prevailing fear.

Myth II: Learning Economics Requires a Lot of Memorising, Since So Many Laws and Theories Must Be Reproduced

Unfortunately, this myth exists due to the rote learning that has become ingrained in traditional systems of degree education. We can fully read your state of mind when a teacher enters the class and announces that he will be teaching you the "Law of Demand" today and puts up the following slide, asking you to note down the following and then goes on to list the underlying assumptions and exceptions:

> Definition: The Law of Demand states that "ceteris paribus," when price of a commodity increases its quality demanded decreases and vice versa.

But once you understand the crux of this dull and dreary statement, you will realise that it is simply a day-to-day observed phenomenon: people tend to buy less at a higher price and more at a lower price. Imagine that the price of a tall size, freshly brewed coffee in Starbucks increases from, say, \$2.50 to \$4.00. All else remaining the same, the demand for Starbucks coffee will fall. In India, at the beginning of the mango season (May) when its price is (say) ₹150 per kg, your family buys only 1 kg (kilogram), but in the next month, when the price comes down to (say) ₹50 per kg, you buy 3 kg or 4 kg. Nothing changed in these two months, except the price of mango: your family income, the season, the family's liking for the fruit, and its quality all remained the same.

We promise to break this myth.

Myth III: Economics Has Too Many Tables, Diagrams, and Formulas

Please note that tables, equations, and diagrams are meant to facilitate the analysis, not to burden you. These are tools of analysis, not an end in themselves. We shall be making use of these techniques along with explanations and plenty of examples.

1.3 What Is Economics about?

In colleges, economics is usually taught as an "arts" or humanities subject. Hence, many perceive that economics is not a science. But, it is; although not exactly like physics and chemistry which are physical sciences. In physical science, labs, equipment, etc. are used heavily. In economics, these are not used as much, but the goals and the methodologies are broadly similar. Physical science attempts to explain physical phenomena around and within us, or in the solar system and the universe. Economics is the study of economic phenomena around individuals, regions, countries, or the world as a whole. In physics, we question the effect of throwing an object with a given force and at a given angle on its trajectory over space. In economics, we question, for instance, the effects of a policy change on the growth path of an economy over time. In physical sciences there are many laws. There are a few in economics too. The only distinction is that economics is a *social science* that deals with the behaviour of individuals and organisations within a society.

In general, science refers to a body of knowledge that leads to "empirically verifiable hypotheses"—meaning the knowledge that generates predictions (effects of some action on something else) that can be tested in the real world. If a prediction cannot be tested, it is not scientific. In economics, one derives predictions or hypotheses that can be tested by using data, statistical/econometric methods, and practical experiments with human beings (including students sometimes).[1]

Many textbooks have attempted to lay down a definition—sometimes a series of definitions—of economics by quoting celebrated economists from the past. In our view, this is rather naïve—actually, and counterproductive—because it demands unnecessary memorisation. It is more useful to have a clear sense of what economics is about via examples. Many non-economists think that economics is all about how to make or manage money. This is not true. Economics is much broader. There are three central tenets leading to an *economic problem*:

(A) Human wants are unlimited (or infinite).
(B) Resources are scarce.
(C) Individuals or decision-making units, called "agents" in economics, are rational.

Point (A) essentially says that, unlike a hermit in a cave, normal humans are seldom materially satiated or fulfilled: they almost always want more. If you own a Maruti car, your next goal may be to have a compact or mid-size SUV (sport utility vehicle). If you own an apartment in Nairobi, your next wish would be to have another for investment or for your child, and so on.

In a lighter vein, inquisitiveness expands our wants even if we may have plenty already. You give a child 49 toys to play with and tell him not to touch the 50th one which is kept in the corner. For sure, the child will go after the "untouchable." In the Biblical story in the Book of Genesis, Adam and Eve were living happily in the Garden of Eden—akin to "Swarg" (heaven) in Hindu mythology. They were free to move anywhere, do whatever they liked, eat or drink whatever they desired, except eat the forbidden apple. However, day in and day out they would move around every now and then and get more and more curious about the forbidden apple. This desire or want arose despite having everything else in abundance.[2]

Point (B) says that availability of resources is limited or scarce. If nothing else, time is scarce. Even some of the richest persons in the world today, Bill Gates, Jeff Bezos, Elon Musk, Mukesh Ambani, or Jack Ma, must make a choice on a particular morning: whether to do yoga for one hour or have a video conference with top executives.[3] Look at yourselves: how hard-pressed for time you become when semester exams knock on your door. Not just time, almost anything else, even pure water, is scarce. The degree of scarcity however varies among countries, individuals, and times. In a typically developed country, labour is relatively scarcer than technology and equipment, while in a developing country it is the opposite. Taking holidays is scarcer for our working children than for semi-retired folks like us, the authors.

Points (A) and (B), i.e., unlimited wants and limited resources, present a fundamental mismatch: they cannot be equated. It is safe to bet that this problem shall remain until eternity. This mismatch leads to what is called trade-off and settling for an affordable choice, permitted by limited means or resources. Recall your childhood when you went to the market with your mom or dad. You were insisting on having a balloon and a candy, while your parent asked you to choose only one. No amount of crying or cajoling on your part worked and finally you were resigned to pick one. For reasons best known to you, you might have chosen candy by giving up balloon. This action is called a *trade-off.* In this example, you have traded off balloon for candy. Remember an off-repeated dialogue in Bollywood movies "Kuchh Paaney ke liye kuchh khona padta hai," that is, "to gain something, we must lose something else." This is the essence of trade-off.[4]

An individual or entity must make a choice in the face of scarcity. If things were not scarce, there would not be a subject ~~matter~~like economics, because "you" or a nation can have anything that is wished or wanted. This may be a possibility in heaven but not on Earth.

The next logical question is, which among the alternatives or options that are available or affordable, will a person or entity choose? Tenet (C) comes into play here. Rationality means choosing one among the alternatives that serves the entity the best according to one's own criterion or objective. A rational student would decide how many hours to study before an important exam, weighing the gain from studying more hours vis-à-vis the loss in terms of physical and mental strain.

In brief, the problem of choice arises because of unlimited wants in the face of limited resources, which is the same as scarcity. The study of rational choice problems at the individual, social, regional, national, and international level is what economics is about.

See Box 1.1 for a perspective on the goal of economic policymaking, which highlights the choice between reducing wants and reducing scarcity to address an economic problem. A moot question is: Can you reduce wants suo moto? In your youthful exuberance, some of you might answer in the affirmative but, believe us, it is easier said than done. Whatever we may have possessed in our lives, still the truth is "yeh dil mange more" (This heart longs for more). All religions preach to us to check our worldly desires and live a frugal life. But very few among us are able to practice it. Such persons are beyond the scope of our study. The alternative suggested in Box 1.1 is to reduce scarcity—yes. This can be done, was done in the past, is being done at present, and will be done in future by finding more resources, technological improvements, inventions, and better organisation. But remember, however hard we may try, resources will be finite, whereas wants will remain infinite. You don't have to be a student of mathematics to know that any finite number, howsoever big, will always remain less than infinity.

BOX 1.1 REDUCING WANTS OR SCARCITY TO SOLVE AN ECONOMIC PROBLEM

How should we "solve" an economic problem of mismatch between wants and resources—by reducing wants or reducing scarcity through increasing resources? Sometimes, policy and decisionmakers, knowingly or unknowingly, emphasise and propagate "reducing wants" as an easy and acceptable method of solution. Their logic is this. If some things are scarce, advise people to reduce consumption, which will then match the limited amount available. But this is, by and large, a negative approach. Think of electricity power or drinking water for instance. In many parts of India, their availability is limited—especially during summer months. There are other countries in Asia and Africa where the situation is similar. For the government or policymakers there are, fundamentally, two options to solve this problem: help increase supply by investing in power and water projects sufficiently or decrease demand by preaching a slogan that we should reduce consumption "in the national interest." If the second option is emphasised repeatedly every year, there will be little incentive to focus on the first option of increasing supply. Over time, the public "learns" to feel guilty about normally consuming power and water; and that tends to further reduce the intent of the policymakers to invest sufficiently in power and water. The supply side will continue to be neglected under some pretext or another. The shortages will continue as if destined.Is this what we really want? Is it any indicator of our endeavour towards growth and development? "No." Reducing wants to solve an economic problem may be justified *only* as a short-run emergency measure in an unanticipated situation like war, famine, drought, etc. It has little rationale over a longer time horizon and in normal times.

You may be willing to heed the government's call to reduce your consumption personally, but it is not necessary that everyone willingly accepts the government directive. If, for instance, a rationing is imposed, it can trigger undesirable side effects like black marketing and other economic and social distortions.

The correct perspective of economics is to recognise—and salute—the unlimited-ness of wants, try *not* to suppress, but strive to fulfil them as best as we can by investing in appropriate technology and making sensible choices among the alternatives. This is the spirit of economics.

In the chapters to come, you may not see the word "scarce" or "scarcity" being used much, but they always remain in the background.

1.4 Constraints and Opportunity Costs

Scarcity implies that an individual, an organisation, or a country cannot have everything in any desired quantity. Some constraints will stand in the way. If you want more of one thing, you must forego some amount of some other thing at any given instant of time (which, over time, may very well change). This is what "cost" means in economics. An iPhone "costing" $950 at a given point of time means that if you want to have the iPhone at that time, you must forego $950 worth of other goods that you could have had otherwise.

The term "cost" in economics refers to what is called *opportunity cost*. The opportunity cost of a given activity is defined by the value of the next best alternative. Consider the following examples.

Example 1.1

Rajnish is a software engineer working for Wipro in Bengaluru, India, earning ₹2 million per year. There are, say, three career alternatives available for him. He can work for Microsoft or IBM in Bangalore for ₹1.8 million or ₹1.85 million per year, respectively. The third alternative is that he can set up his own software firm, expecting to make a profit of ₹1.6 million a year for himself. What is Rajnish's opportunity cost of working in Wipro?

Answer: The next best alternative is to work for IBM, the value of which option is ₹1.85 million per year. This is the opportunity cost of working for Wipro. ■

Example 1.2

An auto-parts company in China wants to establish a plant outside of China. The alternatives are Germany, Indonesia, Japan, or the United States. Given its financial situation, the company is constrained to set up only one plant outside of China. Assume that the setting-up costs and the operating costs of a plant in any of these four countries are the same. The marketing research department offers a projection that if the plant is set up in Germany, Indonesia, Japan, or the United States, it will fetch an annual profit of $2.5 million, $2 million, $2.3 million, or $2.8 million, respectively. What is the opportunity cost of establishing its plant in the United States?

Answer: Among the alternatives available (Germany, Indonesia, and Japan), the maximum profit is $2.5 million (if the plant is set up in Germany). Hence, $2.5 million is the opportunity cost of setting up the plant in the United States. ■

The next example is a bit different.

Example 1.3

Allgood owns a firm that assembles computers and attends to service calls from customers who already have computers (bought from Allgood and elsewhere). He has ten employees. Each of them can assemble a computer or attend a service call. There is no difference in efficiency among the employees. Over a week's period, one employee can assemble eight computers or attend 24 calls. What is Allgood's opportunity cost of assembling computers in terms of attending service calls and vice versa?

Answer: We will develop a long answer. For example, if Allgood uses all his employees to assemble computers, he makes 80 computers, but is able to attend zero service calls. Instead, if he assigns three of them to the assembling job, 24 computers can be assembled and 168 calls can be attended by the remaining 7 employees.

Of course, if all employees are asked to attend calls, there is zero production of computers, and 240 calls are attended. Notice that, as Allgood keeps increasing the production of assembled computers, the number of service-call jobs attended falls.

Because the number of employees is given, there is an opportunity cost of computers assembled in terms of service calls completed and vice versa. Since 1 employee can either assemble 8 computers or attend 24 calls, we can say that 8 computers "cost" 24 calls and thus the opportunity cost of 1 computer is equal to 3 service calls—and equivalently, the opportunity cost of 1 service call equals one-third computers. ■

In the last example, you might argue why Allgood is constrained to employ only ten workers. If the going is good and the company is making profits, why not expand and increase the number of employees? Sure. We will take up such issues in relevant chapters.

1.5 Production Possibility Curve

Rajnish's or Allgood's problems illustrate the constraints faced by a single individual. Interestingly, the entire economy of a country or region faces a similar constraint. This is illustrated by what is called a production possibility curve or a PPC.

Realise that, at any given point in time, the technologies available for producing various goods and services and the resources available for production in an economy—meaning the size of its working population, land, buildings, machinery etc.—are all given. Thus, an economy cannot produce an arbitrary amount of any good or service. If all resources are utilised in producing a single good, say, bicycles, then only a given number of bicycles can be produced. Starting from a given allocation of resources to different sectors of an economy, if more resources are employed in one sector, the output of that sector increases and fewer resources are available for other sectors, reducing the output in some sectors. Before determining which combination of goods may serve the economy the best, we first must look at various combinations of output that "can" be produced.

Consider a hypothetical economy that can produce only two goods: motorbikes and rice. All motorbikes are of the same quality and so is rice. Suppose that, if all resources of this economy (like land, skilled, and unskilled labour, etc.) are used in the rice sector and if they work efficiently, 1.5 million tonnes of rice can be produced (within, say, a year). Assume that the same resources can produce motorbikes too, and if all resources are employed in making motorbikes, suppose that 10 million motorbikes can be made. These are two production possibilities, both of which are rather extreme. Most likely there will be other in-between possibilities. For instance, if the economy is producing 6 million motorbikes, it can produce, say, 0.94 million tons of rice.

Table 1.1 summarises the various production possibilities that are available to this hypothetical economy. Not surprisingly, notice that as the production of one good increases, that of the other decreases. This reflects scarcity of resources.

TABLE 1.1 Production Possibilities

	Motor Bikes (in millions)	*Rice (in million tonnes)*
Possibility A	0	1.50
Possibility B	2	1.40
Possibility C	4	1.22
Possibility D	6	0.94
Possibility E	8	0.57
Possibility F	10	0.00

If we now plot these possibilities (0, 1.5), (2, 1.4), etc. and join the line segments, we get a curve as shown in the left panel of Figure 1.1. It measures motorbikes along the x-(horizontal)axis and rice on the y-(vertical)axis. This is the production possibility curve (PPC) of our hypothetical economy. More realistically, if there are numerous production possibilities, not just six, then we get a smoother curve such as in the right panel of Figure 1.1. This is how a production possibility curve (PPC) is normally exhibited.

Formally, the PPC is defined for a "two-good" economy, *showing various combinations of the two goods that can be produced with available technologies and with given resources, which are fully and efficiently employed.* Equivalently, *a PPC shows the maximum amount that can be produced of one good, given the amount produced of the other good.* It is naturally downward sloping since more production of one good is associated with less of the other.[5]

Mark that the PPC does not show or say the "actual" point chosen in the economy: it only shows the possibilities. The economy may not be even operating on the curve, if, for example, there is unemployment of labour (as true for a country like India) or resources work inefficiently (e.g., if workers go on strike frequently). In that case, the economy will operate strictly within the PPC at a point like G in the right panel. However, by definition, an economy cannot operate anywhere outside of the PPC. Moreover, assuming that the economy is operating on the curve, we cannot, without further information, determine the exact point of production. It depends on preferences of individuals and the government in the economy.

Realise that, although a PPC is defined in the context of a two-good economy, the idea behind it is general and holds for any number of goods: that is, if all resources are used efficiently in production, at any given point of time more production of one good must imply less of some other good or goods.

Although, along any given PPC, an increase in the output of one good is associated with a decrease in the output of the other, it does not imply that an economy can never produce more of both (generally all) goods. The PPC defines the possibilities at a given point in time. Over time, if technology improvements take place and/or more resources are available, the economy will be capable of producing more of both (or all) goods.

As an example, in Figure 1.2, the PPC marked AC may represent an economy in 2024, while the outer PPC marked FH may represent it in 2028. That is, the PPC

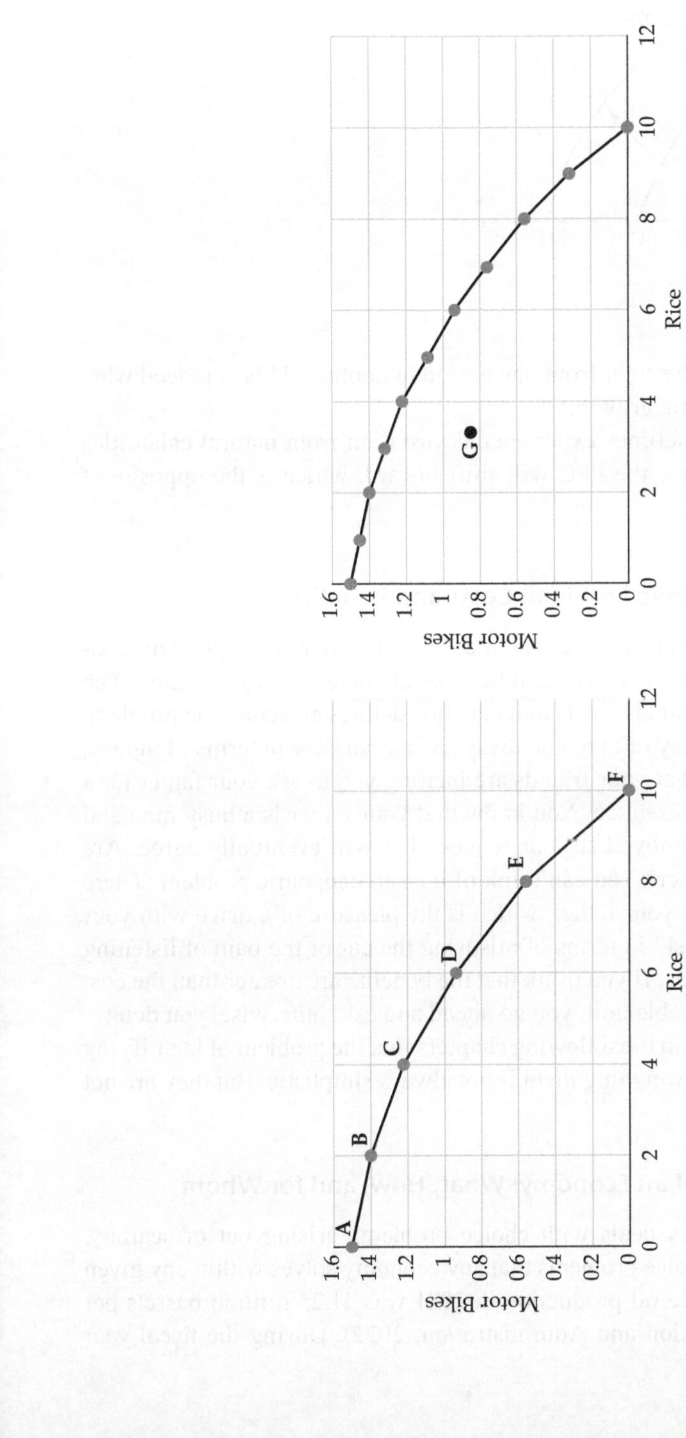

FIGURE 1.1 Production Possibility Curve or Frontier

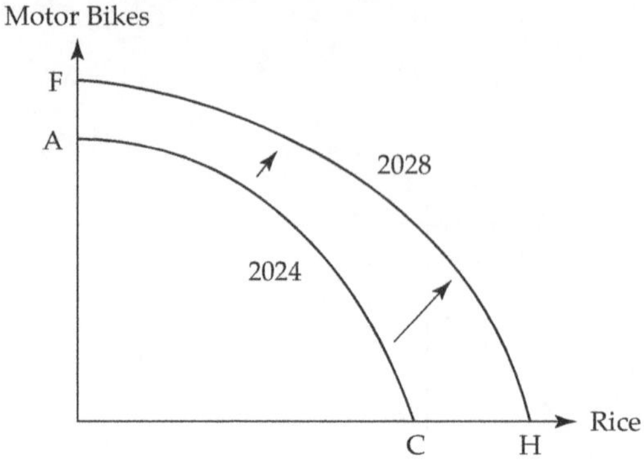

FIGURE 1.2 Shift of the PPC

of a country can shift to the right from one period to another. This is indeed what we understand by economic growth.

Nations or regions sometimes experience devastation from natural calamities or wars. In these situations, the PPC will shift inward, which is the opposite of growth.

1.6 Nature of an Economic Problem: Costs and Benefits

We have illustrated the concept of economic costs in different ways. Any economic problem always involves costs and benefits of some kind to someone. The combination of the two, namely, costs and benefits, defines an economic problem.

The costs or benefits may or may not always be measurable in terms of money. As an example, suppose that your friends are inciting you to ask your father for a ride in his luxury, chauffeured car. You know that your father is a busy man and that initially he will be annoyed at your request, but will eventually agree. Are you going to ask your father? You can think of it as an economic problem. There is a "benefit" from asking your father, which is the pleasure of a drive with your friends. But there is a "cost" in terms of misusing the car or the pain of listening to your father's harsh words. If you think that the benefits are greater than the cost measured in some comparable unit, you go ahead and ask; otherwise, you don't.

Of course, you will see in the following chapters that the problem of identifying the benefits and costs and weighing them is not always simplistic. But they are not inordinately hard either.

1.7 Central Problems of an Economy: What, How, and for Whom

Remember that economics deals with choice problems arising out of scarcity. There are indeed many choice problems that any economy solves within any given time period. The US crude oil production in 2021 was 11.25 million barrels per day (US Energy Information and Administration, 2022). During the fiscal year

2018–2019, 50 million tons of potato was produced in India (Government of India, 2020). The output of any commodity or service in any given time period is not entirely driven by external factors. Production of oil is dependent on technology and manpower employed by companies. Output of any crop does not depend on rainfall only. It is partly influenced by how much of land is used to raise a particular crop and by the applications of fertilisers, power, etc. These are consequences of individual choice as well as government policies. Hence, external factors held constant, the production of oil in the United States or India's production of potato in a given year is an outcome of choice.

Some goods are not produced in an economy either because the technology is unavailable, or it is more economical to import than produce domestically. For instance, India, South Africa, and many other countries do not produce commercial jet planes.[6] This is also a choice problem.[7]

Besides which goods are produced being a problem of choice, how or in which method a good is to be produced is also an issue of choice. Usually, there is more than one method to produce a given commodity. For instance, electricity can be generated by hydro, coal, or nuclear power. Agricultural activity can be undertaken by a relatively labour-intensive method or by a relatively capital-intensive method.

Who earns how much is also a problem of choice facing an economy. There are differences in earnings across occupations and across countries for the same occupation. For example, in 2021, the average annual wage per employee in the United States was $74,738 and the same in the United Kingdom was $49,979 (at US dollar, 2021).[8] In India, the University Grant Commission's (UGC's) gross pay for professors ranged from ₹2.4 to ₹3.2 million annually. As compared to this, in fields like business, economics, or statistics, a senior professor in an American university earns no less than $200,000 a year, which, at an exchange rate of $1 = ₹85, is equivalent to ₹17 million.

Various economic problems facing an economy fall into three categories: "what," "how," and "for whom."

What

What goods and services would be produced in an economy and in what quantities? Figure 1.3 graphs the car production in 2021 by the top ten countries. Not surprisingly, China leads the list. What explains, for example, Germany producing 3 million cars in 2021? In the fiscal year 2019–2020, the Indian economy produced 33 million tonnes of crude petroleum. Why is it 33 million tonnes, not, say 40 million tonnes? In the same financial year, India produced about 15.5 million bicycles (Government of India, 2021). What factors determine the quantities of production?

How

By which methods would the goods and services be produced? Should garments in India be produced by relatively labour-intensive or machine-intensive methods? Cement can be produced by what is called a "dry" process or a "wet" process.

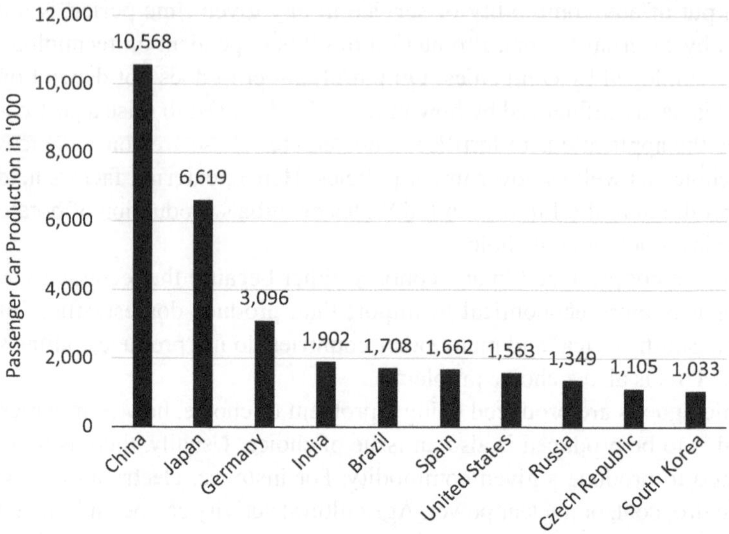

FIGURE 1.3 Passenger Car Production: Top Ten Countries, 2021

Source: U.S. Department of Transportation, Bureau of Transportation Statistics, accessed on November 28, 2022.

Which technology is to be used in a new cement plant to be constructed? These types of questions come under the "how" problem.

For Whom

From various goods and services that are available to an economy, who gets how much to consume? It depends on who earns how much or who has how much of assets. For example, how much an economics post-graduate earns, compared to a political science post-graduate or a chemical engineer? The "for whom" question refers to the issue of income and wealth distribution in an economy.

1.8 Two Alternative Economic Systems to Solve the Central Problems

In a market-oriented or capitalist economy, all three fundamental problems are solved by a "magic" (!) institution called "market." There is a price for any marketed product or service, and the price is influenced by the forces of demand and supply. These forces guide which goods and how much are to be produced and consumed through a signal, that is, price. Samsung of South Korea is the largest TV producer in the world (as of 2022). Samsung has the technology of producing high-quality TVs, which it can sell at a competitive price. There is a large world demand for its TVs, which sustains its production level. Dosa, a mouth-watering South Indian dish, is "produced" in the Indian economy because the technology of making dosa is available, the cost of producing and supplying it is not too high, and there is a demand for dosa. These are examples illustrating how the "what" problem is solved.

Alternatively, in a centrally planned economic system, which was in practice in the former Soviet Union and other East European countries till the late 1980s, these problems are addressed in a direct manner by the government. There was a central planning authority that decide which goods and how much should be consumed and produced in the economy within a given span of time, say a year or five years.[9] These are like short-term and long-term targets that are set according to the overall growth and development strategy for the economy that is considered "desirable" by the planning authority.

Factories are state-owned, and the production methods are dictated by the planning authority. Salaries are also decided by the government. In brief, all three central problems are essentially solved by direct command from the government. That is why a centrally planned economy is also called a *command economy*. The origin of the command-economy philosophy is the Communist social ideal spelt out in Karl Marx's *Das Capital*. See Appendix 1.B for an account of the Marxian philosophy, command economy, and its collapse.

Which system is better in solving the fundamental problems of an economy? This is where emotions sometimes run high. However, the world history till date goes in favour of the market economy—for the simple and stunning fact that the Soviet system collapsed. Even the Chinese economy that used to be centrally planned has vigorously moved towards a market system.

1.9 Economic Agents in a Market Economy

In the chapters to come, we study *the market* or *the capitalistic economy*. Who are the "players," or the economic *agents*, in such an economy? There are three sets of players:

- Consumers/Households
- Producers/Firms
- Government.

Households demand goods and services and supply factors of production like labour, land, machines, etc., whereas the producers supply goods and services and demand factors of production. Even in an economy in which there is no interference by the government in the business, the government plays a critical role in terms of protecting *property rights*. That is, by enforcing laws, the legal rights of consumers and producers are protected, so that they can transact or exchange in the market efficiently. In reality, of course, the government of any country does more than just protect property rights: besides providing national security and other public essentials, its actions affect production and consumption decisions via taxes, subsidies, etc., some of which will be studied in this book.

The threefold classification of agents is functional. The same person can assume the roles of different economic agents in a single day. When you go to the market to buy a loaf of bread, you are a buyer/consumer, whereas when you attend office for work, you are a seller of your professional skills for which you earn salary or wages. If you are self-employed or in a family business, you act as an entrepreneur and do not receive a fixed reward like salary. Can you guess what you get in this case (hint: a residual which can even be negative)? As another example, suppose during lunch time you look at the stock market and find some interesting trends. You call your broker to sell a part of your shareholding in say the banking sector and buy some shares in pharmaceuticals. If so, you are a portfolio manager for yourself in the asset market.

1.10 Positive versus Normative Economics

Apart from the three broad questions, what kinds of more specific questions/issues are addressed in economics? There are several. For instance, what are the various factors that determine the demand for a particular good in the market? What factors determine the supply of a particular good in the market? How would an increase in the price of coffee affect the demand for tea? What should be the government's policy to increase employment in the economy? In a country like India, why does the announcement of a new central budget every year have an impact on the stock market? What should be Argentina's best policy with respect to import of agricultural goods?

Even a problem like terrorism is influenced by economic forces. How do counterterrorism measures like security, preemptive strikes, and financial control affect the behaviour of terrorist organisations? What factors determine the lifespan of terrorist organisations? The reach of economics is far beyond what you might have expected. There are of course many more questions of potential interest and relevance.

However, if you look at the sample of questions outlined above, you will see that all the questions can be grouped into two types. One involves the effect of something or some policy change on some other thing. The other is concerned with how a particular policy should be designed to the best interest of the economy in a given context. The former is called *positive economics* or positive economic issues, while the latter is called *normative economics* or normative economic issues.

The answers to the positive economic questions form the foundation for answering normative economic questions. For instance, if we want to know what should be a government's best policy towards, say, the software industry—a normative question—we have to first know how a certain policy will affect the consumers and the producers of the software and other related industries—a positive question. Activity 1.1 is related to the difference between positive and normative issues facing policymakers.

ACTIVITY 1.1 STATEMENTS BY INDIA'S HEALTH AND WELFARE MINISTER AND THE FINANCE MINISTER ON THE ISSUE OF PROHIBITION

In India, the sale of liquor is a state subject, i.e., it is under the purview of a state government. Hypothetically speaking, the Chief Minister of Bihar is in a dilemma about whether or not he should impose prohibition (of liquor consumption) in his state. He calls a meeting of his cabinet and asks the Ministry of Health and Welfare and the Ministry of Finance to present their views.

The highlights of the two presentations are as follows:

Statement of the Health and Welfare Minister	*Statement of the Finance Minister*
Drinking is injurious to health.	Liquor sale is a source of revenue for the state.
It is a social evil.	The state earns ₹60,000 crore by way of excise and sales tax on liquor, constituting 25% of the total revenue collection.
It causes violence against women and children.	A sudden fall of one-fourth of total revenue will have a serious impact on the ongoing welfare activities of the state.
Family gets neglected and deprived.	We will have to stop financial aid to 4,000 primary schools in villages.
It causes disputes.	2,000 primary health centres will have to be closed.
It poses a threat to law and order.	The drinking water facility for 1,000 poor colonies will have to be discontinued. The child immunisation plan of 1 million children will have to be discontinued.
Hence, we strongly support prohibition.	**Hence, we strongly oppose prohibition.**

Question 1. Who is "Right," the Health Minister or the Finance Minister?

Question 2. If you were the Chief Minister of the state, what would you do?

There is no right or wrong answer. The answer may be written in the normative and positive aspects. The point is that the Health Minister is speaking of the issue in the normative platform, whereas the Finance Minister is viewing it in a positive form.

1.11 Understanding Basic Words and Phrases in Economics

We now introduce some words and phrases which we use in normal communication, but they mean something more precise in economics.

Buyers, Consumers, and Households: In real life it is not necessary that the one who buys a commodity is also its consumer. You buy a toy for a child. A husband may buy flowers for his wife. However, to make analysis simple, we use the terms buyers, consumers, and households, interchangeably.

Sellers and Producers: A seller sells goods and services to the buyers or households. A seller is not necessarily the producer: a seller of iPhone in your local market is not the producer of iPhone. There is a supply chain from production to the wholesale market and then to the final consumers in the retail market. As long as we do not wish to specifically study how wholesale and retail markets are linked, we can collapse them, as we do in this book, and equate sellers with producers.

Goods and Services: Goods are tangible, while services are intangible. Goods have a definite shape, form, and size. They could be in solid, liquid, or gaseous form, and they can be separated from their producers. A car produced in Alabama, USA, is sold in other states. It is not like this in e case of many other services. A doctor's (seller's) skill of looking inside the throat for infection cannot be delivered to a patient (buyer) through Amazon or Flipkart. However, with modern technological advancement it is not necessary that a doctor should be physically present to perform a particular type of operation or to prescribe a medicine. Yet, she/he must be present online if not in person.

Consumables versus Durables: In management, goods are sometimes classified as Fast Moving Consumer Goods (FMCG) and *durables* or *white* goods. Potato chips, vegetables, cold drinks, shampoo, etc. are in the FMCG category, whereas cars and refrigerators are durables. Durables are "consumed" over a long period of time, while providing service flows over multiple periods of time. We may distinguish between *consumer durables* and *producer durables*. The former are the durables that are used by households for consumption, not production, e.g., a toaster, a sports car, etc. Some durables are used for production only, e.g., cement kilns which are used in producing cement and mechanical robots used for assembly line production of automobiles. Of course, the same good can be a consumer durable or a producer durable depending upon the purpose of use. Your parents may have bought for you a motor bike to move around while in college. The motor bike is thus a consumer durable. But if the same bike is used for pizza delivery it is a producer durable.

Intermediate or Ancillary Goods: We distinguish between goods for final consumption and those used as inputs for further production like car air-conditioners, rubber gaskets, motorbike chains, etc. Goods that are used up in the process of production or distribution are called ancillary products or intermediate goods. However, it is not always possible to strictly compartmentalise goods into final consumption and intermediate category: milk purchased by a dairy firm is an intermediate good, whereas the same milk sold to a household for usual consumption is a final good.

A "Good" versus being Good: A good may be bad, good, or neutral from a normative perspective. Cigarettes are not good for health, but they are an economic good like a TV. A good is simply a tangible product.

Utility versus Usefulness: Utility refers to the satisfaction derived from a consuming good or service, regardless of whether it is useful or desirable. As long as a cigarette provides utility or satisfaction and therefore bought and sold in the market, it is a good from an economic perspective. It is a different question whether cigarette or tobacco use is desirable or useful.

Market and Price: Traditionally, the market meant a physical meeting place of buyers and sellers. It could be the village haat in India, a weekly market (you might have heard of terms like *mangal bazaar* (Tuesday market), or a farmer's market in Western countries. A local shopping complex or a shopping mall is also referred to as a market. Nowadays we have physical and online markets that are growing fast.

In the marketplace, physical or virtual, a good or service commands a price. In a monetary economy, the buyer pays a price to the seller in return for a good/service.[10] The price of a good or service is based on its *exchange value* with respect to money, not necessarily the *use value*. A pack of cigarettes commands a price despite having zero or rather negative use value.

This distinction between the exchange value and the use value of a good or service is sometimes illustrated by what is known as the *diamond–water paradox*. We know that water is essential for survival; hence its use value is high. However, its price is virtually zero or small. On the other hand, a diamond has no use value apart from being an item of display of wealth (with due apologies). However, a small piece of diamond commands a high price. We resolve this paradox by stating that the price of a product is based upon the exchange value of a good or service.

Suppose you buy a car from a local dealer for $30,000. Did the producer (seller) get $30,000? No, because this price includes taxes and retailor and whole-seller margin. There is a supply chain between the producer and the final consumer consisting of *intermediaries*. The number and amount changed by the intermediaries may vary from one product to another. These supply-chain issues are important, but not so for what we are interested in the book, which is to help you understand microeconomic and managerial principles. Hence, we make *a simplifying assumption that there are no intermediaries between the buyer and the producer.* With this assumption, we can say that whatever price is paid by the consumer becomes the price received by the producer. This proves quite convenient in economic analysis.[11]

1.12 Microeconomics versus Macroeconomics

Economics has many branches. Of them, there are two core ones: *microeconomics* and *macroeconomics*. The former refers mostly, but not exclusively, to the analysis of scarcity and choice problems facing a single economic unit such as a producer or a consumer. Suppose that you own a barber shop. How many barbers should you hire? How many persons should you serve per day on average? What price are you going to charge for a crew-style haircut? As another example, given your monthly pocket money funded by your parents, how many ice creams and chocolates are you going to buy? These are questions of individual choice. Microeconomics deals with the principles behind such choices.

On the other hand, macroeconomics deals with the behaviour of economy-wide aggregates such as real GDP, employment, interest rate, inflation, etc. What determines the real GDP or inflation rate in an economy? What policies can reduce the rate of unemployment in a developing country like India? And so on.

1.13 Managerial Decision-Making, Managerial Economics, and Economics

We analysed the nature of managerial decision-making and what economics is about. Realise that any managerial decision-making would involve a rational choice based on weighing costs and benefits. If a manager fires an employee, the benefit lies in saving costs associated with the fired person like his salary and other compensations, whereas cost is the value of his work or lost productivity and the expenses incurred in hiring a replacement. If a sales manager opens a new branch in a city, she/he would have to weigh the expected benefits in terms of new clientele and business vis-à-vis the cost of the new establishment. Hence, managerial decision-making, and economics go hand in hand.

Viewed a bit differently, the relationship between economics and managerial/business economics is somewhat similar to that between physics and mechanical engineering, chemistry and chemical engineering, or statistics and econometrics. For example, econometrics is about statistical measurements in economics. It can be interpreted as statistics applied to economics. Thus, in a broad sense, econometrics is all statistics, yet different because of the difference in its focus. Likewise, managerial economics can be thought of as economics applied to managerial or business decision-making.

Although a manager should have a good understanding of the overall functioning of an economy in which the product she is associated with is sold, she is mostly concerned with decision-making with regard to a particular group of individuals within a company, particular group of products, or a particular market.

Hence, managerial economics typically refers to microeconomics rather than macroeconomics.

1.14 A Primer on Schedules, Curves, Mathematical Functions, "Total," "Marginal," and "Average"

Being a branch of social science, analyses, and conclusions in economics are founded on observed human behaviour. Relationships pertaining to human behaviour are postulated or derived. Here are two related examples. In northern India, there are extreme variations in temperature during seasons over a year. In winter, the temperature dips to around 3°C while in summer it crosses 40°C. Shopkeepers find that as the temperature drops, demand for woollen garments increases, and vice versa, and when the temperature soars, demand for cold drinks increases and vice versa. We can thus say that demand for sweaters, D_S, and that for cold drinks, D_C, depend on temperature (T). These are behavioural relations, which can be succinctly expressed in a functional form relating the "variables":

$$D_S = f(T); \quad D_C = g(T).$$

In the language of mathematics, we say that D_S and D_C are functions of temperature, T, where f and g denote the respective functions. In each relationship, there are two variables, D_S and T in the former and D_C and T in the latter. We assume you already know the difference between a "constant" and a "variable." An entity which does not change its value/measure in a particular context is a constant; an entity whose value can change in a context is a variable.[12] A function captures how a change in one variable (e.g., T) impacts on another (D_S or D_C). A word of caution: a change in T may depend on some other factors like the rotation and revolution of earth and the height of the location from the sea level. Thus, it will be wrong to say that T changes on its own. But in our context of demand for sweaters and cold drinks, we are not interested in the reasons behind a change in T. Hence, we consider exogenous changes in T, meaning changes in T due to exogeneous or extraneous reasons like planetary positions, height, etc.

Mathematical functions like f and g defined above merely capture a relationship between variables. There is nothing intrinsically scary about them. Suppose that, based on observed behaviour from a locality, we compile the sales volume of sweaters and cold drinks with varying temperatures and present the data in a table as in Table 1.2. The relationship between columns (1) and (2) and that between columns (1) and (3), respectively, reflect the functions $f(T)$ and $g(T)$. Notice that the numbers in columns (2) and (3), respectively, decrease and increase with those in column (1), as we would expect. *A relationship presented in a tabular form is called* a **schedule**. Table 1.2 presents two schedules: one for demand for sweaters and the other for cold drinks with respect to variations in temperature.

TABLE 1.2 D_S and D_C as Functions of Temperature, T

Temperature in Celsius	D_S	D_C
(1)	(2)	(3)
5	50	5
10	45	7
15	40	10
20	30	20
25	10	40
30	5	60
35	3	90
40	1	150

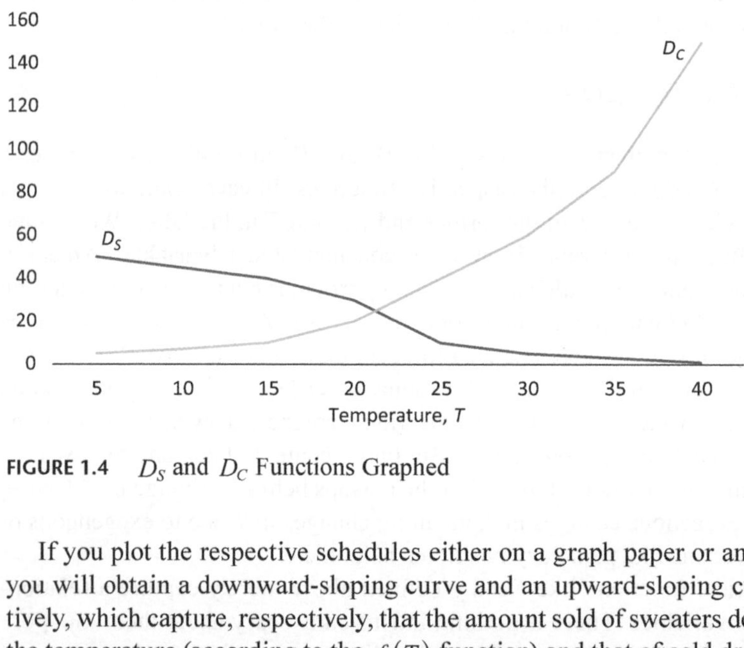

FIGURE 1.4 D_S and D_C Functions Graphed

If you plot the respective schedules either on a graph paper or an Excel sheet, you will obtain a downward-sloping curve and an upward-sloping curve, respectively, which capture, respectively, that the amount sold of sweaters decreases with the temperature (according to the $f(T)$ function) and that of cold drink increases with the temperature (following the $g(T)$ function).[13] Indeed, the graphs of $f(T)$ and $g(T)$ function based on the numbers in Table 1.2 and generated by Excel sheet are shown in Figure 1.4.

The purpose of this section is to dispel your apprehensions about diagrams. Let us not forget the adage "A good picture is worth more than a thousand words." We advise you that whenever you draw a diagram based on a given table, pay attention to the units and proportions. Make sure to properly label the diagram, i.e., mention the units taken on the two axes and name the curves. In due course, we shall be drawing these diagrams without specific data. There, also, please keep the functional relationship in mind. For instance, if we postulate an inverse relationship between the price of a good and its own demand, the resultant curve will slope downward from left to right.

1.14.1 "Total," "Average," and "Marginal" Functions

In microeconomics, there are many types of "total," "average," and "marginal" curves, depending on what is being analysed. We will see them in Chapter 4 and some of the subsequent chapters, especially Chapter 7. We discuss them here *generically* so that we understand the common patterns. This will make it easier for us to learn *specific* types of these curves later.

We are talking about "total," "average," and "marginal" functions associated with something produced, consumed, sold, etc. For example, if it is the amount produced by a firm, we will have total cost, average cost, and marginal cost functions. If a firm produces more, the "total" cost of production will be higher. The total cost of producing three dozen safety pins will be higher than the total cost of producing one dozen safety pins. The total cost of testing 3,000 patients with Covid-19 symptoms will be higher than the total cost of testing 2,000 such patients. Consider Table 1.3 for a **total** cost schedule facing a private medical X-ray lab. Look at column (2) vis-à-vis column (1). Ignore columns (3) and (4) for the moment.

Notice that it costs $15,000 to the lab even when there are no X-rays done. It is because the lab may have to pay rent for the space it occupies, pay instalments towards bank loans taken earlier to buy equipment, etc. These are overhead or fixed costs, regardless of how good or bad the business is (more on this in Chapter 7). For instance, monthly rent is typically fixed as per the rental contract. If it is,

TABLE 1.3 An Example of Total Cost Schedule Over a Month

No. of X-Rays 'in 000 (output)	*Total Cost ($ in '000)*	*Average Cost ($ in '000)*	*Marginal Cost ($ in '000)*
(1)	(2)	(3)	(4)
0	15	∞	–
1	30	30	15
2	40	20	10
3	45	15	5
4	52	13	7
5	80	16	28
6	120	20	40
7	175	25	55
8	240	30	65
9	324	36	84
10	440	44	116

say, $5,000 per month, you must pay, by law, this amount to your landlord regardless of how your business might be doing.

From the "total," we can compute the **average** = Total ÷ Quantity. In this case it is the average cost, shown along column (3). "**Marginal**" is the increment to the "total"—in this case, the cost of increasing output by one unit, which is called the marginal cost, listed in column (4). For instance, the marginal cost of producing 4 units of output = total cost of producing 4 units of output – total cost of producing 3 units of output $= 52 - 45 = 7$. Likewise, the marginal cost of producing 10 units of output = total cost of producing 10 units of output – total cost of producing 9 units of output $= 440 - 324 = 116$. If we graph these schedules, we obtain the "total," "average," and "marginal" curves, shown in Figure 1.5. Notice that while the total cost curve increases monotonically, the average and the marginal cost curves are U-shaped.

As said earlier, in microeconomics, there are many types of total, average, and marginal curves. Generally and algebraically, if we have a function $y = f(x)$ where y is the total with respect to x, then average is simply $y/x = f(x)/x$, whereas the marginal is the derivative of the total, $dy/dx = df(x)/dx = f'(x)$. Note that $f'(x)$ is just a notation for first derivative dy/dx or $df(x)/dx$. These are summarised in Table

Four Properties

There are four properties or patterns concerning the behaviour of total, average, and marginal, which will be of use in some of the chapters to follow. The first one is rather technical, but it will be useful to know it for understanding how the average and the marginal curves are drawn vis-à-vis each other. The remaining three are simpler and, as we will find out, quite useful at the same time.

(A) Compare columns (3) and (4) in Table 1.3 and observe that *as long as the average is increasing or decreasing, the marginal is above or below the average.* The reason behind this pattern is mathematical, not economic. We can understand this through the following example.

Suppose you are an enthusiastic college teacher, very eager to know how your students did in a challenging test you gave last week. After checking each script, you enter the score (marks) into the computer and the computer gives you the average score of all scripts you have checked so far. You have already checked nine scripts and the average is, say, 85 (out of 100).

Suppose that the next (tenth script) receives 91. Without entering this number in the computer, can you say if the new average will be higher or lesser than 85, the old average? Yes: the average will be higher because the average, thus far, was 85 and hence if the last ("marginal") student's score is greater than the old average, it will push the average up. This means that (i) *if the "average" is increasing, the "marginal" must be above the average.*

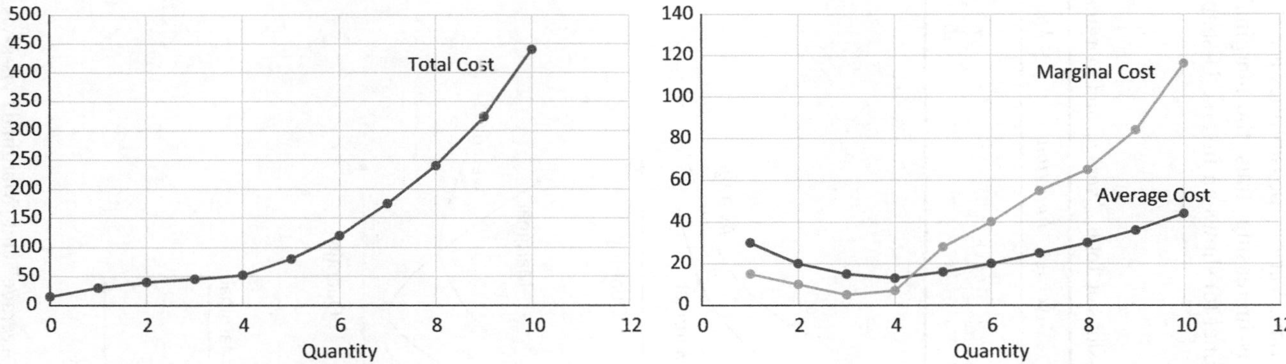

FIGURE 1.5 Total Cost, Average Cost, and Marginal Cost Curves Derived from Table 1.3

If, instead, the tenth student had scored anything less than 85, by the same logic, it would have pulled down the average, implying that (ii) *if the "average" is decreasing, the "marginal" must be below the average.*[14]

In summary, the relationship between average and marginal depends on the shape of the average function. Various possibilities are illustrated in Figure 1.6. In panel (a), the average is increasing; thus, the marginal > the average. Panel (b) shows the opposite. Panel (c) shows an inverse U-shaped average curve. See

TABLE 1.4 Algebraic Expressions of Total, Average, and Marginal Functions

"Total" Function (Given)	*"Average" Function*	*"Marginal" Function*
$y = f(x)$	$\frac{y}{x} = \frac{f(x)}{x}$	$\frac{dy}{dx} = \frac{df(x)}{dx} = f'(x)$

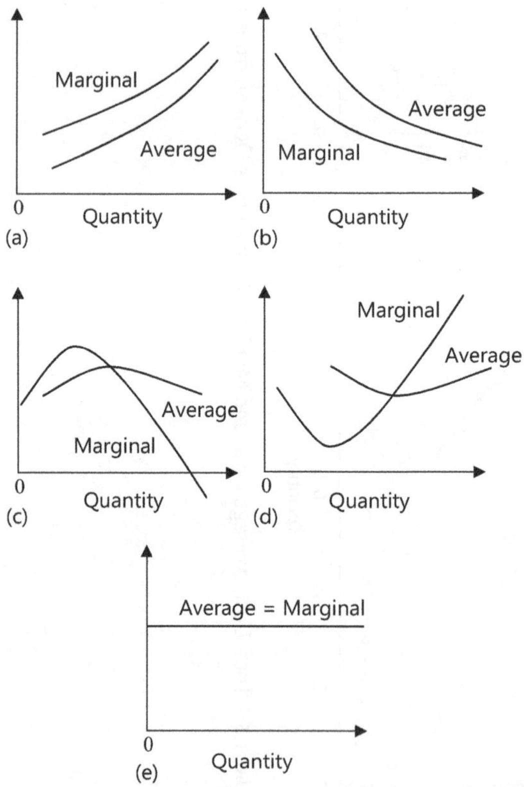

FIGURE 1.6 Behaviour of "Average" and "Marginal" vis-à-vis Each Other

that the marginal curve cuts the average curve at the latter's maximum point, the implication being that when the average is increasing initially, the marginal > the average, and, beyond some quantity, as quantity increases the average falls and the marginal < the average. Panel (d) depicts a U-shaped average curve. In the initial range, the average is falling and the marginal < the average. Beyond a certain point, the average increases and the marginal > the average. The right panel of Figure 1.5 is an example. In panel (e) of Figure 1.6, the average is constant; that is, it does not increase or decrease. Thus, the marginal = the average.

(B) Since the marginal is simply an incremental to the total, *the sum of the marginal must be equal to the variable component of the total.* We can verify this from columns (2) and (4) in Table 1.3. For example, consider output = 6. The total cost is 120, of which the variable component is $120-15=105$. If we sum up the marginal costs for output levels 1, 2, 3, 4, 5, and 6, it is $15+10+5+7+28+40=105$. Such equality holds at *any* level of output.

The marginal being incremental to the total, the total must be increasing or decreasing as the marginal is positive or negative. In Table 1.3 or Figure 1.5, the total cost is increasing and thus the marginal cost is positive. The reverse causality also holds: total cost increases throughout because the marginal cost is positive. In some situations, the total may not be increasing or decreasing throughout; and, thus, the marginal can be both positive and negative depending on the quantity.

(C) To further understand; Figure 1.7 depicts what is called a **Laffer curve**, named after Arthur Laffer. It depicts the total tax proceeds as a function of the tax rate; the point being that if raising tax revenues is an objective, it is not a good idea to fix a tax rate as too high. Realise that when the tax rate is zero, tax proceeds are naturally zero. As we consider higher and higher tax rates, tax proceeds will keep increasing initially. But beyond a certain point, a further increase in the tax rate would have such a dampening effect on the very activity that generates taxes that the total tax proceeds "will" decline. When the tax is near 100%, there will be no tax-generating activity and hence the tax

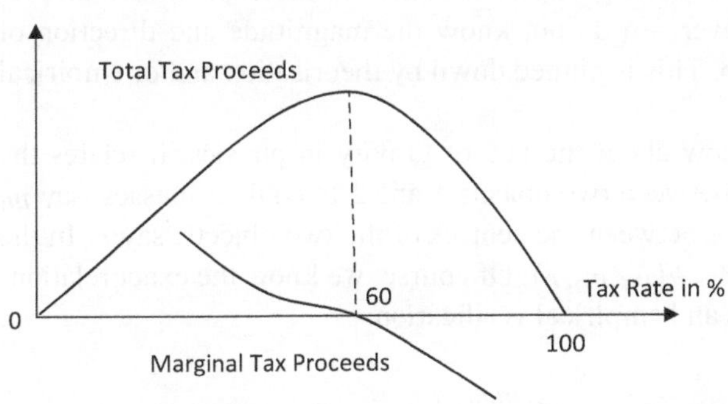

FIGURE 1.7 Laffer Curve

proceeds will approach zero. Combining how tax proceeds change with the tax rate at very low and very high levels of the tax rate, we will obtain a curve as in Figure 1.7. They increase with the tax rate initially, but, after a certain point, fall with any further increase in the tax rate.

This implies that there is a total tax proceeds maximising tax rate. This is shown at 60% in Figure 1.7 as an example. Between 0 and 60% tax rates, the *marginal* tax proceeds (meaning an increase in total tax proceeds for one percentage increase in the tax rate) are positive and thus the total tax proceeds increase with the tax rate, and, beyond 60%, the *marginal* tax proceeds are negative, i.e., the total tax proceeds fall with any further increase in the tax rate. At 60%, the marginal tax proceeds are zero.

(D) *If the "total" curve is smooth, the marginal is the derivative of the total and hence equal to the slope of the total curve.* Figure 1.7 shows a smooth total tax proceeds curve and the marginal tax proceeds curve, which is simply the derivative along the former curve.

As said earlier, we will use the properties (A) to (D) in some of the following chapters in different contexts.

1.14.2 A Function of Many Variables

So far, we have discussed y being a function of one variable x. (A function may be denoted by f, g, or some other alphabet, e.g., $y =$ “ (x), where “ is an uppercase Greek alphabet called "Gamma.") This is appropriate when we want to study how y may change when only x changes. However, changes in y may depend on changes in x and other variables. If we want to study such a situation, we must consider a more general function like $y = f(x, a, b, c)$, signifying that y will change if any or any combination of x, a, b, and c changes.

1.14.3 Deterministic versus Stochastic Functions

A general function like $y = f(x, a, b, c)$ simply conveys that a change in one variable depends on changes in some group of variables in the context of a discussion or an analysis. However, we do not know the magnitude and direction of this functional relationship. This is pinned down by theorisation and/or empirical observations and analysis.

For example, we all know about the law of gravity in physics. It relates the gravitational force, say F, between two objects 1 and 2 to (i) their masses, say m_1 and m_2 and (ii) the distance between the centres of the two objects, say r. In the general functional form, $F = h(m_1, m_2, r)$. Of course, we know the exact relationship based on experiments and empirical verification:

$$\text{Law of Gravity}: F = h(m_1, m_2, r) = G\frac{m_1 m_2}{r^2}.$$

where the additional entity G is the gravitational constant, equal to 6.67×10^{-11}.

Like the example of gravity equation, data analysis in economics leads to functional forms, except for one major difference. Realise that the law of gravity is a **deterministic function**, meaning that if we know the values of m_1, m_2, and r, we know, for sure, what the gravitational force is. In social and behavioural disciplines, however, the cause–effect or dependence relationships are more complex and subject to random factors, which, by definition, cannot be accounted for. For instance, consider how the amount of tandoori roti dough that Shyam, a cook, can make (y) depends on the time available to him, say t. Assume that any quantity of flour he needs can be obtained from the storeroom. We may think of expressing this relation by writing a function $y = f(t)$. But realise that it is *not* like the Newton's law of gravity. How many roti doughs Shyam can roll in say 30 minutes depends on the intensity of his effort, which is not accounted for in the function $y = f(t)$. If he is unwell or in a bad mood, the output is likely to be less. If his wife calls to tell him that she has cooked his most favourite dish, chicken biryani, for him when he returns from work, Shyam's effort level may increase. The point is that, effort is something unobserved and subject to random fluctuations, which, on its own, can influence an outcome y. In this example, y depends on t and a random factor say u, that is $y = f(t,u)$. For instance, u can take, say, three values, 1, 0, and −1 with probabilities 0.25, 0.55, and 0.20. A function, which includes one random variable or many, is called a **stochastic function**.

Unlike the gravity equation, in social or behavioural sciences, the measured functions are stochastic. However, for theoretical or analytical purposes, we will ignore the random factors and consider deterministic functions like the demand function for sweaters or cold drink introduced earlier. But when we want to statistically measure those demand functions from data, we incorporate the effect of random factors and consider stochastic functions.

Facts and Insights

- The hallmark of any managerial post is decision-making.
- The common myths associated with economics as a subject in college are: "Economics is a theory course, I have joined a business school to gain 'practical' knowledge," "Economics requires a lot of mugging since so many laws and theories must be reproduced ditto!" and "Economics has too many tables, diagrams and formulas."
- Economics is a social science.
- There are three central tenets leading to an economic problem: human wants are unlimited (or infinite); resources are scarce; and individuals of decision-making units are rational.
- Infinity of wants and scarcity of resources lead to trade-offs between available choices.
- Economics deals with rational choice in the face of scarcity.

- The opportunity cost of a given activity is defined by the value of the next best alternative.
- At a given point in time the production possibility curve (PPC) is downward sloping, meaning that a higher production of one good implies less production of some other good. But over time the production possibility curve can shift, and an economy can produce more of all goods.
- Unemployment of resources means that the economy is producing inside its production possibility curve.
- Economic growth amounts to a shift of an economy's PPC to the right.
- Problems of economics involve benefits and costs of choices.
- There are three central problems of any economy: what, how, and for whom. The "what" problem refers to what and how much of goods and services are to be produced in an economy. The "how" problem refers to the methods of producing a good. The "for whom" problem refers to income and wealth distribution in an economy.
- Two alternative economic systems are command economy or central planning, and market or capitalistic economy.
- There are three types of economic agents in an economy: consumers/households, producers/firms, and the government.
- Positive economics deals with the effect of a change in a parameter facing an economy on various entities in an economy.
- Normative economics refers to analysing what policies may best serve the interest of an economy.
- Intermediate goods or raw materials are those that are used up in the production process in a single period.
- Durable goods are those that provide service flows over many periods of time. There are producer durables and consumer durables.
- The price of a good or a service is based upon its exchange value with respect to money, not necessarily the use value.
- Microeconomics deals with individual choice problems, whereas macroeconomics studies the behaviour of economy-wide aggregates like GDP, price level, interest rate, etc.
- Managerial decision-making is essentially an economic or a rational choice based on weighing costs and benefits of an action taken.
- Managerial economics refers to the study of economic principles that are relevant or useful in business and managerial decision-making.
- Mathematical functions are algebraic expressions capturing how different variables are related to one another in a precise way.
- In microeconomics, many types of "total," "average," and "marginal" functions arise. They are related to one another in certain ways. Apart from how average and marginal functions are related to each other, the total increases or decreases accordingly as the marginal is positive or negative, and, if the "total" function is smooth, the marginal is its first derivative.

- There are deterministic and stochastic functions.
- In social and behaviour sciences, empirically measured functions are stochastic, while for analytical or theoretical purposes we assume deterministic functions.

Exercises

Descriptive/Analytical

1.1 "Economics cannot be a science. There are no laboratories or tests." Defend or refute.

1.2 Consider an economy in which two goods are produced: (a) computers with the help of labour and specialised machines that can be used in making computers only and (b) wheat with the help of labour and land that again can be used in producing wheat only. In other words, while labour is used in producing both goods, specialised machines are specific to the computer sector and land is specific to the wheat sector. Suppose in such an economy the supply of specialised machines increases. How will this shift the economy's production possibility curve?

1.3 "An economy always produces on, but not inside a PPC." Defend or refute.

1.4 Illustrate the three fundamental problems facing an economy by giving examples not given in the text.

1.5 "Economics as a subject is concerned only with managing one's money." Defend or refute.

Short Answer (Word Limit = Approx. 500)

1.6 Give two examples of "how" problems, other than those given in the text.

1.7 Give two examples of "what" problems, other than those given in the text.

1.8 "How does France's association with World Trade Organization (WTO) affect the production of agricultural goods in France?" Is this a positive or a normative question? Justify.

1.9 "Should Afghanistan try to negotiate a free trade agreement with Japan?" Is this a positive or a normative question? Justify.

1.10 "All else the same, an increase in the rate of unemployment in the economy shifts the production possible curve to the left." Defend or refute.

1.11 Suppose refugees from a neighbouring country settle in a host country. How will it affect the PPC of the host country?

1.12 Bribe taking and bribe giving are not moral, but people do give and take bribes to get various things done—it is an economic decision. Identify the nature of benefits and costs of

   a) bribe giving,

   b) bribe taking.

   (Note: This doesn't justify the presence of bribes.)

1.13 Give two examples of economic questions, through which one can distinguish between micro- and macroeconomics.
1.14 "The relationship between economics and managerial economics is like that between mechanical engineering and chemical engineering." Do you agree or disagree? Give reasons.
1.15 "The government should provide jobs to every adult individual capable of working." It is a noble economic objective for any government. But are there any constraints in meeting this objective? Discuss.
1.16 Given below are two job offers: (A) a higher pay package in a less reputed company vis-à-vis (B) a lower pay package in a more reputed company. Which one will you trade-off: A for B or B for A and why?
1.17 Identify the independent and dependent variable in the following sets of variables: (a) altitude and temperature, (b) leather tanneries and water pollution, and (c) literacy rate and books sales. Also, state whether these are directly (positively) related or inversely related and show these diagrammatically.

Quizzes/Numerical

1.18 You work in Walmart. The following options are available if you quit this job: (a) work as a salesperson in a computer store for \$50,000 a year, (b) an assistant in the local congressman office for \$45,000, or (c) a salesperson job for \$53,000. What is your opportunity cost of working in Walmart?
1.19 In every half hour, a chaatwallah (fast-food vendor) on a street in New Delhi, India, can serve 10 plates of chaat (snack A) or 30 gol guppas (snack B). He works 5 hours a day. Draw his "daily" PPC of serving chaat plates and gol guppas.
1.20 Consider a mathematical function $y = 100 - 5x$. Assume a few values of x, say 2, 5, 10, 15, 18, and 20 and find the corresponding values of y. Plot these with free hand. Comment on the direction (inverse or direct/positive) of the relationship.
1.21 Now suppose $y = 5x$. Once again assume the same values of x as above. Now plot. What do you find?
1.22 Given below are two tables showing values of x and y.

x	y	x	y
0	10	20	0
2	10	20	2
4	10	20	4
6	10	20	7
8	10	20	11
10	10	20	14

Plot these separately and comment on their shapes.

1.23 Consider two functions, $y = 100 - 5x$ and $y = 100 - 2x - 0.2x^2$. If you plot them in the graph paper, you will find that the plot of the first function is a straight line, whereas that of the second is a curve. Why?

1.24 Given the following:

Purely Socialist | Mixed | Purely Capitalist

and based on your understanding of the model of economic management, place the countries, namely, the United States, the United Kingdom, Russia, China, India, Switzerland, and Japan, in their respective category. Justify your answer.

Appendix 1.A Increasing Marginal Opportunity Cost and the Shape of the PPC

Along a PPC, as more production of one good implies some sacrifice of the other good, the rate of this sacrifice is the **marginal opportunity cost** of the expanding good. In Table 1.1, starting from possibility B, if bike production rises by two units (from 2 to 4), $1.40 - 1.22 = 0.18$ million tonnes of rice need to be foregone. Hence, between the production possibilities B and C, the marginal opportunity cost of motor bikes (in thousands) is equal to $0.18/2 = 0.09$ million tonnes of rice. Similarly, between the production possibilities C and D, the marginal opportunity cost (per one lakh bikes) is 0.14 crore tonnes of rice, and so on. Thus, the marginal opportunity cost of a good on a PPC is the amount sacrificed of the other good per unit increase in the production of the good in question.

Compared to Table 1.1, Table 1.5 has an extra column, listing the marginal opportunity cost of motorbikes. Observe that, as the output of motorbikes increases, its marginal opportunity cost increases (from 0.05 to 0.09, 0.09 to 0.14, and so on). Why does the marginal opportunity cost increase? The economic reason is that, as more and more of a good is produced, factors producing it become

TABLE 1.5 Marginal Opportunity Cost along the PPC

	Motor Bikes (in millions)	*Rice (in million tonnes)*	*Marginal Opportunity Cost of Bikes (in terms of rice)*
Possibility A	0	1.50	–
Possibility B	2	1.40	0.05 (between A and B)
Possibility C	4	1.22	0.09 (between B and C)
Possibility D	6	0.94	0.14 (between C and D)
Possibility E	8	0.57	0.185 (between D and E)
Possibility F	10	0.00	0.285 (between E and F)

TABLE 1.6 Production of Sugar and Chilli

Production of Sugar	*Production of Chilli*
0	102
1	100
2	95
3	85
4	73
5	55
6	30
7	0

marginally less and less productive. Thus, more and more of the other good must be sacrificed to ensure a given increase of the former good. This is called the increasing marginal opportunity cost.

Increasing marginal opportunity cost implies that the PPC is concave. To see this, if, instead, the marginal opportunity cost were decreasing, you can check by constructing an example that the PPC will be convex. Finally, if the marginal opportunity cost were constant, the PPC would be a straight line. Typically, however, the marginal opportunity cost of a particular good on the PPC is increasing and therefore the PPC is concave.

Example A1.1

A country named Spice produces two goods: chilli and sugar. The production possibilities of these two goods are given in Table 1.6. Calculate the marginal opportunity cost of sugar in terms of chilli and that of chilli in terms of sugar at various points. Is the assumption of increasing marginal cost satisfied? Draw the PPC by plotting the production possibilities and joining them.

Answer: Between sugar–chilli production combinations (0,102) to (1,100), the marginal opportunity cost of sugar is equal to 102 – 100 = 2 chilli, since 2 units of chilli is sacrificed to obtain 1 extra unit of sugar. The marginal opportunity cost of chilli is the inverse of that of sugar and thus equal to ½: between these combinations 102 – 100 = 2 extra units of chilli are obtained by sacrificing 1 unit of sugar and hence 1 extra unit of chilli can be produced by giving up ½ unit of sugar. Likewise, the marginal opportunity costs at other combinations are calculated and listed in Table 1.7.

As we go down this table, sugar production increases and we see that the marginal opportunity cost of sugar increases. Similarly, as we go up the table, chilli production is higher and higher and its marginal opportunity cost increases (from 1/30 to 1/25, from 1/25 to 1/18, and so on). Hence the assumption of increasing marginal cost is met for both goods. The resulting PPC is graphed in Figure 1.8. ■

TABLE 1.7 Marginal Opportunity Costs at Other Combinations

Between Production Combinations	*Marginal Opportunity Cost of Sugar*	*Marginal Opportunity Cost of Chilli*
(1,100) and (2,95)	100 – 95 = 5	1/5
(2,95) and (3,85)	95 – 85 = 10	1/10
(3,85) and (4,73)	85 – 73 = 12	1/12
(4,73) and (5,55)	73 – 55 = 18	1/18
(5,55) and (6,30)	55 – 30 = 25	1/25
(6,30) and (7, 0)	30 – 0 = 30	1/30

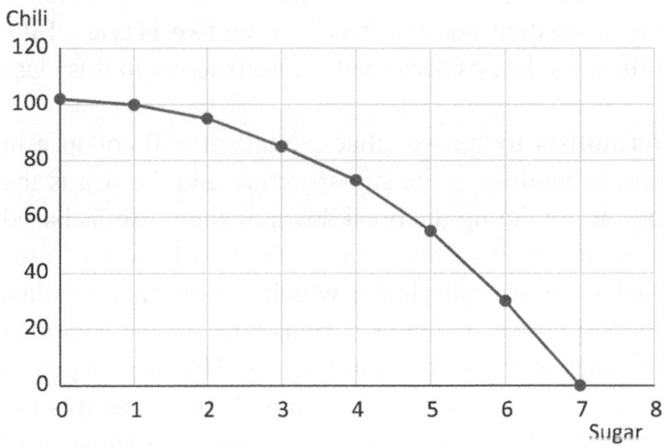

FIGURE 1.8 The PPC

Appendix 1.B Karl Marx, Communist Ideal, and the Command Economy

Karl Marx, a 19th-century German philosopher is the intellectual founder of the command economy or the socialist model. Das Kapital (The Capital) was his magnum opus. The other prominent philosophers of communist ideology include Leon Trotsky, Rosa Luxemburg, Joseph Stalin, Vladimir Lenin, and Mao Tse Tung. Marxian philosophy is based on three pillars.

Dialectical Materialism	Historical Materialism	Economic Determinism

Dialectic refers to inner conflict. There is an inbuilt fission in matter. To every action, there arises an equally strong reaction which is constantly in clash with each other. Alternatively put, to every thesis there arises an anti-thesis. The two clash with each other, resulting in a synthesis. In due course of time, the synthesis becomes thesis against which an anti-thesis arises and the clash of two results once again gives rise to a synthesis. This process goes on as long as the dialectic prevails. The dialectical materialism is reflected in history. In pre-historic times, when man lived in jungles like all other species, there was no inner conflict. Marx calls this primitive communism. In slavery, class conflict emerges between the master and the slave. This conflict gave way to feudalism which again had two conflicting classes: the feudal lord and the serf.

Over time, feudalism led to capitalism, in which once again two classes emerged, the capitalist and the worker. These classes are alternatively termed as bourgeois and proletariat, respectively, the haves and the have-nots. Bourgeois are essentially capitalists plus their friends, i.e., politicians, bureaucrats, and other influential people. Proletariats are essentially labourers plus other small self-employed artisans like blacksmiths, cobblers, small farmers, etc. The bourgeois class owns all means of production except labour, while the proletariats have nothing but their labour. There is a constant conflict between the two classes. Like slavery and feudalism, capitalism too has its own seeds of destruction in this class conflict.

Marx uses economic determinism to "prove" that capitalism will collapse in due course. According to him, economics is the sub-structure and the rest is the superstructure. His reasoning for predicting the breakdown of capitalism is based on his theory of surplus value. It runs like this. Out of the two factors of production, labour and capital, labour is the only factor which can produce surplus. Capital simply reproduces itself. Labour generates surplus because the capitalist pays it less than what it contributes to the production process. The surplus generated by the labour increases the capital owned by the capitalists. It prompts the capitalist to use more capital (as it is free, self-owned) thus replacing labour. But remember, labour is the sole factor of surplus generation. Its lesser use results in the falling rate of profit which ultimately causes its own downfall. The working class can only hasten its own fall. Marx pronounced a clarion call: "workers of the world unite, you have nothing to lose but your chains." We don't propose to write a critique of the socialist model. Let us just have a look at the extent to which this model was practised.

After World War I, Lenin rose to power in Russia, paving the way for Communists to come to rule. In due course of time, Russia along with 15 neighbouring states formed the Union of Soviet Socialist Republics (USSR) in 1922. Thereafter, many East European states like the erstwhile Yugoslavia, Poland, and Hungary too followed the command economy model. The rise of Mao Tse Tung led to the Communist rule in China. Socialism spread far and wide. As stated briefly in the main text, in socialism decision-making is centralised and concentrated at the top of the pyramid. The fundamental problems of the economy, that is, what, how, and for whom, are tackled by the central authority which may either be a single individual or a group of persons. For instance, the central planning authority would decide which crop is to be produced in which field and with which inputs and technology. The rest of the economic agents are supposed to simply carry out the orders. All means of production are centrally owned: there is no right to private property, nor is there any right to inheritance. After deciding what and how to produce, the state will also decide who will get how much.

You can see that such a system cannot be sustained in a democracy. The command economies had to eliminate the multi-party democratic system and replace it with a single party system. In such a system, even if you get the right to vote, who will you choose if all candidates belong to the same political party and follow the same ideology?

The command economy model started to collapse first in China (after the death of Mao) in the mid-1970s. Later with the collapse of the Berlin Wall in 1989, the USSR disintegrated and with this came the demise of the command economy. Please note that it still survives at the political level. We do not propose to go deep into the reasons behind its collapse, except to note the most crucial economic reason for its collapse, namely, its practice of delinking productivity or efficiency from reward, which essentially discourages an individual's incentive. Marxian philosophy believed in the dictum "from each according to her ability and to each according to her needs." It means that a task is assigned to the most efficient worker available for the job, but at the time of giving reward, she/he is paid as per the need, not talent or productivity. Clearly, under this arrangement there was no incentive to be more productive and efficient. No wonder in this system, people became more and more dependent on state largesse and freebies.

We hope that this brief description of the command economy model will help you to better understand and appreciate the market economy.

Notes

1 Experimental economics is an important branch in economics.
2 As the story goes further, Adam and Eve succumbed to their inquisitive nature and ate the forbidden apple. As a punishment, they were expelled from heaven and sent to the earth.
3 It is only a hypothetical example.
4 It does not imply however that the gains must always equal the losses.
5 Notice that the *PPC* is downward sloping *and* concave to the origin; this is discussed in Appendix 1.A.
6 But they might be producing other types of planes. For instance, India produces helicopters, small aircrafts, and some fighter planes.
7 You may argue that India does not produce commercial jet planes because it does not have the necessary technology. However, if a technology is not available domestically, it can be acquired by paying for it. Acquiring a particular technology is also a choice problem. Many technologies can be purchased if we decide to pay for it. But we should not buy any available technology even if we can afford it. The benefits from having a technology must be weighed against the cost of acquiring it from abroad.
8 Source: OECD iLibrary, accessed on November 28, 2022.
9 This is where the notion of "five-year plans" in India came from.
10 In barter system, when money did not evolve, goods and services would be exchanged for goods and services. Let's not get into that.

11 Incorporating intermediaries will bring complications but no change in our central conclusions.

12 A variable is sometimes categorised as a "stock" or a "flow." The distinction between a stock and a flow is typically covered in a macroeconomics or macroeconomic management course.

13 You are welcome to sharpen your understanding by postulating some other functional relationships based either on your gut feeling or observed behaviour.

14 Those who are mathematically oriented can see the relationship between the average and the marginal "in a minute." Using calculus, differentiating the "average" with respect to x. This implies that if average is increasing (or decreasing), i.e., $\mathrm{d}(\text{Average})/\mathrm{d}x$. is positive (or negative), then Marginal > (or <) Average.

Bibliography

Government of India. (2020, April). *Monthly report potato. Horticulture statistics division, department of agriculture, cooperation & Farmers welfare*, Ministry of Agriculture & Farmers Welfare.

Government of India. (2021). *Economic survey 2020–2021.* Ministry of Finance.

U.S. Energy Information and Administration. (2022, November 8). Short-term energy outlook. Retrieved November 28, 2022, from https://www.eia.gov/outlooks/steo/report/us_oil.php

2

FORCES OF DEMAND AND SUPPLY

Price Mechanism at Work

In 1973, the Organisation of Petroleum Exporting Countries (OPEC) collectively curtailed the production of oil considerably. The supply of oil in the world market fell so drastically that the price of oil quadrupled within one year. A barrel of crude oil from Saudi Arabia that cost $2.59 in September 1973 was $11.65 by January 1974. The world economic order changed permanently since then.

Lee was making plans of selling two 100-square-yard plots that he owned in his hometown at $100,000 each, in order to pay for his son's education in America (costing $200,000). Meanwhile, as part of the state government's plan to develop an IT (information technology) Park, IT industries moved into the town. The demand for real estate skyrocketed. Within six months the price of one plot was $220,000. Lee then had to sell only one plot to finance his son's education in the United States.

The preceding examples illustrate how market forces work. In the first example, the price of oil soared because of a drastic fall in supply. In the second, there was an increase in demand, which resulted in a land-price hike. The market system works in accordance with the forces of demand and supply. "Demand" and "Supply" are two fundamental concepts in economics as well as management, which help us to understand and explain simple and complicated situations. Sometimes we jokingly remark, "Tell a parrot two words, demand and supply, and it will become an Economist!"

This chapter is indeed "the" showcase of how the market economy functions. We study demand first.

DOI: 10.4324/9781003452195-2

2.1 Demand

In common usage, demand typically means an emphatic wish. A labour union may demand higher wages. A child kidnapper may demand $1 million as ransom. On a news channel in India, Arnab Goswami may be saying "The nation demands to know … ?" In late 2020 and early 2021, farmers in some parts of India demanded the repeal of farm laws passed earlier by the Central Government of India.

In economics, demand is defined as a measured desire in exchange for a payment: *it is a desire to acquire or buy a commodity backed by one's ability to finance the purchase.* See Box 2.1 for a classroom example in the Indian context.

BOX 2.1 POOR GURUJI (TEACHER)

While teaching this topic, if your teacher states, "I want to buy a Ferrari," and then asks, "Will this statement makes my demand for a Ferrari?" The whole class will most likely respond with a loud "NO" as everyone knows that teachers in India are not so well paid that they could buy such a luxury car! (Incidentally this has happened to us umpteen times). Well! the students are right. The teacher's desire alone doesn't make 'demand.' But if the teacher announces, "I want to buy a scooter, a two-wheeler." Will this announcement makes his demand for a scooter? This time a lot of students would nod in affirmation. Thus, the desire to have a scooter backed by resources and the preparedness to sacrifice these resources to acquire it makes the demand for the scooter.

We first examine the demand for a commodity or service at the individual or household level, not by an entire community or all residents in a region. Suppose that each month your parents give you ₹6,000 as your "stipend" money to spend on food, snacks, stationeries, movies, clothes, etc. In this context, think of your demand for ice cream within a month and ask yourself what factors determine how many ice cream cones you would buy within a month. You may come up with the following:

- Price of Ice Cream Cones: Assume that all ice cream cones are of the same kind and quality. Suppose that they become more expensive than before: from ₹15 a piece to ₹30. Unless you "cannot live without having to eat so many ice-creams per month," you will most likely consume less ice cream than before. (Perhaps you will switch partly to a substitute product, say kulfi.)
- Your Monthly Stipend: As a reward to your having done very well in the exams, your parents raise your stipend from ₹6,000 to ₹8,000. You would probably spend more on clothing, entertainment, and food—including ice cream, i.e., the effect is that you would demand more ice cream.

- Price of Kulfi (A Frozen Dairy Dessert): Suppose that for some very unusual reason, kulfi becomes quite cheap: ₹20 per piece instead of ₹40, while your stipend is unchanged at ₹6,000. Would you buy as many ice creams as before? Given that you do like kulfi (although perhaps not as much as ice cream), you would probably have more kulfi and consume less ice cream.
- Weight-Consciousness: You've become very weight-conscious lately. Since ice cream is "fattening," you may be consuming less ice cream than before, even when there is no change in prices, stipend, etc.
- Future Price Expectation: Imagine a rumour that, within a matter of one week, because of supply problems, ice cream will be doubly expensive. If this rumour spreads, many of you would dash to buy ice cream now and store them in the refrigerator. In other words, your present or current demand for ice cream is affected by future price expectation, while there is no change in the stipend or in any price now.

We have listed above most, if not all, of the factors that may affect your demand for ice cream.[1] We can generalise from this. Call the price of ice cream as "own price," the price of *kulfi* as the "price of a related good," monthly stipend as "income,"—and weight-consciousness as "tastes" in the sense that it has changed your "effective" taste for ice cream.

Now think of consumables like clothing, household items, and other types of food. We can say that the demand for a product by an individual or a household depends on:

- Own price,
- Income,
- Prices of related goods,
- Taste, and
- Future price expectations

where the term "income" refers to the total expenditure on all different goods you may wish to purchase within a given period—not the salary or earnings of a person. Note that such a characterisation applies to not just goods (commodities) but also services. Goods or commodities like fish, jeans, or a lipstick have physical dimensions. Services refer to consultation with a doctor, eating out in restaurants, air travel, house repair jobs, etc., which do not have a definite physical shape *per se*. Yet they command a price like a commodity.

The question now is, how, in general, do these factors affect the quantity demanded of a product or a service?

2.1.1 Own Price

The effect of own price is captured through what is called the **Law of Demand**, stating that, *other things remaining unchanged, the quantity demanded of a* *product by a consumer falls as its own price increases.* This is quite intuitive: if a product becomes more (or less) expensive, you would buy less (or more) of it. Note here that (i) "other things" refer to other factors affecting demand like income, prices of related goods, etc., and (ii) the law applies in the context of a given area and a given period.

Table 2.1 presents a numerical example of this law, and it is interpreted as follows: If the price of an ice cream cone *were* ₹20, Sunita would buy 50 cones; if it *were* ₹22, she would have bought 40 cones, and so on—although at any given point of time (and space) there is a standard price for an ice cream. The Law of Demand presented in a tabular form is called a **demand schedule**. Table 2.1 is a demand schedule.

The numbers in Table 2.1 are graphed in Figure 2.1(a), in which (own) price is measured on the y-axis and quantity demanded along the x-axis. This is the demand curve, corresponding to the demand schedule in Table 2.1. In general, **demand curve** *is a graphical representation of the Law of Demand, measuring the inverse relationship between own price and the quantity demanded.*[2] A general (unspecific) demand curve is typically illustrated as a smooth

TABLE 2.1 Demand for Ice Cream by Sunita during Summer Months

Own Price (₹)	*Quantity Demanded of Ice Cream*
20	50
22	40
25	32
27	26
30	20
32	15

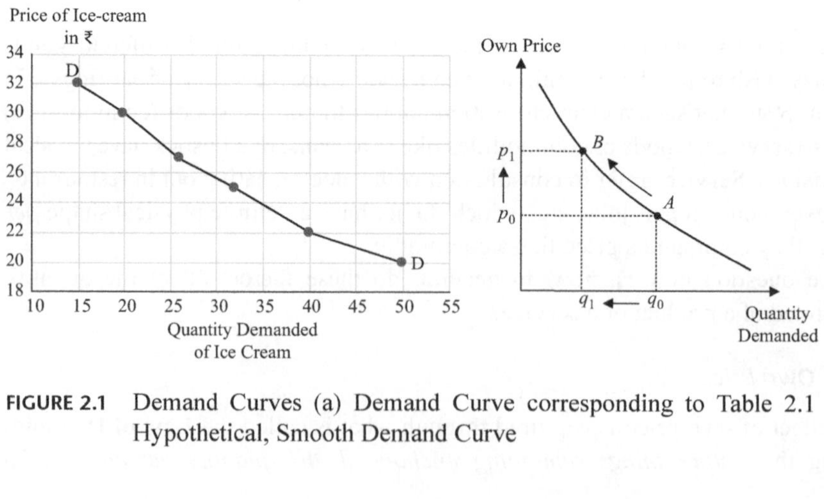

FIGURE 2.1 Demand Curves (a) Demand Curve corresponding to Table 2.1 (b) A Hypothetical, Smooth Demand Curve

downward-sloping curve, as in Figure 2.1(b). At the price $p_0$for example, the quantity demanded is q_0 and the consumer is at the point *A* on the demand curve. At a higher price p_1, the quantity demanded is less, that is, q_1, and the consumer is at point *B*, and so on.

The Law of Demand holds generally but not universally. There are exceptions and we will learn them as we go along. But unless mentioned explicitly, we presume the law holds, i.e., the demand curve is downward-sloping.

2.1.2 Income

Suppose the income of a consumer rises and other things *including the own price* remain the same. Would she buy more or less of a particular good? Normally one would buy more. But it may not be true for all goods. As an example, suppose that your stipend (income) is low. You are probably consuming a fair amount of low-priced snacks like peanuts and biscuits, which you do not like as much as, say, ice cream, but you buy them because that is mostly what you can afford with your low income. But, if your income rises, it is likely that you will buy less of peanuts and biscuits and more of ice cream, because you are able to afford more of what you like.

In this example, as income increases, the demand for ice cream increases and that for peanuts falls. In general, if the demand for a product rises with income, we call it a **superior** or a **normal good**. But, if less of a good is demanded as income increases, it is an **inferior good.**

The effect of income on quantity demanded is illustrated in Figure 2.2. Panels (a) and (b), respectively, show a normal good and an inferior good. In both panels, D_0D_0 represents the original demand curve, and D_1D_1 the new demand curve

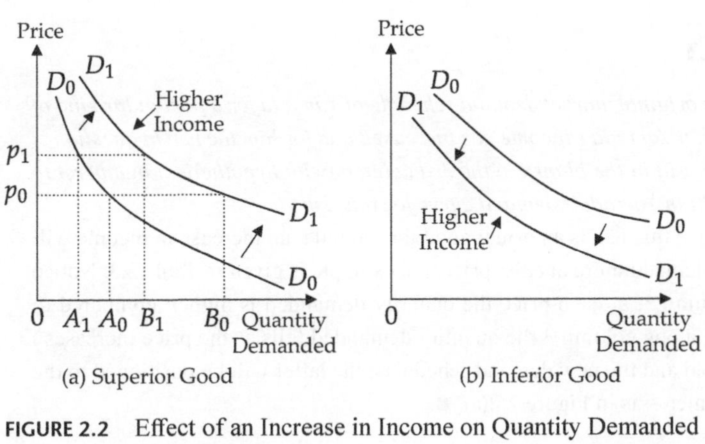

FIGURE 2.2 Effect of an Increase in Income on Quantity Demanded

after an *increase* in income. Panel (a) shows that, at price p_0 , for instance, the quantity demanded originally was A_0. At a higher income but at the same price p_0, it is B_0, which is greater than A_0. Similarly, at the price p_1, the original quantity demanded was A_1, whereas the new quantity demanded with higher income is B_1. The same pattern holds at any particular price: quantity demanded is greater with higher income—which exactly defines a normal or a superior good. We can then say that, *for a normal or superior good, an increase in income shifts the demand curve to the right.* By the same logic, a decrease in income shifts the demand curve to the left.

Panel (b) of Figure 2.2 shows the opposite for an inferior good: *an increase* (*or a decrease*) *in income shifts the demand curve of an inferior good to the left* (*or right*). See Box 2.2c on a brief discussion of inferior goods in reality.

BOX 2.2 WHICH GOODS ARE INFERIOR IN REALITY

Typically, certain food cereals are inferior goods. For instance, in most parts of the world, maize (also called corn) has been found to be an inferior good. Rosegrant et al., (1995) reported that, in Philippines, a 1% increase in income led to a 0.15% decrease in white maize consumed. Minot and Goletti (2000) found that in Vietnam even rice is an inferior good: given that the income of a family exceeds a certain level, an increase in income was associated with a decrease in the amount of rice consumed. According to McKenzie (2002), tortillas in Mexico are inferior goods.

Are cereals inferior goods in India? Most studies such as by Bhalla et al. (1999) and others find that they are not. However, as an exception, Kumar (1998) find some evidence of inferior cereals.

Example 2.1

Table 2.2 is the original market demand schedule of Yamada for a particular kind of fish. Suppose that Yamada's income has increased and for him the fish in question is a normal good. Fill in the blanks in the 3rd column (with hypothetical numbers) to represent a shift of Yamada's demand curve for this fish.

Answer: Since this fish is a normal good for Yamada, an increase in income will induce him to demand more at *each* price. An example is given in Table 2.3. Notice that, along column 3, at each price the quantity demanded is higher, compared to column 2. (Yet along column 3 the quantity demanded falls as the price increases.) If we plot the old and the new demand schedules, the latter will be positioned to the right of the former—as in Figure 2.2(a). ■

TABLE 2.2 Original Market Demand Schedule of Mr. Yamada for a Particular Kind of Fish

Price in Yen (¥)	*Yamada's Demand for Fish*	*His Demand for Fish after an Increase in Income*
100	10	?
200	7	?
300	6	?
400	5	?
500	3	?
600	1	?

TABLE 2.3 Demand for Fish after an Increase in Income

¥	*Yamada's Demand for Fish*	*His Demand for Fish after an Increase in Income*
100	10	13 (>10)
200	7	10 (>7)
300	6	9 (>6)
400	5	6 (>5)
500	3	4 (>2)
600	1	2 (>1)

2.1.3 Prices of Related Goods

In taste, two goods may be related to each other. If so, they may be substitutes for each other or one may be a complement to the other. In drinks, tea and coffee are substitutes. In meat, chicken and mutton are substitutes. In the staple food, rice and chapatti (Indian bread) are substitutes. But consider tea and sugar. Sugar is a complement to tea: if you consume more tea, you consume more sugar (unless, of course, you are diabetic).[3] Substitutability or complementarity is not restricted to food or drinks only. For instance, the demand for auto mechanic services is complementary to the demand for automobiles.

If two goods are related it is natural that a change in the price of one will affect the demand for the other. This is called the *cross-price effect, defined as the effect of a change in the price of one product on the demand for another related product.*

Consider how the demand for tea is likely to be affected by an increase in the price of coffee. It would increase, since a substitute good is now costlier. This implies that, as the price of coffee increases, the demand curve for tea shifts to the right (i.e., at any given price of tea, more tea will be demanded at a higher coffee price). Thus, *an increase (a decrease) in the price of a substitute good shifts the demand curve of a product to the right (left).* This is exhibited in Figure 2.3(a).

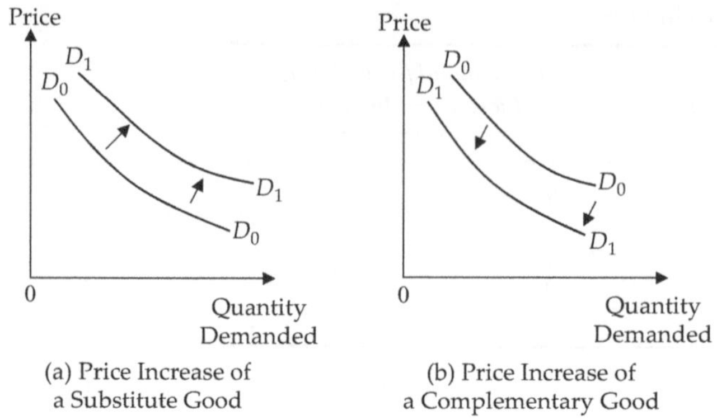

FIGURE 2.3 The Effect of an Increase in the Price of a Related Good

Now ask yourself how an increase in the price of tea would affect the demand for sugar. Tea consumption will decrease—and so will the demand for sugar. It is opposite of what happens when the price of a substitute good increases. Thus, *an increase (a decrease) in the price of a complementary good shifts the demand curve of a product to the left (right).* This is shown in Figure 2.3(b).

2.1.4 Taste

A person's taste for a product may change for various reasons. When younger, you very much disliked bitter gourd; but now your natural dislike may not be that intense. A change in taste may occur even when there is no change in your natural liking. For instance, because of health problems, you may be consuming less chocolate and ice cream, even though your natural liking for them remains as strong as ever. Taste changes can happen with respect to non-food products too.

How does a taste change affect the demand for a commodity? Simple: *a favourable (an unfavourable) change in taste for a product increases (decreases) the demand and hence shifts the demand curve to the right (left).*

2.1.5 Expectations

Suppose there is an unexpected weather prediction that a huge cyclone is going to hit your town in the next three days. This prediction will cause people to anticipate that there will be a shortage of supplies for various daily consumables during and immediately after the cyclone and hence these items will be much more costly. This will prompt them to rush to the stores and stock up on grocery items like milk, oil, bread, potato, and toiletries like paper napkins, toilet paper, etc. in bulk. A similar scenario unfolded during the initial months of the Covid-19 pandemic in 2020. Household essentials got sold in grocery stores in the United States and other countries in minutes or a couple of hours after they were displayed on the shelves. In such situations, there is no change in income, own price, prices of related goods, or tastes, yet there is an increase in the *current* demand for some products. We can then say that *an increase (a decrease) in the expected price of a product increases (decreases) the current demand for it and shifts its current demand curve to the right (left).*

In Chapter 1 you were introduced to the notion of a function. We put it to use here. Various factors affecting the demand for a product, say, A, can be expressed compactly as:

$$q_{AD} = f\left(p_A, p_B, p_C, M, O\right), \tag{2.1}$$

where q_{AD} stands for quantity demanded of good A, p_A its own price, p_B and p_C are prices of related goods B and C (if there are more related goods, they can be included too), M is consumer's income meaning total expenditure, and O represents all other factors like tastes, price expectations, etc.

When we wish to stress the effect of own price, while suppressing or holding constant other determinants, we can express equation (2.1) as a shorthand function:

$$q_{AD} = f\left(p_A\right). \tag{2.2}$$

2.1.6 Other Factors

There are still other factors that can influence a person's demand for a commodity. For example, to impress others and possibly themselves, some people tend to buy more of a good when it becomes more expensive. You can think of this as a (strange) change in taste because of a change in price. This is called a **Veblen effect** and the good in question is called a **Veblen good**.[4] Veblen goods are "conspicuous goods," which others may look at with some envy—like a brand-name car, a fancy jacket, or something similar. As the quantity demanded increases with price, the Law of Demand does not hold obviously for a person whose behaviour is subject to the Veblen effect. This is common among the ultra-rich, not the *hoi polio* (common mass). Imagine the crowd outside leading stores when they announce festival sales, be it Oxford Street in London or Karol Bagh in New Delhi. The page-3 personalities among the ultra-rich are hardly seen with the commoners. A specific example is given in Box 2.3.

There may be a **bandwagon effect**—meaning that if others start to use it in a big way, the product becomes trendy and you go for it too *without looking at the merit*. That is, you "follow the crowd."

There can also a **snob effect,** referring to a situation where you want to be different from others for the sake of being different, i.e., you "go against the crowd." If more people buy something, your demand for it falls. This is the opposite of the bandwagon effect.

BOX 2.3 DEFYING THE LAW OF DEMAND: THE GLITTERATI

A family friend of ours who owns a boutique in Greater Kailash, a posh locality in Delhi, once narrated this story. Her clientele was by and large the very rich ladies living in nearby localities. The dresses (suits, sarees, lehengas) were also priced way above the normal rates in other stores. Inspired by the desire to increase her clientele among others, she placed a small set of designer dresses on one shelf which were reasonably priced (she might have overheard us saying that reduced prices attract more customers.) She even told some of her clients about that shelf. None cared to even look at that. For almost three months not even a single item was sold from that shelf. One day, she simply removed the prices tags of those dresses and put new price tags which were higher than the price of dresses in other shelves. In less than a week, the whole range was sold!

In such cases, the price becomes a symbol of quality and status. "It is NOT for me, if it is cheap."

Still another effect can operate in the form of a **network externality**, *defined as a change in the benefit to a person when the number of other individuals using it increases.* For instance, if your friends stop using Facebook (for some reason), your demand for Facebook will fall. But if they all start to use Facebook, your demand for Facebook will increase.[5] Thus, a person's benefit increases with the size of the network and therefore an increase in the number of consumers in a network increases the individual demand for the product or service. This is a **positive externality.** Note that it is somewhat similar but *not* same as the bandwagon effect, which says that you "go" for the product without looking at the merit.

The opposite can happen: a person's benefit may decrease with the number of users in a network. Consider using the bus service in a city. If the number of bus-riders increases and the buses are overcrowded, it may lower your benefit from a bus-ride and induce you to use less of it. This is a case of **negative externality**. Unless specified, the convention is that network externality refers to the case of a positive externality.

2.1.7 Market Demand

So far, we have analysed the demand for a particular good by a single individual, family, or household. **Market demand** *is the total demand by all individuals combined in the entire market.*[6]

As a simple example, let there be only three individuals in the market: Rekha, Reshma, and Rachel. Figure 2.4 depicts their individual demand curves for

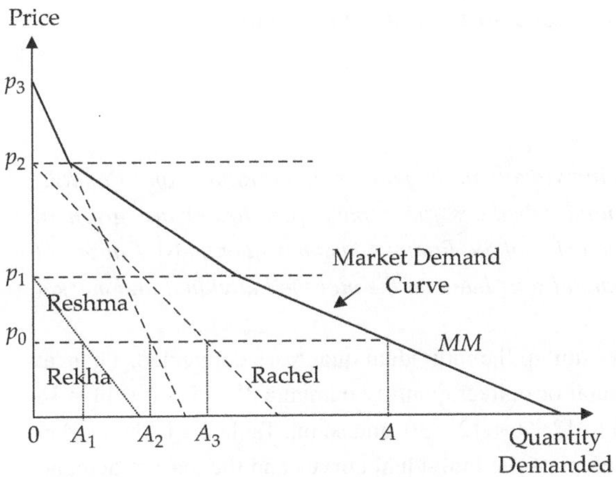

FIGURE 2.4 Market Demand Curve

product A, marked by the respective dotted lines (with vertical intercepts p_1, p_2, and p_3). It is presumed for simplicity that ice cream can be measured continuously as points on a line. For instance, at price p_0, Rekha demands $0A_1$, Reshma $0A_2$, and Rachel $0A_3$. Then the quantity demanded in the market at price p_0 equals $0A_1 + 0A_2 + 0A_3$. This sum is equal to $0A$, where the point A is marked on the curve. Other points on this curve are obtained by similar exercise at other prices.[7] The *MM* curve is then the market demand curve.[8] Algebraically, suppose there are H individuals or households in the market denoted by $h = 1,2,\cdots,H$. Let $f^h(p_A)$ be the demand function for any particular household h. We can sum these individual demand curves as:

$$f^1(p_A) + f^2(p_A) + \cdots + f^H(p_A) \equiv F(p_A). \tag{2.3}$$

Here the new function $F(p_A)$ is simply the summation of individual demand functions and it is the market demand curve.

Note that in obtaining the market demand curve, essentially, the quantities measured along the horizontal, x-axis are added up. Thus, *the market demand curve is the horizontal or lateral summation of individual demand curves.*

What are the factors that can shift a market demand curve? Since the market demand curve is based on individual demand curves and the number of individuals constituting the market, these are:

- Income levels of individuals, i.e., income distribution across consumers in the market.
- Prices of related goods.

- Tastes of individuals (i.e., distribution of tastes).
- The number of individuals or consuming units in the market.

Example 2.2

Suppose that there are three individuals in the market: Ram, Rahim, and Randall. Their individual family demand schedules for apples (per dozen) are given in Table 2.4. For example, at the price of $9, Rahim consumes (demands) 4 dozen of apples. Derive the market demand schedule and the plot the individual and market demand curves.

Answer: At each price, we sum up the individual quantities demanded. Thus, at price equal to $5/dozen, the total or market quantity demanded = 15 + 7 + 14 = 36 dozen. At price $6, it is equal to 12 + 6 + 12 = 30, and so on. Table 2.5 is the market demand schedule. Figure 2.5 depicts the individual curves and the market demand curve. ■

TABLE 2.4 Family Demand Schedules for Apples

Price per Dozen ($)	*Quantity Demanded by Ram*	*Quantity Demanded by Rahim*	*Quantity Demanded by Randall*
5	15	7	14
6	12	6	12
8	10	5	10
9	8	4	9
11	7	3	7
13	6	2	5
15	4	0	3
18	3	0	0

TABLE 2.5 Individual Curves and the Market Demand Curve

Price per dDozen	*Total Quantity Demanded of Apples (in Dozen)*
5	36
6	30
8	25
9	21
11	17
13	13
15	7
18	3

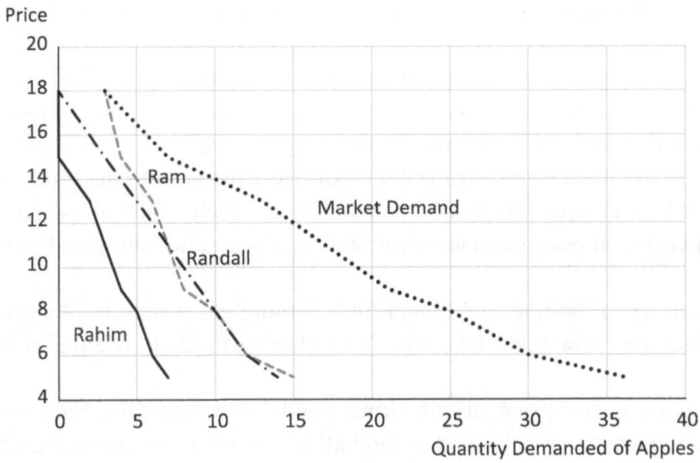

FIGURE 2.5 Market Demand Curve in the Example

2.1.8 *"Change in Quantity Demanded" Versus "Change in Demand"*

Think for a moment about how we have organised the effects of various factors on demand for a particular commodity (for an individual or the entire market). First, the effect of a change in the own price is characterised by the Law of Demand and depicted as the demand curve, and, next, the effects of changes in other factors likes income, prices of related goods, and taste are seen through a shift in the demand curve.

Having understood this, we can differentiate the two terms in the title of this section. Refer back to Figure 2.1(b). Suppose the own price changes from p_0 to p_1. The consumer "moves," so-to-speak, from point *A* to point *B* on the same demand curve. This is called a **change in quantity demanded**—*meaning a movement along a given demand curve due to a change in the own price.* On the other hand, a **change in demand** refers to *a change in the whole demand schedule or curve, which is same as a shift of the demand curve—that occurs due to a change in other factors such as income, prices of related goods or taste.* In other words, the first term refers to the movement *along* a demand curve and the second to a movement *of* it.

2.2 Supply

Whereas the consumers or the households demand various goods and services, it is the producers or the firms who supply them. What factors determine the supply of a particular good to a market within a given time period? Suppose Manuel has a factory in Brazil that produces football (soccer ball). What factors determine how many footballs Manuel produces and supplies to the market in a span of, say, a year?

One is the market price of a football itself (assuming that all footballs are exactly of the same size and quality). All else the same, if the market price of football increases, Manuel would tend to produce and supply more.

Another factor is the cost of raw material, labour, etc., that go into the production of footballs. If leather and other synthetic material in which a football is made become more expensive, it becomes a less profitable business, and you would produce less.

Technology matters, of course. If Manuel finds a more efficient way of combining labour, machines, raw materials, etc., in producing football, Manuel will produce more.

Yet another factor is the price of substitute goods in production. Suppose Manuel's factory makes volleyballs and volleyball becomes more popular than before. It will be in greater demand among women and men in sport and the price of volleyball will rise. How would this affect Manuel's production and supply of football? It would decline, as he would divert more of his resources from producing football towards producing volleyball.

We now state these factors of supply generally and consider their implications.

2.2.1 Own Price and the Supply Curve

All other things remaining the same, the higher the price of a product, the more a firm will produce and supply to the market. This is the **Law of Supply**, counterpart of the Law of Demand. Table 2.6 lists various quantities of football supplied at different prices. Such a table describes a supply schedule. Figure 2.6(a) graphs this table, measuring price and quantity along the y-axis and the x-axis, respectively. The resulting curve is a **supply curve**, *a graphical representation of the Law of Supply or a supply schedule.* It is upward sloping or positively sloped, because a

TABLE 2.6 A Supply Schedule

Price of Football (in Brazilian Real, R$)	*Quantity Supplied of Football (in '000)*
0	0
100	10
200	18
300	24
400	28
500	29

higher quantity of supply is associated with a higher price. Figure 2.6(b) draws a smooth supply curve for analytical purposes.

2.2.2 Shifts of a Supply Curve

Similar to the case of demand, factors other than the own price shift a supply curve.

Input Prices

Consider Figure 2.7 in which S_0 is the original supply curve. At the price p_1, the quantity supplied is q_1; at p_2, the quantity supplied is q_2, and so on. Now suppose there is an increase in the price of an input or in the prices of several inputs that are

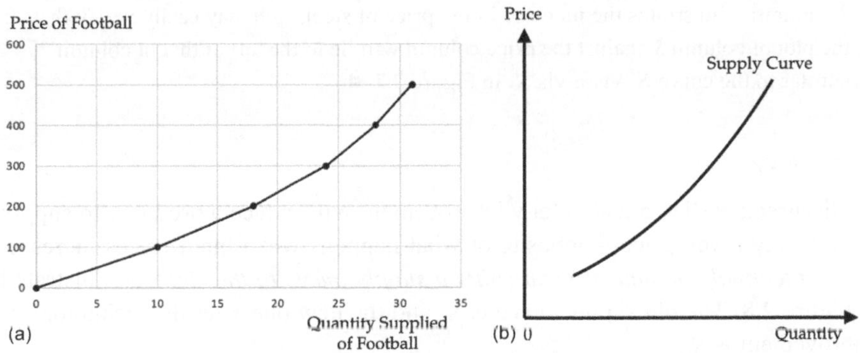

FIGURE 2.6 Supply Curve (a) Supply Curve based on Table 2.6 (b) A General, Hypothetical Supply Curve

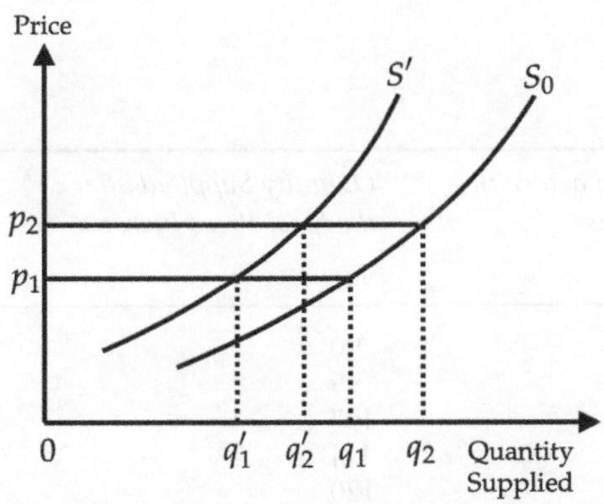

FIGURE 2.7 An Input Price Increase and the Supply Curve

used in making the product. This will raise costs. At any given price, a firm will supply less. At p_1 the quantity supplied now is q_1', which is less than q_1, at p_2, it is q_2', and so on. The resulting supply curve is S', lying to the left of S_0. Hence, *an increase (a decrease) in input prices shifts a supply curve to the left (right).*

Example 2.3

A company produces steel cabinets of a given type, dimension, and quality. The market price of steel rises by 20%. Through a numerical example, illustrate how this would affect the company's supply curve of almirahs.

Answer: An increase in the price of steel reflects an input price increase. This will imply that at the same price for a cabinet, the company will supply less. Table 2.7 offers an example. Column 2 enumerates the original quantities supplied at various prices. In column 3 each entry is less than the corresponding entry in column 2, meaning a decrease in the quantities at each price. Thus, in relation to column 2, column 3 illustrates the increase in the price of steel. You may easily verify that the plot of column 3 against the price column will lie to the left of that of column 2, similar to the curve S' vis-à-vis S_0 in Figure 2.7. ■

Technology

As discussed earlier, a technology improvement will induce a producer to supply more at any given price—opposite of what happens when input prices increase. Thus, *a technology improvement shifts a supply curve to the right*, as illustrated in Figure 2.8. The old supply curve is S_0 and the new one after the technological improvement is S_1.

Price of a Substitute Good

In our football–volleyball example, an increase in the price of volleyball led to a decrease in the production of football. Generalising from this, we can say that *an*

TABLE 2.7 An Example

Price of a Steel Cabinet (€)	*Quantity Supplied before the Steel Price Increase*	*Quantity Supplied after the Steel Price Increase*
(1)	*(2)*	*(3)*
200	100	90
220	110	99
260	115	107
310	122	114
360	128	120
420	132	123

increase in the price of a substitute good in production will shift the supply curve of a given product to the left.

This is illustrated in Figure 2.9. The original supply curve is S_0, whereas the new supply curve is S_1.

Business Taxes

Businesses not only incur the cost of production but they also pay taxes because of their production activity. Unlike the income tax, it is an *indirect tax* as it does not directly affect net income. If a business buys inputs from abroad or from a domestic source, it may have to pay a customs duty, another example of an indirect tax.

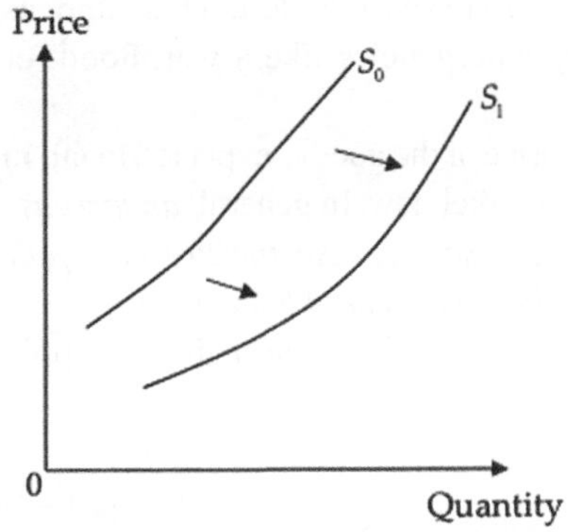

FIGURE 2.8 Technological Improvement and the Supply Curve

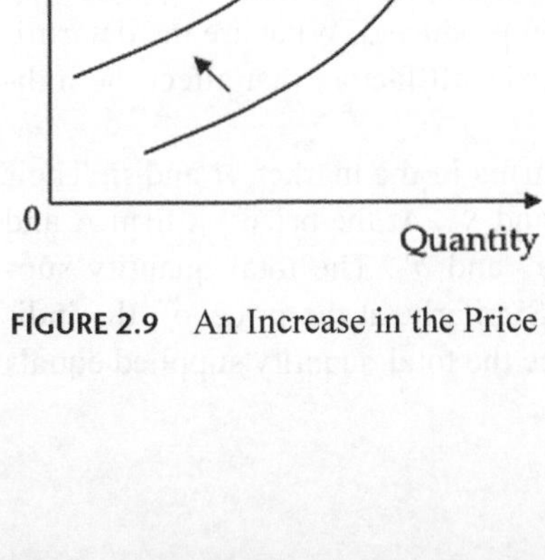

FIGURE 2.9 An Increase in the Price of a Substitute Good and the Supply Curve

If business taxes increase, from a producer's point of view it is like an increase in the price of an input. Thus, *an increase* (*a decrease*) *in business taxes shifts the supply curve to the left* (*right*).

Other Factors

There are other factors that affect the supply curve of a product as well. For producing an agricultural good, weather plays a vital role. We all know how dependent agriculture output in a tropical country like India is to the monsoon.

Another is price speculation—or what is same as—future price expectation. If it is speculated that the price of a good will rise in the near future because of some external factor, suppliers may engage in **hoarding**, not releasing the good to the market, since they expect to make larger profits later by releasing output when the market price is much higher. Hoarding behaviour tends to reduce the *current* supply of the product and shift the current supply curve to the left. This happens typically in the case of essential goods during emergencies like a war, flood, or drought. Hoarding is illegal.[9]

In the same vein, if suppliers perceive that the price of the good is expected to fall in the future, they would tend to supply more to the market now. In general, *an increase* (*a decrease*) *in the expected future price would decrease* (*increase*) *the current supply of a commodity to the market and therefore shift the supply curve to the left.*

Similar to the demand function, we can algebraically write a firm's supply function of the product A as:

$$q_{AS} = g\left(p_A, p_B, p_C, w_L, r_K, T, O\right), \tag{2.4}$$

where q_{AS} is the quantity supplied of product *A*, p_A is the own price, p_B and p_C are prices of related goods, w_L and r_K are prices of the two inputs, say *L* (labour) and *K* (capital) that enter the production technology (other inputs can be easily included), *T* represents technology, and finally *O* stands for other determinants of supply.

2.2.3 Market Supply Curve

So far, we have discussed the supply curve of a single producer. For the entire industry we derive the the market supply curve, analogous to the market demand curve. If there are 50 producers in a market for example, *the market supply curve is horizontal sum of the supply curves* of the 50 producers. What are the determinants of the market supply curve? The answer is: all factors that affect the individual supply curve *plus* the number of firms.

For illustration, Figure 2.10 assumes two firms in the market, *A* and *B*. Their respective supply curves are indicated as S_A and S_B. At the price p_1, firm A and firm B, respectively, supply the quantities, q_A^1 and q_B^1. The total quantity supplied in the market is equal to $q_A^1 + q_B^1 = q_M^1$. Similarly, at the price p_2, the individual quantities supplied are q_A^2 and q_B^2. Hence the total quantity supplied equals

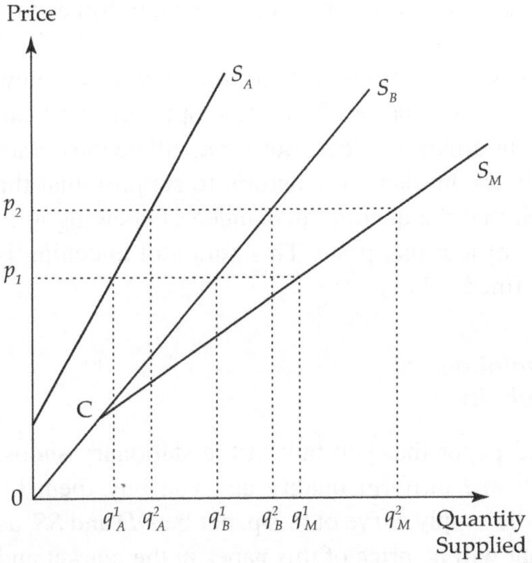

FIGURE 2.10 Market Supply Curve

$q_A^2 + q_B^2 = q_M^2$. If we join the price–quantity combinations like $(p_1, q_M^1)(p_2, q_M^2)$, etc. we obtain the market supply curve, shown as the curve $0CS_M$.

If there are N firms in the industry producing good A and we denote firms by $n = 1, 2, \cdots, N$, we write the market supply function as:

$$g^1(p_A) + g^2(p_A) + \cdots + g^N(p_A) \equiv N(p_A). \tag{2.5}$$

2.2.4 Change in Quantity Supplied versus Change in Supply

The distinction is similar to that between a change in quantity demanded and a change in demand. The former refers to a movement along a given supply curve and this occurs because of a change in the own price. In contrast, a change in supply refers to a shift of an entire supply curve. For instance, a change in technology changes the supply.

These terms essentially distinguish the effect of own price on the supply of a good from the effects of other determinants.

2.3 Price Determination

We have studied demand behaviour by consumers and supply behaviour by producers separately. In a market, consumers and producers interact and therefore their behaviour must be consistent with each other in some sense. Demand and supply are like the twin blades of a pair of scissors. Just as they work in coordination with each other to produce results, so do the demand and supply forces in a market economy.

Consider the market for, say, chewing gum. From its demand curve we know how much of it will be demanded at various prices. From its supply curve we can tell how much of it will be supplied at different prices. But what will be the *actual* price of chewing gum prevailing in the market? It is natural to suppose that the actual prevailing price will be such that the quantity demanded of chewing gum matches with the quantity supplied of it at that price. This notion of matching is called market equilibrium (to be defined below).

2.3.1 Market Equilibrium, Determination of Price and Quantity, and Stability

Consider the market for, say, ruled paper that you buy in the stationary shops. Suppose that they are available in one uniform quality and you buy them by weight. Let the demand curve and the supply curve of this paper be *DD* and *SS*, as in Figure 2.11. The question is: what will be price of this paper in the market and how much of it will be produced and sold in the market?

Suppose that initially the price of this paper is p_1. Notice that at this price the consumers are willing to buy the amount D_1, while the producers are willing to supply the amount Y_1. There is a mismatch: consumers are demanding more than what the producers are supplying. The difference *AB* or Y_1D_1, is the **excess demand**, *defined generally as the excess of the quantity demanded over the quantity supplied.* Will the price of paper stay or remain stable at p_1? No. Excess demand will create competition or bidding among buyers to get hold of the limited amount available and this will raise the price. Suppose that the price rises to p_2. Will it be stable at p_2? The answer is again no. The magnitude of

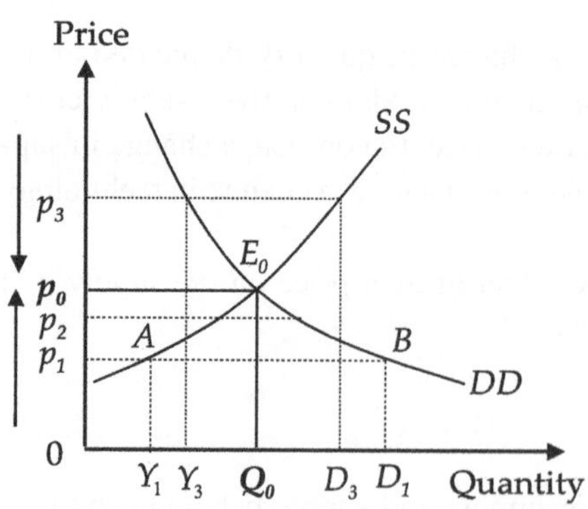

FIGURE 2.11 Market Equilibrium

excess demand is less than before, but it exists nevertheless, which will push up the price further. Indeed, the price will keep increasing as long as excess demand exists. The upward pointing arrow shows this. It is easy to see that this process of price adjustment will finally settle at p_0, at which there is no excess demand.

Instead, if initially the price were above p_0, say at p_3, the producers are supplying more than what the consumers are willing to buy. There is excess supply, *defined generally as the excess of quantity supplied over quantity demanded.* It is equal to Y_3D_3. Excess supply generates competition among the sellers to sell the limited amount that the consumers are willing to purchase. This causes the price to fall. The process will continue until the price converges to p_0, at which there is no excess supply.

At p_0 then, there is **market equilibrium**, *defined as the situation where the excess demand or excess supply is zero.* Put differently, *market equilibrium occurs when the quantity demanded and the quantity supplied of a product are equal to each other, or equivalently the demand and the supply curves intersect* (at E_0 in the example). It is also called **market clearing** and the corresponding price is called the **equilibrium price** (p_0 in the example). The corresponding quantity demanded and supplied (Q_0 in the example) defines the equilibrium quantity exchanged.[10]

Furthermore, the fact that, irrespective of where the price is initially, it eventually settles at p_0 implies that the market equilibrium is *stable.*

This notion of market equilibrium is the basis of how the market economy works. Using this concept, the following sections illustrate how various economic phenomena play out in a market economy.

2.3.2 Sustainable versus Non-sustainable Industry

Figure 2.11 assumes that the demand and supply curves intersect in the positive quadrant. Suppose they don't, as in Figure 2.12. It does not mean that this can never happen or there is no equilibrium. It only means that the industry is not sustainable and the good is not produced, i.e., the equilibrium production and

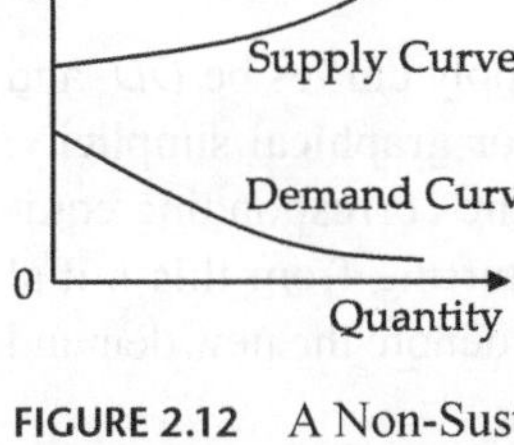

FIGURE 2.12 A Non-Sustainable Industry

consumption are zero—because the cost is too high relative to what the consumers are willing to pay.

However, it does *not* necessarily mean that the consumers cannot buy this product at all. If imports are allowed and the price of imports is low enough, then consumers can have it, although the domestic industry for the product is not sustainable and hence the domestic supply is zero. That is, the good is totally imported. For instance, at this point of writing, products like laser jet printers, computer memory chips, commercial jet planes, and certain kinds of drugs are totally imported by India. Note the following.

- An industry may not be sustainable in one country, but sustainable in another.
- Over time, a product, not sustainable earlier, can become sustainable in a country. For instance, colour TVs were not produced in India till the end of the 1970s. In the 1980s, the technology of producing colour TV became available in India and the market was large enough to start and sustain the colour TV industry.
- If a product becomes sustainable, it does not imply that we should *not* import any of it at all. Domestic production and imports can co-exist.

2.4 Demand and Supply Shifts

We return to the situation where there is an equilibrium with a positive quantity exchanged. Our demand–supply "model" can now be put to work in explaining various phenomena.

In reality, prices and quantities of products and services vary over time and space. A home in Florida, USA, that used to cost around \$300,000 in 2019 sold for much higher than \$500,000 in 2021. An Apple (or any) laptop of same specifications costs less and less over time. The South Indian delight *dosa* of a particular kind and quality may be selling for ₹100 in Delhi, India, whereas in Chennai, India, the same may be costing only ₹30. Our demand–supply analysis helps us to understand such phenomena—and more.

Methodologically, either the demand curve or the supply curve (or both) can shift and as a result price and quantities change. Hence, we need to first understand how such shifts affect equilibrium price and quantity.

2.4.1 Demand Shifts

Turn to Figure 2.13(a). Initially, let the demand and the supply curves be DD_0 and SS_0, respectively. They are drawn as straight lines just for graphical simplicity. The original equilibrium point is E_0, and, p_0 and Q_0 are the corresponding equilibrium price and the equilibrium quantity transacted. Starting from this initial situation, suppose there is an increase in demand. Let DD_1 denote the new demand

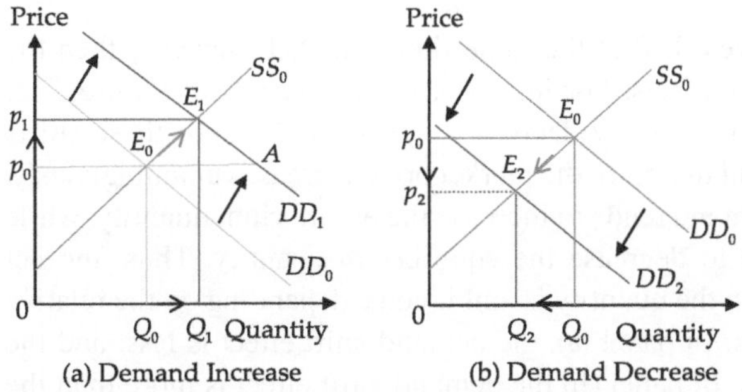

FIGURE 2.13 Effects of Demand Shifts

curve. We see that E_1 is the new market equilibrium point, p_1 is the new equilibrium price, and Q_1 the new equilibrium quantity. Hence an increase in demand raises both equilibrium price and quantity.

The "economic process" behind these changes is the following. As demand increases (from DD_0 to DD_1), at the original price (p_0) there is an excess demand (E_0A). This tends to push up the market price. As a result, the new equilibrium price is higher. There is no change in supply or the supply curve, and, because of a higher price, the producers move up along the (unchanged) supply curve and supply more to the market. Thus, a higher quantity is sold in the new equilibrium.

Panel (b) of Figure 2.13 exhibits a decrease in demand and its effects. As the demand curve shifts to the left from DD_0 to DD_2, at the original price there is an excess supply (equal to E_0B), which pushes the price down. The producers move down along the supply curve. Consequently, both equilibrium price and the equilibrium quantity transacted fall. The price and quantity at the new equilibrium are p_2 and Q_2, respectively.

2.4.2 Supply Shifts

These are shown in Figure 2.14. In panel (a) there is an increase in supply (from SS_0 to SS_1). At the original price this creates an excess supply (E_0B). This pushes the price down. There is no change in the demand curve. As the price falls, the demanders (the consumers) move down and to the right on their demand curve. In summary, the price falls (from p_0 to p_2), while the quantity increases (from Q_0 to Q_1).

Panel (b) of Figure 2.14 demonstrates a decrease in supply. The supply curve shifts to the left from SS_0 to SS_2. Initially, a decrease in supply causes an excess demand. The price rises. Consumers move up on the demand curve and buy less. These implications are the opposite of those of an increase in supply.

2.4.3 Simultaneous Shifts

It is possible that both curves shift at the same time. The net impact is then the sum of the two individual impacts. For instance, in both panels of Figure 2.15, the demand increases and the supply decreases. Individually, both these shifts tend to increase the price and therefore the market price increases unambiguously. However, an increase in demand tends to increase the equilibrium quantity, while a decrease in supply tends to decrease the equilibrium quantity. Thus, the net impact of these two shifts on the quantity is ambiguous, depending on the relative magnitude of the two shifts. In panel (a), the demand-shift effect is less, and the equilibrium quantity is less. In panel (b) the demand-shift effect is more than the supply-shift effect and thus, there is an increase in the equilibrium quantity available in the market.

You can similarly work out the effects of other joint shifts. Various outcomes are summarised in Table 2.8.

We now examine the effects of various *sources* of demand and supply shifts by analysing one at a time.

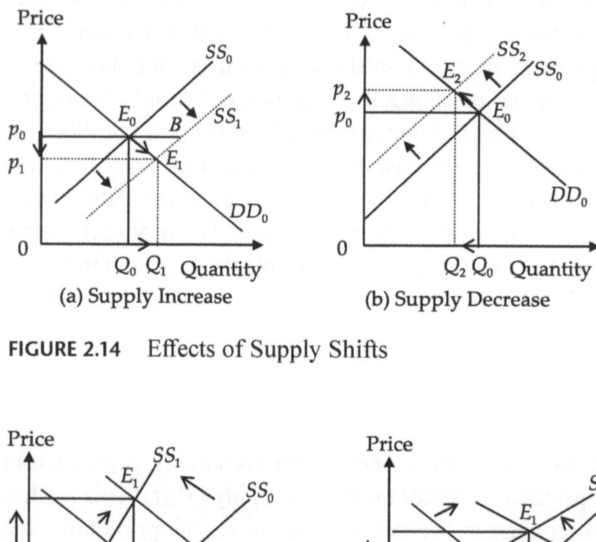

FIGURE 2.14 Effects of Supply Shifts

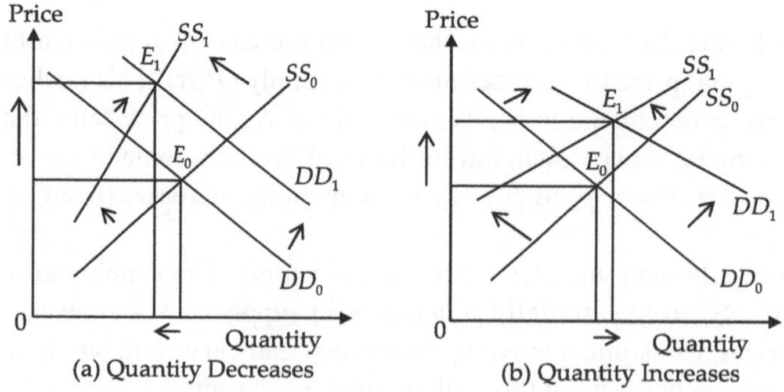

FIGURE 2.15 Effect of an Increase in Demand Combined with a Decrease in Supply

TABLE 2.8 Effects of Demand and Supply Shifts

Source(s) of Shift	*Effect on Price*	*Effect on Quantity*
(A) Demand ↑	↑	↑
(B) Demand ↓	↓	↓
(C) Supply ↑	↓	↑
(D) Supply ↓	↑	↓
(E) Demand ↑ & Supply ↑	↑↓	↑
(F) Demand ↑ & Supply ↓	↑	↑↓
(G) Demand ↓ & Supply ↑	↓	↑↓
(H) Demand ↓ & Supply ↓	↑↓	↓

2.4.4 Sources of Demand Shift

Suppose the total income of consumers in the market increases. If the good is normal, the market-demand curve will shift to the right. Row (A) in Table 2.8 applies. The equilibrium price will increase, and more quantity will be available in the market. If the good is inferior, row (B) applies. The effects are opposite: price and quantity will both decrease.

As a real-life example, in the 1990s, the prices of flats and land in many cities in the state of Kerala, India, skyrocketed. It was because many Keralites went to the Middle East for work and sent back their money to buy real estate. There was a major increase in the income of people in that region. Real estate is obviously not an inferior good. As our demand–supply "model" predicts, the real estate price increased dramatically.

Similarly, if the price of a substitute good increases, the demand curve of the good in question will shift to the right. Row (A) in Table 2.8 applies. Price and quantity will increase. For instance, if coffee becomes more expensive for some reason, people will switch to tea. The demand curve for tea will shift out. The price of tea will increase and more of tea will be sold in the market. Indeed, this happened in the world market of tea in the late 1990s. Brazil is the biggest producer of coffee in the world market. In the mid-1990s, coffee production in Brazil was severely curtailed by bad weather. The coffee price in the world market increased substantially and remained higher than before for a few years. It was observed that during the same years the price of tea also went up in the world market without any supply problems in tea as such. As other examples, (a) all else the same, a decrease in the price of iPhones will shift inward the demand curve for Android cell phones like Samsung and the price of Samsung cell phones will decline; (b) when smart watches by non-brand companies became available at low prices in the mid- and late 2010s, Apple had to lower the price of its iwatches.

On the other hand, if the price of a complementary good rises, the demand curve shifts to the left, (B) in Table 2.8 applies and both price and quantity fall.

If peoples' taste for a product improves (deteriorates), the demand curve shifts to the right (left). As a result, the price and the quantity both increase (decrease) in the market. As a hypothetical example, suppose medical research proves that eating 200 grams of lentil a day significantly improves memory. This will surely increase the demand for lentil. You will soon observe that lentil is costlier and more of it is sold in the market. As a real-life example, the demand for air travel plummeted right after September 11, 2001. This was due to the fear of terrorism, which can be interpreted as a change in taste for air travel. Consequently, the price of airline tickets within the United States went down considerably and there were much fewer scheduled flights. The same happened worldwide in 2020 during the Covid-19 pandemic.

Even if the individual demand curves remain the same, the market demand curve can shift if the number of consuming households changes. An increase (a decrease) in the number of consumers in the market will shift the market demand curve to the right (left). As a result, price and quantity both will increase (decrease). As an example, in the 1980s in Delhi, India, witnessed a surge in the price of land. It occurred because many people migrated from Punjab to Delhi, following disturbances in Punjab, and this shifted the market demand curve for real estate in Delhi. In recent times, due to Covid-19 and subsequent lockdowns, three sectors witnessed a massive increase in number of buyers. These are online shopping portals like Amazon and Flipkart, food delivery chains like Zomato and Swiggy, and, online coaching portals like Byju's. Set up in 2011 by a husband–wife team, Byju's became operational in 2015. Between 2015 and March 2020, it had 45 million users. After lockdown, within a few months, its user base rose to 70 million. Byju's valuation skyrocketed to a whopping $15 billion. On the other hand, sectors like aviation and travel nosedived due to massive fall in the number of users.

2.4.5 Sources of Supply Shift

In section 2.2 we learnt that the market supply curve can shift because of changes in technology, input prices, business taxes, and the number of firms in the market.

As technology improvement shifts the supply curve to the right, row (C) in Table 2.8 applies. The price falls and the quantity increases. Computer chips of any given speed are a prime example. Because of rapid technological progress in producing micro-chips, the supply curve of chips of a given speed has been shifting to the right and thus the price of the same micro-chip has been falling over time. A particular chip becomes obsolete after a few years.

We have also learnt that an increase in input prices shifts the supply curve to the left. How will it affect price and quantity? This is clear from row (D) in Table 2.8: the price will increase, and the quantity sold will fall. The opposite happens if input prices fall. Desktop computers are a good example. It has inputs like memory chip, motherboard, etc., and the prices of these inputs are falling over time. Thus, a computer with same configurations and quality is becoming cheaper over time.

As another example, between 2004 and 2005, the crude oil price in the world market soared. In the United States it led the average retail petrol price to increase from $1.87 in 2004 to $2.90 in 2005, a 55% increase. Petrol is used as an input in many businesses, which typically involve transport. In late 2005, FedEx, the premier courier service company announced that it would increase its air shipment rates by 3.5%.

In 2021, the Directorate General of Civil Aviation in India raised the Aviation Security Fee (ASF) from ₹160 to ₹200 per one domestic passenger. All else the same, it was expected to increase the price of domestic airfare.

An increase or a decrease in business taxes works analogous to an increase or a decrease in an input price. An application of how the price of a service is affected by input prices and taxes, see Box 2.4.

BOX 2.4 UNFAIR AIRFARE

A while ago, on October 13, 2004, a daily newspaper in India, *Hindustan Times*, ran an article "Unfair Air Fare." The main point was that air fares in India were very high compared to rates outside–in some cases it was about *three times* as high. For example, based on 21 days advance ticket booking, a one-way flight from Delhi to Trivandrum was costing ₹13,120 and the flying time was two hours and forty-five minutes. In comparison, Delhi to Singapore was costing ₹15, 750 one-way and the flying time was five hours and thirty minutes.

Why were the rates so high in India? While the airlines blamed it on fuel prices, the article argued that flawed policy and "back-breaking" taxes were factors. For instance, because of government policy on fuel prices, the Air Turbine Fuel (ATF) rates in India were about 2 ½ times more than elsewhere. In Singapore, one kilo-litre of ATF was costing ₹15,100, whereas in India it was ₹30,000. There was also 8% excise tax and sales taxes ranged from 4% to 29% by different states. Furthermore, navigation charges and landing fees constituted about 30% of operating costs whereas in other countries they were about 15% of operating costs.

This is an example of how input prices and business taxes affect the market price of a service.

We also learnt in section 2.2 that an increase or a decrease in the expected future price of a product may motivate sellers to respectively hoard or flood the market with their goods in the current period. In other words, as the price of a product in the *future* is expected to decrease or increase, the *current* supply curve will shift to the right or to the left with a result that the current price will decrease or increase.

As a prime example, think of stocks of various companies, which are sold in the share market—pretty much like other commodities. Investors' expectations about the *future* play a big role in determining a stock price. As a hypothetical example, if investors dream that the price of a stock that they are holding is going to double in the next few weeks (and they believe in their dreams), they are going to buy more of this stock today. If many investors think the same way, it will impact the stock market today—*irrespective* of whether or not their expectations turn out to be correct in the future. Of course, investors have some basis of their expectations. The point is that expectations about the future, regardless of their merits, will impact the stock price in the current period.

As an example, on Monday, May 17, 2004, the "Sensex," an index of selected stocks in the Indian stock market, fell precipitously—by 565 points (11%). This was completely unprecedented in the history of the Bombay Stock Exchange. Why? It was because the UPA (a political coalition in India) registered an unexpected win in the general elections at that time. This led many important investors to think that the country may roll back on the reforms, which would adversely affect business, profits, and the stock price in the future. Thus, there was a decrease in the expected future price of stocks. The investors sold their stocks in huge volumes, which resulted in a huge drop in the stock prices across the board. Some people have called this day as the "Black Monday" of the Indian stock market. More recently, on November 9, 2016, Sensex crashed by 1,624 points (around 6%) due to the demonetisation of big currency notes in India and the fear of crackdown on black money. Again, on February 28, 2020, Sensex crashed by about 5% due to Covid-19 fears. Those of you who are keenly interested in the share market in India must have seen umpteen times the sudden spurt or fall in Sensex based purely on expectations about the future.

A change in the number of firms affects the market supply curve too. An increase in the number of firms, for example, would shift the market supply curve to the right. As a result, the price will fall, and a higher quantity will be sold. In common language, this is the case of *an increase in competition.*

The telecommunication market in India is a good example. In the early 1990s, Mahanagar Telephone Nigam Limited (MTNL) was the sole provider of the International Subscriber Dialling (ISD) facility in Delhi. An ISD call from India to America cost over ₹50 per minute. By 2004/2005, there were other land-line providers like Tata-Indicom, Reliance, and Touchtel which cost only less than ₹10 per minute. Much more recently, in the early 2020s, with another company, Jio coming in landlines have virtually become a thing of the past. *WhatsApp* has further made it possible to connect to anyone in the world at virtually no cost.

When mobile phones came to India in the late 1990s, incoming and outgoing call rates were ₹8 and ₹16 per minute, respectively, besides a huge monthly rental. In 2020s, it is almost unimaginable that such high rates existed two to three decades ago. The rates in the 2020s are much cheaper due to greater number of cell phone carriers.

Domestic air travel in India is another classic example of a massive fall in price due to an increase in competition. Earlier, Air India, or more specifically Indian Airlines, was the sole provider of domestic air travel. As competition was allowed, many private players entered, bringing down airfares to such low levels that it has become cheaper sometimes to fly by air than to travel first class by railways.

Facts and Insights

- The quantity demanded of a product is dependent on own price, prices of related goods, income, tastes, and future price expectations.
- *Ceteris paribus*, an increase (a decrease) in the own price tends to reduce (increase) the quantity demanded of a product. This is the Law of Demand.
- An increase in income may increase the demand for a product (this is the case of a normal good) or decrease the demand for a product (this is the case of an inferior good). Accordingly, the demand curve shifts to the right (left) for a normal (inferior) good as income increases.
- In reality, there are very few goods, which are inferior.
- An increase in the price of a substitute good tends to increase the demand for a given good, i.e., shift the demand curve of a given product to the right, while an increase in the price of a complementary good tends to do the opposite.
- A taste change in favour of a product shifts its demand curve to the right.
- An increase in price expectations shifts the current demand curve for a product to the right.
- The Veblen effect, bandwagon effect, snob effect, and network externality refer to situations where other people's demand affects the demand behaviour of an individual.
- Market demand curve is the horizontal summation of individual demand curves.
- A change in demand refers to a shift of the demand curve, while a change in the quantity demanded refers to a movement along a given demand curve.
- The quantity supplied of a product is dependent on own price, prices of related goods in production, technology, input prices, business taxes, and future price expectations.
- *Ceteris paribus*, an increase (a decrease) in the own price tends to increase (decrease) the quantity supplied of a product. This is the law of supply.
- An increase in the price of a substitute good in production decreases the supply a product in question.
- A technology improvement shifts the supply curve to the right, while an increase in an input price shifts the supply curve of a product to the left.
- Business taxes like GST (Goods and Service Tax) can be seen as a part of the overall costs of production. An increase in the business taxes shifts the supply curve to the left.

- An increase in the expected future price of a product tends to reduce its *current* supply.
- Market supply curve is the horizontal summation of the individual supply curves.
- A change in supply refers to a shift of the supply curve, while a change in the quantity supplied refers to a movement along a given demand curve.
- If at a price, the quantity demanded exceeds the quantity supplied, i.e., there is an excess demand, competition among buyers to acquire the good pushes the price up. Likewise, if there is an excess supply, i.e., the quantity supplied exceeds the quantity demanded, competition among the suppliers drives the price down.
- Market equilibrium is achieved at that price at which quantity demanded is equated with quantity supplied. In this sense, price mechanism co-ordinates the decision-making by consumers and producers.
- A non-sustainable domestic industry does not imply that the consumers are not able to consume the product at all, because they may be able to import the product.
- An increase (a decrease) in demand causes the equilibrium price and the quantity transacted to increase (decrease), whereas an increase (a decrease) in supply causes the equilibrium price to fall (rise) and the equilibrium quantity transacted to increase (decrease). These implications form the basis of how various demand and supply shifts, individually or together, may affect the price and the quantity transacted.

Exercises

Descriptive/Analytical

2.1. What does a demand curve tell? What does it assume as given?

2.2. Explain the determinants of market demand curve.

2.3. Explain in terms of excess demand and supply how equilibrium in a market is established at the price where quantity demanded and quantity supplied are equal to each other.

2.4. "An increase or shift in the market demand curve will shift the market supply curve as well." Defend or refute.

If the demand curve and the supply curve of a product do not intersect, explain what it means or implies.

2.6. How will a simultaneous increase in demand and a decrease in supply affect the market price and quantity transacted?

2.7. How will a simultaneous decrease in demand and supply affect the market price and quantity transacted?

2.8. (A very India-centric question) Do research on Tata Nano Singur crisis in West Bengal in the late 2000s. Explain the controversy in terms of demand and supply forces affecting the price of land.

Short Answer (word limit = 500 approx.)

2.9. How would a speculation that petrol price is going to be doubled in next two days will affect your demand for petrol today and why?
2.10. It is announced that a new steel plant will come up in an area within a year's time. How will it affect the demand for land in that area *now*? Which determinant of demand is at work here?
2.11. Explain the Veblen effect in demanding a good.
2.12. Differentiate between the bandwagon effect and the snob effect.
2.13. What is network externality?
2.14 A furniture manufacturer in Mumbai faces an increase in the price of teak wood. How will it affect its supply curve of furniture to the market?
2.15 Referring to the previous question, the furniture manufacturer has found a new mechanised way of polishing furniture, which reduces costs by 20%. Will this result in a change the quantity supplied or a change in supply by the furniture manufacturer? Give reasons.
2.16 A farmer has some land, a part of which is used for growing wheat and the remaining for corn. Starting with a given supply curve of corn, if wheat begins to fetch a higher price in the market, how will the farmer's supply curve of corn be affected and why?
2.17 Suppose the government reduces the business tax imposed on a particular sector. How will this affect the supply curve?
2.18 All else the same, how will an increase in the business tax affect the market price and quantity of a product?
2.19 A massive flood cuts off supplies of essentials like edible oil, onions, etc. to a particular region. All else the same, how might this affect the current supply of edible oil by local sellers, and, why?
2.20 How will entry of foreign firms into a particular sector shift the individual supply curves by local firms and the market supply curve?
2.21 Illustrate the situation where a domestic industry is not viable or sustainable. Does it mean that the consumers cannot consume a product?

Quizzes/Numerical

2.22 John stays in the college dormitory. He used to get a stipend of $1,000 a month from his father for personal expenses. Recently, his father has become more generous and gives him $1,500. We observe that John is going to a lot more movies than before but eating less at the nearby McDonald's. There are no changes in the prices of movie ticket or food at McDonald's. From this, can we say that both movies and food at McDonald's are normal goods for John? Why or why not?

2.23 There are train and bus services between Tokyo and Osaka (two major cities in Japan). Suppose the train fares between the two cities come down. How will it affect the demand for bus travel between the two cities? Which determinant of demand is at work here?

2.24 Name two pairs of non-food items (besides those cited in the text) such that one is complementary in consumption to the other.

2.25 Because movie tickets have become more costly, Zorba goes out to see movies less often and hence is also eating out less in restaurants. Can we infer from this that there has been a change in demand by Zorba for movies but a change in quantity demanded for restaurant food?

2.26 A local fisherman catches fish from a near-by river early in the morning and sells all his catch by the same day (he doesn't have any storing facility). Consider his daily supply curve of fish to the market, *after* fish is caught in the morning. Is it upward sloping, i.e., will quantity supplied increase if there is an increase in the market price of fish?

2.27 "Under any price below (respectively above) the market price, there is excess demand (respectively excess supply) in a market." Defend or refute.

Given the following market demand and the supply functions: $Q_d = 160 - 4p$ (Demand Function) and $Q_s = -20 + 2p$ (Supply Function), respectively,

a) Find the market clearing price and quantity. Show diagrammatically.
b) What happens if the prevailing market price is 40?

Given the market demand and supply functions, $Q_d = 160 - 4p$ (Demand Function) and $Q_s = -100 + 2p$ (Supply Function), respectively, can you find the equilibrium price and quantity? Why or why not?

Two firms producing an identical commodity are faced with identical demand function in their respective market domains which are mutually exclusive. The demand function is $Q_d = 160 - 4p$. Notice that, at price = €30, both have market quantity demanded equal to 40 units. Suppose that they both plan to increase sales volume to 60 units. One plans to do it by reducing price while the other plans to do so by more advertising. Show these changes with the help of suitable diagrams. Assume that additional advertisement has a positive impact on sales.

Appendix 2.A Solving Market Equilibrium, Mathematically

Suppose the demand and the supply functions are given, respectively, as $q_D = a - bp$ and $q_S = c + gp$, where a, b, $g > 0$ and $a > c$. Because b and g are positive, the demand function is downward-sloping, and the supply curve is upward-sloping.

The restriction $a > c$ ensures that both curves intersect in the positive quadrant (otherwise it is a case of a non-sustainable industry).

Market equilibrium is defined as $q_D = q_S$, that is, quantity demanded equals the quantity supplied. Given the expressions of q_D and q_S, the market equilibrium condition is:

$$a - bp = c + gp.$$

This is one equation in one variable, p. We can solve it and let the solution be denoted as p_0. From the above equation,

$$p_0 = \frac{a-c}{b+g},$$

where p_0 is the equilibrium price. Notice that if a were less than or equal to c, p_0 would have been negative or zero.

Given p_0, we solve the equilibrium quantity, say q_0, by substituting the solution expression of p_0 into either the demand function or the supply function. Substituting into the demand function

$$a - bp_0 = a - \frac{b(a-c)}{b+g} = \frac{ag+bc}{b+g} = q_0.$$

We would obtain exactly the same expression of q_0 had we substituted the expression of p_0 into the supply function, $c + gp$.

Appendix 2.B Business Taxes in India

A business tax is an indirect tax which is levied on the producer/seller but is wholly or partly shifted to the buyers thus causing the price of a commodity to rise. Earlier, in India, there was a multiplicity of tax rates imposed both by the central and state governments and these varied from state to state, thus resulting in different prices for the same commodity. However, in 2017, GST (Goods and Service Tax) replaced the old system, and it was applicable to the whole nation. It proposed five tax slabs (ranging from 0% to 28%) for various commodities. However, petroleum products, alcoholic drinks, and electricity are not in GST and are taxed separately by respective state governments. Service tax is levied on intangibles, which was around 15%.

Notes

1 There may be other factors. For instance, a change in weather is likely to affect your demand for ice cream.

2 An inverse relationship between two entities means that, as one increases, the other decreases.

3 "Chat" is an Indian snack. Chat masala is complementary to chat. That is why, it is called "chat masala" in the first place.
4 It is named after Thorstein Veblen, an American economist and psychologist in the late 19th and the early 20th century.
5 Although Facebook is "free," it has its own cost or price for you like being bombarded with ads for products you browsed elsewhere, less sound sleep at night, greater chance of being admonished by your elders etc.
6 By "market," one could mean an entire city, a province, region, country or even the whole world. It depends on the context of the analysis.
7 Note that at any price equal to or greater than p_2 the quantity demanded of ice-cream by Rekha and Rachel is zero. Thus, the total quantity demanded is same as the quantity demanded by Reshma only. Similarly, at any price between p_1 nd p_2 the quantity demanded by Rekha is zero. Hence the total quantity demanded equals to the sum of quantities demanded by Reshma and Rachel. At any price below p_1 all three individuals demand positive quantities, which are added to obtain the total quantity demanded in the market.
8 Note that if there were 10 or 10 thousand individuals in the market, we would have done the same thing in principle: add up the quantities demanded by all individuals in the market at each price.
9 Households sometimes hoard too, as it happened during the initial phase of the second Covid-19 wave in India. People were hoarding oxygen and vital medicines.
10 Appendix 2.A provides an algebraic solution for the equilibrium price in a linear demand–supply model.

Bibliography

Bhalla, G. S., Hazell, P., & Kerr, J. (1999). *Prospects for India's cereal supply and demand to 2020* (Food, Agriculture, and Environment Discussion Paper 29). International Food Policy Research Institute.

Kumar, P. (1998). *Food demand and supply projections for India* (Agricultural Economics Policy Paper 98-01). Indian Agricultural Research Institute.

McKenzie, D. (2002). Are tortillas a Giffen good in Mexico? *Economic Bulletin, 15*, 1–7.

Minot, M., & Goletti, F. (2000). *Rice market liberalization and poverty in Viet Nam* (Research Report No. 114). International Food Policy Research Institute.

Rosegrant, M. W., Agcaoili-Sombilla, M., & Perez, N. (1995). *Global food projections to 2020: Implications for investment* (Vision Discussion Paper No. 5). International Food Policy Research Institute.

3

ELASTICITY OF DEMAND AND SUPPLY

3.1 Introduction

In Chapter 2, we have learnt that a rational individual will tend to buy less of a commodity if its price increases, all else remaining unchanged or *ceteris paribus*. Aggregating this behaviour over many individuals or households in a village, city, or region gives us a downward-sloping market-demand curve.

In contrast, sellers/producers increase the production and supply of a commodity as its price increases, *ceteris paribus*. Aggregating individual supply curves yields an upward-sloping market-supply curve. However, the laws of demand and supply and how different factors other than own price affect quantities demanded and supplied tell us the *direction* of buyers' and sellers' responses, respectively, and not the *magnitude* of variations in quantities demanded or supplied. This chapter discusses and develops the concept of *elasticity* which is widely used to *quantify* the responsiveness of the quantity demanded or supplied of a good to changes in various factors.

Why is this important? Read the story outlined in *Activity 3.1*. The word "elasticity" does not figure anywhere in it. But, as you will soon realise, it is the concept of elasticity that helps solve the "puzzle" in *Activity 3.1*.

ACTIVITY 3.1

In majority of the business schools in India, three major functional specialisations are offered: marketing, finance, and human resources (HR). Normally, 50% of students opt for marketing, 40% for finance, and 10% for HR. Barring

DOI: 10.4324/9781003452195-3

the top 30–40 from elite business schools, most of the students with marketing specialisation get their first placement in the sales department. In finance and HR, fresh hires are given the task of roping in more clients. Suppose you get placed in a reputed company that sells refrigerators. Naturally, a sales profile is made available to you. Your boss calls a meeting of sales representatives including you to discuss the ways to increase sales and sales revenues. You immediately recall the Law of Demand from this course and distinctly remember the following example of the two goods whose prices are reduced, resulting in an increase in their respective quantity demanded.

Refrigerator Price	*Quantity Demanded*	*Salt Price*	*Quantity Demanded*
10,000	100	50	100
9,000	130	45	105

Based on the data from the first two columns, you recommend a small reduction in price as a strategy to boost sales, and thereby increase revenues from sales. Suppose your boss likes your suggestion and implements it straightway. At the end of the quarter, when sales figures are compiled, there is a big jump in sales and sales revenues. You become a star performer, get the employee of the quarter prize, and a decent bonus. Nothing succeeds like success. Shortly thereafter, a salt manufacturer offers you a job in his marketing division with a handsome pay package which you can't refuse. So, you shift job. In your new company, you are once again faced with the same task: How to increase the sales and revenues from sales? The Law of Demand flashes in your mind again. This time, based on the numbers in the last two columns, you recommend a price cut so that more quantities are sold—as you did in your previous company. Your new boss accepts your recommendation, and the price of salt is reduced. At the quarter's end, you expect praise and bonus from your boss. But, to your utter dismay and shock, nothing like that happens. On the contrary, the response of your boss is rude and shocking. You wonder what went wrong and re-check the above-given table. A fall in price of both the goods causes an increase in the quantity demanded. You still fail to understand why a price cut in both cases resulted in diametrically opposite response from your bosses. "The fault, dear Brutus, lies in ourselves, not in our stars," said William Shakespeare. We suggest that you carefully analyse the table to find an answer to your puzzle.

Hints:

1. Check the percentage change in price and quantity demanded of the two commodities.

2. Remember, the companies are interested in increasing sales volume if and only if it results in an increase in sales *revenues*. Check the sales revenues in both cases. Did you realise your mistake?

Still confused? Then get going on this chapter. Not confused? You will still find many things that are informative and useful.

Indeed, elasticity as a quantitative measure of the response of a variable to changes in related variables is a general concept, not confined to demand and supply. Suppose a variable y changes, in part, due to a change in x. It could be how the exchange rate between two currencies changes with respect to a change in the short-term interest rate in one of the countries, how the real GDP of a country changes with respect to the flow of foreign direct investment (FDI), and so on. In general:

$$\text{Elasticity of } y \text{ with respect to } x = \frac{\text{Proportional change in } y}{\text{Proportional change in } x}. \tag{3.1}$$

Notice importantly that the elasticity is not a measure of absolute change but *proportional* change, hence unit-independent. It does not matter, for example, whether y is measured in metres or kilometres or x is measured in thousands or millions.

How do we operationalise equation (3.1) in the context of changes in quantities demanded and quantities supplied?[1]

3.2 Elasticity of Demand

We know from Chapter 2 that the quantity demanded depends on own price, prices of related goods, income, etc. The quantitative measure of the impact of changes in these determinants on quantity demanded is the respective elasticity.

3.2.1 Price Elasticity of Demand

It measures the responsiveness of the quantity demanded to a change in the own price, and is defined by:

$$e_p = -\frac{\%\text{ change in quantity demanded}}{\%\text{ change in own price}} \tag{3.2}$$

Since own price and the quantity demanded move in opposite ways, the percentage changes in the quantity demanded and own price bear opposite signs. The ratio of the two percentage changes is negative. Adding the negative sign in front of the formula in equation (3.2) makes e_p positive and is indicative of the *magnitude* of response. That is, e_p gives the *absolute* value of the price elasticity of demand.[2] By definition, the greater the responsiveness of the quantity demanded for the same proportionate change in price, the higher is the price elasticity.

There are alternative methods to measure proportional changes, and, accordingly, alternative ways of operationalising e_p.

Simple Percentage Method

This method directly applies the formula given in equation (3.2). Let the original price of a product be p_0, at which the quantity demanded is q_0. Suppose the own price changes to p_1 and accordingly (along the demand curve) the quantity demanded changes to q_1. Then the percentage changes in price and quantity demanded have the following expressions, respectively:

$$\frac{p_1 - p_0}{p_0} \times 100; \quad \frac{q_1 - q_0}{q_0} \times 100. \tag{3.3}$$

The first one goes in the denominator (3.3) and the second in the numerator. Hence,

$$e_p = -\frac{(q_1 - q_0)/q_0}{(p_1 - p_0)/p_0} \tag{3.4}$$

In economics, a change in a variable is typically denoted by the capital Greek letter Δ (pronounced Delta). For example, ” q_d would denote the change in the quantity demanded, equal to $q_1 - q_0$, and, similarly ” p would denote $p_1 - p_0$. Using this notation, we can also write (3.4) as:

$$e_p = -\frac{(\Delta q_d)/q_d}{(\Delta p)/p}. \tag{3.5}$$

Here is a numerical example that uses (3.4) or (3.5) follows.

Example 3.1

Rita used to consume 10 ice creams a month when the price of her favourite vanilla ice cream was \$2. Ice cream has become more expensive, \$3 per cone. Rita now consumes 8 ice creams a month. What is e_p of Rita's demand for vanilla ice cream?

Answer: The original price and quantity are: $p_0 = 2$ and $q_0 = 10$. The new price and quantity are: $p_1 = 3$ and $q_1 = 8$. The percentage increase in price is 50% and the percentage decline in quantity consumed is 20%. Applying equations (3.4) or (3.5), ■

$$e_p = -\frac{-20}{50} = 0.4. \tag{3.6}$$

Arc Elasticity

There is however a problem with the percentage method. Consider the above numerical example, except that the new price and quantity were, respectively, the old price and quantity, and the old price and quantity were, respectively, the new price and quantity. Thus, $p_0 = 3$, $q_0 = 8$, $p_1 = 2$, and $q_1 = 10$. Since the concept of elasticity refers to the magnitude of the response of the quantity demanded to a price change, the order between which is the old and which is the new price–quantity combination should not ideally matter. But it does. Apply (3.4) or (3.5), to this example, and you will find that e_p is *not* what is given in (3.6). It is equal to 0.75.

It is not hard to see why the discrepancy arises. It is because the denominator of the percentage change of price or the quantity is sensitive to which is the original price or quantity. To get around this problem, a compromise is used. Instead of p_0 in the denominator of the percentage change of price, we take $(p_0 + p_1)/2$, the average of the original price and the new price. Similarly, q_0 in the numerator of the percentage change in the quantity is replaced by $(q_0 + q_1)/2$. Then the equation becomes:

$$e_p = -\frac{(q_1 - q_0)(p_0 + p_1)}{(q_0 + q_1)(p_1 - p_0)}. \tag{3.7}$$

This is called the **arc elasticity**. According to this measure, the computed price elasticity is independent of which is the original price–quantity combination. In Example 3.1, the arc elasticity $= 5/9 \cong 0.55$.

Example 3.2

Earlier, Pran, an avid movie-goer who lives in Mumbai, India, was seeing five movies per month, when the price of a movie in his favourite cinema hall was ₹400. In the past year the price came down to ₹300 and he was seeing seven movies per month. Assume that, for Pran, all movies are of the same quality. What is the arc elasticity of demand for movies by Pran?

Answer: Here the original price and quantity demanded are: $p_0 = 400$ and $q_0 = 5$. The new price and quantity demanded are: $p_1 = 300$ and $q_1 = 7$. Thus, $p_0 + p_1 = 700$, $q_0 + q_1 = 12$, $p_1 - p_0 = -100$, and $q_1 - q_0 = 2$. Applying the equation given in (3.7), the arc elasticity is equal to 1.17. ■

Geometric Method and Point Elasticity

Arc elasticity is an approximate formula. It is appropriate when the price change is not small. When the price change is relatively small, we can use a graphical formula or a **geometric method**. This is illustrated in Figure 3.1.

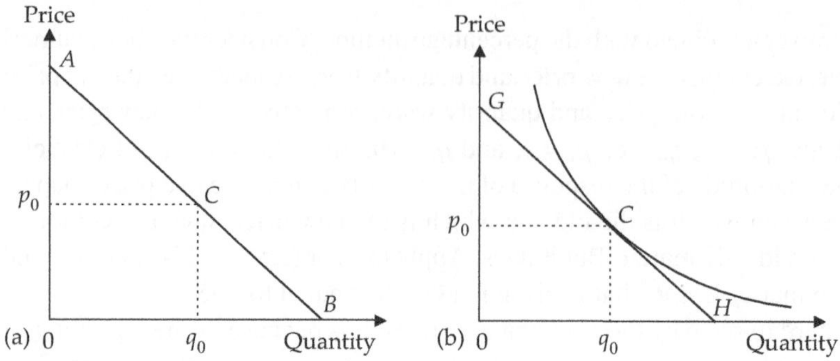

FIGURE 3.1 Point Elasticity of Demand

Consider Panel (a). The demand curve is a straight line with intercepts *A* and *B*. Let the initial price be p_0. At this price, the consumer demands the amount q_0, i.e., she is at point *C* on the demand line. Then, as shown mathematically in Appendix 0.A, for a very arbitrarily small price variation from p_0, either upward or downward, e_p is equal to BC / CA, the ratio of the lower segment to the upper segment of the line *AB*.[3]

If the demand curve is not a straight line, it is a bit more complicated but essentially the same. Suppose the demand curve looks like the one shown in panel (b) and we are asked to compute the price elasticity at the price p_0.Now, draw the tangent of the demand curve at the price where the elasticity is to be computed. At p_0, this is GH. For a very small price change, e_p turns out to be equal to HC / CG, again the ratio of the lower to the upper segment. This is also proven in Appendix 3.A.

This ratio formula is called **point elasticity**, wherein the word "point" refers to a small variation. In general, *the point elasticity at a given price is equal to the ratio of the lower segment to the upper segment of the demand line at that price or the same ratio on the tangent of the demand curve at that price.*

Example 3.3

Suppose the demand curve for a product is a straight line as shown in Figure 3.2. Its intercept on the price axis equals 30. Calculate the point elasticity at the price $p_0 = 9$.

Answer: Since $p_0 = 9$, we have $BE = 0D = 9$ and $AD = 0A - 0D = 30 - 9 = 21$. Hence, $BE / AD = 9 / 21 = 3 / 7$. The triangles *BEC* and *ADB* are similar. Thus, $BE / AD = BC / AB$. Since $BE / AD = 3 / 7$, we have BC / AB, the measure of point elasticity, equal to 3/7.

Suppose there are two intersecting demand curves as shown in Figure 3.3. We can say that at the price where the two curves intersect, the flatter demand curve (D_B compared to D_A) is more price elastic. This is because the flatter demand curve shows greater quantity variation from a given price variation.[4] ■

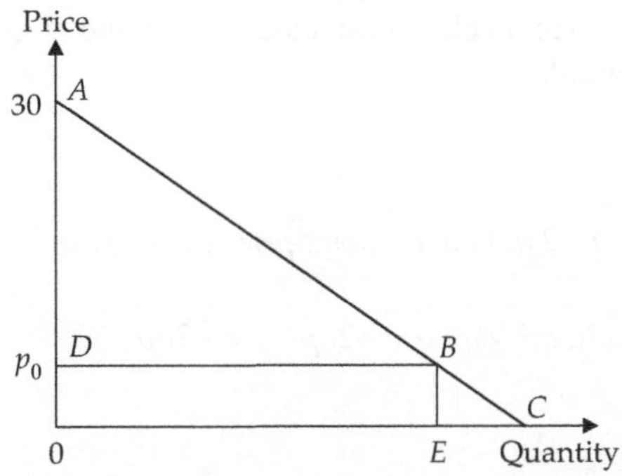

FIGURE 3.2 Computing Point Elasticity of Demand

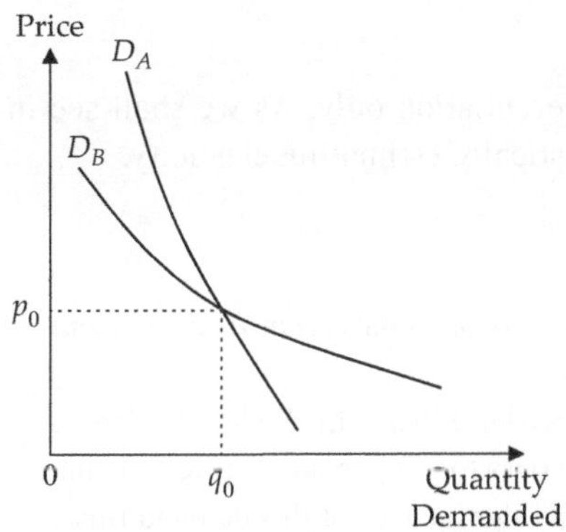

FIGURE 3.3 Comparing Point Elasticities of Demand

Log Formula for Elasticity

Point elasticity has an algebraic expression. Let the small change in price be denoted by the "calculus" symbol *dp* and let the corresponding change in quantity demanded be *dq*. Hence, proportional changes are *dp/p* and *dq/q*, respectively, and we write price elasticity equal to:

$$e_p = -\frac{dq / q}{dp / p}. \tag{3.8}$$

At this point, recall the natural log function from high-school algebra, $\ln x$. If we differentiate it with respect to x, $d\ln x / dx = 1 / x$ and thus $d\ln x = dx / x$. Substituting this into (3.8) for $x = q$ and $x = p$, we can write:

$$e_p = -\frac{d\ln q}{d\ln p}. \tag{3.9}$$

This is a convenient formula. If we are given a demand function algebraically and asked to find price elasticity at some price level, we can easily apply the "log formula" of elasticity (3.9). Here is an example.

Example 3.4

Consider a linear demand function $q = 100 - 2p$. Find the point-price elasticity at a price equal to 30?

Answer: We have $dq = -2dp$. Hence, $d\ln q = dq/q = -2dp/q = -2dp/(100-2p)$, implying

$$-\frac{d\ln q}{d\ln p} = -\frac{-2dp/(100-2p)}{dp/p} = \frac{2p}{100-2p}.$$

Just substitute $p = 30$ into the above. The price elasticity of demand = $2\times 30/(100-2\times 30) = 1.5$. ■

The log formula essentially involves one differentiation only. As we shall see in Chapter 6, the next example is useful for statistically estimating elasticity.

Example 3.5

Consider a nonlinear demand function $q = Ap^{-b}$. What is the algebraic expression for price elasticity?

Answer: Applying natural log to both sides, we have $\ln q = \ln A - b\ln p$. Hence, the price elasticity $= -d\ln q / d\ln p = b$. That is, the exponent of price in this demand function itself is the price elasticity. The significance of this demand function is that the price elasticity is constant: it does not change with a change in price. In Chapter 6, we will discuss how one can statistically estimate b from data. ■

Indeed, the log formula is general, not specific to the price elasticity of demand. Consider any function $y = f(x)$. For small changes in x, the elasticity of y with respect to x equals:

$$e_{yx} = \frac{d\ln y}{d\ln x}. \tag{3.10}$$

Elastic and Inelastic Demand

These concepts relate to whether the (magnitude of the) price elasticity exceeds or falls short of unity. If $e_p > 1$, we say that the product demand is **elastic.** If $e_p < 1$, the demand is said to be **inelastic**. What factors determine whether the product is price-elastic or price-inelastic will be discussed shortly.

In the intermediate case of $e_p = 1$, the demand for the product is **unitarily elastic**, i.e., the demand is neither elastic nor inelastic. In this case, the demand curve has a particular mathematical shape called a rectangular parabola, which is asymptotic to both the x-axis and y-axis, as shown in Figure 3.4(a).

There are two other special cases. If $e_p = 0$, then the product demand is said to be **perfectly inelastic**. This holds when there is no change in quantity demanded as price changes, i.e., the product is absolutely essential to the consumer. A very bad case of addiction is a typical example. If someone is badly addicted to smoking and "has" to smoke a pack a day, he/she may buy 1 pack a day irrespective of what the price of cigarettes is (so long as cigarettes are not too costly). This is shown in Figure 3.4(b), where the demand curve is vertical. Figure 3.4(c) depicts the opposite case when e_p is infinite and the demand curve is a flat (horizontal) line. In this case the demand is **perfectly elastic.** An example will be considered in Chapter 8.[5]

Determinants of Price Elasticity

A major factor dictating price elasticity is *the availability of close substitutes.* If close substitutes are not available to a consumer, a consumer is likely to be too "dependent" on the product and hence her demand for it is likely to be relatively inelastic. Essential items, by definition, do not have very many closed substitutes and therefore the demand for them is typically inelastic.

Price elasticity depends also on *whether the good in question is a narrowly defined product or a broadly defined one.* Suppose the price of Levi's jeans increases, while prices of other brands like Lee and Wrangler are unchanged. This will lead to a large decline in the demand for Levi's jeans because Levi's jeans are a narrowly defined product and there are close substitutes available. But if we are looking at a product like a family's consumption of casual clothing in general, the demand for it is likely to be inelastic since clothing is essential. Thus, all else the same, the price elasticity of a narrowly defined product is likely to be high and that of a broadly defined product is likely to be relatively small.

Whether a good is a necessity, a comfort, or a luxury also has a bearing on price elasticity. Those commodities and services that we "require" for a minimal, normal living are necessities. They include milk, toothpaste, etc. The demand for a necessity is relatively inelastic, i.e., $e_p < 1$. We can define comforts as those which enhance a person's productivity, efficiency, and, to some extent, pleasure.

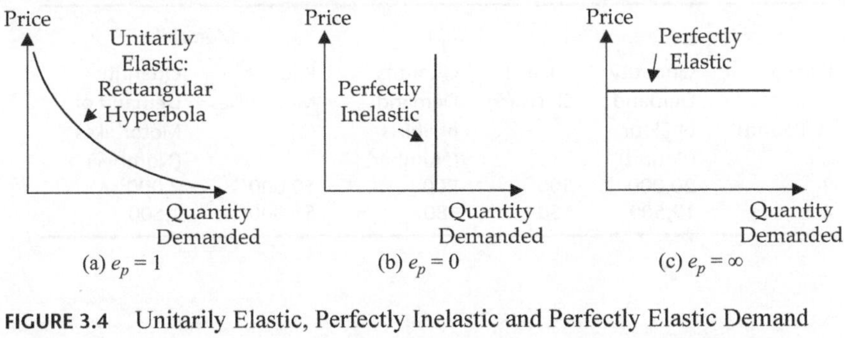

FIGURE 3.4 Unitarily Elastic, Perfectly Inelastic and Perfectly Elastic Demand

They are bought primarily by the middle-income group, which is highly price-conscious. The demand for comforts is normally relatively elastic, i.e., $e_p > 1$.

Comforts stretched beyond a limit become luxuries. A small or midsize car is a comfort, but beyond that it is a luxury like, say, a Mercedes E-Class. Dining in a five- or seven-star hotel like Taj in Mumbai or Lake Palace Hotel in Udaipur, and, keeping a team of gourmet food cooks at home 24×7 are examples of service luxuries. Luxuries are partly things of display and bought typically by the rich, for whom they are necessities. Hence, we can say that the demand for luxuries is relatively inelastic, i.e., $e_p < 1$.

Another determinant is *the proportion of total expenditure spent on the product.* If this proportion is large, a consumer's demand will be quite sensitive to a price change, i.e., the elasticity will be high. But if the proportion of total expenditure spent on the product is small, as for salt for example, the elasticity is likely to be small.

Individual habits also matter. A product may be very "essential" for some but not for others. You may not be a regular jogger and hence your demand for jogging shoes may be elastic. But your friend may be an avid jogger and her demand for jogging shoes may be inelastic.

All else the same, *time period* affects price elasticity. The greater the time horizon, the higher is the elasticity of demand for the same product. It is because if the time period is short, it is hard to find or develop substitutes of a product. In a longer horizon it is easier. The oil price shock experienced by the world economy in the early 1970s is a prime example. Within a year, the price of oil increased by more than threefold. The world economy was badly hit—because almost all countries were greatly dependent on oil and their demand for oil was inelastic. Over time, however, other forms of energy were explored. The demand for oil is less elastic now than it was back in the mid-1970s. In recent times, there has been an increasing emphasis on alternative energy that is likely to reduce our demand for oil in a major way.

ACTIVITY 3.2

Consider the behaviour of buyers in a market with respect to three commodities: flour, T-shirt, and motorbike:

Flour		*T-Shirt*		*Motorbike*	
Price of Flour ($/Pound)	Quantity Demand of Flour (Pound)	Price of Shirts ($)	Quantity Demand of Shirts (Number)	Price of Motorbikes ($)	Quantity Demand of Motorbikes (Number)
3	20,000	500	200	50,000	2,000
4.5	19,500	550	180	55,000	1,500

The first and the second rows indicate the price and quantities in the original and the new situation. What do you notice? In all three cases, an increase in price results in a decrease in the quantity demanded. The Law of Demand operates. Fine! However, do you notice an interesting pattern? We have deliberately increased the price of all commodities by the same proportion, i.e., by 10%. However, we find the responses to this equal price increase in terms of percentage change in the quantity demanded are different.

Calculate the percentage change in the quantity demanded due to an equal percentage change (10%) of price in all three items. (Hint: Change in quantity from the original quantity). What do you find? Can you give reasons for the differences in the percentage decrease in the quantity demanded of the three goods despite the same percentage increase in price?

Price Elasticity, Total Expenditure, and Total Revenue

The information on price elasticity is helpful not just in assessing the responsiveness of the quantity demanded of a product to a change in the own price but also in determining how the total spending on a good, i.e., price × quantity demanded, may change as the product price changes. This is important information for producers who would like to know how a price change may impact on sales revenues.

Suppose that the price of petrol increases from ¥150 to ¥200 per litre in Japan. Is a middle-income Japanese family going to spend more on petrol or less? In the very short run (say within a week's time after the petrol price hike), the demand for petrol is likely to change by a little, if at all. As a result, a family's spending on petrol will be higher. But, over time, the family will look for substitutes. Perhaps the children in the family might consider using bus to go to school rather than go in the family car. Previously, the family almost always used to take the car to go to the hills. Now it may decide to take the train. Since the quantity demanded falls when the price increases, it is not clear whether the *total* spending on petrol will increase or decrease with a price change.

As you can guess, the answer depends on the magnitude of the price elasticity of demand. If the demand for petrol is inelastic, there will not be much decline in the quantity demanded of petrol as its price increases and thus price ×quantity demanded of petrol will increase. More precisely, if $e_p < 1$, the percentage change in price exceeds the percentage change in the quantity demanded, and therefore, the direction of change in price will govern the direction of change of the total expenditure on the product. Thus, if $e_p < 1$, an increase (a decrease) in the price will lead to an increase (a decrease) in the total expenditure on the product.

Similarly, if the demand for a product is elastic, i.e., $e_p > 1$, the percentage change in the quantity demanded is greater than that of price. Hence the change in the direction of the quantity demanded will dictate the change in the direction of total expenditure. As the price increases (decreases), the quantity demanded will increase (decrease) and the total expenditure will increase (decrease).

In the intermediate case where $e_p = 1$, the percentage change in price is equal to the percentage change in the quantity demanded and hence the total expenditure does not change with price.

More precisely, because total expenditure = price ×quantity demanded, we have the mathematic relationship[6]:

$$\begin{aligned}
&\% \text{ increase in the total expenditure} \\
&= \% \text{ increase in price} + \% \text{ increase in quantity demanded} \\
&= (\% \text{ increase in price})\left(1 + \frac{\% \text{ increase in quantity demanded}}{\% \text{ increase in price}}\right) \\
&= (\% \text{ increase in price})(1 - e_p)
\end{aligned}$$

Based on the above algebraic derivation, Table 3.1 summarises the qualitative relationships between a price change and its effect on total expenditure.

The impact of a change in price on the total expenditure on a product is useful information for a business or a seller. Realise that the total expenditure of consumers on a product sold by a seller is equal to the seller's total revenue or what is called the total turnover. Hence, if a seller is contemplating a price change of a product and wants to know whether total revenue or turnover will increase or decrease, the price elasticity of demand is the key. If this elasticity is greater than one, a price increase (decrease) will lower (raise) the total revenue. If it is less than one, a price increase (decrease) will raise (lower) the total revenue. You may revisit Activity 3.1 and figure out why a fall in the prices of refrigerator and salt led to opposite effects on respective revenues from sales.

TABLE 3.1 Price Change and Its Impact on Total Expenditure

Price Change	*Elasticity*	*Total Expenditure*
–	$e_p > 1$	↓
↓	$e_p > 1$	–
–	$e_p < 1$	–
–	$e_p < 1$	↓
–↓	$e_p = 1$	No Change

The above argument has similar implications taxing commodities and the amount of tax collection. If a low-price-elasticity good (such that $e_p < 1$) is taxed, it is likely to increase the tax revenues, equal to the tax rate per unit sold × quantity sold in the market. If it is a high-price-elasticity product, the impact is likely to be the opposite. See Box 3.1 for a problem for a financial minister who is mulling over to increase the tax rate in order to increase the revenues of the state.

BOX 3.1 WHAT TO TAX: NECESSITIES, COMFORTS, OR LUXURIES? THE FINANCE MINISTER'S DILEMMA

This has a lesson for a finance minister. Faced with the ever-increasing resource crunch, finance ministers have to increase taxes. All taxes can be broadly classified into two categories: direct and indirect. Direct taxes (like income tax, corporate tax) are paid by the person or organisation on whom they are levied. In the case of indirect taxes, the tax levied on the person or organisation can be shifted to another person or an organisation, either partially or wholly. Examples are excise duty, customs duty, and goods and services tax (GST). These taxes are levied on the producers but are finally paid by the ultimate buyer (consumer). Finance ministers normally refrain from increasing direct taxes as these are obvious and make democratic governments unpopular. Hence, they typically resort to increasing indirect taxes. An increase in tax on goods is normally passed on to the consumers via raising price. If the elasticity of demand for a product is low, an increase in tax rate (and subsequent increase in price) will not decrease sales much. Hence tax collection will increase. Necessities and luxuries have a low elasticity of demand. But it will be politically unwise to tax necessities. Hence finance ministers normally increase taxes on luxuries. But, as we know, luxury items are purchased by only a select few: the very rich section of the society. In poor countries, this section is even more limited. Thus, very few fall into the tax net, which increases total tax collection only marginally.

3.2.2 Income Elasticity of Demand

So far, we have focused on the responsiveness of the quantity demanded with respect to the own price. It is also useful to know the responsiveness of the quantity demanded to a change in income. This is captured by **income elasticity of demand**, defined by the expression (3.11):

$$e_I = \frac{\%\ \text{change in quantity demanded}}{\%\ \text{change in income}} \tag{3.11}$$

For a normal good, an increase in income leads to an increase in the quantity demanded; hence $e_I > 0$. For an inferior good, the income and quantity demanded are inversely related and thus $e_I < 0$. Henceforth, let us consider only a normal good.

The magnitude of the income elasticity of demand for a product depends on how essential or non-essential the product is, i.e., the nature of the need for the product. Since the demand for essential goods is not likely to vary much, the income elasticity (just as its price elasticity) is likely to be small. Otherwise, it is likely to be relatively large.

Further, there is a relationship between a change in income and the corresponding change in *share* of total expenditure on a product, depending on whether e_I is greater or less than one. Note that the total expenditure on the product has the expression $E = pq$. Thus, the share of total expenditure on the product equals E / M or pq / M, where M is the total expenditure on *all* goods. If $e_I > 1$, by definition, the percentage change in the quantity demanded is greater than the percentage change in income. Hence, the price of the product remaining unchanged, the ratio of the quantity demanded to income—and therefore the ratio of total expenditure on the product to income or which is same as the share of total expenditure on the product—must increase. Similarly, if $e_I < 1$, an increase in income will lead to a decrease in the share of total expenditure on the product.

Income elasticity is important for *targeting of sales* or what is the same thing as formulating a *marketing strategy*. Suppose a company sells its product globally and is looking at two "emerging markets"; meaning, countries where the aggregate income is expected to grow at a decent rate. In one of them the income elasticity of demand for its product is less than one and in the other it is greater than one. Then the company should promote its product more aggressively in the second market. Furthermore, over the long run, income elasticity measures can be used for planning a *firm's growth* in a particular product or service space.

Box 3.2 provides some data-based estimates of price and income elasticities.

BOX 3.2 ESTIMATES OF PRICE AND INCOME ELASTICITY OF DEMAND

There are innumerable econometric studies, which have estimated price and income elasticities for various products and services with respect to various countries. A few of them are reported here.

Commodity or Service	Study	Estimates
	Price Elasticity	
Non-cereal food, India (urban + rural)	(Meenakshi & Ray, 1999)	0.804
Clothing, India (urban + rural)	(Meenakshi & Ray, 1999)	0.560
Electricity, India (urban)	(Filippini & Pachuri, 2002)	0.32 (winter), 0.39 (monsoon), 0.16 (summer)
High-speed Internet access through cable modems, US (residential)	(Kridel et al., 2000)	1.08 to 1.79
Gasoline, India	(Kanjilal & Ghosh, 2018)	2.08 (long run)
	Income Elasticity	
Electricity, India (urban)	(Filippini & Pachuri, 2002)	0.69 (winter), 0.64 (monsoon), 0.66 (summer)
White maize, Philippines	(Rosegrant et al., 1995)	0.15
Gasoline, India	(Kanjilal & Ghosh, 2018)	1.36 (long run)

3.2.3 Cross-Price Elasticity

This measures the sensitivity of the quantity demanded of one good with respect to a change in the price of a related good. **Cross-price elasticity** is defined as:

$$e_c = \frac{\%\text{ change in quantity demanded}}{\%\text{ change in the price of the related good}}. \tag{3.12}$$

If the good in question is a substitute for the good whose price is changing, then $e_c > 0$, since the quantity demanded and the price of the related good both change in the same direction. Otherwise, if the product in question is complementary to the good whose price is changing, $e_c < 0$.

A simple example of the usefulness of cross-price elasticity is where a rival company has reduced the price of its product and you would like to know by how much it would affect the quantity demand of your product in the market, which is a substitute of the rival company's product.

TABLE 3.2 Product Line of Maruti Udyog

Category	*Price of Base Models in India as of June 2021*	*Brands*
A	Around ₹4,00,000	S-Presso, Alto
B	Around ₹6,00,000	Desire, Swift
C	Around ₹8,00,000	Ciaz, S-Cross

Further, if a firm produces a **production line** instead of a single model of a product, knowing the cross-price elasticity of demand can also be quite useful. The following example illustrates this. Most of the auto manufacturers make cars in different segments: low-end, middle-end, and high-end. In India, Maruti Udyog Limited, a major auto manufacturer, also does the same. Let us divide Maruti-manufactured cars into three segments—A, B, and C—as shown in Table 3.2.

Suppose that Maruti finds out that its revenues from new car sales in the B segment have remained stagnant for quite some time. Its management decides to slash the price of B-segment cars by ₹50,000, expecting that it will increase its car sales and revenues from this segment (under the assumption that the demand for B-segment cars is price-elastic). Will this strategy necessarily increase the *overall* total revenues coming from sales in different segments? Not necessarily, because there will be a cross-substitution effect. Some of the new customers, who were thinking of buying an A-segment Maruti car before, will switch over to a B-segment car. Similarly, from the other end, some potential buyers of C-segment Maruti car may also want to switch to a B-segment car. In other words, Maruti will face a decline in the revenues from sales in the A and C segments. This is where information on the cross-price elasticity comes to play. The higher the elasticity of demand for A- and C-segment Maruti cars with respect to the price of B-segment Maruti cars, the greater will be the decline in revenues from A and C segments, and the less likely will it be that a price-cutting strategy of this kind will boost the company's *total* revenues.

See Box 3.3 for some estimates of cross-price elasticity in different parts of the world.

BOX 3.3 ESTIMATES OF CROSS-PRICE EFFECTS ON DEMAND

Like own price and income elasticities, there are many estimates available for cross-price elasticities for different pairs of commodities and for different countries. The following table gives a sample that covers three continents.

Demand for the Commodity or Service	Substitute Good Whose Price Change Is Considered	Study	Estimates
Cable modem for high-speed internet access	Dial-up access	(Kridel et al., 2000)	0.15 (United States)
Poultry	Beef	(FAO Regional Office for Asia and the Pacific, 1999)	0.10 (Indonesia)
Electricity	Firewood	(Kebede et al., 2002)	0.59 (Ethiopia)
Plain water	Soft drinks	(Guerrero-Lopez et al., 2017)	0.63 (Chile)

3.2.4 Advertising Elasticity

By influencing people's tastes, advertising by business firms tends to change the consumers' demand for a particular product or a particular brand of a product. We define:

$$\text{Advertising Elasticity} = \frac{\%\ \text{change in sales}}{\%\ \text{change in the units of advertising}}.$$

There are indeed several studies that have estimated advertising elasticity for various categories of products. For example, in the context of the United States, a study by the Kaiser Family Foundation in 2003, "Impact of Direct-to-Consumer Advertising on Prescription Drug Spending," found that during the period 1996–1999, in the medicines market, a 10% increase in direct-to-consumer advertising and physician promotion activity by medicine companies led to a 1% increase in the medicine sales. Thus, the advertising elasticity in this case is 0.10. Much smaller advertising elasticities are reported by Shapiro et al. (2021) for consumer package goods in the context of the US economy.

What are the factors influencing this elasticity? One is advertising by the rival firms. The more the advertising by rivals, the less will be the advertising elasticity facing a particular firm. Another factor is the stage of the product in the market. If the product is relatively new in the market, the advertising elasticity is likely to be high (as more and more people come to know about it and its quality), but as the product gets old, this elasticity is likely to be smaller.

3.3 Elasticity of Supply

Parallel to demand, elasticity of supply measures the responsiveness of the quantity supplied. The **price elasticity of supply** is defined by:

$$e_p^s = \frac{\%\text{ change in quantity supplied}}{\%\text{ change in own price}}. \tag{3.13}$$

To distinguish between the elasticity of demand and elasticity of supply, we have added the superscript "s." This is the percentage formula. The numerator is equal to (” $q_s / q_s) \times 100$, where ” denotes the change and q_s denotes the quantity supplied. Similarly, the denominator equals $(\Delta p / p) \times 100$, where p denotes price. Hence the percentage formula is alternatively expressed as:

$$e_p^s = \frac{(\Delta q_s / q_s) \times 100}{(\Delta p / p) \times 100} = \frac{p}{q} \cdot \frac{\Delta q_s}{\Delta p}. \tag{3.14}$$

For any change in price which is not very small, e_p^s is sensitive to an interchange between the original price and the new price and the corresponding interchange between the original quantity and the new quantity. This problem is avoided by using the **arc price elasticity of supply** defined by:

$$e_p^s = \frac{p_0 + p_1}{q_0 + q_1} \cdot \frac{\Delta q_s}{\Delta p}, \tag{3.15}$$

where (p_0, q_0) is the old price–quantity pair and (p_1, q_1) is the new one. This is analogous to the arc elasticity of demand.

Example 3.6

A sugar manufacturer was supplying 10 quintals of sugar to the market when sugar was selling for \$3/kg. The price of sugar has increased to \$5/kg and the manufacturer is supplying 15 quintals to the market. All other things are unchanged. What is the arc elasticity of supply?

Answer: The original price and quantity supplied are: $p_0 = 3$ and $q_0 = 10$. The new price and quantities are: $p_1 = 5$ and $q_1 = 15$. Thus, ”$p = 2$,” $q_s = 5$, $p_0 + p_1 = 8$, and $q_0 + q_1 = 25$. Applying (3.15).

$$e_p^s = \frac{8}{25} \cdot \frac{5}{2} = 0.8. \ \blacksquare$$

3.3.1 Point Elasticity of Supply

For a very small change in price there is also a **point elasticity** method. Suppose the supply curve is a straight line. Figure 3.5 shows three possibilities. The supply line has a positive intercept on the price axis, a positive intercept on the quantity axis, and passes through the origin, shown, respectively, in panels (a), (b), and (c). As proven in Appendix 3.C, in panels (a) and (b) the point elasticity is equal to *BC/0C*, the ratio of the horizontal segment to the quantity supplied. In panel (a), $BC > 0C$ and hence $BC/0C > 1$, i.e., the point elasticity of supply is greater than one, or the supply is said to be elastic. In panel (b) it is the opposite: $BC/0C < 1$. The point elasticity is less than one or supply is inelastic.

Panel (c) is a special case, where the point *B* coincides with the origin. We have $BC = 0C$ and thus $e_s = 1$. In other words, a "straight-line supply curve" passing through the origin always has price elasticity equal to one (or "unitarily elastic"), *regardless* of how flat or steep the supply curve is. For instance, in Figure 3.6 all the three supply curves, S_1, S_2, and S_3 have $e_p^s = 1$ at any price.

There are two other special cases of straight-line supply curves: one where it is vertical and the other where it is horizontal, as shown in Figure 3.7. A vertical supply curve has $e_p^s = 0$, since the quantity supplied is fixed. Typically, this holds when we consider the supply of a product at an *instant* of time. For example, during a particular day, the supply of fish in the entire market of Kolkata is fixed. Assuming that fish cannot be stored, that the whole quantity of fish *has* to be sold in the market that day irrespective of how much price it fetches.[7] At the other extreme, along a horizontal supply curve, $e_p^s = \infty$, meaning that a little or a "marginal" change in price will lead to an arbitrarily large change in supply.

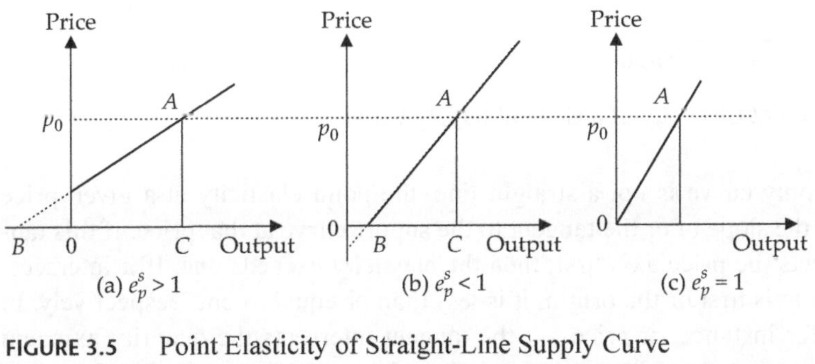

FIGURE 3.5 Point Elasticity of Straight-Line Supply Curve

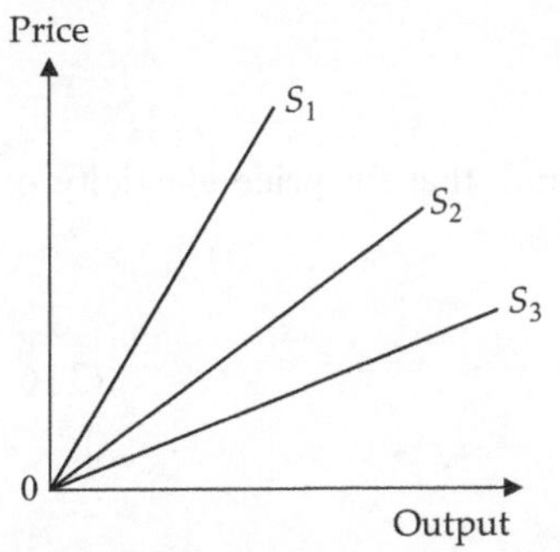

FIGURE 3.6 Unitarily Elastic Supply Curves

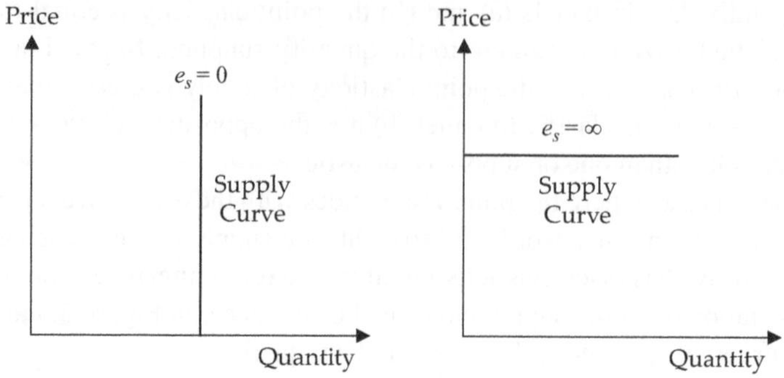

FIGURE 3.7 Special Cases

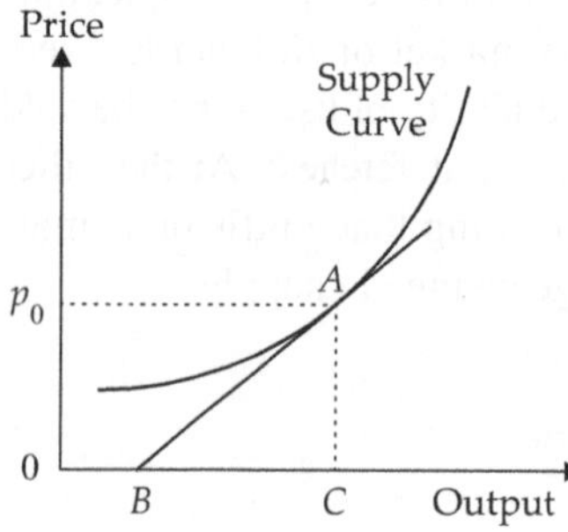

FIGURE 3.8 Point Elasticity of a General Supply Curve

If the supply curve is not a straight line, the point elasticity at a given price depends on the slope of or the tangent to the supply curve at that price. If this tangent intersects the price axis first, then the elasticity exceeds one. If it intersects the quantity axis first or the origin, it is less than or equal to one, respectively. In Figure 3.8 for instance, at price p_0, the tangent intersects the quantity axis and therefore the price elasticity of supply is less than one. Appendix 3.D discusses how the point-price elasticity can be compared between two supply curves.

3.3.2 Log Formula for Price Elasticity of Supply

Just as the log formula for price elasticity of demand, that for price elasticity of supply is given by:

$$e_p^s = \frac{d \ln q^s}{d \ln p}. \tag{3.16}$$

3.3.3 Supply Elasticity with Respect to Other Factors

What about the elasticities of supply with respect to other factors like technology, input prices, or taxes? In principle, one can define them. But there are several kinds of inputs and different types of technological improvement. Therefore, the standard practice is not to specify them as a general category. However, depending on what one wishes to analyse, one can always define and discuss the relevant elasticity of supply. For instance, if we are considering producers who are producing competing goods, we define a cross-price elasticity of supply, e.g., the elasticity of wheat production with respect to the price of sugar cane.

See Box 3.4 for a sample of elasticities of supply.

BOX 3.4 ESTIMATES OF ELASTICITIES OF SUPPLY

In general, compared to demand elasticities, supply elasticities are harder to estimate and hence harder to find (because of data availability problems and because firms operate in different types of market environments). Yet, they are available. The following table presents a sample. Notice that it contains own price elasticities of supply and examples of elasticities with respect to input price changes.

Elasticity of Supply of	With Respect to the Price of	Study	Estimate
Rice	Own	(Chand, 1998–99)	0.25 (India)
Wheat	Own	(Chand, 1998–99)	0.85 (India)
Oysters	Own	(Muth et al., 2000)	1.97: halfshell oysters 2.30: shucked oysters 1.64: shellstock oysters (US)
Broiler Poultry	Own	(Fabiosa et al., 2004)	0.22 (Indonesia)
Rice	Fertilizer (an input)	(Chand, 1998–99)	-0.16 (India)
Wheat	Fertilizer (an input)	(Chand, 1998–99)	-0.02 (India)

Facts and Insights

- The price elasticity of demand measures the responsiveness of the quantity demanded of a product with respect to a change in the own price.
- There are percentage, arc elasticity, and point elasticity formulae for quantities demanded and supplied.
- The magnitude of price elasticity of demand depends whether a good is a luxury or a necessity, availability of substitute goods, how narrowly defined a product is, the proportion of total expenditure on a product.
- All else the same, the longer the time period, the higher will be the price elasticity of a product demand as people tend to discover more substitutes.
- If the demand for a product is price elastic, i.e., price elasticity is greater than one (inelastic, i.e., the price elasticity is less than one), an increase in price leads to a decrease (an increase) in the total spending on the product.
- Income elasticity of demand measures the responsiveness of the quantity demanded of a product with respect to a change in income. It is useful in assessing which markets to emphasise in the overall marketing strategy of a firm.
- Cross-price elasticity of demand refers to the responsiveness of the quantity demanded of a product with respect to a change in the price of a related good. It is positive in case of a change in the price of a substitute good and negative in case of a change in the price of a complementary good. Cross-price elasticity measures are important to estimate the overall revenue implication of a change in the price of a product for a firm producing a product line.
- Advertising elasticity refers to the responsiveness of the quantity demanded of a product with respect to a change in the units of advertising of it.
- The price elasticity of supply measures the responsiveness of the quantity supplied to a change in the own price.
- Cross-price elasticity of supply measures the responsiveness of the quantity supplied of one good with respect to a change in the price of a related good.

Appendix 3.A Derivation of the Point Elasticity of Demand Formula

Consider the straight-line demand curve *AB* in Figure 3.9, same as Figure 3.1(a) except that there are more lines and points. The original price is $p_0 = Cq_0$, and the original quantity demanded is $q_0 = p_0C$. We are to prove that the point elasticity at the price p_0 is equal to BC/AC.

Suppose there is an increase in price and the new price is p_1. The new quantity demanded is p_1F. Consider the triangle *FEC*. The change in price and the change in quantity demanded are, respectively, equal to ” $p = FE$ and ” $q = -EC$. The “-” sign for the quantity change means a *decrease* in quantity. Thus,

$$e_p = \frac{p_0}{q_0}\frac{\text{”}q}{\text{”}p} = \frac{Cq_0}{p_0C}\frac{EC}{FE}.$$

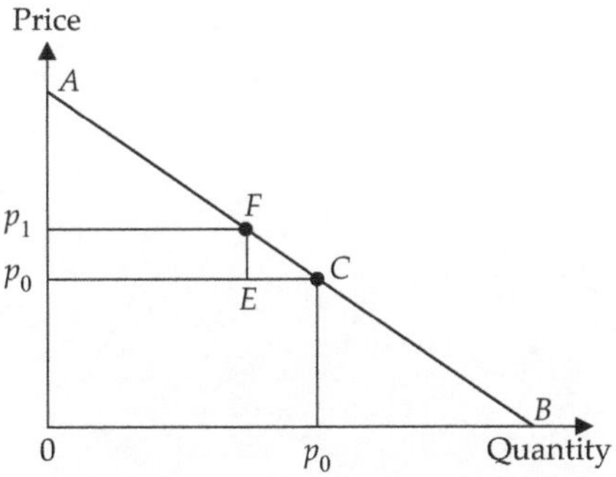

FIGURE 3.9 Deriving the Point Elasticity of Demand Formula

As the triangles FEC and Cq_0B are similar, $EC / FE = q_0B / Cq_0$. Hence,

$$e_p = \frac{Cq_0}{p_0C}\frac{q_0B}{Cq_0} = \frac{q_0B}{p_0C}.$$

The triangles Cq_0B and Ap_0C are similar. Hence, $q_0B / Cq_0 = BC / CA$. Thus, $e_p = BC / CA$. This proves the point elasticity formula for a straight-line demand curve.

If it is a demand curve as in Figure 3.1(b) in the text, for a small change in price, $” p / ” q$ is simply the slope of the demand curve (as price and quantity are, respectively, measured vertically and horizontally). At the price p_0, the slope $= -0G / 0H$. Thus, $\Delta p / \Delta q = -0G / 0H$, or $\Delta q / \Delta p = -0H / 0G$, and

$$e_p = -\frac{p_0}{q_0}\frac{\Delta q}{\Delta p} = \frac{Cq_0}{p_0C}\frac{0H}{0G}.$$

The triangles $G0H$ and Cq_0H are similar. Hence, $0H / 0G = q_0H / cq_0$, and, thus,

$$e_p = \frac{Cq_0}{p_0C}\frac{0H}{0G} = \frac{Cq_0}{p_0C}\frac{q_0H}{Cq_0} = \frac{q_0H}{p_0C}.$$

The last ratio is equal to HC/CG since the triangles Cq_0H and Gp_0C are similar. This proves $e_p = HC / CG$.

Appendix 3.B Comparing Price Elasticity of Two Demand Curves

Consider Figure 3.10, which is same as Figure 3.3 except that it has three extra points. Let p_0 be the original price. At this price, the quantities demanded on

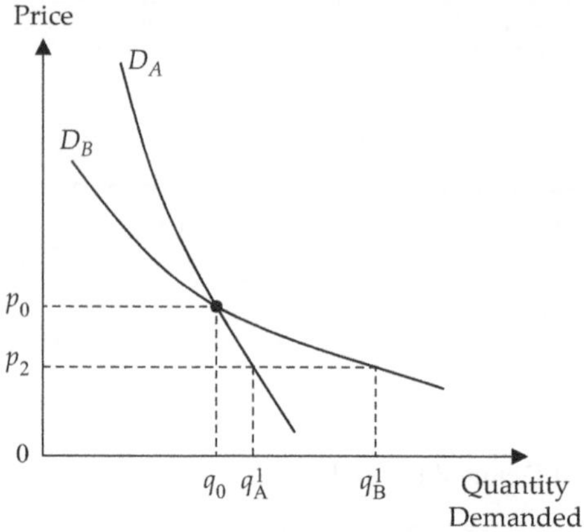

FIGURE 3.10 Flatter Demand Curve Is More Price Elastic

both curves are equal to q_0. Suppose there is a decrease in price from p_0 to p_1. The quantity demanded increases to q_A^1 along D_A and q_B^1 along D_B. Note that the increase in the quantity demanded (" q) along the flatter demand curve D_B is greater than that along the steeper demand curve D_A. On both demand curves, the original price and quantity demanded are the same, and moreover, the price change (" p) is also the same. Hence, the price elasticity is greater along the flatter demand curve D_B. If we had considered an increase in price, you may check that the magnitude of decrease in the quantity demanded is greater along D_B also. Therefore, of the two demand curves, the flatter demand curve is more price elastic than the steeper demand curve at their point of intersection.

Appendix 3.C Formula for the Point Elasticity for Supply in Figure 3.5

Consider a small price change from p_0 in Figure 3.5.

$$e_p^s = \frac{p_0}{0C}\frac{\Delta q_s}{\Delta p}\bigg|_{\Delta p \to 0} = \frac{AC}{0C}\frac{dq_s}{dp}.$$

In panels (a) and (b), dp / dq = rise/run = AC / BC, implying

$$\frac{dq_s}{dp} = \frac{BC}{AC}.$$

Substituting this expression,

$$e_p^s = \frac{AC}{0C}\frac{dq_s}{dp} = \frac{AC}{0C}\frac{BC}{AC} = \frac{BC}{0C}.$$

In panel (c), $dp / dq_s = AC / 0C$, or $dq_s / dp = 0C / AC$. Hence,

$$e_p^s = \frac{AC}{0C}\frac{dq_s}{dp} = \frac{AC}{0C}\frac{0C}{AC} = 1.$$

Appendix 3.D Comparing Price Elasticity of Two Supply Curves

How do we compare elasticities of two supply curves? Of course, if they are straight lines passing through the origin, we know that they will both have elasticity equal to one. We also know that if one (straight line) supply curve has the intercept on the price axis and the other on the quantity axis, the elasticity along the former is greater. But, barring these cases, we cannot compare in general, except at their point of intersection. Turn to Figure 3.11. As in case of two intersecting demand curves, at the price p_0, the flatter supply curve S_B has higher elasticity than the steeper supply curve S_1, because the quantity adjustment to a given price change is greater along the former. The argument and proof are analogous to that behind the comparison shown in Figure 3.10. Thus, *of two supply curves, the flatter supply curve is more elastic than the steeper supply curve at their point of intersection.*

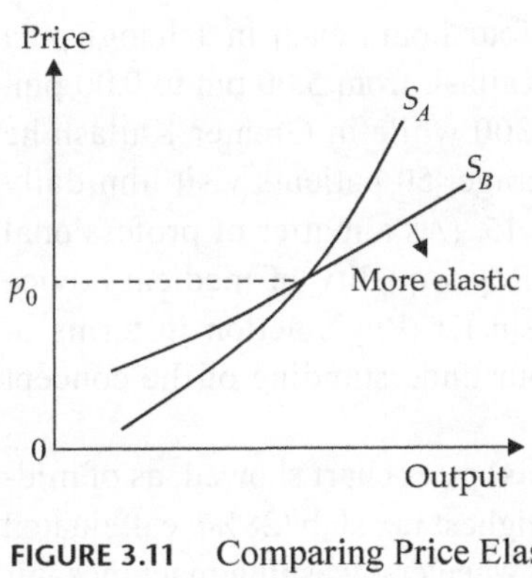

FIGURE 3.11 Comparing Price Elasticities of Supply Curves

Exercises

Descriptive/Analytical

3.1 Explain the concept of price elasticity of demand. What are its determinants?
3.2 Explain with suitable examples the factors on which price elasticity of supply depends.
3.3 Explain the income and cross elasticity of demand. How are they measured?

Short Answer (Word Limit = Approx. 500)

3.4 Petrol price has been increased, but Mr. Gupta's family is spending less on petrol. What can be inferred about the elasticity of demand for petrol of this family?
3.5 Suppose there are two straight-line demand curves, originating from the same point on the price axis. Show that, at any given price, the point-price elasticities of the two curves are equal.
3.6 If there are two straight-line downward-sloping parallel demand curves, then at any price, the price elasticity is greater along the line closer to the origin.
3.7 "The income elasticity of demand for a product must always be positive." Defend or refute.
3.8 "The cross-price elasticity of demand for a product is always positive." Defend or refute.
3.9 "Among two straight-line supply curves, the steeper one is less price elastic." Comment.
3.10 A ladies-clothing manufacturer in India produces *saris* and *shalwars*. How will an increase in the average price of *saris* affect the supply curve of *shalwars*?
3.11 Dr. Roy has his private clinics in two localities in New Delhi, India: Jahangirpuri and Greater Kailash. While Jahangirpuri houses predominantly the low-income people, Greater Kailash is a posh locality. Dr. Roy is available in his clinics every day for four hours each in Jahangirpuri from 9.00 am to 1.00 pm and in Greater Kailash from 5.00 pm to 9.00 pm. His consultation fee in Jahangirpuri is ₹300 while in Greater Kailash he charges ₹500. In Jahangirpuri, on an average, 50 patients visit him daily while in Greater Kailash, this number is 15. (As a matter of professional commitment and personal conduct, Dr. Roy's quality of medical advice remains the same for all patients). Explain Dr. Roy's action in terms of economic rationality in the context of your understanding of the concept of elasticity of demand.

In India, the GST (Goods & Services Tax) rates chart showed, as of mid-2021, the following sectors subject to the highest tax slab (28%): caffeinated beverages; tobacco products, cars and two wheelers, washing machines, air conditioners, dishwashing machines, aerated beverage, yachts, aircrafts, racing club services, food or drinks in 5-star hotels, ballet, go-carting, and sporting events like the Indian Premier League (IPL). Can you reason why these products command high tax rates.

3.13 At the peak of their popularity, many artists start demanding astronomical fee for their shows as they find no rival anywhere near their current status. What could be the short-, medium- and long-term consequences of this behaviour? If you happen to be the adviser of such a star, what pricing strategy would you recommend and why?

Quizzes/Numerical

3.14 Vitamin D whole milk was selling at $4/gallon in New York and the total quantity sold of this brand of milk by a local store per month was 80 gallons. Recently, the milk price has doubled, while the quantity sold has decreased to 60 tonnes. Calculate the arc price elasticity of demand for this brand of milk.

3.15 A private hospital, *Get Well*, was charging ₹600,000 for a double-bypass heart surgery and it was generating ₹10,800,000 of revenues from it per month. It has increased its rate to ₹1,050,000 and now it is generating ₹9,600,000 revenues from it. What can we say about the price elasticity of demand for double-bypass surgery at *Get Well*?

3.16 Mr. Gallagher and his family members are fond of an Indian dessert called *gulab jamun*. Recently, the price of *gulab jamun* has increased by 20% and the total spending by Mr. Gallagher's family on *gulab jamun* has increased by 15%. What is the price elasticity of demand for *gulab jamun* by this family?

3.17 If the advertising elasticity is 0.2, what will be the percentage change in sales from a 15% increase in the units of advertising, keeping everything else constant?

3.18 A pencil manufacturer was supplying 400 dozen of pencil when the price was €6 per dozen. The market price has risen to €8 and the manufacturer is supplying 440 dozen of pencils to the market. Calculate the arc elasticity of supply.

Given the demand function $Q_d = 160 - 4p$, find (a) the price at which point elasticity of demand is (i) infinity, (ii) one, (iii) zero, and (b) the price range in which elasticity of demand is (i) greater than one, (ii) less than one.

Notes

1 The meaning of "operationalising" will be clear as we proceed.
2 Some textbooks define price elasticity as (3.2), except for the negative sign.
3 Note that if we consider a higher price, this ratio will be higher, which means that the higher the price, the greater is the point elasticity. This is intuitive, saying that if a product becomes more expensive, the consumer becomes more sensitive about her demand for it in response to a further price change.

4 Appendix 3.B provides a proof.
5 How we can compare the price elasticity between two demand curves is discussed in Appendix 3.B.
6 This relationship holds exactly only if the price change is very small. Otherwise, it holds approximately.
7 But, if we look at supply of a commodity over a period of time, it will be responsive to a change in price.

Bibliography

Chand, R. (1998–99). Supply responsiveness in India's Redfed agriculture. In *The annual report 1998–99 of the National Centre for Agricultural Economics and Policy Research*. Indian Council of Agricultural Research.

Fabiosa, J. F., Jensen, H. H., & Yan, D. (2004). *Output supply and input demand system of commercial and backyard poultry producers in Indonesia* (Working Paper No 04-WP 363). Center for Agriculture and Rural Development, Iowa State University.

FAO Regional Office for Asia and the Pacific. (1999). *Industries of Indonesia prior to the Asian financial crisis*. FOA for Asia and the Pacific.

Filippini, M., & Pachuri, S. (2002). *Elasticities of electricity demand in Urban Indian households* (Working Paper No 16). Centre for Energy Policy and Economics, Swiss Federal Institute of Technology.

Guerrero-Lopez, C. M., Unar-Munguia, M., & Arantxa Colchero, M. (2017). Price elasticity of demand for soft drinks, other sugar-sweetened beverages and energy defense food in Chile. *BMC Public Health, 17*, 180.

Kanjilal, K., & Ghosh, S. (2018). Revisiting income and price elasticity of gasoline demand in India: New evidence of Cointegration tests. *Empirical Economics, 55*(4), 1869–1888.

Kebede, B., Bekele, A., & Kedir, E. (2002). Can the urban poor afford modern energy? The case of Ethiopia. *Energy Policy, 30*(11–12), 1029–1045.

Kridel, D. J., Rappoport, P. N., & Taylor, L. D. (2000). *The demand for high-speed access to the internet: The case of cable modems*. Presented at the 13th Biennial Conference of the International Telecommunications Society, Buenos Aires.

Meenakshi, J. V., & Ray, R. (1999). Regional differences in India's food expenditure pattern: A complete demand systems approach. *Journal of International Development, 11*, 47–74.

Muth, M. K., Anderson, D. W., Karns, S. A., Murray, B. C., & Dominico, J. L. (2000). *Economic impacts of requiring post-harvest treatment of oysters: Final report*. Prepared for Interstate Shellfish Sanitation Conference, Research Triangle Institute.

Rosegrant, M. W., Agcaoili-Sombilla, M., & Perez, N. (1995). *Global food projection to 2020: Implications for investment. 2020* (Vision Discussion Paper No 5). International Food Policy Research Institute.

Shapiro, B., Hitsch, G. J., & Tuchman, A. (2021). TV advertising effectiveness and profitability: Generalizable results from 288 brands. *Econometrica, 89*(4), 1855–1879.

4

CONSUMER BEHAVIOUR

The Law of Demand tells us that normally people tend to buy less when the price of that commodity increases and vice versa. The Law of Supply states the opposite. These laws tell us the direction of change. The elasticities of demand and supply measure the magnitude of the change in demand or supply in response to a change in price and other respective determinants. So far, so good.

We now raise the question of "Why?" Why do buyers tend to buy less at a higher price and more at a lower price? Why do sellers offer more supplies at a higher price and vice versa? In this chapter, our focus is on the behaviour of buyers. Put differently, we analyse the basis of the Law of Demand. You may think it is silly to ask why someone would buy less of a good when its price rises? Isn't it obvious? Yes, at one level it is. But there are far-from-obvious underlying patterns that lead to this behaviour. We dive deeper to uncover them.

There are three theoretical approaches to consumer behaviour or what is also called **consumer theory** or **demand theory**: namely, the **marginal-utility approach**, the **indifference-curve** approach, and the **revealed-preference approach**. They are different but consistent with one another. The last two explain the basis of the Law of Demand in a deeper way than does the marginal-utility approach. In the main text of this chapter, we'll cover the marginal-utility approach and simply introduce the basics of the more general indifference-curve approach. This caters to the need of many business schools and commerce courses, where the students are generally made to acquaint themselves with consumer behaviour without much rigour or comprehensiveness.

The details of the indifference-curve approach and the revealed-preference approach are relegated to the appendices following the text—which are far more "econ-centric" and should be useful to those studying economics and to those business schools that want consumer behaviour to be taught in depth.

DOI: 10.4324/9781003452195-4

Rest assured however that skipping the detailed analysis of consumer behaviour as outlined in the appendices will in no way be a handicap in grasping the subsequent chapters. It will also *not* diminish your understanding of the tools of economics for managerial decision-making.

4.1 Marginal-Utility Theory

This is the simplest of all, popularised by Alfred Marshall, regarded as the Father of Microeconomics. It involves the concept of utility.

4.1.1 Utility Concepts

An individual buys something because consuming or using it provides her pleasure or satisfaction. You buy an orange because it fulfils your want. A smoker buys a pack of cigarettes as he enjoys it. Satisfaction is personal. You may be averse to smoking but I may not be. Whether consuming a product is good or bad is a separate issue. The notion of satisfaction is captured by **total utility**, *defined as the total satisfaction, measured in some psychological unit, obtained from consuming a given amount of a good.* Let's name this unit as "util." For example, if you consume 10 chocolates then the marginal-utility theory assumes that you can quantify your satisfaction from it, such as 100 utils, 60 utils, or whatever.

In comparison to total utility, **marginal utility (MU)** is defined as the additional or the extra utility obtained from consuming an *extra* unit of a product. (Recall our discussion of "total" and "marginal" in Chapter 1.) To continue our example, suppose that 10 chocolates give you 70 utils of total utility and 11 chocolates give you 80 utils of total utility. We then say that the marginal utility of 11 chocolates, not 11th chocolate, equals $80 - 70 = 10$ utils.

Suppose you are a movie buff. You regularly watch them on HD streaming "on demand" by paying for them. Let Table 4.1 define your total utility (TU) and

TABLE 4.1 Total Utility and Marginal Utility

No. of Movies	*Total Utility*	*Marginal Utility*
0	0	–
1	40	40
2	100	60
3	155	55
4	190	35
5	220	30
6	233	13
7	235	2
8	225	-10
9	195	-30

marginal utility (MU) schedules from seeing these movies. Notice that, at each level of consumption, marginal utility is equal to the extra utility obtained from the last unit consumed. For instance, the MU of three movies is equal to 55 utils, because the 3rd movie gives extra utility equal to 155 – 100 = 55 utils. Four movies accord 35 utils of marginal utility, and so on. Mark that if you consume too many movies, your marginal utility becomes negative, i.e., after a certain point, seeing one more movie becomes a drag rather than an enjoyment.

The decreasing pattern of marginal utility with consumption is called the **Law of Diminishing Marginal Utility**, which states that, *after a certain level of consumption (possibly from the very first unit), the marginal utility falls as more and more of a product is consumed.* The law says something natural to us—no matter how much you like something, after consuming a certain amount, the intensity of desire decreases as you consume more and more of it—whether or not the marginal utility becomes zero or negative eventually.

Another example of the phenomenon of diminishing marginal utility is presented in Box 4.1 *A Hilsa Feast.*

BOX 4.1 A HILSA FEAST

On a pleasant Saturday evening, you accompany your parents to the wedding of a relative. A huge buffet of multiple varieties of food and beverages is laid out for the guests, including fish curry, chicken biryani, vegetable pulao, rasgullas, mishti doi (sweet curd), to name a few. To top it all, the fish is hilsa; a freshwater variety considered a top delicacy in eastern India. Being a Bengali, Odia, or Assamese, your eyes light up! Unlimited helpings of *macher-jhol* (fish curry, that too hilsa) available at no price! Wow! Is it free really?

Some of you may say that it is not free. My parents brought a gift for the wedding couple; so, we are paying a price. In India, a widely prevalent custom is to present a "shagun," an auspicious amount of cash (₹101, ₹501, ₹1,100, ₹5,100, etc.), which in urban parts is normally given in an envelope to the wedding couple. The shagun is society's custom, not really a price. The gift is given not in exchange for a feast. Would you withdraw your gift or reduce the amount of shagun if the wedding feast only had simple "dal-bhat" and vegetable? No. Similarly, would the host turn you out if you did not bring a gift or shagun? Thus, let's agree that food, particularly, hilsa, is free. That is, cooked hilsa price = 0 for you in that evening.

Now, as soon as the dinner time is announced, you grab a plate and serve for yourself a portion, say one piece of fish. You enjoy a lot–a state of bliss. In no time, it disappears from your plate. You quickly indulge yourself in a second helping of the same size. Suppose that, after eating one piece of hilsa, we ask you (each time) to rate your level of satisfaction on a 10-point scale, 10 measuring the highest and zero meaning the lowest level of satisfaction. Mostly likely, after consuming the first portion, your response will be 10. What about your rating after the second portion? Will it be 10 again? Highly unlikely. Almost certainly, you will quote a number lower than 10, say 8. This will further decline as the process of consumption goes on. Depending on how hungry you might be and how much you love hilsa fish, you may have had four servings before you stopped. Why did you stop even if it is free?

The answer lies in the Law of Diminishing Marginal Utility, a natural facet of human behaviour: the more we have of a particular good, after a certain level or right from the start, less and less is the intensity of desire to have an extra unit of that good. If you stopped after the fourth piece, the marginal utility from five pieces of hilsa must be zero or negative.

Returning to Table 4.1, while the MU schedule, by its definition, is derived from a TU schedule, the TU schedule can also be derived from an MU schedule: since there is zero utility from consuming zero amount, *total utility is the sum of marginal utilities.* Please refer to Chapter 1 to verify this. Table 4.1 is graphed in Figure 4.1, showing the total utility (TU) curve and the marginal utility curve. Notice the pattern in the marginal utility column or curve: after the second unit of consumption, it continuously falls, complying with the law of diminishing marginal utility.

Suppose now that an HD movie streaming can be rented for ¥150. There is a trade-off. Acquiring the right to see an additional movie gives you a utility gain. But paying ¥150 for it deprives you from using this money for something else. It is a cost or loss for you. You must weigh the gain against the loss. The question is, how many movies are you going to consume or demand?

From Table 4.1 or Figure 4.1 it is obvious that you are not going to rent more than seven movies: Why would you get movies when they give you negative

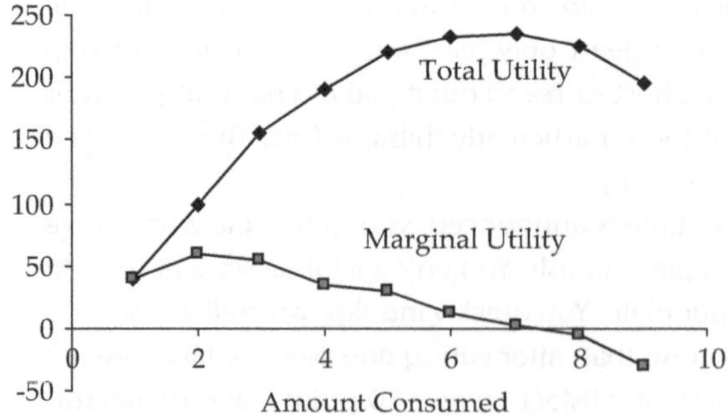

FIGURE 4.1 Total Utility and Marginal Utility Curves

satisfaction? However, below seven, there is a trade-off between benefits (utility) and costs. To compare benefits and costs, the utility must be expressed in terms of money. Assume that, to you, one yen is worth 0.2 utils, i.e., the marginal utility of yen or money is 0.2 utils.[1] Then the TUs and the MUs in Table 4.1 can be converted to those "in terms of money or yen." These are presented in Table 4.2.

Example 4.1

A person's marginal utility from consuming banana is given in Table 4.3. Derive her total utility schedule. If the marginal utility of dollar (i.e., utility of one dollar) is 3 utils, derive the marginal utility schedule in terms of money (dollar).

Answer: Since total utility is the sum of marginal utilities, the total utility of two bananas is equal to the marginal utility of one banana (39) plus that of two bananas (36) = 75 utils. Table 4.4 calculates the total utilities for various units consumed. ■

TABLE 4.2 Utilities in Yen

No. Movies	*Total Utility* ¥	*Marginal Utility* ¥
0	0	–
1	200	200
2	500	300
3	775	275
4	950	175
5	1,100	150
6	1,165	65
7	1,175	10
8	1,125	-50
9	975	-150

Marginal Utility of ¥1 = 2 utils

TABLE 4.3 Marginal Utility

No. of Bananas	*Marginal Utility*
0	–
1	39
2	36
3	33
4	24
5	12
6	0
7	-9

TABLE 4.4 Total Utilities

Number of Bananas	*Total Utility*
0	–
1	39
2	39+36 = 75
3	75 + 33 = 108
4	108 + 24 = 132
5	132 + 12 = 144
6	144 + 0 = 144
7	144 – 9 = 135

TABLE 4.5 Marginal Utility in Money

No. of Bananas	*Marginal Utility in Money ($)*
0	–
1	39/3 = 13
2	36/3 = 12
3	33/24 = 11
4	24/3 = 8
5	12/3 = 4
6	0/3 = 0
7	-9/3 = -3

By definition, the marginal utility in terms of money (or dollar) is equal to the marginal utility divided by the utility of a dollar. Thus, we simply divide column 2 of Table 4.3 by 3. The results are given in Table 4.5. ■

4.1.2 Decision Rule

Returning to our example of renting movies, we are now set to answer how many movies you should rent. Recalling that the on-demand movie rental is ¥150, consider renting the first movie. From Table 4.2, compared to no movies, the first movie gives extra utility in terms of money equal to ¥200. But you pay only ¥150. Hence you should rent at least one movie. Similarly, the second movie gives utility worth ¥300, while, again, you pay only ¥150 for it. Thus, the second movie is worth getting. Extending this logic, it follows that you would buy four movies. Would you buy the fifth? The situation is a bit different. The extra gain in utility in terms of money (¥150) exactly equals how much you pay for it. Thus, the answer is: "you may buy the 5th unit or may not; it doesn't matter." But would you buy the sixth unit? Clearly no, because the extra utility gain is worth ¥65 only, less than the price. Hence the answer is: you would rent either four or five movies. Note importantly that when you rent five units,

Marginal Utility of a Product in terms of Money = Its Price. (4.1)

Realise that, if the units in which the good is consumed can be measured continuously as points on a line of real numbers (e.g., rice in kg, grams etc.), there will be little difference between the fourth unit and fifth unit. Thus, the condition (4.1) is the general rule or the general principle of maximising the surplus of total utility over how much you spend on a particular good. It is optimal rule for purchasing or demanding a good.[2]

The condition (4.1) can be expressed in two alternative ways. By definition, the MU of a product in terms of money equals MU of the product divided by the marginal utility of money (dollar, yen, or whatever currency it is). Thus,

$$\frac{\text{Marginal Utility of a Product}}{\text{Marginal Utility of a Rupee}} = \text{Its Price.} \tag{4.2}$$

We can rewrite the above equation as:

$$\frac{\text{Marginal Utility of a Product}}{\text{Its Price}} = \text{Marginal Utility of a Rupee.} \tag{4.3}$$

Any of the conditions (4.1), (4.2), or (4.3) is called the **consumer's equilibrium** condition. "Equilibrium," a commonly used term in economics, means a position of rest. In the present context, the consumer should "rest" with regard to her purchase of a good as soon as the condition (4.1) is met. Loosely, this is sometimes called the "marginal utility − price" principle, implicitly assuming that the marginal utility of a currency unit is equal to one.

It is important to understand that the law of diminishing marginal utility underlies the condition (4.1). How? Compared to the level of purchase or demand at which (4.1) is satisfied, if you have more, the law implies that the extra benefit will be less than the extra cost (the price) and so the surplus cannot be increased. Similarly, if you buy less the law implies that the marginal utility will be higher and thus the benefit foregone exceeds how much is saved in terms of the cost (the price); hence the surplus cannot be increased. Therefore, the surplus is maximised at that point where the "marginal utility = price" principle is met.

This principle is illustrated in Figure 4.2. Assume that the commodity can be measured on a continuous scale and the law of diminishing marginal utility holds right from the first unit of consumption. The curve AB denotes the marginal utility in terms of money curve. Since MU is the addition to TU, the area under this curve equals the total utility in terms of money. Thus, at the consumption level q_1, the total utility in terms of money is equal to the area $0Am_1q_1$. At q_2, it is $0Am_2q_2$. At q_0, it is $0Am_0q_0$, and so on. Let p_0 be the price of the product. The area under the p_0 line measures the total cost or the total expenditure on the good. If the amount q_1 is bought, the total expenditure = price × quantity = the area $0p_0c_1q_1$. Similarly

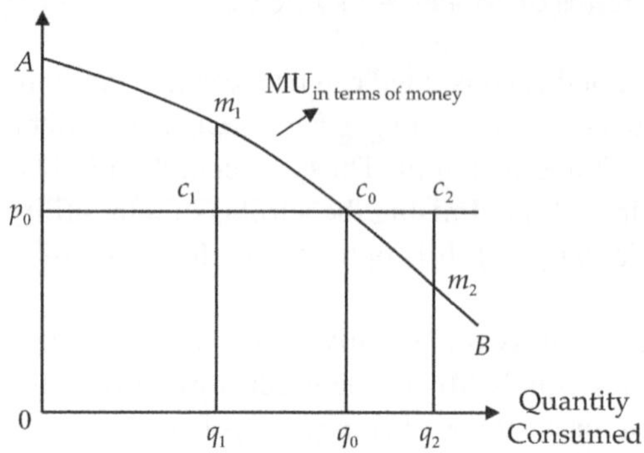

FIGURE 4.2 Optimal Purchase Rule

at q_0, it is $0p_0c_0q_0$, and so on. *Thus, the difference between the area under the MU in terms of money curve and the area below the price line measures the surplus.*

Where is the surplus maximised? The answer is q_0, where the "marginal utility = price" rule holds. The surplus at q_0 equals $0Ac_0q_0 = 0p_0c_0q_0 = Ap_0c_0$. Note that at any point to the left of this level such as q_1, the surplus $= 0Am_1q_1 - 0p_0c_1q_1 = Ap_0c_1m_1 = Ap_0c_0 - m_1c_1c_0 < Ap_0c_0$. At q_2, which is to the right of q_0, similar calculation yields that the surplus $= Ap_0c_0 - m_2c_2c_0 < Ap_0c_0$. This proves that the surplus is maximised at q_0. In general, *the surplus maximising quantity purchased, consumed, or demanded is where the price line intersects with the MU in terms of money curve.*

Example 4.2

Consider the numbers given in Example 4.1. Suppose bananas sell for ₹8 a piece. How many bananas will the consumer buy?

Answer: Compare the marginal utilities in terms of money given in Table 4.5 to the price of banana. Condition (4.1) is met at 4 units of consumption. Hence, the consumer will buy 4 bananas.[3] ■

4.1.3 Why Is the Demand Curve Downward-Sloping?

We can now answer why the demand curve is downward-sloping. Turn to Figure 4.3, which depicts the same "marginal utility in terms of the money" curve *AB* as in Figure 4.2. The "marginal utility = price" rule implies that at the price p_0, the consumer will buy the quantity q_0. At price p_1, she will demand q_1; at the price p_2, her quantity demanded will be q_2, and so on. This means that the points like n_0, n_1, and n_2 must lie on the demand curve. *Hence the marginal utility in terms of money curve itself is the demand curve.* We can simply relabel the *AB* curve in Figure 4.3

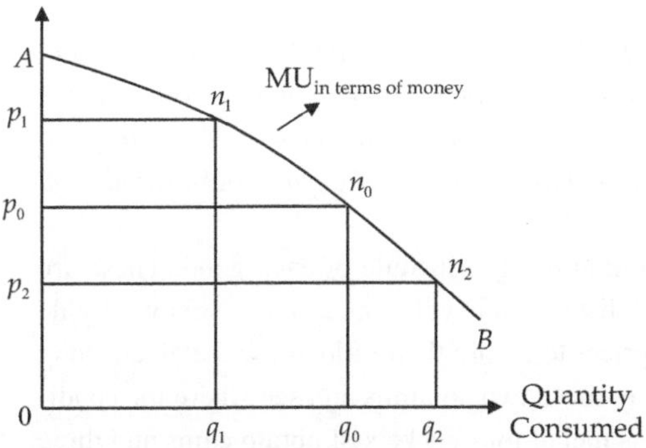

FIGURE 4.3 The Demand Curve

as the demand curve. It follows that *the demand curve is downward-sloping due to the law of diminishing marginal utility.* Simply put, diminishing marginal utility implies that as the consumer buys more of a good, her intensity of desire falls, and she is willing to pay less. That is why when the price falls, she buys more. This is the essence of the marginal-utility theory.

4.1.4 Many Goods

In reality, a consumer buys many goods and services, not just one. In this case, the principle of maximising the surplus is a simple extension of condition (4.3), that is, *the consumer should allocate his spending such that the marginal utility of a rupee must be same for all goods.*

Algebraically, let different goods be named *x*, *y*, *z*, etc. with respective marginal utilities equal to MU_x, MU_y, MU_z, etc. and the respective prices equal to p_x, p_y, p_z, etc. From condition (4.3), the marginal utility of a rupee spent on good *x* equals MU_x / p_x, that on good *y* is equal to MU_y / p_y, and so on. Thus condition (4.3) extends to:

$$\frac{MU_x}{p_x} = \frac{MU_y}{p_y} = \frac{MU_z}{p_z} = \ldots \quad (4.4)$$

This is called the **law of equi-proportional utility.**

The economic reasoning is straightforward. If, for instance, ₹1 brings more marginal utility from consuming say good A than from consuming good B, the consumer's total utility will be increased if more rupees are spent on good A and less on good B. This process should continue till there is no difference between the marginal utility of a rupee spent on different goods.

Example 4.3

Among many things, Sangeeta buys potato chips at ₹20 a packet and comic booklets at ₹30. Her total utility schedules with respect to these two goods are given in Table 4.6. Her marginal utility of money is 2 utils. She has Rs. ₹170 to spend on these two goods. How many potato chips packets and comic books should she buy?

Answer: We first derive the marginal utility schedule of each good. These are additions to the total utility. Table 4.7 lists them in columns 2 and 4. Next we divide the marginal utilities by respective prices to obtain their ratio; these are given along columns (3) and (5). We now compare these two columns and see where the condition (4.4) is satisfied. We see that it is met at four packets of potato chips and three comic books. The cost of this bundle is equal to ₹(4×20 + 3×30) = ₹170, which Sangeeta can just afford. Thus, the answer is that she will buy four packets of potato chips and three comic books. ■

TABLE 4.6 Total Utility from Comic Books

Units Consumed	*Total Utility from Potato Chips Packets*	*Total Utility from Comic Books*
0	0	0
1	60	81
2	116	153
3	163	213
4	203	267
5	239	312
7	271	351
8	300	381

TABLE 4.7 Total Marginal Utilities of the Two Commodities

Units Consumed	*Marginal Utility of Potato Chips*	*Marginal Utility ÷ Price: Potato Chips*	*Marginal Utility of Comic Books*	*Marginal Utility ÷ Price: Comic Books*
(1)	(2)	(3)	(4)	(5)
0	–	–	–	–
1	60	3.00	81	2.70
2	56	2.80	72	2.40
3	47	2.35	60	2.00
4	40	2.00	54	1.80
5	36	1.80	45	1.50
7	32	1.60	39	1.30
8	29	1.45	30	1.0

Although we have got our answer, it is useful to understand the *process* of purchasing these goods sequentially. To start with, Sangeeta has zero amount of potato chips packets or comic books. Should she first buy a potato chips packet or a comic book? Looking at column (3) of Table 4.7, if she buys a potato chips packet, she gets a pleasure equal to 3 utils per rupee. Instead, if she buys a comic book, from column (5), she gets a pleasure equal to 2.8 per rupee. So money is "well spent" on potato chips, i.e., she first buys one packet of potato chips. Her next choice is between buying the second packet of potato chips and the first comic book. Respectively, they offer 2.8 utils per rupee and 2.7 utils per rupee. Hence, Sangeeta will go for her second packet of potato chips. Consider her next choice—which is between the third potato chips packet (yielding 2.4 utils per rupee) and the first comic book (yielding 2.7 utils per rupee). Thus, she will go for her first comic book, which offers higher marginal utility per rupee. Extending this logic, we see that the next two purchases will be a comic book and a packet of potato chips. So far, she has bought three potato chips packets and two comic books. She has spent ₹ $(3\times20+2\times30)=$ ₹120 and is left with ₹50. In the next purchase, both potato chips packet and comic book offer utility equal to 2 utils per rupee. She buys both and spends the remaining ₹50. Her total purchases are four packets of potato chips and three comic books.

4.1.5 A Critique

The marginal utility theory, or, what is sometimes called the Marshallian theory, has some obvious limitations. First, it assumes that the marginal utility of any particular good depends on the amount consumed of that good *only*. In reality, liking or disliking towards one good may depend on how much of some other good is consumed. For example, how much satisfaction you get from buying an extra litre of petrol for your motor bike may depend, in part, on how many times you visit movie theatres near your college. A family's utility from consuming an extra kilogram of rice may depend on how much of wheat it consumes. Second, in explaining how a consumer responds to a price change, it assumes that the marginal utility of money (rupees) is constant. This is not realistic; a change in price would, in general, change a consumer's real income, which, in turn, would change the marginal utility (value) of money. Finally, the marginal utility theory assumes that the consumer can quantify in absolute terms the satisfaction obtained from consuming any given amount of a good. In technical language we say that the consumer measures utility *cardinally*. This is unrealistic, since satisfaction or pleasure is psychological, not something that can be exactly quantified.

Despite these limitations, the Marshallian theory is useful in many ways. First, the basic idea of utility from consuming or experiencing something is used in understanding various economic phenomena. Second, it clearly and simply illustrates the trade-off, or, when you want to demand something but need to pay for it. Third, note that what is critical in understanding demand behaviour is not total utility per se but the *marginal* utility. The "marginal utility = price" rule essentially reflects **marginalism**, *meaning weighing marginal benefit to marginal cost*, which is critical in many economic environments, not just consumer behaviour.

4.2 Indifference-Curve Approach

This is the newer or the "modern" approach to consumer theory, which rectifies the weaknesses of the Marshallian theory outlined above. It features consumer's preference over various goods *together* (as bundles). It also considers how the quantities demanded for various goods are *interrelated* because of the budget constraint facing a consumer. For instance, suppose she has $105 as her income and there are two goods available, say, apples at $15 per dozen and chocolate bars at $12 per dozen. Let a dozen be the unit. We can easily check that this consumer can afford three apples and five chocolates but not five apples and 3 chocolates. In short, how much of different goods a consumer buys depends on her preferences and her budget. The indifference-curve approach looks at the problem of *simultaneously choosing the amounts demanded of several goods.*

Furthermore, it does not assume that the marginal utility of money is constant. Finally, it is not necessary to measure satisfaction or utility cardinally. All that is needed is that the consumer be able to compare or rank utility obtained from any two bundles of goods, without having to assign a number for the absolute amount of satisfaction obtained from consuming a bundle. In formal language, in the indifference-curve approach, utility is measured *ordinally*.

BOX 4.2 "ABSOLUTE" VERSUS "RELATIVE"

Akbar and Birbal figure quite often in north Indian folklores. Birbal was known for his wit and wisdom. Akbar would test him every now and then. Once Akbar drew a straight line on a board and asked Birbal to make it short without erasing it from either side. This was in the presence of all his ministers and noblemen, who thought that it is just not possible to shorten the length of a line without erasing it from any side, they thought Birbal would give up. But look! What did Birbal do? He drew a line bigger than the original one just along it and told the emperor "My lord, it has become shorter." Clever, isn't it?

Suppose your boss calls you in his cabin and asks you to pick one of the two options:

Option A: A 10% increase in your salary and a 50% increase in your colleagues' salaries.

Option B: Nobody gets any increase in salary.

You are not supposed to challenge your boss's wisdom, nor are you allowed to plead. Further, you must decide then and there. You cannot go out of the cabin to communicate or negotiate with your colleagues. *Which option would you pick up and why?*

This experiment has been conducted in the classroom several times in the past. What has been the outcome? Normally, the class is divided into 50–50 with a plus–minus of 10%. Which of the two sides is wrong? Neither. Those who pick option A are considering their absolute gain. Suppose you are one of them. Before you took option A, you and your colleagues were getting the same salary, say ₹50,000 per month. Imagine what will be your salary cheque next month: ₹55,000, whereas your colleagues will receive ₹75,000. Despite an *absolute* increase in your salary, your *relative* salary has declined considerably. But this does not bother you. However, those who took option B are thinking in terms of relative, not absolute, gain. There is nothing rational or irrational about either choice. It depends on the viewpoint or preference of a person.

It is worth noting that, in their standard versions, both the marginal-utility approach and the indifference-curve approach presume that a person's utility depends on that person's consumption only, not that of any other individual. In other words, utility depends on absolute consumption, not relative consumption. If you decide to buy a car made by Honda, your enjoyment from it does not depend on whether your neighbour rides a BMW. In economics, differentiating between "**absolute**" and "**relative**" is important. See Box 4.2 for a further discussion.

4.2.1 Indifference Curve

As suggested by the name, the indifference-curve approach begins with a concept, called the **indifference curve**. It is a very useful geometric construct, describing a consumer's preferences over different "bundles" of goods.

Suppose you (meaning your family) consume only two goods: apples and chocolates. Start with any combination of these goods which you (the consumer) may want to consume without any consideration of whether you can afford it. One possibility is, say, 0 apples along with 40 chocolates. In short, write this "bundle" as (0, 40). Consider another bundle with 1 apple and some chocolates. Ask yourself how many chocolates, along with 1 apple, will give you the same satisfaction as does the bundle (0, 40)?

Assume that you always prefer more of a commodity to less, which, formally, is called the assumption of *non-satiation*, or "greediness."[4] This assumption helps in answering the question posed above. Since you are getting more apples than before (1 instead of 0), you will be willing to give up some chocolates—so as to enjoy the same level of satisfaction as before. Suppose it is 30 chocolates for you.

Then, you are "indifferent" between the bundles (0, 40) and (1, 30). Similarly, suppose that, if you consume 2 apples, you need 22 chocolates to make you indifferent between this bundle and the previous two. Table 4.8 lists various bundles, giving you equal satisfaction, i.e., you are indifferent between any pair of bundles in the list.

Figure 4.4(a) graphs these bundles and joins them. The resulting curve is *an* **indifference curve**, *generally defined as a locus of commodity bundles among which a consumer is indifferent.* If goods are measured on a continuous scale as points on a real line, not as just integers 1, 2, 3, etc., this curve will look very smooth, as drawn in Figure 4.4(b). In what follows, we will, on many occasions, use the short-hand "IC" for indifference curve.

Individual tastes can be different. Your tastes may be similar to your best friend's but not the same. Your brother's tastes may be very different from yours. Figure 4.5 shows ICs showing different tastes for four boys. Look at first Ram and Rahim's. They are downward-sloping as in Figure 4.4(b). But, the difference is that Rahim's is much flatter than Ram's. What does this mean? It implies that Ram has a strong preference, in some sense, for apples and Rahim has a strong preference for chocolate. How? Look at Ram's IC first. He is indifferent between (5 apples, 6 chocolates) and

TABLE 4.8 Bundles among which the Consumer Is Indifferent

Apples	*Chocolates*
0	40
1	30
2	22
3	15
4	9
5	5
6	2
7	0

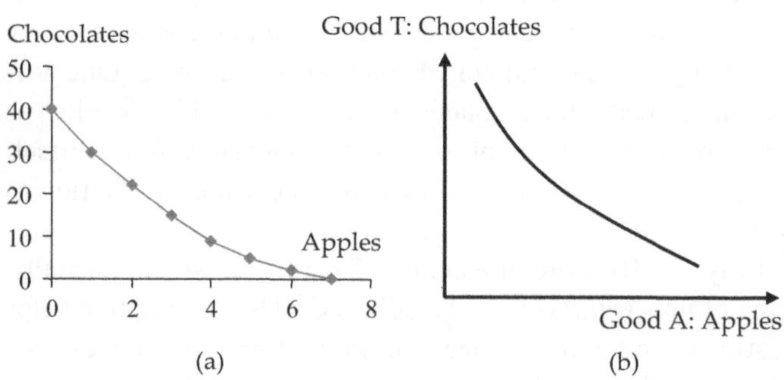

FIGURE 4.4 Indifference Curve

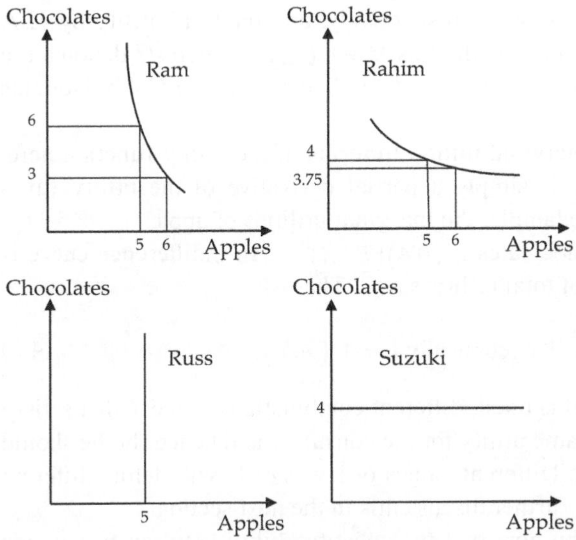

FIGURE 4.5 Various Indifference Curves

(6 apples, 3 chocolates). Compared to the first bundle, if he wants one extra apple, he is willing to give up 3 chocolates. However, notice that if Rahim wants one extra apple, he is only willing to give up 0.25 chocolates. That is, Ram is willing to give up more chocolates than Rahim—which is same as saying that Ram has a weaker preference for chocolate and Rahim has a stronger preference for the same. Put differently, Ram has a strong preference for apples, while Rahim has a strong liking for chocolates. The point is that *steepness or flatness of indifference curves indicates the relative strength of preference towards goods.*

Now look at Russ's IC. It is vertical, i.e., its steepness is absolute. Hence, Russ is an extreme case of Ram. His satisfaction depends only on how many apples he consumes. He is willing to give up any quantity of chocolates to get one more apple. That is why his indifference curve is vertical. Similarly, Suzuki is an extreme case of Rahim. His satisfaction depends only on chocolates, and he is ready to give up any amount of apples for an extra unit of chocolate.

From now on however, we will analyse downward-sloping indifference curves like Ram's or Rahim's and will ignore the special cases like Russ's or Suzuki's.

4.2.2 Basis of the Indifference Curves and the Marginal Rate of Substitution

Indifference curves are based on the notion of a **utility function or a total utility function**, relating total utility to different commodity bundles consumed. This is more general than the total utility function based on consumption of a single good in the marginal-utility theory. Denote the quantities consumed of apples and chocolates as A and T, respectively, and the total utility by V. A general utility function can be specified as $V = U(A,T)$, where U denotes the utility function. An example will be $V = A^{0.6}T^{0.4}$. It is called a Cobb–Douglas utility function.[5]

Recall the definition of marginal utility. In terms of the utility function here, realise that marginal utility is simply a partial derivative of the utility function. In the Cobb–Douglas example, the marginal utilities of apples is $\partial V / \partial A = (0.6)(T / A)^{0.4}$ and that of chocolates is $(0.4)(T / A)^{0.6}$. An indifference curve is defined at some *given* level of total utility, say $\bar{V}$. That is,

$$\text{Indifference Curve defined algebraically } \bar{V} = U(A,T). \tag{4.5}$$

Because the total utility level is fixed, different combinations A and T that satisfy equation (4.5) generate the same utility for the consumer and hence she/he should be indifferent between them. Different values or levels of $\bar{V}$ will define different indifference curves. We will further discuss this in the next section.

You must have realised by now that the substitutability between two goods underlies the downward-sloping shape of the indifference curve. *The rate of sacrifice of one good for the other along a* **given** *indifference curve is called the* **marginal rate of substitution (MRS).** For instance, if you go back to Table 4.8, starting with the bundle (0, 40), one unit increase in apples requires a sacrifice of 10 chocolates. Hence the MRS of apples for chocolates is 10. That of chocolate for apples is the inverse of this, equal to 1/10. Similarly, between the bundles (1, 30) and (2, 22), the MRS of apples for chocolates is 8 and that of chocolate for apples is 1/8, and so on. Marginal rate of substitution is an important concept in the indifference-curve analysis. Let us further understand it via the following example.

Example 4.4

Consider the indifference schedule given in Table 4.9. Between different adjacent bundles, compute the marginal rate of substitution of one good vis-à-vis the other.

Answer: As the consumer moves from bundle A to bundle B, one unit increase in good Y entails a sacrifice of 91 – 87 = 4 units of good X. Hence the MRS of Y for X is 4 units of good X. The MRS of X for Y is the inverse of that of Y for X; this is equal to ¼. Table 4.10 lists the MRSs between various bundles. ■

There is a relationship between MRS and marginal utility. Let the marginal utility of apples and that of chocolate be, respectively, denoted as MU_{apples} and $MU_{chocolates}$. Suppose that the MRS of apples is equal to m (chocolates). Then, by the definition of MRS, the utility from m chocolates must be equal to MU_{apples}. By the definition of marginal utility, the utility gained from consuming m chocolates =

TABLE 4.9 Indifference Schedule

Bundles	*Good X*	*Good Y*
A	91	1
B	87	2
C	75	4
D	61	6
E	53	7
F	23	10
G	1	12

TABLE 4.10 Marginal Rate of Substitution

Between Bundles	*MRS of* X *for* Y	*MRS of* Y *for* X
A & B	¼	4
B & C	1/6	6
C &D	1/7	7
D & E	1/8	8
E & F	1/10	10
F &G	1/11	11

$m.\text{MU}_{\text{chocolates}}$. Hence $m.\text{MU}_{\text{chocolates}} = \text{MU}_{\text{apples}}$, implying $m = \text{MU}_{\text{chocolates}}/\text{MU}_{\text{apples}}$, i.e., *MRS equals the ratio of marginal utilities.*

Importantly, MRS relates also to the slope of an IC.[6] To see this, consider the IC drawn in Figure 4.6(a). Starting with the bundle (A_0, T_0), consider another bundle (A_1, T_1), which has a slightly higher quantity of apples. The MRS of apples is the ratio $T_0T_1 / A_0A_1 = \text{AC} / \text{BC}$. If you now imagine sliding A_1 closer to A_0, so that the increase in apples is very small and the distance *BC* tends to zero, then the ratio *AC/BC* is nothing but the slope of the indifference curve at (A_0, T_0). Hence, MRS is equal to the slope of the indifference curve.[7] Figure 4.6(b) depicts another IC with *M* and *N* as two bundles on it. The MRS of apples for chocolates at *M* is the slope of the tangent line *CMD* and at *N* it is the slope of the tangent line *ENF*. In other words, *MRS is equal to the slope of an indifference curve. Notice that as you move to the right on the apples axis, the indifference curve becomes flatter, i.e., the absolute value of the slope declines. This is called the* **law of diminishing marginal rate of substitution**. *It means intuitively that if a consumer wants more and more of one good, the other good becomes more and more scarce to her and she is willing to sacrifice less and less of the other good. This is the counterpart of the law of diminishing marginal utility in the Marshallian theory. Because of the decreasing slope of the indifference as we move to the right, diminishing MRS underlies the convex shape of the indifference curve.*

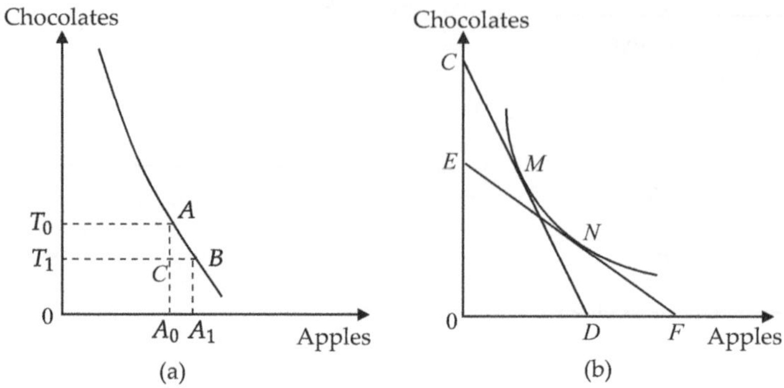

FIGURE 4.6 Marginal Rate of Substitution

If, in general, there are two goods a and b, we have:

$$\mathrm{MRS}_{a\text{ for }b} = \frac{\mathrm{MU}_a}{\mathrm{MU}_b} = \text{slope of the IC on the axis measuring } a. \tag{4.6}$$

4.2.3 Indifference Map

Remember that in attempting to introduce an indifference curve, we started with an arbitrary bundle (0, 40). Had we started with a different one, say (2, 40), we would have obtained a different indifference curve—showing bundles which offer the same utility as does (2, 40). A consumer's taste is represented not by a single indifference curve but by many indifference curves. *A collection of indifference curves is called an* **indifference map.** Each indifference curve in an indifference map stands for some level of satisfaction or utility relative to some other level of satisfaction. In terms of equation (4.5) defining the indifference curve, different values of $\bar{V}$ generates an indifference map, as shown in Figure 4.7.

Nowhere in the indifference-curve analysis, is the consumer assumed to tell or "assign" any particular number to the level of satisfaction obtained from consuming a bundle. She is only required to compare or rank utility between any pair bundles. If two bundles yield the same level of satisfaction (without further quantification), then both lie on the same indifference curve. Otherwise, one bundle lies on a higher indifference compared to the other. In this sense, utility is measured "ordinally," not cardinally.

4.2.4 Budget Line or Price Line

The indifference curve or the indifference map shows a consumer's preferences, tastes, or likes–dislikes. As we move to the right in an indifference map, it means more consumption of goods and more utility or satisfaction, even though we

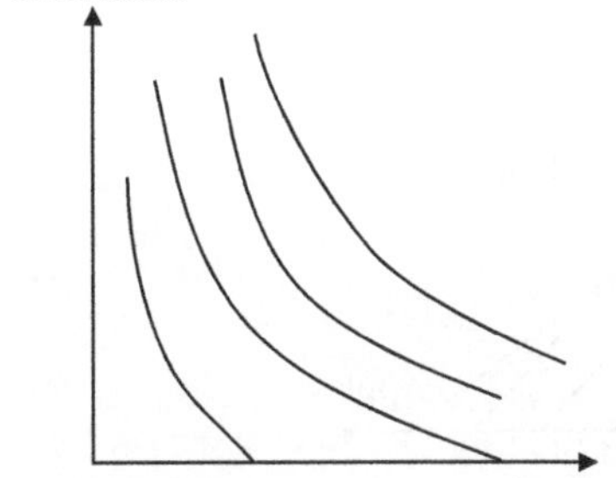

FIGURE 4.7 An Indifference Map

cannot measure utility exactly. However, wishes and aspirations are one thing and affordability is another.

We now bring in how much of goods a consumer can afford to buy. Given what can be bought, a consumer would buy the bundle she/he likes the best. Common sense suggests that affordability should depend on two factors: (a) prices of various goods a consumer wants to consume and (b) her income.[8]

Suppose that the price of apples is \$15 (per dozen) and that of a chocolate bar is \$12 (per dozen). Denote the respective prices as $p_A = 15$ and $p_T = 12$. Suppose Robert's income (say M) is ₹300. What different combinations (bundles) of apples and chocolates *can* he buy with his income and these prices? For simplicity, assume that both these goods can be measured on a continuous scale. Table 4.11 lists some of these bundles. Note that the total cost of each bundle is $M = \$300$.

Figure 4.8(a) graphs the bundles in Table 4.11. Joining them gives us the **price line** or the **budget line**, *defined as the locus of bundles of the two goods the*

TABLE 4.11 Bundles that Robert can Buy, Given Prices and Income

$p_F = 15; p_T = 12; M = 300$

Apples	Chocolates
0	25
4	20
8	15
12	10
16	5
20	0

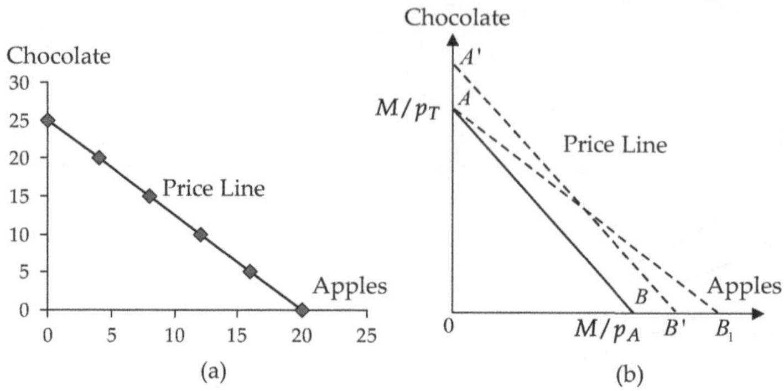

FIGURE 4.8 The Price/Budget Line

consumer can buy by fully spending her income, given the prices and her income. In general, the price line shows the budget equation:

$$\text{Budget Equation } p_A A + p_T T = M. \tag{4.7}$$

This is exhibited in Figure 4.8(b) by a line such as *AB*. (Ignore, for now the dotted lines.) If all income were spent of apples, the consumer would get M / p_A amount of apples. This marks the intercept of the budget line *AB* on the apples axis. Likewise, M / p_T is the budget line's intercept on the chocolates axis. Note that the slope of the budget line, rise/run, is equal to $(M / p_T) \div (M / p_A) = p_A / p_T$. That is, *the slope of the price line is the ratio of prices.*

Note that a consumer can afford to buy any combination of goods on or inside the price line. *The area inside or on the price line is called the* **budget set**. If a bundle is on the line, then buying that bundle exhausts all income. A bundle strictly inside the line means that the income is not fully spent. However, a rational consumer who prefers more to less will consume *on* the budget line.

The question is: Given a budget line like *AB* in Figure 4.7(b), which point on *AB* will a rational consumer choose?

4.2.5 Consumer's Equilibrium

Turn to Figure 4.9. Note that, on the budget line *AB*, the point of tangency *E* ensures most satisfaction to the consumer, the utility level being indicated by indifference curve IC_0. Any other point of the budget line will offer utility such as IC_1. Hence the consumer's optimal consumption or purchase bundle is A_0 of apples and T_0 of chocolates, which is associated with tangency point *E*. We say that the consumer attains equilibrium at point *E*.

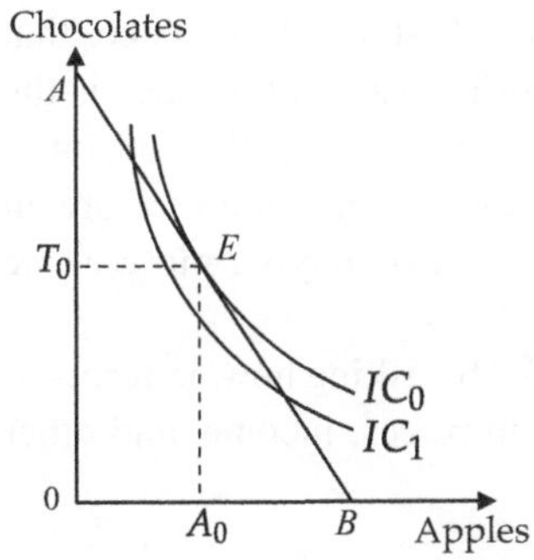

FIGURE 4.9 Consumer's Equilibrium

The point of tangency is where the slope of the indifference curve is equal to the slope of the budget line. Recall that the former is the marginal rate of substitution (MRS), which, in turn, is equal to the ratio of marginal utilities (see (equation 4.6)), and, the latter is the price ratio.

Therefore, the **consumer's equilibrium condition** (over any two goods x and y) is, in general,

$$\text{MRS}_{x\text{ for }y} = \frac{\text{MU}_x}{\text{MU}_y} = \frac{p_x}{p_y}. \tag{4.8}$$

The consumer's equilibrium condition can be approached in a different but an equivalent way. Denote the marginal utility of a dollar (unit of a currency) by $\text{MU}_{\$1}$. Then, if for example, good x costs p_x dollars (i.e., the price of good x is p_x), an extra unit purchased of good x involves giving up p_x dollars and hence giving up utility equal to $p_x.\text{MU}_{\$1}$. On the other hand, the extra unit purchased (and consumed) yields extra pleasure equal to the marginal utility of the good, i.e., MU_x. A rational consumer must allocate his spending on a good such that these *marginal* utility losses and gains at the margin be equal, i.e., $p_x.\text{MU}_{\$1} = \text{MU}_x$. It is because, if, for example, $p_x.\text{MU}_{\$1} < \text{MU}_x$, the consumer will gain by consuming a bit more good x, as the extra utility cost of acquiring it is less than the extra gain in utility from consuming the good. Similarly, if $p_x.\text{MU}_{\$1} > \text{MU}_x$, the consumer is spending "too much" on good x and will be better off by spending less on this good. We can express $p_x.\text{MU}_{\$1} = \text{MU}_x$ as $\text{MU}_x / p_x = \text{MU}_{\$1}$. This condition must hold for any commodity consumed. Hence, in general, if the consumer consumes many goods, $x, y, z, \cdots$, we can write the consumer's equilibrium condition as:

$$\frac{\text{MU}_x}{p_x} = \frac{\text{MU}_y}{p_y} = \frac{\text{MU}_z}{p_z} = \ldots = \text{MU}_{\$1}. \tag{4.9}$$

Note that equation (4.9) is a generalised version of equation (4.8) and same as equation (4.4), obtained in the marginal-utility theory. It states, in essence, that the consumer's equilibrium is attained when the marginal value of a rupee is the same across all goods consumed. As noted earlier, if, for instance, the consumer allocates her spending such that the marginal utility of ₹1 spent on an ice cream is greater than that spent on apples, she will be better off by buying more of ice creams and less of apples.

We now put the indifference-curve theory "to work" by asking how, in terms of the theory, a rational consumer responds to changes in prices, income, and other determinants of demand.

4.2.6 Change in Income

We begin with the effects of a change in income. Consider Figure 4.9 in relation to Figure 4.8(b) and ask yourself what happens if the consumer's income (total spending) increases. As long as prices remain unchanged, an increase in income will shift the budget line to the right (from AB to $A'B'$ in panel (b) of Figure 4.8—which means intuitively that the consumer can afford to purchase more of both goods. With the new budget line, there will be a new tangency point. Compared to the original point E associated with A_0 of apples and T_0 of chocolate in Figure 4.9, will the consumer buy more of both apples and chocolates? The general answer is "no," but the likely outcome is "yes." That is, a consumer will normally buy more of both goods when income rises, but it is possible that she will consume less of one of the two goods. (A rational consumer will never buy less of both goods when income increases so long as she prefers more to less of a good.) Indeed, there are examples of goods, the demand for which falls with an increase in income. Indeed, we have already discussed this in Chapter 2 in relation to income elasticity of demand. These are called **inferior goods**, which are typically necessities that relatively poor families buy because of income constraints, but do not really "like" them. Otherwise, if the demand for a product increases with an increase in income, it is called a **normal good**. Obviously, instances of normal goods far outnumber those of inferior goods.

4.2.7 Price Effect

The IC approach provides a deeper understanding of how price changes affect quantities that are demanded. Suppose the consumer's income and the price of one of the two goods, say, chocolates remain unchanged but apples become costlier. How would it affect the demand of apples and chocolates? A change in the price of a product alters the *relative* cost of products to the consumer, which is called the **relative price.** For instance, an increase in the price of apples together with no change in the price of chocolates makes apples relatively costlier, i.e., raises the relative price of apples. This induces a **substitution effect**: the consumer would tend to buy less of apples and more of chocolates as the relative price of apples increases. The marginal-utility theory also illustrates this substitution effect, although we did not introduce this term then.

In addition, the IC approach reveals that, as the price of a product increases, it also entails a negative **income effect** in the sense that the consumer's buying power is reduced. Imagine what would happen to the consumption of a family whose income remains unchanged, while prices of what it consumes increase. This would shift of the budget line inward. That is, a negative income effect will kick in from an increase in the price of a consumable.

Let us be more specific. Assume as before that Robert's income is \$300 and initially $p_A = 15$ and $p_T = 12$. He was buying 12 apples and 10 chocolates. Suppose the price of chocolates remains unchanged while the price of apples increases from \$15 to \$18. If he continues to buy the same quantity of apples, that is, 12, he must spend an extra $\$3 \times 12 = \$36$. In a way, this is a loss to Robert, which we can interpret as a decline in the real income or purchasing power of Robert. In general then, *a rise or fall in the price of a commodity leads to a decrease or an increase in the real income of a consumer.* Returning to the case of an increase in the price of apples, the resultant negative income effect would tend to reduce or increase the consumption of it accordingly as it is a normal or an inferior good.

Thus, an important insight obtained from the indifference-curve analysis is that a price change exerts two effects on quantities demanded: a substitution effect and an income effect. More precisely,

$$\text{Price Effect} = \text{Substitution Effect} + \text{Income Effect}. \tag{4.10}$$

We may note that the marginal-utility theory with constant marginal value of money captures the substitution effect, not the income effect.

For a clearer understanding, the two effects of an increase in the price of apples on quantities demanded of both goods are shown in Table 4.12 assuming that both apples and chocolates are normal goods. As apples become relatively more costly compared to chocolates, by the substitution effect the demand for apples decreases

TABLE 4.12 Substitution and Income Effects

		Demand for Apples	*Demand for Chocolates*	*Overall Effect on Demand for Apples*	*Overall Effect on Demand for Chocolates*
Increase in the price of apples (Price Effect)	Substitution Effect	Negative	Positive	Negative	Ambiguous
	Income Effect	Negative	Negative		

and that for chocolates increases. Assuming that both goods are normal, a decrease in real income from an increase in the price of apples implies a decrease in the demand for both apples and chocolate. The overall impacts of an increase in the price of apples on the demand for apples and chocolate are summarised in the last two columns of Table 4.12.

If one of the goods happens to be inferior, then the net effects become further ambiguous. For instance, if, for someone, apples are an inferior good (hard to imagine), then the income effect of an increase in the price of apples on its consumption will be positive—which runs opposite to the substitution effect. But if the (perverse) income effect is not large enough, the substitution effect dominates, and the directions of change listed in Table 4.12 hold. But, if apples are strongly inferior, the perverse income effect outweighs the substitution effect, resulting in an overall positive price effect. That is, an increase in the own price would increase the quantity demanded for it, "defying," so to speak, the Law of Demand. In general, such a good, a few exist, is called a **Giffen good**, named after its discoverer, Sir Robert Giffen. Giffen observed this among the poor people in England at that time.[9]

Why the Demand Curve is Downward-Sloping: Once Again

The nature of the price effect explains why the demand curve is downward-sloping. By the substitution effect, the quantity demanded of a good falls unambiguously with an increase in the own price. In addition, if the good is normal, the decline in real income associated with the increase in price implies less demand. Hence the demand falls, that is, the demand curve is downward-sloping on account of both substitution and income effects. If the good is inferior but the income effect is relatively small, the substitution effect outweighs the income effect, and the demand curve is (still) downward-sloping. Only in the case of a good where the product is inferior and the income effect is strong enough, the quantity demanded increases with own price and thus the demand curve is not downward-sloping. This is the case of a Giffen good.

Cross-Price Effects

How does a change in the price of say good x affect the demand for another good say y? We can understand this through our earlier example of an increase in the price of apples, except that we are asking how this affects the demand for chocolate. Substitution and income effects outlined in Table 4.12 are at work here too. The demand for chocolates will increase due to the substitution effect, whereas the income effect on chocolates depends on whether it is a normal or an inferior good. The sum of the two effects measures the cross-price effect. If the two goods are substitutes in taste like tea and coffee, the substitution effect will be dominant. Hence, *the demand for a good would increase with the price of a substitute good.* If they are complementary like tea–sugar or automobile repair +services, the income effect will be dominant and thus *a demand for a good would decrease with the price of a complementary good.*

4.2.8 A Summary of Conclusions from the Indifference-Curve Approach

The IC approach implies the following:

- Own substitution effect is unambiguously negative.
- Own price effect is negative because of both substitution and income effects (assuming normal goods). Even if it is an inferior good, the own price effect is negative as long as the income effect is outweighed by the substitution effect. This explains why the demand curve is downward-sloping.
- In relation to Chapter 2 we learn that Giffen goods are those inferior goods for which perverse income effect outweighs the substitution effect and as a result the law of demand does not hold.
- If two goods are substitutes (e.g., tea and coffee), then an increase in the price of one good will result in the increase in the demand for the other good. If they are complements (e.g., laptop and software packages on a laptop), an increase in the price of one good will decrease the quantity demanded of the other.

The concepts that lead to these conclusions are the diminishing marginal rate of substitution, substitution effect, and income effect.

Further details of the IC analysis and the revealed-preference approach are explored in the appendices to this chapter.

Facts and Insights

- In Marshallian theory of consumer behaviour, satisfaction/utility from consuming a product is assumed to be cardinally measurable.
- Law of diminishing utility is a fundamental assumption. It states that after a certain level of consumption (possibly from the very first unit), the marginal utility falls as more and more of a product is consumed.
- A consumer attains equilibrium with respect to buying a good when the marginal utility of the product in terms of money equals the price of the product.
- A consumer attains equilibrium with respect to buying many goods when the marginal utility of \$1/₹1spent on each good is same across all goods.
- The demand curve is downward-sloping because of the law of diminishing marginal utility.
- In the indifference-curve analysis, the slope of an indifference curve is the marginal rate of substitution of one good for another.
- In the indifference-curve analysis, the law of diminishing marginal rate of substitution is a fundamental assumption and the counterpart of the law of diminishing marginal utility.

- The law of diminishing marginal rate of substitution states that, along an indifference curve, as a consumer consumes more and more of a product, he/she is willing to forego less and less of some other product.
- The slope of the price line (same as budget line) is the ratio prices of two commodities.
- In the indifference-curve analysis, a consumer attains equilibrium when the indifference curve is tangent to the price/budget line, or equivalently, the marginal rate of substitution of one good in terms of another is equal to the respective price ratio.
- An increase in income may increase, decrease, or may not affect the demand for a good. If the quantity demanded of a product increases (respectively decreases) with income, then we call the product as normal or superior good (respectively inferior good).
- An increase (a decrease) in the price of a product increases (lowers) its relative price and lowers (raises) the real income of a consumer—in that his budget line shifts out (shifts in). This leads to a substitution effect and an income effect of a price change.
- Price effect = a substitution effect + an income effect.
- The own substitution effect of a price change on the quantity demanded is always negative.
- As the price of a product increases, the demand for a normal good decreases on account of both the substitution effect and the income effect. Therefore, the quantity demanded goes down unambiguously.
- For an inferior good, as its price rises, the quantity demanded may decrease or increase, since the substitution effect and the income effect exert opposite movements on the quantity demanded.
- A Giffen good is an inferior good such that the perverse income effect outweighs the substitution effect. Hence the Law of Demand doesn't hold.
- Substitution effect and income effect are also at work in the effect of a change in price of one good on the quantity demand of another. The cross-price effect of an increase in the price of a good on another is positive or negative as the two goods are substitutes or complements.

Exercises

Descriptive/Analytical

4.1. How are total utility and marginal utility curves related? "If we know a total utility schedule, we can derive a marginal utility schedule and vice versa." Is this correct? Give reasons.

4.2. Explain in terms of diminishing marginal utility the logic behind the Law of Demand.

4.3. "An inferior good is a Giffen good, but a Giffen good is not necessarily an inferior good." Defend or refute.

Short Answer (word limit = 500 approx.)

4.4. Among many other goods, Mumtaz regularly buys oil for her hair (L) and hand lotions (N). Let MU_L and MU_N denote the respective marginal utilities and p_L and p_N their prices. Both goods are measured continuously. She is spending €200 on hair oil and €140 on hand lotions and the marginal utilities are such that $MU_L / MU_N > p_L / p_N$. Is her spending on these two goods optimal? Or should she reallocate her spending? Give reasons.

4.5. Suppose the two goods are A and B. The respective prices are $p_A = 10$ and $p_B = 15$. Income is 300. Draw the budget line.

4.6. What is meant by "relative price"? Explain it via an example outside of the text.

4.7. How will a decrease in the price of a good shift the price line and why?

4.8. Suppose income and prices of all goods increase by the same percentage. How will it affect the budget line and why?

4.9. How will a decrease in income, coupled with an increase in the price of one good, shift the price line and why?

4.10. Suppose the price of an inferior good falls. Outline how this will affect the quantity demanded of this good via the substitution effect and the income effect.

4.11. "The own substitution effect is always negative, i.e., when the price of a product falls, by the substitution effect the consumer will demand more of it." Defend or refute.

4.12. Explain in terms of substitution and income effect, why the demand curve for a product is normally downward-sloping.

4.13. "The marginal-utility theory considers both the income and the substitution effect of a price change." Do you agree or disagree? Give reasons.

Quizzes/Numerical

4.14. Jim's total utility schedule from buying a phone card for international calls is the following.

Minutes of Call	*Total Utility*
0	0
1	50
2	95
3	135
4	170
5	200
6	225
7	245
8	260

The phone card costs \$0.25 per minute and Jim's marginal utility of a dollar is 96. How many minutes of call will he buy?

4.15. In a small town in Punjab, India, carrot *halwa* (a dessert for the winter) sells for ₹40/kg. A family, whose members love carrot *halwa*, consumes 3.5 kg of carrot *halwa* (over a week) and its marginal utility is 100 utils. Assume that carrot *halwa* can be measured continuously. If for this family the marginal utility of rupee is 2 utils, should it consume more, less, or is its consumption level of carrot *halwa* optimal?

Units Consumed	*Marginal Utility: Chicken Rolls*	*Marginal Utility: Ice Cream*
0	0	0
1	62.5	48.0
2	55.0	40.0
3	50.0	36.0
4	42.5	30.0
5	37.5	24.0
6	25.0	18.0

4.16. An avid eater has \$41 to spend on chicken roll and ice cream, selling at prices \$5 and \$4, respectively. The total utility schedules are given in the following table. How many chicken rolls and ice creams will this person consume?

4.17. Suppose a low-income family has "income" (meaning total spending) of ₹2,000/week. It spends this income on two goods: sugar and potato (highly unlikely but we can imagine). The price of potato is ₹25/kg. Sugar can be bought from the ration shop and the open market. The ration shop price of sugar is ₹10/kg and a consumer can buy a maximum of 5 kg of sugar. In the open market sugar can be bought at ₹40/kg. Draw the consumer's price line.

Appendix 4.A Further Analysis of the Indifference-Curve Approach

Starting with Figure 4.4(b), which depicts smoothly downward-sloping and convex-to-the-origin indifference curve, we first note that in some situations, ICs may look like the ones drawn in Figure 4.10. These are special cases.

4.1A Special Cases

The ICs look rectangular in Figure 4.10(a). This is the case where the consumer always consumes the two goods in a fixed proportion. For instance, if there are only two goods, say tea and sugar, and you are extremely particular about the proportion

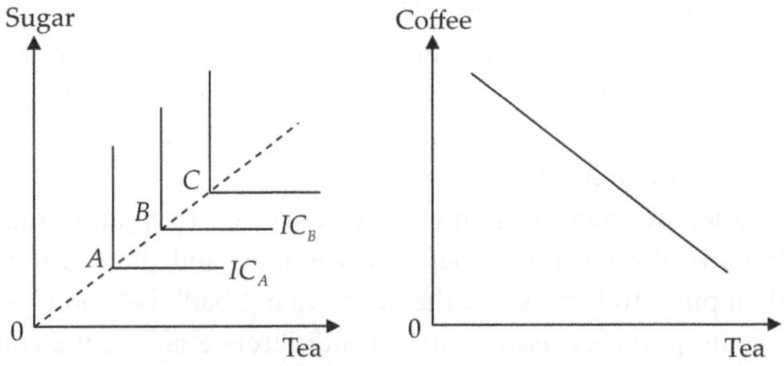

(a) Perfect Complements (b) Perfect Substitutes

FIGURE 4.10 Special Cases

of sugar to tea, then the amount of tea being given, an increase in sugar per se will not add to your utility, or the amount of sugar being given, an increase in tea per se will not make you happier. In panel (a), this proportion is given by the slope of the dotted ray through the origin. For example, if you are initially consuming at point *A* and given more tea (but no more or no less sugar) you get the same amount of satisfaction as at *A*. This explains the horizontal segment of the indifference curve IC_A. Similarly, if you are given more sugar but there is no change in tea consumption you are as well off as at *A*; this explains the vertical part of the same IC. Of course, if you get more sugar and more tea in the same proportion you are happier. For instance, IC_B with more tea and more sugar at *B* than at *A* represents higher utility than IC_A. Panel (a) depicts the case where the two goods are a **perfect complement** of each other. Such indifference curves represent zero substitutability in consumption between the two goods, i.e., the MRS between the two goods is 0.

Next, consider Figure 4.10(b), where the indifference curves are straight lines. Since the slope of a straight line is fixed, it means that a fixed amount of one good is given up for acquiring one extra unit of the other—so that the consumer's utility is unchanged. Thus, the two goods are **perfect substitutes** for each other. It is as if one unit of one good is being sacrificed in order to have one more unit of the other good, when units are defined appropriately. Put differently, the two goods are virtually the same good in the perception or taste of the consumer. It can happen for products like tea and coffee, or more "realistically," say white-coloured pens and pink-coloured pens of the same quality. The MRS between two perfectly substitutes is infinite.

Having noted these special cases, we return to the normal looking downward-sloping, convex-to-the-origin smooth ICs.

4.2A Properties of Indifference Curves

1. They are downward-sloping, which follows from the assumption of non-satiation. However, suppose that one good is an economic "bad" in the sense that the more you consume of it, the worse you feel, e.g., pollution.

In this case, the marginal utility is negative. Non-satiation does not hold obviously—indeed, the opposite of it holds. However, let the other good (say apples) satisfy non-satiation. How would an indifference curve with apples and pollution look like? It will be *upward* sloping, as shown in Figure 4.11, because if you are given more of the "bad," you need to be compensated with *more* of the "good" to be indifferent.

But, unless any specific mention is made, we continue to assume that the assumption of non-satiation (explained later) is met, and the indifference is downward-sloping. Indeed, since the negative of "bad" is "good," if we want to analyse the pollution issue with an indifference curve, we can always think of "environment" as the opposite of pollution and the indifference curve with environment on one axis and apples on the other will be downward-sloping. Thus, essentially, no generalisation is lost if we say that an indifference curve is downward-sloping.

2. Any two indifference curves for a given individual cannot intersect. We "prove" this "by contradiction." Consider Figure 4.12(a). To the contrary, let the two indifference curves, IC_1 and IC_2, intersect, as shown. Mark bundles *A*, *B*, and *C*. The bundle *A* is common in both indifference curves. The bundles *B* and *C* have the same quantity of apples (A_1), but *C* has more chocolates (T_2) than *B* (T_1). The last fact implies that the consumer prefers *C* to *B*. Note also that the consumer is indifferent between *A* and *B* (since both lie on the indifference curve IC_1) and she is also indifferent between *A* and *C* (as both lie on the indifference curve IC_2). The last two statements imply that the consumer must be indifferent between *B* and *C*. This however contradicts that *C* is preferred to *B*. Hence our supposition that two indifference curves intersect cannot be true.
3. An indifference curve to the right of a given indifference curve represents higher utility or satisfaction. This is simple and intuitive. In Figure 4.12(b), IC_2 is to the right of IC_1. Mark bundle *D* on IC_1 and bundle *E* on IC_2. Both have same quantity of apples (equal to A_2), but *E* has more chocolate (T_4 as

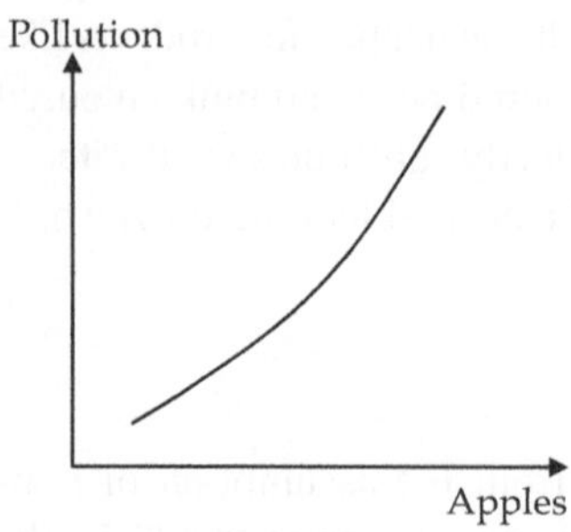

FIGURE 4.11 Indifference Curve with an Economic "Bad"

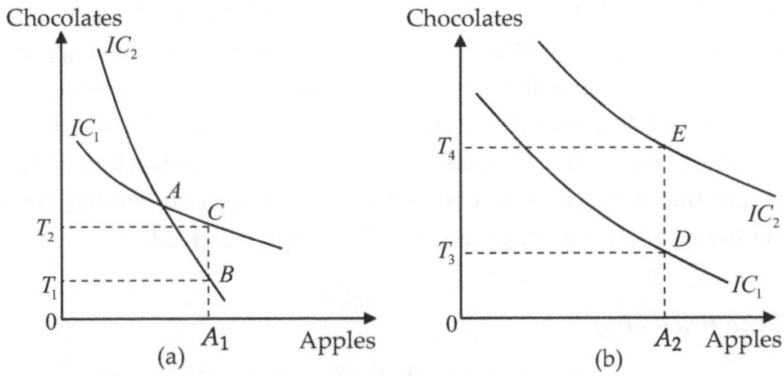

FIGURE 4.12 Some Properties of Indifference Curves

compared to T_3). Hence, E is preferred to D and therefore IC_2 must represent higher utility than IC_1.

4. As discussed in the text, diminishing marginal rate of substitution implies that *an indifference curve is convex to the origin.*[10]

4.3A Structure of Preferences

At a more fundamental (basic) level, the definitions of indifference curve and indifference map and the properties of indifference curve are based on the following assumptions on a consumer's preferences.

Comparability: This states that, given any two bundles, say A and B, the consumer can always compare them: either she prefers A to B, or prefers B to A, or she is indifferent between the two. In other words, she cannot say that "I do not know how to rank these two bundles." What does this assumption imply in our indifference curve analysis? It implies that for any two bundles, one must have an indifference curve passing through each, and by comparing the indifference curves, the consumer can always rank the two bundles.

Consistency: It states that if one bundle is preferred to another, the latter cannot be preferred to the former. This may appear too obvious, but, nonetheless, an assumption.

Non-Satiation: We already know what this is. It is merely stated here in more general terms. That is, if there are two bundles A and B, and, if compared to B, A has more quantities of some goods and no less of any good, then the consumer prefers A to B. In terms of the indifference map, it means that an indifference curve to the right represents higher utility.

Transitivity: If there are three bundles, say A, B, and C, such that A is preferred to B, and B is preferred to C, then A must be preferred to C. Recall that this assumption is used in proving that two indifference curves cannot intersect.

Convexity: Suppose that the consumer is indifferent between two bundles, A and B. The bundle A has 6 apples and 10 chocolates, while the bundle B has 4 apples and 16 chocolates. Take the average of apples in the two bundles, which have 5 apples. Similarly take the average of chocolates in the two bundles; it is 13. Consider a bundle C having the respective average amounts, i.e., 5 apples and 13 chocolates. Convexity of preferences means that the consumer prefers C to A or B. More generally, convexity means that if the consumer is indifferent between two bundles, then the bundle having the respective average amounts is always preferred.

4.4A Equation of the Price Line

As before, denote quantities consumed (demanded) of apples and chocolates as A and T, respectively. The price line is defined by the relation $p_A A + P_T T = M$. We can rewrite this as:

$$T = \frac{M}{p_T} - \frac{p_A}{p_T} A,$$

which is the equation of the price line: T as a function of A. Note that its slope is equal to $\mathrm{d}T / \mathrm{d}A = -p_A / p_T$, which is negative and constant. Hence, the price line is a downward-sloping straight line, with the absolute value of its slope equal to the price ratio.

Example 4.1A

A consumer has an income of €10,000 to be spent on goods A and B. The prices are: $p_A =$ €400 and $p_B =$ €500. Fill in the blanks in Table 4.13 *in terms of how much of the respective good the consumer can buy given the prices and her income.*

Answer: If the consumer is buying 20 units of good B, she spends Rs. €10,000 on good B. Nothing is left for good A. Hence the amount of good A that can be purchased is 0. If 10 units of good A is bought, the amount €10×400 = €4,000 is spent on A. €6,000 is left for good B, which will fetch €6,000/€500 = 12 units of good B. Likewise, as we move down the table, the respective numbers are: 4 units of good B, 21.25 of good A and 0 of good B. ■

TABLE 4.13 Good A Good B

Good A	*Good* B
–	20
10	–
–	8
20	–
–	3
25	–

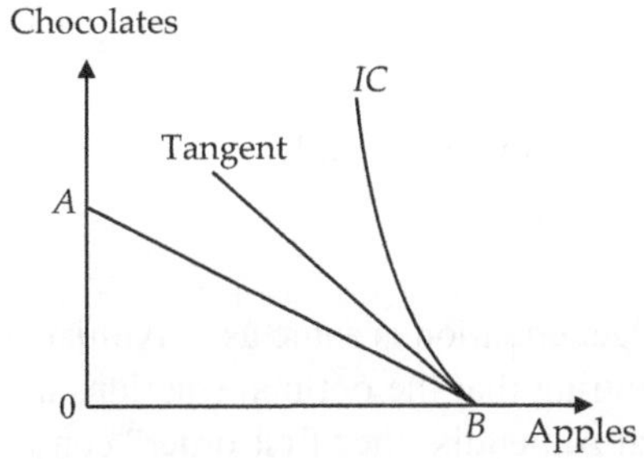

FIGURE 4.13 Corner Solution

4.5A Corner Solution

In the IC approach, we typically consider the situation where the consumer buys a positive amount of each good, shown in Figure 4.9, for example. But, it need not be the case always. It is possible that the highest indifference curve on the price line is reached at a corner point. Figure 4.13 shows the case of a consumer who attains her equilibrium at point *B*, consuming zero chocolate and all apples that can be afforded. A major difference with Figure 4.9 is that if the optimal bundle is a corner "solution" so to speak, the price line may not be equal to the slope of the indifference curve. This is indeed the case in Figure 4.13: the tangent to the IC has a higher slope than does the price line.

4.6A Derivation of Consumer Equilibrium Condition (4.9) and the Demand Functions

Suppose there are *n* goods, 1, 2, 3,..., *n*, the quantities of which are denoted as $x_1, x_2, \cdots, x_n$. Let the utility function be $V = U(x_1, x_2, \cdots, x_n)$. Recall that the partials of this function are the respective marginal utilities, e.g., the marginal utility of good 3 (MU_3) is equal to $\partial U / \partial x_3$. The consumer maximises his total utility $V = U(x_1, x_2, \cdots, x_n)$, subject to the budget equation:

$$p_1 x_1 + p_2 x_2 + \cdots + p_n x_n = \text{M},$$

by appropriately choosing $x_1, x_2, \cdots, x_n$.

We convert the above (mathematical) problem into the following one. Rewrite the budget equation as:

$$x_1 = \frac{M - p_2 x_2 - \cdots - p_n x_n}{p_1}.$$

Next, substitute this expression into the utility function and eliminate x_1 in it. We have:

$$V = U\left(\frac{M - p_2x_2 - \cdots - p_nx_n}{p_1}, x_2, x_3, \cdots, x_n\right) \equiv F\left(x_2, x_3, \cdots, x_n\right),$$

a function of $x_2, \cdots, x_n$.

Maximising total utility subject to the budget equation is same as maximising the function F with respect to $x_2, \cdots, x_n$. Assuming that the optimal solutions are positive, i.e., "interior," in view of the General Appendix, the "first-order" conditions of this maximisation are that the partials of F with respect to $x_2, \cdots, x_n$ are zero. Looking at how the function F is related to utility the function U, we have:

$$\frac{\partial F}{\partial x_2} = \frac{\partial U}{\partial x_1}\left(-\frac{p_2}{p_1}\right) + \frac{\partial U}{\partial x_2}.$$

Hence,

$$\frac{\partial F}{\partial x_2} = \frac{\partial U}{\partial x_1}\left(-\frac{p_2}{p_1}\right) + \frac{\partial U}{\partial x_2} = 0.$$

We can rewrite the above as:

$$\frac{\partial U / \partial x_1}{p_1} = \frac{\partial U / \partial x_2}{p_2} \text{ or } \frac{\text{MU}_1}{p_1} = \frac{\text{MU}_2}{p_2}.$$

Similarly, $\partial F / \partial x_3 = 0$ gives:

$$\frac{\text{MU}_1}{p_1} = \frac{\text{MU}_3}{p_3}.$$

We can do the same for x_4, x_5 up to x_n. With respect to x_n, $\partial F / \partial x_n = 0$ gives:

$$\frac{\text{MU}_1}{p_1} = \frac{\text{MU}_n}{p_n}.$$

We now collect these equations and write them together as:

$$\frac{\text{MU}_1}{p_1} = \frac{\text{MU}_2}{p_2} = \cdots = \frac{\text{MU}_n}{p_n}.$$

Note that this is the same as our consumer's equilibrium conditions (4.9).

To illustrate how the demand functions are derived, consider the Cobb–Douglas utility function as in the main text. More generally, let the utility function be: $U = x_1^{\alpha_1} x_2^{\alpha_2}$, $\alpha_1, \alpha_2 > 0$. We have the budget equation: $p_1 x_1 + p_2 x_2 = M$, which we can write as $x_1 = (M - p_2 x_2)/p_1$. Substituting this into the utility function, we have:

$$U = \left(\frac{M - p_2 x_2}{p_1}\right)^{\alpha_1} x_2^{\alpha_2} = F(x_2).$$

This is maximised with respect to x_2. We have:

$$\frac{dF}{dx_2} = \frac{1}{p_1^{\alpha_1}}\left[-\alpha_1 p_2 (M - p_2 x_2)^{\alpha_1 - 1} x_2^{\alpha_2} + \alpha_2 (M - p_2 x_2)^{\alpha_1} x_2^{\alpha_2 - 1}\right].$$

The first-order condition is: $dF = dx_2 = 0$. Hence, setting the above expression to zero, we obtain the equation: $-\alpha_1 p_2 (M - p_2 x_2)^{\alpha_1 - 1} x_2^{\alpha_2} + \alpha_2 (M - p_2 x_2)^{\alpha_1} x_2^{\alpha_2 - 1} = 0$. This simplifies to $(\pm_1 + \pm_2) p_2 x_2 = \pm_2 M$ and solves x_2:

$$x_2 = \frac{\alpha_2}{\alpha_1 + \alpha_2} \frac{M}{p_2}.$$

This is the demand function for x_2. If we substitute this function into the budget equation, eliminate x_2, and rearrange, we get the demand function for x_1:

$$x_1 = \frac{\alpha_1}{\alpha_1 + \alpha_2} \frac{M}{p_1}.$$

Check for yourself that both goods are normal, i.e., as M increases, both x_1 and x_2 increase. Furthermore, and, interestingly, the cross-price effects are zero, i.e., $\partial x_1 / \partial p_2 = \partial x_2 / \partial p_1 = 0$.

4.7A Change in Income

Having considered the consumer's equilibrium, we can analyse how income and price changes would generally affect the consumer's equilibrium and thereby quantities demanded of goods.

Suppose the consumer's income increases (but prices remain the same). We have already seen that this will shift the price line to the right in parallel. This is illustrated in Figure 4.14. In panel (a), the original equilibrium point is A. As income increases, the price line shifts out. The new equilibrium point is B. Compared to A, the consumption of both goods is higher. That is, as income increases, the consumer demands more of both goods. The effect of a change in income on quantity demanded of a good is called the **income effect**. Our preceding discussion implies that this effect can be positive, defining a normal good, or negative, defining an inferior good.

While Figure 4.14 depicts a single shift of income, Figure 4.15 shows multiple income levels and the associated consumer equilibrium points. By joining these points, we obtain a line called the **income consumption curve** (ICC). In panel (a), E_1, E_2, E_3, etc. are the equilibrium bundles at three different levels of income such as M_1, M_2, M_3, etc. (Ignore for now the markings A_1 and A_2.). Therefore, the line $0C$, joining such points is the ICC. It depicts the case, where both goods are normal. Put differently, if both goods are normal, the ICC is upward sloping.

However, if, over some range of income one good were inferior (both cannot be), the other good would increase. As a result, the ICC curve will have a negatively sloping part, as shown in Figure 4.15(b).

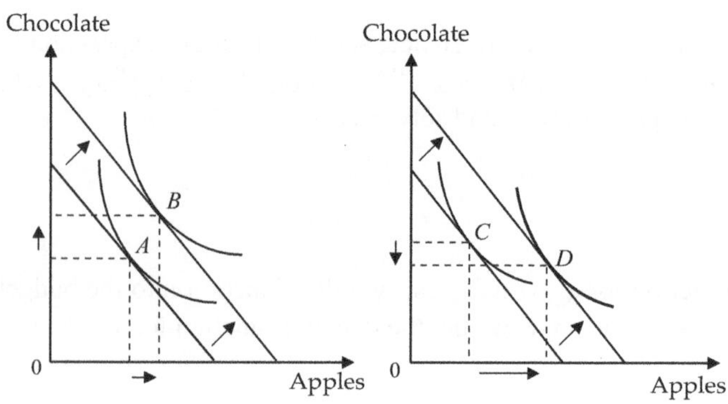

(a) Both goods 'normal' (b) One good inferior

FIGURE 4.14 Income Effect

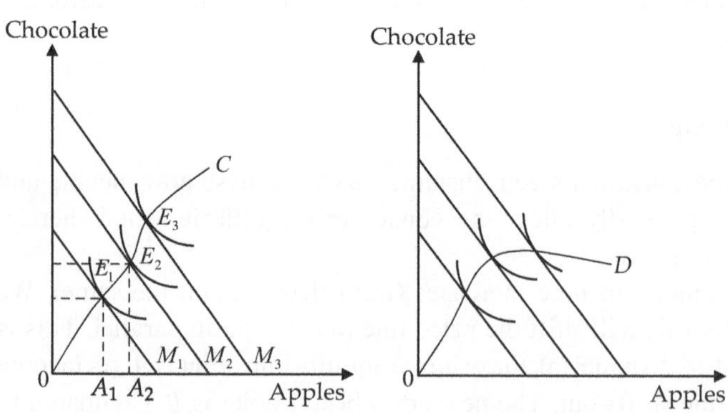

(a) Both goods normal (b) Apples normal; Chocolates inferior

FIGURE 4.15 Income Consumption Curves

From the ICC, we can mark the quantities demanded of a particular good at various levels of income. For instance, in Figure 4.15(a), A_1 of apples is demanded when the income is M_1, A_2 of apples is demanded at income M_2, and so on. If we graph A_1 against M_1, A_2 against M_2, etc., we get what is called an **Engel curve,** a graph showing quantities demanded of a good at various levels of income.[11] Clearly, the Engel curve for a normal good would be upward-sloping and that of an inferior good would have a downward portion. These are illustrated in Figure 4.16. Note that (a) the Engel curve is derived from the ICC and (b), by definition, the elasticity of the Engel curve equals the income elasticity of demand for a product. We next analyse the effects of a change in price.

4.8A Change in Price

Suppose the price of apples falls. The price line shifts out on the apples axis. As shown in Figure 4.17, there are three possibilities: the consumer demands (a) more of apples and chocolate, (b) more apples and less chocolates, or (c) less apples and

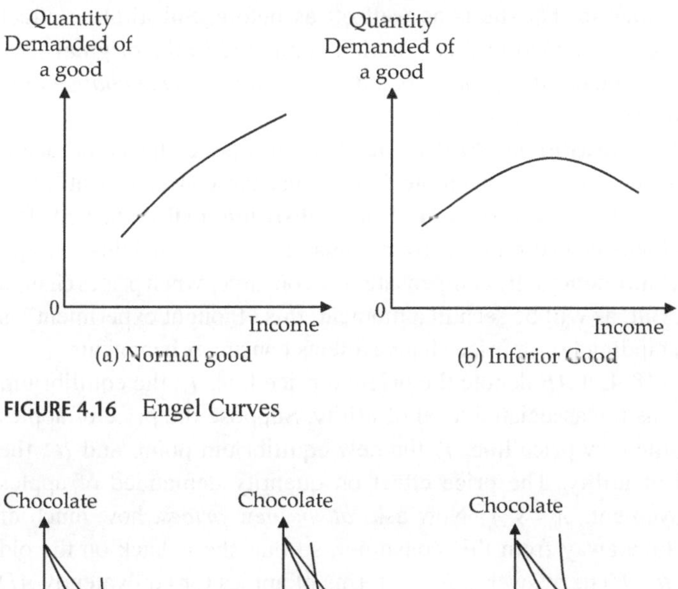

FIGURE 4.16 Engel Curves

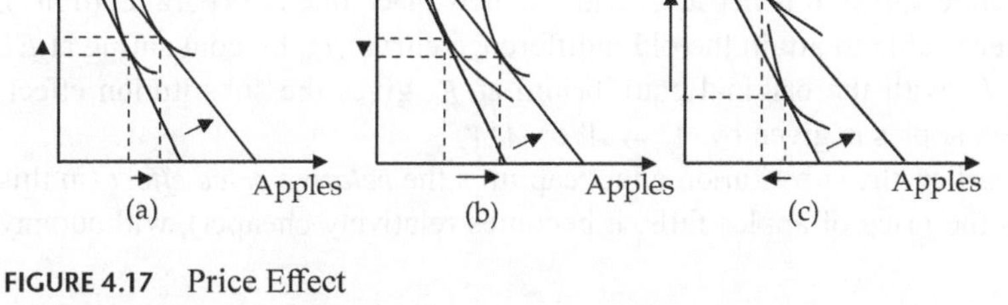

FIGURE 4.17 Price Effect

more chocolates. Thus, the Law of Demand holds in cases (a) and (b), but not in (c). Thus, the own price effect may not be always negative (i.e., a decrease or an increase in own price may not lead, respectively, to an increase or a decrease in the quantity demanded).

How do we explain this? The income effect just considered *and* a substitution effect together characterise the overall effect of a price change.

4.9A Substitution Effect in Detail

When the price of a product falls, the price line shifts out and a consumer can afford some bundles, which could not be purchased earlier. You can interpret this as the consumer being "richer," i.e., her real income or real purchasing power being higher—even though her income hasn't changed. This is why we see in Figure 4.17 that she is always on a higher indifference curve, i.e., better off than before—irrespective of how quantities demanded change.

Now consider the following hypothetical experiment. As the price of a product falls, take away some income from the consumer such that she is "as well off as before." Similarly, if there is an increase in a product price, give some extra income to the consumer so that she is as well off as before. Substitution effect refers to the quantities consumed in this situation compared to the original situation before the price change. *It captures the effect of relative price change only (without the accompanying income effect).*

Differently put, the **substitution effect** is the effect of a price change on quantity demanded when income is "compensated" such that the consumer's utility is unchanged. More precisely, it is called the **Hicksian substitution effect**, named after John Hicks, a Nobel Laureate in economics from England, who analysed this concept.

Note however that no one actually compensates the consumer when prices change in the marketplace. But, as will be seen in a moment, this "thought experiment" is important in understanding how a price change affects consumer behaviour.

Refer to Figure 4.18. Let AB denote the original price line, E_0 the equilibrium point on it with IC_0 as the associated level of utility. Suppose the price of apples falls, so that AC is the new price line, E_1 the new equilibrium point, and IC_1 the new (higher) level of utility. The price effect on quantity demanded of apples is given by the movement, $A_0 \rightarrow A_1$. Now ask, *at the new prices*, how much of income should we take away from this consumer, so that she is back on the old indifference curve IC_0? The answer is FC in terms of apples (or equivalently AD in terms of chocolates). It is because, with the new price line DF (parallel to AC), the consumer is able to attain the old indifference curve IC_0 by consuming at E'. Comparing E' with the original equilibrium at E_0 gives the substitution effect. This effect on apples is given by $A_0 \rightarrow A'$ or A_0A'.

As said earlier, the substitution effect captures the *relative price effect* (in this example, as the price of apples falls, it becomes relatively cheaper), without any

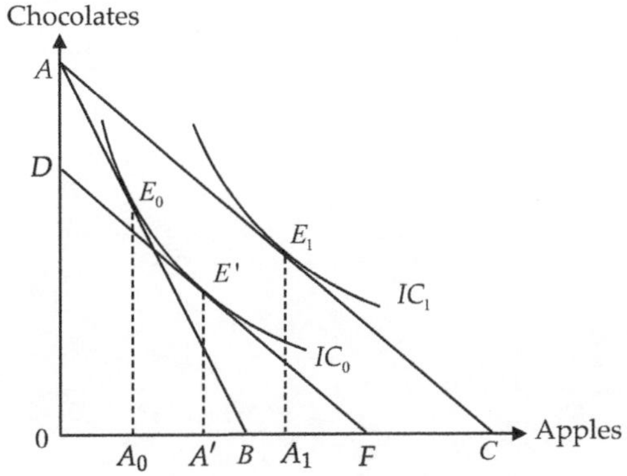

FIGURE 4.18 Hicksian Substitution Effect

change in real income. Moreover, *the own substitution effect is always negative*: as a good becomes relatively more expensive, the consumer (along the same indifference curve) substitutes this good for the other and hence consumes (demands) less of the good in question.

We are now in a position to "understand" the price effect, which contains a substitution effect and an income effect. In our example, as the price of apples falls, by the substitution effect, the consumer buys more of apples, measured by $A_0 \rightarrow A'$. A decrease in price increases the real income (by BC in terms of apples). This leads to an income effect, measured by $A' \rightarrow A_1$. Both effects add to $A_0 \rightarrow A_1$, the price effect. Hence, in general,

Price Effect = Substitution Effect + Income Effect.

This is stated in the main text and the key behind understanding the price effect.

4.10A Slutsky's Substitution Effect

A Soviet economist, Eugen Slutsky, had proposed an alternative definition of the substitution effect, similar to the Hicksian substitution effect. While in the latter the income is adjusted such that the consumer is able to be on the original or the *old indifference curve* at the new set of prices, Slutsky's substitution effect is derived when the income adjustment is such that the consumer is able to buy the *old bundle* at the new set of prices.

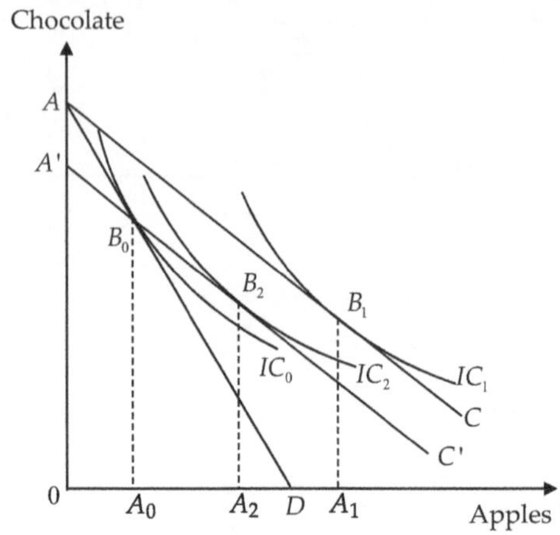

FIGURE 4.19 Slutsky's Substitution Effect

Turn to Figure 4.19. The original price line is *AD*. The consumer's equilibrium point is B_0 and she enjoys welfare indicated by IC_0. The price of apples falls, *AC* is the new price line, B_1 is the new consumption point, and the consumer is on a higher indifference curve IC_1. Let income be adjusted such that at the new set of prices the consumer is able to buy the old bundle B_0. This is indicated by the price line *A'C'*, which is parallel to the *new* price line *AC* and which passes through the old bundle B_0. The amount of income adjusted equals *AA'* in terms of chocolate. With such income adjustment, the consumer would attain equilibrium at B_2. The Slutsky's substitution effect refers to the movement from B_0 to B_2. In terms of demand for apples, this substitution effect is the increase in consumption from A_0 to A_2.[12]

However, Hicks's and Slutsky's substitution effects share the same important property: the own substitution effect is unambiguously negative, i.e., by the substitution effect, as the price of a commodity increases, the consumer demands less of it. Further, the price effect as the sum of a substitution effect and an income effect remains the same.

4.11A Normal, Inferior, and Giffen Goods

Note that, for a normal good, as its price changes, both the substitution effect and the income effect on the quantity demanded work in the same direction and therefore the Law of Demand holds. For instance, if there is a decrease in price, the quantity demanded of the product increases by the substitution effect (as the relative price of it falls). In addition, a fall in price means an increase in real income, and, if the good is normal, the quantity demanded of it increases as real income increases. Hence both the substitution effect and the income effect lead to an increase in the quantity demanded. This holds in the example illustrated in Figure 4.18.

If the good is inferior, the income effect is "perverse" or "negative" (i.e., an increase in income leads to a *decrease* in the quantity demanded) and thus it works opposite to the substitution effect. The Law of Demand may or may not hold. If the perverse income effect is smaller in magnitude than the substitution effect, the latter dominates, and the Law of Demand still holds. But if the perverse income effect is sufficiently strong to outweigh the substitution effect, the Law of Demand fails to hold. Such a good is called a Giffen good and such an unusual situation is called a **Giffen paradox**, named after an English economist and statistician R. Giffen, who studied such goods.

The inferior-good situation is illustrated in Figure 4.20. Both panels illustrate the effect of an *increase* in price of good x, such that the price line shifts from AB to AC. The original consumption bundle and the new one are, respectively, E_0 and E_1. In terms of demand for good x, the substitution effect (*a la* Hicks) is the reduction in quantity demanded from x_0 to x'. The income effect is the *increase* in quantity demanded from x' to x_1. Being an inferior good, the income effect on it is negative (in both panels): the real income has declined (due to an increase in the price of good x) and by the income effect the quantity demanded of good x has increased. However, the difference between the two panels is that in panel (a) the magnitude of the income effect is less than that of the substitution effect (the length $x'x_1$ is less than the length $x'x_0$), whereas the opposite is true in panel (b) with the length $x'x_1$ exceeding the length $x'x_0$. The consequence is that there is a difference in the price effect. In panel (a), the quantity demanded decreases from x_0 to x_1 (and hence the Law of Demand holds), while in panel (b), the quantity demanded *increases* from x_0 to x_1 and hence the Law of Demand does not hold.

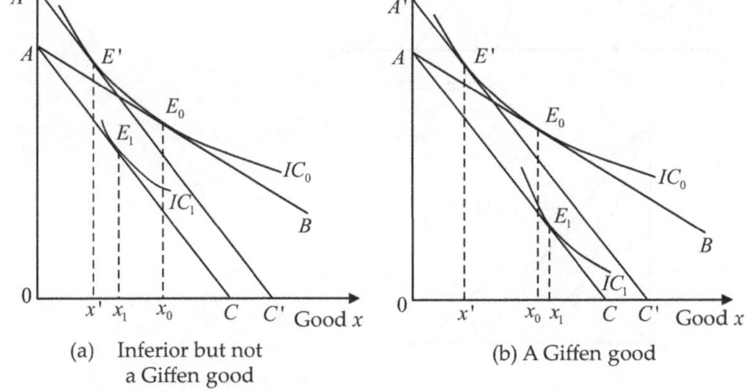

FIGURE 4.20 Inferior and Giffen Goods

In summary, panel (a) depicts the situation in which the good is inferior, but the substitution effect is greater than the income effect, so that the Law of Demand holds. The good in question is not a Giffen good. Panel (b) shows a situation where the good is, again, inferior, but the income effect exceeds the substitution effect, so that the Law of Demand fails to hold. This is a situation of Giffen paradox, and the good x is a Giffen good.

Giffen goods are thus a subset of inferior goods. In reality however, there are not many examples of inferior goods, and there are even fewer examples of Giffen goods.

4.12A Price Consumption Curve (PPC) and the Demand Curve

Suppose there are two goods x and y, and the price of only one good, say good x, changes. Further suppose that good x is not a Giffen good.[13] Consider various cases, depending on the magnitude of the price elasticity e_p.

Suppose $e_p > 1$. Then, if the price of good x falls, the quantity demanded of good x increases more than proportionately and because of that the total expenditure on good x rises. With income unchanged, this implies that the expenditure on the other good, y, must fall. With the price of good y unchanged, this means that the quantity demanded of good y falls too. In summary, as the price of good x decreases, the quantity demanded of good x increases and that of good y declines. The PCC in this situation is illustrated in Figure 4.21(a). The price of good x is falling gradually from p_1 to p_2, p_2 to p_3, and so on (each

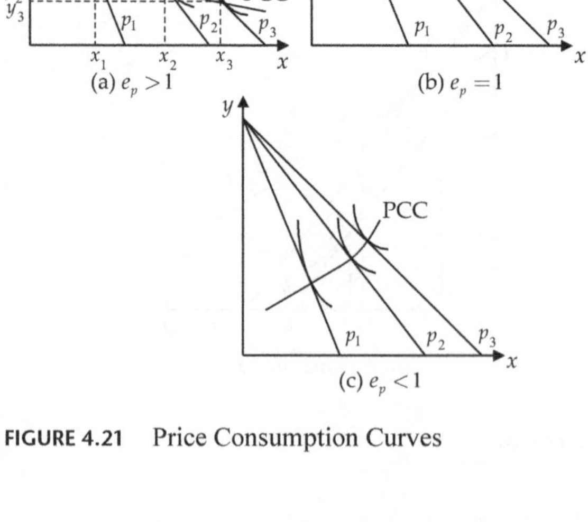

FIGURE 4.21 Price Consumption Curves

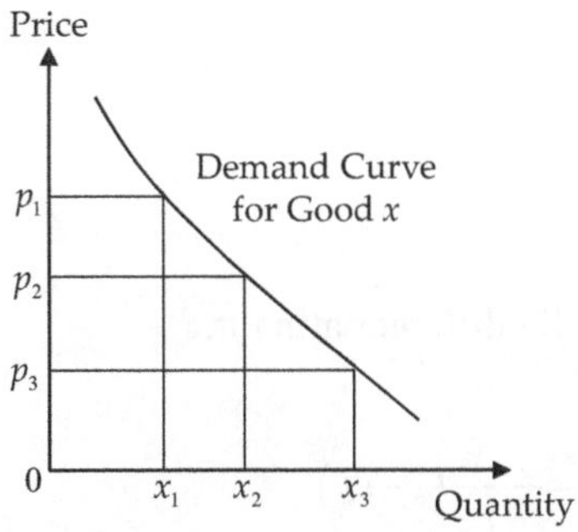

FIGURE 4.22 Deriving the Demand Curve from the Price Consumption Curve

price line is indicated by the price of good x). The quantity demanded of good x increases from x_1 to x_2, x_2 to x_3, and so on. The quantity demanded of good y *decreases* from y_1 to y_2, y_2 to y_3, etc. The PCC, as a result, is downward-sloping.

If $e_p = 1$, as the price of good x changes, the quantity demanded of it changes in the opposite direction and proportionately. The total expenditure on good x remains the same and that means the total expenditure on good y also remains the same. The price of good y being unchanged, there is thus no change in the quantity demanded of good y. This case is illustrated in Figure 4.21(b). As the price of good x keeps falling, the quantity demanded of it keeps increasing, while that of good y is unchanged. The PCC is a flat line.

Suppose $e_p < 1$. Applying similar reasoning, you can deduce that, if the price of good x decreases, the quantity demanded of both goods increase. Hence, the PCC is upward-sloping, as shown in Figure 4.21(c).

Once we know the PCC, we can *derive* the demand curve. How? Look at Figure 4.21(a) for instance. At price p_1, x_1 of good x is demanded. At price p_2, the quantity x_2 is demanded, and so on. And mark that the income and the price of good y are fixed. Hence, "all other things" in the Law of Demand are given. It follows that if we graph the price–quantity combinations (p_1, x_1), (p_2, x_2), (p_3, x_2), etc., it must be same as the demand curve. Figure 4.22 does exactly that and shows the demand curve, derived from the PCC in Figure 4.21(a).[14]

4.13A The Shape of the PCC

We know from Chapter 2 that the price elasticity of demand good x is given by:

$$e_p = -\frac{p_x}{x}\frac{dx}{dp_x},$$

where x is the quantity demanded of good x and p_x is its price. From the budget constraint,

$$y = \frac{M - p_x x}{p_y},$$

where y is the quantity demanded of good y. Totally differentiating it,

$$\frac{dy}{dp_x} = -\frac{1}{p_y}\left(x + p_x \frac{dx}{dp_x}\right) = -\frac{x}{p_y}\left(1 + \frac{p_x}{x}\frac{dx}{dp_x}\right) = -\frac{x}{p_y}\left(1 - e_p\right).$$

Thus dy/dp_x is negative, zero, or positive, i.e., when p_x increases, the demand for good y decreases, remains unchanged or increases, according as e_p is greater than, equal to or less than one. This result governs the shape of PCCs drawn in Figure 4.21.

4.14A Many Goods and a Composite Good

In real life a consumer or a family buys many goods, not just two. If we want to analyse the demand behaviour of a consumer with respect to many goods at a time, the two-dimensional geometry cannot help. But this doesn't mean that the indifference curve analysis is irrelevant.

The indifference curve analysis can be easily generalised to any arbitrary number of goods and services and the main results are generalisations of what we have already learnt in the "two-good case." We have already seen the consumer equilibrium conditions in the many goods case, given in equation (4.9). Also, the income effect, the substitution effect, and the price effect all have the same meaning as in our two-good indifference curve model.

Interestingly, there is a special case where many goods can be effectively represented by two goods and the indifference curve analysis is directly applicable. Suppose that out of many goods we are only interested in the demand for one good *relative to the rest.* For example, we may want to study the food consumption pattern of a family in comparison to its consumption of all goods like housing, clothing, entertainment, etc. Realise that in this case we are essentially looking at two goods: food and "others."

There is a result in the demand theory (which you may learn in detail at the post-graduate level), stating that a group of goods can be lumped together and treated as a single (composite) good for analytical purposes as long as the prices of individual commodities within the group move proportionately. It is called the **composite-good theorem.**

More particularly, this theorem implies that *if the relative prices within a group of goods remain constant, the total expenditure on them can be treated*

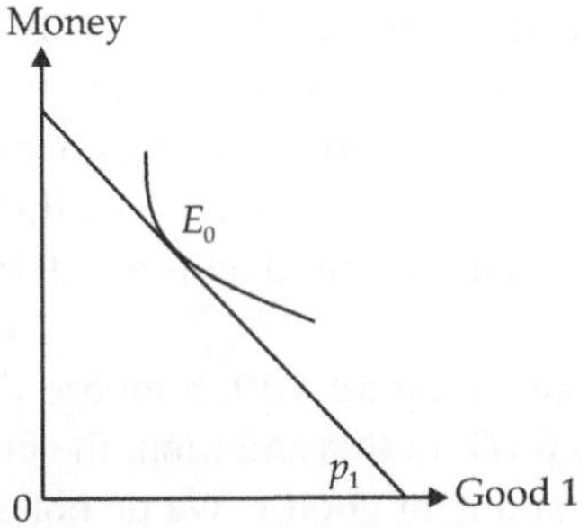

FIGURE 4.23 Composite Good

as a composite good. We can make this more precise. Let there be n goods, namely, 1, 2,..., n. Let p_1, p_2, etc. be their respective prices and let x_1, x_2 etc. be the respective quantities demanded. Then, if the price of good 1 can change but prices of other goods cannot, the total expenditure on other goods, given by $C = p_2x_2 + p_3x_3 + \cdots + p_nx_n$, can be treated as a single good.

The composite-good theorem also implies that we can draw an indifference curve measuring good 1 on one axis and C along the other. This is shown in Figure 4.23. Sometimes the expenditure on all other goods (C) is named "money"—in the sense that C is equal to the total amount of money left to buy the goods other than the one we are focussing on. This is why C is indicated as money in Figure 4.23. We can also define a price line in terms of good 1 and good C. In the equation form it is: $p_1x_1 + C = M$, where M is the total income as before. Figure 4.23 also draws a budget line. Notice that the way good C is defined, its price is equal to one. Thus, the slope of the price line must equal p_1. The consumer equilibrium is attained at the tangency point E_0.As before, we can analyse the income effect, the substitution effect, and the price effect.

Appendix 4.B: Revealed-Preference Approach

In both the marginal-utility and the IC approaches, the starting point is an individual's preferences. In the indifference-curve analysis in particular, her indifference map essentially gives an ordering or ranking of various bundles in taste. Next, the budget set defines those bundles that the consumer can afford to buy at the given prices and income. Among these bundles, she chooses the one that she likes the best. In turn, this defines the consumer's demand for various goods. As prices or income change, the budget set changes and the consumer again chooses the bundle in the new budget set, which yields to her the highest satisfaction. One definite—and central—result is that, as a product price changes, by the substitution effect (i.e., if income is compensated), more of it is demanded. Both approaches are founded on the notion that "preferences lead to choice."

On the other hand, the revealed-preference approach to demand is built on a simple (yet beautiful) idea that we do *not* need to start from preferences.[15] If we simply observe what the consumer is choosing (given prices and income) and assume that the consumer's chosen bundle itself tells (reveals) us that this bundle is the most preferred among all bundles that are available in the budget set, this is *sufficient* to imply that the substitution effect on demand for a product is negatively related to own price. How does this work?

Turn to Figure 4.24, which is somewhat similar to Figure 4.19. Suppose that originally the price line *AD*, i.e., the budget set is $0AD$. In this situation, the consumer chooses a bundle, say z_0, with x_0 of good x and y_0 of good y. We do not ask how she chooses the bundle z_0; we simply observe it.

But, given that a bundle is chosen, we say that it is "revealed preferred" to any other bundle in the budget set (otherwise the consumer wouldn't have chosen z_0). In other words, revealed preference is defined as follows: a bundle z_1 is said to **be revealed preferred** to a bundle z_2 if both belong to some budget set in which z_1 is chosen (and $z_2$is not). In other words, in this theory, preferences are induced from what the consumer chooses rather than vice versa.

Apart from this definition, there is an assumption called the **weak axiom of revealed preference**, that is, if a bundle z_1 is revealed preferred to another bundle z_2, then z_2 cannot be revealed preferred to z_1. It is like a consistency assumption. This axiom by itself implies that the own substitution effect must be negative, a proof of which is given below.

Turning to Figure 4.24 and suppose that the price of good x falls such that the new budget set is $0AC$. However, let the consumer's income be adjusted such that he is just able to buy the old bundle z_0, i.e., let $0A'z_0C'$ be the new budget set. (This is same as Slutsky's income adjustment.) The new chosen bundle must lie in this budget set.

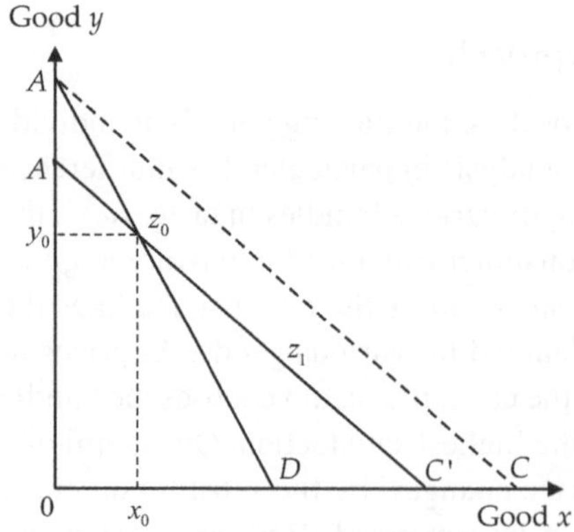

FIGURE 4.24 Substitution Effect in the Revealed-Preference Approach

We now argue that the new chosen bundle must have more (at least no less) of good x than x_0 (which will prove that the substitution effect is negative). First, divide the new budget set $0A'z_0C'$ into two areas: $0A'z_0D$ and the triangle z_0DC'. If the new chosen bundle lies in the area $0A'z_0D$, it must be no other than z_0. It is because, if some other bundle, say z_1 is the chosen bundle, by definition, it is revealed to z_0, since both z_0 and z_1 are in the budget set $0A'z_0C'$ and z_1 is chosen. However, z_1 lying in the area $0A'z_0D$ implies that it is in the old budget set $0AD$ and since z_0 is the chosen bundle in this budget set it is revealed preferred to z_1. Thus we have a situation where z_1 is revealed preferred to z_0 and z_0 is revealed preferred to z_1, contradicting the weak axiom of revealed preference. Hence the new chosen bundle cannot lie in the area $0A'z_0D$ unless it is same as z_0.

The remaining possibility is that the new chosen bundle lies in the triangle z_0DC'. But note that any bundle in this triangle has no less of good x than x_0; indeed, any bundle in the triangle z_0DC' other than z_0 has *more* of good x than x_0.

Combining the two possibilities about where the new chosen bundle may lie, it follows that it *cannot* have less of good x than x_0. This proves that the substitution effect on product demand is (weakly) negatively related to own price.

The fundamental point of this approach/theory is that the central result of the consumer theory, namely, the substitution effect, need not start with preferences over all possible consumption bundles. As long as we maintain that the actual choice behaviour of a consumer reveals her preferences over the bundles available in a budget set, it is enough to imply the negative substitution effect.

We know that, in general, the demand for any particular good may increase, decrease, or remain unchanged as income changes, i.e., there is no systematic sign of the income effect: it can be positive, negative, or zero. Thus, although the income effect is not explicitly looked at in a typical analysis of the revealed-preference theory it is "understood" that it can always be directly added to the substitution effect. The end product is a complete demand theory, not just the substitution effect.

Notes

1 This may vary from one person to another. Comparative to a rich individual, a poor person's marginal valuation of a rupee will be higher.

2 In the hilsa example in *Box 4.1 A Hilsa Feast*, we can interpret that you stopped with four pieces of hilsa, because the fifth piece would have generated for you a negative marginal or incremental utility, while the price of hilsa is zero. It is consistent with the condition (4.1) in that a rational consumer will not consume an amount of a good such that the marginal utility falls short of the price of the good.

3 Another answer is 3 units, as bananas are not being measured on a continuous scale.

4 It amounts to saying that the marginal utility is positive.

5 It is named after Charles Cobb and Paul Douglas, who discovered this functional form in 1928 in relation to production analysis. Later it came to be used in demand theory also. Cobb was a mathematician. Interestingly, Douglas, who started his career as an economist in academia, left academics later and became a senator in the United States.

6 The slope of a curve at a point is the slope of the tangent to the curve at that point.
7 Strictly speaking it is equal to the *absolute value* of the slope of the indifference curve.
8 As stated in Chapter 2, in demand theory, "income" typically refers to the total amount of money allocated for spending. More accurately, income means a consumer's earnings, one part of which is saved and the other spent or consumed. It is the second part that has traditionally been "loosely" called "income" in demand theory.
9 Jensen and Miller (2002) report that in North and South China, rice and noodles were Giffen goods.
10 If we had assumed increasing MRS, the slope would have increased gradually, and the curve would have looked like the production possibility frontier: concave to the origin.
11 It is an important tool in applied consumer theory, named after a 19th-century German statistician Ernst Engel, who made an extensive study of expenditure patterns of families with different levels of income. For example, he (probably the first ever) found that the income elasticity of demand for food was relatively low.
12 The corresponding income effect is from F_2 to F_1.
13 It is not difficult at all to draw the PCC for a Giffen good.
14 The PCCs in Figure 4.22(b) and Figure 4.22 (c) will give rise to different demand curves.
15 Paul Samuelson, a famous American economist and a Nobel Laureate, is the originator of this theory.

BIBLIOGRAPHY

Jensen, R., & Miller, N. (2002). *Giffen behavior: Theory and evidence* (Working Paper, John F. Kennedy School of Government). Harvard University Press.

5

APPLICATIONS OF CONSUMER THEORY

Consumer theory has numerous applications. In this chapter we consider four of them. The first is an application of the marginal-utility theory, while the remaining are based on the indifference curve analysis. In particular, the first application, namely, consumer surplus, will be used to build the concept of social welfare or social surplus in Chapter 9.

This is an eco-centric chapter which is an essential reading for those who have chosen economics honours or minor.[1] However, for students of management, we highly recommend that the broad framework and conclusions of these applications be taught, since these applications have an important bearing on some pricing and marketing strategies. Consider, for instance, our fourth application, namely consumption-savings decisions. When we study the determinants of demand, income, or more appropriately total spending, emerges as the second-most-important determinant of demand. In turn, a person's total current spending depends on her current income and past savings and future income. In most developed countries, there is a sizable number of "senior citizens" (we, the authors, proudly belong to this group), whose current spending is financed by their past savings. Table 5.1 will give you an idea of the magnitude of this section of the population in different countries.

In the IT sector many of the young entrants with unique specialisations are offered astronomical salaries. For some, success gets ingrained in their heads and they spend lavishly on buying apartments, luxury cars, and taking holidays at exotic locations. A chunk of all this is financed with borrowings from banks due to the impressive current pay slip, "against" their future income potential, which

1 In India, a minor in a subject is called a 'pass subject.'

DOI: 10.4324/9781003452195-5

TABLE 5.1 Size of the Older Population in Selected Countries

Country	*Age 65 and Over (in millions)*	*Age 65 and Over (% of total population)*
China	166.37	11.9
United States	52.76	16.0
Japan	35.58	28.2
Russian Federation	21.42	14.6
Germany	17.78	21.4
Italy	13.76	22.8
Spain	8.99	19.1

Sources: United Nations Population Division, *World Population Prospects 2019*, https://population.un.org/wpp/Download/Standard/Population/; (Kaneda et al., 2019).

may or may not play out. In this example, expected future income affects current spending.

To see clearly the market potential among different segments of the population for specific products a manager is concerned with, she/he would benefit from understanding the determinants of a person's spending or consumption and savings—which is our fourth application.

5.1 Consumer's Surplus

We have learnt that if the price of a product falls (rises), all else the same, the consumer is better off (worse off). It is useful to express such "welfare" change in terms of money. Why? Suppose that the government slashes the duty on printers imported from abroad. Obviously, those who purchase printers are better off. We would like to know how much money or purchasing power they gain *from this policy change*?

Suppose that the government increases the Goods and Services Tax (GST) on restaurant food by 10%. Those of you who love restaurant food would not like it, because it means a loss of purchasing power to you. One may want to know how much of purchasing power restaurant goers lose from an increase of GST on restaurant food.

Consumer surplus is a widely used concept to measure in money terms the *net* benefit or surplus from buying a product at a given price and a change in consumer's welfare due to a change in price. It is defined as *the total willingness to pay for a product minus the total payment for the product.* When we come out of a restaurant overly satisfied, we sometimes say that the food was certainly worth the price. If you loved both the main meal and the dessert and particularly enjoyed the dessert, you may say that you got your money's worth just from the dessert. What this says is that the total satisfaction or utility, say (a), was greater than your total payment for the food, say (b). Look back at the definition of consumer surplus. In the present example, it is equal to the excess of (a) over (b). Read Box 5.1 on the background of how the concept was first taught by Dr. J. K. Goyal at the beginning of his career.

BOX 5.1 LEARNING TO TEACH THE ODD WAY

This happened way back in 1975 when Dr. J. K. Goyal, had recently joined as lecturer (an instructor) in a college in New Delhi, India. Microeconomics was one of the subjects he was assigned to teach. Unlike the elite colleges of Delhi at the time, this college was notorious for its student intake quality and indiscipline. Teaching—and that too a diagram and formula 'infested' subject like economics—was a challenge. He was preparing for his lecture for the next day when he had to introduce the concept of consumer surplus. He did not want to introduce this term in the typical dull and clichéd manner. Suddenly, his flatmate persuaded him to leave his class preparation and they went to watch a famous Bollywood movie *Sholay*. It was still some time when the show would start, and they were loitering around outside the cinema hall. Dr. Goyal's mind was still stuck on "Consumer Surplus," when he overheard a conversation between two rickshaw-pullers. One of them was asking the other to go with him to see *Sholay* and the other replied that he had already seen this movie, but he would still go to watch the movie again. The first one asked "But, why do you want to see a movie which you have already seen?" The other replied "*Picture ke paise toh Helen ke dance main he poore ho jatey hai*" (What you pay for the whole picture, you recover in a sizzling dance sequence by the-then dancing queen, Helen.) This made Dr. Goyal realise that if this consumer could get his money's worth (price of the movie ticket) from just a four-minute dance sequence, then what about the rest of the movie that he watches? Needless to say, when he started his lecture in the classroom the next day with this anecdote, the entire lecture on consumer surplus went smoothly.

More precisely, if we are talking about good x, where p_x and x stand, respectively, for the price and the quantity demanded of this good, the total payment for good x is simply price × quantity demanded = $p_x x$. This is the cost to the consumer. Next, we may define the total willingness to pay for good x equal to the total utility obtained from consuming x measured in money. Remember from the marginal-utility theory that the total utility in terms of money is measured by the area under the marginal utility in terms of money curve. Further, this curve *is* the same as the demand curve for the product. *Hence the total willingness to pay is equal to the area under the demand curve.* For instance, in *Figure 5.1*(a), if $p_x = p_0$ and the consumer is demanding x_0, her total willingness to pay is equal to the area $0ABx_0$. Similarly, if $p_x = p_1$ and the consumer demands x_1, the total willingness to pay

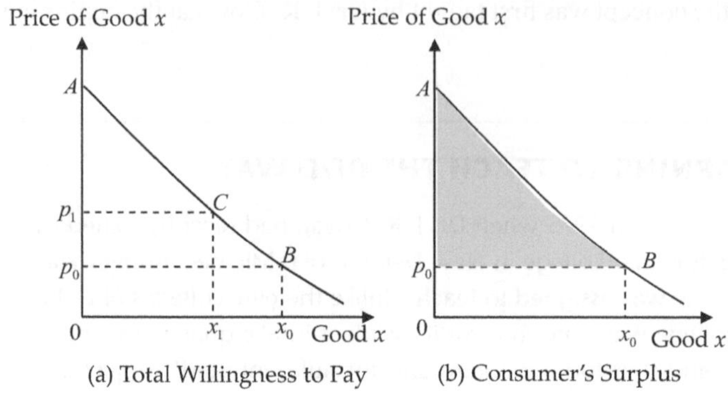

FIGURE 5.1 Consumer Surplus

equals the area $0ACx_1$. Once we know the total willingness to pay and the actual payment, the difference between them is the consumer surplus.

Let's compute the consumer surplus in our example. At the price p_0 for instance, the total willingness to pay $= 0ABx_0$, while the total consumer payment or expenditure on it is the area $0p_0 \times 0x_0 = 0p_0Bx_0$. Thus, the consumer surplus $= 0ABx_0 - 0p_0Bx_0 = p_0AB$. By similar calculation, at the price p_1, the consumer surplus is equal to p_1AC. Thus, in general, *the consumer surplus equals the area under a demand curve over and above the line representing the price.* This is shown more prominently in Figure 5.1(b), where the dotted area is the consumer surplus at the price p_0.

Using consumer surplus, we can measure the *change* in consumers' welfare due to a price change. If, for example, the price of good x increases from $p_0$to p_1, the change in consumer surplus is simply the difference between the consumer surpluses associated with $p_0$and p_1. In Figure 5.1(a), this is equal to $p_0AC - p_1AB = -p_0p_1CB$. The negative sign reflects a welfare *decrease* due to a price increase, which is expected. In absolute value, the change in the consumer surpluses is given by the area between the two respective price lines.

See Box 5.2 for a sample of estimates of consumer surplus.

BOX 5.2 CONSUMER SURPLUS ESTIMATES

Many estimates of consumer surplus are available for various commodities and services in different countries. For instance, Watal (2000) provides estimates of loss in consumer surplus in the demand for patentable pharmaceutical products if intellectual right protections are granted in India following our WTO commitments. Assuming that prices of such products would increase anywhere from 26% to 242%, the consumer surplus loss is evaluated at \$50 million to $140 million. Peck et al., (1999) study the demand for tobacco products in India and China (and other countries). They estimate that, in per capita terms and in 1990 prices, the consumer surpluses in demanding tobacco products were $12 and $9 in India and China, respectively. Mitra (1999–2000) examined the demand for four tourist spots in Arunachal Pradesh, India. Using local transport cost as the price of touring these spots, the consumer surplus per visit by Indians were estimated at ₹995; that by foreigners was estimated at ₹1,232. Cohen et al., (2016) estimate that the consumer surplus from UberX service in 2015 for the United States was $6.8 billion.

Example 5.1

The demand curve facing a consumer is a straight line as shown in Figure 5.2. *Compute the consumer surpluses at prices 6 and 8 and compare them. Which is greater and why?*

Answer: At price = 8, we have $AD = 20 - 8 = 12$. The triangles *ADC* and *A0B* are similar. Thus $DC/AD = 0B/0A$. The last ratio equals 30/20 = 3/2. Thus, $DC = (3/2) \times AD = (3/2) \times 12 = 18$. This is the quantity demanded at a price equal to 8. The total willingness to pay at this price is equal to the area under the demand curve, which, in turn, equals the rectangle *ODCE* plus the triangle *ADC*. These areas are, respectively, equal to $8 \times 18 = 144$ and $(1/2) \times 12 \times 18 = 108$. Thus, the total willingness to pay = 144 + 90 = 234. The consumer surplus is the area of the triangle under the demand curve, equal to 108.

Similar calculation yields the consumer surplus at price 6 equal to 147. This is higher than the consumer surplus at price equal to 8, because the price is lower. ■

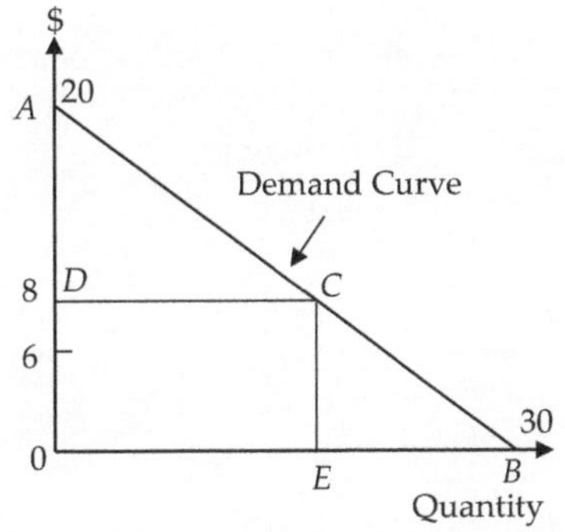

FIGURE 5.2 Calculating Consumer's Surplus

5.2 Cash versus Kind Subsidy

The government offers many types of "kind subsidy" to poor sections of the population or to its employees. For instance, food in the canteens of many government organisations in India is highly subsidised. A decent meal with three chapatis (Indian bread), dal (lentil), a subji (curry) and curd (yogurt) may cost $40 to an employee, whereas the market price of that meal may be ₹120. Another example is leave travel concession (LTC) given to central and state employees. This is again a subsidy in kind: the government subsidises its employees in their "consumption" of travel. In the United States, the poor are given "food stamps" by the government, which can be used as cash *only if* the person is buying food items. These are subsidies on food consumption.

Note that, in each of these examples and in general, providing subsidy-in-kind costs to the government, ultimately to the tax-payers, while the objective behind granting a kind subsidy is to improve the welfare of the recipients.

There is however an alternative, which will cost the same to the government and will also please its recipients: that is, let the government pay a cash subsidy to the recipients, equal to the amount it was spending on the subsidy programme in kind. The issue is: *which programme is better for the consumer, given that both programmes cost the same to the government?*

Consider Figure 5.3, which measures food on one axis and "other goods" along the other. Suppose that without any subsidy on food the budget line of the consumer is *AB*, the slope of which measures the relative price of food. The consumer

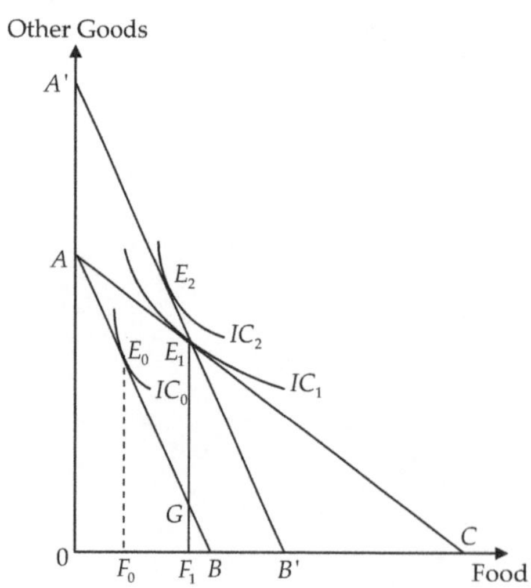

FIGURE 5.3 Cash versus Kind Subsidy

attains his equilibrium at E_0. He consumes $0F_0$ of food and E_0F_0 of other goods. His welfare is indicated by the indifference curve IC_0.

Start with a food subsidy programme. Suppose that the government now subsidises the consumption of food (i.e., food becomes cheaper to the consumer), such that the new budget line is AC. The person would now consume F_1 of food and E_1F_1 of other goods. Mark the point G, where E_1F_1 intersects AB. We now argue that E_1G is the cost of this kind-subsidy programme. How? Suppose the consumer was buying the same amount of food he is consuming now (F_1) at the *unsubsidised* (old) price, i.e., along the old budget line AB. He would then have been left with GF_1 of other goods. But with the subsidy programme in place he is left with E_1F_1 of other goods. Since the prices of other goods are unchanged, the difference between E_1F_1 and GF_1, equal to E_1G, must be what the government is paying as the subsidy.

Consider now the alternative programme of giving the amount E_1G, by cash to the consumer. Mark the line $A'B'$ drawn parallel to AB and passing through E_1. It has the property that $E_1G = AA'$. With the cash subsidy in place, in terms of the other goods the consumer's disposable income (inclusive of the cash subsidy) is now $0A + E_1G = 0A + AA' = 0A'$. Since there is no subsidy on food, the new budget line must have the original slope, AB. Thus $A'B'$ is the budget line. What is then the consumer's optimal point of consumption? It is E_2. Note that the optimal consumption point in the subsidy-in-kind programme, which is E_1, is still available to the consumer in the cash-subsidy programme (as E_1 lies on $A'B'$ too). But, *E_1 is no longer the equilibrium point.* Importantly, at E_2 the consumer is on a higher indifference curve (IC_2) as compared to that at E_1 (IC_1).

The conclusion is that *the consumer is better off by the cash-subsidy programme than the kind-subsidy programme.* The underlying reason is the following. The cost of the kind-subsidy programme (E_1G) *depends* on the equilibrium choice of the consumption bundle in that programme; hence in a cash-subsidy programme whose cost is equal to the kind-subsidy programme, the above consumption bundle is also available (i.e., the bundle E_1 is available along the budget line $A'B'$). This implies that the consumer cannot be worse off in the cash-subsidy programme as compared to the kind-subsidy programme, because he always has the option of choosing E_1 in the cash-subsidy programme. Moreover, since the relative price of the good in question facing the consumer is different between the two schemes, he *will* choose a different bundle in the cash-subsidy programme (E_2) than the one in the kind-subsidy programme (E_1) and be strictly better off. Put differently, moving from the kind-subsidy programme to the cash-subsidy programme provides "trading opportunities" to the consumer in terms of choosing its consumption bundle. This opportunity to trade enhances his utility.[1]

Our conclusion raises a question: if cash subsidy is better, why do we observe kind-subsidy in practice? One explanation is that the consumer, in accordance with his own preferences, may spend the cash-subsidy on items that the government does not want him to spend on, e.g., alcohol. Many poor people, especially men, are indeed addicted to drinking and any extra cash given to them that is intended to be spent on food is very likely spent instead on alcohol. Our indifference-curve model and our conclusion that a cash-subsidy programme is better than a kind-subsidy programme assume implicitly that the pattern of preferences of the targeted recipients is not "perverted" from the viewpoint of the government or the society.

The kind-versus-cash subsidy comparison can shed light on our gift culture. We all exchange gifts with our near and dear ones on various happy occasions. Sometimes, we spend a lot of time in deciding what to gift. A gift is an expression of one's love, affection, respect, and regard for the recipient. Various goods like flowers, dresses, jewellery, watches, cars, etc. are commonly given as gifts. Suppose you buy a dress for ₹2,000 to be given as gift at a wedding, a "gift in kind." Alternatively, you could gift ₹2,000 in cash, which is a "gift in cash." As far as you are concerned, it makes no difference to you as the "cost" remains the same for you. What would, you think, a recipient mostly likely prefer? We bet it is the gift in cash. Why, because the recipient has more choices open to him/her with cash than with a physical gift. It may surprise you that barring the urban, rich sections of India, cash is typically given as gift on social occasions.

See Box 5.3 for a perspective on cash or kind as gift in a lighter vein.

BOX 5.3 THE UNROMANTIC ECONOMIST

Some of you must have read a very moving short story by O Henry titled "The Gift of the Magi." It's the story of a couple who is very much devoted to each other. Unfortunately, this couple is very poor. Christmas is just a few days away and both of them want to surprise each other by giving them gifts on Christmas day, but neither has any money. The husband had a guitar whose strings were broken and he could not afford to buy new strings. But he loved his guitar very much. The wife knew it. The wife had nice long black hair. One day, when both of them were together in the market, the wife saw a beautiful comb, but she couldn't afford to buy it. The husband knew it.

On Christmas eve, they sit together and give their packed gifts to each other. The wife was wearing a scarf on her head. The husband opens his gift, and lo! It's a pack of nice guitar strings! He is stunned; the wife opens her gift, and lo! It's that beautiful comb which she could not afford to buy. Both look at each other. The husband had sold his guitar to buy the comb, the wife had sold her long black hair to buy the guitar strings.

The economist would jump and say: "See didn't I tell you that gift in cash is always better than gift in kind?" How unromantic!

In-kind subsidies are not uncommon in the business world, such as distribution of sweets to employees during festival times, and, free automobile for home use, free ayurvedic massage and body relaxation programmes etc. offered to business executives as perks. Sometimes, employees also prefer these perks to avoid income tax. Our analysis can potentially help a manager choose between these programmes and cash bonuses.

5.3 Direct versus Indirect Tax

Taxes are of two kinds. One is a **direct tax**, *referring to a tax on an individual or an organisation.* Direct taxes include personal income tax, corporate income tax, wealth tax, property tax, and gift tax. In India, only the Central Government imposes personal income tax. There are no state income taxes. In some countries like the United States, some states also levy income tax over and above the central (federal) income tax. Corporate income tax is levied on the profits of private companies. After this tax is paid, a company may invest a part of the remaining profits in building assets for the company with the remainder paid out to shareholders as dividends. Dividend income, just as wage income, is subject to the personal income tax. Direct taxes are those that cannot be shifted to other parties.

The other is an **indirect tax**, *referring to taxes, which alter the cost or price of a good or service to either producers or consumers.* There are many types of indirect taxes used in India and other countries, such as import or customs tariff, excise tax, sales tax, service tax, value-added-tax, or VAT and GST.

Suppose that the government wants to generate a given amount of revenues from consumers or households (for spending on national defence, building a dam, subsidising the poor, etc.). There are two options: an income tax as a direct tax and an indirect tax on a commodity or service. Which is the better option for the sake of consumer's welfare?

In many ways this issue is symmetric to the earlier one of kind versus cash subsidy, which involved the method of disbursing among a class of people a given amount of tax revenue already raised, rather than raising revenue itself. Note that an indirect tax increases the price of a product to the consumer and hence is the opposite of a kind subsidy. Further, an income tax is the opposite of a cash subsidy. But, interestingly, the answer to both issues is similar. *Income tax is a better option in terms of consumer's welfare*, just as the cash subsidy was better to the consumer than the kind subsidy.

The economic reason behind this is also similar to that in the case of kind versus cash subsidy. In the income tax programme, the equilibrium bundle of goods which is available with the indirect tax programme is always available to the consumer, but not the vice versa. Thus, the consumer cannot be worse off than in the indirect tax programme. The details of deriving this conclusion are given in Appendix 5.A.

Why do governments then use indirect taxes? The prime reason is that an income tax is politically unattractive in that it is visible, affects an individual's "pocket" directly, and thus is likely to be politically unpopular, whereas the cost of an indirect tax is less "visible" to the public and hence more convenient to use politically. Moreover, in many countries the authority to impose a direct tax like an income tax lies with the central or the federal government only, not with state governments. Hence, to raise revenues for their expenditure and commitments, the state governments resort to indirect taxes.

5.4 Consumptions-Savings Decisions

Chapter 4 dealt with the consumer's decision-making on how much to consume of different goods and services once she has allotted how much to spend. At a more aggregate level, we can think of two decision problems facing an individual or a household. After it receives its "income" in terms of wages, profits, rents, etc. and from the sale of previously held assets, a part of it is spent and the remainder is saved. How much to spend and how much to save is one problem. The other is to allocate the total spending on different goods and services—which we studied in Chapter 4.[2]

Interestingly, the approach to analyse the second problem can be applied to understand the first problem of choice between consumption and savings—which is our goal here.

Assume for simplicity that a consumer lives only two periods, present (period 1) and future (period 2), i.e., there is only one future period. (More advanced models allow for multiple periods.) She consumes two goods, namely, current (period 1) consumption and future (period 2) consumption. Each of these is a basket having many goods and services in the respective periods. Let's call them C_1 and C_2, respectively, the total expenditure/spending or "consumption" in periods 1 and 2.[3]

Realise that a person's savings in the current period partly or wholly finances future consumption. Assume for simplicity that the consumer does not save anything in period 2 for children and other dependents at the end of period 2. Let Y_1 (≥ 0) denote the person's income and wealth in the beginning of period 1 and Y_2 (≥ 0) be her future period 2 fresh income and wealth. Let us refer to Y_1 and Y_2 *as present and future "income."* It is possible that Y_1 or Y_2 is zero. For instance, if a person is currently unemployed and has zero savings or wealth from the past, then $Y_1 = 0$. If the person plans to retire in period 2, then $Y_2 = 0$.

Notice that in this framework, savings in the current period, say S, equal $Y_1 - C_1$, the excess of income over consumption. Savings can be positive, zero, or negative, whereas negative savings mean that a person is a borrower in period 1. As an example, suppose you are just stepping out of college, confident of getting a good job in the next quarter, while, at the moment, you have no income, i.e., $Y_1 = 0$. However, based on the expectation of future potential earnings you may be able to buy a mega-screen 70" TV by borrowing from your parents or possibly from a financial institution. In this case, $Y_1 - C_1 < 0$, i.e., your savings are negative. Let's assume that if savings are positive, they are invested in an interest-earning asset like a savings account. You are then a lender. In the real world, lending and borrowing interest rates almost always differ. But let us assume for simplicity that both interest rates are the same, equal to r. Realise that your carry-over to period 2 is equal to $S(1+r)=(Y_1-C_1)(1+r)$, which is positive or negative accordingly as you are a lender or a borrower.

A rational consumer's problem is to choose present and future consumption, i.e., C_1 and C_2, so as to maximise utility from C_1 and C_2, given the income flows in the two periods, Y_1 and Y_2, and the interest rate r. From Y_1 and the choice of current consumption, C_1, we know what the savings are. Hence, the choice of current consumption is equivalent to the choice of savings.

This is somewhat similar to the consumer choice problem analysed in Chapter 4, where we analysed how a consumer would allocate his total expenditure on apples and chocolates. Here we consider how a consumer allocates his "lifetime" income on present and future consumption. This is called an **intertemporal choice**, or over-the-time choice.

We begin with characterising the "intertemporal budget," which will tell us various combinations of present consumption and future consumption that the consumer can afford.

5.4.1 Intertemporal Budget Line

Think of what future consumption, C_2, is equal to. Given that nothing is left for anyone at the end of period 2, future consumption must equal future income Y_2 plus the carry-over from period 1, i.e., $C_2=Y_2+S(1+r)$. Remembering that $S=Y_1-C_1$, we can write the above equation as:

$$C_2=Y_2+(Y_1-C_1)(1+r), \text{ or}$$
$$C_1+\frac{C_2}{1+r}=Y_1+\frac{Y_2}{1+r}. \tag{5.1}$$

This is the **intertemporal budget** equation. The left-hand side is the *discounted* value of present and future consumptions, whereas the right-hand side is the *discounted* value of present and future incomes. The word "discounted" means that future consumption and future income are discounted to make it comparable to present consumption and present income. For instance, while C_2 is the future, period 2, consumption, it is worth only $C_2/(1+r)$ in terms of the period 1 in the sense that if you forego $C_2/(1+r)$ amount of consumption today (period 1) and save it, that will fetch you $(1+r)C_2/(1+r)=C_2$ of consumption in period 2.

We can compare the intertemporal budget with the consumer's budget studied in Chapter 4. In view of the budget equation (5.1), the "price" of present consumption is $p_1=1$ and the price of future consumption is $p_2=1/(1+r)$.

Figure 5.4 depicts the intertemporal budget line as *AB*. If $C_2 = 0$, then $C_1 = Y_1 + Y_2/(1+r)$; this is the intercept of the budget line on the x-axis measuring C_1. Likewise, you can determine that the intercept on the y-axis measuring C_2 is $C_1 = Y_1(1+r) + Y_2$. The absolute value of the slope of *AB* is then,

$$\frac{\text{rise}}{\text{run}} = \frac{Y_1(1+r)+Y_2}{Y_1+Y_2/(1+r)} = 1+r.$$

The term $1+r$ is indeed the relative price of present consumption in terms of the future consumption, as $p_1/p_2 = 1/\left[1/(1+r)\right] = 1+r$. This has straightforward interpretation. That is, if the interest rate is r, as you sacrifice or save one unit of present consumption €1, you get future consumption equal to €$(1+r)$.

There is a particular point, *N*, on *AB*, which is of special significance. At this point, $C_1 = Y_1$ and $C_2 = Y_2$, i.e., the present consumption is exactly equal to the present income and future consumption matches with future income. This is the point at which there is no borrowing or lending, i.e., savings are zero. If the consumer chooses a point on *AB* and below the point *N*, like *G*, then $C_1 > Y_1$. This means that he is a borrower. Similarly, if he chooses a point on *AB* lying above the point *N*, he is a lender.

Shift of the Intertemporal Budget Line

However, before looking at which point the consumer will choose (in principle), let us consider how the budget line shifts when the current income (Y_1), future income (Y_2), or the interest rate (r) changes. Suppose Y_1 increases. Then the intercept on

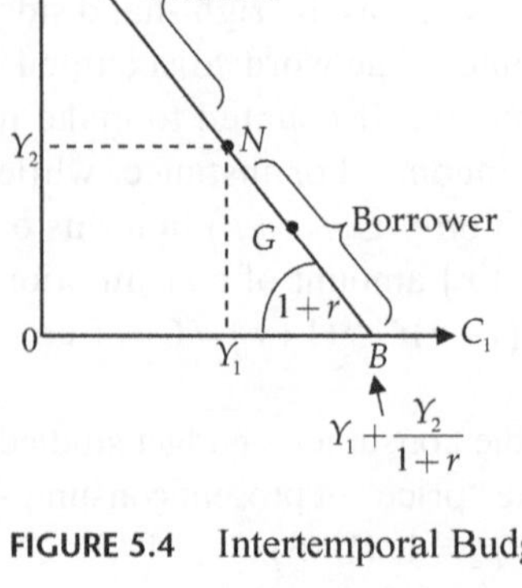

FIGURE 5.4 Intertemporal Budget

the x-axis moves to the right and that on the y-axis moves up. Thus, the budget line shifts to the right. The same holds for an increase in Y_2. But an increase in the interest rate has a different kind of effect. Note three things.

(1) A higher r means a lower value of $Y_1 + Y_2/(1+r)$, implying that the intercept on the x-axis shifts towards the origin.
(2) It means a higher value of $Y_1(1+r) + Y_2$; thus the vertical intercept moves up.
(3) Think about the point N. Since it is the zero borrowing–lending point, it must remain unaffected by any interest rate change. Put differently, the choice of $C_1 = Y_1$ and $C_2 = Y_2$ always satisfies the budget *irrespective of what the interest rate is*. Therefore, the point N does not move when the interest rate changes.

These three features imply that the budget line shifts neither to the right entirely, nor to the left entirely. Instead, *an interest rate increase moves the intertemporal budget line clockwise, pivoting on the point N*. This is shown in Figure 5.5.

5.4.2 Preferences and Consumer's Equilibrium

We now ask, which point on the budget line will be chosen by the consumer? Apart from the budget, this would partly depend on the consumer's preferences over present and future consumption. All else the same, if he is very impatient, he would have a lot of present consumption and a little of future consumption. If he is very patient, he would choose an opposite combination. We can define a utility function over present and future consumption: $U(C_1, C_2)$, similar to the one defined in Chapter 4. Based on this, we can draw indifference curves (ICs) in C_1 and C_2. Figure 5.6 shows two such ICs. As in Chapter 4, we define the marginal rate of substitution of the present consumption for future consumption as the units of future consumption the consumer wants to forego in order to have one extra

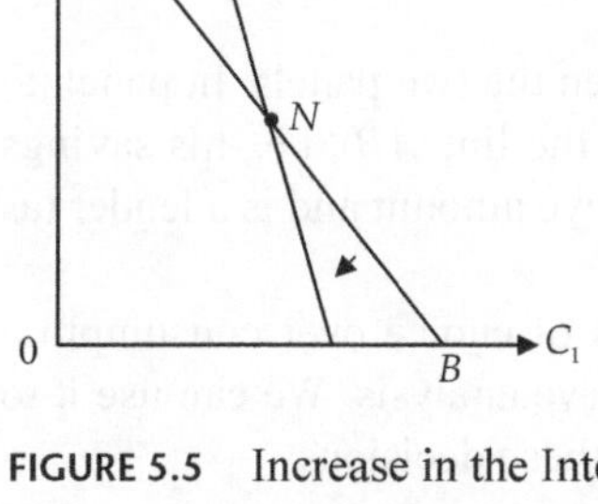

FIGURE 5.5 Increase in the Interest Rate and the Budget Line

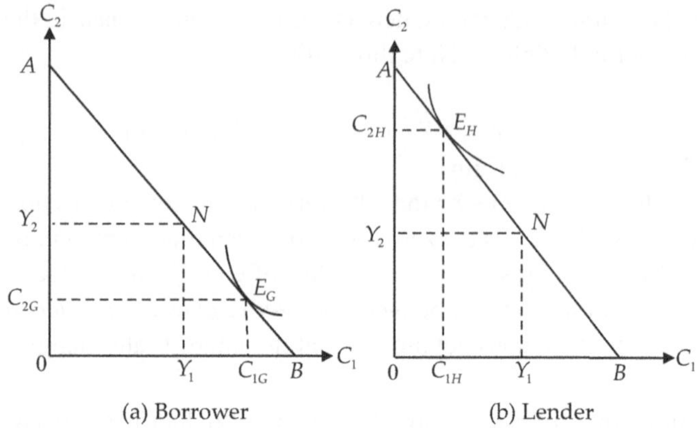

FIGURE 5.6 Consumer's Equilibrium

unit of present consumption. This is called the **intertemporal rate of substitution**. Denote this as MRS_{12}. Recall that, in general, MRS is equal to the slope of the indifference curve. Here, MRS_{12} is equal to the slope of the IC in the present and future consumption.

Once all this is understood, it is easy to characterise the consumer's equilibrium. Turn to Figure 5.6 again. Given his budget, the consumer maximises his utility from the present and future consumption at the point of tangency between the budget line and the IC. In panel (a) this is the point E_G. Panel (b) represents a different individual with a generally flatter indifference curve and the equilibrium point is E_H. In both cases, the tangency point between the indifference curve and the budget line is the equilibrium point. What is the general condition of consumer's equilibrium? The tangency point has the property that the slope of the IC = the slope of the budget line. Or,

$$MRS_{12} = 1 + r. \tag{5.2}$$

This is the same as the marginal principle of consumer equilibrium studied in Chapter 4, since $1+r$ is the inter-temporal price ratio, p_1 / p_2, where, as we have seen earlier, $p_1 = 1$ and $p_2 = 1/(1+r)$.

Notice an important qualitative difference between the two panels. In panel (a) the consumer is a borrower (as E_G lies below N on the line AB), i.e., his savings are negative. In panel (b) the consumer saves a positive amount and is a lender (as E_H lies above N on the line AB).

What we have outlined above is a simple model of choice over consumption and savings as an application of the indifference curve analysis. We can use it to understand how income and interest changes affect these decisions.

5.4.3 Changes in Incomes and the Interest Rate

Suppose there is an increase in the present/current income. This shifts out the budget line. This is analogous to the income effect studied in Chapter 4. It is reasonable to assume that *both current consumption and future consumption are normal goods* (since these are broad aggregates rather than specific goods). This implies that, as the present income increases, current consumption and future consumption both would increase. What about savings? Since future consumption also increases with present income, only a fraction of an increase in present income goes towards present consumption. This implies that savings would increase too.

In macroeconomics, you learn concepts like the **marginal propensity to consume** (*MPC*) and **marginal propensity to save** (*MPS*). *MPC* is a ratio of increase in consumption expenditure due to an increase in income. For example, if your income rises from 100 to 200, and, as a result, your consumption expenditure rises from 80 to 150, then *MPC* is 70 divided by 100 that is 0.7 and your $MPS = 1 - MPC$ is 0.3. In the present context they are defined respectively as the increase in present consumption and savings per unit increase of present income. Our consumption-savings model's implication that current consumption and savings increase with current income implies that pre $MPC > 0$ and $MPS > 0$. Both *MPC* and *MPS* being positive, and $MPC + MPS$ being equal to one, it follows that $0 < MPC, MPS < 1$.

We thus have a "micro-economic foundation" of why *MPC* and *MPS* are positive and less than one. The important underlying assumption is that both current consumption and future consumption are normal goods.

Consider an increase in *future* income. This also shifts out the budget line, and, given our assumption of "normality," it means an increase in present and future consumption also. However, as the present consumption increases while the present income is unchanged, it implies a *decrease* in the savings.

Since the budget line shifts out in each case, the consumer is always on a higher indifference curve. That is, a consumer always benefits from an increase in the present income or the future income.

Finally, we analyse an increase in the interest rate. As we have earlier seen, the budget line rotates clockwise, pivoting on the point of no-borrowing-no-lending. How present and future consumptions change depends on whether the consumer is a borrower or a lender. Consider Figure 5.7. Note that in both panels, the equilibrium points, before and after a change in the interest rate, lie below the point N, showing that the consumer is a borrower. Observe that in panel (a) both present and future consumptions fall as the interest rate increases, whereas in panel (b) the present consumption falls whereas the future consumption rises. Combining the two, we say that, *if a consumer is a borrower, an increase in the interest rate leads to a decrease in the present consumption, while future consumption may increase or decrease.*

This result can be explained in terms of substitution and income effects that we learnt in Chapter 4. An increase in the interest rate increases the relative price of

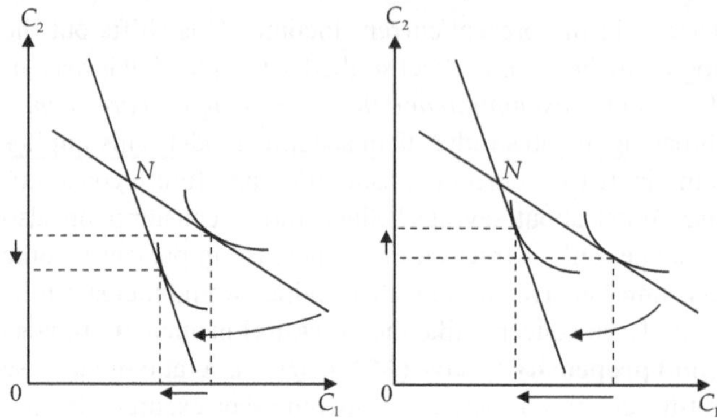

(a) Present and Future Consumptions Fall (b) Present Consumption Falls But Future Consumption Increases

FIGURE 5.7 Effect of a Change in the Interest Rate on a Borrower

present consumption in terms of future consumption (i.e., present consumption is now more "expensive" relative to future consumption than before). By the substitution effect, the consumer will reduce current consumption and increase future consumption. Furthermore, since he is a borrower, an increase in the interest rate reduces his real income. Assuming normality, this would tend to reduce both present and future consumptions. Hence, the net effect is that present consumption decreases unambiguously, whereas future consumption may increase or decrease.

How does an increase in the interest rate affect savings? Mark that present consumption falls, while there is no change in the present income. This implies that savings, equal to the excess of present income over present consumption, increase.[4] Does the consumer benefit or lose, in terms of welfare? See that in both the panels the consumer moves to a lower indifference curve. Thus, he is worse off. Why? Because he is a borrower, an increase in the interest rate tends to reduce his real income.

The lender's case is shown in Figure 5.8. Combining the effects shown in both panels we see that, *as the interest rate rises, present consumption may increase or decrease, while future consumption increases unambiguously.* It is because, by the substitution effect, the present consumption falls and future consumption rises—as in case of a borrower. But, being a lender an increase in the interest rate tends to *increase* real income. Given normality, this would tend to increase consumption in both periods. Therefore, the net effect on present consumption is ambiguous, while that on the future consumption is positive.

How are the savings affected? Since the present income may increase or decrease while the present income remains the same, unlike for a borrower, the lender's savings may increase or decrease. The reason lies in the underlying substitution and income effects. Finally, we notice from Figure 5.8 that a lender is

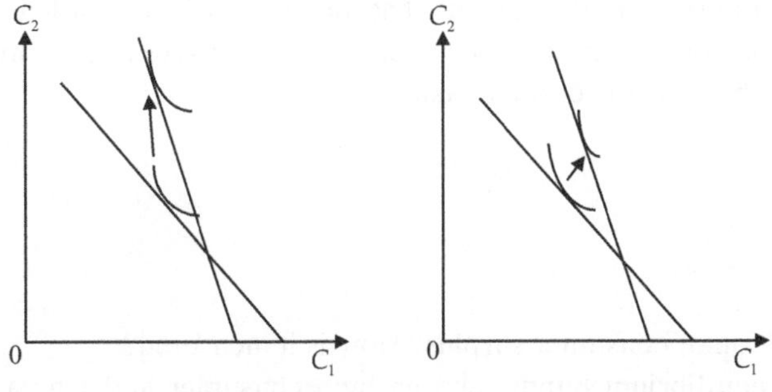

(a) Present Consumption Falls but Future Consumption Increases

(b) Present and Future Consumptions Increase

FIGURE 5.8 Effects of a Change in the Interest Rate on a Lender

always better off with a higher interest rate. This is expected, since an increase in the interest rate tends to increase the real income of a lender.

Facts and Insights

- Consumer surplus measures the level of consumer welfare associated with a particular price of a commodity.
- An increase (a decrease) in the price of a product leads to a decrease (an increase) in the consumer surplus.
- Equilibrium consumption bundle in a kind-subsidy programme is always available in a cash-subsidy programme but not vice versa (presuming that both programmes involve the same amount of subsidy). Hence, the latter programme offers more trading opportunities compared to the former and hence is preferred by the consumer.
- Equilibrium consumption bundle in an indirect tax programme is always available in an income tax programme, but not vice versa (presuming that both programmes yield the same amount of revenues). Thus, the latter programme offers more trading opportunities compared to the former and hence is preferred by the consumer.
- A person's savings can be interpreted as his future consumption.
- The interest rate reflects the relative price of present consumption in terms of future consumption.
- Assuming that both the present consumption and future consumption are normal goods, an increase in the present or future income implies more present and future consumption. Moreover, $0 < MPC, MPS < 1$.
- An increase in the interest rate tends to increase (decrease) the real income of a lender (borrower) and therefore exerts a positive (negative) effect on present consumption. Together with the substitution effect, it implies an ambiguous

effect of an increase in the interest rate on savings by a lender and a positive effect on savings of a borrower. This means that the amount lent by a lender may increase, decrease, or remain unchanged as the interest rate rises, while the amount borrowed by a borrower falls unambiguously.

Exercises

Descriptive/Analytical

5.1. What is the definition of consumer surplus? How is it measured?
5.2. Explain why the equilibrium bundle chosen by a consumer under a cash subsidy or a direct tax programme is always available under a kind subsidy or an indirect tax programme, given that the budgetary implications of the two subsidy or tax programmes are the same to the government.
5.3. What is intertemporal rate of substitution and how does it explain how much of present and future consumption a rational consumer will choose.

Short Answer (word limit = 500 approx.)

5.4. Your housemaid asks you for her Diwali (a premier festival in India) gift. You offer her either ₹1,000 or some item of ₹1,000 that she can use. Which will she prefer and why?
5.5. Will a cash subsidy scheme and a reduction in income tax shift the budget line of a consumer in a similar way? Explain.
5.6. Will a programme of kind subsidy and a reduction in indirect tax shift the budget line of a consumer in a similar way? Explain.
5.7. Differentiate between direct and indirect taxes with suitable examples.
5.8. Intuitively explain why an individual would prefer a cash subsidy programme to a kind subsidy programme.
5.9. If individuals prefer cash subsidy to kind subsidy and both programmes cost the same to the government, why in reality do we see examples of kind subsidy?

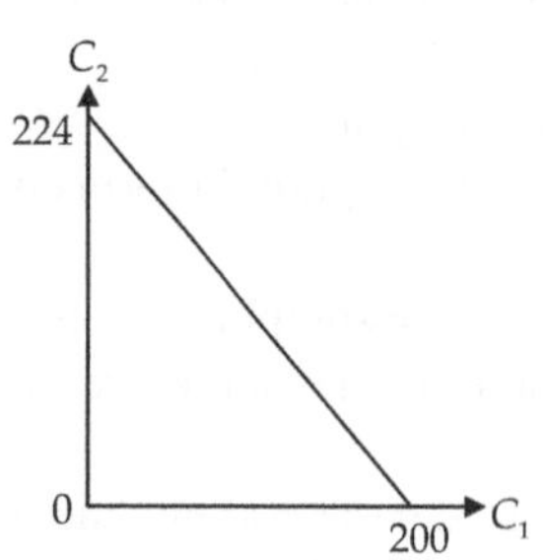

FIGURE 5.9 Exercise

5.10. Intuitively explain why an individual may be better off with a direct tax like income tax than with an indirect tax on the consumption of a good.

5.11. Derive that the sum of the marginal propensity to consume and the marginal propensity to save is one.

5.12. The intertemporal budget line is given as follows. What is the interest rate?

5.13. "Increases in present income and future income have similar impacts on a person's current savings." Defend or refute.

5.14. Explain how a decrease in the interest rate would change the intertemporal budget line of an individual.

5.15. Explain in words how a decrease in the interest rate would affect the amount lent by a lender through income and substitution effects.

5.16. Explain in words how a decrease in the interest rate would affect the amount borrowed by a borrower through income and substitution effects.

5.17. Consumer's surplus is only a figment of imagination of the economists in situations where the prices of the products are clearly displayed and there is no bargaining. Defend or refute.

5.18. Suppose you happen to be working at the retail counter of a high-end designer wear outlet where there are no price tags on the dresses. However, you have been told the minimum price at which a dress can be sold. Apart from your fixed monthly salary, you get as incentive 50% of the excess price (over and above the minimum) on the dresses sold. You have a monthly sales target as well to meet. What will you do to retain your job and earn decent incentive?

5.19. Why do shopkeepers find it more lucrative to offer some 'add-ons' with the main commodity instead of simply reducing the price equivalent to the cost of "add-ons"? (Add-ons are items which you get "free" when you buy a commodity, e.g., a bowl with every purchase of a cornflake packet, a gold coin with a car and a handkerchief with a shirt.

5.20. You are the HR manager of an IT firm, most of whose employees are highly skilled workers with rare technical skill. Poaching is not uncommon and employee retention is your key concern. You have recently spotted a high-skill worker, earning ₹4 million per year, in your rival firm who is willing to join your firm. You have been given the permission to poach this employee for a ₹5 million Cost to the Company (CTC) and you have the liberty to design his pay packet, not exceeding the sanctioned amount. Recently, two interns from a nearby business school have joined you to do their summer internship. You ask them to design his pay packet separately. One of them tells you to offer him ₹4 million as salary and the rest of the amount in perks such as chauffeur-driven car for office and personal use, membership subscription for local club, two fully paid family holidays every year, keeping the total amount on these perks within ₹1 million. The other intern suggests giving him ₹5 million as salary. His argument is based on his learning from economics that cash reward is better than reward in kind. Whose recommendations would you accept and why?

Quizzes/Numerical

5.21. Suppose we compare an income tax programme with an indirect tax on a good, which a consumer doesn't consume. Which programme would he prefer?

5.22. Consider the consumption-savings model. The present and future incomes are \$30,000 and \$45,000 respectively. The interest rate is 10%. Draw the intertemporal budget line indicating the intercepts and the slope.

5.23. Referring to the previous question, suppose that the consumer's present consumption is \$36,000. What is then his future-period consumption?

5.24. What is meant by intertemporal rate of substitution? Does it increase with an increase in the interest rate? Explain.

5.25. What impact will an increase in the interest rate likely have on the current demand for goods and services for the following consumers, named A, B, C, and D. (a) A earns \$5,000 a month in a secure job and hardly saves anything. (b) B too earns \$5,000 a month with job security (till 60) and regularly saves 15 per cent of her income. (c) C is a software engineer who has just started on a monthly pay package of \$7,000. He is upbeat about his job and buys an expensive flat in a posh locality for \$700,000 by taking a bank loan. (d) D is also a software engineer having a 10-year work experience with no job security and variable income in the past. In this current job, he is getting about \$3,000.

Appendix 5.A Direct versus Indirect Tax: Details

Consider Figure 5.10. There are two goods: clothing and "others." Suppose that there is no tax to begin with. The price line is *AB*. The consumer's equilibrium

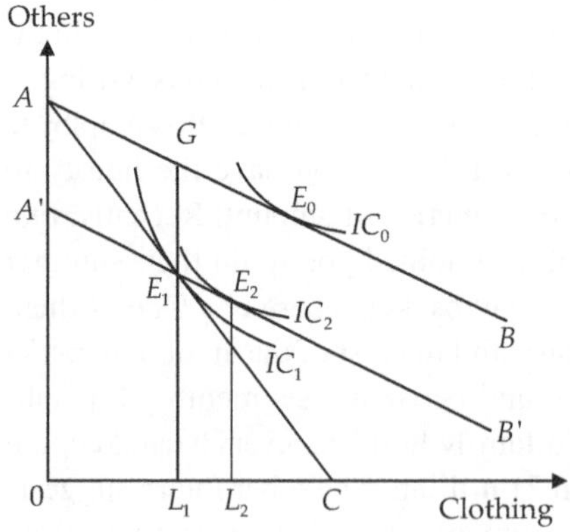

FIGURE 5.10 Direct Tax versus Indirect Tax

is at E_0.First consider a sales tax on clothing. The price of clothing is higher to the consumer because of this tax. Let *AC* be the new price line. The consumer chooses the tangency point E_1. She consumes L_1 of clothing and E_1L_1 of others. The indifference curve passing through E_1 is at a lower level than the one passing through E_0 : as you would expect, the consumer is worse off than before. How much revenue is the government collecting? The answer is GE_1. It is because if the consumer didn't have to pay the sales tax, she would have had GL_1 of others but she actually has E_1L_1 of others. Therefore, the difference, equal to GE_1, must be the sales tax proceeds.

If, instead of the indirect tax, the amount GE_1 is taken away from the consumer as income tax, her budget line is *A'B'* that is parallel to *AB*. The point E_2 is the equilibrium point. Notice that the consumer is on a higher indifference curve (IC_2) in comparison to the sales tax programme. Thus, for the consumer, an income tax is preferable to an indirect tax.

As explained in the main text, the economic reason is analogous to that behind why cash-subsidy may be preferable to subsidy in kind. The equilibrium bundle chosen by an individual in the indirect tax programme (E_1) is always available to the consumer in the equivalent income tax programme. A wider set of choices cannot make someone worse off. The relative price of clothing is different between the two programmes. In the income tax programme, the consumer will pick a bundle (E_2) other than (E_1) and be strictly better off compared to the indirect tax programme.

Notes

1 To further complete the argument, the equilibrium bundle in the cash-subsidy programme is not available in the kind-subsidy programme (i.e., E_2 is not available along the budget line AC).
2 We remind you again that the term "income" in the last chapter meant total spending.
3 How we can lump many goods and treat them as one composite good is explained in detail in the appendix to Chapter 4.
4 That is, the amount borrowed decreases.

Bibliography

Cohen, P., Hahn, R., Hall, J., Levitt, S., & Metcalfe, R. (2016). *Using big data to estimate consumer surplus: The case of Uber* (Working Paper 22627, NBER Working Paper Series).

Kaneda, T., Greenbaum, C., & Patierno, K. (2019). *World population data sheet*. Population Reference Bureau.

Mitra, A. (1999–2000). *Environmental conservation and demand for nature-based tourism in Arunachal Pradesh*. Final Report submitted to EERC (Environmental Economics Research Committee, IGIDR, funded by World Bank project: Environmental Management Capcity Building Technical Assistance Project.

Peck, R., Chaloupka, F. J., Jha, P., & Lightwood, J. (1999). A welfare analysis of tobacco use. In R. Peck and F. J. Chaloupke, Eds, *Curbing the epidemic: Governments and the* economics of Tobaco control, pp 131–152, Oxford University Press.

Watal, J. (2000). Pharmaceutical patents, prices and welfare losses: Policy options for India under the WTO TRIPS agreement. *The World Economy*, *23*(5), 733–752.

6

DEMAND FORECASTING

Management is all about decision-making. One way of decision-making would be to take a decision when a problem actually occurs. There is a phrase in English: "Don't cross the bridge until you come to it." Is this necessarily a smart management strategy? Before jumping to an answer, let us distinguish between two types of contingencies: unforeseen and foreseen. Natural calamities like floods, hurricanes, fire, and epidemics are mostly unforeseen. Who could have foreseen the global economic disaster that Covid-19 pandemic brought with it? In this class of situations, it makes sense to adopt: "I'll cross the bridge when I come to it."

However, there are other contingencies (mostly human-made) about which you have an inkling, but you cannot foresee the approximate time or magnitude of their happening. Nor have you any control over them as a micro-level decision-maker. It could be environmental degradation, global warming, wars, political upheavals like military coup, and so on. In such contingencies as well, you could take little pre-emptive action. There is still another set of unforeseen contingencies which relate to scientific discoveries and inventions. These are presently more relevant than ever before owing to the pace of developments in information technology. One fine day, you may suddenly find your product to have become obsolete due to the arrival of an altogether new product.

Barring such instances, there is a wide range of foreseen contingencies for which taking a laidback stand and saying, "I'll cross the bridge when I'll come to it," wouldn't be smart management. In such cases, a prudent manager should carefully gather past and present information, even generate information or data points about various dimensions of the issue, and make a data-based analysis to equip his organisation accordingly. For instance, you know that the Indian government is allowing more foreign direct investment (FDI) in the sector your product

DOI: 10.4324/9781003452195-6

is. So, you anticipate more intense competition. It is not wise to have a strategy of no-strategy until FDI projects are complete and running.

Data analysis is a prerequisite for planning and strategising. A good manager or one who aspires for a management position should have a working knowledge of data analysis, inference, prediction, and forecasting, while mastering these tools may not be a part of their skillset.

For instance, you are hired as a marketing manager of an AC (air-conditioner)-producing company operating in the four major cities of India. Soon after joining, the monthly sales data for Delhi, Mumbai, Kolkata, and Chennai are given to you in a spreadsheet from January of 2017 to December of 2023. The expectation is that you will devise ways to improve total sales by 10% by the year end. You have a bunch of numbers in front of you, actually $4 \times 12 \times 7 = 336$ data points. What do you do with this data? Do you need to have some other data in conjunction with what you have in order to come with a forecast which is consistent with the stated goal?

Suppose that, as a manager of a light bulb manufacturing company that has several plant locations in Peru, you have felt that providing a gym facility would increase the productivity of workers, say measured by how working (as opposed to defective) light bulbs are produced. Keeping this in mind, you have constructed, as an experiment, a gym room in 10 plants out of 30 in Peru. Suppose that you have a collection of monthly data on workers' productivity in the 10 plants with a gym and 20 without a gym over the last 12 months. That is, you have 12 observations on each of the 30 plants. Table 6.1 summarises the data.

Such a table is called **data summary** or **summary statistics**. Summary statistics is *not* data analysis. It is just a data presentation, a prelude to any data analysis. We see that the average productivity is higher in plants with gym facilities (60,000 as opposed to 50,000). Can we then conclude without hesitation that the experiment has succeeded? The answer is, "not yet." Why? Notice that not just the average productivity, the variation of productivity is also higher in plants with a gym. That is, in some sense, the data on plants with a gym is less reliable. So, how do we balance between a higher average and a higher variability and conclude with reasonable confidence that the average productivity in plants with a gym facility is higher? This is in the domain of data or statistical analysis.

TABLE 6.1 An Example of Data Summary

	Gym Facility	*No Gym Facility*
Average plant output per worker (number of working bulbs produced/ number of workers).	60,000	50,000
Standard deviation of plant output per worker.	5,000	3,000
	Sample size = 10	Sample size = 20

Data analysis and conclusion/inference do not necessarily require you to gather data and do the analysis yourself or by your staff. You can rely on other studies as long as you know how to use them. For instance, as you are about to decide your career choice, you may want to know established cause–effect relations between different variables like age, experience, education, and gender on wage earnings in different segments of companies.

This chapter is a short introduction to data analysis, inference, prediction, and forecasting. The meaning of these terms will be clear as we proceed. More specifically, we will learn about:

(a) Different types of data;
(b) Some elementary statistical concepts;
(c) Inference in terms of comparing averages from different datasets;
(d) Estimation of cause–effect relations using regression analysis; and
(e) Forecasting.

A manager should be at least aware of various concepts and how to "read" the data and the conclusions.

6.1 Types of Data

Typically, data on variables are available in one of three formats: cross-section, time series, and panel.

Cross-section: It refers to data at a point or interval of time across different units, for instance, the volume of sale of your product in different cities in Italy during the 1st quarter of 2023.

Time-series: This is data on the same variable over a period of time in a daily, weekly, monthly, quarterly, or an annual basis, e.g., quarterly sales of your product in Germany and GDP of Germany from the 1st quarter of 2015 (2015Q1) to the 4th quarter of 2023 (2023Q4).

Panel: This is a combination of cross-sectional and time-series data.[1] An example will be the sales of your product in the four major cities of India (Delhi, Mumbai, Kolkata, and Chennai) on a quarterly basis from 2018Q2 to 2022Q3.

Depending on "how" a variable is introduced, we can divide data into quantitative data and qualitative data. Quantitative data are given in units like kg, distance, etc., that is, in terms of weight and other dimensions. Some can be measured on a continuous scale in decimals and fractions. Some are available in whole numbers only, e.g., number of TVs sold, number of students in a class, etc. The latter is called **count data**.

Some relevant variables may be qualitative in that we cannot attach a unit or natural number. But information on them is important. For example, in fixing premiums say against car accidents, an insurance company would like to know whether you are married or not. It has, actually, been found that married people are less prone to committing auto accidents than unmarried folks. (Please don't get married in a hurry for this reason.) Thus, we may want to know the impact of marital status on premiums charged. But we cannot "quantify" marital status: either a person is married or not married (legally). Similarly, we may want to know if there is gender discrimination in salaries in private firms. A person's gender can usually take two values, male and female. It cannot be quantified. A qualitative variable can however be incorporated into statistical analysis, prediction, and forecasting by its conversion to what is called a **dummy variable**, which takes two values, 0 or 1. We can describe marital status by a dummy variable, say D_1, which takes values 0 and 1 according to whether a person is unmarried or married. A male–female gender distinction can be introduced by dummy variable say D_2 that takes values 0 or 1 if a person is a male or a female. Put differently, a dummy variable captures a binary outcome: male versus female, married versus unmarried, private sector versus public sector, above 18 years of age and below 18 years of age, smokers versus non-smokers, employed versus unemployed, etc. It does not matter which of the two is assigned 0 or 1.[2]

Dummy variables are widely used in prediction and forecasting.

6.2 Elementary Statistical Concepts

Range, mean, median, mode, variance, and standard deviation are some of the elementary concepts in statistical analysis. We're sure that all these must be getting covered in your course or courses on quantitative analysis. So, we are not discussing them here, except to note that *a manager must know what these statistical concepts measure.*

6.3 Inference on Comparing Averages

Comparing results from two (or more) samples is very helpful in decision-making. The example of introducing gyms in light bulb manufacturing plants illustrates this. As another example, a manager may want to compare the lifetime of light bulbs from two plants, A and B. Suppose that sample sizes, sample averages, and sample standard deviations are as summarised in Table 6.2.

Can we confidently say that Plan B produces more durable light bulbs? Similar to the earlier example of comparing worker productivity, here also we cannot,

TABLE 6.2 Summary Statistics on Lifetime of Light Bulbs

	Plant A	*Plant B*
Mean lifetime (hours)	200.5	220.6
Standard deviation of lifetimes (hours)	50.3	60.9
Sample size	150	200

a priori, say that plant B produces more durable bulbs, because its output has higher variance. We simply note here that there is a statistical-test-cum-inference technique that can settle the comparison issue in precise terms. This is called the *Student t-test*, or simply the *t*-test. Knowing what a *t*-test is should be a part of the toolkit of a good manager.

6.4 Introduction to Regression Analysis

This is a very common, yet powerful tool to estimate a cause–effect relationship for predictive purposes. There are literally tens of regression types. Our purpose is to merely acquaint you with the basics. For instance, you want to know how work experience affects wage earnings in a given profession. You have data on work experience of several individuals, say X_i, in terms of years of working and their annual gross compensation (inclusive of other benefits), say Y_i, where i stands for the individual i or the sample i. How do we determine or measure the impact of a change in X on Y?

We begin with what is called a scatter plot.

6.4.1 Scatter Plots

Suppose you plot available data on work experience (X) and wage earnings (Y) of individuals in a region on a graph paper or in a spreadsheet like Microsoft Excel. Different observations or data points would look something like in Figure 6.1(a).

As another example, suppose that a local small-scale garment company in India makes jeans of its own unique brand and sells them in various outlets in several cities. The sales manager of this company has collected data from different outlets on the price charged and the number of a particular brand of jean sold over a month. This is given in Table 6.3. The various price–quantity combinations are plotted in Figure 6.1(b).

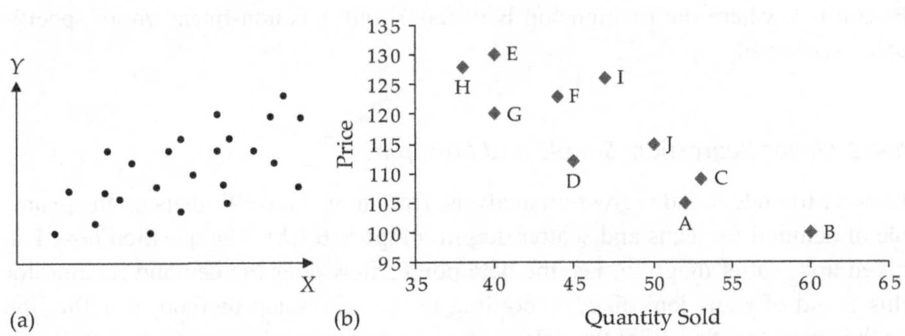

FIGURE 6.1 Scatter Plots

TABLE 6.3 Data on Price and Quantities Sold

Outlet	*Price (₹)*	*Number of jeans sold*
A	105	52
B	100	60
C	109	53
D	112	45
E	130	40
F	123	44
G	120	40
H	128	38
I	126	47
J	115	50

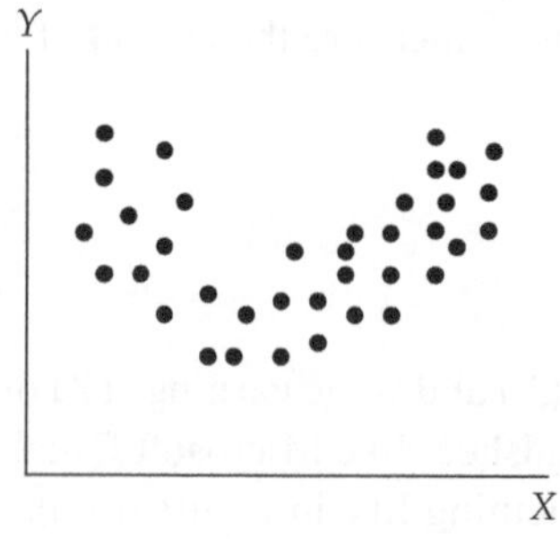

FIGURE 6.2 Another Scatter Diagram

Both panels (a) and (b) are scatter diagrams. A **scatter diagram** is generally defined as *the plot of data on various combinations of two variables.* It indicates the nature of the relationship between the two variables. Figure 6.1(a) tells us that higher wage earnings are associated with more experience; according to Figure 6.1(b), the quantity demanded of jeans decreases with own price.

These are examples of positive and negative X–Y relationships, respectively. A scatter diagram may look more complicated or "non-linear." See, for instance, Figure 6.2, where the relationship between Y and X is non-linear, more specifically, U-shaped.

6.4.2 Linear Regression: Simple and Multiple

In order to understand regression analysis, from now on, we'll focus on the example of demand for jeans and scatter diagram Figure 6.1(b). The question posed is: given this scatter diagram, i.e., the data points, how does the demand relation for this brand of jeans look like? According to the regression method, it is the line or the curve "that best fits the data in the scatter diagram" in some mathematical sense.

Regression analysis typically *assumes* a straight-line, i.e., a linear relationship between the two variables involved. If so, it is called **linear regression.** Thus, in our example, assuming linear regression, we look for a straight line that best represents the points A, B, C, … , J. In Figure 6.3, MN is shown to represent this line, and hence *is* interpreted as the estimated demand function. In terms of regression, MN is called the **regression line.**

In general, if we want to estimate the effect of a variable X on another variable Y by regression, X is called the **independent** or the **explanatory variable** and Y the **dependent variable.** For example, in estimating a demand function, X, the own price, is the independent variable and Y, the quantity sold/demanded, is the dependent variable.

The basis of a regression line like MN in Figure 6.3 is the following. Let the observations on X and Y in the sample be denoted as $(X_1, Y_1), (X_2, Y_2)$, etc. In Table 6.3, these data points refer to entries A, B, C, … up to J. Next, we postulate that the data on X and Y are related by a linear equation *and* a 'random term.' Supposing that the sample data have n (could be 20, 300, or any other number) pairs of observations on X and Y, we write

$$Y_i = a + bX_i + u_i, \quad E(u_i) = 0, \tag{6.1}$$

where $i = 1, 2, \cdots, n$ denote the observations, a and b are constants, and u_i is the error term. A random term captures unforeseen, un-measurable, or unavailable relevant variables. It is a must in any regression analysis, and, because of this, equation (6.1) is a stochastic equation (introduced in Chapter 1), as opposed to a deterministic equation. Requiring $E(u_i) = 0$ implies that a captures the effect of unaccounted factors on Y. An equation like (6.1) defines a linear regression equation. The regression analysis refers to estimating the coefficients a and b

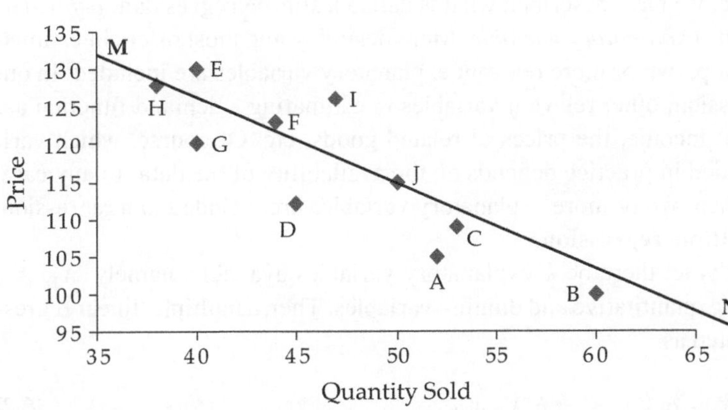

FIGURE 6.3 The Linear Regression Line

from the sample data, where a is called the **intercept coefficient** and b (the multiplicative term with the independent variable) is called the **slope coefficient.**[3]

Intuitively, you can see that the regression line must be the one that passes through the scatter points such that the "aggregate distance," in some sense, of the regression line from the data points is minimised. More precisely, a and b are chosen such that the sum of the squares of the distance, along the axis measuring the dependent variable, between the scatter points and the regression line is minimised. Accordingly, the estimates of a and b are called the **least-squares estimates**. Mathematically speaking, the least-squares estimates of a and b are such that the sum of the squares of the error terms,

$$\sum_{i=1}^{n} u_i^2 = \sum_{i=1}^{n} (Y_i - a - bX_i)^2,$$

is minimised. Note that $Y_i - a - bX_i$ is the distance from the actual data point to the regression line for the ith observation.

How do we interpret a and b? Since b is the coefficient of X, its magnitude and sign capture the marginal effect of the explanatory variable X on Y. However, Y may be affected also by factors other than X. As said earlier, the coefficient a represents the average of the effects of other possible explanatory variables together outside of the regression analysis.

In our example in Table 6.3, the least-squares regression estimates, denoted by a "hat," turn out to be $\hat{\alpha} = 115.645$ and $\hat{b} = -0.588$[4] Note that $\hat{b}$ is negative, reflecting a negative relationship between the price and the quantity demanded, as can be visually inspected in Figure 6.3. If, instead, we have a scatter diagram as in Figure 6.1(a), $\hat{b}$ would be positive, indicating a measured positive relationship between work experience and wage earnings. In general, *in the regression analysis a positive or a negative relation between two variables will imply the estimate of slope coefficient to have a positive or negative sign, respectively.*

In the above, we have described what is called a **simple regression**, *defined as one that has one explanatory variable.* More desirably and most often, in estimating a relationship, two or more relevant explanatory variables are included. In our example regression, other relevant variables in estimating a demand function are the consumers' income, the prices of related goods, etc. Of course, which variables are included in practice depends on the availability of the data. In any case, in principle when two or more explanatory variables are included in a regression, it is called **multiple regression.**

Algebraically, let there be k explanatory variables available, namely, X_1, X_2, $\cdots$, X_k including quantitative and dummy variables. Then a multiple, linear regression can be stated as

$$Y_i = a + b_1 X_{1i} + b_2 X_{2i} + \cdots + b_k X_{ki} + u_i, \tag{6.2}$$

where i denotes observations as before, b_1 captures the marginal effect of X_1 on Y, b_2 is the marginal effect of X_2 on Y, and so on. The task is to estimate the coefficients $a, b_1, b_2, \ldots, b_k$.

However, the general principle behind multiple regression is the same as that of simple regression. The idea is to choose the coefficients such that the regression equation best fits the data points, that is, the sum of squares of the error terms:

$$\sum_{i=1}^{n} u_i^2 = \sum_{i=1}^{n} \left(Y_i - a - b_1 X_{1i} - b_2 X_{2i} \cdots - b_k X_{ki}\right)^2$$

is minimised.

In summary then, the regression analysis has the following elements:

1. It requires data on the dependent variable and some of the explanatory variables.
2. A stochastic equation describing the relationship between the dependent variable and the available explanatory variables is postulated. Typically, a linear relationship is assumed. If so, it is called linear regression.
3. In the linear regression, the intercept coefficient and the slope coefficients are estimated on the criterion that the sum of squares of the difference between the actual values of the dependent variable and its values according to the regression equation is minimised. (In simple regression, it reduces to the sum of squares of the distance along the axis measuring the dependent variable, between the scatter points and the regression line.) Such coefficient estimates are called the least-squares estimates.
4. The sign and the magnitude of a slope coefficient show the sign and magnitude of the marginal effect of the corresponding explanatory variable on the dependent variable. In case of a demand estimation, the slope coefficient of the own price should turn out to be negative (unless it is a Giffen good).

Does the regression method give a "perfect" estimation of what the true relationship (e.g., demand relationship) is? Never. However, there is a general question of how well the regression line fits the data and reliability of the estimates obtained from the estimation. It depends, for instance, on the explanatory variables chosen (or found data on) and the variation in the values of the explanatory variables. If a relevant explanatory variable is missing (for data problems or because it hasn't occurred to the researcher that a particular variable is pertinent), then the fit and estimates will be poor. However, there are ways to get around such problems.

Despite some limitations, regression is a very useful tool of statistical analysis. Don't lose sight of the fact that nothing in this world is perfect.

6.4.3 Log-Linear Regression

In a cause–effect relationship, an estimate of elasticity is desirable, because it is unit-independent. In Chapter 2, we studied elasticities for demand and supply. For instance, if we want to know the elasticity of demand with respect to own price or price of a related good, i.e., how a proportional change in X affects Y proportionally, we may want to estimate a *non-linear* function, $Y = AX^b$. Why? It is because, from Chapter 3, we know that b is the elasticity of Y with respect to X.

Very usefully, however, we do not need to perform non-linear regression. If we apply log, we have $\ln Y = \ln A + b \ln X$, which is a "log-linear" equation in that $\ln Y$ is a linear function of $\ln X$. Hence, we can apply linear regression to $\ln X$ and $\ln Y$. The regression equation, called log-linear regression, is

$$\ln Y_i = a + b \ln X_i + u_i, \tag{6.3}$$

where b is the measure of elasticity of Y with respect to X.

We can specify a multiple log-linear regression equation with many explanatory variables, parallel to equation (6.3). Remember however that the log function is not defined for zero or any negative number. Thus, make sure that Y and the X's must take positive values only.[5]

An example of elasticity estimates based on a regression equation similar to equation (6.3) is given in Box 6.1.

BOX 6.1 PRICE ELASTICITY OF DEMAND FOR HOUSEHOLD APPLIANCES BY USING REGRESSION EQUATIONS SIMILAR TO EQUATION (6.3)

A regression equation like (6.3) is postulated by Fujita (2015) to study the price elasticity of household appliances in the United States over the period 1989–2009. The data points are annual. Hence, the sample size 21. The estimates when energy efficiency indicator, median household income, and stock failures are included as additional explanatory variables besides own price are presented below.

Cloth-washers	Dishwashers	Refrigerators	Freezers	Room Air Conditioners
0.34	0.61	0.47	0.46	0.71

Note: These are absolute values of price elasticity of demand. The estimates are statistically significant at 5% except for refrigerators and freezers.

In some situations, we can normally talk about a percentage change in Y, but not for X. For instance, Y can be wage earnings and X could be education measured by the number of years in school and college. We can say a 10% increase or 8% decrease in earning, but if we consider 5 years of education compared to 4 years of education, we do not normally express this as 25% increase in education. It does not make sense and is, actually, misleading. In this situation, instead of equation (6.3) we can specify:

$$\ln Y_i = a + bX_i + u_i. \tag{6.4}$$

An application of log-linear regression is briefly outlined in Box 6.2.

BOX 6.2 EDUCATION AND WAGE EARNINGS: AN ILLUSTRATION OF LOG-LINEAR REGRESSION

As an example of log-linear regression estimation, you may look at (Woolridge, 2013) Chapter 3, equation (3.19). It provides an illustration of a multiple regression version of equation (6.4), which uses cross-sectional data and where the dependent variable is log of hourly wage across individuals and independent variables include years of education, experience, etc. The estimated coefficient of log of hourly wage with respect to years of education is 0.092. It means that, all else remaining the same, one extra year of education fetches, on average, a 9.2% increase in hourly wage.

We should note however that with increasing availability of data over time, various elasticities are measured by using panel data and advanced regression analyses, of which log-linear specifications are a part.

6.4.4 Non-Linearities

If the scatter plot looks "nonlinear" as in Figure 6.2, a simple linear regression or a log-linear regression may not be a good choice. But non-linear effects of explanatory variables can be estimated by specifying either (a) a regression equation that is linear in parameters but non-linear with respect to explanatory variables or (b) a non-linear equation in variables. A couple of examples are in order.

$$\text{Type}(\text{a}) \quad Y_i = a + bX_i + cX_i^2 + u_i \tag{6.5}$$

$$\text{Type}(\text{b}) \quad Y_i = \exp(a + bX_i) + u_i \tag{6.6}$$

Note that in equation (6.5), Y is quadratic in X but linear in the parameters a, b, and c. Hence, we can treat X^2 as a separate explanatory variable and apply linear regression to equation (6.5) to account for non-linearity. In equation (6.6), Y is an exponential function in X and thus it is non-linear with respect to X and the parameters a and b. We cannot simply take a log of the determinant part of equation (6.6) and transform it to a regression equation like equation (6.4) if Y has negative values in the available data.

Further details on non-linear regression are beyond our scope.

6.5 Forecasting

Note that we are using the word "*forecasting*," not "*prediction*." A prediction model like regression is founded on existing data and used to estimate outcomes for unseen, counterfactual data. If it is simple regression like equation (6.4) and we have the least-squares estimates of a and b, equal to say $\hat{\alpha} = 0.5$ and $\hat{b} = -2.1$, then a prediction involves asking, for example, "what is the predicted or expected value of Y if $X = 10$?" where $X = 10$ may or may not be a data point in the sample. If it is not in the sample, i.e., if $X = 10$ is a counterfactual, it is more precisely called **out-of-sample prediction.** Applying equation (6.4), the predicted value of $\ln \text{Y} = 0.5 - 2.1 \times \ln 10 = -4.33$. Hence that of Y, say $\hat{Y}$ equals $\exp(-4.33) = 0.013$. Forecasting is a sub-discipline of prediction in which we make predictions about the future, based on time-series data.

Sensible forecasting requires **lead time**, *defined as the time gap between the day/date of forecasting of an event and the day/date of its happening.* Consider a situation where a meteorological department forecasts the occurrence of a massive typhoon in the next 12 hours, potentially endangering the lives of thousands of people living in coastal areas. Even if this forecast were by and large precise, very little concrete action can be taken in such a short notice, except warning the people through mass media. Had the meteorological department given three days of lead time, the authorities could have moved the most vulnerable sections to shelters. Likewise, the longer the lead time, the better it would be for the manager as she will get ample time to prepare the organisation to deal with an anticipated issue.

Prudent managers keep track of forecasts of a list of factors or variables. Many of these may be beyond the control of the managers like changes in tax rates, lending rates, inflation, etc. But some actions will be in the span of managerial scope and control. The company can plan those actions based on their forecasts.

Forecasting, in and of itself, is a vast subject. In what follows, we limit ourselves to **demand forecasting**, which is of immense utility to a company with growth aspirations. The modern production pattern is such that there is no direct communication between the buyer and the seller. The buyers of your firm may be in thousands or millions scattered over nationally and (sometimes) internationally. A steel manufacturer in India would be interested to obtain a forecasting on the demand for steel in India, given the extent of competition from imported steel from South Korea and other countries. To make production plans, Maruti Udyog (an auto manufacturer in India) would be interested in the forecasting of demand for autos in the next few years to come. Forecasting is also important not just at the national level but also at a local or regional level in deciding for example whether to open a local or regional office. A multinational firm would need to decide whether or not to open a branch in a particular foreign country. Demand forecasting at an international level can also be useful for a manager.

It is particularly essential in case of perishable goods. As an example, electricity cannot be stored. Any excess supply of it goes waste and any excess demand causes power cuts, thereby affecting production adversely. Even in the case of non-perishable goods, correct forecasting is important to avoid unnecessarily large volumes of inventories, that is, the costs in terms of storage charges and blocked capital.

Actual demand forecasting requires interdisciplinary skills, involving quantitative techniques. In what follows, we aim to present a broad outline of some elementary methods of forecasting.

ACTIVITY 6.1

Suppose after completing your management course with a marketing major, you are employed in a well-known marketing research company. A reputed FMCG Company (established 50 years ago) hires your marketing research company to forecast the demand for its branded potato chips in the short term (next year), medium term (next 5 years), and long term (next 10 years). Your boss asks you to prepare a blueprint of the task and make a power-point presentation. How will you go about this task?

What if your client is a new entrant in the branded potato chips industry who wants to enter this market with a bang and seeks the demand forecasts of his recently launched product in short, medium, and long terms?

Demand forecasting can be useful not just for managerial decision-making within a firm but also for the government in policymaking. For example, a forecasting on the demand for petrol may guide the government's policy towards petrol pricing, building of reserves, etc. A good demand forecasting for HIV vaccine is important for developing countries where AIDS is a growing phenomenon. The same is true for Covid-19 vaccine.

There are different kinds of demand forecasting depending on (a) the time horizon and (b) the method involved. In the business world, quantity decisions that ought to change periodically in response to demand will benefit from a **short-run forecasting**. Examples include forecasting on inventory demand and demand for various raw materials. As a rough approximation, a forecasting up to six months ahead is regarded as a short-term forecasting. A **medium-term forecasting** on demand (say up to 2/3 years hence) will be useful for decisions like a plant expansion or contraction, entering a new market, etc. A **long-term demand forecasting**, over say five years, will be critical in decision-making such as setting up of R&D (research and development) infrastructure for the introduction of a new product or product line, setting up a new major plant, etc.

Of course, whether it is a short-, medium-, or long-term demand forecasting, in order for it to be useful to a manager, the results of it must be provided with a sufficient lead time. Various demand-forecasting techniques or methods exist. We discuss four of them: expert opinion, consumer polls and surveys, use of elasticity estimates, and time-series analysis.

6.5.1 Expert Opinion

Many businesses rely often on expert opinion. Experts are presumably knowledgeable about the pattern of demand for certain products or industry in a certain region. In giving an opinion, an expert may use his intuition only or some data analysis. If the manager who seeks the forecasts is constrained to obtain one expert opinion, then that expert's opinion is most likely the forecast to be used by him.

But a manager may be in a position to ask more than one expert. Suppose different experts give very different opinions. How does the manager process this information? There is a method called a **Delphi technique**, which essentially involves asking the experts repeatedly. It can be understood through a simple example. Suppose that there are three experts A, B, and C. Over the next five years, according to A, the market demand for a product will grow at 10%. B says that this growth rate will be 0%, while C thinks that the market will grow at 6%. There are thus huge differences in the expert opinion. Delphi method involves asking each expert again to submit revised estimates by providing him what others have predicted. For instance, A will be told that two other experts have projected the growth rate at 0% and 6%. The grounds on which B and C have made these forecasts will also be shared with A. However, the identity of B and C will be kept confidential to avoid personal bias. The same will be done with B and C. Given a chance to re-evaluate, A may lower his projection taking into account what others have said. Similarly, C may revise his projection upwards. Suppose that in the next round, the numbers obtained are 7%, 4%, and 5%. These are closer than the earlier numbers. This technique involves obtaining re-evaluations until the opinions converge or nearly converge. In the current example, a manager may think that the numbers 7, 4, and 5 are close enough for the purpose and he may decide the number say 5 or 5.5 (something very close to the average). Or the manager may decide to go for one more round.

There are problems with the Delphi method, however. First, good experts are typically very busy people, who command very high fees. This may be a major constraint. Second, it is not necessary that experts may want to revise their estimates. Because, if they do it frequently, it may reflect that they are not very confident about themselves, projecting a negative image that they may not possess a high expertise. They surely do not wish to hamper their reputation.

Despite these limitations, expert opinions on forecasts are much sought after in the business world.

6.5.2 Consumer Polls and Surveys

Various consumer surveys are used for forecasting. For example, the National Council of Applied Economic Research (NCAER) based in New Delhi, India, conducts an annual survey called the Market Information Survey of Households (MISH). A sample of 300,000 households is gathered covering all districts in India. The survey gathers data from the household about their income, their purchase of various products, both durable and non-durable, among other things. Surveys of Consumers at the University of Michigan ask consumers about their current and future financial status and their opinions/thoughts on the economy at the present time and in the near future.

There are market research companies which conduct consumer polls and surveys on specific products and sell their forecasting to their clients. Currently a lot of marketing research companies are recruiting management graduates from reputed B Schools with attractive pay packets. Their clients include well-known companies in both the FMCG sector and in consumer durables. Even a lot of political parties hire them to get genuine feedback from the masses. Since the buyers of these companies and the electorate of the political parties run into millions it is neither feasible nor viable to seek the opinion of all. Sampling techniques are used. Ideally, a sample should be picked in such a manner that it represents the population. You must have learnt terms like **random sampling** and **stratified sampling**. The questionnaire should be framed in such a manner that it is not loaded, and it enables you to compile quantitative data. In some cases, instead of the consumers, retailers' opinion is sought as they are the first ones to know the feedback of the product.

However, please remember that despite all these precautions, surveys/polls remain less reliable for a variety of reasons. The consumers are not very serious when they answer the survey questions since there is nothing at stake for them. Many curtly refuse as the enumerator approaches them. You will learn this soon when your teacher sends you to the nearby mall for conducting a primary survey of a product or sector in your course on business or marketing strategy. Sometimes the enumerator may simply fudge the data with bogus respondents. Some of your colleagues will do that claiming to be "*smart, not hard workers*." (We strongly discourage you to be "smart" this way.) There are online surveys too. These are cost-effective, but their response rate is very poor.

6.5.3 Using Elasticities

We can understand the use of elasticities in forecasting via the following example. Suppose you are the boss of the international division of an American auto manufacturer and contemplating to sell compact-size cars including sports utility vehicles (SUVs) in Cambodia. A well-known study on the automobile market in Cambodia finds an estimate of income elasticity of demand for new compact-size cars equal to 2.5. You also find the World Bank's projection of Cambodia's real GDP at 6% on average for the next eight years. From these two numbers, you may estimate that the new compact-size car sale will grow at the rate $2.5 \times 0.06 = 0.15 = 15\%$. If, currently 2 lakh compact-size cars are being sold in Cambodia, the expected numbers for the next six years will be 2.3, 2.6, 3, 3.5, 4, and 4.6 lakh. Realise that the forecasts are based on available elasticity estimates.

If there are two sellers of compact-size cars in Cambodia and you will be the third seller if you enter the Cambodian market and you expect no other entrant in the next six years, you may arrive at a back-of-the-envelope forecast of expected sales of your car in India, which are the numbers above divided by three.

You can, of course, consider other scenarios where you expect some other new manufactures to sell compact-size cars in the Cambodian market and arrive at different forecasts. After this, you would have to consider costs of production, transport, taxes, etc. to arrive at a decision on whether to enter the market in Cambodia.

6.5.4 Time-Series Analysis

In the regression analysis introduced earlier, we learnt how one can estimate, for example, a demand function by using data on quantity demanded of a product in say different locations in a country and a set of independent variables, e.g., own price, consumers' income, etc. in those locations. This is an example of cross-sectional regression.

In a time-series analysis, the idea is not to "only" emphasise the relationship of one variable with some others, but to rely on the behaviour of the variable itself over time in the past – and extrapolate from that the likely future values of the variable. The existing pattern of change in a variable over time can be seen from a **time-series plot or graph**, which measures calendar time along the x-axis and the variable on the y-axis. For instance, *Figure 6.4*, based on (Tutun, 2016), shows the time-series plot of monthly data on gross electricity consumption of Turkey from January 2006 to December 2010.

In general, let time be denoted by t. Suppose that we have time-series data on variable Y (e.g., quantity demanded of a product) for $t = 0, 1, 2, \ldots, T$. The question is: what is the forecast of Y for $t = T + 1, T + 2$ and so on.

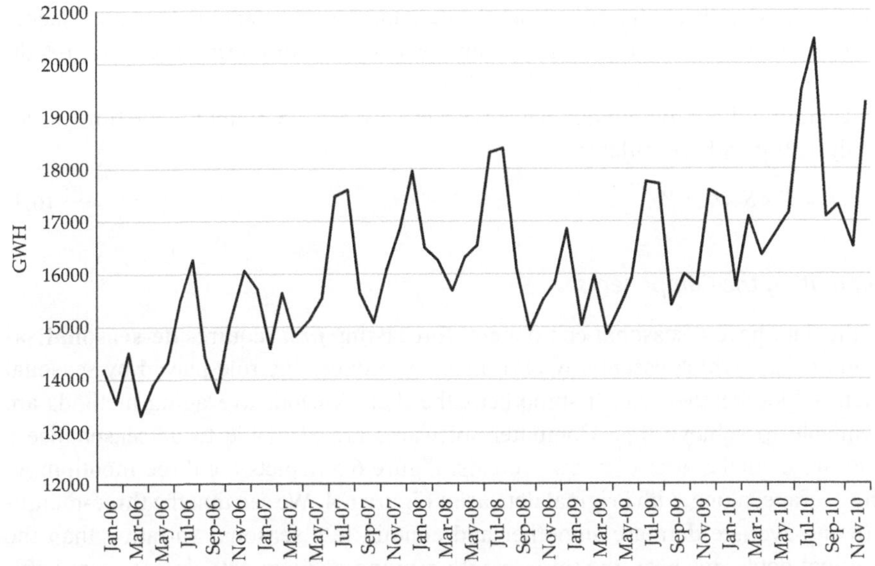

FIGURE 6.4 Monthly Gross Consumption of Electricity in Turkey: 2006–2010

Components of Time-Series Data

Time-series analysis interprets the values that a variable takes at different points of time as having four components.

Trend: It captures any long-run trend of growth or decline of the variable. For instance, if we have a time-series plot of the total number of cell phones sold in India in the recent years, we are certain to see an upward, i.e., a positive trend. But if we look at the total number of 14" TV sets sold we expect to see a negative trend.

Seasonal Component: For many products and services, among other factors, the quantity demanded depends on the prevailing season. Consider the demand for bottled mineral water. The demand for it is much higher in summer than in the winter months. The demand for visits to general physicians for common sickness like cold, cough, and flu is higher in the winter than in the summer months. Refrigerator sales are likely to reach their peak in months approaching or during summer. Electricity consumption is expected to peak in the winter and the summer months as it is used for heating and cooling. See the seasonal pattern of electricity consumption in Turkey as shown in Figure 6.4. In general, seasonal variations are present in "high-frequency" data like monthly, bi-weekly, daily, or possibly quarterly in some cases, but not in "low-frequency" data like annual or decadal.

Cyclical: This relates to business-cyclic variations. For example, if the economy is passing through a recession, the demand for real estate is typically slack.

Random Component: The last component is just **randomness** or error, resulting from unanticipated or unexplained events.

Denoting these four components, respectively, by T, S, C, and R, the time-series analysis typically postulates:

$$Y = T \times S \times C \times R. \tag{6.7}$$

Separating the Components

If the data have a seasonal component, forecasting *first* requires **de-seasonalisation** of data, which essentially eliminates or reduces the role played by seasonal factors like weather, etc. It smoothens the data. Various averaging methods are available to achieve this. Computer softwares are available to de-seasonalise a data series in a matter of a few seconds. Figure 6.5 depicts the three-month moving average, along with original data as in Figure 6.4. We see that the three-month-moving-average data are smoother and contain less seasonal variation than the original data. However, the three-month-moving-average data do not seem sufficiently de-seasonalised. In general, there are other methods of doing so like using seasonal dummy variables, which we shall not get into.

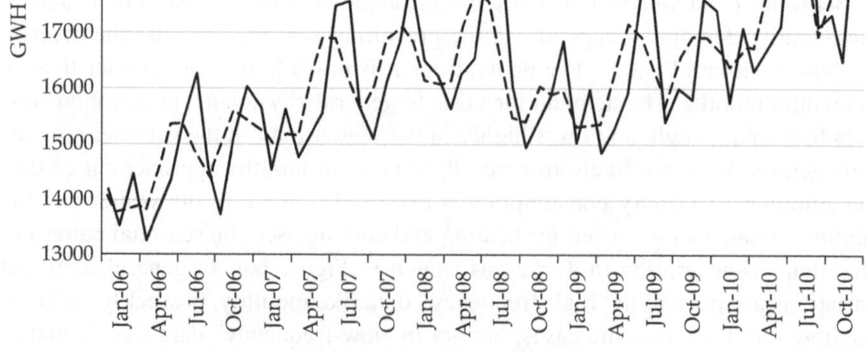

FIGURE 6.5 Raw and Deseasonalised Data on Gross Electricity Consumption in Turkey, January 2006 to December 2010

Once the data are de-seasonalised, there are several methods available to filter out the T (trend) and the C (cyclical) components separately or jointly. Whatever is left as a residual is the R (random) component.

The forecasting obtained in an actual situation depends on the sophistication of the methodology used, tools, computer software, time available—and not to mention, the skill of the individual entrusted with the task of forecasting.

As an illustration, a very simplistic procedure will involve fitting a linear trend line to a de-seasonalised time-series data by the regression method and then extrapolating from it to a future date. That is, a regression equation of the form:

$$Y_t = a + bt + u_t \tag{6.8}$$

is assumed, where t denotes calendar time (the independent variable) and Y_t is de-seasonalised variable under consideration (e.g., quantity demanded of a product). Using the least-squares estimates of a and b, we can set t to any future date (e.g., a month or a quarter hence) and compute the corresponding value of Y, which is its forecast for that date.

In many situations, the past values of the dependent variable also have considerable explaining power. This has been confirmed by numerous empirical studies. For example, an equation like:

$$Y_t = a + bt + c_1 Y_{t-1} + c_2 Y_{t-2} + u_t \tag{6.9}$$

may be a good fit for the available time-series data. Equation (6.9) is a simple example of what is called a **time-series model**.

Typically, a variable like, say, the real GDP would not only depend on its own past but also other variables like interest rate, money supply, etc. A more general time-series model will be:

$$Y_t = a + bt + c_1 Y_{t-1} + c_2 Y_{t-2} + d_1 X_{t-1} + d_2 X_{t-2} + d_3 X_{t-3} + u_t, \tag{6.10}$$

where the history of the variable X (say short-term interest rate) is believed to influence the time-path of Y (real GDP). Notice that both X and Y are "lagged." How far into the past a variable should be lagged can be judged by statistical criteria. Big financial companies have their own macro model to generate forecasting.

If Y is a variable that is expected to grow over time, except for brief intervals of downturns, e.g., real GDP of a country, sales of a company in an emerging market like India, it is statistically problematic to use the "level" of the variable as in equation (6.9) or (6.10). Instead, the first difference $\left(Y_t - Y_{t-1}\right)$ or the first log-difference $\left(\ln Y_t - \ln Y_{t-1}\right)$ is used. It is beyond the scope here to elaborate these procedures. If X is also a growth variable, a time-series model might be:

$$\Delta Y_t = a + b + c_1 \Delta Y_{t-1} + c_2 Y_{t-2} + d_1 \Delta X_{t-1} + d_2 X_{t-2} + d_3 \Delta X_{t-3} + u_t, \tag{6.11}$$

where Δ stands for the first ln-difference, e.g., $\Delta X_{t-2} = \ln X_{t-2} - \ln X_{t-3}$. Note importantly that *the first log-difference of a variable approximates its growth rate.*[6] We have suppressed time t as a separate explanatory variable because the time trend of Y is already built in its first log-difference.

Facts and Insights

- Data summary or summary statistics is a prelude to statistical analysis.
- There are three types of data: cross-section, time-series, and panel.
- Count data refers to those entities (e.g., number of cars, number of students, etc.) that can be measured only in whole numbers like 0, 1, 2, and so on.
- Qualitative variables like whether a person is married or not, whether a country is in the African continent or not, whether a school is public or private are captured by a dummy variable, which takes values 0 or 1.
- The scatter diagram indicates the nature of relationship between two variables.
- Regression analysis estimates, from available data, how changes in one variable called the dependent variable (e.g., quantity demanded of a product) is affected by changes in another variable or a group of variables, called the independent or the explanatory variables (e.g., own price, prices of related goods, income, etc.).
- Simple and multiple regressions refer to the cases where there is one explanatory variable or more than one explanatory variables.
- In linear regression the slope coefficient measures the marginal effect of the respective explanatory variable on the dependent variable.
- If the slope coefficient is positive (negative) it indicates a positive (negative) relationship between the independent variable and the dependent variable.
- The intercept coefficient estimates the average effect of other variables not included in the regression.
- Least-squares estimates are those estimates of coefficients that minimise the sum of squares of the difference between the actual values of the dependent variable and its predicted values.
- Log-linear regression refers to where the natural log of a variable is regressed against the explanatory variable or the natural log of the explanatory variable.
- Out-of-sample prediction refers to using an estimated regression equation to predict a variable from unobserved, counterfactual values of the explanatory variables.
- Lead time is the time gap between the day/date of forecasting of an event and the day/date of its actual happening.
- The regression method does not yield the perfect estimation of the true relationship between the dependent variable and the set of independent variables.

- Demand forecasting is achieved by soliciting expert opinion, using consumer polls and survey, using elasticities, or by using time-series techniques.
- Delphi technique involves asking each expert again to submit revised estimates by providing him what others have predicted.
- In the time-series method, the idea is not to overly emphasise the relationship of one variable to some others, but to rely on the existing behaviour of the variable itself over time—and extrapolate from that the likely future values of the variable.
- Time-series data are typically multiplicatively decomposed into four components: trend, seasonality, cyclical, and random.
- Seasonal data may be present in variables whose values are observed daily, weekly, monthly, or quarterly. Examples will be the sale of woollen garments, electricity consumption in a region, rainfall, etc.
- In the time-series method, the data are de-seasonalised (by using smoothing techniques) before the trend and the cyclical component are extracted.
- Linear trend line is obtained by regressing the de-seasonalised time-series data with respect to time.
- Time-series modelling refers to using past values of a variable to predict its present value.
- In time-series analysis, variables that grow over time are entered into the regression model by their first differences or first log-differences.

Exercises

Descriptive/Analytical

6.1. Briefly explain what a dummy variable is.

6.2. Give two examples each of cross-section, time series, and panel data other than what is given in the chapter.

6.3. "A non-linear relationship can be estimated only by non-linear regression." Defend or refute.

6.4. What is log-linear regression and what is its advantage over simple regression in levels?

6.5. "The regression method does not give a perfect fit of the estimated line for the dependent variable. Therefore, it is unreliable." Comment.

6.6. How is demand forecasting useful to a manager? Substantiate your answer with suitable examples.

6.7. Briefly describe the Delphi method of forecasting demand.

6.8. What are the various methods of conducting an opinion poll for the purpose of demand forecasting? Examine their relative strengths and weaknesses.

6.9. Briefly describe various ways of demand forecasting.

Short Answer (word limit = 500 approx.)

6.10. What is linear regression? Which coefficient of linear regression does indicate whether there is an increasing or a decreasing relationship between the two variables and why?

6.11. Suppose the data on price and quantity demanded for a commodity are plotted as a scatter diagram and the fitted regression line has a positive slope. Does it imply necessarily that the regression is yielding an illogical result?

6.12. What is the criterion on which the least-squares regression coefficients are estimated?

6.13. In linear regression, what is the interpretation of the "intercept coefficient"?

6.14. In linear regression, what is the interpretation of the "slope coefficient"?

6.15. "In a multiple linear regression there are several intercept coefficients and several slope coefficients?" Comment.

6.16. In the context of a multiple linear regression of estimating a demand function, the data on quantity demanded, own price, the price of a substitute good, and income are used. Which sign will we expect of the slope coefficient of the variable representing the price of a substitute good and why?

6.17. What is the essential difference between the regression method and the time-series method?

6.18. Briefly describe what is meant by the "trend component" of a time-series data.

6.19. What are the different components of a time-series data?

6.20. Briefly describe any simple procedure to obtain the trend line fitting a time-series data.

Quizzes/Numerical

6.21. Consider the following scatter diagram. If a regression line is fitted to this data, would it be positively sloped or negatively sloped? Explain.

6.22. A log-linear demand estimation yields:

$\ln D = 0.5 - 1.5 \ln p + \text{other factors},$

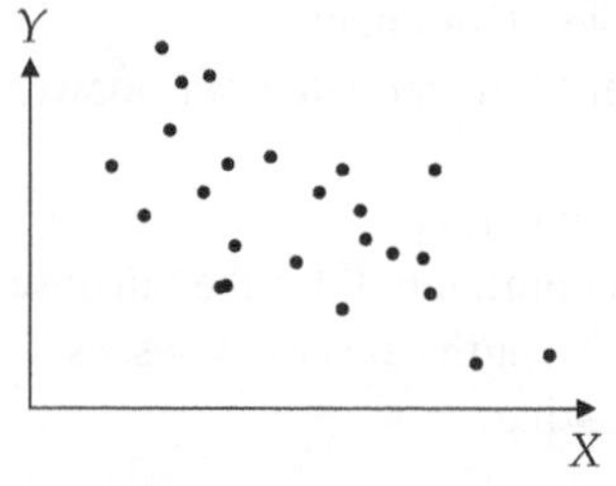

FIGURE 6.6 Scatter diagram

where the effect of other explanatory variables like income, prices of related goods are suppressed. If the objective is to increase sales by 12% through price reduction, by what percentage should the price be reduced?

6.23. A log-linear regression gives:

$$\ln Y = 2.3 - 0.3 \ln X_1 + 1.5 \ln X_2.$$

If X_1 and X_2 change by 5% and 6%, respectively, what is the percentage change in Y?

6.24. The following table gives monthly time series data on the number of colour televisions sold in a region (in 100,000) in India. Plot this data. Show that there is some seasonality, that is, during some months sales are either very high or low relative to the rest of the months in a year. Give a probable reason for the presence of seasonality.

Month/Year	*Sales*	*Month/Year*	*Sales*	*Month/Year*	*Sales*
May 2021	5.8	May 2022	4.3	May 2023	7
June 2021	5.7	June 2022	4.61	June 2023	6.8
July 2021	4.9	July 2022	5.74	July 2023	7
Aug 2021	5.62	Aug 2022	7.07	Aug 2023	7.25
Sep 2021	5.2	Sep 2022	9.82	Sep 2023	10.5
Oct 2021	8.82	Oct 2022	10.77	Oct 2023	11
Nov 2021	5.7	Nov 2022	6.2	Nov 2023	7.5
Dec 2021	6.8	Dec 2022	6.8	Dec 2023	6.68
Jan 2022	7.86	Jan 2023	7.05	Jan 2024	7.07
Feb 2022	7.9	Feb 2023	7.3	Feb 2024	7.36
Mar 2022	5.37	Mar 2023	8.27	Mar 2024	5.65
Apr 2022	4.18	Apr 2023	6.75	Apr 2024	6.97

Notes

1 There is also a fourth type of data called repeated cross-sectional data that refers to survey on new cross-sectional units at successive points of time.
2 More than two qualitative categories can be accommodated by creating more dummy variables. We don't however get into this.
3 This is because if we graph X and Y, respectively, in the x-axis and y-axis, a is the intercept on the y-axis and b is the slope of the line.
4 Any standard textbook on statistics will have the least-squares formulae for computing a and b.
5 For instance, we cannot have the current account balance of a country as an explanatory variable and apply a log-linear equation. It is because the current account balance may be negative.

6 Consider the natural-log function, say $f(z) = \ln z$. Taking the first-order Taylor's approximation at $z = 1$, $f(z) \approx 1 + f'(z)\big|_{z=1} + (z-1)$. If $f(z) = \ln z$, then $f'(z) = 1/z$. Thus, $\ln z \approx z - 1$. Letting $z \equiv Y_t / Y_{t-1}$, we have $\ln(Y_t / Y_{t-1}) = (Y_t - Y_{t-1}) / Y_{t-1}$. Notice that the left-hand side expression is the first log-difference, whereas the right-hand side is the growth rate.

Bibliography

Fujita, K. Sydny. (2015). *Estimating Price Elasticity using Market-Level Appliance Data.* Report. Lawrence Berkeley National Laboratory.

Tutun, S. (2016). The monthly electricity dataset for Turkey. Mendeley *Data.* https://doi.org/10.17632/2y4zftpmx4.1

Woolridge, J. M. (2013). *Introductory econometrics: A modern approach* (5th ed.). Cengage Learning.

7

PRODUCTION, COSTS, AND REVENUES

Chapters 4 and 5 and most of Chapter 6 dealt with consumption and demand for commodities by households. In this chapter, we begin analysing the behaviour of firms, whose principal activity is to produce goods or services. To keep matters simple, we assume that one firm produces one good or service, although, in reality, many firms produce and sell two or more products.

To produce, the firm hires inputs like different types of workers or labour, machinery, land or space, and raw materials. Sometimes, machinery and land/space are combined and called 'capital.' Production, on the one hand, entails the costs of the inputs, but on the other, leads to sales and revenues. A firm produces something to sell in a market and get revenues to cover costs and hopefully make profits.

This causal chain is exhibited in Figure 7.1. Inputs and output are linked by technology-cum-organisation, briefly referred to as "technology," and output or production leads to revenues via demand. Thus, a firm faces two types of markets: input markets, e.g., for skilled workers, trucks, land or space, etc., and the product market. In this chapter, we learn some general features/concepts about the firm itself, the costs of production, and revenues.

We may caution you that this chapter covers quite a few concepts. We have tried our best to explain and relate them to each other, and as you will see, they will be used in the subsequent chapters.

7.1 Firms versus Industry versus Sector

A **firm** is a single producer of a commodity or service, the basic unit or organisation where production takes place. A collection of firms producing the same or

DOI: 10.4324/9781003452195-7

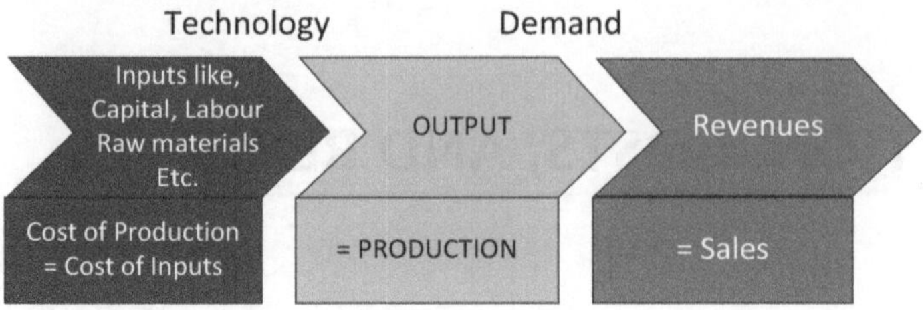

FIGURE 7.1 Inputs, Output, and Revenues

similar products is an **industry**. In international shipping services, there are DHL, FedEx, UPS, DTDC, Blue Dart, and many other companies. These are firms and a collection of them constitutes the international shipping industry. In India, JK Tyres is a firm. So are Apollo, Ceat, Modi Continental, etc. All tyre producers taken together constitute the tyre industry. In some cases, the word "Industry" figures in the name of a company. This does not, however, make it an industry. For instance, Reliance Industries Ltd. is a firm.

A **sector** is a collection of industries, covering a broader group of products. The manufacturing sector refers to all industries producing manufactured goods. The agriculture sector covers production of wheat, rice, corn, etc. Sometimes, an industry is loosely referred to as a sector, e.g., the telecom sector. However, in the context of discussion, it is clear whether we mean an industry or a sector in a broader sense.

Finally, an economy consists of various sectors.

7.2 Types of Firms

What types of firms operate in an economy *in terms of ownership, management, and liability*? Surely, the business of an ice cream vendor paddling his cart is different from that of a firm that produces ice cream, like Mother Diary, Amul, Kwality, Vadilal, Baskin-Robins, or Nirulas in India.

There are mainly three types of firms:

- Individual proprietorship
- Partnership
- Corporation

Individual proprietorship refers to any single-owner or single family-owned business. Most small businesses are of this kind. If you own a small stationary shop, then you are an individual proprietor. Management typically lies with the owner or the entrepreneur. If anything goes wrong with the business like defaulting on loans, negligence in paying taxes, etc, as the owner, you are entirely responsible legally or "liable."[1]

A **partnership** is one in which a group of people run a business as partners. They are the co-owners and they directly manage the firm. A partnership typically involves a small business. Many professional groups like lawyers and chartered accountants form partnerships. The key feature of a partnership firm is that each partner is totally liable, i.e., has **unlimited liability**, as does the owner in an individual proprietorship. It means, for example, that if there is an outstanding payment that needs to be made, and other partners cannot pay for some reason, then you as a partner are entirely liable.

In a **corporation**, *there is a difference between ownership and management.* The shareholders are the owners, and they appoint a board of directors, among whom some (like the CEO, Chief Executive Officer) are directly responsible for the operations of the enterprise. **Limited liability** *is a crucial feature of a corporation*, meaning that a shareholder is responsible/liable for payments only to the extent of his ownership share in the company. For example, if some outstanding payment must be made, say, ₹1 crore, and there is no other way to finance it other than collecting it from the owners, and you own 5% of shares in the company, then your liability cannot exceed ₹5 lakh. Among the corporations, there are private limited companies and public limited companies. In the former, the shares are held among a few, and any new shareholder must be approved by the existing shareholders. Shares are not traded in the stock market. A private limited company can "go public"—and become a "public limited company" by offering an initial public offering (IPO). The general public can buy its shares. There are tens of thousands of public limited companies around the world. Almost any big company name you read or hear about are public limited companies. All big private companies in India (e.g., Reliance, Infosys) fall into this category. Some public sector firms, like BHEL, Air India, and Indian Oil are also public limited companies. In public sector firms, the government holds a large percentage of shares and appoints its own people to manage the company. Unlike private limited companies, public limited companies are supposed to follow more norms and are subject to more scrutiny.[2]

7.3 Goal of a Firm

In consumer theory, the basic behavioural assumption is that consumers maximise their surplus or utility. What is the objective of a firm? In economics, the predominant assumption is that a firm's goal is to maximise its profit. This is intuitive, since the entrepreneurs' or the owners' benefit lies in the profit income the firm generates.

However, for corporations in which ownership is separated from the management, it is arguable that the management may not be necessarily maximising profits for the shareholders. Typically, the shareholders are in large numbers and do not have good information about the true merits and demerits of important decision-making. Thus, the management can survive and do well for itself as long as it provides some minimum acceptable returns to the shareholders, "keeping them happy," so to speak. Rather, the argument goes that managers make decisions so as to maximise sales or revenues—to which their remuneration, perks, and reputations are linked—subject to some minimum profit constraint.

However, which assumption one should make for analysing firm behaviour must rest ultimately not on how intuitive or reasonable the objective of the firm may appear to an individual or an expert, but on whether the assumption leads to good predictions about the firm's behaviour in terms of the observables. By this criterion, it turns out that profit-maximisation assumption is as good as any other alternative assumption that has been proposed in the literature. Therefore, profit maximisation remains the dominant assumption regarding the goal of a firm and this will be assumed in this chapter and elsewhere in the book.

While the goal of profit-making is certainly pertinent for a private firm, how about a public sector firm in countries like India? The very adjective "public" and its ownership (at least a large fraction of it) by the government strongly suggest that such a firm is supposed to work in the "public interest," not always to maximise profits. Whether in India such firms have worked in the true public interest or not is debatable, but it is a fact that majority of them were incurring heavy losses consistently over decades. It is an open secret that a significant fraction of employment in these sectors, especially from the 1950s to the 1980s, was politically rather than economically motivated. Surely, these firms were not operating on the principle of profit maximisation. In the last few decades, many losing public sector enterprises in India have been disinvested (sold to private parties). The remaining public sector firms are under pressure to show results in terms of revenues raised *and* profits earned. Thus, profit maximisation is a good working hypothesis for the functioning of existing public sector firms as well.

Analysis of production marks the beginning of our study of a firm's profit-maximising behaviour.

7.4 Factors of Production or Inputs

Our starting point is to understand the technology—not in an engineering sense but in terms of the patterns of relationship between various inputs used in the production process and output under a given technology.

Of course, different goods have different technologies of production. Wheat and computers are not produced by the same technology. Even the same good is not produced by a single technology. Rice or paddy is produced in many parts of India by relatively labour-intensive methods, whereas highly mechanised method of agriculture is common in many advanced countries.

Even though specific technologies may differ, there are common elements across the production processes of various goods. For instance, whether it is donuts, hair-cutting, bicycles, or rockets, the amount produced within a given time depends, among other things, on how many workers are employed and how many hours they work. Similarly, it may depend on machinery, equipment, building, land, raw material, and so on. Various things that go into a production process are called, in general, **factors of production** or **inputs**.

Among the inputs, **raw materials** are a bit different from others in the sense that they are purchased from some other sectors of the economy as other "goods" and they are used up in production. Therefore, raw materials are also called **intermediate goods** or **services**. A bicycle industry uses steel as a raw material. Fertilizers are used as raw materials in agriculture.

Attaching the terms, raw material or intermediate good/service, depends on whether the product is used for production or consumption by individuals or households. If you buy coffee beans for home consumption it is not a raw material, but for a coffee shop, which sells coffee as a drink, it is a raw material.

Other inputs are not used up in production. When someone works for a firm, he or she is not "used up" like lumber or coal. A worker provides her *service* to a firm. The same is true for land. If you are running a software firm in a ground-floor flat you have taken on rent, you are using the service of some space or land. It is not totally used up in your production process. Keeping this in mind, economists define three **primary factors of production** (or primary inputs) whose services are used in production: namely,

- Labour
- Capital
- Land

Labour refers to hours of work by workers or employees. This is a **human input**, whereas capital and land are **non-human inputs**. Various equipment, machines, etc., are termed as **capital. Land** refers to land (like in agriculture) or space (room, flat, or building). Capital and land are distinguished in that the former is man–woman-made or person-made, while the latter is essentially provided to us by nature. Of course, in modern times, humankind has "invaded" nature to "make" land. Reclaiming land from sea is an example. In this case, land is person-made too.

If the objective is to simply distinguish between primary human inputs and primary non-human inputs, one may combine capital and land, calling it capital. Here and elsewhere, we shall use the terms "factors" and "inputs" interchangeably.

In summary then, inputs can be divided broadly into two categories: (i) raw material or intermediate goods and services and (ii) primary factors of production. In turn, the latter can be broadly of two types: human (labour) and non-human (capital and land). Each of these can be sub-divided into many categories depending upon the purpose of the study. We can distinguish between skilled labour and unskilled labour. In the skilled labour category, we can distinguish between civil engineers, chemical engineers, accountants, software engineers, designers, writers, etc. There are different types of capital as well, like computers, trucks, trackers, cargo planes, various types of medical equipment, and a whole array of other machines that are not simply used up in one or a few rounds of production. If the purchase of various forms of equipment is financed by loan, the loan itself can be interpreted as capital, whose reward is the interest paid to the lender (e.g., a bank).

The earnings of the three primary factors are:

• Wages or salaries for labour	• Rental or interest income for capital	• Rental income for land

What about the person who employs people, machinery, etc., i.e., the employer? She is not rewarded any wage, interest income, or rental income. She gets profit income, equal to the difference between revenues a firm generates and costs of various inputs. This is the return for her entrepreneurial effort and the risk of doing business itself. It could be a profit or a loss, not income in the ordinary sense. Profit or loss is a residual. Some authors treat the firm owner as an additional factor of production, calling it **entrepreneurship**, whose reward is a **residual payment**, namely, **profit/loss**.[3] We prefer not to do so, because the nature of reward to entrepreneurship is fundamentally different from that to labour, capital, or land. Profits/losses will be studied in subsequent chapters.

See Box 7.1 for a brief account of how different factors of production came into existence.

BOX 7.1 EVOLUTION OF FACTORS OF PRODUCTION

We can look at factors of production from an evolutionary perspective. In prehistoric times when man lived in jungles along with all other species, he had to survive like others. If he killed a deer, the whole of it belonged to him. The deer was the reward for his labour. It was not shared by anyone else, except perhaps his family members if there were any. In due course of time, jungles came under the occupation of feudal lords. When this person would now try to enter the jungle for hunting a deer, he would be stopped. The feudal lord would allow him to hunt only if he was given a portion of the deer. In such a situation when a deer is killed it is shared by two parties, the hunter and the feudal lord. Over time the hunter realised that killing a deer with a spear would be a lot easier and more precise than killing it with bare hands or a stick. So, the hunter approached the village blacksmith and requested him to lend him a spear for a day. Naturally, there is no free lunch. The blacksmith would lend him his spear only on the condition that he too gets a portion of the deer. Now the reward (deer) is shared by three: the hunter, the feudal lord, and the blacksmith. The hunter provides the **labour** input, feudal lord his **land,** and the blacksmith his physical **capital**.

We can take the story further. Suppose after the landlord's permission to "operate" in "his" jungle and borrowing spear from blacksmith for a day, the hunter failed to kill a deer, came back empty-handed, and informed the landlord and the blacksmith. There is no reward (deer) to be shared. But what if the hunter was telling a lie? He may not have put in his effort. He may have simply relaxed or collected some fruits and wood. Alternatively, he may have killed a deer and hid the same somewhere. Now while granting permission to use land and lending a spear, the landlord and the blacksmith would insist on a pre-determined, fixed reward for granting permission to use their land and spear for a day. In such a situation, if the reward is based on the assumption that one deer would be killed in a day, there could be three possibilities. If actually one deer is killed, all three would share one-third of it equally. If two deer are killed, the landlord and blacksmith will get only one-third of one deer each (pre-determined/fixed) and the remainder 1.33 deer will remain with the hunter. What if no deer is killed? The hunter will still have to pay two-third deer (or an equivalent amount of some other commodity) to the other two. In all these cases, the hunter's reward is a **residual** which may be positive or negative.

All hunters may not be so courageous and risk-taking. Hence, there emerged another class of people who will hire the hunter (labour) for a pre-determined reward (wages), procure permission from the landlord for a pre-determined reward (rent), and borrow spear from the blacksmith for a pre-determined reward (interest). In this setup, the hunter is not taking any risk. His "job" is to hunt deer. At the end of the day whatever he kills, no deer, one, or more deer, his reward (and those of landlord and blacksmith) is fixed. The residual, which can vary and even be negative, remains with the risk-taker, called the **entrepreneur** whose reward is **profit/loss**.

7.5 Production

In day-to-day usage, production means the creation of a commodity or service which did not exist earlier. A new car that you bought was manufactured/produced in the workshop of a company. Cars existed but the exact car you bought didn't. The crop grown by a farmer did not exist until the field was cultivated, seeds sown, watered, tendering done, and finally harvesting was completed. In economics, we use the term production as an antonym of consumption. You'd recall that we defined consumption as a process of destruction of utility. In contrast, production can be seen as a process of adding utility potential. Suppose a trunk of a fallen tree is lying in a jungle. If someone picks it up and brings it to the local sawmill, it is production. The shape and size of the log remain the same, and only the location has changed.

In economics, there are various concepts associated with production.

7.5.1 Gross Production and Value-Added

Production is defined in gross or value-added terms. The former refers to the quantity produced, whereas the latter is the value of the quantity produced less the payments made to raw materials, all measured in real terms using a price deflator.

Value-added means the value that is added to the value of raw materials purchased for production. Suppose a weaver weaves five bedsheets in a day which are sold at a price of \$20 per piece. We can say that his production in a day is five bedsheets in quantity or \$100 in value. This is his gross production. Remember that, in producing bedsheets, yarn is used. Suppose in these five bedsheets he has used 10 kg of yarn which he bought from the market for \$70. Given this information, we say that in the production of five bedsheets, his value added is \$100 –\$70 = \$30.

In what follows, *by production we would mean the quantity of gross production in respective units like yards of clothes, number of bicycles, etc.*

7.5.2 Production Function

This is the central concept in respect of production. The technical and organisational process that links inputs to output of a good/service is called the **production function** of that good/service. It is defined as *the technological/organisational relationship between inputs and output, giving maximum outputs that can be produced from various input combinations.*

Suppose that a firm employs two inputs, say, labour and land, measured, respectively, in hours and thousand square feet. Various input-to-output combinations are given in Table 7.1. One hour of labour and 2,000 sq. feet of land produce, at the maximum, 4 units of output, 5 hours of labour and 7,000 sq. feet of land produce 19 units of output at the maximum, and so on. Table 7.1 describes a production function. Note the following:

1. It is assumed that inputs work to the best of their efficiency in the normal sense of the term. Hence, instead of "maximum output," we just say output.
2. The notion of production function is not limited to two inputs. There can be many, including several types of capital and different skills of labour.
3. Table 7.1 lists only some, not all, possible combinations of inputs and output.

Compactly, one can write a production function as a mathematical function. If we denote various input levels as $x_1, x_2, x_3, \cdots, x_n$ and the output by y, then, we can write

$$\text{Production function: } y = f\left(x_1, x_2, \cdots, x_n; T\right). \tag{7.1}$$

TABLE 7.1 Production Function

Labour (hours)	*Land ('000 sq. feet)*	*Output (units)*
0	0	0
1	2	4
1	3	6
3	6	14
4	6	16
5	7	19
6	10	21

Besides the x's being the inputs, T represents technology "parameters." A concrete example is $y = A\left(\sqrt{x_1} + x_2\right)$. Here, T refers to the parameter A. If $A = 10$, then the actual production function is $y = 10\left(\sqrt{x_1} + x_2\right)$. It means that, if, for example, a firm employs 9 units of input 1 and 5 units of input 2, i.e., $x_1 = 9$ and $x_2 = 5$, the firm, with its technology remaining fixed at $A = 10$, produces $y = 10\left(\sqrt{9} + 5\right) = 80$.

There can be more than one technology parameters. For instance, a commonly used production technology for economic analysis called Cobb–Douglas, named after its discoverers, Charles Cobb and Paul Douglas. In a two-input scenario with say L (labour) and K (capital), the Cobb–Douglas production function is:

$$Cobb - Douglas: \; y = AL^{\alpha}K^{\beta}, A > 0, \alpha > 0, \beta > 0. \tag{7.2}$$

Here technology, T, consists of three parameters: A, α, and β. If $A = 10$, $\alpha = 0.7$, and $\beta = 0.5$, the actual Cobb–Douglas production function is $y = 10K^{0.7}L^{0.5}$.

Realise that the parameter set T is not directly observed. For many firms in the real world, efficiency results often from superior internal organisation, which is hard to quantify. T could be a result of learning by doing over time, which is also difficult to measure. The incorporation of inventions and discoveries cannot be measured numerically. In addition, the technology for large manufacturing is defined by the type of the main plant around which production is organised. For example, a cement plant may be defined by a kiln, a large rotary object which must run 24 × 7 non-stop with virtually no downtime. A cement production unit may be defined by the number of kilns it has. Once set up, it is extremely costly to add kilns to a cement-producing facility. Hence, there is no variation in technology—unlike the number of people employed or the number of trucks a company owns/hires for transport.

However, using regression analysis, already explained in Chapter 6, a production function can be statistically estimated, given data on inputs and output. In the Cobb–Douglas case for example, we can estimate the technology parameters A, α, and β.

7.5.3 Returns to an Input

A production function given in a tabular form as in Table 7.1 or in an algebraic form does not say much about how any single input contributes to production. This is assessed by varying one input, while keeping all other inputs fixed. There are three important concepts here.

Total Physical Product, Marginal Physical Product, and Average Physical Product

The general notions of "total," "marginal," and "average" are already explained in Chapter 1. In the present context, the **total product** or **total physical product** of an input, denoted by *TPP*, is defined by the total output associated with a given level of employment of the input in question. Another is the **marginal product** or the **marginal physical product** (*MPP*), defined as the increase in the total physical product per one-unit increase in the employment of an input. In both these definitions, it is presumed that *other input levels are unchanged.* Let the input in question whose employment is varying be called a "*variable input.*"

Finally, the **average product** or the **average physical product** (*APP*) is defined as the *TPP* per unit of the variable input, i.e., $APP = TPP \div L$, where *L* stands for the variable input.

The three notions just defined are also, respectively, called total, marginal, and average returns to an input, and they are very much related to the production function. As a matter of fact, they characterise it. The concepts of *TPP*, *MPP*, and *APP* apply to all inputs, not just labour. But the important point is that they measure how output changes with respect to any particular input, *one at a time*, when the other input levels are fixed.

Table 7.2 offers a numerical example showing a *TPP* schedule, where the variable input, *L*, is labour. The graph of a *TPP* schedule gives the **total physical product curve**. Figure 7.2 shows the *TPP* curve for the *TPP* schedule in Table 7.2. Why the *TPP* curve shapes this way will be discussed later.

As explained in Chapter 1, the marginal physical product, *MPP*, can be obtained from the total physical product, *TPP*, just as marginal utility is derived from total utility.[4] The *MPP* schedule corresponding to Table 7.2 is given in column (2) of Table 7.3. The *APP* schedule is given in column (3) of Table 7.3; for each value of *L*, it is equal to *TPP* divided by *L* in Table 7.2.

The graphs of an *MPP* schedule and an *APP* schedule are, respectively, called the **marginal physical product curve** and the **average physical product curve**. These graphs based on Table 7.2 are shown in Figure 7.3. Both are "inverse U-shaped" since *MPP* and *APP* initially increase and then decrease.

TABLE 7.2 Total Physical Product

*Labour Hours Employed (*L*)*	*Total Physical Product (*TPP*)*
0	0
1	20
2	44
3	66
4	86
5	102
6	112
7	112
8	100
9	80

FIGURE 7.2 Total Physical Product Curve Corresponding to Table 7.2

TABLE 7.3 Marginal Physical and Average Physical Product Schedules

*Labour Hours Employed (*L*)*	*Marginal Physical Product (*MPP*)*	*Average Physical Product (*APP*)*
(1)	(2)	(3)
0	–	–
1	20	20
2	24	22
3	22	22
4	20	21.50
5	16	20.40
6	10	18.67
7	0	16
8	-12	12.50
9	-20	8.89

If the variable input can be measured continuously like decimal points on the real line—rather than as "discrete" numbers like 1, 2, 3, ... only—the *TPP, MPP*, and *APP* curves will look smooth. Figure 7.4 depicts such curves. Because *MPP* is incremental to *TPP*, the slope of *TPP* drawn in panel (a) is equal to the *MPP* at different levels of *L*.

The *MPP* curve in panel (b) shows that it is positive or negative to the left or right of L_0, which is consistent with panel (a).[5] It follows that *TPP increases, remains constant, or decreases as MPP is positive, zero, or negative.*

Recall from Chapter 1 that the variable part of a "total" is the sum of the "marginal." Here the "total" is zero when $L = 0$. Hence, there is no fixed component of the "total." Thus, *TPP* is the sum of the *MPP*s. This translates to the area under

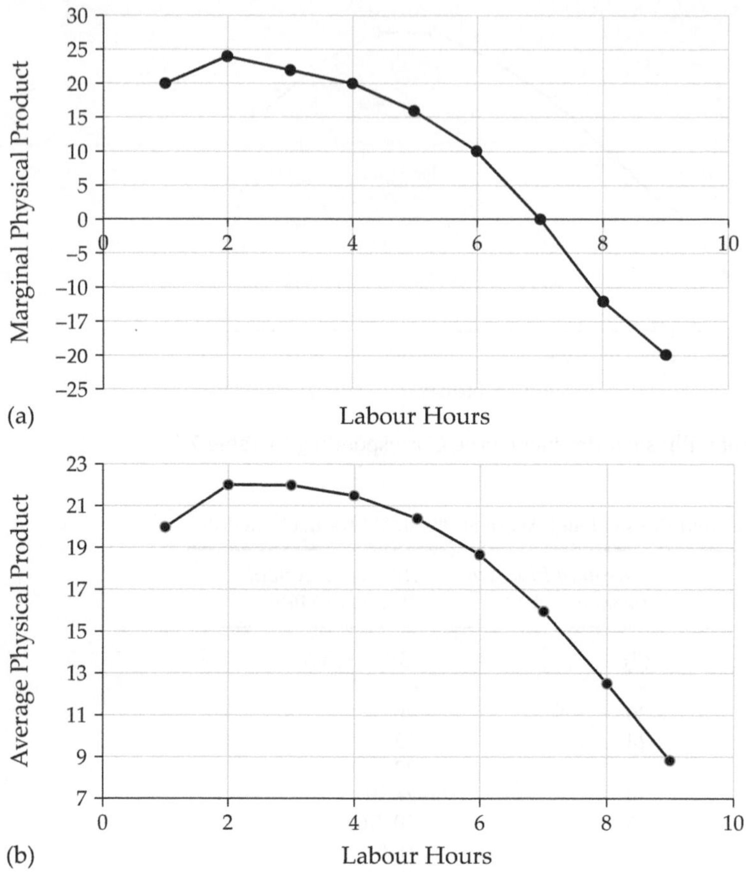

FIGURE 7.3 Marginal Physical Product Curve and Average Physical Product Curve Corresponding to Table 7.3

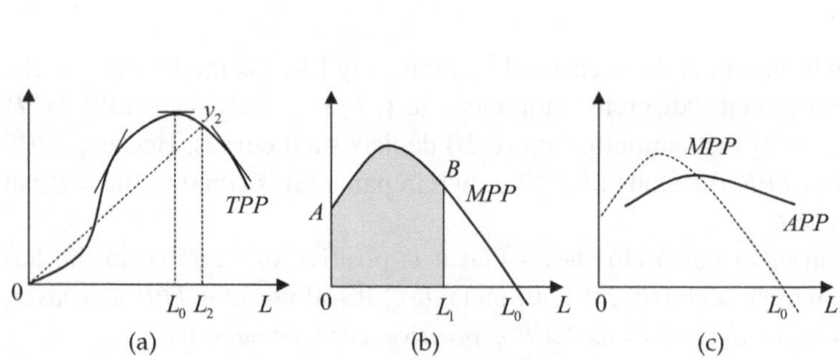

FIGURE 7.4 Smooth *TPP*, *MPP*, and *APP* Curves

the *MPP* curve when L is measured on a continuous scale. For instance, in panel (b), at $L = L_1$, the *TPP* is equal to the shaded area $0ABL_1$.

From *TPP*, we can readily obtain *APP* by applying its definition. Similarly, if the *APP*s are known, we get *TPP* by multiplying *APP* with the level of employment. Then, *MPP*s are obtained by applying their definitions. Geometrically, *APP is equal to the slope of the ray from the origin to the point on the TPP curve.* For instance, in Figure 7.4(a), at $L = L_2$, $TPP = y_2$. Thus, $APP = L_2y_2 / 0L_2$, which is simply the slope of the ray $0y_2$ from the origin.

Note in Figure 7.4(c) that the *MPP* curve cuts the *APP* curve at the maximum point, i.e., as *APP* rises (to the left of the maximum point), $MPP > APP$ and as *APP* falls (to the right of the maximum point), $MPP < APP$. The reason behind this is mathematical, not economic, and this is already discussed in Chapter 1.

Various relationships among *TPP*, *MPP*, and *APP* are "summarized," so to speak, in Figure 7.5. The top part graphs the *TPP* curve and the bottom part the corresponding *MPP* and the *APP* curves. Between the levels of employment from 0 to L_2, *TPP* is increasing at an increasing rate (i.e., the slope is rising). Accordingly, in the bottom half, *MPP* is increasing. From L_2 to L_1, *TPP* increases at a decreasing rate (i.e., the slope decreases) and accordingly in the bottom part the *MPP* falls. At $L = L_0$, the slope of the *TPP* curve, equal to the *MPP*, is zero. Beyond L_0, *TPP* slopes downwards and thus $MPP < 0$. The *APP* being equal to the slope of the ray from the origin to the point on the *TPP* curve, we see in the top part that it increases between 0 and L_1 and falls thereafter. We also see that, at $L = L_1$, *APP* is maximum and equal to the slope of the *TPP* curve (*MPP*) as well; in other words, $MPP = APP$, where *APP* achieves its maximum.

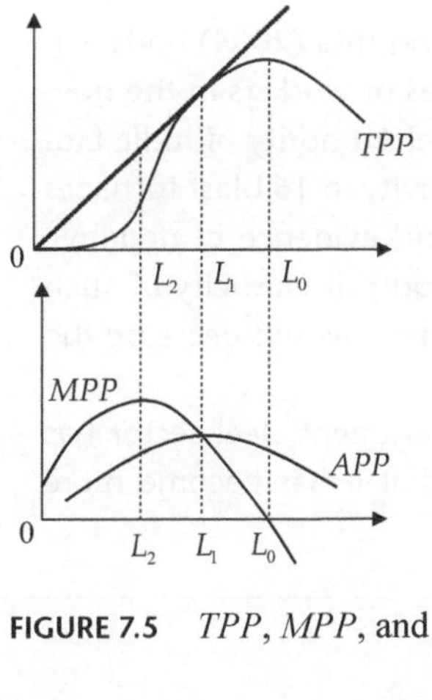

FIGURE 7.5 *TPP*, *MPP*, and *APP* Curves in a Single Graph

Law of Diminishing Returns

Why are various curves shaped the way they are? As it turns out, the pattern that *MPP* initially increases, then diminishes, and finally may become negative is the key. This pattern has a few names: the **law of diminishing marginal product**, the **law of diminishing marginal returns**, or briefly, the **law of diminishing returns**. *It says that*, keeping the employment of other inputs fixed, as more of a particular input is used in production, after a certain level, its marginal physical product decreases as more and more of it is employed.[6]

The logic behind this law is the following. When the employment of a single input gradually increases while all other inputs are kept unchanged, the factor proportions among other inputs and the input in question become initially more suitable for production, because the scarcity of the (needed) variable input gradually falls. This tends to increase the marginal product. But, after a certain level, the variable factor can work with other given inputs only less efficiently (as other inputs become relatively scare), i.e., factor proportions become increasingly unsuitable for production. This implies that the marginal product of a factor would fall as more of it is used.

BOX 7.2 EVIDENCE ON NEGATIVE MARGINAL PRODUCT

It is an open secret that in the "before-reforms" era from the 1950s to the mid-1980s in India, there used to be excess employment in public sectors run by the government. The reason behind this is not hard to seek: some jobs are/were handed out based on political rather than profit considerations. Can such excess employment be so high that the marginal product of a certain kind of labour employed be negative? It is very easy to conjecture yes, yet very difficult to back it up with "hard" evidence.

However, an econometric study by Das and Sengupta (2004) finds evidence of negative marginal product of certain types of workers in the government steel sector—in steel plants under the Steel Authority of India Ltd. (SAIL). Based on data on employment and productivity in 16 blast furnaces over the period 1991–1997, the authors have found evidence of negative marginal product for non-executive workers. The output elasticity of such workers was –0.17, i.e., 10% increase in such workers would *decrease* the output by 1.7%.

The good news however is that, lately, the government steel sector has become profitable and casual empiricism tells us that it has become more efficient.

The *MPP* initially increasing and then falling implies an inverse U-shaped *MPP* curve, i.e., the law of diminishing returns explains this shape of the *MPP* curve. In turn, this implies the shape of the *TPP* curve and the inverse U look of the *APP* curve. Note the following:

1. Diminishing returns to a factor may set in right from the beginning, i.e., *MPP* may be diminishing throughout. In that case, the point L_2 in Figure 7.5 essentially coincides with the origin.
2. A profit-maximising firm will never hire so much of any input such that its *MPP* is negative. Why? Because, if it does, it always can employ a bit less of the input in question, and this would increase output and revenue from sales, at the same time save costs (as less of the input is employed and paid) and thus increase profits. A firm will continue to do this until the *MPP* is no more negative. However, see Box 7.2 for statistical evidence on the existence of negative marginal product in a public sector enterprise in India.

Example 7.1

The MPP schedule of a variable input is given in Table 7.4. *Assuming that the TPP at zero level of the input is zero, derive the TPP and the APP schedules.*

Answer: Since *TPP* is the sum of *MPP*s, *TPP* at the employment level equal to 1 is equal to *TPP* at zero level of employment (which is 0) plus the *MPP* of input at the employment level 1 (which is 40); it is equal to 0 + 40 = 40. Likewise, the *TPP* at the employment level of 2 units is equal to 40 + *MPP* at this level of employment (which is 35) = 75. *TPP*s at higher levels of employment are calculated sequentially and listed in the middle column of Table 7.5. Once we know the *TPP*s, *APP*s are obtained by dividing *TPP*s by the respective levels of employment. These are listed in the last column of Table 7.5. (At zero level of employment, *APP* is not defined.) ■

TABLE 7.4 MPP Schedule

Employment Level of an Input	MPP
0	–
1	40
2	35
4	29
5	21
6	11
7	0

TABLE 7.5 TPP and APP

Employment Level of an Input	TPP	APP
0	0	–
1	40	40
2	75	37.5
4	104	26
5	125	25
6	136	22.267
7	136	19.428

7.5.4 Relevance of Time Horizon

We know that an increase in the price of a commodity induces producers to produce more and vice versa. A question may arise: Can the production be increased or decreased as easily as we open a tap and close it? Certainly not.

Suppose a fast-food cart vendor, Ramgopal places his cart every day outside a locally known historical monument visited by a limited number of people. He brings a certain quantity of semi-prepared raw material (e.g., dough, boiled potatoes, chopped salad, etc.) based on his experience of the past. One day when he arrives at his usual time with his usual quantity of raw material, he finds a great rush of people. Soon he comes to know that there is a shooting for a commercial advertisement by a prominent film star. The local people got the news through *WhatsApp* and rushed. Ramgopal finds the demand for his fast-food skyrocketing in the next one hour. The shooting will be over in an hour or so. Can he increase his supply, i.e., production of fast food? Unfortunately, it is not possible as time is too short. He can only start charging a price slightly higher than usual or may start giving a lesser quantity per plate than usual (which is effectively the same as increasing the price). *A time-period that is too short for changing the output is called* **a market period** in economics.

What if Ramgopal comes to know that a film shooting will take place at this monument during the entire next week? Foreseeing this (temporary) increase in demand, can he increase supplies (production)? Certainly he can, by bringing a bigger quantity of ingredients in his wares. Maybe he will temporarily hire additional help. However, the maximum limit to which he can increase his production will be subject to the size of his cooking utensils and his cart. This is an example of a **short period** or a **short run** from the viewpoint of production: the period is short but not too short, so that a producer can change some of the inputs (e.g., raw material and labour in the example), but not all. Ramgopal has not been able to buy cooking utensils or a new cart (these are capital for him).

What if Ramgopal finds that this "little known" historical monument has been declared a UNESCO Heritage monument attracting everyday visitors, not only from India but also from abroad. What will he do now? He will procure bigger utensils, buy a big-size cart, and apply for requisite municipal permissions to park and occupy municipal space. We can call this a **long period** or a **long run**, defined as a long period such that a producer can vary all the inputs of production. Finally, if Ramgopal wants to stay in the business for the foreseeable future, he may decide to mechanise the production of fast food, by buying mixers, grinders, etc., so that he can produce more with the same number of workers. We may call this a **secular period** or a **very long run**.

We hope you have understood the significance of time horizon in production. Compactly put, if we have a production function as specified in equation (7.1), the four time periods are defined as follows:

Market period	Levels of all inputs remain unchanged, i.e., the values of $x_1, x_2, x_3, \ldots, x_n$ are fixed.
Short run	Levels of some inputs, not but all, vary, e.g., x_1, x_2, and x_3 vary, while x_4 to x_n remain fixed.
Long run	Levels of all inputs can vary, i.e., the values of x_1 to x_n can change.
Secular period	Levels of all inputs as well as technology parameters T can change.

7.5.5 Returns to Scale

We have studied the concepts that capture the contribution of any single input towards production. This does *not* mean at all that a firm can vary only one input at a time. When market conditions or technologies change, a firm would very well adjust many inputs. For instance, if a garment factory finds a cheaper source of getting cotton, it would like to expand its production by hiring more workers (labour) and buying more sewing machines (capital) as well. There are concepts capturing the *joint contribution* of inputs towards output.

Assume that a firm is not employing any input to the level such that its marginal product is negative (a profit-maximising firm would not do it anyway). Suppose that it increases the employment of all inputs by a given proportion, e.g., by 10%. The output will surely increase since the marginal product of each input is positive. But, by how much? If it increases more than proportionately, e.g., by more than 10%, we say that there are increasing returns to scale. If the output rises but less than proportionately, there are decreasing returns to scale. Finally, if it increases exactly proportionately, there are constant returns to scale. Formally, we say that there are **increasing returns to scale, constant returns to scale**, or decreasing/diminishing returns to scale, when, as all inputs increase proportionately, the output increases more than, exactly, or less than proportionately. See Appendix 7.A for the mathematical definition of the three types of returns to scale. Note the following:

1. The words "diminishing" or "decreasing" above do *not* mean that output decreases when all inputs increase.

2. These concepts relate again to the production function. A production function may exhibit one type of returns to scale at all input levels or may exhibit any combination increasing, constant, and decreasing returns to scale.
3. If a production function satisfies constant returns to scale throughout, it is called a **linearly homogeneous production function**. For example, suppose there are two inputs, labour (L) and capital (K) and the production function is Cobb–Douglas, given by $y = L^{0.6}K^{0.4}$. Starting with any initial values of L and K, check that if L and K are doubled, y is also doubled. (It is because the exponents of L and K in the production function add up to one.)

More exactly, these concepts of scale are "internal" in that the returns to scale are something internal to the firm and its technology, not dependent on other firms in the industry. Thus, it is more appropriate to attach a prefix "internal," e.g., there are internal increasing returns to scale instead of just increasing returns to scale. As opposed to internal economies of scale and diseconomies of scale, there are external economies and diseconomies of scale. We shall not cover them however.

The basis for internal economies or diseconomies of scale will be discussed in the next section. A word of caution is in order: *do not get confused between (the law of) diminishing returns and diminishing returns to scale.* The former is related to the incremental output effect of "one" input keeping other inputs fixed, whereas the latter refers to an output change when all factors vary proportionately. Furthermore, diminishing returns can operate when the returns to scale are decreasing, constant, or increasing. That is, diminishing returns to a factor and returns to scale are different, yet compatible with each other (see Activity 7.1).

ACTIVITY 7.1

Suppose you are given a Cobb–Douglas production function: $Q = \sqrt{LK}$, where L is labour and K is capital. Based on this, calculate the various levels of output when either L is increased, or K is increased, or when both L and K are increased in the same proportion. Complete all boxes in the following table.

$K \rightarrow$	1	2	3	4	5	6	7
$L \downarrow$							
1	?						
2		?					
3			?				
4				?			
5					?		
6						?	
7							?

a) Read the output numbers diagonally (boxes marked by "?"). What do you find in terms of returns to scale?

b) Keep one input constant (say K at 1 unit). Check the *TPP* of L by increasing it from 1 to 7. Enter the numbers obtained in a table. Also compute another column for *MPP*. What do you notice?

c) Are constant returns to a scale compatible with diminishing returns to a factor? Verify.

d) Repeat this exercise for the production function $Q = 50L^{0.7}K^{0.5}$. What are the qualitative differences in your answers to (a) through (c)?

7.5.6 Isoquants

If there are two inputs, the production function can be shown graphically by *an* **isoquant**, *defined as the locus of combinations of inputs, giving rise to the same level of output.* If, for example, the two inputs are labour and capital, various combinations of L and K that produce, say 60 units of output, define the isoquant for output = 60. In principle, it is like an indifference curve. That is why an isoquant is also called a **production indifference curve.** Like indifference curves, isoquants are quite useful constructs to understand a firm's rational choice of inputs.

How does an isoquant look like? Suppose the *MPP*s of both inputs are positive. Then, starting from a given combination of inputs producing a given amount of output, if the employment of one input is increased, there is more output. Thus, if the output must be brought down to its original level, the amount used of the other input must be reduced. In other words, an increase in one input must be matched with an appropriate decrease in the other—so that the output is unchanged. This implies that the isoquant will have a negative slope. If we consider a very high level of employment of an input such that its *MPP* is negative, then an increase in one input must be associated with an increase in the other such that the output remains the same. Accordingly, the isoquant will have a positive slope. Overall then, an isoquant will look like the line *ABCD* drawn in Figure 7.6(a). However, as discussed earlier, a profit-maximising firm will never use an input such that its *MPP* is negative. Thus, the segments *AB* and *CD* on the isoquant *ABCD* are not operational. The segment *BC* is the only **economic region of production.** For this reason, from now on, an isoquant will be assumed to be a downward-sloping curve, as shown in Figure 7.6(b).

A whole isoquant reflects technology, whereas *a* **technique** *refers to the proportion of inputs used at a given point on the isoquant.* For example, at point E in Figure 7.6(b), $0L_E$ of labour and $0K_E$ of capital are used. The capital/labour ratio is $0K_E / 0L_E$.Since $0K_E = EL_E$, this ratio is equal to $EL_E / 0L_E$, which is the slope of the ray from the origin $0E$. Similarly at point F, the capital/labour ratio is the slope of the ray $0F$. Clearly, the ratio is higher at point E than at point F (as $0E$ is

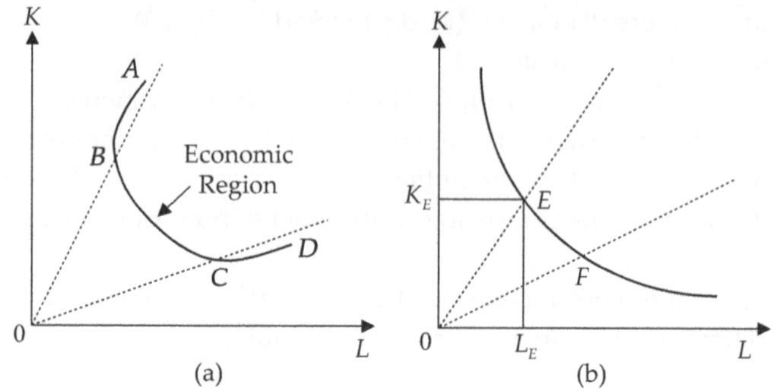

FIGURE 7.6 An Isoquant

steeper than $0F$). We say that, compared to F, E involves a relatively more capital-intensive or a relatively less labour-intensive *technique*.

Once you see the similarity between an isoquant and an indifference curve, you realise that the economic analysis of production has some similarity with that consumer behaviour. A collection of isoquants in a single graph is called an isoquant map. An isoquant to the right of a given isoquant represents a higher output. Two isoquants cannot intersect. Recall from Chapter 4 the definition of marginal rate of substitution of one good for another. Its counterpart here is *the* **marginal rate of technical substitution** (*MRTS briefly*), *referring to the rate of substitution between inputs so that the output is unchanged.* For instance, the *MRTS* of input 1 for input 2 equals the amount of input 2 that needs to be foregone per unit increase in input 1 so that the output remains unchanged. *MRTS is equal to the ratio of marginal products*—just as the *MRS* in consumer theory is equal to the ratio of marginal utilities. If, for example, there are two inputs, labour and capital, then the *MRTS* of labour for capital is equal to the *MPP* of labour divided by the *MPP* of capital. In general,

$$MRTS_{\text{Input 1 for Input 2}} = \frac{MPP_1}{MPP_2} \tag{7.3}$$

$$= \text{slope of the isoquant on the axis measuring Input 1.}$$

An algebraic proof of it is given in Appendix 7.B.

In Chapter 4, we saw that diminishing MRTS between two goods implied an indifference curve being convex to the origin. Here *we assume diminishing MRTS, which implies that an isoquant is convex to the origin, as shown in* Figure 7.6(b).

Two special kinds of isoquants are drawn in Figure 7.7. In panel (a), the two inputs are perfect complements of each other in that they are used in fixed proportion to each other. This proportion is indicated by the ray $0C$ from the origin. This implies that if the employment of one input is increased and yet the output is to

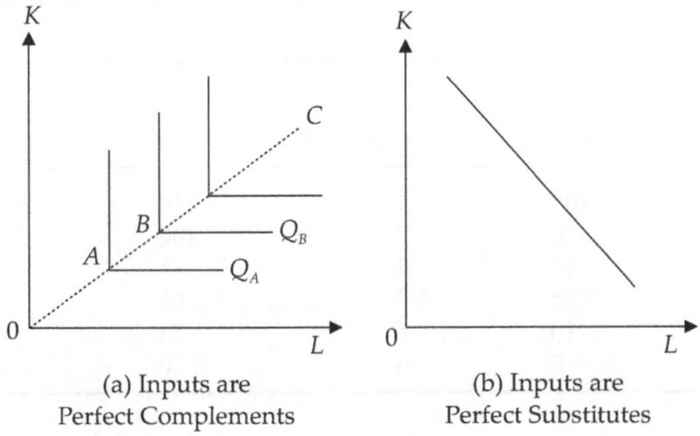

FIGURE 7.7 Special Cases of Isoquants

be kept unchanged, no amount of other input can be sacrificed. Thus, *MRTS* = 0. This explains the vertical and flat portions of the isoquants. Such a technology is called the **Leontief technology**, named after Wassily Leontief, a Nobel Laureate in Economics, who extensively used the assumption of this technology in his research on what is called the **input–output analysis**. Perfect complementarity also means that the ratio of an input to output, called the **input coefficient**, is constant. On the other hand, when an isoquant is a straight line, as shown in panel (b), its slope is fixed. Thus, *MRTS* is constant. Since, irrespective of how much of each input is being used initially, a given amount of one input needs to be sacrificed per one-unit increase in the other input in order to keep the output unchanged, the inputs are perfect substitutes of each other (when the isoquant is a straight line).

However, from now on, we shall disregard the two special cases, assume diminishing *MRTS* and accordingly use the downward-sloping, convex isoquants as in Figure 7.6(b).

Example 7.2

In Table 7.6 *the input bundles in columns U and V define isoquants for two different levels of output. Derive the marginal rates of technical substitution of capital for labour on both isoquants. Is the assumption of diminishing marginal rate of technical substitution satisfied?*

Answer: *MRTS* measures the rate of sacrifice of an input when the employment level of another input increases. The *MRTS* of capital for labour is the amount of labour sacrificed per unit increase in capital as we go down the input bundles in Table 7.6. Along isoquant *U*, from input bundle A to B, it is equal to 100 – 70 = 30 units of labour. From the input bundle B to C, it is 70 – 45 = 30 units of labour, and so on. Table 7.7 lists the *MRTS*s. We observe that *MRTS* is decreasing along the isoquant *U*, but not decreasing along the isoquant *V*. (For our analysis, we rule out isoquants of type *V*.) ■

TABLE 7.6 The Input Bundles in Columns U and V Define Isoquants for Two Different Levels of Output

	U		V	
Input Bundles	*Capital (K)*	*Labour (L)*	*Capital (K)*	*Labour (L)*
A	1	100	1	110
B	2	70	2	100
C	3	45	3	85
D	4	25	4	65
E	5	10	5	35
F	6	0	6	0

TABLE 7.7 MRTSs

Input Bundles	MRTS *of Capital for Labour along Isoquant* U	MRTS *of Capital for Labour along Isoquant* V
A to B	30	10
B to C	25	15
C to D	20	20
D to E	15	25
E to F	10	30

7.5.7 Factor Productivity

The starting point of our economic analysis of production was the notion of a production function, which tells us the amount produced from various combinations of inputs with a given technology. The concepts like total product, marginal product, and returns to scale characterise the contribution of inputs towards output, given technology. We can broadly say that output depends on inputs "and" technology. An important difference between inputs and technology is that inputs are directly visible and measurable, but technology broadly interpreted as an integration of the physical process, organisation, learning, motivation, etc., is hard to measure.

How much of output change in a sector or in an economy can we ascribe to changes in the use of factors on the one hand and technological progress on the other? This question was asked and answered in the 1950s by Robert Solow, a Nobel Laureate in Economics, in the context of long-term growth of the US economy. The output was the real GDP of the United States over the period 1909–1949, while the inputs were the use of labour and capital in the corresponding years. Regression method (explained in Chapter 6) was used to estimate the contribution by labour and capital. Since technology or technological progress could not be measured, the residual of the regression of GDP with respect to labour and capital was interpreted as the contribution of technology. Later, it came to be known as

Solow residual or **total factor productivity** (TFP). Solow residual is like "manna from heaven," as we get more output without increasing measurable production inputs. To his own surprise, which also took the profession by surprise, the contribution of technology was huge relatively to contributions by labour and capital.

Total increase in output	= 5.0%
Contribution of labour	= 2.1%
Contribution of capital	= 1.5%

For illustrative purposes, suppose the findings are as shown in the side table. That is, out of 5% increase is output, 2.1 + 1.5 = 3.6% is explained by an increase in the use of inputs. The remainder is then 1.4%, which is the TFP or the contribution of technological advancement.

TFP has become a common measure of productivity growth. Estimated initially in a macroeconomic context, it has found widespread applications at the sectoral and industry levels. How is all this relevant for a manager? The thinking is that it is no big deal to produce more by increasing inputs. Who doesn't know that? Moreover, the increase in output will also increase input costs. A smart manager is one who, with the same resources available, can increase output by increasing productivity through technological, organisational, and motivational innovations. There are many examples of new CEOs who have brought a "turn around" in the fortune of a company in terms of sales and profits. This is not much explained by an increase in inputs. Rather, implementing productivity-enhancing new ideas and strategies is the key.

7.6 Cost of Production

Economists refer to many types of cost of production. To begin with, **explicit costs** *are those, which are directly paid to other parties by an entrepreneur or a company running a business.* They include for example the cost of labour, raw material, machinery purchased, etc. In contrast, **implicit costs** *are those for which there is no direct payment but indirectly there is a cost involved.* Suppose you own a two-storey building. You live on the first floor, while on the ground floor you operate a small publishing company. Obviously, you do not have any rental cost for business operations. But there is an implicit cost. If you had otherwise rented out the ground floor to some other party, you would have obtained some rental income. By using it for your own business, you are effectively losing that income—and that is an implicit cost. Similarly, if you use your own savings in the business, the interest income foregone is an implicit cost.

Explicit costs are more commonly known as **accounting costs**. Accounting costs plus the implicit costs of the kinds described above reflect the true cost of running a business and are called **economic costs**. *In economic analysis, costs almost always refer to economic costs.*

Costs that are already incurred are referred to as **sunk costs**. These costs are fixed and can never be changed since one cannot change history. In what follows, we will be concerned with cost concepts from a forward-looking perspective, based on the time horizon of an entrepreneur, e.g., short run and long run. There is no specific calendar time like a month, quarter, or year that distinguishes between short run and long run. Rather, as will be seen, the distinction is drawn based upon a production-planning perspective.

7.6.1 Short Run

If you look at a firm at a given point of time like a snapshot, everything is fixed. The firm is producing a given amount by using given levels of inputs and the inputs are paid their prices. All costs are given or fixed. But if we imagine the functioning of a firm over a relatively short length of time (like a movie), we can distinguish between costs that are fixed and that are not. Suppose you run a clothing store. In a span of say one month or two months, it is likely that the rental costs of the room or rooms you use are "fixed," in the sense that how much you pay as rent is not tied to how much you sell or produce. The landlord will keep knocking at your door and ask for rent money, even if you are not generating any revenue from your business. That is why, generally, the rental cost is considered fixed in the short run. But, typically, labour costs are not fixed, because workers can be hired and fired on a short notice by a firm. Costs of raw materials (e.g., clothes you buy in the wholesale market) are not fixed–as you can buy more or less of them depending on the state of your business.

As another example, suppose Dr De Silva owns a diagnostic centre in his hometown in Portugal. It is located in a one-storey flat, inherited from his father. He employs about 30 people including nurses, technicians, management employees, and manual workers. By taking loans from a bank, he has bought several high-tech machines that do CAT scan, MRI, ultrasound tests, etc. Every month he repays the bank €5,000 in instalment towards his loan and interest. These payments to the bank are an example of fixed cost, because it is independent of how many patients are served by Dr. De Sliva's diagnostic centre. There is also an implicit rental cost of the flat, equal to the rent foregone by using the flat for the diagnostic centre. This is also a fixed cost. However, depending on how this venture is going, Dr. De Silva can hire more or less number of nurses or manual workers within a short notice. Hence, payment to nurses and other workers are variable.

In a longer horizon however, an entrepreneur can think of explicitly or implicitly renting a different amount of space, choosing a different plant size, different number of machines, etc. In other words, *in the long run there are no fixed costs.*

Returning to the short run, we then say that a firm has two types of costs:

- Fixed costs
- Variable costs.

Fixed costs are those costs that do not change with output. In more common, business, terminology fixed costs are called **overhead cost**. One should not confuse between fixed costs and sunk costs. Recall that sunk costs refer to costs incurred in the past, whereas fixed costs refer to the present or future.

Variable costs refer to those that vary with the output. Typically, rental costs of land and capital are fixed, whereas labour and raw material costs are variable.

Formally, fixed and variable costs are more fully called **total fixed cost** (*TFC*) and **total variable cost** (*TVC*), respectively. The sum of the two costs is called simply the **total cost** (*TC*). That is,

$$TC = TFC + TVC. \tag{7.4}$$

These costs, graphed against the output, are the respective curves; see Figure 7.8 (but ignore for now the tangents, the point *a* and the dotted lines from this point). The *TFC* curve is a horizontal straight line (having zero slope) since *TFC* is independent of the output level. The *TVC* curve is upward-sloping, because producing more would cost more.[7]

Since *TC* = *TFC* + *TVC* and costs are measured along the vertical axis, *the TC curve is the vertical sum of TFC and TVC curves.* That is, at any output level, if we measure the *TFC* and *TVC* on the vertical axis and add them up, we get the corresponding point on the *TC* curve.

Like the marginal product and average product, we define marginal cost and average cost. **Marginal cost** *(MC) is the addition to the total variable cost per one extra unit produced. It is also equal to the addition to the total cost per one extra unit produced,* because the difference between *TVC* and *TC* is fixed. In graph, *MC* is the slope of the *TVC* and the *TC* curves. You see in Figure 7.8 that, as the output increases, the slope of *TVC* initially falls and then rises. This means that the *MC* curve (measuring *MC* against output) will be downward-sloping first and then

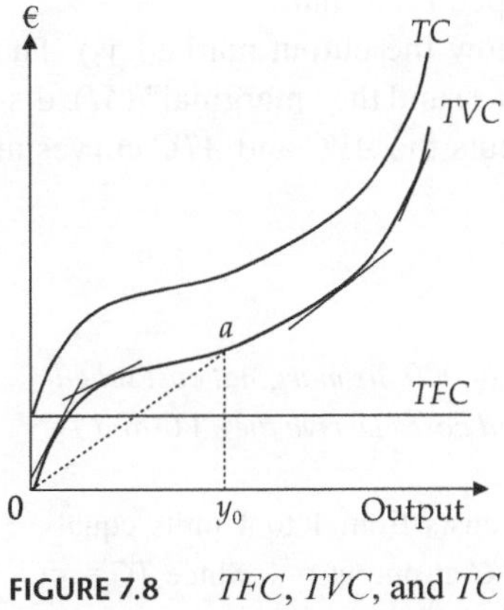

FIGURE 7.8 *TFC*, *TVC*, and *TC* Curves

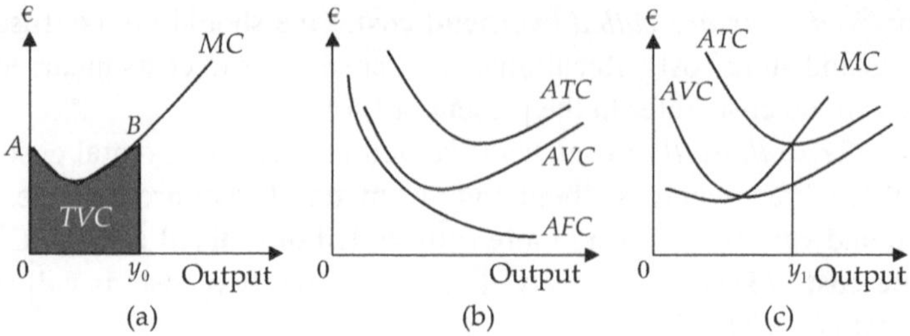

FIGURE 7.9 *MC*, *AVC*, and *ATC* Curves

upward-sloping. Put differently, it is U-shaped as shown in Figure 7.9(a). Also, since *MC* is the addition to the *TVC*, *the area under the MC curve equals the TVC*. Since the summation of *MC*s does not account for fixed costs, the area under the *MC* curve does not equal to the total cost (unless, of course, the fixed cost is zero).

Similarly, we can define,

Average Fixed Cost (*AFC*)	$\equiv TFC \div$ Output
Average Variable Cost (*AVC*)	$\equiv TVC \div$ Output
Average Total Cost (*ATC*)	$\equiv TC \div$ Output,

where the symbol "≡" means "equal to by definition." The *AFC*, *AVC*, and *ATC* curves are drawn in Figure 7.9(b). The *AFC* is uniformly downward-sloping by its definition: as output increases, the denominator of it increases while the numerator remains unchanged.[8] The shapes of the *AVC* and *ATC* curves depend on the shape of the *TVC* or the *TC* curve. Referring back to Figure 7.8 again, see that at output y_0 for instance, $TVC = y_0a$ and thus $AVC = y_0a/0y_0$, which is the slope of the ray $0a$. If we let output gradually increase from zero, this slope decreases up to a point and then increases. This implies that the *AVC* curve will be U-shaped. The argument behind the *ATC* curve being U-shaped is similar.

Finally, turn to Figure 7.9(c) (and ignore for now the output marked y_1). The mathematical relationship between the "average" (*A*) and the "marginal" (*M*), discussed in Chapter 1, implies that the *MC* curve cuts the *AVC* and *ATC* curves at their respective minimum points.

Example 7.3

A firm's total cost of producing 4 units of output is €70,000. Its marginal cost schedule is given in Table 7.8. *What is the firm's total fixed cost? Derive the TVC and TC schedules for outputs from 0 to 7.*

Answer: From Table 7.8, the sum of marginal costs from 1 to 4 units equals $(10+7+5+6)\times 1{,}000 = ¬28{,}000$. This is the *TVC* at output = 4. Since *TC* = ¬

TABLE 7.8 Marginal Cost

Output	*Marginal Cost ('000 €)*
0	–
1	10
2	7
3	5
4	6
5	8
6	11
7	14

TABLE 7.9 Total Cost and Total Variable Cost

Output	TC *'000 €*	TVC *'000 €*
0	42	0
1	52	10
2	59	17
3	64	22
4	70	28
5	78	36
6	89	47
7	103	61

70,000 at this level of output, the difference, equal to €42,000, is the total fixed cost. Likewise, we can calculate the *TVC*s at other levels of output. These are given in the middle column of Table 7.9. We already know the total fixed cost. Adding it to *TVC* for each level of output gives us the *TC* schedule. This is the last column of Table 7.9. ■

Why Are MC, AVC, *and* ATC *Curves U-Shaped?*

The U-shape of the *MC*, *AVC*, and *ATC* curves follows from the *TC* and *TVC* curves drawn in Figure 7.9. But there is no basic, economic reason behind why the *MC*, *AVC*, and *ATC* curves are U-shaped: we could have drawn these curves first and then obtained the *TC* and the *TVC* curves from them. The underlying reason lies in the law of diminishing returns, studied earlier.

Recall that the law states that initially the *MPP* of a factor may be increasing but after a certain point it must start to diminish. This means that if some other inputs are kept unchanged, i.e., there are fixed factors and hence there are fixed costs in the short run, initially when a factor's *MPP* is increasing, a gradual increase in output by a given amount would require *a decrease in the rate of increase* of the variable inputs, therefore a decrease in the rate of increase of total cost of variable inputs. But the rate of increase of the total cost of variable inputs is equal to *MC*, by definition. Thus, initially, *MC* decreases with output. After a certain point when diminishing returns set in, a gradual increase in output by a given amount would require an *increase in the rate of increase* of the total cost of variable inputs. This translates into *MC* increasing with output. In summary, *MC* initially decreases with output and then increases with it after a certain point. That is, the *MC* curve is U-shaped.[9] The U-shape of the *MC* curve implies that the *AVC* and *ATC* curves are U-shaped also.

The U-shape of the MC curve also explains why *TC* and *TVC* curves look the way they do in Figure 7.9: initially concave, and, from a certain level of output and higher, convex. As a special case, if the *MPP* of each factor starts to decrease right from the beginning of its employment, then the *MC* curve will be upward-sloping throughout and so will be the *AVC* and *ATC* curves. Moreover, the *TC* and *TVC* curves will be convex-looking over any output range.

Shift of the Short-Run Cost Curves

What factors shift the short-run supply curves? They are technology, input prices, the level of fixed factors, and business taxes. A technology improvement enables more output to be generated from the same levels of inputs. It would lower costs and, in general, shift down *TC*, *TVC*, *AVC*, *ATC*, and *MC* curves. An increase in the price of fixed factors would shift up the *TFC*, *AFC*, *ATC*, and *TC* curves, while *TVC*, *AVC*, and *MC* curves will remain unchanged. An increase in the price of variable factors would not shift *TFC* and *AFC* curves, but would shift other curves up.

The positions of the short-run variable and marginal cost curves depend crucially on the levels of fixed inputs. Since fixed inputs typically are heavy machinery, land, etc., the levels of fixed inputs define what is briefly called the **plant size**. Hence, we can say that the plant size determines the positions of *TVC*, *AVC*, and *MC* curves. In particular, the output at which the *ATC* attains its minimum can be interpreted as the most efficient output level, corresponding to the plant size. For instance, if you go back to Figure 7.9(c), the most efficient output level relative to the underlying plant size is y_1. An output higher or less than y_1 means over-utilising or under-utilising the plant, so that the unit cost exceeds the minimum *ATC*.

Now consider an increase in the plant size. With a bigger plant, the most efficient level of output will be higher. This is illustrated in both the panels of Figure 7.10. However, will it mean a lower minimum *ATC* or a higher minimum *ATC*? That depends on the initial plant size. If it is relatively small, an increase in plant size would reduce the minimum *ATC* because of increasing returns to scale (to be discussed later). Otherwise, if the initial plant size is sufficiently large, a further increase in the plant size will raise the minimum *ATC* because of decreasing return to scale (to be discussed later). These possibilities are shown, respectively, in panels (a) and (b) of Figure 7.10.

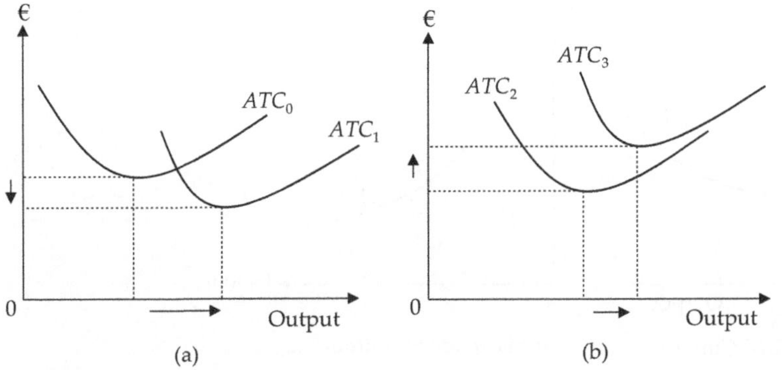

FIGURE 7.10 An Increase in the Plant Size

Businesses around the world pay various taxes to the government like VAT or GST. Such tax payments add to the direct production costs of firms. Thus, an increase in the rate of business taxes will shift up the short-run *ATC* and *MC* curves.

7.6.2 Long Run

In the long run, a producer has more options compared to the short run. Contracts can be changed. Plant sizes can be increased or decreased. In fact, the quantity of any input can be varied. There are no fixed costs. All costs are variable. Thus, we simply say "total cost" instead of "total variable cost." The *TC* curve shapes like the *TVC* curve, passing through the origin. This is shown in Figure 7.11(a) and marked as the *LTC* curve ("*L*" standing for "long run").

What is the basis of the position of *LTC* curve? That is, at a production level, say y_0, what determines that the point *T* on the *LTC* curve? This is not a trivial question, because a given level of output can be produced from different combinations of inputs. Recall the concept of isoquant. The one that is shown Figure 7.11(b) for the output level y_0 has many points or input combinations on it like *A*, *B*, *C*, *D*, etc. Different input combinations for the same output may cost differently. For instance, let point A represent 10 units of labour and 3 units of capital and point B stand for 7 units of labour and 6 units of capital. Suppose per-unit labour and capital costs are €100 and €150, respectively. Then the input bundle *A* will cost €100 × 10 + €150 × 3 = €1,450. Similarly, you can check that bundle *B* will cost €1,600. Obviously, a rational firm would prefer input bundle *A* to input bundle *B*. Since there are other combinations, their costs must be evaluated too. In order to maximise profits, a rational firm will minimise total costs at any given level of output. If *C* in Figure 7.11(b) is the cost-minimising input bundle, then the total cost associated with it will define the point *T* in Figure 7.11(a). Hence, *LTC is the*

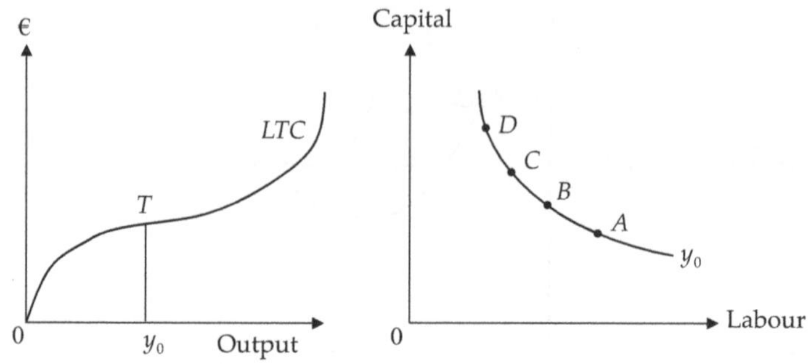

(a) The *LTC* Curve (b) Isoquant for output = y_0

FIGURE 7.11 Long-Run Total Cost Curve

locus of total costs of cost-minimizing input bundles at different levels of output. A detailed mathematical treatment of the cost-minimisation problem facing a firm is outlined in Appendix 7.C.

Example 7.4

Consider the input bundles along the isoquant U back in Table 7.6. *Suppose the price of capital services is* r = €600 *and that of labour services, the wage rate, is* w = €50 *Which one of the input bundles among A to F minimises the total cost of producing the output associated with isoquant U? Suppose capital becomes more expensive: r increases from €600 to €800. Now, which input bundle minimises the total cost? Compare the new input cost-minimising input bundle to the old cost-minimising input bundle.*

Answer: This is straightforward. For each bundle, we know the level of each input and its price. Multiplying them gives the total cost of hiring that input. Summing it over the two inputs gives the total cost of the input bundle. For instance, consider input bundle B having 2 units of capital and 70 units of labour. With r = €600, 2 units of capital will cost €1,200 and with w = €50, 70 units of labour will cost €3,500. Thus, the total cost of input bundle B = 1,200 + 3,500 = €4,700. Table 7.10 enumerates the total cost of all input bundles. When r = €600 and w = €50, the total cost is the minimum at the input bundle E: the minimised total cost is equal to €3,500. When r = €800 and w = €50, the total cost is minimised at the input bundle D and the minimised total cost equals €4,450. ■

Compared to the input bundle E in the initial situation, the input bundle D has less capital and more labour. It is because the *ratio* of the price of capital to the price of labour is 800/50 = 16, which is higher than 600/50 = 12, the corresponding ratio in the original situation. That is, in the new situation, capital is relatively more expensive, and labour is *relatively* cheaper and hence the firm hires less capital and less labour. Furthermore, in the new situation, in absolute terms, one input price is the same, while the other one is higher. Therefore, the minimised cost in the new situation (€4,450) is greater than that in the original situation (€3,500).

The concept of marginal cost remains the same however. We call it the long-run marginal cost or *LMC*. There is no difference between *AVC* and *ATC*. Instead, we call it the long-run average cost or *LAC*.

In general, both *LMC* and *LAC* curves are U-shaped, similar to the short-run marginal and average cost curve, as shown in Figure 7.12. But the underlying reason is different, not the law of diminishing returns. This does *not* mean that, for any factor, this law is only a short-run concept and does not hold in the long run. The difference however is that since all factors are variable, it is the nature of returns to scale which determines how the long-run costs may change with output. For instance, if there are increasing returns to scale (*IRS*), a proportionate change in all inputs leads to a more-than-proportionate change in the output. This means, for example, that a 10% increase in output can be obtained by say a 7% increase

TABLE 7.10 Cost Minimisation along the Isoquant U

Input Bundles	*K* =, *L* =	*Total Cost:* $r = €600$; $w = €50$	*Total Cost:* $r = €800$; $w = €50$
A	1, 100	5,600	5,800
B	2, 70	4,700	5,100
C	3, 45	4,050	4,650
D	4, 25	3,650	**4,450**
E	5, 10	**3,500**	4,500
F	6, 0	3,600	4,800

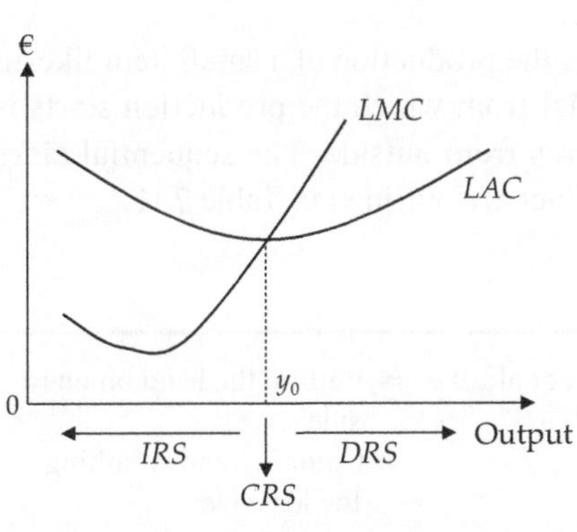

FIGURE 7.12 Long-Run Average and Marginal Cost Curves

in all inputs. In terms of costs, it means that a 10% increase in output will lead to a 7% increase in the total cost, and it implies a decline in the average cost. Hence,

I. Increasing returns to scale (*IRS*) ⇒ *LAC* falls with output;
II. Decreasing returns to scale (*DRS*) ⇒ *LAC* rises with output;
III. Constant returns to scale (*CRS*) ⇒ *LAC* remains constant with respect to output.

Therefore, a U-shaped *LAC* curve, as shown in Figure 7.12, which means that *LAC* first declines, then remains constant (at the minimum point), and finally increases, is built on the assumption that as a firm contemplates higher and higher output in the long run, it is expected to experience *IRS* first, *CRS* next, and *DRS* finally. The reason behind such a sequence is the following.

Why Is the Long-Run Average Cost Curve U-Shaped?

Starting from a small scale of output or plant size, an expansion enables a firm to reap the benefits from two sources of internal economies of scale: (a) division of labour and specialisation in tasks and (b) large overhead costs.

Division of Labour

When a firm operates at a small scale, the same person (or a few) must do multiple tasks in the production chains as the firm cannot afford more people, whereas the same person may not be efficient in multiple tasks. When the scale of operations increases, the division of labour is possible. For instance, if initially a firm has one secretary who does typing as well as answers customers, then, as business improves and the firm is able to hire, say, two secretaries, it can hire one who is really good at typing and the other good at dealing with the public. Labour is divided into doing different tasks, so to speak, i.e., there is a division of labour.

A classic example of division of labour is the production of a small item like an all-purpose steel pin. The basic raw material from which the production starts is a bundle of steel wires that the firm procures from outside. The sequential tasks leading to pins coming out as the final product are outlined in Table 7.11.

TABLE 7.11 An Example of Division of Labour

Straightening the wire	⇒ Cutting it into equal pieces	⇒ Putting the head on one side
⇒ Sharpening the other side	⇒ Polishing	⇒ Counting and weighing the lost size
⇒ Packing		

The idea is to let one or more individuals do one task (or a very limited number of tasks), while no individual does more than one task (or a very limited number of tasks). It has been observed that division of labour and specialisation increases the productivity of workers because of repeated action.

Have you ever seen the chef making *roomali roti* (a bread) in the nearby popular Irani *dhaba* (roadside hot-food vendor)? The ease with which he spreads the dough into a thin round disc-like size without breaking it from anywhere and tosses it in mid-air to let it land exactly on the inverted tawa—exquisite, isn't it? Or a bartender mixing cocktails with liquor bottle doing multiple somersaults in his hand without falling! These are all magics of the division of labour and specialisation. As the size of operations increases, the division of labour is possible at the managerial level as well. A small firm cannot afford managers with various functional specialisations. The same person hires, manages the staff, looks after the finances and accounts, does the marketing work, etc. However, a big firm can afford to employ experts in every functional area which in turn improves productivity.

In short, the division of labour generates internal scale economies via productivity gains, tending to reduce average costs.

Spreading Overhead Costs

In some situations, the technology itself is defined by the land on which the production unit is located and the main plant, and, furthermore, it is astronomically costly for a firm to vary these even in the long run. The technology itself entails huge overhead or fixed cost even in the long run. These are *not* the kind of fixed costs that can be varied in the long run. A typical example is a large-scale blast furnace that produces steel. A whole steel plant is built around such blast furnaces, and they must run 24 hours a day, irrespective of the actual amount of production of raw steel. In this case, an expansion of output tends to "spread" the fixed cost of technology and lower the unit cost.

Consider a simple production technology with one factor of production only, that is, $y = -T + 2L$, where T is the technology parameter and L is the labour time used in production. Suppose $T = 8$, i.e., $y = -8 + 2L$. The negative sign in front of T does not mean that technology is a bad thing. It simply means that for any output to be generated, a minimum threshold level of labour time is required. Note that in the example, to generate any positive output, the level of labour employment must exceed 4. Check that any given percentage increase in L leads to a more-than-proportionate increase in output, implying internal scale economies. As an example, if L increases from 10 to 15, y increases from 12 to 22; that is, a 50% increase in inputs leads to 83.3% increase in output. Note that the source of the internal scale economies lies in the presence of a minimum threshold level of employment, which is simply an overhead cost dictated by technology.[10]

However, after a certain point when the output reaches a critical limit, any higher size of operation brings with it a bagful of problems that were hitherto alien to a firm when it was small. A small organisation works as an organic whole. The manager knows her staff and workers very well. Everyone is on a first name-calling basis. Decision-making is quick. However, when the scale of operations expands, the firm gets divided into multiple units. Decision-making gets delayed as "passing the buck" culture creeps in. In-fighting and disagreements are not uncommon. Sometimes, there could be a clash between organisational goals and personal goals. Trade unionism and collective bargaining may cause impediments in the production process. In short, inefficiency in management and control creeps in due to overcrowding and congestion of inputs, etc., as the size of the firm and output exceed a threshold. These are called diseconomies of scale, because of which any further expansion of output leads to an increase in the plant size accompanied by an increase in the long-run average cost.

In-between *IRS* and *DRS*, there are neither economies nor diseconomies of scale: a firm experiences *CR*S. If this happens for an interval of output, the *LAC* will have a flat segment. Otherwise, it will be just a point.

Our reasoning for why the *LAC* curve is U-shaped is complete. *The U-shape of the LAC curve implies a similar shape to the LMC curve.*[11]

Shift of Long-Run Average and Marginal Cost Curves

A change in technology, a change in an input price or a change in the rate of business taxes shift the long-run average and marginal cost curves too. As one would expect, a technology improvement shifts them down, while an increase in an input price or business taxes shifts them up.

Relationships between Short-Run and Long-Run Cost Curves

The plant size is given in the short run, whereas it can be varied in the long run (by definition). Hence, the long-run cost at any given level of output should consider the firm's choice of the plant size. Figure 7.13 depicts a family of short-run *AC* and *MC* curves. As discussed earlier, a larger plant size is associated with a higher level of the most efficient output. But the minimum *AC* decreases or increases with plant size as the initial plant size is relatively small or large. Figure 7.13 exhibits this pattern.

Note that (1) the long-run *AC* cannot be independent of the short-run *AC*. (2) At any given level of output *cannot* exceed the short-run *AC*, because there is more flexibility in the long run; put differently, the firm always has the choice, in the long run, to select the plant size chosen in the short run and hence the *LAC* cannot be higher. (1) and (2) imply that *the LAC curve must be tangential to or an envelope of the family of short-run ACs.*

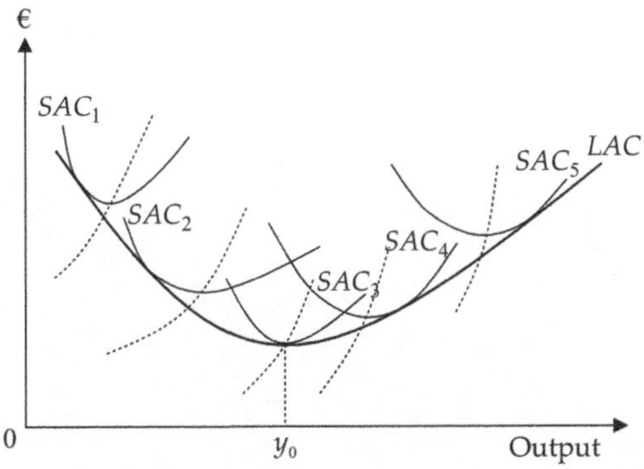

FIGURE 7.13 Short-Run and Long-Run Cost Curves

Notice the output level y_0 at which the *LAC* as well as the associated short-run *AC* (*SAC*) is minimised. At any output level below (or above) y_0, the tangency point lies to the left (or right) of the minimum point on the corresponding *SAC*.

Social and Private Cost of Production

The cost curves we have studied thus far relate to firms in an industry. Do they also reflect the society's cost of producing the same good? Of course, the firm or the industry in question is a part of the society and thus its costs must be included in society's cost. But a firm's and society's costs may not always be the same, because productive activity by one firm or industry may affect other firms, other industries, or the households.

Typically, the production of many industrial goods generates industrial waste, causing pollution. Many steel plants emit smoke, which has a very high carbon dioxide content. Wastes from chemical plants are highly dangerous. Suppose that a chemical plant doesn't have a proper disposal system and it simply channels its waste to a nearby river.[12] Many people and other living beings use the river water for a variety of purposes. Obviously, polluted water causes health problems – it is an environmental concern.

Are, in this hypothetical example, the chemical plant's marginal and average costs the same as the society's marginal and average costs? The answer is no. The plant's own costs of producing output in terms of payments to labour, raw material, capital, land, etc., are its private costs. But they *do not* include the environmental cost of the output to the society at large. The social costs, which must include the cost to the environment, are higher.

In this example, we say that an increase in the firms' output causes **an** externality to the society and it is a **negative externality** in that the firm's output, via creating or increasing pollution, adversely affects the society.

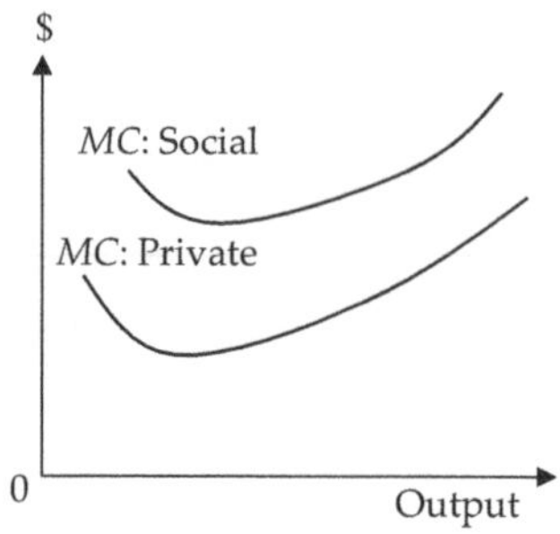

FIGURE 7.14 Private and Social Costs

We term the firm's own cost as the **private cost**, whereas the **social cost** *is defined as the sum of the private cost and the cost of the externality caused to the society.* Figure 7.14 illustrates these curves in terms of the marginal cost in the presence of a negative externality.

In some cases, there may be a **positive externality**. Suppose a new nursery has come up close to your neighbourhood. You, as the general public, enjoy the smell of flowers and the greenery from plants and small trees. This is an example of positive externality and in this case, the social marginal is less than the private marginal cost.

7.6.3 How Do Firms Finance Their Costs?

We have covered several cost concepts. But you may ask a basic, yet relevant, question that we haven't touched yet. How does a firm finance its costs? Put differently, what are the sources of funds from which a firm can pay the factors of production?

An Existing Firm

For an existing firm, there are four sources in general. One is the **plough-back of profit** or what is called **retained earnings**, referring to a part of its own accumulated profit being used towards covering some costs. It simply means using the firm's own money. A small entrepreneur may use part of his profit income for his own consumption and invest the rest in his firm. A corporation pays out a part of its profit earnings to shareholders, who are the owners of the firm. The rest are retained earnings, which are "ploughed back" to the firm.

Businesses do not always however use their own money to cover costs. **Loans from financial institutions** are another source. A loan is a financial contract between the lender (the financial institution like a commercial bank) and the borrower (the firm), specifying the duration of the loan and an interest rate. The lending institution typically reviews the project for which the loan is being requested.

Further, as security to itself, it holds some property of the firm (borrower) as the **mortgage**. If, for some reason, the firm is not able to pay back the loan, the lending institution has the right to sell off the mortgaged property and use the proceeds to recover its loan. If the sale of the mortgaged property doesn't fully recover the loan, the firm owners are personally liable to pay the rest.

New stocks and bonds are the remaining two other ways of financing. Through issuing these, the firm raises funds from the general public. These instruments will be described in Chapter 12. Basically, stocks offer ownership of the firm, whereas bonds do not. Stocks and bonds are, respectively, **equity** and debt instruments issued by a firm.

There are trade-offs between raising funds through these alternative ways. It is not in the interest of the company's management to always plough-back a large fraction of profits – because this would mean less dividend payments and a smaller return to stockholders. Hence, the public wouldn't want to invest much in the company by buying its stocks. It will be harder for the company to raise money in the future through issuing stocks. On the other hand, it is not wise to always pay back most of the profit earnings to the shareholders, because all else the same, this would leave less amount for plough-back and expansion of the company's operation. A balance must be struck between dividend payments and retained earnings.

Raising funds through stocks on the one hand and loans and bonds on the other have their advantages and disadvantages. It is interesting to observe that, while, for an investor, stocks are riskier than bonds, for the firm it is the opposite. Since lenders to the firm and bondholders must be paid, even when the times are bad, it is risky for the firm to raise funds through loans and bonds. On the other hand, if profits are high, stockholders will be paid more in the long run (as they are the owners), while lenders and bondholders will be paid only to the extent of the interest rate inherent in a bond. Thus, bonds are "cheaper" to the firm than stocks but riskier.

A Start-Up Firm

How would a start-up firm finance itself? Nobody will subscribe to its equity or debt instruments. No traditional commercial bank or financial institution will lend its money without collaterals. If it is your start-up firm, you don't want to pressurise your parents to help you, as their hard-earned money is saved for their old age and illness. We too would not advise you to do that, nor would we advise you to fall into the trap of traditional, unscrupulous moneylenders. You may tap your own savings, inheritance, or help from friends and relatives. However, chances are that you have none or little of these.

You should also be aware that even if a start-up is started up, the chances of failure are high. According to a survey in 2017 conducted by the IBM Institute for Business Value (IBV) in collaboration with Oxford Economics, it is found that

90% of Indian start-ups fail within the first five years due to lack of motivation and unique business models. The high-failure rate of start-ups is a global phenomenon, not confined to India. According to Eisenmann (2021), more than two-thirds do not show a positive return to the investors.[13]

Are all doors closed virtually for a young entrepreneur without adequate funds? No. Fortunately, over the past two decades or so, a new class of lenders is emerging globally who primarily finance start-ups and risky ventures. They are aptly called **venture capitalist**, **angle investors**, or **private equity**. The very purpose of venture capital is to provide finance (mostly in the form of private equity) to start-ups and emerging firms with growth potential. There are no predefined terms and conditions. They vary from case to case. The venture capitalists are aware of the high rate of failure of start-ups. Hence, their terms are stringent. They may give you some degree of freedom in the initial years, but in due course of time, they tend to extract their "pound of flesh." As a rule of thumb, 80% of returns of venture capitalists come from 20% start-ups. As a budding entrepreneur, you should know that you are to offer them high returns to compensate them for their investment in your venture and in three others in your peer group who failed. Venture capitalists not only insist on taking a fat equity share but also some degree of interference in managerial decision-making. We are not saying that this interference is always bad; sometimes the advice could be sound and timely. After all, there is a commonality of interest between you and angel investor. Since you are faced with the TINA factor (There Is No Alternative), you can take a calculated risk in incorporating venture capitalist along with you.

In the context of India, over the past one decade or so, the Government of India has come out with various schemes that promote skill development and entrepreneurship. Some of these are especially meant for students and faculty members. The favourable government schemes and cheap mobile data have resulted in a massive growth of start-ups in India. According to the Start-up India Portal (as of December 2020), India has about 50,000 start-ups. The best part is that you don't have to wait for starting your firm till you finish your studies. You can set up a start-up of your own in your B-School. Some B-Schools have set up **incubation centres** for these start-ups. Two government schemes are worth mentioning. These are:

- Atal Innovation Mission (2017)
- National Innovation and Start-up Policy (2019) for Students and Faculty.

Under the Atal Innovation Mission, higher-education institutions (HEIs) are encouraged to set up Atal Incubation Centres in their respective premises. The government provides initial financial support as well. The other scheme is also meant to do so.

Last but not least, by any means, apart from grooming you to be employable in industry, commerce, and business, many business schools encourage the spirit of entrepreneurship. The catchphrase is "Don't be a job seeker, be a job provider." The students can establish their start-ups inside B-School under the mentorship of their teachers. This reduces the need for huge initial capital expenditure. The start-up gets nurtured. We advise you to check in your B-School the facilities available for the promotion of start-ups.

It is heartening to note that in recent years, a small number (not insignificant) of you are seriously thinking of setting up your own company. In your graduation years and now, you may have participated in several Business Plan Competitions and won awards for your unique business idea which has the potential to be turned into a robust start-up.

7.7 Revenues

Revenues or sales are the lifeblood of business. If the output produced and sold doesn't bring enough revenues, a firm has no choice but to close or file bankruptcy. For the sake of simplicity, let us continue to suppose that a firm sells only one product or service. Like in the case of productivity and costs, there are three main revenue concepts: total, average, and marginal.

7.7.1 Total Revenue, Average Revenue, and Marginal Revenue

If a firm sells quantity q at price p, then

$$\text{Total Revenues} = TR = pq. \tag{7.5}$$

More generally, if a firm sells its output in multiple markets 1, 2,…., n, and the quantities sold are $q_1, q_2, \cdots, q_n$ at prices $p_1, p_2, \cdots, p_n$, respectively, then

$$TR = p_1 q_1 + p_2 q_2 + \cdots + p_n q_n. \tag{7.6}$$

We've implicitly assumed no volume discounts—which is that, if a customer buys a greater amount, she gets a better deal at a lower price.

Suppose 1, 2,…, n denotes different customers *in a single market*, who buy quantities $q_1, q_2, \cdots, q_n$ at prices $p_1, p_2, \cdots, p_n$. In this case, the revenue expression is the same as equation (7.6) except that the summation is over individuals or buying units, not markets.

However, to understand various revenue concepts, we ignore multiple markets and volume discounts and *focus on a single market with a uniform price.* Accordingly, we return to equation (7.5).

The first question we pose is, aren't price charged and quantity sold in a market by a firm related? The answer is generally yes, except for the case of a very small seller or vendor of a homogeneous product. Since, by definition, the producer is small and he is selling something like, say, baked corn and there is nothing special about the baked corn by the vendor compared to any other on nearby streets, it is reasonable to suppose that he can sell as many baked corns as he can at going market rate of say ₹10 a piece. If he sells 20 in a winter afternoon, his TR is ₹10 × 20 = ₹200. If he sells more say 30, TR = ₹300 and so on. Being small, he cannot sell baked corn in hundreds so as to influence the market price of ₹10 per piece. We graph this vendor's total revenue curve in Figure 7.15, which simply relates total revenue to output. It is a straight line since the price is constant.

In the above example, the seller has no market power in terms of controlling price. We cannot expect a small baked-corn vendor with no speciality to command any market power to determine the corn price. It is given to him at ₹10 "by the market."

In other situations, a firm may have some market power. To understand further revenue concepts, it will be very convenient to consider a monopoly market, i.e., a market served by one seller only, who sells something that does not have a close substitute. (Such a market will be analysed in detail in Chapter 10.) At the end, we will argue that the concepts to be developed are quite general, applying to *any* market, not just monopoly.

Since there is only seller of a product that people want, we may jump to a conclusion that the monopolist can charge any arbitrarily high price it wants. This is false. Suppose that Amul is the only ice cream vendor in your small town or village in India, i.e., it is a monopoly in selling ice cream. Can it hope to sell a reasonable number of ice cream at ₹500 a cone? The obvious answer is no, because at this price the quantity demanded might be zero or near zero in a small town.

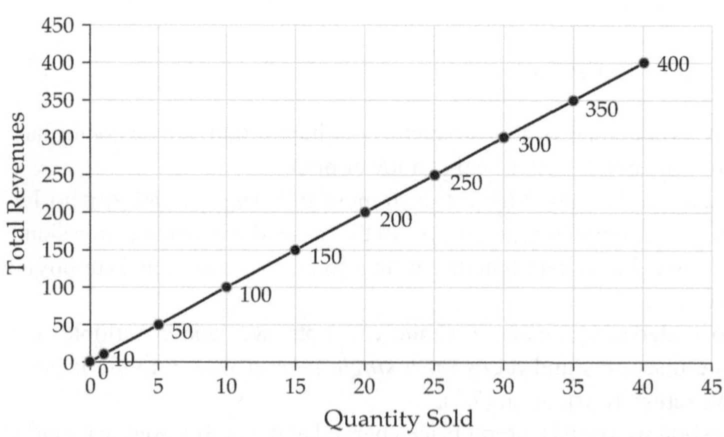

FIGURE 7.15 Total Revenue Curve at Price = ₹10

The availability of no substitutes does not necessarily mean that people have to "demand" it unless it is absolutely essential for existence.

However, by "arbitrarily high price," one might have meant a price higher than what it would be if there were competing sellers of the same or similar products. This is correct. So, what price will Amul charge? The answer is that Amul will charge a price keeping in view the market demand curve for Amul's ice cream, because people will buy ice cream based on the demand curve. The general point is that *a producer with market power must however respect the market demand curve.* Put differently, the *market demand function is a* **constraint** *facing any firm with market power.* It cannot charge "any" high price arbitrarily, unless people cannot live without the product, i.e., the demand curve for the product is (unusually) vertical.

We now consider the market demand schedule given in Table 7.12. Along this schedule, if the seller wants to sell 5 units for example, she (the monopolist) *must* charge a price = ₹9. The reason is the following. At any price higher than this, she will be able to sell only less than 5 units. Further, she can always sell 5 units by charging ₹9 each—since 5 units are demanded at price = ₹9. Thus, there is no reason to sell 5 units for any price less than ₹9. By a similar argument, if the monopolist wants to produce and sell 6 units, the price charged will be ₹6, and so on.

We now write "Output" in place of "Quantity Demanded" and present the same demand schedule with output listed in increasing order from 0 to 7. Column (1) of Table 7.13 does it, while column (2) lists the price. These columns represent the demand schedule in Table 7.12.

Next, we multiply the output by price and get the total revenue (*TR*) at each level of output. This is given in column (3). Analogous to average cost, we define **average revenue** (AR) as *total revenues divided by the output or the amount sold.* That is, $AR = TR \div output$. Notice that in equation (7.5), $TR/Output$ = price.[14] Hence, *AR is always equal to price*: they are one and the same thing, except that *AR* refers to the firm, while price refers to the consumers and the firm. In the example, *AR* is shown in column (4) of Table 7.13, the entries of which are the same as those in column (2).

TABLE 7.12 A Demand Schedule

Price (₹)	*Quantity Demanded (units)*
3	7
6	6
9	5
12	4
15	3
18	2
21	1
24	0

Our next and final concept is **marginal revenue**, MR. Like marginal cost facing a firm, the *marginal revenue of a firm is the addition to the total revenues from one extra unit produced and sold.* In the example, the *MR* schedule is shown in column (5) of Table 7.13.

Panels (a) and (b) of Figure 7.16, respectively, graph the *TR* and *AR–MR* curves corresponding to Table 7.13. The *TR* curve is inverse U-shaped as *TR* initially increases and then decreases with output. Panels (c) and (d) of Figure 7.16 depict a smooth, hypothetical *TR* curve and the associated *AR* and *MR* curves. As you notice, *TR* reaches its maximum when $MR = 0$. This follows from the relationship

TABLE 7.13 *TR*, *AR*, and *MR*

Output	*Price (₹)*	*TR (₹)*	*AR= p (₹)*	*MR (₹)*
(1)	(2)	(3)	(4)	(5)
0	24	0	–	–
1	21	21	21	21
2	18	36	18	15
3	15	45	15	9
4	12	48	12	3
5	9	45	9	-3
6	6	36	6	-9
7	3	21	2	-15

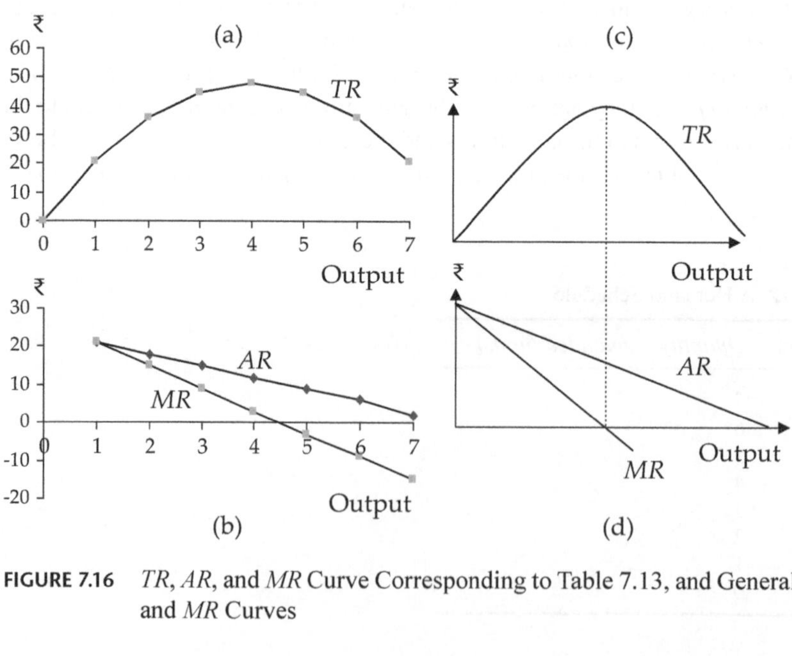

FIGURE 7.16 *TR*, *AR*, and *MR* Curve Corresponding to Table 7.13, and General *TR*, *AR*, and *MR* Curves

between a "total" and a "marginal" explained and illustrated in Chapter 1, Chapter 4, and previous sections of the current chapter.

There is a popular saying that a picture is worth a thousand words. What is not well-advertised, however, is that sometimes equations are worth tens of pictures. (Einstein once remarked—in reply to question asking him to join politics as he was so renowned and well-respected—politics is for the present, but an equation remains forever.) Economists follow both these principles seriously. Note that, in our example in Tables 7.12 and 7.13, the demand function is linear, i.e., $q = A - bp$. This implies $p = (A-q)/b$, and hence,

$$TR = pq = \frac{(A-q)q}{b} = \frac{Aq}{b} - \frac{q^2}{b}.$$

This is the expression that governs the shape of the *TR* curve shown in Figure 7.16(c). The parameter values are $A = 8$ and $b = 1/3$. Since $AR = p$, we have $AR = (A-q)/b$, and by taking the derivative of the *TR* function, $MR = (A-2q)/b$.

Consider another example, a non-linear demand:

$$q = 5p^{-1.5}. \tag{7.7}$$

Given this, we can derive

$$AR = (q/5)^{-0.67};\ TR = 2.94q^{0.33};\ MR = 0.97q^{-0.67}. \tag{7.8}$$

One can think of many other forms of non-linear demand functions.

It will be useful to know how *TR*, *AR*, and *MR* relate to one another. We make use of the pattern of entries in Table 7.13 and the general relations between "total," "average," and "marginal" to learn them. They are however not specific to Table 7.13 or a linear demand function.

i) *MR decreases with the output. Initially it is positive and after a certain level of output it turns negative.* See the last column of Table 7.13.
ii) *TR increases or decreases with output, as MR is positive or negative.*
iii) (i) and (ii) imply that *TR* first increases and then it decreases with output. Thus, the graph of *TR* against output, the *TR* curve, rises initially and then falls. It means that *if output is measured on a continuous scale, TR reaches the maximum when MR = 0.*
iv) Since *AR* = price, *the AR curve is the same as the demand curve facing the firm.*
v) Notice in Table 7.13 that, except for the first unit, at all other levels of output, *MR* < *AR*. This follows from the relationship between the "average" and the "marginal": that is, if the "average" is falling (rising), the "marginal" is less (greater) than the "average."

vi) Consider the range of output over which $MR > 0$. Since the discrepancy between MR and AR arises because the average revenue is falling with quantity, the rate of decrease in the AR determines the proportional difference between MR and AR. In turn, the rate of decrease in AR, meaning the rate of decrease in price as quantity demanded increases, depends on the price elasticity of demand. Hence, the higher the price elasticity of demand, the flatter the demand curve and thus the less the decrease in the price or AR. It then follows that *the higher the elasticity, the smaller the ratio, AR/MR.* In fact, as shown in Appendix 7.D:

$$\frac{AR}{MR} = \frac{e_p}{e_p - 1}, \tag{7.9}$$

where e_p is the price elasticity of demand. You can easily verify that the ratio on the right-hand side of equation (7.9) decreases with an increase in e_p. This "proves" that the AR/MR ratio decreases with the price elasticity of demand.

vii) There is an important relationship between the sign of the MR and the magnitude of the price elasticity of demand, which is not apparent from Figure 7.16. In the range of output where $MR > 0$, an increase in output or quantity sold results in an increase in the total revenue. This is the same as saying that a decrease in price (as quantity sold increases) is associated with an increase in the total expenditure (= total revenue). Now, go back to Chapter 3 and check the relationship between a price change, elasticity, and the change in total expenditure: a decrease in price is associated with an increase in total expenditure if and only if the price elasticity is greater than unity. Thus, *$MR > 0$ means that the price elasticity is greater than one.* Similarly, *$MR < 0$ means that the price elasticity is less than one.*

7.7.2 Generality of the Revenue Concepts

It is worth reemphasising that the three revenue concepts, their qualitative behaviour, and interrelationships are not confined to a monopoly market. This was assumed only for the sake of simplicity and understanding. To see the point, suppose there are two competing products in the market, say, only *Patanjali Dant Kanti (K)* and *Vicco Vajradanti Ayurvedic (V)* produced, respectively, by the Ramdev Group and Vicco Group in the toothpaste market of India. They are basically the same product with slightly different ingredients and perceived differences. Suppose the respective demand curves are: $q_K = 5p_K^{-1.5}p_V^{0.7}$ and $q_V = 2p_K^{1.1}p_V^{-1.3}$. Note that the own price effect is negative, and the cross-price effect is positive since the two brands are substitutes of each other. Given these demand functions facing the respective firms, suppose that the price of *Vicco Vajradanti Ayurvedic* is set at ₹1, i.e., $p_V = 1$ (chosen for calculation simplicity) by the Vicco Group *before* the Ramdev Group produced or priced *Patanjali Dant Kanti.* What are the revenue prospects from selling *Patanjali Dant Kanti?* Just substitute "1" for p_V in the demand function for *Patanjali Dant Kanti.* We have $q_K = 5p_K^{-1.5}$. Once we know the demand function, we can compute the *TR*, *AR*, and *MR* functions and curves in the way explained earlier. Indeed, we already know these functions!! Just check the expressions in equations (7.7) and (7.8).

Facts and Insights

- Most businesses are individual proprietorships.
- In individual proprietorship and partnership firms, each owner has unlimited liability, meaning that if the company is due for a payment and other owners are not able to pay, e.g., someone dies or currently resides in a foreign country, then an owner who is available is liable for the entire amount due.
- Limited liability and separation of management from ownership are the salient features of a corporation.
- In predicting the firm's behaviour, profit maximisation has worked as good as other alternative assumptions on the goal of a firm.
- In India, public sector firms are becoming more and more revenue- and profit-oriented.
- Primary factors provide their services to production activity, whereas raw materials are totally used up in a production process.
- The contribution of an individual input to output is measured by the notions of total physical product, marginal physical product, and the average physical product.
- The marginal physical product and the average physical product curves are "inverse U-shaped" because of the law of diminishing returns.
- The law of diminishing marginal returns states that, keeping the employment of other inputs fixed, as more of a particular input is used in production, after a certain level (possibly from the beginning) its marginal physical product decreases as more and more of it is employed.
- The basis of the law of diminishing returns lies in that as more and more of a single factor is used in production, the proportion of this factor with other factors becomes less and less suitable for production.
- In economics, a market period is defined as that short period in which a producer or a firm cannot vary the level of employment of any input.
- A short period is that period in which a firm can vary the employment of some inputs, but not all, whereas a long period is where a firm can vary the employment of all inputs.

- Returns to scale refers to the proportionate increase in output when all inputs are changed in the same proportion. A production function is said to exhibit increasing, constant, or decreasing returns to scale as output increases more than proportionately, proportionately, or less than proportionately when all inputs are increased by a given proportion.
- A production function satisfying constant returns to scale is also called a linearly homogeneous production function.
- Isoquants are similar to indifference curves. They represent combinations of inputs that produce the same level of output.
- Leontief technology refers to the production function or technology where proportions of inputs used are fixed.
- Total factor productivity is a common measure of productivity growth.
- A profit-maximising firm will not use any input to the level where its marginal product is negative.
- In economic analysis, costs always refer to economic costs—the sum of explicit (accounting) costs and implicit costs.
- Sunk costs are the costs incurred in the past.
- Fixed costs are independent of the output, while variable costs are not.
- Fixed costs, which refer to the present or future are very different from the sunk cost, which is a thing of the past.
- The total variable cost in the short run or the total cost in the long run is the minimised total cost in the cost-minimisation problem.
- The short-run average variable and average total cost curves are U-shaped because the short-run marginal cost curve is U-shaped. The latter follows from the law of diminishing returns.
- A technological improvement shifts the cost curves down, while input price increases or increases in business taxes shift them up.
- An increase in the plant size may increase or decrease the minimum average total cost accordingly as there are increasing or decreasing returns to scale.
- The concepts of marginal product and the law of diminishing returns are valid even in the long run when all factors are variable.
- In the long run, all costs are variable.
- The long-run average cost is U-shaped because a firm typically experiences increasing returns of scale, followed by constant and decreasing returns to scale. The U-shape of the long-run average cost curve implies the U-shape of the long-run marginal cost curve.
- A profit-maximising firm will employ input combinations that minimise total cost at any given level of output.
- Given output, an increase in an input price would lead a firm to use less of that input. Thus, an increase in the wage rate will lead a firm to use a less

labour-intensive (i.e., more capital-intensive) technique. Similarly, an increase in the rent or interest rate will induce a firm to use a less capital-intensive, i.e., more labour-intensive technique.

- Divisions of labour and volume discounts on the purchase of inputs are sources of economies of scale, whereas management inefficiency due to large scale of operations, overcrowding, and congestion of inputs cause diseconomies of scale.
- Negative (positive) externalities imply that the social marginal cost is higher (less) than the private marginal cost.
- Pollution imposes a negative externality on the society.
- Existing firms finance their costs through retained earnings, loans from financial institutions, and issuing new bonds and stocks.
- As a means of financing its costs or operation, issuing bonds are cheaper but riskier to a firm than issuing stocks.
- Issuing new bonds and stocks or applying for sizeable loans from financial institutions are generally subjected to an outside scrutiny of a firm's performance.
- In most economies, the failure rate of start-up companies is high.
- Financing a start-up is rather difficult unless there are private funds already available to an entrepreneur.
- A separate class of investors has emerged in recent decades who primarily invest in start-up companies, namely, venture capitalists, angel investors, or private equity.
- The Government of India has various schemes to help start-ups. Several B-Schools encourage entrepreneurship as a career option. Even the students can establish their own start-ups inside a B-School under the mentorship of their teachers.
- It is not true that a firm with some market power can choose any price arbitrarily because it is the sole producer of the product or service. The market demand curve acts as a constraint.
- There are three main revenue concepts: total revenue (*TR*), average revenue (*AR*), and marginal revenue (*MR*). Revenues are generated from market demand for a product.
- By definition, average revenue = price.
- The market demand function is a constraint facing any firm with market power. It cannot charge "any" high price arbitrarily, unless people cannot live without the product, that is, the demand curve for the product is (unusually) vertical.
- The relationships between the three revenue concepts are governed by those between "total," "average," and "marginal." In addition, the relation between *AR* and *MR* depends on the price elasticity of the product, as given in equation (7.9).

Exercises

Descriptive/Analytical

7.1. What are the differences between a partnership form of business and an individual proprietorship?

7.2. What is the difference between a partnership business and a corporation?

7.3. "In the real world, many firms go out of business. Thus, profit maximisation is a bad assumption." Defend or refute.

7.4. Briefly discuss the reason behind diminishing marginal returns to an input.

7.5. Consider the Cobb–Douglas production, specified in the text. Suppose $\alpha + \beta > 1$. What does this imply towards the returns to scale? How would your answer change if $\alpha + \beta$ equals one or less than one?

7.6. Explain total factor productivity and its implications.

7.7. Explain why the short-run *MC*, *AVC*, and *ATC* curves are U-shaped?

7.8. Briefly state and explain the relationship between *MC*, *AVC*, and *ATC* curves.

7.9. Briefly describe the relationship between the short-run average cost curve and the long-run average cost curve.

7.10. Briefly explain the relationship between the returns to scale and the shape of the long-run average and marginal cost curves.

7.11. What are the reasons behind a firm experiencing economies of scale first, followed by diseconomies of scale?

7.12. The production activity of a firm causes a negative externality. How will the social marginal cost be different from the private marginal cost?

7.13. What are the different sources available to a corporation to finance its operations/costs?

7.14. What are the different funding sources available to a start-up company?

7.15. "For a start-up company, the chance of failure is high. It is thus not advisable for a young professional to start a new business." Defend or refute.

7.16. "By virtue of being the only firm, a monopoly firm in a market would charge any arbitrarily high price for its product." Defend or refute.

7.17. Some years ago, a minister of a particular province in India made a comment to the effect that some private sector firms incur losses in the business, and hence, what is wrong with public sector firms making losses? Do you agree or disagree? Give reasons.

Short Answer (word limit = 500 approx.)

7.18. "A private firm makes its decisions with the objective of maximising its profits." Comment.

7.19. How defensible is the assumption of profit maximisation as the main objective of a public sector firm today in India? Briefly discuss.

7.20. Many large, private firms contribute regularly to charity and other social causes. Is the behaviour consistent with the profit-maximisation hypothesis? Briefly discuss.

7.21. Why is the *MPP* curve of an input either downward-sloping throughout or inverse U-shaped?

7.22. Differentiate between diminishing returns (to an input) and diminishing returns to scale.

7.23. In terms of an isoquant, what is the economic region of production and why?

7.24. Why is a typical isoquant convex to the origin?

7.25. What does Leontief technology mean? What shape of an isoquant does it imply?

7.26. "If the technology is Leontief, the returns to scale are constant." Defend or refute.

7.27. "Cost is zero if a firm doesn't hire any input. Hence cost minimisation essentially means shutting down the operation of the firm." Comment.

7.28. Differentiate between sunk costs and fixed costs with suitable examples.

7.36. Through a hypothetical, yet relating to the real world, give an example of an implicit cost.

7.37. What is an overhead cost? Give two examples.

7.38. A firm's total cost schedule in the short run is the following. What is its total fixed cost? Derive the marginal cost schedule.

Output	*Total Cost ($)*
0	10
1	25
2	35
3	43
4	54
5	69
6	91
7	121
8	161

7.39. How does an increase in business taxes shift the marginal and average cost curves?

7.40. How does a technical progress shift the marginal and average cost curves?

7.41. How would an increase in input prices affect the marginal and average cost curves?

7.42. Briefly describe the link between the cost-minimisation process in the short-run and the long-run cost curves.

7.43. Suppose the long-run average cost is constant (independent of the output). That is, the *LAC* curve is a horizontal line. Draw the long-run marginal cost curve relative to this *LAC* curve. Give reasons.

7.44. A firm experiences increasing returns to scale initially over a range of output, constant returns to scale over another range, and decreasing returns to scale thereafter. Draw the firm's long-run average cost curve.

7.45. "Increasing and decreasing returns to scale respectively imply the downward portion and the upward portion of the long-run average cost." Defend or refute.

7.46. What do positive and negative externalities mean?

7.47. A chemical plant owned by an Indian company operates in Ghana and it causes pollution in that country. Is there a difference between private cost and social cost in terms of this company's production of chemicals in this plant?

7.48. What are retained earnings?

7.49. In raising funds from the public through issuing stocks and bonds, which is the riskier way for the firm? If it is riskier, then why would a firm choose that way to finance its expenses?

7.50. Intuitively explain why for a monopoly firm the total revenue curve will be concave rather than a straight line.

Quizzes/Numerical

7.51. Name four public sector firms in India that have been disinvested, i.e., sold to the private sector.

7.52. "A profit-maximising firm will never hire so much of an input, such that its marginal product is negative." Defend or refute.

7.53. A 15% increase in all inputs leads to only a 5% increase in the output. Are the returns to scale increasing, constant, or diminishing?

7.54. Some input combinations and the respective outputs associated with a given production function are given in the following table. What are the returns to scale (increasing, constant, or diminishing) if the firm moves from input combination ______ to input combination _____?
(a) B, C; (b) C, D; (c) D, E; (d) E, F; and (e) F, G.

Input Combination	*Labour*	*Capital*	*Output*
A	0	0	0
B	1	2	5
C	2	4	11
D	3	6	18
E	4	8	24
F	5	10	30
G	6	12	35

7.55. Suppose that a firm is committed to produce a given amount of output. There are two factors of production: capital and labour. Let rent and wages be their prices. Suppose this level of output is produced by an input combination such that the ratio of the marginal product of capital to that of labour exceeds the ratio of rent to wages. How should the firm change the input combination so as to lower the total cost of producing this level of output and why?

7.56. "Economic cost is a part of accounting costs." Defend or refute.

7.57. "Marginal cost is the addition to the total cost, not to the total variable cost, per one extra unit produced." Defend or refute.

7.58. What is the area under the marginal cost curve equal to, total cost or total variable cost?

7.59. *AVC* is minimised at a level of output, which is ______ than that at which *ATC* attains its minimum value. Fill in the blank and give reasons.

7.60. What is the vertical difference between the *TC* and *TVC* equal to and why?

7.61. A potato chips vendor sells one packet for \$2. Draw his total revenue curve for one evening over 1 to 50 plates.

7.62. A monopoly firm faces the following demand curve. Draw his total revenue, average revenue, and marginal revenue curves.

Price (€)	*Quantity Demanded (units)*
3	7
6	6
10	5
15	4
21	3
28	2
36	1
45	0

7.63. For a monopoly, the price elasticity of demand at price \$12 is 1.5, and at price \$12, he sells quantity 20 along the market demand. What is the firm's marginal revenue at quantity 20?

Appendix 7.A Mathematical Definitions of Returns to Scale

Let $y = f(x_1, x_2, \cdots, x_n)$ be the production function. Suppose all inputs increase by a proportion λ. Increasing, constant, or decreasing returns to scale are distinguished on the basis of whether $f(\lambda x_1, \lambda x_2, \cdots, \lambda x_n)$ is greater than, equal to, or less than $\lambda y = \lambda f(x_1, x_2, \cdots, x_n)$. The three types of returns to scale are defined by

Increasing Returns to Scale if $f(\lambda x_1, \lambda x_2, \cdots, \lambda x_n) > \lambda f(x_1, x_2, \cdots, x_n)$

Constant Returns to Scale if $f(\lambda x_1, \lambda x_2, \cdots, \lambda x_n) = \lambda f(x_1, x_2, \cdots, x_n)$

Decreasing Returns to Scale if $f(\lambda x_1, \lambda x_2, \cdots, \lambda x_n) < \lambda f(x_1, x_2, \cdots, x_n)$.

Appendix 7.B Proof of Equation (7.3)

With two inputs 1 and 2, we can write the production function as $y = f(x_1, x_2)$. Isoquants refer to input combinations that produce a given amount of output, say $\bar{y}$. Thus, $\bar{y} = f(x_1, x_2)$ defines an isoquant, relating input amounts x_1 and x_2 at some given level of output. If we totally differentiate the production function, $dy = (\partial f / \partial x_1) dx_1 + (\partial f / \partial x_1) dx_2$. Along an isoquant, there is no change in output, i.e., $dy = 0$. Hence, $(\partial f / \partial x_1) dx_1 + (\partial f / \partial x_1) dx_2 = 0$. We can rewrite it as,

$$\frac{dx_2}{dx_1} = -\frac{\partial f / \partial x_1}{\partial f / \partial x_2} < 0. \tag{A7.1}$$

Hence, an isoquant is downward-sloping and its slope = MRTS is, in absolute value, equal to the ratio of marginal products. The expressions in equation (A7.1) prove equation (7.3).

Appendix 7.C Iso-Cost Lines and Cost Minimisation

The key to understanding the cost-minimisation problem of a firm is the iso-cost line.

7.1.C Iso-cost Line

Similar to a firm's technology being characterised by isoquants, its total costs of employing factors can be represented by what is called an iso-cost line. Suppose labour and capital are the two inputs. Labour costs ₹w per hour and renting capital (e.g., a truck) costs ₹r per unit. These are respective factor/input prices. We define an **iso-cost line** as the locus of combinations of inputs whose total costs are the same.

In our two-input model, the total cost = wL (cost of labour) + rK (cost of capital). Consider the iso-cost line for total cost equal to say ₹1,000. Let w = ₹50 and r = ₹40. Various combinations of L and K such that $50 \times L + 40 \times K = 1{,}000$ define the iso-cost line for total cost = ₹1,000.

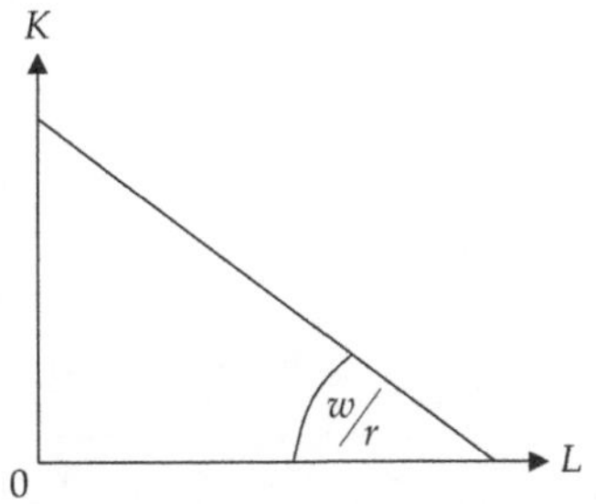

FIGURE 7.17 An Iso-Cost Line

Clearly, along an iso-cost line, if the firm hires more of one input, it must hire less of the other. You can see that the iso-cost line is identical to the price line studied in consumer theory, except that total cost substitutes income, factor prices substitute product prices and we are talking about demand for inputs rather than demand for goods. Thus, like the price line, the iso-cost line is a downward-sloping straight line. Figure 7.17 shows an arbitrary iso-cost line. Just as a slope of the price line equals the ratio of product prices, *the slope of the iso-cost line is equal to the ratio of factor prices.* In Figure 7.17 where labour is measured along the x-axis and capital along the y-axis, it is equal to the wage/rental ratio, w/r.

While an iso-cost line is defined for a given total cost, the total cost itself may change, depending on how much a producer is willing to spend on inputs. In other words, iso-cost lines can be shift—just as the price line in consumer theory does. Different levels of total cost imply different iso-cost lines.

Consider an increase in the total cost. This will lead to a parallel rightward shift of the iso-cost line. Similarly, a decrease in total cost will lead to a parallel leftward shift of the iso-cost line. A change in a factor price can shift an iso-cost line too. Suppose there is an increase in the wage rate, w. If the firm hires labour only, with the same amount of total cost, it can hire less only as labour is more expensive. This will shift the intercept of the iso-cost line on the axis measuring labour towards the origin. In Figure 7.17, the iso-cost line will become steeper.[15]

7.2.C Cost Minimisation

Equipped with the various concepts and assumptions at our disposal, we now analyse the decision problem facing a firm. Suppose a firm has committed itself to produce a given amount of output.[16] Which combination of inputs should it choose?

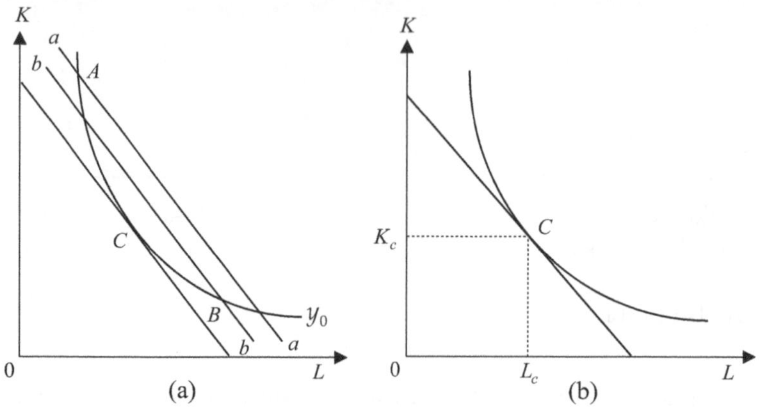

FIGURE 7.18 Cost Minimisation

Turn to Figure 7.18(a). Suppose the output to be produced is y_0. The firm can choose any point on the isoquant representing y_0. Suppose it selects the input combination at point *A*. The total cost of this is indicated by the iso-cost line passing through this point, namely *aa*. Consider another combination *B*. Its total cost is shown by *bb*. Since the line *bb* lies to the left of the line *aa*, the combination *B* costs less than the combination *A*. Similar calculation can be made from any other combination on the isoquant.

As stated earlier, the firm's ultimate objective is to maximise profits. Profits, by definition, are equal to total sales revenues minus the total cost of inputs. Obviously, the higher the costs, the less are the profits. Hence, *maximising profits implies that the firm must choose that input bundle which costs the least among those that can produce the output.* We now go back to Figure 7.18(a) and ask which input bundle entails the minimum total costs, given that the firm is producing y_0. The answer is the tangency point *C*, because at any other combination of inputs (such as *A* or *B*), the iso-cost line will be at a higher level compared to that at *C*. The input levels, L_c of labour and K_c of capital associated with the tangency point *C* then constitute the cost-minimising choice of inputs as shown in Figure 7.18(b).

In general, we say that the optimal or the cost-minimising choice of inputs is governed by the condition that the iso-cost line is tangential to the isoquant. Since the slope of the former is the input price ratio and that of the latter is the MRTS (equal to the ratio of MPPs), we can write the condition more fully.

Cost-Minimisation Condition: MRTS = ratio of *MPP*s = factor price ratio. (A7.2)

When the factors are denoted by *L* and *K*, with *w* and *r* as the respective factor prices, we can write this condition as:

$$\frac{MPP_L}{MPP_K} = \frac{w}{r}. \tag{A7.3}$$

The condition (A7.3) can be derived algebraically. Revert to calling the two inputs as input 1 and input 2. Cost minimisation states that $C = w_1x_1 + w_2x_2$ is minimised along an isoquant. Keeping in view equation (A7.1),

$$dC = w_1dx_1 + w_2dx_2 = w_1dx_1 + \left(dx_2 / dx_1\right)dx_1 = \left[w_1 + w_2\left(-\frac{\partial f / \partial x_1}{\partial f / \partial x_2} \right) \right] dx_1.$$

If C is minimised, $dC / dx_1 = 0$. This implies that the term inside the brackets [] is zero, i.e.,

$$w_1 + w_2\left(-\frac{\partial f / \partial x_1}{\partial f / \partial x_2} \right) = 0, \text{ or } \frac{\partial f / \partial x_1}{\partial f / \partial x_2} = \frac{w_1}{w_2}.$$

The last equation is the same as the cost-minimisation condition stated in equation (A7.3).

7.3.C A Change in an Input Price

Having derived the cost-minimising condition, we can analyse how a change in a factor price or the output level can affect the optimal choice of inputs. Suppose, labour becomes cheaper.[17] This will make iso-cost line flatter (since its slope equals w/r). Turning to Figure 7.19, suppose C is the original point of choice and cc is the associated iso-cost line. With a lower value of w, the new iso-cost lines will be flatter

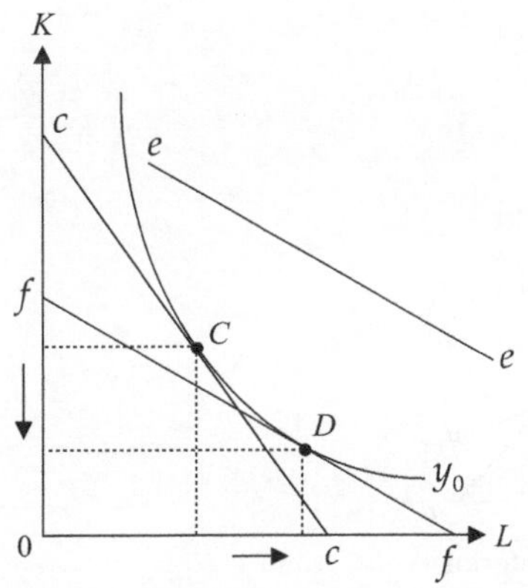

FIGURE 7.19 An Input Price Change

than *cc*: *ee*, *ff*, etc. which are parallel. The new cost-minimising input bundle is the tangency point between the isoquant y_0 and the iso-cost line *ff*. This is the bundle *D*. Compared to *C*, the new input combination has more labour and less capital. This makes sense, because, labour being relatively cheaper now, the firm is hiring more labour and less capital i.e., it is employing a more labour-intensive technique.

7.4.C A Change in Output

Suppose the firm decides to produce a higher quantity, y_1, than the original output y_0 (while input prices are unchanged). This means a higher isoquant. The effects are shown in Figure 7.20. In both panels, the point *C* is the original cost-minimising input bundle. In panel (a) the new bundle is indicated at *A*. Compared to the original input bundle, the firm hires more of both inputs. Panel (b) illustrates the case where the firm employs more of one input and less of the other. You may notice that the effect of an increase in output "works like" an income effect in demand theory. Like normal and inferior goods, we define normal and inferior inputs. *An input is said to be* **normal or inferior** *as, at constant factor prices, the demand for it increases. An input is said to be* **normal** *or* **inferior** *as, at constant factor prices, the demand for it increases or decreases with output.* In panel (a) both inputs are normal, whereas in panel (b), labour is the normal while capital is the inferior input.

Note however that irrespective of whether some inputs are inferior, a higher output is always associated with a higher iso-cost line, i.e., total cost always increases with output.

Suppose we extend this exercise and let output increase continuously. The effects are shown in Figure 7.21. The cost-minimising points are C_1, C_2, C_3, etc. If we join these points the line ($0E$) is called *the* **expansion path**, *defined generally as the locus of cost-minimising input bundles at different levels of output, given the input prices.* The expansion path indicates a firm's pattern of hiring inputs as it plans to expand its production.

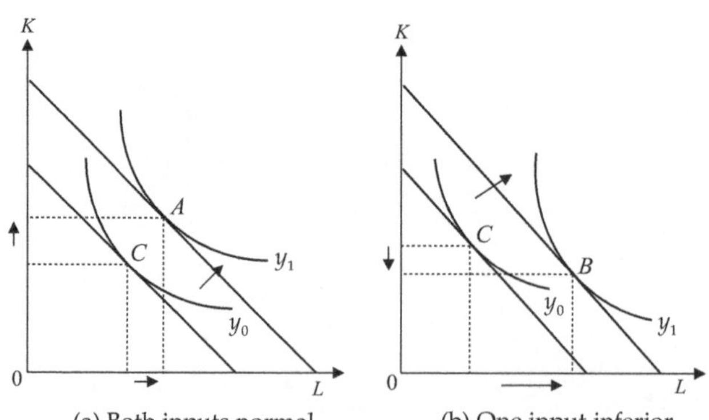

FIGURE 7.20 An Increase in Output

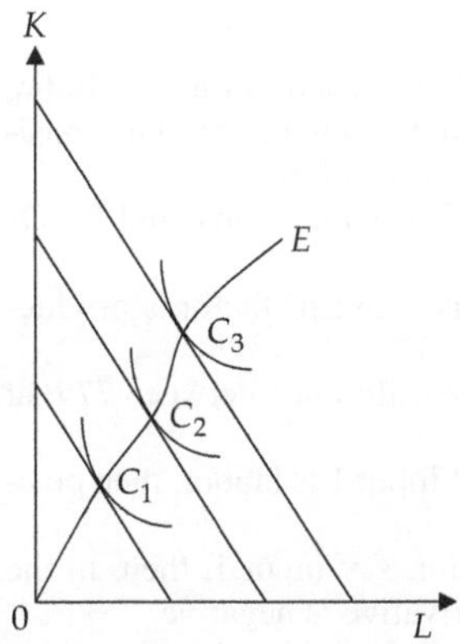

FIGURE 7.21 An Expansion Path

Appendix 7.D Derivation of the Relation (7.9)

Let $q = q(p)$ denote the demand function. By definition, the price elasticity of demand has the expression,

$$e_p = -\frac{p}{q}\frac{dq}{dp}.$$

Hence,

$$\frac{1}{e_p} = -\frac{q}{p}\frac{dp}{dq}. \qquad \text{(A7.4)}$$

Recall that marginal revenue is the incremental effect of an increase in quantity on total revenue, that is, $MR = d(TR)/dq$. Since $TR = pq$, we have

$$\begin{aligned} MR &= \frac{d(pq)}{dq} \\ &= p + q\frac{dp}{dq} \\ &= p\left(1 + \frac{q}{p}\frac{dp}{dq}\right) \\ &= AR\left(1 - \frac{1}{e_p}\right) \\ \Rightarrow \frac{AR}{MR} &= \frac{e_p}{e_p - 1}, \end{aligned}$$

where we have made use of equation (A7.4). This proves the relation (7.9).

Notes

1 For a business to operate legally (whether it is an individual proprietor or not) in India, it must be registered with the Registrar of Companies (ROC). There are many businesses, which are unregistered, e.g., road-side vendors of various kinds.
2 There are other entities like some co-operatives, non-profit organisations, and NGOs that operate like a business.
3 If so, it seems more appropriate to view entrepreneurship as a "quasi" factor of production since its reward is a residual payment.
4 For example, the *MPP* at $L = 2$, which is 24, is equal to the difference between *TPP* at $L = 2$, which is 44, and *TPP* at $L = 1$, which is 20.
5 Mathematically, in terms of the production function (7.1) if input 1 is labour, then positive or negative *MPP* is indicated by $\partial f / \partial x_1 \gtrless 0$.
6 Mathematically, if the marginal returns are diminishing for, say input 1, then, in the production function (7.1), $\partial^2 f / \partial x_1^2 < 0$, i.e., the second derivative is negative.
7 Recall that in Chapter 1, we presented a total cost schedule (or table). The *TC* curve here is based on some total cost schedule like the one in Chapter 1.
8 Indeed, the *AFC* curve shapes like, what is called in geometry, a rectangular parabola. This is similar in shape to a unitarily elastic demand curve mentioned in Chapter 2.
9 In other words, the *MC* curve is the mirror image of the *MPP* curve.
10 Apart from internal scale economies, there is another reason for the unit cost to decline with output. That is, when hiring or purchasing more inputs to produce a higher quantity, a producer may get quantity discounts. This would tend to lower the average cost as output expands.
11 This stands in contrast to the short run where the shape of the marginal cost curve determines the shape of the average variable and average total cost curves.
12 In reality, many chemical plants do have proper disposal systems.
13 Eisenmann (2021) identifies six factors for failures of start-ups. To name them, there are three early-stage factors: "good idea, bad-bedfellows," "false starts," and "false positives." There are three late-stage factors too: "speed trap," "help wanted," and "cascading miracles."
14 This is true except when output is zero. At zero output, *TR*/output = 0/0 is not defined.
15 Similarly, an increase in *r* will shift the intercept of the iso-cost line on the measuring capital and in Figure 7.17 the iso-cost line will become flatter.
16 In subsequent chapters we will study how a firm decides to choose its output.
17 It could happen when, for example, workers from outside migrate into the area.

Bibliography

Das, S., & Sengupta, R. (2004). Project pursuit regression and disaggregate productivity effects: The case of Indian blast furnaces. *Journal of Applied Econometrics*, *19*(3), 397–418.

Eisenmann, T. (2021). *Why startups fail? A new roadmap for entrepreneurial success.* Currency. €100 × 10 + €150 × 3 = €1,450.

8

PROFIT MAXIMISATION AND PERFECT COMPETITION

Given our understanding of various concepts relating to production, costs, and revenues, we are ready to analyse the profit-maximising behaviour of a firm. As utility maximisation leads to the demand curve, profit maximisation leads to the supply curve, introduced in Chapter 2, if the market structure is perfectly competitive—something we will define and analyse in detail in this chapter.

8.1 Accounting Profit and Economic Profit

Profits, by definition, are equal to the difference between the total revenues generated from selling output and the total costs of producing output. Depending on which part of the cost is included in calculation, there are two notions of profit. One is **accounting profits**, meaning total revenues minus total explicit costs. The other is **economic profits, abnormal profits, producer's surplus**, or simply **profits**, *equal to the total revenues minus the economic costs* (*the sum of explicit and implicit costs*).

Here is an example.

Example 8.1

George owns the ground floor and basement of a building in Nairobi. He lives on the ground floor and was renting the basement to a bank for KES12,00,000 (Kenyan Shilling) a year. He used to work for a local hospital. Last year, he decided to take the basement off rent and opened a clinic of his own there. Over one year, the annual "turnover," a common business term meaning total revenues collected from services offered to patients, is KES45,00,000. The salary expenses paid to his employees amounted to KES10,00,000. The cost of electricity, phone, and other

DOI: 10.4324/9781003452195-8

utilities ran into KES3,00,000. The cost of medical supplies and other raw materials was KES400,000. These are all the expenses he had to incur for the business over the year. What are his explicit costs, accounting profit, and economic profit?

Answer: Salary expenses, utility costs, and costs of medical supplies and raw materials sum up to explicit costs, equal to 10 + 3 + 4 = KES17,00,000. The foregone rental income is KES12,00,000, which is the implicit cost. Hence, the total (economic) costs, including explicit and implicit costs, are equal to 17 + 12 = KES29,00,000. Hence the accounting profits = Revenues – Explicit costs = 45 – 17 = KES28,00,000. But the economic profits = Revenues – Total Costs = 45 – 29 = KES16,00,000.■

It is possible that while the accounting profits are positive, the economic profits are negative. In what follows, we will refer to the economic profit.

8.2 Revenues

In Chapter 7, we have discussed how revenues are related to a firm's sale of output. We elaborate upon this by noting here that the relationship between revenues and output depends on the **market structure**—referring to the number of firms operating in the market, the nature of competition between them, the ease of entry into and exit from the industry by a firm, and the nature of the product. In this chapter, we focus on a market structure, called **perfect competition**, which is of central importance in economics.

8.2.1 Perfect Competition

Perfect competition or a **perfectly competitive industry** is defined by the following characteristics.

(a) All firms sell a very homogeneous, i.e., an identical product.
(b) There is a large number of buyers and a large number of small sellers (producers or firms) in the industry.
(c) There is free entry and exit for firms.

Consider for instance wheat or onion. These are homogeneous products—same or identical everywhere (unlike cars that come in various designs, quality, etc.). The same is true of leather football or cooking gas. In general, by a "homogeneous" or "identical" product we refer to a standardised item for which inherent quality differences are minimal and which does not come in different designs or on which consumers do not have different perceptions.[1]

As additional examples of which goods are homogeneous and which are not, various computer-related items have become standardised items these days, which was not true in the 1980s or even in 1990s. A pen drive with 128 GB space and usb-c port for example is almost the same everywhere in the world and quality differences among different brands are rather minor. In contrast, TVs come in different sizes, features, and looks. They are not homogeneous. Different types of cotton shirts may have the same "quality" but looks may be different, so that they are not necessarily homogeneous from the perspective of consumers. Sometimes, products like toothpaste or lipstick may be the same basically, but through advertising, consumers see them differently—and their perception matters. Such products are not considered homogeneous from the viewpoint of economic analysis.

The important implication of a product being homogeneous is that all firms that produce and sell it *must* charge the same price. It is because, between two firms, if one charges a higher price than the other, no one will buy from the former.[2]

Product homogeneity and the existence of a large number of firms imply that (i) each firm is very small compared to the market and (ii) no single firm can influence the price. In other words, *a firm in a perfectly competitive industry is a* **price taker**: it takes the market price as given. Still put differently, the market price is *exogenous* to any individual firm. This is another way of saying that *in a perfectly competitive market no firm possesses any market power.*[3]

The last feature leads to a simple relationship between a firm's output and a firm's total revenues, equal to price (p) times the quantity sold/produced (y), i.e., $TR = py$. Since p is given to the firm, its total revenues must equal $p \times 1$ if one unit is sold, $p \times 2$ if two units are sold, and so on. Plotting these points against the output, we obtain the *TR* curve in Figure 8.1. It is a ray from the origin with slope equal to p everywhere, because p is given to the firm.[4] A decrease or an increase in p rotates this curve clockwise or anti-clockwise, respectively.

We know from Chapter 7 that marginal revenues (*MR*s) are additions to the total revenues (*TR*). In Figure 8.1, notice by how much *TR* increases as one extra unit is produced. As output is increased from 0 to 1, $MR = p - 0 = p$. Similarly, if output increases from 1 unit to 2 units, $MR = 2p - p = p$. Thus, *under perfect*

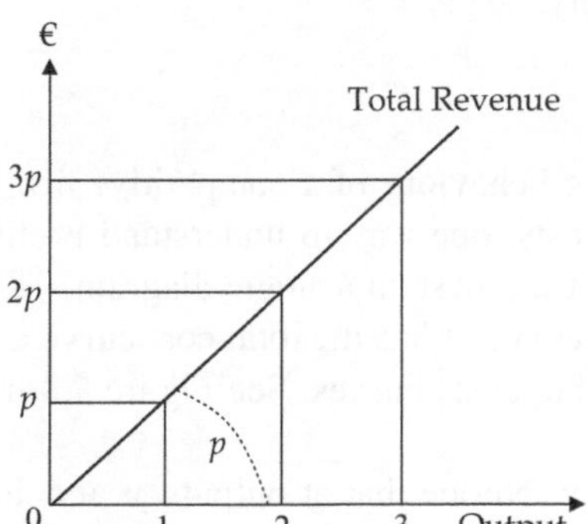

FIGURE 8.1 The Total Revenue Curve Facing a Perfectly Competitive Firm

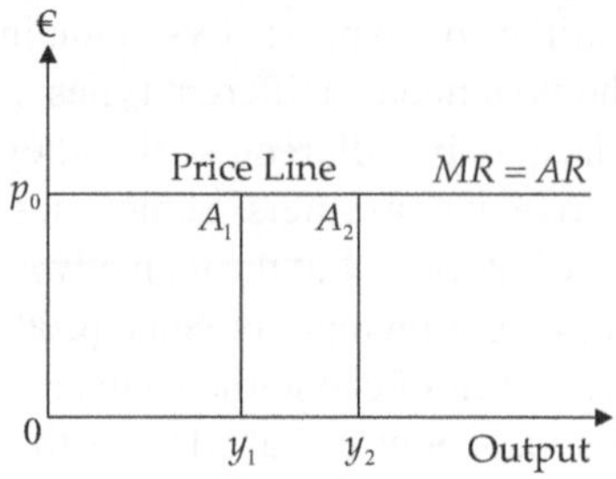

FIGURE 8.2 The Price Line

competition, $MR = p$, the price. This is because product price is given or is exogenous to a firm.[5]

What is the expression for average revenues (AR)? It is total revenues (pq) divided by the quantity produced and sold (q), equal to p. That is, $AR = p$. Note that this has nothing to do with price being given to a firm. It holds in general, regardless of whether the firm is perfectly competitive.

As you will see shortly, it will be useful to have another graph called the **price line**, defined as a plot of price facing a competitive firm against its output. However, since p is exogenous to the firm it is simply a flat line as in Figure 8.2. From the price line, we can measure the total revenues. If, for instance, the output $= y_1$, $TR = 0p_0 \times 0y_1 =$ the area $0p_0A_1y_1$. Similarly, at $y = y_2$, the total revenues equal the area $0p_0A_2y_2$, and so on. *Hence, the (rectangular) area under the price line measures total revenues for a perfectly competitive firm.*

Sometimes the price line is referred as the "demand curve facing a competitive firm," in the sense that irrespective of how much a firm wants to sell or equivalently how much the consumers are buying from the firm, the price they are paying does not change.[6] If the firm charges any price greater than the market price, it faces the prospect of zero demand for its output. Hence, the demand curve facing a competitive firm has an infinite price elasticity, i.e., $e_p = \infty$.

8.3 Producer's Equilibrium: Short Run

We are ready to analyse the profit-maximising behaviour of a competitive firm. Since profits are total revenues minus total costs, one way to understand profit maximisation is to look at the curves representing these in a single diagram—as in Figure 8.3. Along with the straight-line TR curve, it has the total cost curve as the vertical sum of total fixed and total variable costs curves. See Figure 7.8 in Chapter 7.

We can "read" profits at any level of output. Notice that at outputs $\underline{y}$ and $\bar{y}$, the two curves intersect, implying that $TR = TC$ and thus profits are zero. In other words, these are the "break-even" levels of output. If the output is less than $\underline{y}$ or

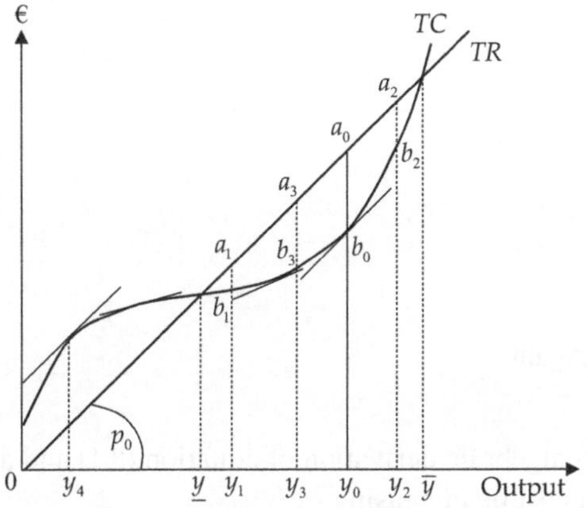

FIGURE 8.3 Profit Maximisation by a Competitive Firm

greater than $\overline{y}$, $TR < TC$ and hence profits are negative, i.e., there are (abnormal) losses.

However, in-between $\underline{y}$ and $\overline{y}$, $TR > TC$ and there are (abnormal) profits. Obviously, the firm would produce somewhere in this range. By visual inspection, note that producing y_3 generates profit (equal to a_3b_3), which is higher than the profit (a_1b_1) associated with y_1 or the profit (a_2b_2) associated with output y_2.But what is the level of output at which the profit is the maximum? Realise that it *has* to be the output y_0 at which the slope of the *TR* curve (= the price p_0) is equal to the slope of the *TC* curve (= the marginal cost), i.e., at which the tangent to the *TC* curve is parallel to the *TR* line. Any output higher or less than y_0 yields less profit compared to y_0. We can then say that profit is maximised at that level of output at which price equals marginal cost.

This condition does not however completely identify the profit-maximising output. It is because, notice that at the output y_4 also, the slope of the *TR* line is equal to the slope of the *TC* curve, i.e., $p = MC$ holds. However, obviously, profit is not maximised at y_4. Indeed, there is a loss at this output. Apart from profit and loss, there is another difference between y_4 and y_0. That is, the *MC* (the slope of the *TC* curve) decreases with output around y_4, while it increases with output around y_0. This is the basis on which we differentiate between y_0 and y_4, and identify the profit-maximising output y_0. In general then, the profit-maximising or the **optimal output** of a competitive firm is characterised by the following conditions:

$$p = MC; \; MC \text{ is increasing in output.} \tag{8.1}$$

Often, the condition that *MC* is increasing is implicitly understood by economists and the profit-maximisation condition for a competitive firm is (loosely) stated as

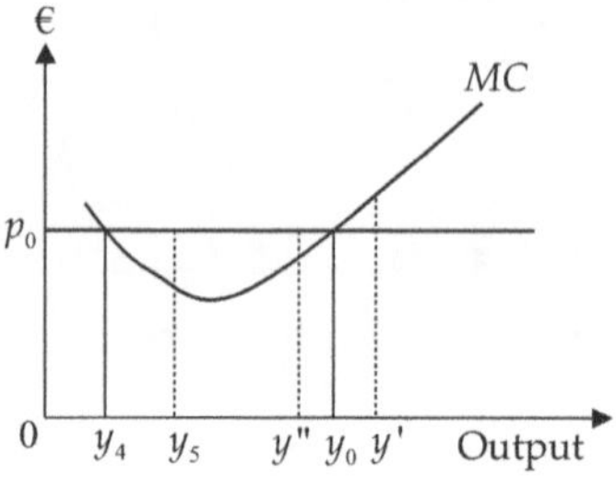

FIGURE 8.4 Profit Maximisation Once Again

"$p = MC$." Appendix 8.A contains an algebraic derivation of equation (8.1) and a discussion on condition that marginal cost be increasing.

The economic reasoning behind the profit-maximising conditions of equation (8.1) can be understood via Figure 8.4, which depicts the price line at $p = p_0$ and a firm's *MC* curve corresponding to the *TR* and *TC* lines in Figure 8.3.

We see that $p = MC$ holds at outputs y_0 and y_4 which correspond to the same points in Figure 8.3. Around y_4, *MC* is decreasing, while around y_0, it is increasing in output. Applying economic reasoning, we now argue that profit is maximised at y_0, not at y_4. Suppose that the firm is producing at y_0. Consider an alternative of producing a slightly higher amount say y'. Since *MC* is increasing, $MC > p_0$. By definition, *MC* is the cost of producing the additional amount. Similarly, $MR = p$ is the additional revenue. Thus $MC > p_0$ means that the additional cost is greater than the additional revenue. It implies that producing an amount slightly higher than y_0 yields less profit. Similarly, if the firm produced a bit less than y_0, say y'', $MC < p_0$. This holds also because *MC* is increasing in output around y_0. That $MC < p_0$ as output is reduced from y_0 means that savings in cost are less than revenues foregone. It is also a worse situation compared to producing at y_0. This proves that around y_0, producing y_0 yields maximum profit.

On the other hand, suppose the firm is producing at y_4. Because *MC* is decreasing, if the firm produces a slightly higher amount (say y_5), the market price would exceed *MC*, i.e., extra revenue to be earned would be higher than extra cost to be incurred. This will bring more profits. Therefore, producing at y_4 cannot be maximising profits. This completes the argument that out of the two output levels where $p = MC$, the profit-maximising one is where *MC* increases with output.

8.4 Profit–Loss Calculations and the Shut-Down Condition

Profits and losses can be seen in a different diagram, which is quite useful. Turn to Figure 8.5, which depicts various price lines and the firm's *MC*, *AVC*, and *ATC* curves. At price p_0, the profit-maximising output is y_0, as the *MC* at this output is equal to p_0 and the *MC* curve is rising. The firm is making profits. The *ATC* is

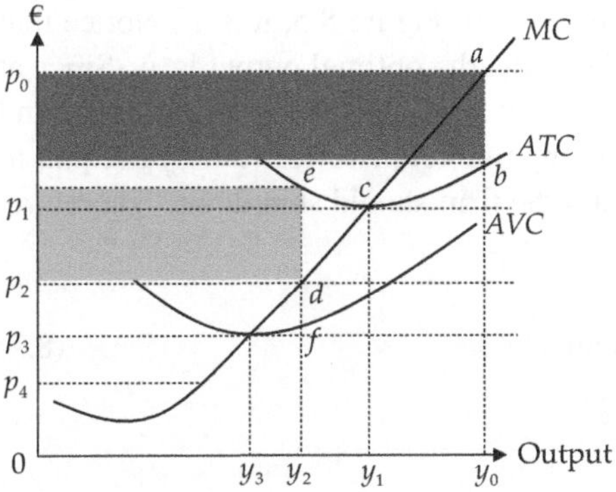

FIGURE 8.5 Profits, Losses, and the Shut-Down Condition

indicated at b and the profit per unit of output, $p - ATC$, is the line segment ab. Total profits are shown by the rectangular dotted area, equal to output times the profit per unit of output.

Consider next the price p_1. The price line goes through the minimum point on the ATC curve, i.e., p_1 equals the minimum ATC. The optimal output is y_1. Notice that at this output price equals the average total cost and thus profits are zero; in the business language, the firm is "breaking even." We can generally define **break-even price** as that price at which profits are zero, and, say that the break-even price for a competitive firm is equal to the minimum ATC.

It is clear that at any price less than p_1, the firm incurs losses. Consider p_2 for example. The optimal output is y_2. The ATC is indicated at the point e and ed measures losses per unit. Total losses are shown by the stripped rectangular area. Similarly, you can calculate losses at the price p_3. They will be greater. At a further lower price such as p_4, losses will be even greater than at p_3.

A natural question arises here: Shouldn't the firm shut down (i.e., produce nothing) if there are losses? The answer is: "not necessarily." Why? It is because in the short run the firm *must* pay the fixed cost even if it decides not to produce any amount. For example, it must pay the rent as per a signed lease, repay loan to the bank, and so on. In other words, shutting down does not necessarily imply that profits are zero. In the short run, it involves a loss, equal to TFC. It is then possible that in not shutting down the firm's losses are less, compared to shutting down. If the firm shuts down, its losses are TFC. Instead, if it operates (and produces where $p = MC$), the losses are $TC - TR = TFC - TVC - TR = TFC - AVC.y - py = TFC - (AVC - p)y$. Therefore, the difference between the two levels of loss $= (AVC - p)y$. It then follows that the firm shuts down if $p < AVC$, i.e., if the market price is less than the average variable cost at the profit-maximising output.[7]

It turns out that the above condition can be stated with more precision. Consider the price, which is equal to the minimum *AVC*. In Figure 8.5, it is p_3 Notice that at this price if the firm follows the $p = MC$ rule, the optimal output is y_3. Since at this output $p = AVC$, the firm should be indifferent between shutting down and not shutting down. It then follows that at any market price less than p_3 (equal to the minimum *AVC*), we have $p < AVC$ and the firm should shut down. Therefore, we can state

$$\text{Shut} - \text{Down Condition}: p < \text{minimum}\, AVC. \tag{8.2}$$

Example 8.2

A competitive firm has a short-run total cost schedule as given in Table 8.1. *What is the market price at which it will break even? What is the market price at which it will decide to shut down?*

Answer: Dividing the total cost by output gives the *ATC*. See at which level output *ATC* is minimised. The minimised *ATC* itself is the break-even price. As we go down the Table 8.1 from output equal to 1 to output equal to 9, the *ATC*s are respectively $4,000, $2,400, $1,800, $1500, $1,360, $1,300, $1,385, $1,425, and $1,600. Hence, the break-even price is $1,300.

Next, note that at zero output, the total cost is $3,000. Hence, $3,000 is the total fixed cost. If we deduct this from the total costs, we get the *TVC*. As we increase output, starting at 1, the *TVC*s are, respectively, equal to $1,000, $1,800, $2400, $3,000, $3,800, $4,800, $6,500, $8,500, and $11,400. Dividing these by the respective output, *AVC*s are, respectively, equal to $1,000, $900, $800, $750, $760, $800, $927, $10,625, and $1,267. The minimum *AVC* is the price at which the firm will shut down and this is equal to $750.■

TABLE 8.1 Short-Run Total Cost

Output	*Short-Run Total Cost ($)*
0	3,000
1	4,000
2	4,800
3	5,400
4	6,000
5	6,800
6	7,800
7	9,500
8	11,500
9	14,400

TABLE 8.2 Short-Run Marginal Cost

Output	*Short-Run Marginal Cost ($)*
0	–
1	1,000
2	800
3	600
4	600
5	800
6	1,000
7	1,700
8	2,000
9	2,900

Example 8.3

Consider a competitive firm whose short-run total cost schedule is given in Table 8.1. *The market price it faces is $2,000. How much should it produce in order to maximise its profits? Is the firm making profits or incurring losses?*

Answer: We first derive the marginal cost schedule from the total cost schedule. This is given in Table 8.2. The price = marginal cost condition is satisfied at output = 8. We also check that marginal cost is increasing around this level of output (it is $1,700 at output = 7, $2,000 at output = 8 and $2,900 at output = 9). Thus, profit is indeed maximised at output = 8. The maximised profit is equal to $TR - TC$ = $2,000 ×8 – $11,500 = $4,500.[8]■

8.5 Short-Run Supply Curve

Having understood profit maximisation and the shut-down behaviour, it is "easy" to "derive" the supply curve, introduced back in Chapter 2. Recall that a firm's supply curve is one showing various quantities it is willing to produce and supply to the market at various prices, given technology, and input prices. It is the counterpart of the demand curve in consumer theory. As said earlier, in consumer theory, the demand for a commodity was derived from the consumer's optimal choice of the consumption bundle. Likewise, the supply curve is derived from the producer's optimal/rational choice of output.

Refer to Figure 8.5. If the market price is p_0, we know that the profit-maximising output is y_0, where $p_0 = MC$. Thus , y_0 is what the firm would supply to the market at price p_0. This price–quantity pair is simply the point *a*. Similarly, at the price p_1, the firm would supply the quantity y_1, and the corresponding point on the *MC* curve is *c*. The locus of points *a*,*c*, and so on along the *MC* curve is then the supply curve. However, not all the points on the *MC* curve would lie on the supply curve. We have just seen that the firm does not operate below the minimum *AVC*, which is also a point on the *MC* curve. We can then say that *a firm's short-run supply curve is its short-run marginal cost curve over and above the minimum AVC point.* Since *MC* is rising, over and above the minimum *AVC* point on it, the supply curve is upward-sloping. This is the economic foundation behind the supply curve.

What factors can shift a firm's supply curve? Since it is a part of the *MC* curve, whatever shifts the *MC* curve would shift the supply curve. From what we have learnt in Chapter 7 about the shift of the short-run *MC* curve, it follows that a technological improvement shifts the supply curve to the right, whereas an increase in an input price or in the rate of a business tax shifts the supply curve to the left. These shifts were discussed back in Chapter 2. Here we see their micro basis.

8.5.1 Time Horizon and the Market Period

Remember that we are considering a short-run period, meaning an interval of time during which a firm can vary some inputs, but not all inputs. As a result, the supply is upward-sloping to the right.

However, if time period is very short, it is only natural that a firm cannot vary the employment of *any* input. Such a short period is called **market period** in economics. How does the supply curve in a market period look like? For instance, think of an agricultural good like paddy. It takes months between preparing the soil for the seeds and getting paddy ready for sale in the market during the spring season. How does the supply curve of paddy look like during the spring time? Given that it is already harvested and ready for sale, the quantity is fixed, *irrespective of the price it is going to fetch.* Accordingly, the supply curve for paddy during spring would be vertical, as shown in Figure 8.6, where $\overline{YY}$ is the given quantity available for sale.

In sum, *a period so short that no inputs and output can change is called the* **market period** and *the corresponding supply curve in the market period is vertical.*

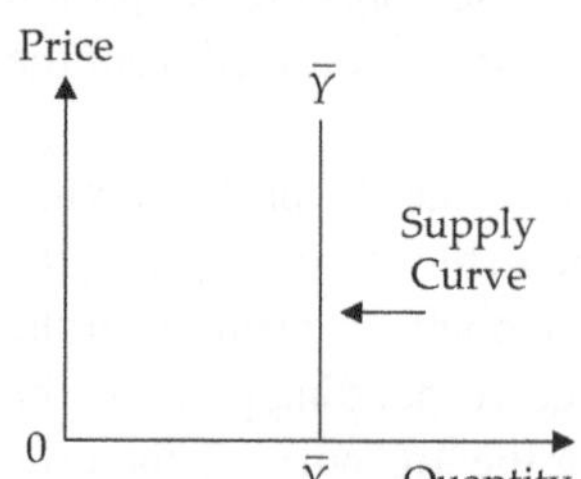

FIGURE 8.6 Supply Curve in the "Market Period"

8.6 Long Run

In the long run when all—rather than some—inputs are variable, the profit-maximising behaviour of a perfectly competitive firm remains nearly the same qualitatively as in the short run. Profit is maximised at the output where the *long-run* marginal cost (*LMC*) is equal to price and *LMC* is increasing in output. For instance, in Figure 8.7 that depicts the *LMC* curve and the *LAC* (long-run average cost) curve, if market price is p_0, the firm produces y_0 and there are abnormal profits (see panel (a)). At p_e, the firm produces y_e and the profits are zero (see panel (b)). This is the break-even price, equal to the minimum *LAC*.

However, there is one important difference with the short run. Since there are no fixed costs, the firm would shut down—and leave the industry—as long as *any* loss is made in the long run. Why would a rational firm stay if it expects to lose in the long run? In view of Figure 8.7(b), we see that losses occur if $p < p_e$. Hence, the output or the quantity supplied is zero as long as price is less than the minimum average cost: *the long-run supply curve of a firm is the long-run marginal cost curve over and above the minimum long-run average cost point.*

8.6.1 Comparison with the Short-Run Supply Curve

Although both short-run and long-run supply curves are upward-sloping, there is a qualitative difference between them (apart from which part of the respective *MC* curve they belong to). Recall that in the market period no inputs can be varied, and the supply curve is vertical. Over the short run, the firm has some flexibility, i.e., some input level can be changed, and the supply curve is upward-sloping rather than vertical. Thus, the short-run supply curve is more elastic than the market-period supply curve. In the long run, the firm has even more flexibility, as it can change the level of *any* input. Therefore, it can adjust its output more with respect to a given change in the product price. Accordingly, the long-run supply

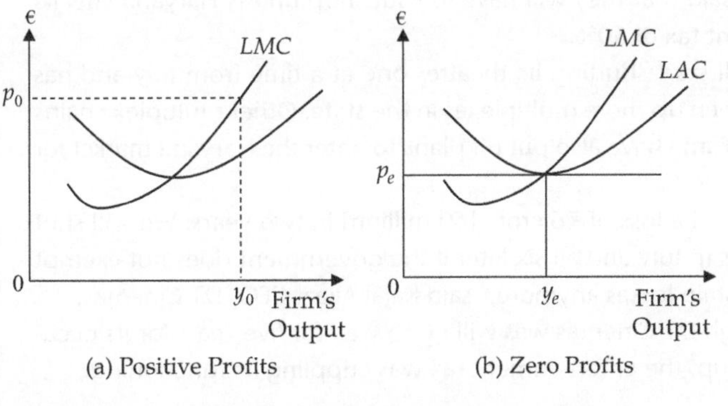

FIGURE 8.7 Competitive Equilibrium in the Long Run

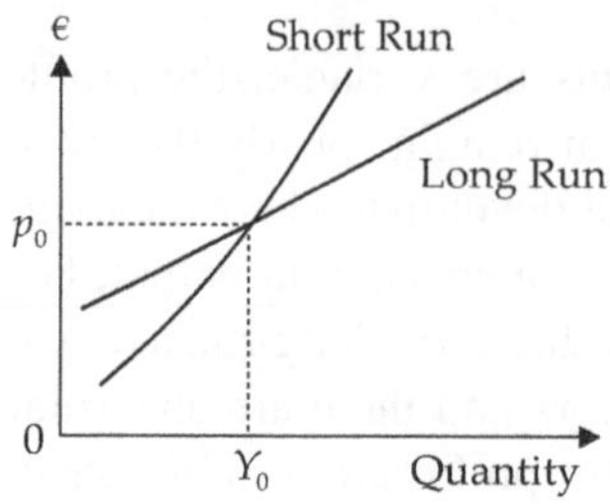

FIGURE 8.8 Short-Run versus Long-Run Supply Curves

curve is more elastic than the short-run supply curve, meaning graphically that *the long-run supply curve is more elastic and hence flatter than the short-run supply curve.*

This is illustrated in Figure 8.8. Suppose that initially in a long-run equilibrium the firm was producing Y_0 at price p_0. If there is a price change from p_0 (upward or downward), the output or supply adjustment is greater along the long-run than along the short-run supply curve.

8.6.2 Free Entry and Exit

BOX 8.1 HINDUSTAN TIMES, MAY 21, 2005

Gurgaon Cinemas Give up, Plan Exit

By S. K. Ahuja

Gurgaon, 20 May

The show is over Gurgaon multiplexes. Grappling with heavy losses, multiplex players have said that they will have to shut shop unless Haryana cuts its steep entertainment tax of 50%.

DT cinemas will start shutting its theatres one at a time from July and has shelved plans to open up more multiplexes in the state. Other multiplex chains such as INOX and Fame have also put off plans to enter the Haryana market for the same reason.

"We have suffered a loss of ₹6 crore [60 million] in two years. We will shut two of our theatres in July and all six later if the government does not exempt tax. We cannot sustain losses anymore," said Kajal Aijaz, CEO, DT Cinemas.

Aijaz said though DT Cinemas was willing to wait for five years for its occupancy rate to pick up, the entertainment tax was crippling its functioning.

Ajay Bijli, of PVR Cinemas, which has seven screens in Gurgaon, confirmed that PVR was losing ₹2 crore [20 million] a year and demanded that the state's entertainment tax be done away with. "Looking at the mounting losses, we will have no option but to shut down in due course," he told HT [*Hindustan Times*].

With cinemas being big crowd-pullers, this is not good news for the malls-cum-multiplexes that have seen a spate of closures by stores recently.

Admitting that the high tax was a big deterrent to entering the market, Shyam Shroff of Fame said: "We had plans to set up a multiplex in Gurgaon but we backed out because of the high tax structure."

DT and PVR have formed an association, the Multiplex Association of Haryana, to take up their cause with the government. But though Ajiz, its president, has already me Haryana Chief Minister B. S. Hooda, there has not been any progress on the tax front so far.

Recall that free entry and exit is a central characteristic of a perfectly competitive market, and we haven't said anything about it yet. But in the long run it is relevant—because in the long run new firms are likely to enter the industry or some existing firm would exit depending on whether they are earning (abnormal) profits or incurring (abnormal) losses. See Box 8.1 for a newspaper write-up in the 2000s in New Delhi, India, namely (*Hindustan Times*) on how taxes forced entrepreneurs in the multiplex movie-theatre industry to quit a market in the satellite city of Gurgaon in the state of Haryana.

Industry equilibrium in terms of entry and exit is attained in the market when no firms have any incentive to enter or quit. This happens when economic profits are zero. That is, entrepreneurs earn only their opportunity cost or what is called **normal profit**.

What is the zero-profit condition? We can write long-run profits = (price − *LAC*) × output, and, thus, these profits are zero if and only if price = *LAC*. Combining this with the profit-maximising condition of a firm, the overall firm-cum-industry equilibrium conditions are:

$$\text{Price} = LMC = LAC. \tag{8.3}$$

The firm–industry equilibrium is illustrated in Figure 8.7(b). The equilibrium price is p_e, equal to the long-run minimum average cost, and the equilibrium firm-output is y_e. We see that at this price-output combination, both the profit-maximising (price = *MC*) condition and the zero-profit (price = *AC*) condition are met. What is implicit here is that there is some definite, equilibrium number of firms operating in the market. It is because, relative to market demand, too many firms would mean abnormal losses and too few firms would imply abnormal profits. A diagram such as Figure 8.7(b) cannot however show the equilibrium number of firms.

Realise that in the presence of entry and exit, an individual firm's supply curve remains the same as before. But the nature of the industry supply curve—the horizontal sum of individual supply curves—is quite different—because the number of firms in the industry changes in response to profits or losses being made. It is interesting that *the long-run industry supply curve with free entry and exit of firms is a horizontal straight line* (rather than an upward-sloping curve). How is that?

Given the cost curves, we know the minimum *LAC*, say, equal to *m*.[9] Consider the following possibilities. (i) Suppose the long-run market price is less than *m*. Then, no firm will be present in the industry in the long run; the industry output will be zero. (ii) Suppose the price is greater than *m*. New firms will keep entering and thus the industry output will be arbitrarily large. In the language of mathematics, it is *infinity* (∞). (iii) If the price is exactly equal to *m*, the industry output is indeterminate from the supply side. Of course, in the last case the equilibrium quantity supplied to the market must equal to the quantity demanded along the market demand at the price equal to *m*.

By combining the possibilities (i), (ii), and (iii), the industry supply curve is then a horizontal line whose height is equal to the minimum *LAC*, as shown in Figure 8.9.

The practical implication of such long-run equilibrium with free entry and exit is that the price is driven down to its unit cost. Note that the unit cost of a product depends, in part, on technology. Thus, in the long run the price of a product is essentially dictated by its technology—an important remark made by Alfred Marshall long time ago.

A good example of competition driving down the price to the unit cost as firms enter and leave the industry is the personal-computer market. The technology is so standard that assembling a computer takes no more than an hour and loading software is normally a two-to-three-hour job. Entering this business and getting out of it are rather easy. As you can look around and see, there are many computer

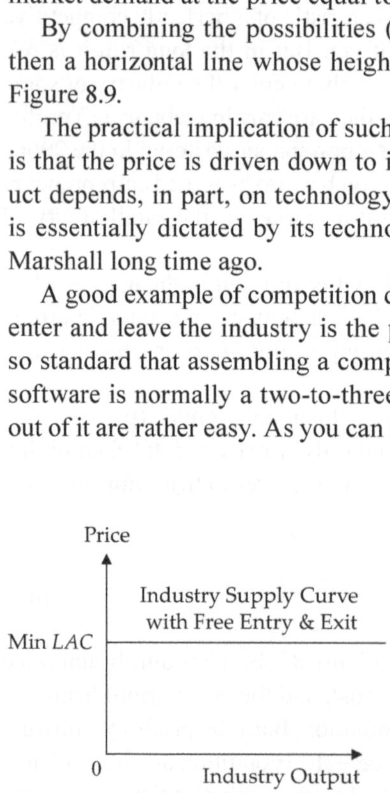

FIGURE 8.9 Long-Run Industry Supply Curve with Free Entry and Exit

vendors in the market in most parts of India. You ask any vendor today about how much profit they make per one unit sold. The business is so competitive that it is a few hundred rupees at the most.

However, in some other businesses the entry and exit processes are costly and time-consuming. In the old era of *licence raj* in India, to start any major business one was supposed to obtain a licence and a series of clearances from the government. Any experienced, aged entrepreneur will tell you how painful it was to obtain these permissions in terms of crossing numerous layers of bureaucracy, corruption, and delay. However, in the post-liberalisation era it is a much simple process. However, compared to many other countries, it is still more difficult and costly to start a business in India.

Of course, getting a licence may be just one deterrent of entry into a business. Another may be initial capital needed to set up a plant and getting production going. When the technology is such that the initial capital requirement is huge, it works as a natural deterrent to entry. Typically, in these industries, those who can enter and survive, earn abnormal profits over a long period of time (as it is hard for others to enter).

Example 8.4

A competitive industry has many identical firms. Each firm's long-run marginal cost schedule is given in Table 8.3. *The market demand schedule for the product is given in* Table 8.4. *In the long-run equilibrium, how many firms would operate in this industry?*

Answer: From the long-run marginal cost schedule, we can derive the long-run total cost schedule by adding up marginal costs. From the latter we can derive the long-run average schedule through dividing the total cost by output. The *LAC* schedule is given in Table 8.5. Notice LAC is minimum at output = 4. Hence, in the long-run equilibrium each firm produces 4 units. The (minimised) *LAC* = ₹8.5; this is the long-run market price, as in the long-run equilibrium the market price is equal to the minimum *LAC*. We now utilise Table 8.4. At price = ₹8.5, 440 units are demanded. In equilibrium, 440 units are produced in the industry. Since each firm produces 4 units, the number of firms in operation must be equal to 440/4 = 110.■

TABLE 8.3 LMC

Output	LMC *(₹)*
1	10
2	9
3	8
4	7
5	9
6	11
7	12

TABLE 8.4 Quantity Demanded

Price (₹)	*Quantity Demanded*
5.5	468
6	465
7.5	460
8	450
8.5	440
9	420
9.5	400

TABLE 8.5 LAC

Output	Lakh *(₹)*
1	10
2	9.5
3	9
4	8.5
5	8.6
6	9
7	9.43

Facts and Insights

- Economic analysis and decision-making consider economic profit, not accounting profit.
- A perfectly competitive market structure is defined by three central characteristics: (i) the product is homogeneous, (ii) there are large number of buyers and small firms, and (iii) there is free entry and exit.
- The product being homogeneous, and the industry being populated with large number of firms imply that an individual firm is a price taker in a competitive market, and no single firm has any market power.
- A perfectly competitive firm maximises profits by producing at a level of output such that the market price equals the marginal cost, and the marginal cost is increasing in output.
- In the short run a firm may be making profits or incurring losses.
- Even if a firm is making losses in the short run, it should not necessarily shut down because the firm must pay the fixed cost whether or not it shuts down.
- The shut-down price equals the minimum average variable cost for a competitive firm.
- The supply curve of a competitive firm is a part of its marginal cost curve.
- In the market period the supply of a product is fixed, and the supply curve is vertical.

- The long-run supply curve is more price elastic than the short-run supply curve.
- In the long run with free entry and exit, the firms make zero economic profits, or, which is the same thing, make normal profits.
- The long-run firm-cum-industry equilibrium is characterised by the market price being equal to the long-run marginal cost as well as the long-run average cost.
- The long-run industry supply curve with free entry and exit is a horizontal straight line.
- In the long-run competitive equilibrium the price of a product is essentially governed by its technology.

Exercises

Descriptive/Analytical

8.1. What is the difference between accounting and normal profits? Illustrate it through an example.
8.2. What are the features that characterise a perfectly competitive market?
8.3. Define break-even price and what is this price equal to (in principle) for a perfectly competitive firm in the short run? What is this price equal to in the long run?
8.4. What is the shut-down condition? How is this condition derived?

Short Answer (word limit = 500 approx.)

8.5. Give three examples of products or services (different from those in the text), which are not homogeneous.
8.6. Give two examples of products or services (different from those in the text), which are homogeneous.
8.7. Which assumptions of perfect competition imply that individual firms in perfect competition are price takers?
8.8. What is the shape of the total revenue curve of a perfectly competitive firm and why?
8.9. Why is $AR = MR$ for a competitive firm?
8.10. Assume that the marginal cost increases with output. Briefly explain why "price = marginal cost" is the profit-maximising condition?
8.11. At a given level of output the "price = marginal cost" condition is met, but the marginal cost is decreasing in output. Why isn't profit maximised at this level of output?
8.12. "A firm's short-run supply curve is its marginal cost curve over and above the minimum AVC point." Defend or refute.

8.13. "A firm's long-run supply curve is more inelastic than its short-run supply curve." Defend or refute.

8.14. Which conditions characterise the long-run equilibrium in a competitive industry (with entry and exit) and what is the rationale behind them?

8.15. Considering the entry and exit of firms in the long run, how does the long-run supply curve of a competitive industry look like and why?

8.16. Explain why Marshall observed that the long-run price in a competitive market is determined mainly by technology, not demand.

8.17. Briefly discuss some of the deterrents of entry into a market.

Quizzes/Numerical

8.18 Guha owns a publishing company in the basement of the building that he owns. Within a quarter (three months), the company earns ₹17 lakh (1 lakh = hundred thousand) revenues. The salary payments to employees are ₹6 lakh. Raw material and machine maintenance costs are ₹5 lakh. Machines were bought previously by taking a loan from the bank, the principal and interest cost per quarter is ₹4 lakh. If Guha would have rented his basement, he would have earned a rental income of ₹5 lakh. What are his quarterly accounting and economic profits?

8.19 "In the short run a competitive firm always makes abnormal profits." Defend or refute.

8.20 A competitive firm's total variable cost schedule is given as follows. What is the shut-down price in this example?

Output	*Total Variable Cost ($)*
0	0
1	5
2	9
3	12
4	18
5	25
6	33
7	42
8	54

8.21 "At the shut-down price, the firm breaks even." Defend or refute.

8.22 "If a firm shuts down, its short-run profits are zero." Defend or refute.

8.23 What is "market period"? What is the elasticity of the supply curve in the market period?

8.24 A firm's *LAC* curve is minimised at output equal to 20 and the minimum *LAC* is equal to €50. The market demand schedule is given as follows.

Price (€)	Quantity Demanded
10	1,950
20	1,700
30	1,400
40	1,200
50	1,000
60	900
70	800

In the long-run equilibrium with free entry and exit, how much is sold in the market and what price? How many firms do operate in the market? (It is implicit here and in the text that all firms have the same cost function.)

8.25 A competitive firm's total cost is given by the mathematical relation $y^2 - 10y + 28$, where y denotes the output. Considering its profit maximisation in the short run, if the market price is 20, how much will this firm produce?

Appendix 8.A Profit Maximisation by a Perfectly Competitive Firm, Mathematically

A competitive firm's total revenue has the expression, *py*. Let $C(y)$ denote the total variable cost function and F the total fixed cost. The marginal cost is the first derivative of the total variable cost function, equal to $C'(y)$. Let $C''(y)$ denote the second derivative of the total variable cost function. If $C''(y)$ is positive (or negative), the *MC* increases (or decreases) with output. We express profits, π, as a function of y:

$$\text{À} = py - C(y) - F.$$

The firm chooses y to maximise π. The first-order condition of this maximisation is:

$$\frac{d\text{À}}{dy} = p - C'(y) = 0. \qquad \text{(A8.1)}$$

This says that $p = MC$, a necessary condition of profit maximisation by a perfectly competitive firm. The second-order condition of profit maximisation is that $d^2\text{À}/\,dy^2 < 0$. (The first-order and second-order conditions of unconstrained maximisation such as this are outlined in the General Appendix.) Totally differentiating $d\text{À}/\,dy$ with respect to y,

$$\frac{d^2\pi}{dy^2} = -C''(y).$$

Thus, the second-order condition is met if and only if:

$$C''(y) > 0. \tag{A8.2}$$

Equations (A8.1) and (A8.2) prove the conditions of profit maximisation summarised in equation (8.1).

Notes

1 Some people prefer purplish-red to light skin onions. Wheat from Australia may a bit different from that from Punjab. But these differences are very minor.
2 This is of course barring transport costs and ignoring informational problems.
3 While no single firm has any market power to dictate or influence price, a price, nonetheless, prevails in the market through interaction between sellers and buyers. This is sometimes referred to as "an invisible hand" of the market that sets prices and changes them.
4 If the firm had any influence on price the total revenue curve will not be a straight line.
5 If market structure were not competitive, MR will not be equal to p.
6 This is not however contrary to the law of demand, because here we are talking about the demand for the product by consumers from only one firm, *not* their total demand for the product.
7 If $p = AVC$, the firm is indifferent between shutting down and not shutting down.
8 Another way to check whether the firm is making a profit or loss is to compare the price with the break-even price. We already know from the Example 8.1 that the break-even price = \$1,300. Thus, the market price is greater than the break-even price and therefore the firm must be making profits. Moreover, note that profit is maximised at output = 7 also. Two alternative answers arise because output is not measured on a continuous scale in this example: output only takes integer values, not decimals.
9 In *Figure 8.7*(b), $m = p_e$.

9

EFFICIENCY OF COMPETITIVE MARKETS AND CORRECTIVE MEASURES

In the preceding chapters, our analysis has been positive, not normative. In this chapter, we turn to the normative question on the "efficiency" of the market economy we have studied thus far.

In a perfectly competitive market economy, both buyers and sellers are atomistic, very small compared to the whole market. No single agent wields any market power, that is, no buyer and seller can influence the market price singlehandedly. Based on this assumption, in Chapter 8, we studied in detail the behaviour of a perfectly competitive firm, which gives rise to its supply curve, introduced back in Chapter 2. Aggregating the supply curves gives the market supply curve. Consumer behaviour studied in Chapter 4 also assumed that a buyer or a household was a price taker and it leads to the demand curve. The interaction of supply and demand curves was analysed in Chapter 2. All this amounts to how a perfectly competitive market structure functions through a (perfectly) competitive price mechanism. To elaborate, a price serves as a beacon and guides the allocation of resources. If people begin to like a product and demand more, it tends to increase the market price. This is a signal for producers to produce and supply more to the market. Resources of the economy are reallocated towards the sectors with growing demand. The competitive price mechanism "smoothly" solves the three fundamental problems of an economy: what, how, and to whom, in an invisible manner, so to speak, by "an invisible hand" in the words of Adam Smith, regarded as the Father of Economics.

As discussed in Chapter 1, unlike in socialism, in a capitalist, private economy there is no apex decision-making body. The decisions are atomised and scattered among numerous economic agents trying to further their own self-interest. The

DOI: 10.4324/9781003452195-9

means of production are privately owned. There is a right to private property for everyone. One can inherit and bequeath wealth as one wishes.

In this chapter, we take a panoramic view of the price mechanism as the driving force of capitalism without getting into the nitty-gritty of it. This is akin to conducting a 360-degree appraisal as an HR manager does. It can also be seen as an internal audit of the working of the price mechanism under perfect competition. An alternative terminology would be the oft-repeated management tool of a SWOT analysis that identifies strengths, weaknesses, opportunities, and threats in a particular internal system or procedure.

Is a perfectly competitive economy the best or most efficient—in some sense—for the society or the economy? This is our central question in this chapter. And the answer is yes—under certain conditions. It is a profound result as it means that, in some situations at least, a decentralised, *laissez faire* (meaning complete freely operating), competitive market economy in which no economic agent has any market power, serves the society the best. Provocatively put, *in a perfectly competitive market-oriented economy, there is no clash between private self-interest and the society's interest.* There is no need for any policy intervention. It is most efficient from the perspective of the whole economy or society.

Because this result holds under some—rather ideal—conditions, it is very useful for a deeper understanding of practical economies where these conditions do not hold, since the implication is that when the actual conditions deviate from those "ideal conditions," a basis for economic policy intervention arises. The nature of the deviation dictates the required nature of policy intervention or corrective measures by the state or the government. Thus, in this chapter *we probe normative economics and the rationale behind economic policy intervention.* Put differently, when and how should we depart from unbridled capitalism or a complete *laissez fare*?

Furthermore, by being "best" under some conditions, a perfectly competitive market structure serves as a valuable benchmark against which we can approach to look at other forms of more realistic markets to be studied in the subsequent chapters. This is the reason behind our diversion to normative analysis in this chapter.

A few words about what we mean by the "state" and "government." By "state," we do not mean a province or state in a nation. It is a generic term used in political science in place of government. *For our purpose, state and government are synonyms.*[1]

9.1 Functions of a State

What are the functions of a state? First, it is security, law, order, and taxation. The nation must be defended against external aggression. It must ensure law and order. Those who flout rules of law must be apprehended and punished. The state needs funds to perform these tasks. This is where taxation comes in. It is a well-accepted practice in market economies. In this chapter we will see another rationale for certain kinds of taxation. Second, the market system is often criticised for creating massive disparities in wealth and income. Galbraith coined the term *crony capitalism*, which states that there exists a nexus between business class and the political class in order to help each other. At the same time, as a welfare state, governments often take upon themselves the task of redistribution. It can simply be expressed in the phrase **rob Peter to pay Paul**. Governments tax the rich and provide subsidies and freebees to the relatively poor. However, it has been observed that in the name of redistributive justice governments are very good at robbing Peter but very inefficient in paying Paul.[2] Third, the state produces or provides infrastructure and facilities that provide public goods such as highways, parks, etc. We will study the characteristics that distinguish a public good from a private good. Fourth, the government in some countries including India gets involved in a production activity directly, often as a public monopoly. For instance, railway services in India are provided by the Railway Department of India. Domestic air travel was a monopoly of Indian Airlines for many decades. The state was the only provider of telephony in India for many, many years. State production of a product or service as a monopoly is rationalised when competition is thought to lead to inefficiency in terms of higher costs or that private monopolies may take undue advantage of the consumers. We will discuss this in Chapter 10. However, the advocates of free-market system hold the view that "*Governments have no business to be in business*."

9.2 Social Welfare

Since we are talking about the society's interest, we must define some notion of social welfare. In the context of a market for a single good, in equilibrium a certain amount is produced, which, on the one hand, costs the society in terms of resources used, and, on the other, benefits the society in terms of providing consumption and utility. We may thus define

Social Welfare or Social Surplus (W) = Total social utility obtained from consuming a good − Total Social cost of its production. (9.1)

It can be expressed in another way. Assume that the total social utility is the same as the total utility to the consumers of the product. Similarly, assume that the total social cost of production is equal to the total cost of production faced by the producers. Under these assumptions, we can write

W = Total utility to the consumers − Total cost to the producers.

Next, recall from Chapter 5 that consumer surplus is defined as the total utility measured in money − the total expenditure on the product. Substituting this into the last expression of W,

W = Consumer surplus + {Total expenditure on the product − Total cost to the producers}.

Note that, by definition, the total expenditure on the product = the total revenues accruing to the firms. Hence, the term inside the curly brackets is simply the profits or producer surplus of the firms. Therefore, we can rewrite

Social welfare or Social surplus (W) = Consumer's surplus + Producers' surplus. (9.2)

This is intuitive. In the market for a good there are two types of economic agents: consumers and producers. Social welfare, as defined in equation (9.2), is simply the sum of the welfare of the two sets of parties. The question is: How do we measure social welfare?

9.2.1 Measuring Social Welfare

Figure 9.1 depicts the market demand curve and the market supply curve of a particular good. The competitive equilibrium is at the point E, with the price p_0 and the quantity exchanged y_0.

Focus first on the demand curve. Remember from the consumer surplus analysis in Chapter 5 that the total utility from consuming a product measured in money, which may be termed as the total gross benefit, is equal to the area under the demand curve. Thus if, for example, the amount y_1 is consumed, the total gross benefit = area $0ACy_1$.If y_2 is consumed, it is equal to $0ADy_2$, and so on. This is the first term in the right-hand side of in equation (9.1).

In Chapter 8, we learnt that the supply curve reflects the marginal costs at various levels of output and also that the area under the marginal cost curve is the total variable cost. Thus, the area under the supply curve equals the total variable cost. For instance, at the output y_1, it is equal to the area $0BGy_1$, and so on.

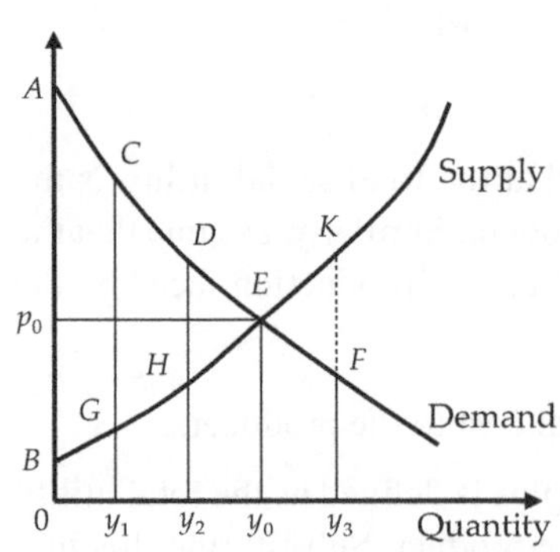

FIGURE 9.1 Measuring Social Welfare

Hence, applying the definition equation (9.1) social welfare at any given quantity = Area under the demand curve – area under the supply curve – total fixed costs (*TFC*).

Being a given amount, *TFC* does not matter in comparing social surplus associated with different quantities. Thus, we can ignore it for convenience (i.e., assume $TFC = 0$) and say that the *social welfare or the social surplus (W) = Area between the demand curve and the supply curve.*

In Figure 9.1, at y_1, $W = ACGB$ and at y_2, $W = ADHB$. At any point to the right of y_0, the measurement of *W* looks a bit different. For instance, at y_3, $W = 0AFy_3 - 0BKy_3 = AEB - EFK$.

9.2.2 Socially Optimal Output and the Perfectly Competitive Equilibrium

Now we can easily compare social surplus at various quantity levels. For instance, *W* at y_2 is greater than *W* at y_1. More generally, as we consider higher and higher levels of output to the left of y_0, the social surplus is greater. At y_0, it is equal to area *ABE*. Moreover, if we consider any level of output higher than y_0 (such as y_3), *W* is less. It then follows that the social surplus is maximised at y_0. Recalling that the supply curve is the marginal cost curve, we see that at y_0, price is equal to marginal cost, i.e.,

$$P = MC.$$

This is the condition for social surplus maximisation, or for, what is called, *social efficiency.*

The economic rationale behind it is that having an extra unit of a product provides utility to the society equal to the marginal utility, which, in turn, is equal to the price of the product, and, the extra cost of having it costs the society its marginal cost. Therefore, the social surplus is maximised when the extra benefit or extra utility (= *P*) is equal to the extra cost (= MC).

Realise that the condition $P = MC$ holds under perfect competition, i.e., in terms of Figure 9.1, y_0 is the amount produced in competitive equilibrium. Thus, *the social surplus is maximised, i.e., social efficiency is attained at the competitive equilibrium.* That is, a *competitive market structure serves the society the best or most efficiently*—when social welfare is defined and measured the way we have. Known as the **First Fundamental Theorem of welfare economics**, it is indeed a central result in the whole of economic science.

And no one yet has described the beauty of this result more tellingly than Adam Smith. According to him, in a perfectly competitive market, everyone, a producer or a consumer, is maximising his/her self-interest (either utility or profit), being guided by the market price on which he/she has no control. No one is doing anyone else any direct favour. Yet pursuing self-interest serves the society's interest. Thus, as mentioned earlier, in a perfectly competitive market of the kind we have studied, there is no conflict between individual interest and social interest. While we have "proved" this geometrically, it can be proven in a very general setting (which is beyond our scope).

9.3 Market Failures

The practical implication of the First Fundamental Theorem is profound, because it implies that an *actual* or a real-life market "fails" to perform in the best interest of society—i.e., there is a **market failure**, if

a. either the market structure is not perfectly competitive,
b. or, there are (special) conditions in a competitive market economy such that private interests do not match with the interests of the society.

Some of the non-competitive market structures and the policy implications in such markets will be discussed in the following chapters. In this chapter, we identify some of the situations in which the "market fails" *even when it is perfectly competitive.*

In the presence of market failure, *laissez faire* is obviously not the best system. Corrective measures in most situations of market failure fall squarely in the hands of the government through various tax-subsidy-transfer schemes. Those who are avid promoters of free market do not really deny a role of the government in managing the economy, but their objection lies in the extent or scope of state interference. This is like if a patient is sick, we all agree that she/he needs intervention by a doctor. But too much of medical intervention is harmful to a patient. (During the second wave of Covid-19 in India in early/mid-2021, some patients harmed themselves by taking antibiotics and steroids indiscriminately (Shelar, 2021).) If a government controls business, a side business of corruption, nepotism, etc. that are harmful to the economy can very well develop and stay, and, sometimes they—the side effects—do more harm than the originally intended benefit from a government's policy.

In what follows, we identify sources of market failure in competitive markets and discuss what the right policy intervention is, *in principle.*

9.3.1 Externalities

In Chapter 7, a distinction was drawn between private cost and social cost, based on the presence of externalities. If such a situation exists, the quantity at which social welfare is maximised differs from the competitive equilibrium—and the "*market fails.*"

Recall the example of a negative externality, where a set of factories are emitting pollution and causing health problems for the surrounding neighbourhoods. The social marginal cost (*SMC*) at each level of output is greater than the private marginal cost (*PMC*). Figure 9.2 illustrates this. The *PMC* curve is the competitive supply curve as in Figure 9.1 and the competitive equilibrium holds at the quantity y_0. However, the total social cost is the area under the *SMC* curve. Thus, the social surplus is maximised at the intersection of the demand curve and the *SMC* curve. The corresponding quantity is y_s, which is the socially optimal level of output. Clearly, the market fails. More precisely, the market "overproduces" compared to what is best for the society (by the amount $y_s y_0$ in Figure 9.2). The economic reason is clear. That is, private producers, in the pursuit of their self-interest, do not take into consideration the negative externality they are causing to the society. In the process, they overproduce compared to what is most efficient for the society.

What is then the corrective measure? *It is to tax the producers such that their own (private) cost, equal to the marginal production cost plus the tax per unit of output, coincides with the social marginal cost.* Such a tax shifts their supply curve to the left and the equilibrium from y_0 to y_s. In other words, the optimal policy intervention is to impose a tax on output, exactly equal to the marginal externality cost (in the example the health cost of pollution) being imposed to the society. Put simply, the optimal policy is to make the producers pay for the health cost of the society that their actions cause.

Mark however that if the government imposes a very heavy tax such that the tax-inclusive marginal private cost curve lies to the left of the social marginal cost curve, the social surplus is *not* maximised. It is because the product, although causing pollution on the one hand, is used nonetheless for society's consumption that generates obvious benefits, and, taxing it too much leads to such a large reduction of this benefit that it may outweigh the extra benefit from reduced pollution. Some well-minded yet overenthusiastic environmentalists seem to sometimes overlook this and clamour for draconian measures to curtail production of

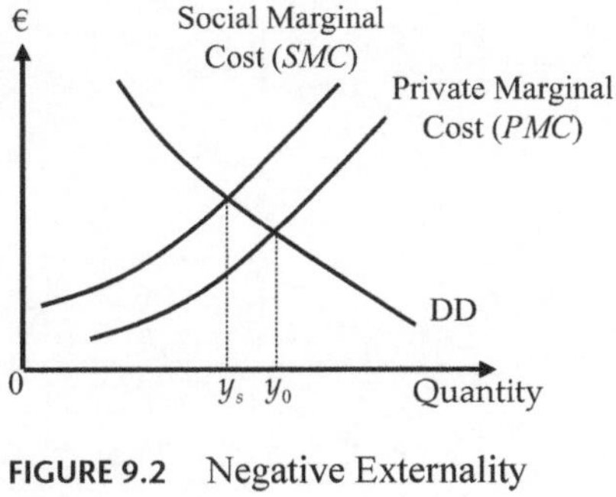

FIGURE 9.2 Negative Externality

goods that cause pollution. Our economic analysis says that in designing policy we should of course take into consideration the pollution cost to the society, but the benefit side of industrial goods should not be ignored. What is called for is a measurement of the (health) cost of pollution, or the cost of a negative externality and a policy that is commensurate with the measured cost. Of course, a long-term policy would be to encourage new, environment-friendly technology.

Figure 9.3 illustrates the optimal intervention issue in a different way. It measures the production tax along the x-axis. Increasing the tax rate, on the one hand, has the benefit of reducing production and thereby reducing pollution or the negative externality. This defines the marginal benefit curve resulting from increasing the tax rate. On the other hand, less output means less consumption of the good, which is a cost to the society. In our example, the chemicals produced by the chemical factories may be used in various useful drugs, so that the lesser the output, the lesser is the availability of useful drugs for various ailments. This is captured by marginal cost curve. The intersection of the two curves defines the magnitude of the optimal tax rate in principle—and this is the tax rate at which the private producers' tax-inclusive marginal cost curve coincides with the social marginal cost curve as in Figure 9.2. Such an optimal tax rate is called a **Pigovian tax**, named after a famous English economist Arthur Pigou, who was the first to distinguish between the private cost from the social cost and analyse how the government, by mixing taxes and subsidies, can correct market failures.

There is still another way to look at a Pigovian tax, as in Figure 9.4. It measures the tax rate on the x-axis, and social welfare on the y-axis. When the tax rate is zero, social welfare is measured at $0A$, which is the free-market, *laissez faire*, level of welfare. As the tax rate is gradually increased, the gap between the private and the social cost gets narrowed, and, as a result, social welfare gradually improves. It attains maximum at the tax rate t_s; this is where the social marginal cost is equal to the private marginal cost. Beyond, there is again a discrepancy between social and private costs and the social welfare falls with an increase in the tax. At any tax rate above $\overline{t}$, the associated level of welfare is even less than

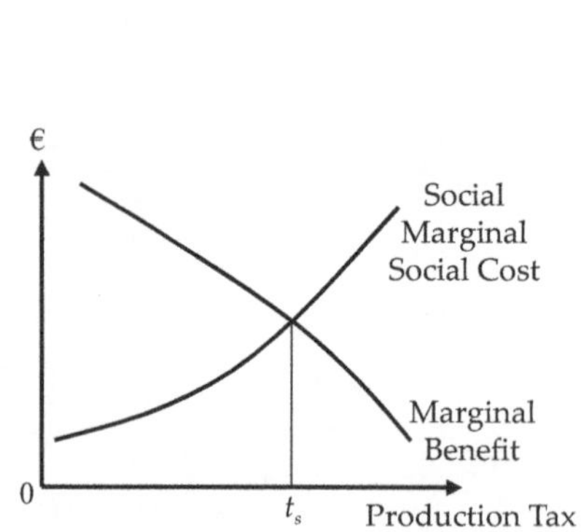

FIGURE 9.3 Negative Externality and Pigouvian Tax

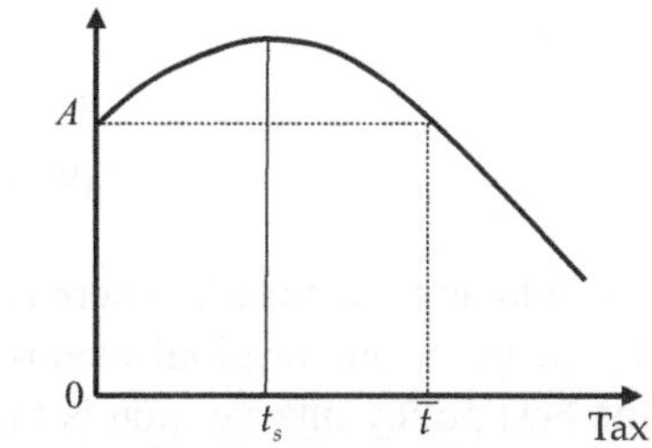

FIGURE 9.4 Pigouvian Tax Again

the *laissez faire* welfare level $0A$. The point is that *high-handed, heavy policy interventions have the potential of making the matter worse compared to a free-market approach, even if there exists a reason for policy intervention.*

While we have concentrated on negative externalities, positive externalities exist. Consider the nursery industry in a town. Suppose that there are many nursery firms spread out within a city. While they sell plants to customers, their very presence cleans air and offers greenery. In this case, the social marginal cost curve for plants and saplings produced and sold by nurseries lies below the private marginal cost, implying that the socially optimal output is higher than the free-market level of competitive output. The market fails. What is the optimal policy intervention? It is a production *subsidy*, i.e., a *negative* Pigovian tax for the nurseries.

Consider a slightly different situation. Suppose a competitive industry has two groups of firms: one having technology that is environment-friendly, i.e., it doesn't cause pollution problems, whereas the other does—as in our original example. Both types of firms coexist. Without loss of generality, let there be one firm in each group. Let these firms be called firm 1, the "clean" firm, and firm 2, the "dirty" one.

Here also the social marginal cost exceeds the private marginal cost for the industry as a whole. Figure 9.2 applies. A free, competitive industry will produce more at a point like y_0 than what is socially efficient like y_s. Some kind of a production tax is required to improve social efficiency.

Consider first a uniform production tax on both firms such that their marginal cost curves shift upward and the amount y_s is produced in equilibrium by both firms together. That is, this tax policy leads the industry to produce a total amount that is consistent with social efficiency. Is this policy intervention the most efficient or simply the efficient? The answer is "no," because in this case efficiency is governed not just by the total amount produced but also by an *allocation* of this total output.

More precisely, the overall social efficiency requires the condition $p = SMC_1 = SMC_2$, where SMC stands for the social marginal cost associated with a firm's activity. Since firm 1 doesn't pollute, $SMC_1 = PMC_1$, where PMC is the private marginal cost. But for firm 2, $SMC_2 = PMC_2 + MC_x$, where MC_x is the marginal cost of pollution. Thus, the efficiency condition is

$$p = PMC_1 = PMC_2 + MC_x. \tag{9.3}$$

That p must equal PMC_1 implies that firm 1 should not be taxed, whereas $p = PMC_2 + MC_x$ means that firm 2 should be taxed as in our original example, with the marginal tax equal to MC_x. Hence the best policy intervention is to impose an appropriate Pigovian tax *only* on firm 2, which pollutes and thus causes negative externality. There is no need to tax firm 1, which isn't causing harm.

We have looked at externalities caused by some production activities and the externalities are imposed on the consumers or households. There are externalities caused by one production activity towards another, or by one type of consumption activity towards others. A prime example of the latter is smoking. Smoking by smokers cause health problems for others too who inhale it. Therefore, a free-market equilibrium in terms of producing and consuming cigarettes is not socially optimal. There is over-consumption of this **de-merit good**. What is the nature of optimal policy? A tax on the consumption of cigarettes. Also, various public-area restrictions for smokers can be viewed as taxing cigarette consumption (insofar as it increases the inconvenience of smoking in the public).

We should also note that externalities can be caused by nature, an invisible hand of a different kind, like natural disasters that adversely affect economic activities. The appropriate corrective measures are relief packages, which are quite different from Pigovian subsidy programmes. An example is narrated in *Box 9.1*.

BOX 9.1 THE INVISIBLE HAND CAUSES MARKET FAILURE

Adam Smith invoked the "Invisible Hand" to explain the efficient working of market mechanism without visible (government) interference. Diego Maradona ascribed Argentina's epic win over England in 1986 (where his deciding goal was controversial) partly due to "the hand of God." In reality, however, markets fail due to various imperfections that invite government interference. Externality is one of the major reasons of market failure—negative externality to be more precise. These externalities are man-made. Pollution is one such example of market failure where governments penalise the polluters by putting a tax. What if the negative externality is not man-made? What about the pandemic caused by Covid-19?

This pandemic caused a strange situation for majority of colleges and universities across the United States, Canada, the United Kingdom, and other developed countries where the bulk of the student intake comes from countries like China, India, and other developing countries. With declining government help and local students' enrolment, most of these institutions survived on tuition-paying foreign students who wanted the social campus experience. Why should a parent in India pay ₹50,00,000 fee for his child if he studies online even when admitted in, say, Boston University?

Cohodes and Dynarski (2020) write: "Schools that chose not to open their campus risked losing customers to those that did." In the absence of government intervention, "schools did what they could to survive" and as a result, many educational institutions became hotbeds of pandemic spread.

9.3.2 Public Goods

Governments intervene in different markets not just by taxing or subsidising a product or service, but also by becoming the supplier. We are referring here not to a public-sector business, but to providing basic services like national defence, administrative services, etc.

The latter are **public goods**, as opposed to private goods which we buy normally in the market. By definition, a pure public good is one having two characteristics:

- Non-rivalry
- Non-excludability.

Non-rivalry *means that, if a fixed amount of the good is available for consumption, one person's consumption of it does not reduce the amount available for others.* Think of national defence. We "consume" national defence in that it provides us a service of safety. A fixed magnitude of national defence is enjoyed by all of us. The availability of national defence to you doesn't reduce the availability of it to me. In other words, we are not "rivals" in consuming the national defence service. As another example, think of plantation of trees along national highways to prevent soil erosion as well as provide greenery and clean environment. This is a service to all. My enjoyment of looking at the greenery doesn't reduce anything of what is available to you. Formally, if you and I each demand a public good equal to say y, our total demand for this good is equal to y, not $2y$.

Non-excludability *means that if it is available to one it is available to all.* No one can be excluded. Please do not confuse this with non-rivalry. Consider for example a fenced enjoyment park, which is only available to those who pay an entrance fee. Non-excludability doesn't hold here because those who don't pay can be excluded. But it is non-rival. If you and I both pay and enter the park, your consumption of the services of the park doesn't reduce mine (unless of course it is too crowded, so that the presence of other people hinders my enjoyment).

As we will now see, both these characteristics together create a situation where a public good cannot be provided by a private entrepreneur in that producing and pricing it will entail a loss, not profit.

Consider non-excludability first. Since no one can be excluded, everyone will expect others to pay for it and once the service is available consume it free. That is, everyone will have incentive to "free-ride" on others—a **free rider problem**—*meaning that everyone recognises that if others pay for a product or service, she/he doesn't have to pay and therefore no one has an incentive to pay.* It is like saying that "I prefer more of police protection in trains. But, I don't want to pay for it, because I know that if others somehow pay, I will enjoy the benefit too." The end result is that only a few end up paying for it. Thus, it will not be profitable for a private entrepreneur to supply the service. The market fails.

The problem caused by the non-rivalry property of the public good can be understood in the light of Figure 9.5. Suppose there are two individuals, Sachin and Brian. Their demand curves for the public good are given, respectively, by the lines *AB* and *DE*. How does the aggregate demand curve look like? Unlike that of a private good, *the aggregate demand for a public good is the vertical, not the horizontal, summation of the individual demand curves.* In Figure 9.5, the lines *AB* and *DE* are added vertically to obtain the line *GFE*, which is the aggregate demand curve. How?

Suppose that the total available quantity is y_0. Because it is a public good, non-rivalry implies that y_0 is available to Sachin and Brian each. From Sachin's demand curve, his total utility is equal to $0Aay_0$, the area under his demand curve. Similarly, the total utility to Brian is equal to the area $0Ddy_0$. The total utility to the two individuals together is equal to the area $0Ggy_0$, under the line *GFE*, which has a kink at the point *F*. The same holds at any other level of total quantity available for

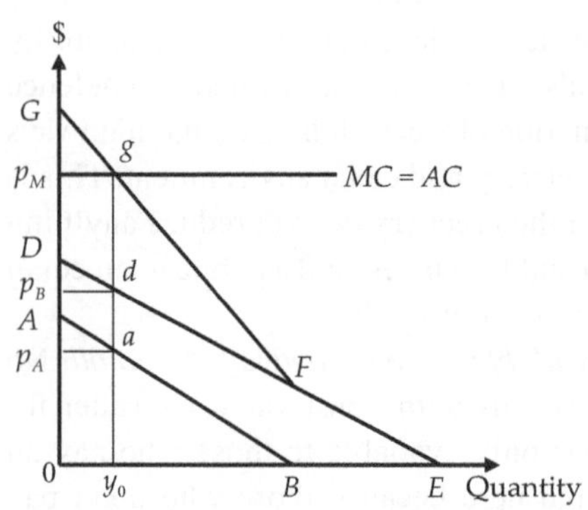

FIGURE 9.5 Non-Rivalry of Public Goods and Market Failure

consumption: the total utility of the individuals together equals the corresponding area under the line *GFE*. It follows that the height of *GFE* at any given level of consumption, e.g., gy_0, measures the society's marginal willingness to pay—which is the price. Thus, *GFE* is the aggregate or the market demand curve.

Assume that there is no difference between the private cost and the social cost (i.e., there are no externalities of the kind discussed earlier). Let *MC* be constant, which is shown by the horizontal line. (If *MC* is constant and there are no fixed costs, it must be equal to the average cost, i.e., $AC = MC$.)

Where is social surplus maximised? It occurs at point *g*, with the total quantity equal to y_0. The question is: Will this quantity be provided by a competitive, private market?

The answer is no. The problem is that a private producer cannot charge the "right" price to each consumer—because at the common quantity consumed (as it is a public good), each consumer has a different marginal valuation: it is p_A for Sachin and p_B for Brian. If the price p_A is charged to both consumers, it is too low for Brian and hence social surplus is not maximised; if p_B is charged it is too high for Sachin and thus at this price also, the social surplus is not maximised. Any other price is not right for any individual, and hence not right for society.

How about Sachin being charged p_A and Brian being charged p_B? In principle, this will maximise social welfare. But there are two problems. First, almost surely, the private producer will not have information about the true valuation by each and every individual—because everyone has an incentive to reveal a near-zero valuation for the product in order to free-ride. Second, even if it is possible to know their true valuation, it will be extremely costly to exercise such price discrimination across so many consumers. The implication is that the market fails.

Therefore, the government steps in such situations and provides public goods by financing it through (compulsory) taxes.

We must note that there is a class of goods or services that are ***local public goods***, meaning that these are not open to all, but it is non-rival for those who have access or who are members. In other words, non-rivalry condition is met while the non-excludability is not. Examples include private clubs (e.g., India International Centre and Gymkhana in New Delhi, India), neighbourhood security personnel, swimming pool for residents of a townhouse complex, etc.

9.3.3 Minimum Consumption of Food by the Poor

The total social utility measured by the area under the market demand curve drawn in Figure 9.1 neither tells us or "cares," so to speak, who consumes how much. If Figure 9.1 depicts the market for an essential product like food, it is possible that out of the total quantity consumed y_0, the poor are able to consume—rather afford—only a small portion of it, less than what is needed for normal nourishment. In other words, undernourishment may be present in a competitive equilibrium as depicted in Figure 9.1.

However, any reasonable notion of social welfare shouldn't ignore the problem of undernourishment of individuals in a society or market. It must place a higher weight on a poor person's consumption of a necessity like food than that on a relatively rich person's consumption of food. Then, clearly, the competitive equilibrium doesn't maximise social welfare, i.e., the market fails. The best corrective measure must involve subsidising the food consumption of the relatively poor such that no one is under-nourished. Put differently, a targeted food subsidy programme is the best policy option. This is indeed the rationale behind the public distribution system (PDS) and targeted public distribution system (TPDS) in India.

How should such a programme be operationalised however? This is where lies the problem of PDS/TPDS programme in India. If the government itself takes upon the task of procuring and distributing food for the poor (as it has been thus far), inefficiencies including corruption are bound to creep in. Instead, some sort of a food stamp programme is likely to be a more efficient way of executing the scheme—because such a programme can be implemented through the private market system and wouldn't require resources needed for the tasks of separate procurement and separate distribution via fair price shops.

9.3.4 Redistribution

Equation (9.2) and the corresponding Figure 9.1 presume that the marginal valuation of one rupee is the same for everyone. But in a society where there is a lot of economic inequality this is not a good assumption. A very poor man's valuation of $100 is very different from that of a millionaire. Thus, some consideration of distribution of income and wealth is desirable in any concept of social or collective well-being. A free competitive market, resulting in a very unequal society with career opportunities not affordable to many cannot be construed as working in the best interest of society.

If redistribution is an objective, what is the right policy intervention? The answer is a progressive income tax system, meaning a relatively high rate for the rich and a relatively low rate for the poor. It is good to know that most countries do follow a progressive income tax system.[3]

9.3.5 Asymmetric Information and Adverse Selection

There is another important class of market failure due to various forms of **asymmetric information**, which leads to the problem of **adverse selection**: a situation *where the informed individuals essentially take advantage of those not informed.* We will understand this via a handful of examples below.

Used-Car Market: This is probably the most famous example put forward by George Akerlof, a Nobel laureate in economics, who was among the first to formally identify such a problem and characterise them. Consider the market for used (second-hand) cars. We know that all second-hand cars are not in the same condition even if they are of the same brand and have the same year of manufacturing.

One vehicle may be that of a single owner and driver, whose driving habits may be exemplary, and who might have kept his car in mint condition. Another vehicle may be company-owned and driven by many and put to rough use. In case the buyer and seller know each other, it is likely that the first car will fetch more price than the other. But the second-hand car market is so vast (both physically and online) that it is impossible for a buyer to know the usage details of every piece offered for sale. Under the circumstances, all used cars (of same brand and manufacturing date/year) will be priced almost in the same range. Devoid of the usage and maintenance information, how much would a buyer be prepared to pay?

To fix ideas, suppose there are two types of used cars: bad (B) and good (G). B-cars are lemons (bad) and G-cars are peaches (good). Suppose that a B-car is worth \$10,000, while a G-car is worth \$15,000. Further, suppose that 70% used cars in the market are B-type and 30% are G-type. Since a buyer does not know which car is of which type, it is reasonable to suppose that she/he will be willing to pay the weighted average of the two prices $= \$10{,}000 \times 0.7 + \$15{,}000 \times 0.3 = \$(7{,}000 + 4{,}500) = \$11{,}500$. An owner of a B-type car will be very happy with this price. But what about the owner of a G-type car? Obviously, she will not be happy at all to get \$11,500 for her good car. She will be discouraged from participating in the second-hand market. In equilibrium, most cars sold will be lemons. The market "fails." Realise that in this situation the buyers and G-car owners are essentially exploited because of asymmetric information, assuming that the owners of B-cars are selfish and do not wish to reveal the true condition of the car to a potential buyer.

Medical and Life Insurance: In these markets, the buyer is better informed than the seller, the opposite of the nature of asymmetric information in the used-car markets. When you buy a medical insurance for yourself or your family, you're asked to furnish detailed information on your past medical problems (if any), say for example, whether you suffer from a chronic disease or you have hereditary issues (like diabetes). As a buyer, you have an incentive to conceal such information. Although the insurance provider gets your medical examination done before selling you a policy, these tests do not always detect pre-existing conditions. Moreover, human beings have different lifestyles: some are health and diet conscious, while others are not. Suppose there are two persons, A and B, of the same age group, gender, and weight. Both have no medical problems. But their lifestyles are opposite. A follows a strict daily routine, which includes doing exercise, walk, and yoga, taking proper balanced diet at regular intervals and sleeping properly. His job is also not very stressful. On the other hand, B leads a hectic, stressful lifestyle without much exercise or yoga. As a result, the probability of A falling ill (and requiring medical expense reimbursement) is much less than that for B. The insurance company would love to offer insurance to folks like A but not to someone like B. However, it is difficult to keep track of the lifestyles of thousands or millions of clients. In this situation of asymmetric information, the insurance provider typically charges a price which is higher than what a good client would be willing to pay.

Credit Market: Asymmetric information is prevalent in credit markets. A lender may not know the credit record of a potential borrower. That is, a borrower knows his/her credit record or behaviour, but the lender may not be able to distinguish a good borrower from a bad borrower. The result is that all borrowers, good and bad alike, will be rationed in some ways by the creditors.

Health Care: In healthcare, the patient, the buyer of health care services, typically knows very little about the cause and remedy of his ailment. He must rely completely on the doctor (seller). A heart patient has no competence to know whether he needs a stent or not to unblock an artery. Theoretically, a rogue doctor or hospital can exploit a patient. We regularly hear about such cases, both confirmed and unconfirmed, in the media.

Higher Education: The higher-education service too has asymmetric information problem between its buyers (students and their parents) and sellers (educational institutions). In this sector, the buyer may have little competence to judge the quality of an educational institution. This may not be a huge concern if the school, college, or university is funded by the state and the buyer pays only a nominal amount of fee.[4]

Let's turn our attention to privately managed self-financed institutions that have grown rapidly over the last three decades in India. These, so-called "public schools" ironically, are in high demand by parents with some economic means. And they charge hefty fees which is their sole source of revenue. They employ glossy advertisements flaunting their physical infrastructure, faculty quality, and placement record. However, the prospective students or their parents can only check their buildings and government approvals. They cannot measure the quality of teachers and their teaching pedagogy, which is the most important aspect. Furthermore, in most cases the placement records' claims are exaggerated and misleading. It is hard to sometimes distinguish between "bad" and "good" private schools.

Adverse Selection and Corrective Measures by the State

In all the examples above, there is asymmetric information: one party is better informed than another. This causes a problem of what is called **adverse selection**. It refers to a situation where an uninformed or less informed party cannot separate wheat from chaff and as a result the "good" get penalised for the behaviour of the bad types. This is like your childhood days when you got punished (along with your brother) by your dad for some mischief committed by your brother and not you—because you both were together at the time of the mischief and your dad had no way to knowing who actually did it. An adverse selection situation is obviously not ideal or optimal for the society. The market fails. Should the government intervene?

For instance, it can pass a law that sellers of second-hand cars must disclose major defects in a declaration form; otherwise, vehicle ownership cannot be changed. But this will generate its own problems. A seller may not genuinely know some of the major defects even after getting it checked by a car mechanic. Is such a law meant to protect the interest of buyers of used cars desirable?

Used-car markets may not be very important from a public interest perspective, and, thus, perhaps, are ignored from a public-policy perspective. But, education is an important sector which cannot be ignored. To protect the buyers or student–parents, the state does intervene. Private-sector higher-education institutions (HEIs) have to adhere to government norms related to the quantity and quality of physical and educational infrastructure like land, building, number of classrooms, computer facilities, library, number of qualified teachers, etc., failing which approval is denied. Moreover, the approval is periodically renewed. There are regulating bodies that perform annual checks and surprise visits. So, the students and their parents need to ensure that the HEI they seek admission into has secured the requisite government approvals. In reality however, state certification is not as effective as it appears since substandard HEIs (the lemons) manage to get approval by bribing the inspectors.

Moving to the health sector, how about the high price being charged for stents? Since this impinges on public health, there is a more solid case for government intervention. Indeed, the Government of India did something about it in 2017. See Box 9.2.

BOX 9.2 THE STENT STUNT

In February 2017, the Government of India passed an order to regulate stent price. By this order, stent prices of all varieties were slashed by about 80%. Prior to this move, the cost of imported metallic stents ranged anything between ₹85,000 to ₹1,60,000. However, it was well known that the manufacturing cost was much lower than the price. There existed a nexus between the manufacturer and end users (Mostly private hospitals and the manufacturers would keep a very high maximum retail price (MRP)) which the doctors would charge from the patients. The resultant huge margin will then be shared by all. Remember the elasticity of demand of such lifesaving items is very low. So, the patient would pay this price. And added to this the asymmetric information, the patient had no other option but to get *fleeced*.

The Government of India fixed the metal stent price in the range of ₹7,500 to ₹30,000. The move was meant to provide big relief to patients needing coronary procedures. However, most of the private hospitals negated this gain by hiking up the operation cost substantially thus leaving the patients as helpless as before.

Let us consider one more example of adverse selection and intervention by the government. Suppose a Bangladeshi firm producing a good-quality product is trying to enter the international market. The firm knows that the quality of its product is very good. But the customers in the international market are not convinced since the firm is new in the market. Hence, they will not be willing to pay a price commensurate with the cost of producing a high-quality product. It is a situation of asymmetric information where product quality is known to the producer but not to the consumers. It is quite possible that, without any support, the Indian firm will incur a loss and therefore may not be able to enter and sustain itself in the international market. This is not an optimal situation from Bangladesh's standpoint. Subsidising such a firm until it is able to establish its quality reputation in the international market will improve social welfare.

Measures by Concerned Parties

State intervention is not always available or without its own problems. Consider insurance companies. Although they are the disadvantaged parties, many of them are well-off and it is hard to justify state assistance to them. However, the insurance companies devise ways to protect themselves from the adverse selection problem. For instance, they can set up stringent tests to detect common pre-existing conditions. Given this information, they may deny insurance or charge high rates to people with pre-existing conditions. However, this way of dealing with the adverse selection problem is unfair to individuals with pre-existing conditions and the society at large. The government must step in to regulate the insurance companies to some extent. This is a case where there is a rationale for the government to regulate parties that adopt private ways to counter an adverse selection problem.

Consider the credit market, where the lenders do not know the quality of project or the effort level of an entrepreneur. They try to solve the adverse selection problem by requiring a collateral against a loan. In recent years, credit records of individuals can be accessed by using their social security number or the Aadhar card number. This tends to alleviate the problem of adverse selection.

Let's go back to the market for used cars. There is a way out for owners of peaches to credibly signal a potential buyer that their cars are of good quality: a voluntary offer of a legally executable warrantee for say six months or one year. Note that the cost of such warrantee will not be high for peach-car owners since they know that their cars are good. But this is not so for lemon-car owners. They will surely hesitate to offer any warrantee. This would enable buyers to separate peaches from lemons. Although the practice of offering warrantee is unusual for individual sellers (unless the car is still under the manufacturer's warrantee), used-car dealers often provide them.

9.4 First-Best and Second-Best

If you go back to our earlier example of two groups of firms, one of which causes a negative externality to households, we conclude that a uniform tax on both groups of firms reduces pollution no doubt but taxing only the group of firms that pollute was the best policy intervention. In the literature the latter is an example of a **first-best policy intervention**—generally defined as that policy intervention that addresses the source of market failure head-on in the most efficient manner. In comparison, a general production tax on both firms, which brings about the correct amount of total output but not the optimal allocation of it among the firms, is welfare-improving, but not the best. It is an example of what is called a **second-best policy intervention**.

The distinction between the first-best and second-best policies is important—since it clearly brings out which is the best among alternative policy options that work towards a particular goal (e.g., reducing pollution). Indeed, in the real world, the governments do adopt, in many situations, the second-best, *not* first-best policy measures.

For example, tax revenues are important for any government to function and provide public goods like national defence, highways, administrative system, etc. Recall the discussion in Chapter 5 on direct versus indirect tax. Our conclusion was that income tax is a better method to raise revenue than an indirect tax. If raising revenue is the objective, then taxing income is the first-best option. Yet, for decades, India partly justified its use of heavy import-tariff regime on the ground that tariffs are "necessary" for revenue purposes. An import tariff is an indirect tax as it changes the price of the imported goods for the consumers and producers. Thus, tariffs are a second-best solution to raise revenues.

If we go back to our discussion of the PDS system in India, a blanket policy where almost every household is entitled for some amount of grains at low prices is only a second-best policy, whereas, a targeted PDS system (TPDS) is, at least in principle, the first-best.[5]

Consider a macro example. In the yester decades of a pegged exchange rate system, India used various policies to help our export sector. One of them was to use a favourable exchange rate for an export-oriented production unit. However, manipulating the exchange rate has implications towards a country's balance of payments. Thus, it is only a second-best policy, whereas the most direct and the first-best policy option is to provide a direct production subsidy—if promoting this sector is the objective.

In general, the first-best intervention is one that addresses the "problem" most directly and specifically without affecting other sectors or units in the economy.

9.5 A Sum-Up: Conservatism versus Liberalism

We started out by saying that a freely functioning competitive market structure serves the society's interest the best. But we also saw how competitive markets may "fail" and how a role for government intervention arises. What are we advocating then? Should the government, as a matter of practice, regularly interfere with the markets or not? Those who say "yes" are labelled as liberals and those who say "no" are the conservatives. The former charge that the latter's argument for free operation of a market is justified only in case of a competitive economy without problems like externalities, public goods, etc. But actual economies do have problems that markets cannot correct on their own. Therefore, it is imperative that government intervene in the markets on a regular basis.

To be fair, the conservatives are generally aware of the concern of the liberals. But their worry is that in the name of intervention, the government may make things even worse, i.e., there is a problem of **government failure** also. It can arise due to lack of information and political imperatives.

Turn to Figure 9.4. Suppose the government doesn't have good information on the marginal social benefit and marginal social cost functions. Then it is quite possible that the government may "overshoot." Not only that it may select a tax (in the example) higher than what is truly optimal, but it may even exceed $\bar{t}$, with the result that intervention is worse than what the free market delivers despite its problems. This is a generic problem, not specific to the tax example. Another source of lack of information is that the government may not have the administrative set-up to correctly identify the beneficiaries of a programme or those that cause externalities. The outcome could very well be, at best, a second-best situation with net benefit being less than the cost of administering a programme or regulation.

Even if the government may have precise information, political imperatives may force policy-makers to overshoot. If, for example, a liberal government is coming to power after a gap, it may wish to please its constituency by going overboard—beyond what may be the optimal degree of intervention or by deliberately choosing a second-best option. As an extreme example, in the name of redistribution of income, it may impose such a heavy tax on the relatively rich that it effectively "kills" entrepreneurial incentive for the society. In such a society, equality will be achieved no doubt, but everyone will be poor. Put differently, *a sufficiently heavy intervention to redistribute a pie has the potential of reducing the size of the pie itself.* To summarise, lack of information and political imperatives may lead to **over-intervention** or a second-best intervention.

In sum, there is no simplistic answer to whether conservatism or liberalism is the way to follow in advocating economic policy within the framework of a market economy. A careful statement will be something like the following.

> Yes, there is a role for the government to play in the economy, but only in a very selective manner. However, if there isn't enough information about the parameters of a market, the benefit of doubt should go to the free market, *not* to policy activism, unless the problem is visibly acute.

This sounds a bit conservative, but most economists are likely to agree to this assessment.

Facts and Insights

- In measuring social welfare or surplus, consumers' benefit is represented by consumer surplus and producers' benefit by the producers' surplus or profits.
- Social surplus (as the sum of consumers' and producers' surplus) in case of a single good is measured by the area between its demand curve and supply curve. It is maximised when price equals the social marginal cost.
- The social surplus is also maximised at the competitive equilibrium since the price = marginal cost condition is met.
- Market failure occurs when a market is not perfectly competitive.
- Even when markets are perfectly competitive, market failure may occur because of externalities, public goods, minimum consumption requirement by the poor, asymmetric information, etc.
- A Pigovian tax/subsidy corrects the market failure due to the presence of negative/positive externalities.
- In case of a public good, non-excludability leads to a free rider problem.
- The market demand curve for a public good is the vertical summation of individual demand curves.
- Market can fail because of adverse selection in an asymmetric information situation, such as second-hand automobile markets, health insurance, higher education, etc. Adverse selection means that parties with private information can exploit the market to their advantage at the cost of less informed parties.
- Second-best interventions also emerge because of political compulsions.
- High-handed policy interventions have the danger of making the matter worse compared to a free-market approach, even if there is a valid reason for policy intervention. This is because of informational problems and political imperatives.
- There is a rationale for the state to intervene in the functioning of markets, but state interventions must be selective, not pervasive.

Exercises

Descriptive/Analytical

9.1. How is social welfare/surplus defined in relation to production and consumption of a particular good and how does it relate to consumer surplus and profits?

9.2. Explain the adverse selection problem via two examples not covered in the text.

9.3. Examine the role of information technology in bridging information asymmetry between buyers and sellers. Give suitable examples.

9.4. What is meant by government failure in terms of policy?

9.5. What are the hurdles in the efficient functioning of market system? How can these be overcome?

Short Answer (word limit = 500 approx.)

9.6 What is the condition of maximising social welfare and what is the logic behind it?
9.7 "Equilibrium in a competitive market attains a social optimum or efficiency." Defend or refute.
9.8 "In a market economy, all are 'selfish' in the sense that they wish to maximize their own benefit without being directly concerned about the benefit of others. Yet, their selfish behaviour may lead to a socially desirable outcome." Agree or disagree? Give reasons.
9.9 What does the term "market failure" mean?
9.10 Diagrammatically explain how the market fails in the presence of a positive externality.
9.11 What is a Pigovian tax? Explain the concept through an example (other than the one given in the text).
9.12 "If an industry is causing pollution, in the interest of social well-being it should be taxed as heavily as possible." Comment.
9.13 What are the two characteristics of a public good? Briefly explain them.
9.14 What problem does the non-excludability characteristic of a public good cause towards paying for the good?
9.15 What problem does the non-rivalry characteristic of a public good cause towards paying for the good?
9.16 Give two instances of asymmetric information (other than those given in the chapter) from your personal experience in which buyer was better informed than seller; and two instances where seller was better informed than buyer. Justify your answer.
9.17 What is meant by a first-best policy intervention? Explain it through an example.
9.18 What is meant by a second-best policy intervention? Explain it via an example.

Quizzes/Numerical

9.19 The production process of an industry causes a negative externality to the society. Then the socially optimal output is _____ than the output in the unregulated market equilibrium. Fill in the blank and give reasons.
9.20 "The market demand curve for a public good is obtained by horizontally adding the individual demand curves for such a good." Agree or disagree. Give reasons.
9.21 Give your opinion on whether the following policies are first-best or second-best.
   a) The steel industry in a country suffers in terms of employment and output, because of cheap import of steel from abroad. On the grounds

of protecting national interest, the government bans the import of steel into the country.

b) There is a fair amount of cheating detected in a city in Gujarat during the entrance exams to civil services. As a result, the government plans to ban all civil service entrance exams in Gujarat. If anyone from Gujarat wants to appear in these exams, he/she has to travel to a neighbouring state.

c) Some criminals in a country were able to escape from the country because they had passports. To reduce such problems, the government decided to ban the issue of passports to all its citizens for the next two years.

d) Some private hospitals in a large city failed to comply with some government regulations for several years. To respond to such problems, the government bans the establishment of new private hospitals for the next three years.

9.22 Classify the consumption/use of the following good/service into private and public goods. Give reasons for doing so.

a) You buy an apple.
b) You book a berth in a railway coach.
c) You go for a walk in a public park.
d) You go for tennis practice in a club.
e) You put on a nice perfume and attend your class.
f) Thief enters the hours of your neighbour at night, your pet dog barks and wakes up the neighbours. The thief is caught.
g) Police patrol in your locality.
h) Guard at the gate of your group housing society.

Notes

1 Governments can be of different types: monarchy (often hereditary), oligarchy (rule of a few), dictatorship, and democracy. The earlier concept of state was of an authority that was to be feared. The citizens obey the state because it is like a *leviathan*—a kind of monster to be feared. From the mid-19th century onwards, political philosophers developed the concept of a *welfare state* in which the citizens were not to be afraid of the government. The government was to assure its people that it existed for their well-being. The obedience to the law should come out of respect, not fear. It was quite natural that such a government be chosen by the *general will* of the public. This paved the way for the emergence of democracy.

2 Rajiv Gandhi, a former Prime Minister of India, once admitted that out of every ₹1 that the government spends on subsidies, hardly nine paisa (9%) reach those who deserve assistance. The rest 91% are cornered by a chain of corrupt politicians, bureaucrats, and middlemen.

3 If a tax system is too progressive it creates negative work incentives and induces tax-evasive behaviour.

4 One can argue that the buyer also pays indirectly through direct and indirect taxes that fund, among other public services, educational institutions.

5 As we discussed earlier, there are costs involved and difficulties in running a TPDS system.

Bibliography

Cohodes, S. and Dynarski, S. (2020). *Colleges Are Fueling the Pandemic in a Classic Market Failure*. New York Times, Oct 8, 2020.

Shelar, J. (2021, May 8). Mumbai: Doctors flag indiscriminate use of steroids, antibiotics in covid-19 treatment. *Hindustan Times*.

10

MONOPOLY

In Chapter 8 we studied a perfectly competitive firm and a perfectly competitive market, a central feature of which is that no single firm has any market power. All other forms of market structure in which some firms or economic agents have some market power go under the rubric of **an imperfectly competitive market** or briefly **an imperfect market**. Market power manifests in the ability to charge a price higher than the marginal cost. There are two sources of market power.

1. One is the presence of limited number of sellers (or buyers to be more general). Lack of competition bestows market power.
2. The second source is a bit subtle, that is, **product differentiation**, meaning that, irrespective of whether there a few or a large number of competitors, a firm will have some market power if it produces a brand or a product which is "different" from what others produce, even though it may be basically the same product. For instance, in the soap market, there are many varieties in India like Lifebouy, Lux, Dove, Pears, etc. They are basically the same product, yet slightly different from each other in terms of look and feel. Each one is unique in some sense and this uniqueness confers some market power.

Because of market power, in the terminology of Chapter 9, an imperfectly competitive market is sub-optimal from the perspective of economic efficiency.

10.1 Types of Imperfect Markets

Depending on the specific features, there are different types of imperfectly competitive markets, a nomenclature of which follows.

DOI: 10.4324/9781003452195-10

Monopoly: "Mono" means "one" and "poly" means "seller." Thus "monopoly" means one seller. The Xerox company producing copying machines back in the 1960s is a classic example of private monopoly. In providing domestic flights, Indian Airlines was a state monopoly for many decades.

Monopolistic Competition: This refers to a market where there are a large number of sellers, but each produces a different variety: brands are not perfect substitutes of each other. Examples are different types of restaurant food, toothpastes, soaps, etc.

Monopsony: It is a market with one buyer only.

Duopoly: This is defined by two firms or sellers only.

Duopsony: It has two buyers only.

Oligopoly: This is a market where there is limited number of sellers. For instance, in the global commercial aircraft market, the producers are Boeing (United States), Airbus (Europe), Aeroflot (Russia), Comac (China), and Embraer (Brazil).

Oligopsony: It is a market where the number of buyers is limited.

In this chapter we study monopoly.

10.2 How Monopoly Arises

By definition, there is little competition in a monopoly market. It is the opposite of a perfectly competitive market in which there are infinitely many sellers. It is implicit that entry into a monopoly market is very difficult or very costly (otherwise, monopoly cannot last long in the first place).

The term "monopoly" should be understood in the context of a given geographical location and time. You hear people use the term "xeroxing" to mean using a photocopying machine. Xerox Corporation is an American company, which discovered the plain-paper photocopying machine in 1959. In the 1960s it was the only company that manufactured and sold plain-paper photocopying machines.[1] This is an example of a private monopoly. For a long time (till its breakup in the 1980s), AT&T had monopoly power in providing telephone services in the United States.

In India, before liberalisation in the power sector got underway in the 1990s, the generation, transmission, and distribution of electricity were in the hands of State Electricity Boards (SEBs). These were monopolies in the respective states. In providing air travel inside the country, Indian Airlines had a monopoly for a long time. Both are examples of "state monopolies." A little different, BCCI (Board of Control for Cricket in India) is a monopoly in providing international-level cricket games having the Indian team. It generates revenues from various sources: the public who go to see these matches by purchasing tickets for ODI or T20, sale of TV rights, commercial sponsorships, IPL franchise owners, and guarantee money for the Indian team's participation abroad. Back in 1998–1999 its profits were about ₹83.7 million. In 2020, its earnings from IPL matches played in UAE (due to Covid-19 situation in India), reported by Timenownews.com dated November 23, 2020, was around ₹40 billion.

There are several reasons behind the emergence of monopoly in a market.

(a) The government gives licence to only one company for providing a product or service in a given locality or space. For instance, in India till 2002, Videsh Sanchar Nigam Limited (VSNL) had monopoly in India in providing international telephony service.
(b) Big private companies—typically in developed countries—engage in research and come up with new products or new technology in producing an existing product. As a reward for their risk of investing in research, they apply to their government for a patent, which is an official recognition that they are the originators of the new product or technology. If a firm is granted the patent, no one else can use its technology without obtaining licence from it. Hence, the firm can exercise monopoly power. Xerox was an example in the 1960s.

A patent or what is called a **patent right** is not granted forever. It is valid only for a certain number of years (after which other firms can freely copy the technology if they can). This period is called **patent life**. In most developed countries, the patent life ranges from 15 to 20 years. In Australia it is 20 years; in the United States it is currently 17 years. In India patent laws were relatively weak. But recently, because of its commitment to the World Trade Organization (WTO), they have become stricter. See Box 10.1 on patent laws in relation to the world economy and India. As examples, an international drug company called Eli Lilly had a patent on a very widely used anti-depressant called *Prozac*. This patent expired in 2003. A Swiss pharmaceutical company, Roche group's patent on Rituxan, which is used for certain types of cancer and autoimmune diseases, expired in 2018.

BOX 10.1 PATENT LAWS

Most developed countries have comprehensive patent laws. During the patent life the patent holder can sell licence to other firms for using its technology (legally). Typically, the licence is sold to firms who operate in markets other than where the patent holder operates, e.g., in a different country. The enforcement of patent law is also strict in developed countries. A patent holder can take to court some other firm, who may be using its technology without a licence, and get a fairly quick decision.

In India, the patent law and its enforcement are relatively passive. This is because historically research and development, discoveries and inventions were not in the focus of Indian firms. Barring a few exceptions, we generally imported technology from abroad. The most important patent legislation in

India is the Indian Patent Act of 1970. It provided that any invention of a new product or a process of production, which is useful and not obvious, is patentable. But it did *not* explicitly allow product patents in the drug and food sector.

However, as an obligation of being a member of WTO, India and other countries had to revamp their patent laws. In India, a major amendment to the Patent Act of 1970 was legislated in 1999, by which both product and process patents are allowable in the food and drugs sector. The amended law became operational in 2005 and it was further amended in 2006. Indian Patent law permits a patent life of 20 years.

Patent filing by Indian entities in the international area remains miniscule compared to many other nations. Back in 2009, India had filed 761 patent applications vis-à-vis 7,946 applications from China. This gap has widened over time. According to the World Intellectual Property Organization (WIPO), a United Nations (UN) watchdog, in 2019 India filed 2,053 patent applications, which is less than 1% of the global total and less than 50% of the number of applications filed by one Chinese company, Huawei and way below China's total applications numbering 58,990 (which surpassed the United States).

A major factor behind India's poor show is its lack of emphasis on R&D. R&D spending in India is less than 1% of its GDP, whereas it is 2.1% in China, 2.8% in the United States, 4.2% in South Korea, and 4.3% in Israel. See Pattanayak (2020).

(c) The expiration of a patent right does not mean that other firms possess the technology automatically. Sometimes, a firm can maintain its technical and organisational superiority that is hard to be copied by others. Thus, technical superiority can be a source of monopoly power. For example, IBM (International Business Machines, an American firm) had virtual monopoly in the computer business for a fairly long time.

(d) The production processes of certain products have large economies of scale relative to demand, meaning that the average cost curve is downward-sloping up to a very high level of output relative to market demand. In such a case, producing a small amount entails a high average cost, whereas a large volume can be produced at a fairly low average cost. If many firms enter the industry, each one will have to produce a relatively small amount, incurring a high average cost and therefore unable to sustain itself in the market. As firms exit from the market, competition among the surviving firms will continue to eliminate the relatively small firms. In the end, one firm survives. Once the only firm is established in the market enjoying a low average cost, it is mostly immune from entry by others since new entrants are typically small in size. In other words, in the presence of strong economies of scale, monopoly emerges "naturally." Such a monopoly is called a **natural monopoly**. Providers of utilities like electricity and water are typical examples. For instance, running two sets of electric poles, wires, and cables for a given area will be much costlier compared to running one.[2]

BOX 10.2 OPEC AND THE WORLD OIL MARKET

OPEC was formed originally in 1960 by Iran, Iraq, Kuwait, Saudi Arabia, and Venezuela. Qatar joined in 1961, followed by Indonesia and Libya in 1962, United Arab Emirates in 1967, Algeria in 1969, and Nigeria in 1971. Currently, there are two additional countries in OPEC, namely, Ecuador and Gabon. The aim of the OPEC countries is to set production quotas, so as to manipulate the price of petrol in the world market.

The oil shortage of 1970s motivated many other countries to explore oil. By mid-1980s there were other countries that used to be importers of oil earlier but became net exporters, e.g., Mexico, The Netherlands, and Russia.

Besides the OPEC, there are other major producers of oil. For example, as a single country, the United States is currently the largest producer of oil with 20% of the world production of oil, followed by Saudi Arabia with 12% of the world production as of 2020. The United States is also the largest consumer of oil, sharing 20% of world consumption of oil as of 2020, followed by China (with 14% of world consumption of oil). The United States consumes more oil than it produces, hence a net importer of oil. India is not among the top 10 producers of oil, but it is the third largest consumer of oil and thus a large net importer of oil.

(e) Sometimes, firms retain their individual identity but they co-ordinate their outputs and pricing policy to act *as if* it is a monopoly. This is called a **cartel.** The Organization of Petroleum Exporting Countries (OPEC) in the 1970s is a prime example of a cartel that led to a virtual monopoly in the world market for oil.[3] See Box 10.2 for how the constitution of OPEC evolved over time.[4] The OPEC's market power is less today than it was in the 1970s and early 1980s.

10.3 Profit Maximisation

For any firm, profits equal the difference between total revenues and total costs. The cost structure facing a monopolist is similar to that of a competitive firm because like a competitive firm a monopoly has to pay for the use of many inputs, e.g. labour and raw material, and, assuming that these inputs are used in other sectors of the economy as well, a monopoly has to buy these inputs competitively.[5] The concepts like total cost, average cost, marginal cost, etc., and their general shapes apply to a monopoly firm as well. Moreover, in a monopoly industry, there is no issue of entry and exit (as long as the monopoly power continues). Hence, except that there are differences between the short-run and long-run cost curves, there isn't much behavioural difference of a monopoly between the short run and the long run.[6] Typically, the two time periods are not differentiated. We just say average, marginal, and total costs without referring to short run or long run.

From our discussion on revenues in Chapters 7 and 8, we know that the revenue structure facing a monopolist is quite different from that of a competitive firm. A perfectly competitive firm is very small compared to the market and thus behaves as a price-taker. This is obviously not true for a monopoly. Being the only firm serving the market, it has market power, which enables a monopolist to be a **price maker** so to speak. Referring to the section on revenues in Chapter 7, a monopoly firm faces the entire market, and, therefore, as it increases or decreases its output and the quantity sold, it cannot expect that the market price would remain unchanged: price will change according to what consumers would be willing to pay along the demand curve. As already noted in Chapter 7, *the market demand curve is a constraint facing a monopoly firm.*

To sum up from our revenue analysis in Chapter 7,

a) The average revenue (*AR*) curve facing a monopolist is the market demand curve itself.
b) The marginal revenue (*MR*) decreases with output. Therefore, the MR curve decreases with output too.

At any level of output, $MR < AR$. Thus, the *MR* curve lies below the *AR* curve.

d) The total revenue (*TR*) increases or decreases with output as *MR* is positive or negative.
e) $MR > 0$ (< 0) means that the price elasticity of greater (less) than one.

These curves are illustrated in parts (a) and (b) of Figure 10.1. The *AR* and *MR* curves need not be straight lines.

Figure 10.2 depicts a *TR* curve and the total cost (*TC*) curve facing the monopoly firm. Once we know the positions and shapes of these curves, we know that the profit is measured by the vertical distance between the two curves. We see that profit is maximised where this vertical distance is the maximum: at a point like y_0, at which the slope of the *TR* curve equals the slope of the *TC* curves. The slopes are, respectively, equal to the *MR* and the *MC*.

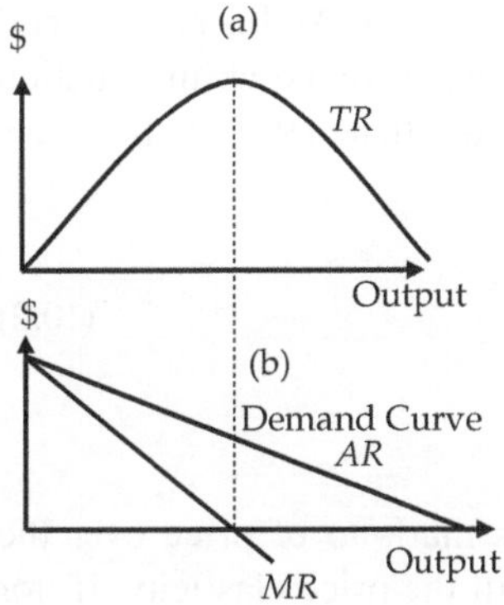

FIGURE 10.1 Revenue Curves Facing a Monopoly Firm

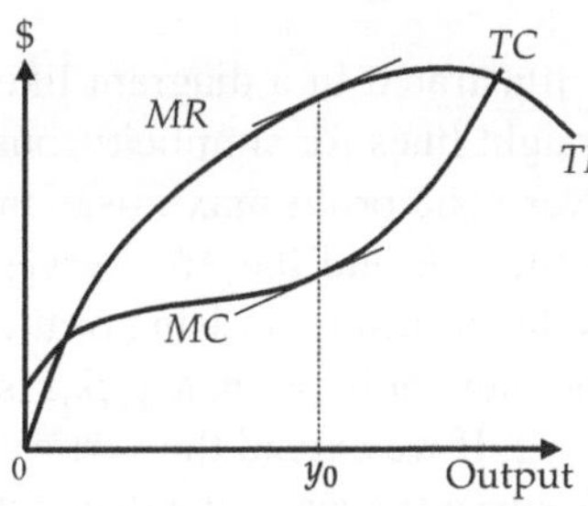

FIGURE 10.2 Profit Maximisation by a Monopoly Firm

Thus,

Profit Maximisation Condition:

$$MR = MC. \tag{10.1}$$

This is indeed a very general condition of profit maximisation by any firm. A mathematical derivation of equation (10.1) is given in Appendix 10.A.

The $MR = MC$ condition is intuitive. At very low levels of output, $MR > MC$. Adding output by one unit generates additional revenues greater than the additional cost. Thus, the firm will obtain more profits if it increases its output. On the other hand, at a very large level of output, $MR < MC$. This means that, if the firm reduces output, the savings in cost will be greater than the revenues lost and hence profits will be higher. Thus, profit reaches its maximum at the level of output, where $MR = MC$. Recall that for a competitive firm $MR = P$ and thus the condition $P = MC$ is a special case of the general condition $MR = MC$.

Note that at the profit-maximising output, $MR = MC$, which together with $MC > 0$ implies that $MR > 0$. We have discussed earlier that $MR > 0$ if and only if the price elasticity of demand, say e_p, is greater than one. Hence, *at the monopoly equilibrium the quantity and price are chosen such that* $e_p > 1$. At this point, recall the relationship between average revenue and marginal revenue as in equation (7.9) in Chapter 7, i.e., $AR/MR = e_p/(e_p - 1)$. We know that $AR = P$, the price. Hence, $MR = MC$ implies $P/MC = e_p/(e_p - 1)$, or,

$$P = \underbrace{\frac{e_p}{e_p - 1}}_{mark-up} \times MC. \tag{10.2}$$

In equation (10.2), the ratio $e_p/(e_p - 1)$ is the gross mark-up of price over the marginal cost. Notice that the mark-up decreases with the price elasticity. If, for example, $e_p = 2.5$, the mark-up is 3.5/(3.5 – 1) = 1.4. That is, there is a 40% (net) mark-up. The mark-up is an outcome of the firm's market power. In a perfectly competitive industry, a firm's market power is zero, $e_p = \infty$, and the gross mark-up is one and thus the (net) mark-up is zero.

A monopolist's profit maximisation is typically illustrated in a diagram like Figure 10.3. It has *AR* and *MR* curves (drawn as straight lines for simplicity, but they need not be). It also has the *AC* and *MC* curves. The profit-maximisation condition *MR* = *MC* is met at the point *E*, where the *MR* and the *MC* curves intersect. The corresponding level of output, y_m, is the profit-maximising or the optimal output. The firm also chooses the price. The monopoly price, say p_m, is the one at which the quantity demanded is equal to y_m. If we extend the vertical line passing through *E*, its intersection with the *AR* curve (which is the demand curve) marks p_m. The profit per unit of output is the difference between *AR* and *AC* at the optimal output. This is equal to the vertical distance *AB*. Thus, total profit = AB × quantity produced = $AB \times 0y_m$ = the area $ABCp_m$. This is shown by the shaded area. (Ignore for now the output level marked y_c and the price p_c.)

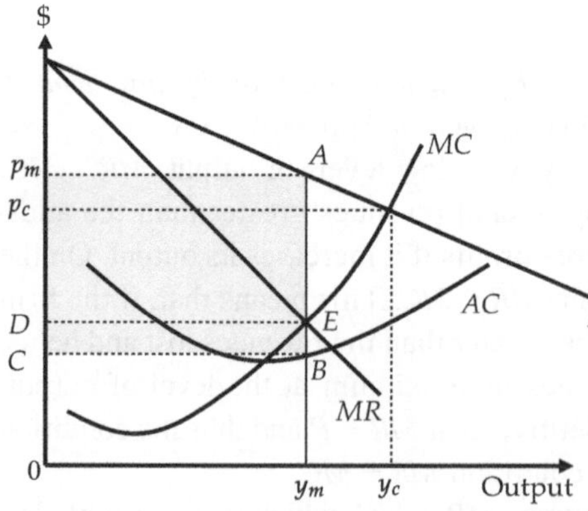

FIGURE 10.3 Profit Maximisation by a Monopolist Once Again

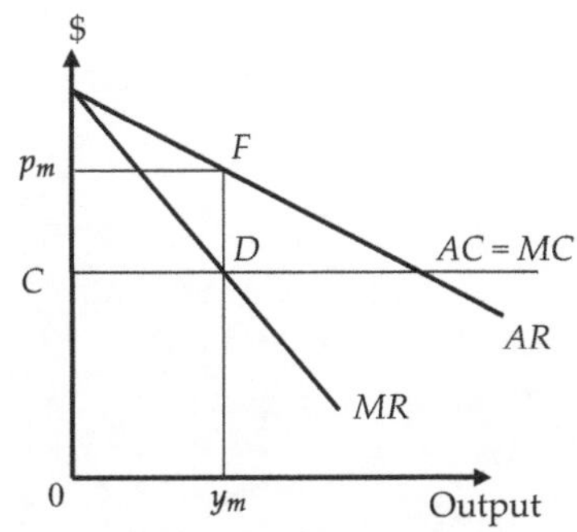

FIGURE 10.4 Monopoly Equilibrium when AC = MC

Sometimes, the monopoly equilibrium is shown in terms of a simpler diagram like Figure 10.4. Suppose that the firm's average cost is constant (independent of the output). This implies that the marginal cost is constant and equal to the average cost, i.e., $AC = MC$. The monopoly output is shown at the intersection of the *MR* curve and the horizontal *MC* curve. The monopoly price is read off the *AR* curve and the profit is indicated by the rectangle $CDFp_m$.

Can a monopolist incur a loss? Yes, but unlikely, since it is the only firm supplying the product, for which, by definition, there are no close substitutes available.

Example 10.1

A monopoly firm faces the demand schedule given in Table 10.1 and the total cost schedule given in Table 10.2. What is its profit-maximising output and price?

Answer: The demand schedule is the *AR* schedule. Multiplying the quantity demanded with price gives the *TR* schedule. The *MR*s are derived as additions to the *TR*. The *AR*, *TR*, and *MR* schedules are given in Table 10.3. From the total cost schedule, the *MC* schedule can be derived; this is given in Table 10.4. ■

TABLE 10.1 Demand Schedule

Price ($)	*Quantity Demanded*
50	8
60	7
70	6
80	5
90	4
100	3
110	2
120	1

TABLE 10.2 Total Cost Schedule

Output	*Total Cost ($)*
1	30
2	75
3	125
4	185
5	250
6	320
7	395
8	475

TABLE 10.3 *AR*, *TR*, and *MR*

Output	*AR ($)*	*TR ($)*	*MR ($)*
1	120	120	120
2	110	220	100
3	100	300	80
4	90	360	60
5	80	400	40
6	70	420	20
7	60	420	0
8	50	400	-20

TABLE 10.4 *MC*

Output	*MC ($)*
1	30
2	45
3	50
4	60
5	65
6	70
7	75
8	80

We see that the condition $MR = MC$ is met at output = 4. Hence, it is the profit-maximising output. Since this amount is sold in the market, from Table 11.3, the corresponding market price (i.e., the monopoly price) is $90.

10.4 Monopoly versus Perfect Competition

In Chapter 9 we learnt that at the equilibrium under a perfectly competitive market structure, social surplus is maximised (under certain conditions). It is therefore imperative to know how other market structures compare with perfect competition. The following are the general features of monopoly vis-à-vis perfect competition.

In perfect competition, profit maximisation leads to a supply curve—telling how much a firm produces at different market prices that are exogenous to the firm. In monopoly however the firm decides the output *and* the price. There is no question of the optimal level of monopoly output at different prices. Strictly speaking, *there is no supply curve as such under monopoly*, because price is not exogenous to a monopoly.

It does *not* mean however that the demand and supply forces do not operate or interact in a monopoly market. Shifts in the demand (*AR*) curve or in the *MC* curve do affect a monopolist's choice of output and price.

For a monopoly, $P > MR$, and, it selects an output level where $MR = MC$. These two relations imply that $P > MC$, which is verified in Figure 10.3 or Figure 10.4. At the profit-maximising output y_m, the price charged $= 0p_{\mathrm{m}}$, which is greater than the marginal cost $= 0D$. *It is the market power possessed by the monopolist, which enables him to charge a price higher than the marginal cost.* In comparison, recall that the price is equal to the marginal cost in perfect competition. We can thus say that a monopoly charges "too high a price" for its product. Moreover, the monopoly price being higher than the competitive price, it follows that, along a given demand curve, less is sold—and therefore less is produced—under monopoly than under perfect competition. In summary, the fundamental behavioural difference between monopoly and perfect competition is that *the monopolist produces less and charges a higher price compared to perfect competition.*

Recall from Chapter 9 that the social surplus maximised at that level of quantity where $P = MC$ and this condition holds at the competitive equilibrium. The monopoly price being different from the marginal cost implies that *the social welfare or surplus is less under monopoly than under perfect competition.*

Example 10.2

Let Table 10.1 describe the total demand schedule facing a competitive industry, and, let Table 10.4 be the supply schedule of this industry (given price = marginal cost). How much will be produced and what will be the price of the product in equilibrium? How does this equilibrium compare with the corresponding monopoly equilibrium worked out in Example 10.1?

Answer: Plotting the demand and supply schedules yields that the quantity demanded is equal to the quantity supplied at price = \$70. The equilibrium quantity produced is 6 units. In *Example 10.1*, the monopoly price is \$90 and the monopoly output is 4 units. Hence, in the monopoly equilibrium, the price is higher, and the quantity sold is less. ■

10.5 Merits of Monopoly

The points (b) and (c) above summarise what is wrong with a monopoly market and form a rationale for restricting monopoly power in practice. Indeed, these features are sometimes played up high enough so as to generate a strong negative public sentiment against a monopolist. Some people even think that a monopolist is an evil that exploits the public.

Before rushing to such a conclusion, one must note some positive aspects of a monopoly. Suppose that initially there are two firms in an industry and both are somewhat inefficient. Their *MC* curves are at a high level and consequently they charge a higher price and produce less than what they would if the *MC* curves were at a lower level. They realise however that if they merge with each other—and thereby become a monopoly—they can reduce their costs. For instance, one firm may have excellent technical manpower but may not have good marketing skills, whereas the other may not have good technical manpower but possesses superior marketing knowledge. By merging, the resulting monopoly firm's *MC* curve will be at a lower level and thus it will be more efficient. In the business language it is called **synergy**. This, by itself, will induce the monopoly to charge a price, which is less, and produce a quantity, which is greater than what it would be if both firms were competing.

Another major benefit from encouraging monopoly to a certain extent is that monopoly power and profits provide incentives for inventions and innovations. In reality, these activities are very risky propositions. They often materialise from individual efforts and persistence. Why would someone invent a product if he/she is not allowed to enjoy monopoly profits for a few years? This is indeed the rationale behind granting patent rights.

Finally, recall natural monopoly. If there are huge internal economies of scale, the presence of a single (monopoly) firm will imply lower unit costs, compared to the situation where there are many small firms. Hence, there is a natural benefit arising from a natural monopoly.

10.6 Price Discrimination

In the real world, there are examples where for the same product or service, a producer charges different prices to different consumers. For the same movie, a movie hall owner prices the afternoon show lower than the evening show. Utility companies, like telephone, electricity, etc., fix different rates for household and industrial (business) customers. In the international markets, the same company, for the same product, may charge different prices to consumers in different countries. For instance, famous Japanese electronics companies typically price their products lower in the American market than in the Japanese market itself.

This practice is called **price discrimination**, *meaning different prices being charged in different markets for essentially the same product.* Why does a firm do it? It is because the demand conditions may vary across markets. Typically, the demand for an evening cinema show is stronger than that for an afternoon show. Therefore, the movie hall charges a higher price for an evening show. In what follows, we make this observation more precise by (a) identifying the conditions under which a firm *can* price-discriminate, (b) deriving the profit-maximising rule under price discrimination, and (c) deducing from this rule the exact nature of the difference between markets that tell us why in one market the price charged may be higher than in another by the same firm.

Suppose there are two markets a monopolist is serving, A and B. Let p_A and p_B denote the prices charged in these two markets, respectively. If $p_A = p_B$, there is no price discrimination. Now suppose the firm price-discriminates and charges a higher price in market B, i.e., $p_A < p_B$. Then the consumers in market A have an incentive to buy the product in their own market, sell it themselves in market B for a higher price, and make a profit. In economics, this is an example of an **arbitrage** *behaviour—meaning the act of weighing the cost or price of a product/service in two different markets, buying or selling accordingly and making a profit.* If the consumers in market A can actually do it, i.e., if reselling from the low-price to the high-price market is feasible, the price of the product in market A will keep rising and that in market B will keep falling until $p_A = p_B$. Therefore, *price discrimination is feasible only if there is no opportunity to resale the product from a low-price market to a high-price market.* We assume this.

In reality, consumers are often not allowed to resell. In the movie ticket example, an afternoon-show ticket is no good for an evening show. In case of differential electricity consumption rates for household and business purposes, it is illegal for businesses to buy electricity from households and vice versa. Also, the physical distance between two markets may be very far, such that the transport cost of goods may be high enough to deter any profitable arbitrage by consumers.

10.6.1 Profit-Maximising Condition under Price Discrimination

We now analyse how a monopoly firm maximises profits given that price discrimination is feasible. Denote the total revenues generated from the two markets by TR_A and TR_B.The grand total of revenues from the two markets equal $TR_A + TR_B$, and the firm's profit can be expressed as $TR_A + TR_B - TC$. We can indeed "breakup" the firm's profit-maximisation problem into two sub-problems: (i) How should the total amount already produced be allocated between the two markets so as to maximise the grand total revenue? (ii) What is the optimal level of the (total) output? Price discrimination essentially relates to problem (i) as it pertains to selling the product in the two markets. So, the question before us is: How should a monopoly firm allocate its sales between the two markets, given that the total amount of the quantities sold in the two markets (= output) is fixed?

The answer is simple: allocate the sales such that $MR_A = MR_B$. That is, *the total revenues across more than one market are maximised if the marginal revenues are equalised across the markets.*

The logic behind this principle is straightforward. Suppose the sales in markets A and B are such that $MR_A > MR_B$. Then let the firm move one unit of the product from market B to market A. By doing this it will lose revenues = MR_B in market B and gain revenues = MR_A in market A. Since $MR_A > MR_B$, the total revenues as the sum of revenues in the two markets will be higher by this reallocation. Moreover, we know that the MR in any market falls with the quantity sold in that market; thus, if the firm shifts sales from market B to market A, MR_B will keep rising and MR_A will keep falling. But as long as $MR_A > MR_B$, this sales-reallocation process will continue to increase the total revenues. Hence, total revenues are maximised at that sales allocation where $MR_A = MR_B$.

Once we understand the answer to the sub-problem (i), the answer to (ii) is an extension of the $MR = MC$ principle, namely,

$$MR_A = MR_B = MC. \tag{10.3}$$

This is the overall profit-maximising condition for a price-discriminating monopolist.[7]

10.6.2 Ranking of Prices

The $MR_A = MR_B$ condition can be used to derive the ranking of prices across the markets. Suppose the demand for the product is more elastic in market A than in market B. Recalling the relationship between AR/MR and the price elasticity of demand discussed earlier, it follows that $AR_A / MR_A < AR_B / MR_B$. This can be restated as $AR_A / AR_B < MR_A / MR_B$. By definition, $AR_A = p_A$ and $AR_B = p_B$. Moreover, $MR_A = MR_B$ means $MR_A / MR_B = 1$. Hence, the inequality $AR_A / AR_B < MR_A / MR_B$ implies that $p_A / p_B < 1$, i.e., the price charged in market A is less than that charged in market B. Remember that the demand in market B is less elastic. Thus, *a price-discriminating monopolist charges a higher price in a market in which the demand is less elastic.* Put differently, *the ranking of prices across the markets is the inverse of the ranking of price elasticities across the markets*.

We can now explain various price discrimination phenomena in the real world. Afternoon movie tickets are cheaper because the demand for movies is more elastic in the afternoon time than in the evening time. Business customers are charged more for power than households, because the demand for power by the former is less elastic.[8]

Example 10.3

A monopolist has already produced 9 units of output, which will be sold in two markets, A and B, between which price discrimination is feasible. The marginal revenue schedules are given in Table 10.5. Suppose the monopolist allots 4 units to be sold in market A and 5 units in market B. Show that this does not maximise the monopolist's total revenue from the two markets combined. Should the monopolist sell more in market A and less in market B, or vice versa? What is the sales allocation which will maximise its total revenues and what will be the prices charged in the two markets?

Answer: If 4 units are sold in market A and 5 units in market B the respective marginal revenues are 15 and 7, respectively. These are unequal and thus cannot maximise total revenues. Moreover, since the marginal revenue is greater in market A than in market B, total revenues are higher if more (less) is allocated to market A (B). When 6 units are sold in market A and 3 in market B, the marginal revenues are equalised and all 9 units are sold. Hence, total revenues must be maximised at this allocation of sales. (Note that marginal revenues are also equal when 7 units are sold in market A and 6 in market B. But this cannot be the answer since the monopolist has only 9 units to sell in the two markets.) To determine the prices charged, we need to first derive the total revenue schedules in the two markets (by adding the respective marginal revenues). Given the total revenue in market A at 6 units and that in market B at 3 units, we then divide them by 6 and 3, respectively, to get the average revenues; these are the respective prices. Computing these you can get $p_A = 16.5$ and $p_B = 10$. ■

TABLE 10.5 Marginal Revenue Schedules

Output	MR_A(€)	MR_B(€)
0	–	–
1	24	11
2	21	10
3	18	9
4	15	8
5	12	7
6	9	6
7	6	4
8	3	2
9	0	0

10.7 Regulating a Private Monopoly

As a monopolist charges a price higher than the marginal cost, the monopoly output is not socially optimal, i.e., a monopoly market fails to perform in the best interest of the society. Hence, there arises a case for regulating a monopolist. More specifically, since the monopoly price exceeds the marginal cost and as a result it produces a quantity less than what is socially optimal, *any policy or regulation that induces the monopolist to produce more is social-welfare improving.*

One idea is to control the price to be charged by a monopolist. In Figure 10.3, the competitive, social-surplus-maximising price is p_c, equal to the marginal cost. Hence, if the regulatory body sets the price equal to p_c, the monopoly problem, from the perspective of social welfare, is solved. This is called a policy of **marginal cost pricing.** Of course, the monopolist is not happy with such a price control, as its profits are less compared the situation where it can set price such that $MR = MC$.

However, the matter is not this simple. Suppose that the monopoly market in question prevails because of a patent right. If, as a regular practice, the price is controlled after a new product or process is introduced into the market, it would act as a disincentive towards R&D (research and development) and innovation. Monopoly profit can be seen as returns to investment in R&D and innovation. Why would an entrepreneur take the risk of such investment if the returns are low? On the other hand, innovations improve product quality, bring new products, and therefore constitute a fundamental source of enhancement of the standard and quality of life. Therefore, while $P = MC$ principle may be the best policy at a given point of time, after the product is available, from a long-term perspective, such a policy of controlling monopoly price may not work in the best interest of the society.

Now consider an industry in which a monopoly does not arise due to R&D. A "natural" candidate is a natural monopoly, defined earlier, which is characterised by a decreasing average cost for a sufficiently long range of output. *Figure 10.5* exhibits this case. Without any regulation, the natural monopolist produces y_m, at which the condition $MR = MC$ is met.

Suppose the regulator sets the price p_c, forcing the monopolist to produce y_c, such that price equals MC. There is a problem, i.e., at this output, the monopolist is incurring a loss as the average cost ($= Cy_c$) exceeds the price p_c. This is indicated by the shaded area. If such a situation persists, the monopolist will leave the industry. The product will not be available at all for consumption. This is bad news for social welfare. Put differently, regulating price equal to the marginal cost is not sustainable.

There is another option. This is to set price equal to the marginal cost *and* provide a lump-sum subsidy to the monopolist, covering its loss. One way to make it operational to some extent is to charge a fixed fee to the consumers and a relatively low rate for actual usage. This is essentially what is called a **two-part tariff.**

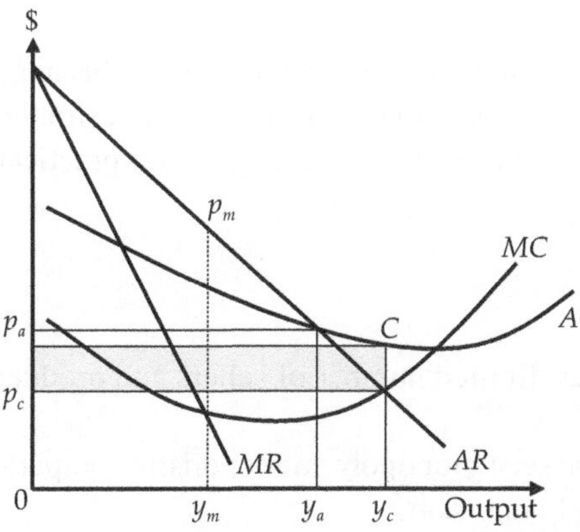

FIGURE 10.5 Regulating a Natural Monopolist

However, there is a difficulty here too. A relatively large amount of a fixed fee effectively discriminates against small users, who are typically the poor.

The next best alternative is to set price equal to the average cost, shown as p_a in Figure 10.5. This is called **average cost pricing**. Compared to the monopoly equilibrium, the monopolist produces higher quantity (equal to y_a) and the social surplus is greater. And the monopolist earns no more than its normal profits.

Indeed, such a regulation is widespread in many countries, especially for public utilities like electricity and water. In practice the price is not set exactly as is depicted in Figure 10.5. There are variations. Historically, a **fair-rate-of-return method** has been used extensively. Essentially there is a regulatory body that assesses the unit cost of production by the firm. A "fair" rate of return for investment by the monopolist is added to this price. The resulting price is the regulated price that the firm is entitled to charge.[9] There is a problem with fair-rate-of-return regulation also. That is, since the regulated price is made dependent on the cost of production, the monopolist has an incentive to inflate its cost in the eyes of the regulator. The cost shown to the regulator may very well exceed the true cost. On the other hand, it is very difficult for the regulatory body itself to have information on all transactions made by the firm and an accurate estimate of the firm's costs of production. By jacking up the costs shown to the regulator, the firm can ensure a price higher than its true unit cost and thereby earn an abnormal profit. Social welfare is less than otherwise.

There is still another option: let the government do the business itself. A prime example in almost any country is postal service, which is typically subsidised. In India, the rail-transport is another example of a subsidised government-run business, controlled by the Ministry of Railways. Interestingly, there have been suggestions for establishing a tariff commission for railways, but the Railways

Ministry, so far, has remained opposed to it. See Appendix 10.B for a short review of the state of affairs of Indian railways.

A general point of this discussion is that regulating a monopoly—because it charges a price higher than the marginal cost—may not be always desirable. Even if it is desirable, executing a regulation effectively is fraught with practical problems.

Facts and Insights

- There are two sources of market power: limited number of sellers and product differentiation.
- There are many types of imperfect markets: monopoly, monopolistic competition, duopoly, duopsony, oligopoly, and oligopsony.
- The Board of Control for Cricket in India is a monopoly of its own kind (as there are no other rival institutions organising competition in cricket in India).
- In India, patent laws were relatively weak. But recently because of our commitment to WTO they have come stricter.
- Monopoly in a market can arise due to various reasons, such as exclusive government licence, patent, technological superiority, economies of scale, etc.
- It is not true that a monopolist can choose any price arbitrarily because it is the sole producer of the product or service. The market demand curve acts as a constraint facing a monopoly firm.
- $MR = MC$ is a general condition of profit-maximisation of a firm.
- The monopolist charges a price higher than the marginal cost. This is because of the market power possessed by the monopolist.
- The mark-up of price over marginal cost depends on the price elasticity of demand facing the monopolist.
- Compared to perfect competition, a monopolist produces less and charges a higher price.
- Since the monopoly price exceeds the marginal cost and as a result it produces a quantity less than what is socially optimal, any policy or regulation that induces the monopolist to produce more is social-welfare improving.
- Merits of monopoly lie in synergies exploited from joint activity, R&D, and economies of scale.
- Under price discrimination, a monopolist charges a higher price in a market in which the demand is less elastic. The ranking of prices across the markets is the inverse of the ranking of price elasticities across the markets.
- Marginal cost pricing would imply losses for a natural monopoly.
- Utilities are typically subject to a fair-rate-of-return regulation by the government.
- Regulating a monopolist is not easy. There are theoretical and practical problems associated with any form of regulation.

- The financial state of the Indian Railways (IR) remains unhealthy. While the Government of India does not plan to "sell" the ownership of IR to the private sector, it plans to lease private parties for providing services like running platforms and trains in some sectors of IR.

Exercises

Descriptive/Analytical

10.1 What are the different types of imperfectly competitive market structure?
10.2 Why is a monopoly firm a price maker?
10.3 The *MR* schedule of a monopoly firm is given below. Derive the TR and *AR* schedules.

Output	MR *($)*
1	26
2	20
3	15
4	11
5	6
6	0
7	-5
8	-7

10.4 What is the condition of profit maximisation by a monopoly firm? What is the logic behind it?
10.5 Compare price and industry output under perfect competition and monopoly.
10.6 What are the merits of monopoly?
10.7 What is meant by price discrimination? What is the condition under which price discrimination is feasible?
10.8 What is the condition of revenue maximisation when a monopoly can price-discriminate between different markets? Give reasons.

Short Answer (word limit = 500 approx.)

10.9 What are patient rights?
10.10 What is a natural monopoly?
10.11 "For a monopoly firm, the *MR* may exceed the price." Defend or refute.
10.12 At the monopoly equilibrium, why is the price elasticity of demand greater than unity?
10.13 "At the monopoly equilibrium social welfare is not maximised." Defend or refute.
10.14 What is meant by synergy from a merger of two firms?

10.15 In the text we have outlined the benefit of synergy from a merger or an acquisition (briefly called M&A in the business language). Can you think of a demerit of M&A in terms of management and efficiency of a company?

10.16 Under price-discriminating monopoly, how are prices across markets correlated with the price elasticities of demand? Give reasons.

10.17 What is marginal cost pricing?

10.18 Explain why a marginal-cost pricing regulation may lead a monopoly firm to incur losses.

10.19 Under marginal cost pricing, will a monopoly earn any abnormal profits? Give reasons.

10.20 What are the problems associated with regulating a natural monopolist?

10.21 What is a two-part tariff?

10.22 What is a fair-rate-of-return regulation?

Quizzes/Numerical

10.23 Collect information on the Board of Control for Cricket in India (BCCI) from the internet and other sources and write a short essay on how far BCCI is a private monopolist.

10.24 "Because there is no competition, a monopoly firm can charge any arbitrarily high price of its product." Defend or refute.

10.25 Since, by definition, a monopoly firm is the only seller of a product, if it wants to sell more, compared to a given quantity being sold, why would it have to charge a lower price to be able to do so?

10.26 "Average revenue is less than the price for a monopoly firm." Defend or refute.

10.27 The higher the price elasticity, the _____ is the ratio of AR to MR. Fill in the blank and explain.

10.28 Suppose the price elasticity of demand facing a monopolist is 3.00. What will be the gross mark-up of monopoly price over marginal cost?

10.29 Compared to a perfectly competitive industry, a monopoly produces ___ and charges a ___ price. Fill in the blanks and give reasons.

10.30 In a chilly late night, you get down from train on a suburban small, isolated station. This is the last train to halt at this station and you are the only passenger to alight. The next train will stop only next day. You come out of the station and find that there is only one autorickshaw available at this hour of the night. Your home is not at a walkable distance, but you don't have any luggage. There are no mobile taxi services (like Ola, Uber) available in this area. Identify this market form. Cite a similar situation from your personal experience.

10.31 In the example given in the previous question, suppose the normal fare to your destination is ₹100 when during daytime, a lot of auto rickshaws and passengers are available. The cost of petrol for that destination is ₹40.

Suppose that the auto rickshaw driver lives in the vicinity of your destination and is planning to go back home empty (i.e., without passenger). When you approach him, he demands ₹500 to take you to your destination, whereas the normal fare is ₹100. You have made up in your mind not to pay more than ₹300, failing which, you are willing to walk.
In such a situation, what will be the likely outcome on negotiated fare if:

a) Both of you (you as the buyer and the driver as seller) know that the distance and destination (i.e., your home and driver's home) to travel is the same.
b) The driver knows your destination; you do not know where the driver lives.
c) The driver does not know your destination, but you know where he lives.

Appendix 10.A Mathematical Derivation of a Monopolist's Profit-Maximising Condition

Let the industry demand function be given by $y = f(p)$, where y is the quantity sold and p is the price charged. We can "invert" this function and write $p = g(y)$ and interpret y as the quantity produced. The function $g(y)$ is called the inverse demand function. For example, if $y = f(p) = a - bp$ is the demand function, the inverse demand function is

$$p = g(y) = \frac{a-y}{b}.$$

The total revenue = quantity produced × price = $yg(y) = R(y)$. This is the total revenue function, and $MR = R'(y)$ is the derivative of the function $R(y)$. Similarly, let the total cost function be denoted by $C(y)$. We have $MC = C'(y)$.

The monopolist's profit = $TR - TC = R(y) - C(y) \equiv \Pi(y)$. This is maximised with respect to y. The first-order condition is

$$\Pi'(y) = R'(y) - C'(y) = 0, \text{ or}$$

$$R'(y) = C'(y), \text{i.e., } MR = MC.$$

Appendix 10.B State of Indian Railways as a Monopoly

Almost everyone in India has grown with Indian Railways (IR). We, the authors, remember our childhood excitement from looking at a train, counting its bogeys, and our very first ever train journey. Reflecting back over time, we observe that the number of trains has increased substantially, and services have improved. But what is the IR's overall record in terms of meeting the need in the modern age of growing business and competing modes of transport? What is its financial state?

Over the years after India's independence in 1947, IR become virtually a sole source of travel for the poor and the common man. Increasing passenger fare is akin to committing political *harakiri* (ritualistic suicide) for any political party. Railway passenger fares in India are one of the lowest in the world, particularly in the non-air-conditioned, general, and suburban classes. The fares in these categories are subsidised to the tune of around 60%. IR cross-subsidises the passenger fares partially by keeping the freight fares high. This is not a prudent financial practice.

How about the overall financial position? In 1998–1999 the total working expense was ₹27, 835 crores (1 crore = 10 million), while the revenues were ₹29, 619 crores. The ratio of the two, called the "operating ratio," was 93%. Of course, the higher the operating ratio, the greater is the degree of *inefficiency*. Since then, barring a brief phase between 2005 and 2010 (in 2008–2009 it was 76%), the operating ratio has remained very high. In the last few years (2014–2020) it has stayed consistently above 95%.

On the face of it an operating ratio less than 100% may not appear bad. But note that these calculations do *not* include *all* normal operating costs like, for instance, the cost of overdue equipment and railway tracks (they wear out over time). If these are included, it is a "heavy-loss making entity in normal commercial accounting terms."

The experts advocate that the IR's freight market share should be improved by rationalising freight rates and providing separate dedicated corridors for freight and passenger trains. An operating ratio of around 80% is considered healthy. For that to happen, the working expenses should increase on an average around 8% (assuming a 5% inflation rate), while the revenues should grow at 12–15%.

In the post-1991 liberalisation era, the Indian government has been selling several public sector undertakings (PSUs) to the private sector. But selling IR is not so easy. The common man is emotionally connected with railways. That is why the government has repeatedly stated that the railways will "never" be privatised. What is meant is the ownership of railways will remain with the Government of India, not private firms. However, IR is being "liberalised," in the sense that private parties are being allowed to provide more services on lease, like running platforms and some trains. Think of railways food catering services. These are private parties, who do not have any "ownership" of railways. Similarly, running platforms and direct train services do not make private firms the owners of railways. The evolving IR structure can be best characterised as a more active public–private–partnership (PPP).

Sources: (Arora, 2021), (Jain, 2021), (The Hindu, 2021).

Notes

1 Plain-paper photocopy machine has been considered, by far, as the most successful commercial product in history. Today there are many well-known companies, besides Xerox, in the world market that produce photocopying machines, e.g., Canon, Mita, Panasonic, Ricoh, Royal, Sharp, and Toshiba.
2 Until a few decades ago, natural monopolies were present in providing telephone services. But this has changed because of new technologies.
3 There are other reasons for monopoly or near-monopoly also, e.g., merger and acquisition. In the early 1990s, in the Indian tea industry, Brooke Bond and Lipton merged and subsequently they merged with Hindustan Lever. It left out Tata, another large tea firm.
4 These are not an exhaustive list of factors leading to monopoly power. For instance, some firm may be a sole possessor of a scarce input and thereby enjoy monopoly power in the product market. The diamond syndicate of South Africa is an example.
5 That is, a monopoly has market power in the product market but not in the input markets.
6 This doesn't imply that monopoly power continues indefinitely. For example, if the monopoly power is obtained by virtue of a patent, it expires with expiration of the patent. The point here is that as long as there is monopoly, there is little analytical difference between short run and long run in terms of output and price determination.
7 If there are more markets like *C*, *D*, etc., the profit maximising rule is that $MR_A = MR_B = MR_C = \cdots = MC$.
8 For various reasons, the Japanese market is more closed to foreign competition, compared to the American market. Thus, the Japanese firms face more competition in the latter market. Hence, the demand for their product is more elastic in the American market than in the Japanese market. Therefore, they benefit from charging a lower price in the American market than in the Japanese market.
9 In India, various state electricity regulatory commissions are in charge of regulating electricity tariffs.

Bibliography

Arora, R. (2021, March 10). View: Passenger fare hike must be to push Indian railways on reform track. *Times of India.*

Jain, S. (2021, January 30). In 5 charts railways poor finances and how to fix it. *Times of India.*

Pattanayak, B. (2020, August 24). Global patents applications: India puts up a poor show, even Huawei has more filings. *Financial Express.*

The Hindu. (2021, March 16). Indian railways will never be Privatised: Goyal in Lok Sabha. *Hindustan Times.*

11

MONOPOLISTIC COMPETITION AND OLIGOPOLY (WITH AN INTRODUCTION TO GAME THEORY)

After going through the chapters on perfect competition and monopoly, you may have become impatient, wondering about the relevance of such detailed analysis of the two market forms which are nowhere near to reality. Perfectly competitive markets may be ideal for social welfare, but they don't exist. While the number of producers of a commodity is very large, there is no variety: every producer produces a homogeneous commodity, which is quite unrealistic. On the other hand, private monopolies are rare, if any. Most of the goods or services produced in monopoly market are public monopolies, which are not guided by profit motive alone.

We understand your discomfort and appreciate your patience for carefully going through these "impractical" market forms. However, the study of these extreme market forms is essential because they constitute the benchmarks, in order to better understand and interpret the "practical" market structures. It is like having an ideal daily exercise and diet plan in front of you to reduce your body weight by 5 kilogram in 6 months—which is important in order to assess how good your actual exercise and diet routine are.

It is time to take a tour of the "real world" of imperfectly competitive, non-monopolistic markets, which are intermediate between perfect competition and monopoly. Indeed, there are many types of markets in between perfect competition and monopoly. We shall discuss two such market forms, namely, monopolistic competition and oligopoly. Under oligopoly itself, there are different forms of markets as sub-categories.

If you happen to join the private sector after finishing your degree course, there is a good chance that your employer-firm, whether it operates in a manufacturing or a service sector, is in an oligopoly market.

DOI: 10.4324/9781003452195-11

11.1 Monopolistic Competition

This market structure is defined by three features: (a) a large number of sellers and buyers, (b) free entry and exit in the long run, and, importantly, (c) **product differentiation**. Product differentiation means that each firm produces a brand or variety (of the same product) that is unique in some sense, i.e., different from what any other firm produces. The varieties produced are supposed to be very close substitutes of one another. Products like toothpaste, soap, and lipstick are good examples.[1] Service providers like tailors who make suits, fancy hair-cut salons are also good examples; each of these provides the same service "basically," yet each one is slightly different from the other in terms of style, feel, look, etc. it offers.

The characteristics (a) and (b), respectively, imply that each firm is small relative to the market and must earn zero abnormal profits in the long run. These are competitive features. However, (c) is a monopoly feature in the sense that any given brand is produced only by one firm; hence each firm has "some" monopoly. Put differently, *product differentiation confers some market power to a monopolistically competitive firm, even though it is small compared to the entire market.* Monopolistic competition is hence a market form that is a mixture of monopoly and competition.

11.1.1 *Equilibrium in the Short Run*

The product differentiation feature offering some market power implies that a monopolistically competitive firm faces *AR* and *MR* curves for its brand like a monopolist. Thus, it maximises profits at the level of output where $MR = MC$, and, it charges a price that exceeds marginal cost.

Analytically, all this is analogous to monopoly, except for one *qualitative* difference. That is, since there are close substitutes available for any particular brand, the demand curve facing a monopolistically competitive firm (unlike that facing a monopoly firm) is very elastic, implying that the *AR* curve must be quite flat. Figure 11.1 draws a short-run situation of a representative firm in monopolistic competition.

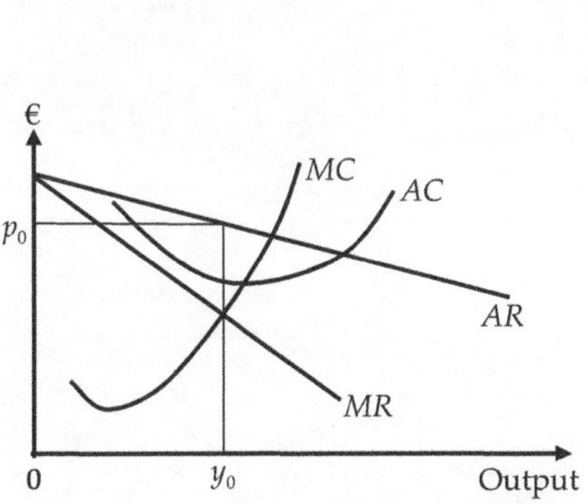

FIGURE 11.1 Monopolistic Competition in the Short Run

The *AR* curve is relatively flat. The *MR* curve corresponds to the *AR* curve. The firm maximises where *MR* equals *MC*, producing the amount y_0 and charging price p_0.

11.1.2 Long Run Equilibrium

There is however a major difference between monopolistic competition and monopoly in the long run. Unlike in monopoly, there is free entry and exit, implying that abnormal profit is driven to zero. This is equivalent to $P = LAC$, where the letter "*L*" refers to the long run. Together with the profit-maximising condition $MR = LMC$, we can compactly write the long-run equilibrium conditions under monopolistic competition as:

$$\begin{aligned} MR &= MC; \\ P &= LAC. \end{aligned} \tag{11.1}$$

Figure 11.2 illustrates the long-run equilibrium. Mark that at the point where $MR = LMC$, AR is also equal to LAC; therefore, profits are zero. The representative firm produces output y_L and charges price p_L.

Even though the long-run profits are zero, the situation is not exactly analogous to the long-run competitive equilibrium. Notice in Figure 11.2 that, whereas under perfect competition, a firm would have produced at the minimum point of the long-run average cost (i.e., at y_c), in monopolistic competition, the equilibrium output lies to the left of where the *LAC* is minimised—such as at y_L. That is, *under monopolistic competition in the long run there are increasing returns to scale and unit cost is not minimised.* This result is known as an *excess capacity theorem* in the sense that in equilibrium the production is not optimised from the viewpoint of using up all economies of scale without stepping into the range of diseconomies of scale.

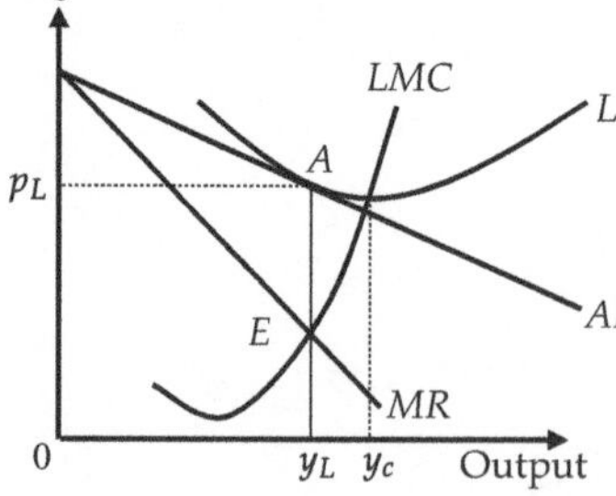

FIGURE 11.2 Monopolistic Competition in the Long Run

11.1.3 Social Welfare Implications

The excess capacity theorem may lead one to think that, compared to the social optimum, there are too many firms so that an individual firm is not able to produce enough to fully utilise the economies of scale. But that is not a definitive conclusion. A smaller number of larger firms would imply lower unit cost and lower price (which tends to increase social welfare), but, also mean lesser number of varieties as well. It is natural to assume that the society values product variety. Imagine a world where one colour or limited-colour T-shirts are sold or a single brand or two brands of car are produced.

If so, then reducing the number of firms will lower social welfare via reducing the number of varieties. Therefore, we cannot generally say whether, compared to the social optimum, the monopolistically competitive equilibrium entails too many or too few firms and varieties. In any event, to the extent that price is not equal to marginal cost, there is some welfare loss compared to what is the first-best for the society.

11.1.4 Advertising

Although the features of monopolistic competition are a combination of perfect competition and monopoly, in terms of decision-making, there is one aspect that is different from both perfect competition and monopoly. That is, monopolistically competitive firms typically engage in advertising, i.e., they incur **advertising costs** or what is also called **selling costs**. It is because of the need to maintain a perception in the mind of the potential consumers that their respective brands are somewhat different (and more tasteful or classy), compared to other brands. This is **persuasive advertising**, the purpose of which is to lure away consumers from other brands. In perfect competition, the product is perfectly homogeneous, hence there is no scope to engage in persuasive advertisement. The same holds for monopoly, but for a different reason: there is no or little competition.

Realise that such selling costs do not benefit the consumers as a group; they only switch consumers from one brand to another. But they involve resources, which could have been potentially used for production. Competitive advertising is a big industry without adding a large value to the society in terms of higher consumption. These costs are "wasteful" from the viewpoint of the society.

However, not all advertising costs are wasteful. On many occasions there is **informative advertisement** (e.g., about health) which are useful for the consumers. Further, even if it is persuasive advertising, an opportunity to advertise may increase competition, reduce prices, and thereby improve social welfare. Indeed, a classic study by Lee Benham found that in America the price of eye-glasses was cheaper on the average by $20 (at 1963 prices) in the states that allowed advertising than in the states that didn't allow advertising.

Is all advertising, which is supposed to be hypothetical like a movie, ethical? Box 11.1 offers a viewpoint.

BOX 11.1 ADVERTISING AND ETHICS

What do you think about the claims made in the following advertisement?

- Apply our cream and you will become fairer in less than 15 days.
- Use this perfume and a dozen young boys/girls will throng you as bees throng the queen bee.
- Take this energy tab and you (a 60-year-old) will instantly feel as agile and manly as a 30-year-old.
- Apply this oil or shampoo and your hair will grow thick and strong.

The list is endless. Tall, unsubstantiated claims, virtually bordering on the absurd, are dished out to us *ad infinitum* in the media. To top it all, all this is presented to us with pomp and show, razzmatazz and glitter by roping in the top stars from films, sports, and other walks of life. In our preceding section, we stated that excess capacity reduces social welfare because firms don't benefit (they get only normal profit) whereas consumers pay more. This is an inherent wastage of monopolistic competition. However, we tried to defend this wastage as it gave us a lot of variety to choose from. In perfect competition, all firms would be producing a single /monotonous homogenous loaf of bread. But in monopolistic competition, we get a wide range of breads differing in size, taste, fragrance, and ingredients. Thus, it is okay to pay a little more for such indulgence.

What about selling costs? Remember as consumers we are the ones who are paying for these costs. In fact, there are a lot of examples where product cost is only a fraction of the total cost. Aerated beverage is a classic example. How will you feel if you are told that the price of a bottle of cola that you just bought for $3.50 could have been available to you for $1.10, had the producers not roped in that international film star in the advertisement or had the producer not sponsored the T20 world cup in cricket? As a matter of fact, you have indirectly paid $2.4 per bottle of your favourite cold drink to watch those matches. Thus, selling cost is the other wastage of monopolistic competition like excess capacity. Can it be justified? We can say that spending on glossy advertisements, sponsoring events such as sports, award functions, soap operas, multi-episode serials, religious functions, etc. makes our life colourful, entertaining, and spicy. As a counter, a critic may argue, what about that buyer of cola who doesn't watch cricket or who does not like that film star? Why is she being forced to pay $1.4 extra every time she buys a bottle of cola she likes?

Besides wastage, there is another issue related to selling costs, that is, ethics. Is it morally right to befool impressionable minds with claims which are utterly false (as cited in the beginning)? Recently there was a lot of hue and cry against a "fairness" cream as it promoted racial discrimination; ultimately the manufacturer had to drop the term "fair" and reposition its advertisement.

This may be an isolated instance. By and large, the producers get away with their baseless claims. You may have noticed in very small font size, fast-disappearing statements like, *results may vary*; *under test conditions*; don't try these stunts at home, statutory warnings, etc. Above all, sellers cite a standard legal term in commerce and trade: CAVEAT EMPTOR—let the buyer beware. The seller will carry out all the tricks at his disposal to lure the buyers to his product. It is up to the buyers to be vigilant. Whether it is ethical or not depends on which side are you on. There is always very large grey area in between "right" and "wrong."

In the famous Hindu epic Mahabharata, Guru Dronacharya, the teacher of both the Pandvas and Kaurvas, was fighting the war on the side of Kaurvas. He was so powerful and knowledgeable that it was virtually impossible for Pandvas to defeat him. Krishna, the master strategist of Pandvas, knew that. It was also well-known that Guru Dron was very much attached to his son Ashwathama, who was also very powerful. Krishna thought that if somehow false news of the death of Ashwathama reaches Dronacharya during the warfare, he would lay down his weapons and then Arjuna (one of the Pandvas) could kill him. However, there was a glitch. Guru Dron would not believe such news unless it came from a very truthful person. And who could be more trustworthy than the eldest of Pandva brothers, Yudhishtra, reputed to be the epitome of truth and righteousness? He had never told a single lie in his lifetime. Thus, when Krishna reached Yudhishtra with this proposal, he flatly refused. Krishna found a way out. There was an elephant named Ashwathama in the army. Krishna got that elephant killed and asked Yudhishtra to pronounce loudly in front of Dronacharya that Ashwathama has been killed. This way he could (Yudhishtra) keep his reputation as he "did not" tell any lie in saying so. Yudhishtra finally agreed on the condition that he would make the following statement (in Sanskrit).

"Ashwathama Hoto; Naro wa Kunjaro?" meaning thereby that Ashwathama has been killed, whether a man or an elephant (he doesn't know). Well, you know this story and what happened thereafter. Yudhishtra was brought in front of the Guru where he pronounced loudly that Ashwathama has been killed, but the moment he stated stating the second part, i.e., whether a man or an elephant, Krishna arranged a loud noise with the blowing of conchs, beating of drums, and the latter part remained unheard by Guru Dronacharya. He simply surrendered himself.

Now the question is, what is ethical? The same ethical dilemma arises when persuasive advertising is used with highly imaginative, sometimes physically impossible claims, that can be potentially imitated by young folks, endangering their health and lives. We leave the debate open.

11.2 Oligopoly

An **oligopoly** *market is one that is populated by a limited number of sellers or producers.* A special case where there are only two firms is called a **duopoly** market. In oligopoly the product may be homogeneous or differentiated. The number of firms being limited means that entry and exit processes are limited. It is not necessary that the government regulates entry or exit. The technology of the product or the service provided may involve such huge fixed or overhead costs that many firms cannot enter or survive.

There are numerous examples of an oligopoly market such as passenger aircrafts, air-conditioners, cars, cellular telephone services, etc. The most crucial behavioural difference of oligopoly with other market structures studied thus far is that each firm in the industry is big enough to hold market power to the extent that a change in the price or output decision by any single firm can significantly affect the profit of any other firm. Put differently, each firm is "important" for any other firm, implying that *in oligopoly there is a game-theoretic, strategic interaction among firms.* In deciding price, quantity, etc. each firm must take into consideration the effects of its own action on the actions to be chosen by others and vice versa. As said earlier, whether the product is homogenous or differentiated does not have any bearing on whether the market is oligopoly or not. One can talk about a homogeneous-product oligopoly or an oligopoly with product differentiation.

As a result, the analysis of oligopoly is a bit complicated, albeit more interesting. Unlike perfect competition, monopoly or monopolistic competition, *there is no single unified "model" of oligopoly.* Instead, there are several "models" of oligopoly.

In what follows, we present the basic elements of game theory, which can be read on its own and whose scope is *not* confined to oligopoly. Next, we outline a few elementary oligopoly models that should suffice for understanding how such markets work from a managerial perspective. In the process, we will see how game theory is relevant for studying oligopoly markets.

11.2.1 Game Theory: A Primer

Game theory is not concerned with how or what factors are important to win a game like cricket, football, or baseball. There is a branch of economics called **economics of sports** that analyses actual games and strategies from an economic or a statistical perspective. *Game theory deals with strategic behaviour or choice in a situation of interdependence among individuals, species, or organisations, i.e., in a situation where the behaviour of one party* ***directly*** *affects the well-being of another.* Technically speaking, it is a branch of mathematics, which has wide applications in various subjects. It is in the domain of economics to examine the behaviour of people and organisations vis-à-vis other people and organisations in a strategic environment. This is why game theory is relevant for economic analysis. In the last few decades, it has become an integral part of economics and is considered "essential" for any higher study in the subject. Since 1995, many among the Nobel laureates in economics have won the prize for their contributions to game theory.

Numerous economic problems can be meaningfully posed in game theory. For instance, firms compete in advertising. One firm's advertising strategy depends on a rival firm's choice of an advertising strategy. One country's economic policy may affect another's welfare and therefore the latter's choice of an appropriate policy.

Our strategy to make you understand game theory lies in laying out examples.

Ice Cream on the Beach

Think of a sea beach as a straight line from 0 to 1, as shown in Figure 11.3. On a sunny, warm day it is crowded. Assume that the crowd is evenly spread out and everyone wants to consume one ice cream. Assume further that there are exactly two ice cream vendors to serve. Both sell one type of ice cream only and there is no quality difference between ice creams sold by them. This implies no preference as such for ice cream from any particular vendor over that of the other. Hence the price of ice cream bought from either vendor will be the same. The central question is: Where are the vendors going to situate themselves on the beach?

It is a "two-person" or a "two-player game," a game between the two vendors. There are many possible, indeed infinitely many possible strategies available for a vendor—i.e., choose a point on the real-line interval [0, 1]. Are both going to select the same spot, i.e., stand at the same location on the beach like at *A*, *C*, *M*, *D*, *B*, or any other point? Or, are they going to locate themselves at different points like the one at *A*, the other at *B*, or one at *C*, the other at *D*, or at any other pair of points? There is an important but natural assumption to be used. That is, people on the beach incur a discomfort to walk to and from the ice cream vendor on the hot sand and the longer they have to travel to get their ice cream, the greater is their total discomfort. This can be viewed as an additional cost of having an ice cream.

Let us try to figure out the answer. One possible answer is that one vendor stands at *C* (marked ¼) and the other is at *D* (marked ¾). It is natural to think that this is the right answer, because with these locational choices people in the left-half of the beach go to the vendor at *C* and those in the right-hand half of the beach

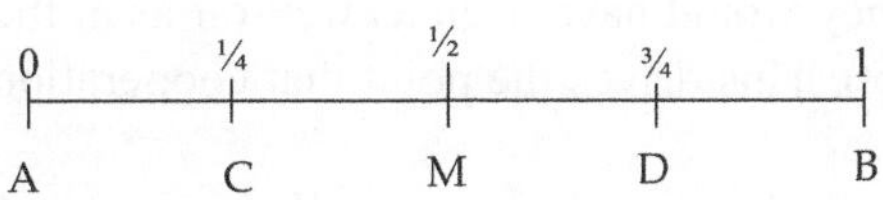

FIGURE 11.3 Location of Ice Cream Vendors

go to the vendor at *D*. No one has to travel more than half of the beach length. Each vendor serves half of the market.

However, we will now argue that the strategies (*C*, *D*) are *not* the answer. It is because, starting with (*C*, *D*), suppose the vendor at *D* moves a little to the left. He will then have all his previous customers (from *M* to *B*) plus a few more in the immediate left of the mid-point *M*, to whom this vendor will now be nearer. As a result, the right-hand vendor captures more than 50% share of the market. Will the left-hand vendor continue to stay at the point *C*? Unless he is a fool, he will move rightward and recapture, perhaps extend his market share.

Where will this process end? The answer is the point *M*. That is, *both vendors will locate themselves in the middle.* This is the answer. It is an *equilibrium*—in the sense that if both vendors are at *M*, neither has any incentive to change its position. Indeed, it is the Nash equilibrium of this game, named after a Nobel laureate in economics, John Nash. *In general, a collection of strategies by the players constitutes* **Nash equilibrium** *if no single player has any incentive to change his strategy, that is, differently put, no single player benefits (i.e., receives a greater payoff) from unilaterally choosing a different strategy.*

This example explains something we observe in the marketplace. In providing a service or a product, the providers (shops) have an incentive cluster geographically rather than spread themselves out. For example, you must have somewhere noticed two petrol pumps side by side on the road and wondered why they didn't locate themselves separately. You may also find two similar eating joints side by side in virtually the same location.

Our example illustrates a very general and important point as well. Notice that in our example the socially most desirable solution is that the vendors locate at points C and D—because this will minimise the total discomfort from travelling by all people on the beach, while each firm keeps its natural market share of one-half. But the strategic equilibrium is not consistent with this, i.e., unlike in a competitive market, *the social welfare is not maximised at the Nash equilibrium.* You can tie this up with our analysis in the last chapter by noting that here there are only two players, not infinitely many, and hence each player has some power. Therefore, the Nash equilibrium entails market failure. Pursuing self-interest is not consistent with the best interest of the society.

To further understand this point, also note that, in our example, the vendors play what is called a **non-cooperative game**, i.e., the players do not select their strategies jointly to maximise their joint profits. But had they acted cooperatively, they would have selected the points *C* and *D* as well, which would have served the interest of the society the best and they would have been as well off as at the point *M* (each serving 50% of the market). This drives the point that cooperation is valuable for a society.

We next consider the most famous example of game theory, called **prisoners' dilemma**.

Prisoners' Dilemma

Two guys, *A* and *B*, have committed a murder. The police "know" it, but they only have circumstantial evidence, no solid proof. The police want confession, without which they expect to extract from the court of law only a mild, two-year, prison sentence for each.

In attempting to make them confess, the police keep *A* and *B* in two separate cells—so that they cannot communicate (no cell phones) or cooperate—and offer them a deal. Each one is told separately, "If you don't confess, while 'your friend' does, you get 20 years in prison and your friend gets only 7 years. If you both confess, each of you will get a 12-year prison sentence."

In this game note that there are two strategies available to each player: "confess" (C) or "hang tough" (T). The question is: What would the prisoners choose? To arrive at an answer let us consider utility to a player from various combinations of strategies. In game theory a player's utility is typically called his payoff. For instance, if *A* confesses (chooses C), while *B* hangs tough (chooses T), *A* gets a 7-year sentence (his payoff is −7) and *B* gets 20 years (his payoff is −20). Various payoffs associated with various strategy combinations in the game are listed in Table 11.1. For each combination of strategies there are two numbers, showing the payoffs. The first number is *A*'s payoff and the second is that of *B*. Table 11.1 is a **payoff matrix.**

To determine which of the four strategy combinations will be chosen, we must use a criterion. The standard assumption in game theory is to accept the notion of Nash equilibrium. That is, we seek that particular combination of strategies such that no player has an incentive to deviate from it.

What about (T, T)? It is not a Nash equilibrium, since either player can deviate (i.e., move to C) and be better off (prison sentence will be reduced by 13 years). What about (C, T), i.e., *A* plays C and *B* plays T? From this combination, *B* would want to deviate and gain: by choosing C instead, he can reduce his prison sentence by 8 years. Indeed, you can check that the Nash equilibrium is (C, C), i.e., both players confess. This is the solution to the Prisoners' dilemma game.

The point of this example is that, from the players' perspective the best strategy combination is of course (T, T). But they are unable to attain it, as they are denied

TABLE 11.1 Payoffs in the Prisoners' Dilemma Game

Prisoner *A*	*Prisoner B*		
		C	*T*
	C	(−12, −12)	(−7, −20)
	T	(−20, −7)	(−2, −2)

any opportunity to communicate and cooperate. In general, *a non-cooperative game does not achieve the best for the players.*

An Advertising Game

Suppose there are two firms, *A* and *B*, in an industry. Each produces a product, which is a direct substitute of the other. There are two strategies available to each firm: advertise and don't advertise. Assume that advertising costs are £10 thousand, although this is not directly relevant. When neither firm advertises, each firm earns a profit of £50 thousand. If one firm advertises and the other doesn't, some customers switch from the latter to the former. The advertising firm's (net) profit is £60 thousand, while the other firm earns a profit of £30 thousand. If both firms advertise, then their profits are £40 thousand each.

The payoff matrix is given in Table 11.2. The left-hand number in the four cells is the payoff of firm *A* and the right-hand number is that of firm *B*.

What is the Nash equilibrium of this game? Applying its definition, you can deduce easily that (advertise, advertise) is the Nash equilibrium. Notice that this game is similar to the Prisoner's dilemma. Compared to the Nash equilibrium, both players can be better off—and the society will benefit—if they choose (no ad, no ad) instead. Yet, they cannot do it—because they are "behaving" (choosing their strategies) in a non-cooperative manner.

World Trade

Almost all countries in the world engage in international trade. They export certain items and import some. Divide all trading countries of the world into two types: developed countries and developing countries and think of them as two countries. Table 11.3 shows their payoffs from various combinations of trade policy.

TABLE 11.2 Advertising Game (Payoffs in Thousands of £)

Firm A	*Firm B*		
		Ad	*No Ad*
	Ad	(40, 40)	(60, 30)
	No Ad	(30, 60)	(50, 50)

TABLE 11.3 Payoffs in the International Trade Policy Game

Developing Countries	Developed Countries		
		Free Trade	Trade Restrictions
	Free Trade	(100, 100)	(30, 160)
	Trade Restrictions	(160, 30)	(60, 60)

If both countries impose trade restrictions against each other, their benefits are (60, 60), measured in some units, where the first entry is the benefit to the developing countries and the second entry is that to the developed countries. On the other hand, suppose they cooperate and eliminate trade restrictions against each other. Both would benefit from specialising and exporting products that they are relatively better at producing. The benefits associated with free trade (zero trade restrictions) are denoted as (100, 100). Note that the same numbers for both developing and developed countries do *not* mean that both gain equally. For instance, for one country the gains may be measured in terms of dollars and for the other it may be in terms of some other currency. Indeed, a fundamental lesson learnt from international economics is that there are many, many sources of benefits from free trade to a nation as a whole. While this is not our subject matter here, simply note that, compared to both countries choosing trade restrictions, each country's payoff is higher under free trade permitted by each other. However, if one country follows trade restriction, while the other doesn't, the former gains at the expense of the latter. For instance, if developing countries "play" "trade restrictions," while the developed countries play "free trade," the former is better off than under free trade (i.e. 160 versus 100) and the latter is worse off.

What is the equilibrium in this game? You can check that it is "trade restrictions" by each country. This is again analogous to the Prisoners' Dilemma game! The implications for cooperation are also similar. If both are able to cooperate, they will choose free trade, and be better off.[2]

Apart from the examples already given and will be given in the exercises, there are numerous economic problems where the tools of the game theory are applied. For instance, the interaction between labour unions and firms can be thought of as a game where the union sets the wage rate and the management of the firm decides the level of employment. In a political-economy context, two parties, as players, choose the economic policies so as to please their own party member and win votes from rival party sympathisers.

Formal Nature of a Game

Game theory goes far beyond the two-player or two-strategy examples we have studied. In general, a **game** (as in game theory) is defined by three things:

(a) A set of players;
(b) A set of strategies available to each player; and
(c) A list of payoffs for each player from each combination of strategies by all players.

A game is "solved" by using some notion of an equilibrium, e.g., the Nash equilibrium.

Zero-Sum and Non-Zero-Sum Games, and Non-Cooperative and Cooperative Games

In general, there are two kinds of games: zero-sum game and non-zero-sum game. Zero-sum game *is one in which the sum of the payoffs to players in all combinations of strategies is zero.* This is equivalent to saying that in a two-player or a two-team game, one wins and the other loses; there are no other possibilities. Any game, which is not a zero-sum game, is *a* **non-zero-sum game**, *defined by the property that the sum of payoff do not always add up to zero.*

None of the examples given so far is zero-sum games. Indeed, *most economic situations in which strategies are important are not zero-sum in nature.* This is important to know, because, for example, there are still some people who erroneously think that international trade is a zero-sum game: if there are two countries and one country benefits from free trade, the other must, by definition, lose. Instead, in most trading situations *all* trading partners benefit, although they may not equally benefit. Similarly, some think that allowing multinational companies to make profits in a country is zero-sum game: since these companies are making profits, the host country must be losing. This is also a mistaken notion. While the multinationals may be making profit, they may be creating employment or at least enhancing the salary of some workers. Is this not good for the workers? Also, they may be making and selling a product, which otherwise would not be available at a reasonable price in the market. Isn't this good for the consumers? While we formally discuss the merits and demerits of international trade and investment in Chapter 15, not in this chapter, the general point is that such economic activity is generally non-zero-sum in nature.

In all the examples given above, there is a unique Nash equilibrium. But this need not be the case; there may be two or more equilibria. In some games, a Nash equilibrium may not even exist; this does not mean however that game theory cannot be used. There are many other equilibrium notions, different ways of using strategies, etc. Indeed, game theory is vast, rich, and fascinating.

We end up our introduction to game theory by noting a different classification of "game situations." There are **non-cooperative games** (all the above examples and those in the exercises are of this kind) and **cooperative games**. Non-cooperative games are those in which players act, i.e., choose their strategies, on their own without any direct understanding or communication with other players. In cooperative games, the players maximise their joint payoff or surplus and distribute it in a way that benefits them all (not necessarily equally). Thus, *in a cooperative-game equilibrium, players are better off than in the corresponding non-cooperative-game equilibrium.*

This raises a question: Why don't then the players or economic agents always play a cooperative game? There are two problems. In some situations, cooperation is not permitted. Think of the prisoner's dilemma game. Will the police allow the murder suspects to cooperate in admitting or not admitting to the crime? As we shall see later in this chapter, firms or companies are not allowed to cooperate or collude in deciding the prices for their products (because it would undermine competition). Cooperation may be permissible in other situations. For instance, two neighbouring countries may be engaged in a situation of potential conflict with each other, each spending enormous amounts on defence. They always have the option of cooperatively downscaling conflict and improving their welfare. But the availability of the option of cooperation does not mean that the players will necessarily choose it over a non-cooperative game (the preceding example should make it clear). It is because there may be issues of reputation and commitment: one player may not expect to obtain a credible commitment towards cooperation from another. This is where social or political institutions come in. Our aim here is not to get deeper into these aspects, but just note that notions of reputation and institutions are studied in the framework of game theory.

We now begin our analysis of oligopoly markets.

11.2.2 Kinked-Demand Curve Model

It is observed that prices in industries with small number of firms (i.e., in oligopoly industries) fluctuate less than prices in industries with a large number of sellers and buyers. Compare for instance the prices of products like television, telephone services, washing machines on the one hand and those of stocks of different companies and different metals on the other. The latter vary from day to day, even from one minute to the next, whereas the former category of prices is relatively stable. Such price stability in an oligopoly market is explained by what is called the kinked-demand curve model.

Consider an oligopoly industry in which the firms produce a differentiated product. Think of a particular firm, say firm X, which is initially producing y_0 and charging the price p_0. This quantity–price combination is shown at the point A in the left panel of Figure 11.4. Starting from this initial situation, suppose that the firm cuts its price, say to p_1. Will the other firms "keep quiet" and not change their prices? No, because if they do not, they will lose customers to firm X, reducing their profits. Their optimal response will be to lower prices too. Thus, the firm initiating the price cut (firm X) will gain only a modest increase in sales (to the extent that there is a decline in the price of *all* brands, which encourages the consumers to buy more of the product across the board). At p_1, the quantity sold by firm X is marked by y_1. The key point is that below the price p_0, the demand curve is relatively inelastic and steep—reflecting a price-cut response by other firms. This is illustrated by the relatively steep line segment AB.

What happens if firm X, instead of lowering its price, increases it, say to p_2? The other firms will not mind this at all as they stand to gain. Since the brand produced by firm X is costlier, it is likely to lose a lot of sales to other firms. That is, the quantity sold by firm X will decrease by a relatively large amount: from y_0 to

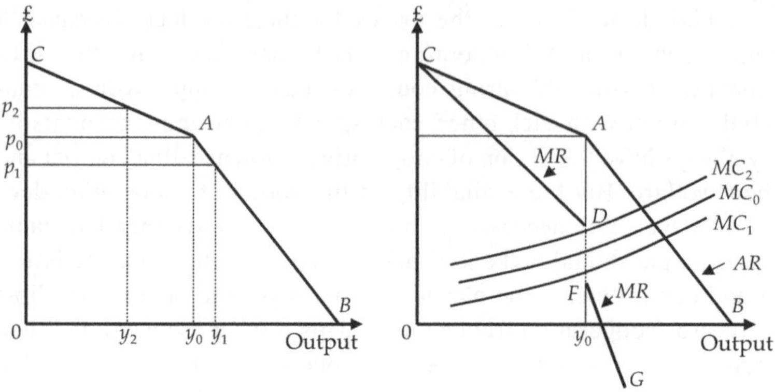

FIGURE 11.4 The Kinked-Demand Curve Model

y_2.Hence, above the price p_0. the demand curve facing firm *X* will be very elastic (flat). This is indicated by the segment *AC*.

Combining what happens with a price cut and a price hike, *CAB* is the entire demand curve facing a particular firm *X*. (The two segments are drawn as straight lines only for simplicity only, but they need not be so.) Note the "kink" (sharp edge) at the point *A*. What is the economic rationale behind such a kink? It is the sharp difference in the price elasticity along the demand curve on the two sides of the price p_0. which arises because of the asymmetry in the response of other firms with regard to a price cut and a price rise initiated by a particular firm.

As the demand curve facing a firm is its *AR* curve, the line *CAB* in the left panel of Figure 11.4 is marked as the *AR* curve in the right panel. What is the corresponding *MR* curve? See the right panel. In the output range from 0 to y_0, the *MR* curve will have a segment like *CD* which corresponds to the segment *CA* on the *AR* curve. In the output range beyond y_0, the *MR* curve has the segment *FG*, corresponding to the segment *AB* on the *AR* curve. Hence, the *MR* curve is discontinuous, with discontinuity occurring at the kink.

Now let the curve MC_0 denote firm *X*'s marginal cost curve. At what level of output is the firm's profit maximised? The answer is y_0 and the reason is as follows. At any level of output below y_0, $MR > MC$ so that profit can be increased by increasing the output. Similarly, at any output above y_0, $MR < MC$, and therefore, profit will increase by decreasing the output. These two statements imply that the profit is the maximum at the output level corresponding to the kink.

Suppose that there is some variation in the cost conditions facing the firm such that the *MC* curve shifts to say MC_1 or MC_2. Notice that this has *no* impact on the firm's profit-maximising output. It continues to produce at the kink and charge the price p_0. In other words, the price chosen by the firm is insensitive to a change in cost conditions—at least to some extent (i.e., as long as the *MC* curve passes between the points D and F). This is how the kinked-demand curve model explains why price variations are not likely to be large in oligopoly markets.

While this model is useful, it has two major drawbacks. First, the model does not explain the position of the kink on the demand curve. It starts with an arbitrarily given output-price combination and then argues that it is the profit-maximisation combination. Second, although it appeals to the notion of strategic interaction (i.e., how one firm responds to a change in strategy by another), it is still not grounded on equilibrium concepts in game theory. We may call this a "quasi"-game theory model.

11.2.3 Quantity Competition: The Cournot Model

Cournot, a French economist and mathematician in the 19th century, formulated a model of duopoly competition in quantities produced and sold, which could be founded on the notion of Nash equilibrium and therefore is consistent with game theory.[3]

Let the two firms be called A and B. Assume that the product is homogeneous. Figure 11.5 depicts the industry demand curve DD. The questions are: (i) What will each firm produce? (ii) What will be the market price? Of course, if we have the answer to question (i), the answer to question (ii) is immediate: add up the two firms' outputs to get the industry-level output and the equilibrium price is the one at which the total quantity demanded is equal to the industry output. Let y_A and y_B denote the output produced and sold by firm A and firm B , respectively. For instance, if $y_A + y_B = Y_0$, the market price is p_0.[4]

Recall that Nash equilibrium is defined by a set of strategies chosen by the players such that any single player will not benefit from changing his strategy. In the present context, the players are firms A and B. The strategies are (the individual)

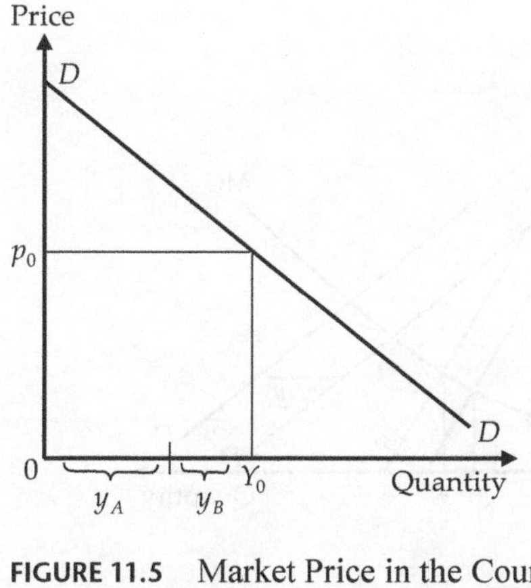

FIGURE 11.5 Market Price in the Cournot Model

outputs chosen by the firms. A particular combination of outputs, say (y_A^0, y_B^0), will qualify as a Nash equilibrium if, given y_B^0, firm A has no incentive to choose any output other than y_A^0, i.e., the y_A^0 is the profit-maximising output of firm A when $y_B = y_B^0$, and likewise y_B^0 is the profit-maximising output of firm B when $y_B = y_B^0$. How are y_A^0 and y_B^0 determined?

Consider first the profit-maximising behaviour of firm A at various possible value of y_B. Suppose that $y_B = 0$. Then firm A has the entire market, i.e., it is a monopoly. The market demand curve is its AR curve. The left panel of Figure 11.6 illustrates this. (The AR curve drawn is the same as the demand curve in Figure 11.5.) It also depicts the marginal cost curve of firm A. Its profit-maximising output is y_m, at which $MR = MC$. Put differently, at $y_B = 0$, the best response of firm A is to produce output equal to y_m.

Now suppose firm B produces a small quantity. Then, compared to $y_B = 0$, at any given quantity sold by firm A, the total quantity sold in the market will be higher and hence the market price will be less. That is, the average revenue will be smaller. Thus, the AR curve facing firm A will lie to the left of its AR curve when $y_B = 0$. This is shown in the right panel of Figure 11.6, which depicts the same market demand curve as in the left panel. The AR curve of firm A is $D'D'$, such that the horizontal difference between DD and $D'D'$ is the amount produced by firm B. The corresponding MR curve is marked by MR'. The associated profit-maximising output by firm A is equal to y_1. This is the best response of firm A.

Note that y_1 is less than y_m, that is, a higher output by firm B implies a smaller profit-maximising output by firm A. Why? It is because if one firm is able to sell a higher quantity than before, it is equivalent to a decrease in the demand curve facing the other firm. Hence the other firm produces less in equilibrium. Such reasoning implies that the equilibrium output of firm A decreases with the output of firm B. This relationship is graphed in Figure 11.7(a). The curve is marked R_A,

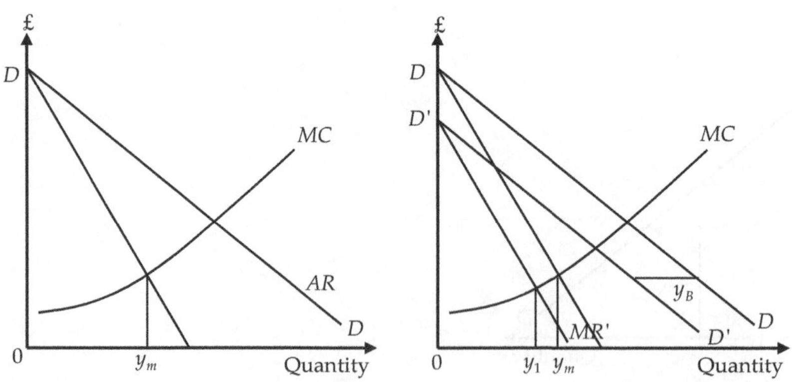

FIGURE 11.6 Output Choice in Cournot Duopoly

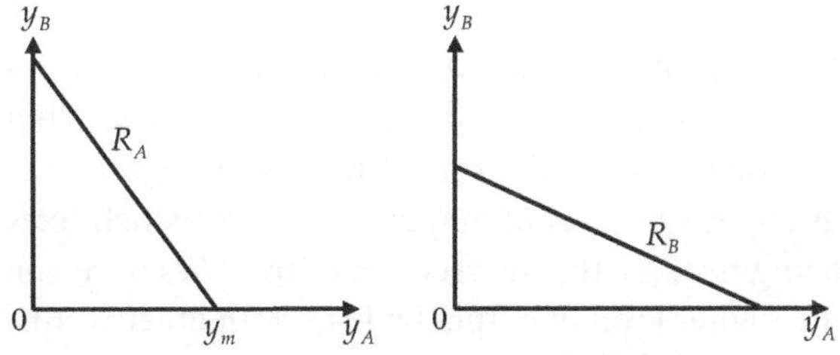

(a) Firm A (b) Firm B

FIGURE 11.7 Best Response Curves

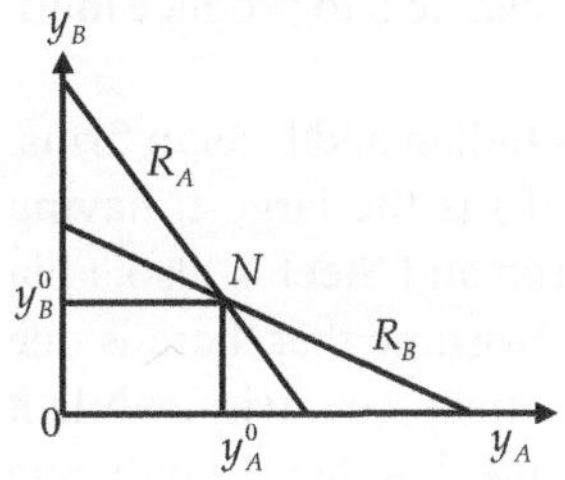

FIGURE 11.8 Nash Equilibrium in Quantity Competition

which we can call the best response curve of firm *A*. In general, *the* **best response curve** *shows a player's best (optimal) strategies corresponding to different strategies chosen by other player(s).*

Similarly, we can analyse the profit-maximising behaviour of firm *B* at various levels of output by firm *A*. By the same logic, the equilibrium output of firm *B* decreases with the output of firm *A*. This relationship is shown by the R_B curve in Figure 11.7(b). This is the best response curve of firm *B*.

Figure 11.8 graphs the best response curves of the two firms together. Mark the point of intersection, *N*. This is the Nash equilibrium point, solving the Nash equilibrium outputs, y_A^0 and y_B^0 , respectively, for firm *A* and firm *B*. Why does the intersection point constitute Nash equilibrium? The point *N* being on R_A means that when $y_B = y_B^0$, firm *A* maximises its profit by producing y_A^0 and thus it has no incentive to choose any output other than y_A^0. The point *N* also lies on R_B, meaning that when $y_A = y_A^0$, y_B^0 is the profit-maximising output of firm *B* and thus firm *B* has no incentive to choose any output other than y_B^0.

We can now use this quantity competition framework to determine the effects of changes in "parameters" facing the industry. The term "parameter" here means a basic condition or state of the industry, which is not influenced by the choices made by producers or consumers, but which can change due to extraneous factors.

For example, suppose that firm A is able to discover a new way of organising workers in the production activity such that its MC curve shifts down. How will it affect the equilibrium quantities produced by both firms? Turn first to Figure 11.6. If the MC curve shifts down, at any given level of output by firm B (which fixes the position of the MR curve facing firm A), the intersection of the MR curve and the new MC curve will occur at a higher level of output by firm A. In other words, the profit-maximising output of firm A is higher than before at any given level of y_B. This implies that the R_A curve in Figure 11.7 will shift to the right (but there will be no shift of the R_B curve).

This shift is shown in Figure 11.9(a). In the new (Nash) equilibrium, firm A produces more and firm B produces less. These are reasonable outcomes. A cost reduction method discovered and executed by a firm will enable it to produce more in the market and force its rival to produce less.

Consider another application. In India, steel is sold by Indian and foreign firms. Among Indian firms, the Steel Authority of India (SAIL) is the largest, having plants at Rourkela, Durgapur, Vilai, and Bokaro. Tata Iron and Steel is also a big manufacturer of steel. However, for analytical purposes, assume that there is one domestic producer of steel. India also imports steel from many countries, while it imposes an import duty. For the sake of arguments, assume that there is only one foreign firm who sells steel in India. Hence, ignoring quality difference between domestic and foreign steel, we can depict the Indian steel market as a duopoly, having a domestic firm and a foreign firm. Note that paying import duty adds to the marginal cost of selling steel in India by the foreign firm. Go back to Figure 11.7 and interpret $R_A$and R_B as the best response curves of the domestic firm and the foreign firm, respectively, keeping in mind that R_B considers the tariff cost facing the foreign firm. As in Figure 11.7, in equilibrium the former sells y_A^0 of steel and the latter sells y_B^0.

Suppose that, starting from a situation of 10% import duty on steel, the Indian government slaps a higher tariff at 15%.[5] How would it affect the firms? The tariff

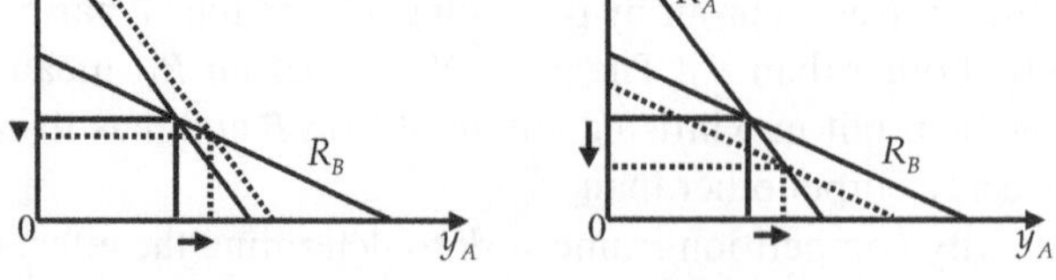

(a) Cost Cutting Innovations (b) Tariff Protection

FIGURE 11.9 Changes in Parameters

hike would shift the foreign marginal cost curve up. As a result, the foreign firm, firm *B*, will produce and sell less at any given level of output by the domestic firm. Hence the R_B curve will shift in, as shown in Figure 11.9(b). As we see, at the new equilibrium the domestic firm produces more, while the foreign firm produces and sells less. Thus, the domestic firm benefits from import protection, while the foreign firm is worse off.

Example 11.1

Two firms, Assam-Chicken (firm A) and Bengal-Chicken (firm B) supply broiler chicken to the city of Guwahati, India. They compete in quantities, i.e., play a Cournot game. Chickens sold by both firms are of the same size and quality, and quantity is measured by the number of chickens produced and supplied to the market. Suppose that the best response function of Assam-Chicken is given by $y_A = 5{,}000 - 3y_B$, *e.g., if* $y_B = 500$, *Assam-Chicken produces* $5{,}000 - 3 \times 500 = 3{,}500$ *chickens. Similarly, let the best response function of Bengal-Chicken be specified by* $y_B = 2{,}000 - (0.5)y_A$. *(a) How many chickens will be supplied to the market by each firm and both firms together in equilibrium? (b) Suppose that* $\mathrm{Q} = 3{,}150 - \mathrm{p}$ *spells the market demand curve for chicken in Guwahati. What will then be the market price of broiler chicken?*

Answer: Rewrite the best response functions as

$$y_A + 3y_B = 5{,}000$$

$$y_A + 2y_B = 4{,}000.$$

These are two equations in two variables: y_A and y_B. Subtracting the second equation from the first, we get the solution of the output supplied by Bengal-Chicken: $y_B = 5{,}000 - 4{,}000 = 1{,}000$. Substituting this value in either equation gives the solution of output by Assam-Chicken: $y_A = 2{,}000$. Thus both firms together sell

$$y_A + y_B = 2{,}000 + 1{,}000 = 3{,}000.$$

This is equal to the total quantity sold in the market, i.e., $\mathrm{Q} = 3{,}000$. Substituting this into the demand function, $\mathrm{p} = 3{,}150 - \mathrm{Q} = 3{,}150 - 3{,}000 = 150$, i.e., a broiler chicken will be sold in the Guwahati market for ₹150.■

11.2.4 Price Competition: The Bertrand Model

The Cournot quantity competition model assumes that firms strategically choose their quantities of production, while the price adjusts to clear the market (as shown in Figure 11.5), after quantities are chosen. It is easily arguable however that firms strategically choose prices instead. This view was advanced forcefully in the late 19th century by a French mathematician, named Joseph Bertrand. It turns out that different outcomes follow under price competition as compared to quantity competition.

Suppose again that there are two firms, and, both sell a homogeneous product. Let p_A and p_B denote the prices charged by firm *A* and firm *B*, respectively. Realise that, because the product is homogeneous, if $p_A < p_B$, for example, no one would buy the product from firm *B*: Why would anyone pay a higher price for exactly the same product? Thus, firm *A* would capture the entire market. Similarly, if $p_A > p_B$, firm *B* will acquire the whole market. Once we understand this, finding Nash equilibrium is a simple task.

Look at Figure 11.10. The curve *DD* depicts the market demand. For simplicity it is assumed that the marginal cost and the average cost are constant (independent of the output), i.e., $MC = AC$. The left panel assumes that the average cost is the same for both firms, equal to c_1. This is the symmetric-cost case. The right panel depicts the asymmetric-cost case, where the average cost of firm *B* ($= c_2$) is less than that of firm *A* ($= c_1$).

Let us begin with the symmetric-cost case. Suppose any of the two firms, say firm *A*, charges a price higher than c_1, say equal to p_0. What is the optimal pricing strategy of firm *B*? There is no need to "calculate" profits by weighing marginal revenue and marginal cost. The answer is "charge a price slightly less than p_0." Why? It is because by doing so firm *B* will capture the entire market. Of course, firm *A* can recapture the entire market by charging a price slightly less than what firm *B* is asking. This reasoning implies that the firms will continue to cut the price till no firm makes any abnormal profit. Thus $p_A = p_B = c_1$ constitute the Nash equilibrium. Given $p_A = c_1$, firm *B* has no incentive to charge a higher price (thereby losing the entire market) or a lower price (thereby incurring losses). Similarly, given $p_B = c_1$, firm *A* has no incentive to change its price from $p_A = c_1$. In summary, *when the product is homogeneous and average costs are the same across the firms, in Bertrand price competition, price = average cost is the Nash equilibrium.* This implies that no firm makes any abnormal profits, i.e., the profits are zero. Which firm sells how much? This is indeterminate. A natural assumption is that since the firms are symmetric, they will have equal shares in the market – each firm will have

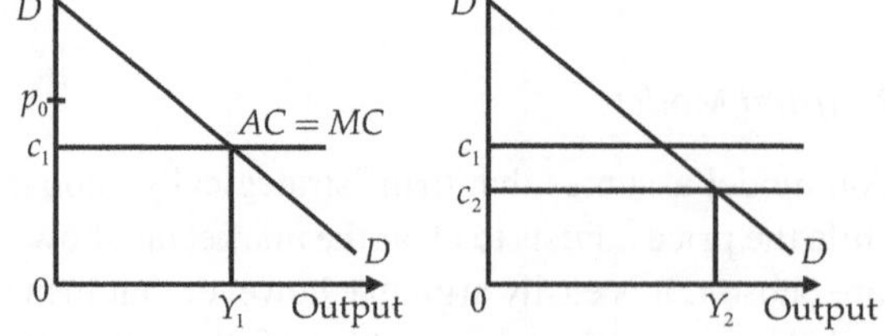

FIGURE 11.10 Bertrand Price Competition

50% of the market, i.e., sell $0Y_1/2$ in the left panel of Figure 11.10. However, irrespective of who sells how much, the total quantity sold is determined by the market demand curve at the price equal to the average cost ($0Y_1$ in Figure 11.10).

It is noteworthy that under the same market and technology parameters, if the firms were competing in quantities, they would have made abnormal profits, as, in Cournot competition the price is not driven down to the average cost. This yields a fundamental insight that *price competition is more severe on the profits of firms in oligopoly than competition in quantity.*

Consider now the asymmetric-cost case. By the same logic, no price above c_1 can be in Nash equilibrium. But unlike the symmetric-cost case, $p_A = p_B = c_1$ do not constitute the Nash equilibrium. It is because firm B can still charge a price lower than c_1, drive firm A out of the market and yet make a profit higher than that at $p_B = c_1$. Hence *in Nash equilibrium, only the more efficient firm survives, and the market price is the one, which is marginally lower than the average cost of the less efficient firm.*

We can indeed generalise the above conclusion to the case of many firms. Rank the firms starting from the most inefficient to the most efficient. Under the price competition, only the most efficient firm survives, because it can "under-cut" in terms of price any other less efficient firm, thereby drive all other firms out and capture the entire market.

It must be noted that the result that only the most efficient firm survives is dependent on the product being homogeneous. If, instead, the product was differentiated, then each firm would have some market power (as in monopolistic competition), and unless the cost differences are very large, the relative more efficient firms and the relative less efficient firms (at least some of them) would co-exist in the market.

Example 11.2

There are two companies, Acquafill and Fizz, which supply bottled water in your hometown. In procuring, processing, and packaging water bottles, each firm incurs a constant average cost of $3 per bottle. The demand curve of bottled water in your hometown is given by the equation $Q = 10{,}000 - 400p$. *If the two firms play the Bertrand price competition game, what will be market price and quantity sold?*

Answer: This is a case of symmetric Bertrand competition. Hence the equilibrium price will be driven down the (common) average cost, i.e., $p = \$3$. Substituting this into the market demand function, the total quantity sold equals:

$$Q = 10{,}000 - 400 \times 3 = 8{,}800. \blacksquare$$

11.2.5 Whether Cournot or Bertrand?

Because quantity and price competition yield very different outcomes, one may ask which one is more appropriate. There is no single answer to this question. It depends on whether in the industry concerned the firms commit to quantities they produce and let prices clear the market or commit to prices and let quantities clear the market. In producing steel for instance, it is relatively time-consuming to change production levels (within say month or a quarter). Thus, steel firms must commit to a production level, and it is reasonable to suppose quantity competition. But, in selling name-brand furniture for example, the prices are quoted in catalogues and websites, which are not changed frequently. Thus, it is reasonable to assume price competition, i.e., treat price as the strategic variable.

11.2.6 Cartel Issues

The Nash equilibrium in quantity or price competition is comparable to the Nash equilibrium in the prisoner's dilemma game. Hence, essentially, oligopoly competition is a prisoner's dilemma situation. In oligopoly, the firms compete with one another rather than collude.

Colluding or collusion means jointly deciding the total output for the industry and the market price, and, formulating an allocation rule as to who will produce how much. If the firms do collude, collectively they behave like a monopoly or a **cartel**. A cartel essentially raises the price of the product by restricting output. Under the cartel, the total (monopoly) profits are higher than the sum of the profits in oligopoly competition (irrespective of the form of oligopoly competition). The quota system dictating who produces how much is devised such that every member (firm) of the cartel is better off, i.e., enjoys higher profit, compared to oligopoly competition.

If so, in the real world, why do firms not always collude or form a cartel on a regular basis? One obvious answer is that colluding or forming a cartel is illegal in many countries because of its anti-competitive (high-price) effects, which hurt the consumers. However, for products that are primarily exported by a country, there is no such concern because higher prices would hit the consumers in the foreign countries, not the domestic consumers. Therefore, over time many cartels have surfaced typically in international markets. OPEC is, of course, the best example. But cartels have been formed in many products including steel and vitamin.

However, there is an inherent problem with any cartel, even if it may be legal. That is, *a member of a cartel has an incentive to "cheat"*—i.e., secretly break the already-agreed cartel rules. This can be understood in view of Figure 11.11. The *MC* curve denotes the marginal cost curve of a cartel member. The cartel has fixed the price of the product at p_r, which is presumably higher than the price that would prevail under oligopoly competition. Such a high price is made sustainable by following a production (an export) quota rule in which each member is asked to produce a limited quantity (less than what it would have produced in oligopoly competition). Let this quantity or quota for the member in question be y_r. In the cartel regime this member's total revenues are thus equal to the area $0p_rCy_r$. Its total costs are measured by the area under the *MC* curve, equal to the area $0ABy_r$. Hence, profits are equal to the area $ABCp_r$.

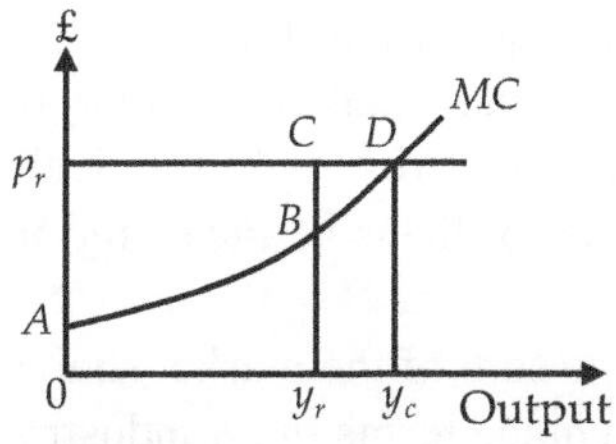

FIGURE 11.11 Cartel Problems

Suppose that this is the original situation: there is a cartel, in which the member firms are charging the price p_r, and each member is producing a limited quantity, with y_r being the output of a particular member firm. Now observe that *as long as the market price is given at* p_r, the particular firm we are looking at can actually increase its output and sale up to y_C and make higher profits because if the market price is given it is equal to the marginal revenue and over the output range 0 to y_C, $MR > MC$. Indeed, by producing y_C, the firm's profits will be equal to ADp_r, which is greater than $ABCp_r$. In other words, this member firm will have an incentive to break the cartel rules, over-produce, and make greater profits.

Of course, once the cheater sells more, there will be downward pressure on the market price. This will be "felt" by the rest of the cartel members (who are "honest" to the cartel) because they will have to face difficulty in selling their quota output at the cartel price p_r (since there is more quantity in the market than before—thanks to the cheater). Whether the cheater is identified or not, others will come to infer that someone among them has broken the rules. What happens next? A strong possibility is that cartel is abandoned, and the industry reverts to the oligopoly competition.

In summary, insofar as the cheater is concerned, it gains in the short run and loses in the long run. If the firms value the future or trust each other very much then no firm may decide to cheat in the first place. If not, cheating is an inherent problem in a cartel and *cartels are inherently unstable.* Hence, in the real world, it is hard to find an example of a cartel that has lasted successfully for a long stretch of time. Even OPEC has had its problems over the years. *The average cartel life (before it busts itself due to cheating and enforcement problems or busted by authorities) is around 4 to 6 years.*

11.3 Measuring Concentration and Anti-Trust Regulations

A common feature of almost any form of an imperfectly competitive market is that price exceeds marginal cost and therefore such a market entails a loss of social surplus. This is of concern especially from the viewpoint of consumers' welfare.

After all, the social purpose of businesses is to create/produce goods and services for meeting our consumption needs and enhancing our standard of living.

Therefore, increasing concentration of firms (meaning smaller number of larger size firms) in an industry is worrisome—insofar as it results in relatively higher prices for the consumers. How can concentration of firms be measured in an industry?

Concentration ratio is a common measure. It is the sum of the market shares of a pre-specified number of the largest firms in percentage terms in an industry. Suppose an industry has N firms. Let us denote the largest firm in terms of market share as firm 1, similarly the second-largest firm in market share as firm 2, and so on. Let the respective market shares in percentage be $s_1, s_2, \ldots, s_N$. By definition, these market shares are in decreasing order. It is common practice to consider 4- or 8-firm concentration ratios. They have the following expressions:

$$4-\text{firm Concentration Ratio} \equiv C_4 \equiv s_1 + s_2 + s_3 + s_4. \quad (11.2)$$

$$8-\text{firm Concentration Ratio} \equiv C_8 \equiv s_1 + s_2 + s_3 + \cdots + s_8. \quad (11.3)$$

Herfindahl–Hirschman Index (HHI) is another commonly used measure of concentration. Let h_i denote the market share of the i-th firm, not necessarily the i-th largest firm. Then,

$$\text{HHI} \equiv h_1^2 + h_2^2 + h_3^2 + \cdots + h_N^2. \quad (11.4)$$

What is the rationale behind this formula? Consider two extreme cases: (a) monopoly and (b) N firms of the same size. In the monopoly case, $h_1 = 1$ and all other h's zero; thus, HHI = 1. In the same-size-firms case, each h is equal to $1/N$. Hence, $\text{HHI} = \text{N} / N^2 = 1/\text{N}$. If there are five equal-size firms, HHI = 1/5; if there are 8 equal-size firms, HHI = 1/8, and so on. The formula yields intuitively appealing numbers. The US Department of Justice uses HHI in evaluating merger–acquisition proposals.[6]

Example 11.3

The printing industry has eight firms, whose sales proceeds (total revenues) in 2023 are given in Table 11.4. *Compute the 4-firm concentration ratio and the HHI for this industry.*

Answer: Given Table 11.4 we computer individual market shares (in fractions) and their squares. The total revenue for all firms together are €200 million. Hence, dividing the total revenues of each firm by 200 we obtain market shares, given in the third column from in Table 11.5. The entries in the last column of Table 11.5 are simply the square of respective numbers in the previous column. The largest four firms are DEF, MNO, PQR, and STU, indicated in boldface font. The sum of their market shares is 0.73, implying the 4-firm concentration ratio of 73%. HHI is simply the sum of all entries in the last column of Table 11.5, equal to 0.159.■

TABLE 11.4 Sales Proceeds of Printing Industry in 2023

Firms	*Total Revenues (in Millions of €)*
ABC	15
DEF	45
GHI	20
JKL	6
MNO	25
PQR	36
STU	40
VWX	13

TABLE 11.5 Market Shares

Firms	*Total Revenues (in Millions of €)*	*Market Share*	*Square of Market Share*
ABC	15	0.075	0.006
DEF	45	0.225	0.051
GHI	20	0.100	0.010
JKL	6	0.030	0.001
MNO	25	0.125	0.016
PQR	36	0.180	0.032
STU	40	0.200	0.040
VWX	13	0.065	0.004

Box 11.2 presents estimates of these measures for the cement industry and the auto industry in India.

BOX 11.2 ESTIMATES OF CONCENTRATION RATIO AND HERFINDAHL–HIRSCHMAN INDEX

Numerous estimates of these are available across many industries, countries, and time periods. We present estimates for the Indian cement industry and the automobile industry in the accompanying diagrams.

You may be surprised to know that India is the second-largest producer of cement, following China. The first cement factory in India came up in 1914. In their study of the changing structure of the cement industry in India from 1989 to 2006 Mukhopadhyaya et al. (2012) present the time series of annual 4-firm concentration ratio and HHI, which is reproduced in the left panel of the diagram. The left-hand and the right-hand vertical axes measure the 4-firm concentration ratio and the HHI. We see that the two measures are highly

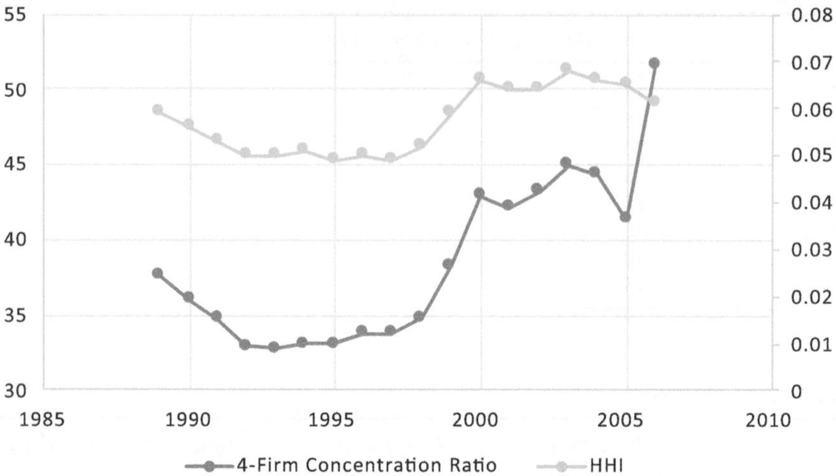

FIGURE 11.12 Indian Cement Industry

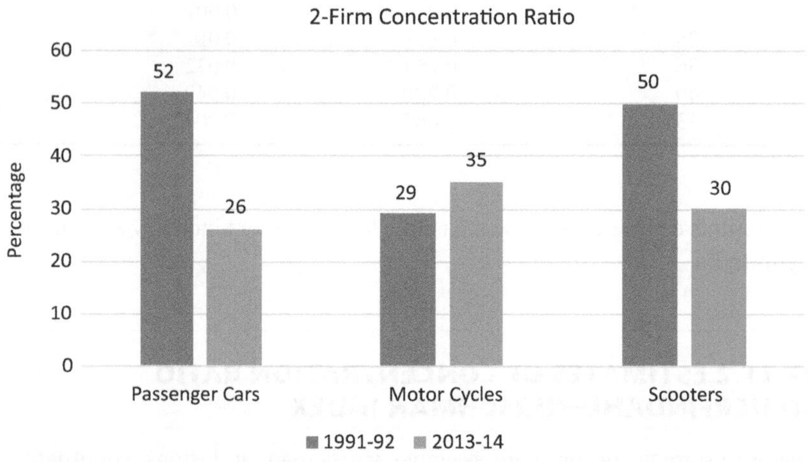

FIGURE 11.13 Indian Automobile Industry

correlated (correlation coefficient is 0.86). Observe that concentration in the Indian cement industry declined from 1989 to the mid-1990s, and, since then till 2006 it had a rising trend.

Kumar and Choudhary (2019) present 2-firm concentration ratios in the Indian automobile industry for two financial years: 1991–1992 and 2013–2014, shown in the right panel of the diagram. See that firm concentration has drastically declined in the passenger car sector. In 1991–1992, there were only three firms. This number increased dramatically to 17 in 2013–2014. The concentration ratios for these two years testify that this sector became much more competitive in the mid-2010s than it was in early 1990s. The same is true for scooter, although it is less dramatic. In contrast, the concentration in the motorcycle industry has moderately increased from early 1990s and to the mid-2010s.

It is not our objective here to analyse the reasons behind the changes in firm concentration in the cement and auto industries. Our aim is to illustrate how the measures of firm concentration in an industry are computed.

11.4 Anti-Trust Regulations

Concentration is indeed the basis of monopoly regulation, which we discussed in Chapter 10. It is also the rationale behind the so-called **anti-trust regulations** with respect to oligopoly markets.

The origin of anti-trust regulations lies in the economic history of the United States. During the decades following the civil war in America, a selected group of aggressive entrepreneurs became extremely powerful, e.g., Andrew Carnegie, Jay Gould, John Rockefeller, and others. These men created huge empires of business for themselves and were accused of exploiting labour and using unfair labour practices. They were portrayed as ruthless businessmen who could do anything to increase their wealth, and, later became branded as "robber barons." Intense public sentiments led to the first major anti-trust law in the form of the Sherman Act of 1890. This marked the beginning of anti-trust regulation in the United States and in the rest of the world. The initial aim of these regulations was to contain market concentration on the presumption that this is bad for the consumers—for the reasons described above.

However, recall from Chapter 10 that there are a few merits of monopoly too—and they apply to an oligopoly market as well. Hence, *the modern philosophy behind anti-trust laws and their enforcement is that being big in business may not be necessarily bad by itself. The key issue that an anti-trust body looks at is whether merger and acquisitions or product/pricing strategies by big firms that tend to eliminate competition serve the interests of consumers.* See Box 11.3 for an account of anti-trust problems faced by Microsoft.

BOX 11.3 ANTI-TRUST WOES OF MICROSOFT, GOOGLE, AND FACEBOOK

The software giant Microsoft has faced anti-trust lawsuits since the mid-1990s. Its rivals have claimed and brought attention to the anti-trust authorities in the United States and Europe that the firm has been essentially either tying its products with its operating system or making it relatively difficult for products from other companies to run efficiently on the Windows platform. For instance, in the early- and mid-1990s Microsoft would "force" computer makers to use Internet Explorer (IE) as a part of licensing Windows. The company however argued that IE was an "integrated part" of its operating system. But in 1997, Microsoft was asked by the anti-trust authorities to un-bundle IE from its operating system. In mid-2000s, the European Commission asked Microsoft to un-bundle Windows Media Player. Sun Microsystems, which developed Java technology, alleged that Microsoft was breaking its contractual obligation by not using Java in IE. Novell Corporation, which developed the server software "NetWare" (and the Word Perfect package), argued that the Windows server operating system didn't allow NetWare to run efficiently. In 2004 and 2005, Microsoft reached out-of-court settlements with Sun, Novell, and others (like Gateway) by paying them compensations, running into hundreds of millions of dollars. Overall, Microsoft has spent well over $3 billion in settling anti-trust litigations.

In more recent times, Google and Facebook have faced anti-trust issues. As of December 2020, several anti-trust lawsuits around the world from government agencies (including more than 30 states in the United States) and private companies have been filed against Google. The Federal Trade Commission (FTC) and at least 46 states in the United States have registered anti-trust litigations against Facebook. According to FTC, Facebook "is illegally maintaining its personal social networking monopoly through a years-long course of anti-competitive conduct." Many of these litigations are yet to reach their verdicts (as of 2023).

11.5 Remarks

Where does this detailed analysis of oligopoly market lead us to? In case of cut-throat competition, price may come down to as low as in perfect competition. You must have notified this several times in case of international and domestic airlines. On the other hand, if cartelisation is strict and honest, price may go up to as high as in monopoly market. However, cartels are fickle as there is always a tendency to cheat and cheaters earn more than the honest partners. Moreover, cartelisation

TABLE 11.6 A Four-Firm Industry Example

Firm	*Market Share as % of Total Sales Volume*
A	10
B	65
C	20
D	5

is illegal. A price war benefits none among the sellers. Similarly, expenditure on competitive advertising is counterproductive. Hence, oligopoly market is fluid. It provides sub-optimal and sometimes indeterminate solutions.

Is there any way to bring some order on stability in such market? The price-leadership model is a framework, where the price is determined by the "leader," while others follow and fix a price almost equal to what the "leader" has finalised. You may ask how to determine who the leader is and why others should follow him. Yes, a very valid question. In some cases, a dominant firm acts as a leader while others follow it. Dominancy can be identified by its market share. For example, suppose there are four firms in an oligopoly, namely, A, B, C, and D, and, their market shares are as given in Table 11.6.

Clearly, firm B is the leader, so firms A, C, D will follow the price fixed by firm B. What if they don't? Theoretically nothing compels A, C, D to follow the price diktat of B. But if they do not follow the leader, then the alternatives are either to adopt a price higher or lower than the one set by the dominant firm, i.e., firm B. None of them would dare to fix a higher price. It would be akin to committing suicide. The market share of A, C, and D combined together being a meagre 35%, a higher price will simply turn away the buyers who would switch to the leader firm. The market share of small firms will only reduce further. What if anyone of the three, say A, charges a lower price? Fine. In short run, A will attract more buyers, but soon his entire stock of product will be sold at lower price. But A will be able to provide only 10% or say a bit more, i.e., 15% of the total market demand. Soon his inventories will vanish. Remember, in products traded in oligopoly it is not easy to increase output drastically. As a result, A will be unable to meet the buyers' demand. They will be forced to go to others. In case C and D also follow A and reduce price, they will exhaust their stock too still leaving 50–60% market demand unfulfilled. In such a condition B, with a huge unsold stock, will exercise virtual monopoly. It will not take long for firms A, C, and D to realise their folly.[7]

Another related question can be: How does a firm become a dominant firm? There can be several reasons for it. One of the most plausible reasons for attaining dominance could be the low cost of production of the leader by innovative ideas, both technological and marketing. For instance, a firm can devise ways to achieve internal economies of scale, which can lead to leadership. Other firms will think twice to enter a price war with such a leading firm, because it can outlast long price war, whereas smaller firms cannot.

BOX 11.4 IT IS A CORPORATE JUNGLE OUT THERE

In an Indian context, in ancient times, a mahatma (Great Soul) once visited a king's palace. The king treated him with respect, offered a seat of a higher pedestal than his throne in his court. The king politely requested the mahatma to say some words of wisdom for himself and his ministers. The mahatma said "O noble king! There are four types of mangoes. The first type appears to be ripe (and sweet) and are actually ripe. The second type of mangoes appears to be unripe (and sour) but are actually ripe. The third kind appears to be unripe and are unripe. The last type are those which appear to be ripe but are unripe."

By that time, the king and his folks were confused. What does this discourse imply? They were too afraid to question the mahatma's wisdom. After a brief pause, the mahatma resumed his sermon. O king similarly, the persons with whom you come in contact are of four types: first, those who appear to be friendly and are actually friendly; second, those who appear to be unfriendly and are actually unfriendly; third, those who appear to be unfriendly but are actually friendly; and finally the fourth category of people appear to be friendly but are actually unfriendly.

There is no harm from the first category, the mahatma said. In fact, they are very helpful. In case of the second category, there is no hidden danger as they appear to be your enemies and are actually so. Hence you can remain vigilant on them. In case of the third category too there is no harm. Such a person, who may appear to be unfriendly are actually friendly and warm-hearted. The problem lies with the fourth category. These persons are sweet-talkers and appear friendly, but are actually harmful, a "hidden danger." You may not be fully equipped to deal with this category.

As a fresh entrant to the business school, we know you have a very colourful, romantic image of the "corporate world" which you plan to join soon. But believe us, it's a corporate jungle out there with many belonging to the fourth category. Darwin works there. Learn and equip yourself to survive and excel. Of course, you may come across warm-hearted nice people: everyone is not a villain. We bring this example here, because many corporates operate in the oligopoly market.

What if there is no clear-cut dominant firm in a market? Suppose that there are four firms in an industry with market shares of 20%, 28%, 25%, and 27% for firms A, B, C, and D, respectively. Clearly, no firm can claim to be dominant. In such a situation, "barometric price-leadership model" works. In this model any firm can take a lead and determine the price. Prudence suggests that this firm will consider the cost of production (which is likely to be similar for all firms) and the prevailing market conditions. It will fix the price which is neither "too high" nor "too low." The other firms will have no option but to charge a similar price.

Please recall that in the beginning we stated that a large majority of you are likely to get placed in products/services traded in oligopoly markets. We have tried to inculcate in you some general skills to help you in your decision-making. You must expect that the real-life situations will be much more complex and varied. No two situations may be identical. We cannot provide you cut-and-dry solutions for every situation. In fact, we, ourselves, have none. You will have to not only survive but excel in that corporate "jungle,", so to speak. Read Box 11.4

Facts and Insights

Game Theory

- Game theory deals with strategic behaviour in a situation of interdependence among individuals, species, or organisations, i.e., in a situation where the behaviour of one party affects the well-being of another.
- Social welfare is not maximised at the Nash non-cooperative equilibrium.
- A non-cooperative game does not achieve the best for the players.
- Game theory illustrates that cooperation is valuable to the society.
- Most economic situations in which strategies are important are not zero-sum in nature.
- Nash equilibrium is where no single player benefits (i.e., receives a greater payoff) from unilaterally choosing a different strategy.
- In a cooperative-game equilibrium, players are better off than in the corresponding non-cooperative-game equilibrium.

Monopolistic Competition and Oligopoly

- In monopolistic competition, an individual firm, even though very small compared to the entire market, has some market power, because its product is differentiated. This implies that the firm is able to set a price above the marginal cost.
- Even though monopolistically competitive firms have market power, they make normal profits, i.e, zero abnormal profits in the long run.
- In the long-run equilibrium in a monopolistically competitive market, the scale of output by a firm is such that economies of scale in production are not fully utilised or exhausted. In this sense, there is an excess capacity.
- Besides setting output and prices, firms in monopolistic competition and oligopoly engage in advertising.
- Persuasive advertising is a social waste, whereas informative advertising is useful.

- There is no unified theory of oligopoly.
- An oligopoly market is characterised by game-theoretic, strategic interaction among firms.
- Essentially, oligopoly competition yields a Prisoner's Dilemma situation.
- The kinked-demand curve model attempts to explain why in some oligopoly markets, prices may be relatively stable.
- Under quantity competition, an increase (a decrease) in the costs faced by one firm leads, in equilibrium, to less output by this firm and more output by the rival firm.
- If the product is homogeneous and firms compete in prices, then the market sustains only the most efficient firm(s).
- Price competition is more severe on the profits of firms in oligopoly than competition in quantity.
- In a cartel where quantities to be produced by firms are restricted, i.e., each firm has a quote, an individual firm has an incentive to cheat—in terms of producing and selling more than its quota. This implies that cartels are inherently unstable.
- The average life of a cartel in the international market is between four to six years.
- Firm concentration in an industry is measured by concentration ratios and the Herfindahl–Hirschman Index (HHI). The Department of Justice of the United States uses HHI to evaluate merger and acquisition proposals.
- The modern philosophy behind anti-trust laws and their enforcement is that being big in business may not be necessarily bad. Central is the issue of whether merger and acquisitions or product/pricing strategies by big firms tend to serve the interests of consumers.
- In India, the recently constituted Competition Commission oversees anti-trust issues. The telecom sector however has a separate regulatory body: Telecom Regulatory Authority of India (TRAI).

Exercises

Descriptive/Analytical

11.1. "Monopoly and competition are opposite forms of market structure. Hence a monopolistically competitive market doesn't make much logical sense." Defend or refute.

11.2. "Like a perfectly competitive or a monopoly market, there is a single model of oligopoly." Defend or refute.

11.3. Explain why in the kinked-demand curve model, the demand curve facing a firm is very elastic (inelastic) at prices below (above) the kink.

11.4. "Firms making abnormal profits in an oligopoly market is the main concern of modern anti-trust bodies." Defend or refute.

11.5. Suppose you work as a manager of a state monopoly (e.g. railways). Would you recommend a budget for advertising on travel in railways even if it is monopoly? Why or why not?

Short Answer (word Limit = 500 approx.)

11.6. Briefly explain the excess capacity theorem in monopolistic competition.

11.7. Give two examples each of competitive advertising and informative advertising which are different from the examples given in the chapter.

11.8. In major cities in India getting water supply by illegally using booster pumps attached to city water line is not an uncommon practice. Consider two neighbouring households *A* and *B*. If none switch on the pump, each gets 10 units of supply. If both turn on the pump, each gets 7 units (implicit here is that the electricity cost of using the pump in terms of buying water is 3 units). But if one switches on while the other doesn't, the former gets 15 units and the latter gets 5 units. Construct the payoff matrix. Using Nash equilibrium, what does the game theory predict in terms of behaviour towards switching on the booster pump?

11.9. You and Yusuf play the following game. Each one of you hide a one-rupee coin in your palm. Both of you choose whether you want head or tail up inside your palm. Then you open your palms at the same time. If there is a matching of head–head or tail–tail, you win, meaning that Yusuf must give his one rupee to you. If there is no matching (i.e., you have head up, while Yusuf has tail up or vice versa), then Yusuf wins (you give one rupee to Yusuf). Construct the payoff matrix and show that there is no Nash equilibrium in this game. Such a game is called a *penny-matching game*.

11.10. Construct two hypothetical examples (not any extensions of examples given in the text or exercises) relating to real-word situation in which the number of players is greater than two.

11.11. Intuitively explain what best response curves are.

11.12. Why are the best response curves downward-sloping under quantity competition?

11.13. Suppose in Kolkata, India, fish is supplied by two firms only: a local firm and an outside firm from another province, Andhra Pradesh. While the local firm incurs the costs of production only, the outside firm incurs the costs of production and the costs of transport by trucks from Andhra Pradesh to Kolkata. Assume that the two firms engage themselves in Cournot competition. (They both sell one type of fish and there is no quality difference.) Starting from an equilibrium situation, suppose that there is a diesel price hike. Using a diagram, demonstrate how this will affect the quantities sold by two firms.

11.14. In a small town, there are two taxi stands serving the whole town. One has a fleet of cars all running on diesel and the other has cars all running on

CNG. Think of this as a duopoly market, each "producing" "kilometres of travel." Starting from a given situation, suppose CNG becomes more expensive, while the cost of diesel remains unchanged. Assuming that the two taxi stands play a Cournot duopoly game, how will this affect the best response curves and the amount produced by the two taxi stands?

11.15. Consider the symmetric Bertrand competition case, in which the average cost is constant. Is the social surplus maximised at the equilibrium?

Quizzes/Numerical

11.16. There are two players in the game: P1 and P2. P1 has three strategies: (a_1, a_2, a_3). P2 also have three strategies: (b_1, b_2, b_3). Their payoffs are given in the following table. Is this a zero-sum or a non-zero-sum game? Which strategy combination is a Nash equilibrium?

			P1	
		a_1	a_2	a_3
P2	b_1	(−2,2)	(−2,2)	(−2,2)
	b_2	(2, −2)	(1, −1)	(2, −2)
	b_3	(−2,2)	(−2,2)	(−2,2)

11.17. There is a game, called the *Battle of Sexes.* The story of this game is that a man and his wife are deciding how to spend the evening. There are two options: go to a movie and go to a dance programme. The husband prefers a movie to the dance programme but it is the opposite of what the wife prefers. At the same time, both want to be together, irrespective of whether they go to the movie or to the dance programme. The payoffs are shown in the table. Show that in this game there are two Nash equilibria. Which are they?

		Husband	
		Movie	Dance
Wife	Movie	(5,3)	(0,0)
	Dance	(0,0)	(3,5)

11.18. Suppose that there are two multinational firms *A* and *B*, contemplating to outsource a component of their production process to a small developing economy: Sunderland. If both enter, they recognise that competition among them in a relatively small market would raise local wages to the extent that outsourcing is not profitable and their global profit will fall by 2 units. If one enters and the other doesn't, then the global profit of the former increases by one unit and that of the latter falls by one unit. If none enters, their profits are unchanged. The table represents the payoff matrix. What is the Nash equilibrium or what are the Nash equilibria, and why?

		Firm *A*	
		Enter	Don't enter
Firm *B*	Enter	(−2, −2)	(1, −1)
	Don't enter	(−1,1)	(0,0)

11.19. In game theory it is an example of what is called a *Hawk–Dove game.* The Hawk and the Dove, respectively, stand for an aggressive and a passive strategy. In our example, "enter" is the Hawk strategy and "don't enter" is the Dove strategy. The Hawk–Dove game has the property that if both players play Hawk, then both are damaged. If both play Dove, then both are better off. If one plays Hawk and the other play Dove, then the Hawk benefits and the other loses, compared to both playing Dove. Is there any Nash equilibrium in this game? If yes, how many and which are they?

11.20. The *LAC* schedule of a representative firm under monopolistic competition is given as follows. In the long-run industry equilibrium, this firm produces an output, which is ____ than ____. Fill in the blanks and give reasons.

Output	*LAC*
0	–
1	20
2	16
3	13
4	11
5	14
6	18
7	24

11.21. "In a monopolistically competitive industry there are no abnormal profits earned in the long-run equilibrium. Therefore, the price must be equal to the marginal cost." Defend or refute.

11.22. "The kinked-demand curve model is used to explain price instability in some oligopoly markets." Defend or refute.

11.23. Suppose that a cartel fixes the price at p_r = ₹150. A cartel member's quota of production is fixed at $y = 35$. This member's marginal cost function is $MC = 50 + 2y$. If this firm decides to cheat, by how much will it like to increase its output (from 35)?

11.24. Suppose that at a given point of time a monopolistically competitive firm faces the *AR*, *MR*, and the cost curves as shown in Figure 11.1. Is this a situation of long-run equilibrium? If not, will some new firms enter into or some existing firm exit from the industry?

11.25. Consider Example 11.2. Suppose that Acquafill is able to cut its average cost from \$3.00 to \$2.50 per bottle, while the average cost of production by Fizz remains unchanged. What will be the market price and quantity sold in the new Bertrand equilibrium?

11.26. An industry consists of six firms, A to F. Their market shares in two calendar years are given in the side table.

   a) Can you simply tell by looking at the numbers if in 2025 the 4-firm concentration is higher or lower than in 2024?

   b) Compute the 4-firm concentration ratio and HHI for 2024 and 2025.

	Market Share in Percentage	
	2024	*2025*
Firm A	10	26
Firm B	25	28
Firm C	27	13
Firm D	15	9
Firm E	12	8
Firm F	11	16

Appendix 11.A Anti-Trust Practice in India

In India, the Monopoly and Restrictive Trade Practices (MRTP) Act of 1969 was the initiating legislation, whose aim was to restrict monopoly power. However, the MRTP interventions were nothing close to what is outlined above as the objective of a standard anti-trust legislation in a market-oriented economy. They were mostly in the form of controls, licence, and permits. It was also largely ineffective, as both public-sector and private-sector monopolies thrived under it. Why? Because in terms of having real punitive powers, it was nearly toothless. To enforce its orders, it had to depend on courts entirely, which would take years to reach any final decision. It didn't have power to impose, on prima facie grounds, any initial penalties for breach of its directives, before the matter could be moved to the courts. It didn't even have powers to enforce the attendance of a witness. The personnel at the disposal of MRTP didn't have the right skills to deal with investigations of economic transactions.

The MRTP Act was repealed, and the MRTP Commission was dissolved in 2002/2003. It was replaced by a new Act called the Competition Act of 2002, which led to the creation of a new anti-trust watchdog, Competition Commission of India (CCI), in 2003. The Commission's aim was to prevent "anti-competitive practices, promote and sustain competition, protect the interests of the consumers and ensure freedom of trade"—as the website of the Competition Commission states. Both goods and services sectors and the private and public sector firms come under its purview. The CCI has the mandate to impose penalties initially on the erring parties, and, to provide relief to firms that are adversely affected by the anti-competitive strategies adopted by other firms.

In 2014, the CCI appraised that the proposed merger of Ranbaxy and Sun Pharmaceuticals was likely to have an appreciable adverse effect on competition. It directed the two companies to make public the details of the proposed merger and sought the feedback of stakeholders. Based on these, the CCI directed the two parties to suitably modify the agreement, thus protecting the interests of other producers and consumers. The merger took place during the same year.

In 2016, it received a notice of merger of Dish TV India Ltd. and Videocon D2h Ltd. This would make the merged entity a dominant firm with 45% market share, leaving Tata Sky (21%), Airtel (20%), and Sun Direct (10%) far behind. But Dish TV is owned by Essel Group, which also owns Zee TV. This merger would have given undue advantage to Zee TV as it could get more advertisement revenue by offering bulk discounts. Hence, the CCI stipulated some restrictions on this merger, which became effective in 2018.

Regulating the Telecom Sector

It is interesting that the telecom sector in India is oligopolistic, yet it is not subject to the "standard" anti-trust regulations. Instead, there is a separate body called the Telecom Regulatory Authority of India, or briefly TRAI, established way back in 1997. Why is there a separate regulatory body for this industry only? It is because (a) this sector provides a "basic" utility, like telephony, which is unlike automobile or an internet browser and (b) there are a few special features of this sector.

Because the industry offers a basic utility, TRAI regulates telecom prices, similar to electricity regulatory commission fixing electricity tariffs. But there is much more. That is, the government recognises the vital role of the telecom sector in the growth and development of almost any other sector of the economy and therefore its objective is to ensure a telecom sector that is world-class.

As we all know and experience, the technology of this sector changes almost "day by day." Along with its benefits, it poses new problems and challenges. For instance, internet services are facilitating telephony. Telephone and broadcasting industries step into each other's markets. There is an issue of "spectrum management" or "frequency allocation." As the demand for frequency is increasing dramatically, it should be used in an efficient manner, without interfering with those used by the national defence sector. It is believed that dealing with these complex issues in a vital sector like telecom requires a separate regulatory and anti-trust body like TRAI.

Remember that in the 2000s, mobile number portability (MNP) was not available. If one wanted to switch from one carrier to another, one "had" to give up the old number. This was quite a nuisance. Initiated by TRAI, the MNP process started in 2009/2010. It is now available nationwide.

Notes

1 There are more than two dozen brands of lipstick in the US market like Revlon, Cover Girl, Maybelline, L'Oreal, Avon, etc. At least seven brands of lipstick are available in the Indian market: Avon, Elle, Lakme, Loreal, Maybelline, Revlon, and Tips & Toes. There are many more brands of toothpaste, e.g., Acquafresh, Anchor, Amar, Babool, Cibaca, Close-Up, Colgate, Forhans, Meswak, Neem, Pepsodent, Promise, and Vicco Vajradanti.

2 In the best of spirits, WTO can be seen as an organisation that attempts to induce cooperation and discipline across countries so as to ensure global free trade.

3 The duopoly model is capable of being easily generalised to the case of more than two firms.

4 We are *not assuming* that the market price is p_0. Individual quantities and the market price are determined within the model.

5 Under the WTO system, a country can unilaterally increase import tariffs on industrial goods only on a temporary basis.

6 There are other indices like the Index of Ginevicius and Cirba, among others.

7 In the global market for smart phones, Apple and Samsung are dominant firms. In India, Maruti Suzuki Ltd. in cars and State Bank of India in commercial banking are standard examples of dominant firms.

Bibliography

Kumar, N., & Choudhary, P. (2019). Concentration in the Indian automobile industry. *Pacific Business Review International*, *11*(9), 103–113.

Mukhopadhyaya, J. N., Roy, M., & Raychaudhury, A. (2012). An analytical study of the changing structure in the cement industry of India. *Indore Management Journal*, *4*(1), 11–23.

12

DECISION-MAKING UNDER UNCERTAINTY

Introduction

Be it a consumer or a producer, the decision-making we have analysed thus far has assumed an environment of certainty. For instance, a consumer "knows" his preferences (utility function), "knows" the prices of goods and services he intends to consume, and is sure about his total income or expenditure. Given and knowing all of this, he finds the consumption bundle that maximises his utility. A competitive firm "knows" what the market price of the product he sells is and "knows" what the costs of production are. With the knowledge of all this, the profit-maximising output is decided where the marginal cost of production equals the market price.

As we all know, *un*certainty is a fact of life. A consumer may not know his total spending, if his income is not certain. A firm may not be sure of the price at which its product will be sold in the market. An automobile manufacturer would not have information on how many cars it would be able to sell exactly in a city or a country in the forthcoming year at a given price. See Box 12.1 for a brief write-up on the pervasiveness of decision-making under uncertainty.

> **BOX 12.1 DECISION-MAKING UNDER UNCERTAINTY AND RISK, EVERYWHERE**
>
> You are in a hurry to go to the opposite side of a street. Are you going to cross the street in the middle or walk to the nearest stoplight to cross? The next day, you have two final exams: Math and English. How many hours would you study for each subject when you are not sure about how helpful an extra hour of studying either subject will be in answering questions? You have some

DOI: 10.4324/9781003452195-12

money to invest in stocks. Are you going to buy them in energy, health care, or IT sectors? An army general with a limited number of soldiers and facing attacks from multiple directions must decide how to allocate his soldiers. Leonel Messi had to decide which way to kick the ball, left or right, in the penalty shootout during the 2022 soccer World Cup final. A manager must decide how many programmers to hire in order to insulate its server from cyberattacks. All these situations involve decision-making in an environment of uncertainty and risk.

As you all realise, uncertainty can create fear, worry, panic, and chaos forcing one to take hasty decisions. Even the most level-headed person would sometimes resort to measures which he/she would never have taken in normal times. Moreover, the larger the stakes involved in such times, the more bizarre could be the reaction! Have you ever thought of the umpteen ways of strange decision-making tools which we all resort to sometimes in the face of uncertainty?

One class of such tools include astrological predictions, zodiac signs, stars, tossing a coin, the fortune tellers sitting on the pavement looking at the lines on your palm, letting the parrot pick your future course of action out of several cards lying in front of it, asking your family priest to read your *janamkundli* (birth chart). Some people stop midway if a black cat crosses their path! We have neither the intention nor the competence to comment on these modes of decision-making.

Another is to "dig the past." "What did my predecessor(s) do under similar circumstances? And with what consequences?" Under a highly volatile, uncertain, complex, and ambiguous (VUCA) world of modern times, can you be certain that the present-day situation is identical (or similar) to what was the situation in the past? This question assumes added relevance in the face of IT revolution these days. Look at what ChatGPT is doing to school- and college-going youngsters and professionals at work place! Creative talent is getting suppressed.

Still another, the third, way in decision-making under certainty is to turn to your "ideal," "role model," or "bench mark." "I am buying 'x' stock in bulk. Why? Because George Soros is buying it." In India, Rakesh Jhunjhunwala used to wield such fellow-following in Indian bourses (Bombay Stock Exchange (BSE) & National Stock Exchange (NSE)). Stocks will start moving northward on the sheer rumour that Rakesh Jhunjhunwala was buying these. Who cares for the fundamentals! The argument is simple—"my role model has more relevant information and can do no wrong." In the beginning of this century, a lot of new business schools were set up in the private sector in India. It was due to an unprecedented number of admission seekers in management programmes. Many promoters of these schools had little idea of the syllabi and teaching pedagogy to be adopted for these "professional courses." What is to be done? Simple enough, find out what and how Harvard is teaching; or nearer home, what IIM-Ahmedabad is doing.

Well, if Harvard is following the "case-study" method of teaching, let us also follow likewise. These promoters forgot that Harvard admits students who have reasonable work experience, whereas in India, a large majority of students admitted are *freshers*, who just finished their undergraduate programmes.

Does all this mean that choice under uncertainty is always a random exercise, devoid of any rational underpinning? The answer is no. In some very unexpected or unfamiliar one-off kind situations or where you have little information about something, you may resort to some ad hoc tool of the kinds described above.

But in the vast many other situations, you may have probabilistic beliefs on relevant parameters based on reading, listening, watching, or past experiences, which may lead you to make a choice in the face of an uncertain environment in a rational way. Within this framework, there are various concepts and guidelines towards understanding the process of rational decision-making under uncertainty—which constitute the subject matter of this chapter.

12.1 Random Variable and Probability Distribution

These are the very basic concepts. Uncertainty about something means that it is "random." In the preceding examples, consumer prices and income, the market price for the producers and the volume of auto sales are random.

In general, we define a **random variable** *as one which is believed to have different possible realisations in the future.* At the time of sowing paddy seeds in the field, a farmer in India may think that rice will be sold in the market at ₹70, ₹75, or ₹84 per kg. In this example, the price of rice is random with three values or possible realisations. Another farmer may think differently. He may believe that the price of rice will take one of four values: ₹65, ₹70, ₹72, ₹80, and ₹85. At the price tag of say $120,000 for a particular model of Mercedes-Benz, a dealer in Chicago may not be sure how many she will be able to sell in the next quarter. Note that these are possible realisations in the *future*, based on one's beliefs prior to the actual realisation. This is called *ex ante* (referring to before something is realised), while only one realisation will materialise, which is an *ex post* occurrence. After a situation or an outcome has occurred or is known, it is no more random.

A random variable is sometimes said to be **stochastic**. It can be quantitative or qualitative. All preceding examples are quantitative, i.e., the variable is associated with a number. If a quantitative variable is measured in integers only, e.g., the number of automobiles sold, the number of offers one may obtain after completing a degree, etc., it is a **discrete random variable**. If a random variable is measured on a continuous scale, e.g., weight of wheat production, time to be taken by an athlete to complete a 100-meter run or temperature of a patient in the hospital, it is a **continuous random variable**.

In contrast, consider, say, the weather for tomorrow. If we are going to characterise it as either sunny or rainy, then the weather is associated with a quality or attribute, not a number. It is a qualitative random variable. In an impending election, we do not know for sure which party will win: Democratic or Republican in the United States; Labour or Conservative in Britain; BJP, Congress, or AAP in New Delhi; and so on. Here, the winning party is a qualitative random variable. A **qualitative random variable** is one whose possible realisations are qualities or attributes, not numbers.

To assess an uncertain situation, we assign probabilities for different possible outcomes. You must have heard a weather forecast like "there is an 80% chance of rain tomorrow," where "chance" means "probability." You may interpret the 80% chance of rain as an assessment that it is very likely that it will rain tomorrow. Probability is a measure of likelihood, based on beliefs or past experiences. We don't get into how an individual or an entity arrives at probabilities of future events. We simply assume them.

For instance, based on the market price of rice observed by a farmer in previous years, she may formulate a probabilistic belief for this year's price like the following:

	₹70	with probability = 0.45, i.e., 45%	
Price of rice per 1 kg. =	₹75	with probability = 0.30, i.e., 30%	(12.1)
	₹84	with probability = 0.25, i.e., 25%.	

The following points are important.

1. Probability is a number between 0 and 1. It cannot be negative or exceed one.
2. The probabilities of different realisations of an event must sum up to 1, i.e., 100%.
3. It is not that probability of *all* events or occurrences is a matter of assumption. Assuming the probabilities of some events, we can "derive" the probabilities of other related events. In the above example, we may ask: *What is the probability that the market price of rice will be greater than ₹70?* Since there are two possible prices greater than ₹70, namely, ₹75 and ₹84, we simply add their probabilities, and the answer is: $0.30 + 0.25 = 0.55$, i.e., 55%.

Once the probabilities are assigned to different values of realisation of a random variable, it is sometimes referred to as a **probability distribution**. Various probabilities assigned to the price of rice in the preceding example constitute an example of probability distribution. Consider the tossing of a coin. There are two outcomes: head or tail. If the coin is fair, then we would assume the probability distribution:

Head	with probability 0.50, i.e., 50%
Tail	with probability 0.50, i.e., 50%.

For a quantitative random variable, the associated probability distribution is said to be discrete or continuous as the (quantitative) random variable itself is discrete or continuous. For instance, the probability distribution in equation (12.1) is discrete.

Suppose you are waiting on the platform for the next train. Assume that waiting-time is continuous and it will vary from 1 minute to 9 minutes. For a continuous random variable like the waiting-time here, the probability is expressed by what is called a **density function**. For a random variable in general, say *x*, which varies over an interval *a* to *b*, we define a density function, say $f(x)$, over this interval, such that (i) $\int_a^b f(x)dx = 1$ and (ii) the probability of occurrence of *x* over any sub-interval in [*a, b*], say *c* to *d*, is equal to $\int_c^d f(x)dx$, which is constrained between 0 and 1.

For the waiting-time example, one may assume a density function, $f(x) = (10 - x)/40$, where $a = 1$ and $b = 9$. You may check that it satisfies the two properties (i) and (ii). Because $f(x)$ decreases with *x*, the probability of the train approaching between equal successive intervals of time from 1 to 9 minutes falls. For instance, the probability that the train arrives between 1 and 2 minutes is 8.5/40 21.25% and that between 2 and 3 minutes is 7.5/40 18.75%.[1] A density function like $(10 - x)/40$ is rather uncommon but is perfectly permissible. A very common density function used for a continuous random variable that can take positive and negative values is the **normal distribution**, which is symmetric and bell-shaped, as drawn in Figure 12.1.[2]

A random variable along with a probability distribution is also called as an **uncertain event**, an **uncertain bundle,** or a **lottery**, all meaning the same thing depending on the context. We can think of the results from the tossing of a coin as an uncertain event. If a monetary payoff or utility is ascribed to an uncertain event, it is referred to as an uncertain bundle or a lottery. For instance, suppose that you agree to play a game with your friend, Alexa. You or Alexa toss a fair coin. If it is head, then you pay her $10. If it is tail, she pays you $10. It is thus a lot tery, and we write it as ($10, –$10; 0.5, 0.5), where the entries to the left and right of the semicolon are the payoffs and the respective probabilities.

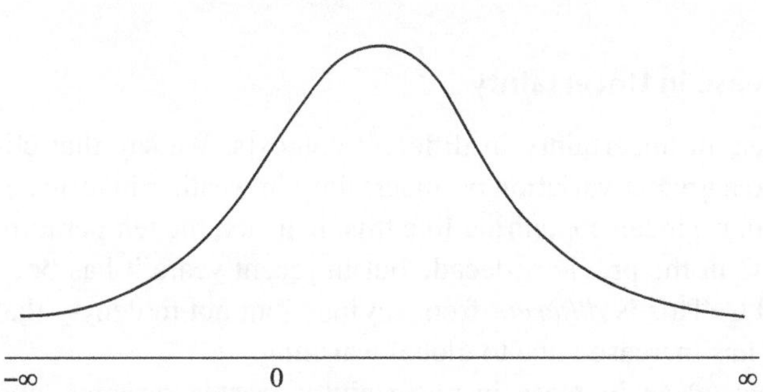

FIGURE 12.1 Shape of Normal Distribution

The above lottery's payoffs are the gains and losses. Sometimes, depending on the context, a person's initial wealth is added to the gains/losses and the lottery's payoffs are expressed in terms of final wealth. Suppose you have $400 before you play this game. This is your initial wealth. If we add this to your gains/losses, the payoffs are $410 and $390. The final wealth lottery or uncertain bundle is ($410, $390; 0.5, 0.5).

In a micro-theoretic context, consider the probability distribution (12.1) of the market price of rice. Suppose the farmer plans to produce 5,000 kg of rice, whose cost of production is ₹4 lakh (one lakh = one hundred thousand). Then the farmer's profits or payoff, will be $70 \times 5{,}000 - 4{,}00{,}000 = -50{,}000$ if the market price is ₹70, $75 \times 5{,}000 - 4{,}00{,}000 = -25{,}000$ if the market price is ₹75 and, by similar calculation, ₹$20{,}000$ if the market price of rice is ₹84 per kg. The uncertain bundle or the lottery is thus (–₹50,000, –₹25,000, ₹20,000; 0.45, 0.3, 0.25).

From two or more uncertain bundles or lotteries, one can construct a compound bundle or a compound lottery, which is essentially a lottery of the lotteries. Consider an ice cream vendor. Suppose that if it is a sunny day and he expects to sell 100 cones and 80 cones with probabilities 0.6 and 0.4. If it is a rainy day, he thinks he would be able to sell 82 or 65 cones with probability 0.2 and 0.8. Assume, for simplicity, that the cost of production is zero, and, whether it is a sunny or a rainy day the vendor expects to sell one ice cream cone for €2. In this example, if it is a sunny day, the vendor's lottery or uncertain bundle is (€200, €160; 0.6, 0.4). In case of rainy day, the lottery is (€164, €130; 0.2, 0.8). Think now of the prospects facing the vendor *as of today* regarding tomorrow. He hears a weather forecast of tomorrow being a rainy day with a probability of 60%. It implies that the probability of tomorrow being a sunny day is 40%. The ice cream vendor is essentially facing a lottery of lotteries. What are the payoffs? In a decreasing order, they are €200, €164, €160, and €130. What are the associated probabilities? The probability that it is a sunny day, *and* he will sell 100 cones $= 0.4 \times 0.6 = 0.24$.Likewise, the probability of a rainy day, *and* he will sell 82 cones $= 0.6 \times 0.2 = 0.12$; that of a sunny day and a sale of 80 cones is 0.16 and that of a rainy day *and* a sale of 65 cones is 0.48. Hence, the compound lottery is: (€200, €164, €160, €130; 0.24, 0.12, 0.16, 0.48).

12.2 Defining an Increase in Uncertainty

We talk about an increase in uncertainty in different contexts. We say that climatic changes have led to a greater variation or uncertainty in weather in terms of temperature. In saying so, we mean something like this: in a city, the temperature varied from 20°C to 35°C in the previous decade but in recent years it has been varying from 15°C to 40°C. This is *different* from saying—but not to deny—that the average temperature has increased due to global warming.

Let us understand that (a) an increase in uncertainty, greater variance, and more fluctuations mean the same thing, and (b) this is *different* from saying that the average has increased or changed. Keeping this in mind and separating the two, an **increase in uncertainty** is defined *as an increase in the variance of a quantitative random variable while the arithmetic mean or average remains unchanged.* Intuitively, an increase in variance without a change in the mean is possible only when the values or the realisations are more spread out. Thus, an increase in uncertainty is also defined as a **mean-preserving spread.**

Example 12.1

Consider the coin-tossing game as earlier with a difference. The stakes are higher: instead of gains and losses equal to \$10 with 50% probabilities, these are of \$12 with 50% probabilities. Is there an increase in uncertainty?

Answer: The mean is unchanged at zero, while the spread is greater. In exact terms, the variance of payoffs in the original game, say $\sigma_A^2 = 0.5\times10^2 + 0.5\times(-10)^2 = 100$. In the new game, the variance is $\sigma_B^2 = 0.5\times12^2 + 0.5\times(-12)^2 = 144$, which is greater than σ_A^2. Therefore, the new game or uncertain bundle carries more uncertainty. ■

Example 12.2

Consider a local neighbourhood lottery, A, that gives €100 if you win (and nothing otherwise) and the chance of winning is 2%. There is another local lottery B that gives €160 if you win (and nothing otherwise), while the chance of winning is 2%. Does lottery B carry more uncertainty than A does?

Answer: You can calculate that the variances: $\sigma_A^2 = 200$ and $\sigma_B^2 = 256$. Lottery B has greater variance. But the means are different. For A and B, respectively, they are $E(A) =$ €2 and $E(B) =$ €3.2. Hence, we cannot say that lottery B is more uncertain. ■

12.3 Expected Utility Hypothesis

At one level, we all understand what we mean by decision-making under uncertainty: What action is to be chosen when the outcomes are uncertain? There is nothing wrong in this understanding. But the real, deeper question is: What is the principle behind making a rational choice under uncertainty?

So far, we have characterised uncertainty by defining an uncertain bundle or a lottery—which is, essentially, a probability distribution of possible outcomes or realisations. The first thing to understand is that *decision-making under uncertainty amounts to choosing an uncertain bundle or a lottery among a set of uncertain bundles or lotteries.* What do we mean?

Consider a perfectly competitive firm which faces price uncertainty. Suppose that, at the time of production, it believes that the market price, p, will have two possible realisations, $p_1 = €10$ and $p_2 = €16$, with respective probabilities 0.6 and 0.4. Further suppose that, technologically, the firm can produce output, y, at three levels only: 10, 15, or 20, i.e., there are only three output possibilities. (We can easily generalise and consider more, even infinitely many, output possibilities.) Let the production cost be $C(10) = 40$, $C(15) = 80$, and $C(20) = 150$. In general, profits $= W = py - C(y)$. Notice that for each level of output there are two profit realisations, depending on whether the market price will be €10 or €16, which you can easily calculate. The probability distribution of profits for the three levels of output are as follows:

Output (y)	*Probability Distribution of Profits* (W)
10	(€60, €120; 0.6, 0.4)
15	(€70, €160; 0.6, 0.4)
20	(€50, €170; 0.6, 0.4)

Therefore, choosing output equal to 10, 15, or 20 amounts to choosing from the three uncertain bundles of payoffs: (€60, €120; 0.6, 0.4), (€70, €160; 0.6, 0.4), or (€50, €170; 0.6, 0.4). In this sense, decision-making under uncertainty is about choosing an uncertain bundle among different possibilities.

The next question is: Because profits are not a unique number for any given level of output, how do we compare them across different levels of output?

One sensible answer might be to calculate the *expected* profits, $E(\pi)$, for each level of output, and compare. Applying the formula for the mean, we have

Output (y)	$E(W)$ in €
10	$60 \times 0.6 + 120 \times 0.4 = 36 + 48 = 84$
15	$70 \times 0.6 + 160 \times 0.4 = 42 + 64 = 106$
20	$50 \times 0.6 + 170 \times 0.4 = 30 + 68 = 98.$

Expected profits/payoffs assign a number to a specific uncertain bundle, which reflects how good that bundle is in some sense. In the present example, they are at the maximum (equal to €106) at output 15. Thus, output = 15 solves the decision-making under price uncertainty.

As it turns out, decision-making based on maximising expected payoffs is the correct approach under a certain condition (namely when the decision-maker is risk-neutral, which will be defined later). In general, we first define a utility function with respect to the payoffs or outcomes, say $U(W)$. It is reasonable to suppose that the higher the payoff, the greater is the utility. That is, $U'(W) > 0$. Next, take the expectation or arithmetic mean of the utilities for each bundle. Thus, *for each uncertain bundle, we assign a number equal to the expected utility of payoffs.* It is the overall utility associated with an uncertain bundle. This is the expected utility hypothesis.

More precisely, let us define a general uncertain bundle with n payoffs or wealth, $W_1, W_2, \ldots, W_n$ along with respected probabilities $b_1, b_2, \ldots, b_n$ (which are non-negative and add up to one). Given a utility function, $U(W)$, the expected utility of an uncertain bundle is

$$V = \sum_{i=1}^{n} b_i U(W_i). \tag{12.2}$$

The **expected utility hypothesis** states that *the overall valuation of an uncertain bundle is equal to the expected utility of the payoffs/wealth associated with that bundle.*

This implies that, *under uncertainty, a rational individual's objective is to maximise the expected utility.*

12.4 Attitude Towards Risk

Before putting the expected utility hypothesis to work, one would think that one's attitude towards risk must play a role in decision-making under uncertainty. If you are averse to risk, you may want to keep all your money in a government interest-bearing asset which is considered very safe; or, as a producer, you may want to sign a contract with a retail buyer to sell your product at a guaranteed price, which is likely to be somewhat at a lower level, rather than sell later and expose yourself to low and high prices. If you are a risk-lover (like an avid gambler) you may want to do the opposite.

The notion of whether one is averse, loving, or neutral towards risk can be made precise by defining a fair bet and whether the person is willing to accept or reject the fair bet. Consider a simple bet, i.e., a lottery which gives you \$1,000 with a probability of 30% and \$2,000 with probability of 70%. The expected payoff from this lottery is $0.3 \times 1{,}000 + 0.7 \times 2{,}000 = 300 + 1{,}400 = \$1{,}700$. Suppose the price to participate in this lottery is $-\$1{,}700$. We then say that it is a fair bet, gamble, lottery, or uncertain bundle. That is, a **fair bet** or a **fair lottery** *is one whose price/cost is equal to the expected payoff.* If a person rejects it, we say that she/he is averse towards risk, i.e., risk-averse. If she accepts a fair bet, we say that she is risk-loving or risk-preferring. If she is neutral or indifferent between accepting and rejecting, she is said to be risk-neutral.

These ideas can be cast more precisely by referring to the utility and the expected utility functions. Consider the lottery

$$(W_1, W_2, \ldots, W_n; b_1, b_2, \ldots, b_n).$$

The expected payoff and the expected utility of payoffs have the respective expressions $E(W) = b_1 W_1 + b_2 W_2 + \ldots + b_n W_n$ and $EU(W) = b_1 U(W_1) + b_2 U(W_2) + \ldots + b_n U(W_n)$.

If a person accepts the fair bet, it means that she prefers the gamble that yields an expected utility $EU(W)$ to having the expected payoff for sure, which gives utility $U(E(W))$, that is, $EU(W) > U(E(W))$.This is the same as saying that the expected utility of payoffs exceeds the utility from the expected payoff—a bit of a tongue-twister. In the earlier numerical example, it means that the person buys the lottery by paying \$1,700, or put differently, the person prefers the lottery to having \$1,700 for sure. If so, the person is said to be risk-loving.

Instead, if $EU(W) < U(E(W))$, the person is rejecting a fair bet and hence said to be risk-averse. Finally, if $EU(W) = U(E(W))$, she is indifferent between accepting and rejecting the fair bet and hence risk-neutral. Therefore, using the concepts of utility and the expected utility hypothesis, we can define *attitude towards risk* as follows: *a person is risk-loving, risk-neutral, or risk-averse according to* $EU(W) \gtreqless U(E(W))$.

If you look again at the definitions, you may guess that one's attitude towards risk depends on the shape or the curvature of one's utility function $U(\pi)$. That is correct. We can see it clearly by analysing Figure 12.2. All three panels exhibit the same uncertain bundle with two payoffs, W_1 and W_2. The respective probabilities (b_1 and b_2) are such that the expected payoff is at the point $E(W)$. However, the curvatures of the utility functions vary. You may think of these for three individuals (a), (b), and (c). In panel (a), the utility function is convex, i.e., the second derivative of the utility function is positive: $U''(W) > 0$. That is, utility increases with the payoff at an increasing rate. It is equal to A_1 and A_2 for payoffs W_1 and W_2, respectively. The expected utility $= D_A$, which is the average of A_1 and A_2 weighted by probabilities b_1 and b_2 and must correspond to the point $E(W)$. Consider the individual (a)'s choice between having this lottery versus having a sure payoff equal to $E(W)$ giving utility $U(E(W)) = \bar{A}$. We see that $D_A > \bar{A}$, that is, the expected utility is greater than the utility from the expected payoff. Thus, individual (a) prefers the risk. She is risk-loving or risk-preferring. Move on to panel (b) where the utility function is linear, i.e., $U''(W) = 0$. We see that the expected utility is the same as the utility from the expected payoff. This person is indifferent between the lottery and a sure payoff of $E(W)$. Hence, she is risk-neutral. Under risk-neutrality, the linearity of the utility function implies that maximising expected utility is equivalent to maximising expected payoffs/wealth.

Finally, consider panel (c), where the utility function is concave, i.e., the second derivative $U''(W)$ is negative. The expected utility is the probability-weighted average of C_1 and C_2, equal to D_C, which is less than the utility from the expected payoff, $\bar{C}$. This person avoids a fair bet and prefers a certainty payoff, $E(W)$, hence is risk-averse.

Given the one-to-one relationship between the curvature of the utility function and attitude towards risk, we can also say that *a person is risk-loving, risk-neutral, or risk-averse according to whether his utility function is strictly convex, linear, or strictly concave with respect to the wealth/payoff.*[3] Note that $U'' \gtreqless 0$ is equivalent to saying that the marginal utility of wealth/payoff increases, remains unchanged, or decreases with wealth/payoff. Therefore, still another way to define attitude towards risk is to say that *a person is risk-loving, risk-neutral, or risk-averse*

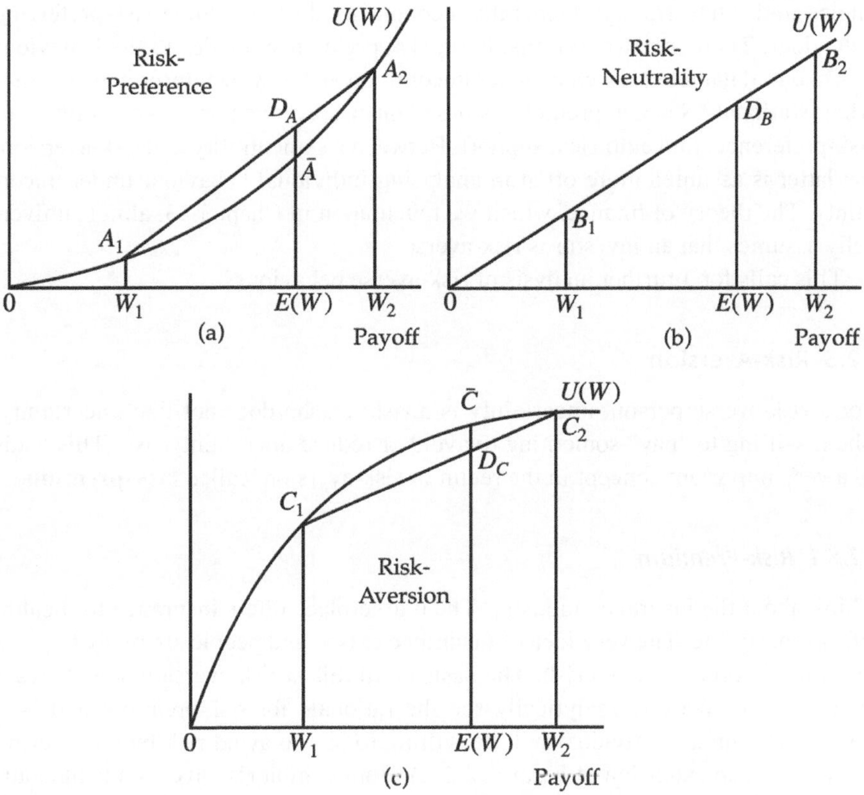

FIGURE 12.2 Attitude towards Risk and Curvature of the Utility Function

according to whether his marginal utility of wealth/payoff increases, remains the same, or decreases with wealth/ payoff.

Example 12.3

Consider the following utility functions, $U(W) =$

W^2	$\ln W$	$W/(1+W)$
$A - e^{-3W}$	$10 + 0.5W$	$\sqrt{W}$

In (iv), *e* is the exponential. Which attitude towards risk do they represent?

Answer: The second derivatives, $U''(W)$, are respectively $2 > 0$, $-1/W^2 < 0$, $-1/(1+W)^3 < 0$, $-9e^{-3W} < 0$, 0, and $-1/(4W^{1.5}) < 0$. Hence, they respectively represent risk-preference, risk-aversion, risk-aversion, risk-aversion, risk-neutrality, and risk-aversion. ■

Given three possible attitudes towards risk, which one do we assume for analysing choice under uncertainty? Generally, economists do *not* assume risk-preferring behaviour. There are two reasons. First, risk-preference alludes to the behaviour of a habitual gambler, which is rather uncommon and may be interpreted as somewhat irrational.[4] Second, predictions based on risk-aversion or risk-neutrality, not risk-preference, find empirical support. Between risk-neutrality and risk-aversion, the latter is assumed more often in analysing individual behaviour under uncertainty. The theory of finance, which we touch upon in Chapter 13, almost universally assumes that an investor is risk-averse.

This calls for a further analysis of risk-averse behaviour.

12.5 Risk-Aversion

For a risk-averse person, uncertainty is a risk: he/she does not like uncertainty. She is willing to "pay" something to avoid or reduce uncertainty/risk. This leads to a very important concept in the realm of risk-aversion, called **risk-premium**.

12.5.1 Risk-Premium

Think about the insurance industry. The marketplace offers insurance for health, life, property, etc. The very idea of insurance exists, and people are ready to pay a premium in order to avoid risk. The basis of all this is risk-aversion: people want to avoid risk. We can analytically see the rationale for risk-premium and how much premium an individual will be willing to pay to avoid risk by considering Figure 12.3, an extension of Figure 12.2 (c). Both exhibit risk-aversion behaviour.

Notice that, as in Figure 12.2(c), the expected utility from the lottery = D_C. Ask this question: What is the certain (with no uncertainty) amount you would like to have that would make you indifferent between that amount and the uncertain

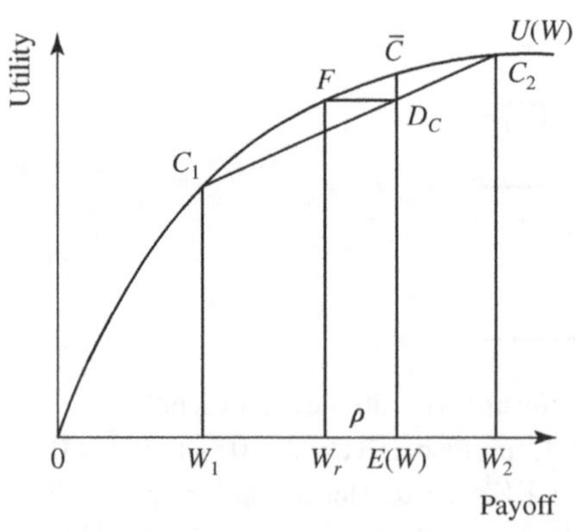

FIGURE 12.3 Risk-Aversion and Risk-Premium

bundle giving you an expected utility = D_C? Draw a horizontal line from D_C and see where it intersects the utility curve. That point is F. Which level of payoff will give utility = $F = D_C$? It is W_r. We can call W_r the **certainty equivalent** of the exhibited lottery. Notice the difference between the expected payoff, $E(W)$, and the certainty equivalent, W_r, shown as ρ, is the maximum that the individual would like to pay to avoid uncertainty because of risk-aversion. How? If she were risk-neutral (which she is not), she would not pay anything, i.e., pay zero to avoid the risk. But, because she is risk-averse, she is willing to accept an amount less than the expected value (rather than the lottery), unless that amount is too small. The minimum acceptable amount is W_r. The difference (= ρ) between the expected value $E(W)$ and W_r is called the risk-premium. That is,

$$\text{Risk-premium} = \text{Expected payoff} - \text{Certainty equivalent of the risk.}$$

12.5.2 Measures of Risk-Aversion

Given that an individual is risk-averse, can we measure the person's degree of risk-aversion? It is intuitive that the risk-premium that a risk-averse person is willing to pay would measure her degree of risk-aversion. It is also intuitive that risk-premium is intimately related to the curvature of the utility function. Depending on how we define the risk or the uncertain bundle vis-à-vis the initial wealth of the person, the corresponding risk-premium is related to the curvature of the utility function. Accordingly, there are different measures of risk-aversion. An interested reader would find them in advanced books on microeconomics and specialised books on finance or uncertainty and risk.

For instance, there is a notion of absolute risk-aversion, which is measured by $-U''(W)/U'(W)$. That is, given a utility function $U(W)$, $-U''(W)/U'(W)$ is the measure of absolute risk-aversion. If we further suppose that the degree or the measure of absolute risk-aversion remains unchanged, say at α, as a person's initial wealth W changes, i.e., we have $-U''(W)/U'(W) = \alpha$ for any W then the corresponding utility function happens to be $A - e^{-\alpha W}$, where e is the exponential. It is called a constant-absolute-risk-aversion utility function, which is widely applied in the theory of portfolio choice in the field of finance.

Empirical estimates of the degree of risk-aversion are available too.

12.5.3 Two Ways to Reduce Risk

A risk-averse person would like to reduce her exposure to risk. There are two ways to do so. One is to pay an insurance premium if an insurance market for the risk exists. Please know that insurance markets do not exist for all types of risk. If a risk is idiosyncratic, meaning that if the adverse event is likely to hit in a random fashion only a relatively minor proportion of the population, then insurance may be available in the market. For instance, insurance is available for burglary and theft in a home. It is because it is highly unlikely that a large fraction of homes in a region will be targets of such crimes at the same time. Therefore, it is profitable for insurance companies to offer home insurance. Premiums collected from homes not affected by these crimes are essentially transferred to the company itself as profits *as well as* towards homes that are affected by these crimes. The whole population that buys such insurance for "peace of mind"—including those who face these crimes and those who do not—essentially share the risk. Put differently, insurance is about risk-sharing.

If, instead, there is a good chance that the adverse event can affect a large section of the population at the same time, the insurance company cannot sustain itself, because there will be too many claimants. That is why, you cannot buy insurance for just being unemployed—because it may be a macro, economywide phenomenon.

Another way to reduce risk is to diversify one's ventures or portfolio. If you are an investor in the security market, you will be well-advised not to invest in just one stock or a few stocks only. If you do so, you will expose yourself to large swings in returns, from a large negative number to a large positive number. It is like putting all your eggs (money or wealth) in one basket. Diversification reduces variations in returns and hence lowers risk.[5]

12.6 Economic Decision-Making/Choice under Risk-Aversion

We have covered many concepts relating to uncertainty and risk but haven't discussed a person's or an entity's economic choice of actions under uncertainty. We will learn it through some examples.

12.6.1 Output Decision by a Perfectly Competitive Firm

Consider a small, perfectly competitive firm, which is a price taker. Suppose that its cost function is known with certainty, i.e., it is non-stochastic, given by $C(y) = 0.25y^2$. Thus, marginal cost has the expression, MC = 0.5y. To begin with, let the price is certain, p = 15. The profit function is:

$$W = py - C(y) = py - (0.25)y^2. \tag{12.3}$$

From Chapter 8, we know that the profit-maximising condition is $p =$ MC $= 0.5y$. Thus, the profit-maximising output is $y_c = 2p = 30$. This is illustrated in Figure 12.4, which plots the profit function (12.3). The profit-maximising output (= 30) is shown at the base of the vertical line.

Now suppose the same firm faces price uncertainty. Moving from certainty to uncertainty amounts to a discrete jump or an increase in uncertainty. Consistent with the definition of an increase in uncertainty discussed earlier, let the expected

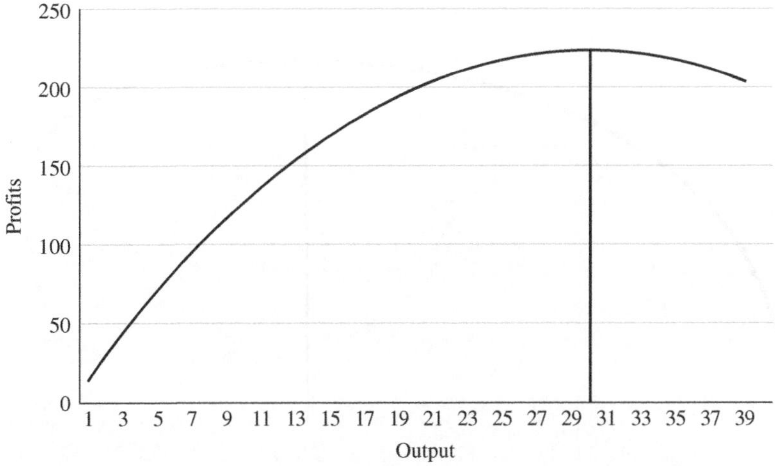

FIGURE 12.4 Profit Function and Optimal (Profit-Maximising) Output

price be the (earlier) certainty price, $p = 15$, while the price under uncertainty assumes two possible values, say $p_1 = 10$ and $p_2 = 20$, with 50% probability of each. That is, $b_1 = b_2 = 0.5$. For any particular level of output, there are two profit outcomes: $W_1 = p_1 y - C(y) = p_1 y - 0.25y^2$ and $W_2 = p_2 y - C(y) = p_2 y - 0.25y^2$. Assuming that the firm is risk-averse, we must specify a concave utility function, say $U(W) = W^{0.25}$.

The expected utility of profit is $E\left(W^{0.25}\right)$, which can be expanded as

$$0.5\left(10y - 0.25y^2\right)^{0.25} + 0.5\left(20y - 0.25y^2\right)^{0.25} \tag{12.4}$$

Although complicated, we can write down the first-order expected-utility-maximising condition and solve the optimal output, say y_u, by using any of the non-linear-equation solvers available in different software.

For our purpose however, we use a more direct and simpler approach. That is, by using (12.4) we numerically compute the expected utility of profits for different levels of output. Next, by simple inspection of the table or plot generated, we determine the output at which the expected utility is the highest. Figure 12.5 presents the numerical plot of expected utility of profits at various levels of output. The highest point is reached at output = 25, i.e., $y_u = 25$. This is the solution for the firm's choice of output under price uncertainty. It is an approximate solution since the outputs at decimal levels are not included in the plot, but sufficient to serve our purpose.

Note that the optimal output under (price) uncertainty (≈ 25) is less than that under certainty. This is an expected implication: compared to no uncertainty, in the face of uncertainty and risk, a risk-averse firm would scale down

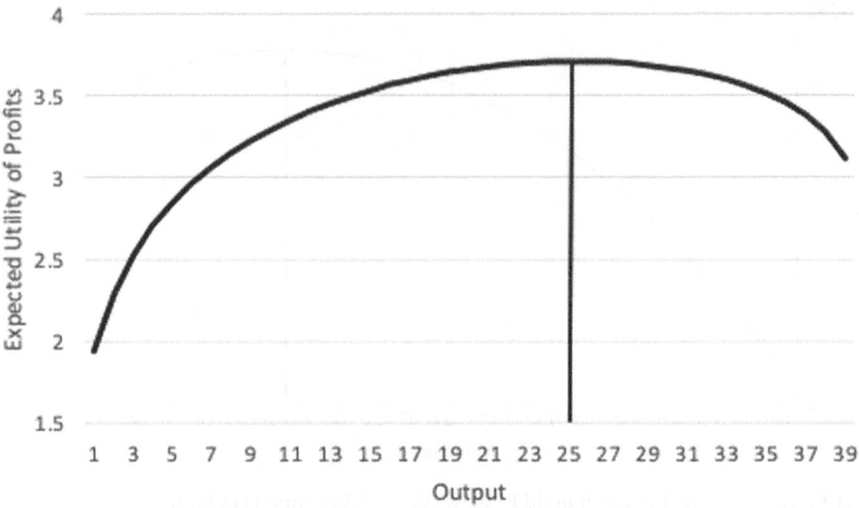

FIGURE 12.5 Expected Utility of Profit Function and Optimal Output

its production. Does the "price = MC" condition"—in this case "expected price = MC" condition—hold? No. At $y_u = 25$, MC $= 0.5y_u = 12.5$, whereas expected price $= 15$. Thus, the expected price exceeds MC. That is, under price uncertainty, a risk-averse competitive firm will produce less than that under price certainty and at the optimal output, the marginal cost is less than the expected price. These are the general implications, not dependent upon the particular utility function and the cost function we have assumed for the sake of illustration.

This example is illustrative of how decision-making under uncertainty works. *We need to know the utility function and the probability distribution of the parameter which is uncertain. Given these and other information typically available under certainty, we obtain the expression of the expected utility. Choose that action or the value of the decision variable which maximises the expected utility.*

12.6.2 Insurance Market

Suppose an individual, say, Rahul, having initial wealth $W > 0$ faces the risk of his car meeting with an accident (a bad state). Let the probability of this happening be $b > 0$. In that event, let $L > 0$ denote the individual's loss (in terms of cost of repair or getting a new car, cost of injuries, possibly death, cost of mental stress, etc.). For simplicity, suppose that L is non-stochastic, i.e., known with certainty.

Without any car insurance, the individual faces two prospects of final wealth, $W - L$ in the event of accident (the bad state) and W in the event of no accident (the good state) with respective probabilities b and $1 - b$. Suppose that insurance is available, and the premium schedule is linear: to ensure one rupee or one dollar, the premium is q fraction of a rupee or dollar. The decision variable is the amount of insurance coverage to be purchased, say $S(\leq L)$. In the presence of insurance being purchased, the prospects of final wealth or payoffs are different. The total insurance payment is qS which must be paid irrespective of whether the car gets into an accident. If the accident does occur, he loses L but recovers S from the insurance company. The payoffs and their probabilities are: $(W_1, W_2; b, 1-b)$, where:

$$W_1 \equiv W - L + (1-q)S \text{ and } W_2 \equiv W - qS.$$

The expected utility is $bU(W_1) + (1-b)U(W_2) =$

$$bU(W - L + (1-q)S) + (1-b)U(W - qS). \tag{12.5}$$

Note that buying insurance has the benefit of increasing the payoff in the bad state, together with a cost of lowering the payoff in the good state.

Differentiating the first term in (12.5) with respect to S, the marginal benefit (MB) of S is $b(1-q)U'(W_1)$. The interpretation is straightforward. In the bad state, one extra rupee/dollar coverage brings to the insurance holder $1-q$ rupee/dollar, whose marginal utility of valuation is $(1-q) \times U'(W_1)$. This is multiplied by the probability of this state, b, to yield MB $= b(1-q)U'(W_1)$. Likewise, differentiating the second term in (12.5) with respect to S gives the marginal cost of insurance coverage, MC $= (1-b)qU'(W_2)$. One extra rupee/dollar coverage leads to a loss of q rupee/dollar in the good state since q is the insurance premium for one rupee/dollar. Its marginal valuation is $q \times U'(W_2)$. This is multiplied by $1-b$, the probability of the good state, and leads to the above expression of MC.

The first question we ask is: whether the person would buy any insurance at all, i.e., whether $S > 0$. To determine this, we evaluate MB and MC of insurance coverage at $S = 0$, i.e., when there is no insurance in the initial situation. Rahul will buy some insurance if and only if (briefly "iff") MB > MC at $S = 0$. Substituting $S = 0$ in the respective expression, MB at $S = 0$ is $b(1-q)U'(W-L)$ and MC at $S = 0$ equals $(1-b)qU'(W)$. Thus, Rahul will buy (some) insurance iff $b(1-q)U'(W-L) > (1-b)qU'(W)$, or,

$$\frac{1-q}{q} > \frac{1-b}{b} \cdot \frac{U'(W)}{U'(W-L)}. \tag{12.6}$$

To understand this condition, let's work with some numbers. Under risk-aversion, the marginal utility of wealth decreases with wealth, implying $U'(W) < U'(W-L)$. Let $U'(W)/U'(W-L) = 0.75$. Further, let $b = 0.2$. Hence, the right-hand side of equation. (12.6) is equal to 3 and therefore, this condition is met iff $(1-q)/q > 3$

or $q < 0.25$. Comparing $q = 0.25$ with $b = 0.2$, we can say that Rahul will *buy some insurance as long as the insurance premium per rupee/dollar is less than or does not far exceed the probability of the bad state occurring.* This makes economic sense. You would buy insurance against a bad state if and only if the premium per rupee/dollar is not way too high relative to the probability of the happening of the bad state.

The next question we pose is whether Rahul will buy full insurance, i.e., choose $S = L$. For this, we evaluate MB and MC at $S = L$. If the former is equal to or exceeds the latter, he will buy full insurance; otherwise, he wouldn't. Substituting $S = L$ into the respective expressions, we have MB $= b(1-q)U'(W-qL)$ and MC $= (1-b)qU'(W-qL)$. Thus, MB > MC iff $b(1-q)U'(W-qL) \geq (1-b)qU'(W-qL)$, which is equivalent to a very simple and intuitive condition:

$$q \leq p. \tag{12.7}$$

That is, a person will *buy full insurance if the insurance premium per rupee/dollar does not exceed the probability of the occurrence of the bad state.*

12.7 Mean-Variance Utility Function

We have earlier talked about measuring risk-aversion and a particular measure called the constant absolute risk-aversion. Recall that, if α denotes the measure of constant absolute risk-aversion, the utility function is $U(W) = A - e^{-\pm W}$, where e is the exponential. There is a well-known result that if (a) the utility function satisfies constant absolute risk-aversion and (b) the probability distribution of wealth is normal, then the expected utility can be expressed as a linear function of the expected or mean wealth, $\bar{W}$, and the variance of wealth, say σ_W^2. More specifically, $EU((W)) = \bar{W} - (\alpha/2)\sigma_W^2$. Intuitively, the expected utility increases with the mean, and, because of risk-aversion, decreases with the variance. It is generally termed as the **mean-variance utility function**. We simply note here that the mean-variance utility function is widely used in the theory of finance.

Facts and Insights

- A random variable may be qualitative or quantitative.
- Quantitative random variables can be discrete or continuous.
- Discrete and continuous random variables are characterised by a discrete or continuous probability distribution.
- A compound uncertain bundle/lottery is a lottery of lotteries.
- An increase in uncertainty is defined as an increase in the variance of a quantitative random variable while the arithmetic mean or average remains unchanged.
- An increase in uncertainty is also defined as a **mean-preserving spread.**

- Decision-making under uncertainty amounts to choosing an uncertain bundle or a lottery among a set of alternative uncertain bundles or lotteries.
- The expected utility hypothesis states that the overall valuation of an uncertain bundle is equal to the expected utility of the payoffs/wealth associated with that bundle.
- Under uncertainty, a rational individual's objective is to maximise the expected utility.
- A fair bet or a fair lottery is one whose price/cost is equal to the expected payoff.
- A person is risk-loving, risk-averse, or risk-neutral as according to how he accepts or rejects a fair bet.
- A person is risk-loving, risk-neutral, or risk-averse according to how the expected utility exceeds, is equal to or less than the utility of the expected payoff/wealth.
- A person is risk-loving, risk-neutral, or risk-averse according to how his utility function is strictly convex, linear, or strictly concave with respect to the wealth/payoffs.
- Under risk-neutrality, maximising expected utility is equivalent to maximising expected payoff.
- Certainty equivalent is that payoff, the utility from which is equal to the expected utility of an uncertain bundle.
- For a risk-averse person, uncertainty is a risk: he/she does not like uncertainty.
- Risk-premium for a risk-aversion person is the difference between the expected payoff and the certainty equivalent payoff.
- Insurance markets exist for idiosyncratic risks, not for economywide risks like unemployment which may be an economywide problem.
- A risk-averse person can reduce risk in two ways: buying insurance if it is available or by diversification of one's ventures or portfolio.
- Decision-making or choice under uncertainty works as follows. We need to know the utility function and the probability distribution of the parameter which is uncertain. Given these and other information typically available under uncertainty, we obtain the expression of the expected utility. Choose that action or the value of the decision variable which maximises the expected utility.
- Compared to price certainty, under price uncertainty, a risk-averse competitive firm produces less and at the optimal level of production, marginal cost is less than the expected price.
- Insurance is about risk-sharing.
- A risk-averse individual will buy some insurance against the occurrence of a bad state as long as the insurance premium per rupee/dollar is less than or does not far exceed the probability of the bad state occurring.
- A risk-averse person will buy full insurance against the possibility of a bad state if the insurance premium per rupee/dollar does not exceed the probability of the occurrence of the bad state.

- If the utility function satisfies constant absolute risk-aversion and the probability distribution of wealth is normal, then expected utility can be expressed as a linear function of the expected or mean wealth, and the variance of wealth.

Exercises

Descriptive/Analytical

12.1 By constructing numerical examples on your own, describe in your own words the differences between risk-preference, risk-neutrality, and risk-aversion.

12.2 "In the presence of uncertainty, decision-making is a random choice." Defend or refute.

12.3 Giving examples out of the text, describe the expected utility hypothesis.

Short Answer (word limit = 500 approx.)

12.4 Giving examples outside of the text, differentiate between discrete and continuous random variables.

12.5 Giving an example outside of the text, explain the concept of mean-preserving spread.

12.6 Intuitively explain what risk-premium is.

Quizzes/Numerical

12.7 "Lottery A offers payoffs of $10 and $100 with respective probabilities 0.7 and 0.3. Lottery B has payoffs $0 and $110 with respective probabilities 0.65 and 0.35. Given these, Lottery B is more uncertain than Lottery A." Defend or refute.

12.8 There are two uncertain bundles:
A = ($10, $20, $30; 0.4, 0.2, 0.4);
B = ($14, $17, $20, $23, $26; 0.24, 0.16, 0.16, 0.16, 0.24).
Can we say which of the two is more uncertain and why?

12.9 Consider the two uncertain bundles in the previous question, and a lottery of lotteries: C = (A, B: 0.3, 0.7). What are the payoffs and probabilities for the compound lottery C?

12.10 A lottery offers €0, €10,000, €50,000, €100,000, and €200,000 with probabilities, 0.9, 0.04, 0.03, 0.02, and 0.01. What is the fair price of this lottery?

12.11 Suppose $U(W) = W^{0.2}$. An uncertain bundle has three payoffs, 25, 36, and 64. The respective probabilities are 0.3, 0.5, and 0.2. What is the risk-premium associated with this bundle?

12.12 Consider the previous question with one modification. The utility function is different, $U(W)=\sqrt{W}$, but the uncertain bundle is the same. Find the risk-premium and compare it with that in the previous question. Is it larger or smaller? Offer an intuitive reason.

12.13 In the car insurance example in the text, suppose that utility function is $U(X)=X^{0.2}$. Furthermore, $W=50{,}000$, $L=15{,}000$, $b=0.1$ and the insurance premium per one rupee/dollar is $q=0.12$. Will this person buy insurance? If yes, will he buy full insurance?

12.14 Refer to the previous question. Using a spreadsheet software, compute the expected utility for different values of S (insurance coverage) ranging from 0, 200, 400,….., 15,000. What is the person's optimal choice of the insurance coverage?

12.15 A person's mean-variance utility function has his degree of constant absolute risk-aversion parameter equal to $\alpha=1.2$. Which of the following uncertain bundles will he choose?

A = (20, 30, 40, 50; 0.2, 0.3, 0.1, 0.4)

B = (15, 30, 40, 50; 0.2, 0.25, 0.1, 0.45)

C = (20, 30, 40, 42; 0.2, 0.3, 0.2, 0.3).

Notes

1 We have $\int f(x)dx=\int(10-x)/40dx=(10x-x^2/2)/40$. Hence, $\int_1^2 f(x)dx=(10\times 2-2^2/2)/40-(10\times 1-1)/40=8.5/40=0.2125$. Similarly, $\int_2^3 f(x)dx=7.5/40=0.1875$, and so on.

2 The mathematical expression of a normal density function is complicated and not of direct use to us.

3 It is possible that the utility function of a person may be convex, linear, and concave over different intervals of payoffs. In this case, we locally define risk-preference, risk-neutrality, and risk aversion. We abstract from these possibilities for the sake of simplicity and clarity.

4 Going to a casino and gambling small amounts for fun once in a while without addiction is a different behaviour.

5 This is a good thing. There is flip side however: it reduces the average return.

13

ASSET MARKETS AND PORTFOLIO CHOICE

Markets exist not just for goods and services and productive inputs, but also for assets, meaning material assets. We can divide (material) assets into financial and physical or non-financial. The former includes cash at home, bank deposits, fixed deposits, stocks and bonds, etc., while the latter includes real estate, antiques, famous paintings, etc. A detailed classification of assets is shown in Figure 13.1.

Technically speaking, anything you possess of value is your asset. You can say that the food items in your kitchen and store, clothes in your wardrobe, TV, refrigerators, laptop, mobiles, motorbike, and small car (for personal use) are your assets. But normally many of these are consumables in that they are consumed away in the current period or can last only for a short while. This is why they are not normally regarded as assets.

From the perspective of how much a person or an entity is worth in rupee or dollar terms, the other side of the coin for assets is **liabilities**. Liabilities are others' claim on you, e.g., a bank loan that you took in buying your house or automobile. Assets minus liabilities constitute your wealth, **net assets** or **net-worth**.

As an example, suppose you have assets worth \$5 million. Some of these assets may be in physical form (land, building, precious metals, antiques, etc.) and others in financial forms like cash, mutual fund investments, etc. Can you claim that your **wealth** is \$5 million? In other words, are the terms asset and wealth synonymous? No. For example, if the loan outstanding on you is \$4 million, your wealth or net-worth is only \$1 million. A person's net-worth can be negative. Because of bad investments, even some very wealthy individuals at some point of time in the past may have a negative net-worth and thus become a pauper. Michael Jackson, the famous pop star, apparently had a negative \$400 million net-worth just before he passed away in 2009. In a lighter vein, read through our unsolicited advice below.

DOI: 10.4324/9781003452195-13

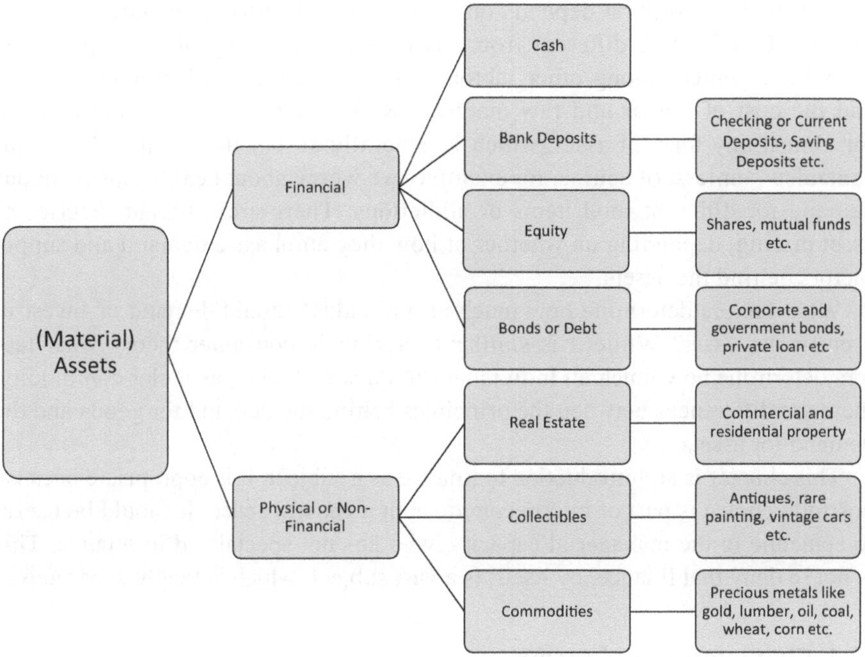

FIGURE 13.1 Classification of (Material) Assets

> **A PIECE OF UNSOLICITED ADVICE.....**
>
> Very soon many of you, students in India, may be entering the "marriage market." In India, barring some exceptions, marriages are finalised between families. If in one such meeting your perspective spouse or his/her father boasts "I have **assets** worth ₹900 million." Please don't get overawed immediately. Politely ask "How much are your liabilities?"

The next question is, how do you choose your assets? This is called **portfolio choice** in finance. In Chapter 5, we analysed how a rational individual allocates his earnings over consumption and savings. The amount earmarked for consumption is spent on different goods and services, whereas savings build assets like cash, gold coins, stocks, etc. This is the same as saying that she "acquires" or "demands" assets, or, what is the same thing, she makes investments. Put differently, *a person's or a family's assets are acquired from the past and present savings* (while some assets may be obtained from others as gifts).

Like in markets for goods and services, asset prices are determined by demand and supply forces. However, the environments affecting demand and supply of assets are different. For instance, the supply of shares to the share market by a corporation depends on how it wants to finance its operation and growth. This is quite different from saying that the supply of shoes produced by Nike depends, among other factors, on the technology of producing shoes and the cost of labour and raw material. Risk is a factor behind the demand for almost any form of asset, which is generally absent from demand for consumables—unless, of course, for example, we worry about health aspects in our demand for different food items or addictions. There are different theories of asset pricing, depending on whether or how they emphasise demand and supply factors behind the assets.

What factors determine how much an individual should demand or invest in a particular asset? While it is similar to asking in consumer theory what factors determine how much an individual should spend on a particular commodity, there are differences between the principles behind the demand for goods and the demand for assets.

This chapter is an introduction to finance as a subject. It is appropriate because portfolio choice is part of microeconomics in a general sense. It should be useful to someone in the managerial capacity, who has not specialised in finance. This is not to deny that finance, by itself, is a vast subject, which is taught separately.

13.1 Characteristics of Assets

In demanding a good (for consumption), the benefit is measured in one dimension, namely, the psychological satisfaction from consuming the good, typically called utility. In contrast, assets do not generate utility directly, but via their capacity to generate purchasing power that can be used for consumption. The benefit from having an asset depends on three dimensions or characteristics of the asset.

13.1.1 Liquidity

It means the ease with which a particular asset can be exchanged for money at face value. Liquidity is important, because people need money on a short-term basis to meet unforeseen needs. Obviously, your money "invested" in a bank in the form of a current or a saving deposit is more liquid than money invested in real estate. You can walk to your bank and cash a check in a matter of minutes. You can withdraw money from your deposit by using ATM machines. But if you have a piece of property, and you want cash immediately by selling it instantly, you are likely to lose significantly relative to its market price. That is, you don't get back its face value. To get its worth, you need to advertise or spread the word that your property is for sale. Following this people approach you, some people may make offers, and this whole process can take weeks or sometimes even months.

13.1.2 Returns

An investment can generate earnings only after a certain period. Hence, time is an important element. Suppose you have put €1,000 in your savings account, the annual interest rate on the savings deposit is 6% and the bank pays interest after one year.[1] Then, the interest income of €60 accrues to you after one year. The principle behind someone or some institution paying you an interest for the use of your money is that there is a *time value of money*: if you are not using your money for a given length of time, someone else can borrow it, use it for some purpose, and therefore is willing to pay you something for the use of that money.

Going back to the example, if you continue to maintain your deposit, the interest earnings accrue year after year. This is called the **yield** of an asset, meaning the periodic income or earnings generated by an asset. In our example, the yield is €60 every year.[2] The yield and the initial amount invested determine the **rate of return** from an asset. In our example, the rate of return equals 60/1000 = 0.06 or 6%, which is same as the interest rate.

Consider another example.

Example 13.1

Suppose that Oniki took $1 million out of his savings to buy a luxury flat for the purpose of renting. It is given on rent for $6,000/month. Assume that $1,000/month is spent on maintenance. The net rental income is then $5,000/month, translating into an annual yield of $60,000. It is expected that after one year the flat will be sold at $1.1 million. What is the rate of return?

Answer: Note that the initial investment or the initial cost of investment is $1 million. Over the year, the return on this investment is calculated as:

$$\frac{60,000}{1\,\text{million}} + \left(\frac{1.1\,\text{million}}{1\,\text{million}} - 1\right) = 0.06 + 0.10 = 0.16 = 16\%$$ ■

The first term is the ratio of yield to the cost of the investment, as in the earlier example. The term inside the brackets is new and equals what is called **capital gains or losses**. If the expected sale value in the future exceeds (falls short of) the initial cost, there is a capital gain (capital loss).[3] In general,

$$\text{Rate of return on an asset} = \frac{\text{yield} + \text{expected sale value}}{\text{cost of the asset}} - 1. \tag{13.1}$$

There is an intuitive way to look at the return from an asset—namely, as an internal or implicit interest rate received. To understand this, consider the same example. The cost of investment is $1 million, whereas, after one year the asset pays back the rent ($60,000) plus the sale value ($1.1 million), equal to $1,160,000. Ask yourself the following question. Suppose you deposit \$1 million in a bank. At what interest rate would you obtain \$1,160,000 a year after (as principal plus interest)? That is, you set up the equation:

$$1,000,000(1+r)=1,160,000.$$

and solve r, which is the internal or the implicit interest rate. We obtain $r=0.16$, i.e., an interest rate of 16%. This is same as the rate of return calculated by considering the yield and the capital gains. Indeed, this way of calculating the rate of return of an asset can be generalised to more than one period; see Example 13.2 below.

In layman terms, the rate of return from holding an asset is the ratio between the excess money or the purchasing power it generates per period and the initial cost of the asset (investment). An asset's rate of return is one of its most important characteristics. Ceteris paribus, the higher the rate of return the greater will be demand for an asset.

Example 13.2

Ahmed, located in Mumbai, India, is in the business of buying and renting state-of-the-art cell phones to tourists from abroad. A new cell phone costs ₹40,000. The rental incomes over a year are ₹12,000. By the end of a year, Ahmed expects to sell this phone in the second-hand market at ₹30,000. Having cell phones and using it in this business can be thought of an asset. What is Ahmed's rate of return from this asset?

Answer: The cost of the asset = ₹40,000. Its yield = ₹12,000 and the expected sale price = ₹30,000. Applying equation (13.1), the rate of return is equal to:

$$\frac{12,000+30,000}{40,000}-1=0.05=5\%.$$

■

Example 13.3

Consider the earlier example of Oniki, investing \$1 million in a rental property. Suppose that he sells the property two years after he bought it at \$1.3 million and during these two years it generated a net rental income of \$60,000 each year. What is the rate of return of this investment by Oniki?

Answer: Let r denote the implicit interest rate. Since the asset is held for two years, we consider a two-year time horizon. A deposit of \$1 million in the bank at the interest rate of r would transform into $\$1,000,000(1+r)^2$ at the end of two years. On the other hand, if this asset is held, the net rental income of \$60,000 obtained after one year becomes $\$60,000(1+r)$ after two years. Add this to the net rental income and sale value received by the end of the second year (\$60,000 +

\$1,300,000). Altogether it amounts to $\$60,000(1+r)+\$1,360,000$. Hence, set up the equation:

$$1,000,000(1+r)^2 = 60,000(1+\text{r})\text{v}+1,360,000.$$

Use a non-linear equation solver (available on internet) to solve r. The solution is $r \cong 0.196$, i.e., a rate of return of 19.6%.[4]■

13.1.3 Risk

Unless we are talking about deposits in a current/savings account or in a fixed deposit, almost any other investment carries some uncertainty and risk on its return. In the last example, the rental income was given and known, equal to \$60,000/year. But it may not be known for sure before the flat is bought. Similarly, the price at which it will be sold a year or two years after is only "expected," not known for sure. On most investments, there is some degree of uncertainty and risk associated with its return. We have already studied risk in Chapter 12.

The concept of **risk** can be understood further via the following example. Suppose that you have a given amount of money for investment and you are looking at two options: Investment A and Investment B. The former provides a return of 0.10 (10%) with a probability of 50% and 0.06 (6%) with a probability of 50%. We can then calculate the **expected return**, defined as the weighted average of possible returns. For Investment A it is equal to $0.10 \times 0.50 + 0.06 \times 0.50 = 0.08$ (8%). Investment B offers a return of 0.13 with probability 50% and 0.03 with a probability of 50%. This also has an expected return of 8%. Mark however that while both options have the same expected return, the variability (measured by the statistical formula for variance) of return is greater with Investment B. Hence, we say that Investment B is riskier than Investment A. In the terminology of Chapter 12, Investment B amounts to a mean-preserving spread relative to Investment A. The higher the degree of variation of returns relative to the average, the greater is the risk associated with an asset.

Obviously, risk is an important consideration in acquiring an asset. All else the same, the higher the risk associated with an asset, the less will be the demand for it.

Example 13.4

Consider two stocks C and D. C gives a return of 10% with a probability of 40% and 15% with a probability of 60%. D offers a return of 12% with a probability of 50% and 14% with a probability of 50%. Calculate the expected return of each of these assets and determine which is riskier.

Answer: The expected returns of stocks C and D are, respectively, equal to:

$$E(C) = 0.10 \times 0.4 + 0.15 \times 0.6 = 0.13 = 13\%;$$

$$E(D) = 0.12 \times 0.5 + 0.14 \times 0.5 = 0.13 = 13\%.$$

That is, both stocks give the same expected or mean return. Hence, the stock whose variance of returns is higher is the riskier one. Denoting variance by V, and applying the statistical formula for the variance,

$$V(C) = (0.10 - 0.13)^2 \times 0.4 + (0.15 - 0.13)^2 \times 0.6 = 0.00006;$$

$$V(D) = (0.12 - 0.13)^2 \times 0.5 + (0.14 - 0.13)^2 \times 0.5 = 0.00001.$$

Hence, stock C is the riskier asset.■

13.2 Further Understanding the Rate of Return: Discounting and Present Value Analysis

Putting your money in an interest-earning safe deposit like a bank account or a government bond is considered as a benchmark investment in the sense that it guarantees a minimum return on your investment. If you are thinking of some other forms of investment, then, apart from the risk factor, you must compare its return to the minimum return (the interest rate). The comparison is not trivial however if the yield on the asset varies from one period to another. A method called the present discounted value or simply a present value analysis is typically used.

This method is illustrated via the following example. Suppose that you are an established businessman in your hometown. You can borrow \$3.3 million from a bank at 15% annual interest rate, which must be paid in three years from now. You are contemplating to use this money to organise a two week-long trade-show. You expect that contacting business firms, making local arrangements, etc. will take two years. At the end of the second year, you expect to hold the first trade-show and at the end of the third year the second trade-show. When the show is on, you expect to get payments from businesses that commit to participate and from potential customers who would come to sample the products. Let us say that these payments or receipts will be \$600,000 in the second year and (after the news of the success of the first trade-show spreads) ₹4.3 million in the third year. For simplicity, suppose that there is no uncertainty or risk: you know for sure that you would "raise" these amounts. Also suppose that liquidity is not an issue. Your only consideration is returns. Holding the trade-shows can be seen as an asset, which is going to provide yields for two years.

You must weigh the rate of return of this asset or investment against the cost of borrowing. The benefits and costs of acquiring this asset are given in Table 13.1, where notice that interest cost of \$3.3 million at 15% is \$495,000 per year. Adding

TABLE 13.1 Benefits and Costs ($)

	End of 1st year	End of 2nd year	End of 3rd year
Benefits	**0**	**600,000**	**4.3 million**
Costs	495,000	495,000	495,000
Interest	0	0	3.3 million
Principal	495,000	495,000	3.795 million
Total Repayment			

up the principal and the interest costs over the three years comes to $4.785 million. The benefit at the end of the third year is higher, equal to $4.9 million ($4.3 million plus $600,000). Does it mean that it is a profitable investment?

Unfortunately, this simplistic comparison of benefits and costs is flawed. This is because the value of a dollar one year from now is *not* the same as that of a dollar two years from now—as long as there is an interest payment involved. Hence a simple adding of figures over the two or more years is something like adding apples and oranges. To obtain a correct comparison between benefits and costs, we must convert them to equivalent dollars in the same year. This is done through **discounting** and a **present value** analysis.

Discounting means converting a given sum of money to be paid or received in some future date to an equivalent sum of money in an earlier period. For instance, consider a sum of $121,000 to be paid or received in 2026. What is its discounted value as of 2024? To answer this, we first ask how much one dollar in 2024 will be worth in 2026. Suppose that the annual interest rate, expected to prevail between 2024 and 2026, is r. Then one dollar lent in 2024 will fetch $1+r$ rupees in 2025 and $(1+r)^2$ in 2026. That is, one dollar in 2026 is worth $1/(1+r)^2$ in 2024. Thus, $121,000 in 2026 discounted back to 2024 is equal to $121,000/$(1+r)^2$. If the interest rate is, say, 10%, i.e., $r = 0.1$, this sum is equal to $121,000/$(1.1)^2$ = $100,000.[5] In general, the **present value** or the **present discounted value** (PDV) is *the sum of the discounted values of payments to be made or received in future periods when the sums are discounted back to the present period.*

We now go back to the example given in Table 13.1 and ask, what are the PDV of the costs and benefits of investing in the trade-show? Note that the first-period payment of $495, 000 discounted back to the current period at the interest rate of 15% is equal to $495,000/(1.15) = $430,434. Similarly, the discounted value of the payment of $495,000 in the second period as of the present period is equal to $495,000/$(1.15)^2$ = $374,291. The discounted value of the third year payment = $3.795 million/$(1.15)^3$ = $2,495,274. Hence, the PDV of the costs = $430,434 + $374,291 + $2,495,274 = $3.3 million (after taking into rounding errors), the amount of the loan taken. This should not be surprising, because the loan is incurred in the current period and the interest rate associated with the loan is being used in the discounting process.

Let us now calculate the PDV of the benefits. In period 1 the benefits are zero and thus its discounted value is zero. The discounted value of the second-period benefit of \$600,000 (as of the current period) = \$600,000/(1.15)^2 = \$453,686. That of the third-year benefit = \$4.3 million/(1.15)^3 = \$2,827,320. Therefore, the PDV of benefits = 0 + 453,686 + 2,827,320 = \$3,281,006. In summary,

PDV of Costs = 3.3 million;

PDV of Benefits 3.28 million.

The latter is *less*. We therefore conclude that it is *not* a profitable investment. (If we consider risk, the conclusion is only strengthened.)

Equivalently, we can calculate the (internal) rate of return of the project, say, ρ, as that internal discount rate at which the discounted value of the costs is equal to the discounted value of the benefits. At the discount rate ρ,

$$\text{The discounted value of costs} \equiv A = \frac{495{,}000}{1+\rho} + \frac{495{,}000}{(1+\rho)^2} + \frac{3{,}795{,}000}{(1+\rho)^3};$$

$$\text{The discounted value of benefits} \equiv B = \frac{0}{1+\rho} + \frac{600{,}000}{(1+\rho)^2} + \frac{4{,}300{,}000}{(1+\rho)^3}$$

Setting up the non-linear equation $A = B$ gives the solution of $\rho \approx 0.121$. That is, the rate of return (= 12.1%) falls short of the interest rate (= 15%), which is the cost of borrowing, leading to the same conclusion that it is not a profitable investment.

Note that we would arrive at the same conclusion even if no money were borrowed, and, instead, the businessman had used \$3.3 million from his own funds—as long as he would have obtained 15% interest from lending this amount in the market.

Two more examples follow.

Example 13.5

A used truck, if bought today, is expected to generate a rent of \$10,000 this year and every year over the next ten years. Beyond the 10th year it will cease to operate and the scrap value of it will be \$1,000. Find the PDV of owning this truck if the interest rate is 8%. Find the same if the interest rate is 11%. In which case is the PDV less and why?

Answer: Choose \$1,000 as the unit. Then, the discounted sum of the values of the yields over first year and the next years at 8% interest rate is equal to:

$$10 + \frac{10}{1.08} + \frac{10}{(1.08)^2} + \cdots + \frac{10}{(1.08)^{10}} = 77.1.$$

The discounted value of the scrap value $= 1/(1.08)^{10} = 0.463$. Adding these,

$$\text{PDV at } 8\% = (77.1 + 0.463) \text{ thousands} = \$77,563.$$

Doing the same calculation, at the interest rate of 11%,

$$\text{PDV at } 11\% = \$69,240,$$

which is less than the PDV at 8% interest rate. It is less because the higher the interest rate, the smaller is the present discounted value of any future year's yield and the smaller is the present discounted value of the (future) scrap value as well.■

Example 13.6

A multinational firm A has a patent for the technology of product, which it wants to sell. There are two potential buyers from India: firm B and firm C. Firm B is willing to pay ₹175 million for it upfront (instantly), while firm C is willing to pay ₹400,000 each year for five years including the current year. For company A, selling the technology also involves sending its technical team at its own cost (= ₹100 million) to set up the operation, which is the same whether firm B or firm C buys the technology. There is no uncertainty about the future payments from firm C. The interest rate is expected to prevail at 10%. Furthermore, suppose that A is not able to sell to both firms. It simply does not have the manpower and resources to set up the technology at two locations. To whom would it sell its technology?

Answer: Technology selling can be regarded as an asset. The cost of both assets is the same, equal to the cost of sending a technical team. Since Firm B has agreed to offer ₹175 million upfront, Firm A will sell to firm B or firm C according as the PDV of payments from Firm C falls short of or exceeds ₹175 million. At 10% rate of interest, the PDV of payments (in lakh) from firm C equals:

$$400,000 + \frac{400,000}{1.1} + \frac{400,000}{(1.1)^2} + \ldots + \frac{400,000}{(1.1)^4} = 166.79 \text{ million.}$$

This is less than ₹175 million. Hence, firm A will sell the technology to firm B.■

13.3 Assets Offered in the Market

We discussed above the profitability of holding a particular asset vis-à-vis holding a loan—a safe asset. We didn't consider the fact that in reality there are many assets available in the market. Thus, even if the holding of an asset is profitable in the manner demonstrated above, it does not necessarily mean that a person should invest in it, because there may be more than one profitable investment prospects. Profitability is a necessary, *not* sufficient, condition of making a rational investment. Also, we ignored the issues of liquidity and riskiness. The marketplace offers various assets with various degrees of liquidity, expected return, and riskiness.

Ceteris paribus, the less liquid an asset the higher is its return. For instance, a five-year fixed deposit (same as certificate of deposit) offers a higher interest than a savings account deposit. Why? It is because if a savings account deposit did offer the same interest as a five-year fixed deposit, no one would invest in the latter: such a fixed deposit scheme would not exist. The market cannot sustain a low-liquidity and low-return asset together with a high-liquidity and high-return asset. This means that, from an individual investor's viewpoint, there is a trade-off between liquidity and returns. Similarly, there is a trade-off between expected return and risk. Among the assets of equal liquidity, the market will offer high-expected-return-cum-high-risk assets together with low-expected-return-cum-low-risk assets.[6]

A list of asset types is depicted in Figure 13.1. In what follows, some of the financial assets are briefly introduced.

Cash: This is the simplest form of a financial asset. It is the most liquid asset. What is the return? It is zero.[7]

Current and Savings Accounts: These refer to the money kept in your bank account. There are minor differences between the two: the former is slightly more liquid than the latter but less liquid than cash. You have access to cash kept at home 7 days a week, 24 hours a day; this may not be true with your bank.[8] Generally, these accounts pay a modest rate of interest, which is their return.

Fixed Deposits or Certificates of Deposit: They don't offer any *yields* in a period-by-period basis (e.g. annually). Money is locked over a longer period. Compared to a bank account, these are less liquid and carry a higher interest rate. The principal and the accumulated interest earnings are paid together at the end of the maturity date.

Shares or Stocks: *These are ownership certificates issued by firms or companies.* Suppose a company X offers 2,00,000 shares to the public for the first time. This is called **IPO**, standing for **initial public offering**. (An IPO by a company is advertised through banks and sometimes through news media.) Suppose that, through your bank or broker, you buy 10,000 shares at a given price (say €10 each). Physically, in olden days it involved writing a cheque to the company's bank for the said purpose, and, in return, a certificate (a piece of paper) was issued saying that say Mr. Z owns 10,000 shares of the company X. After the IPO, the same company's or a firm's shares are readily bought and sold in the stock exchange. A **stock exchange** is where listed shares of various private and public limited companies are traded. Appendix 13.A provides a brief description of stock exchanges in India.

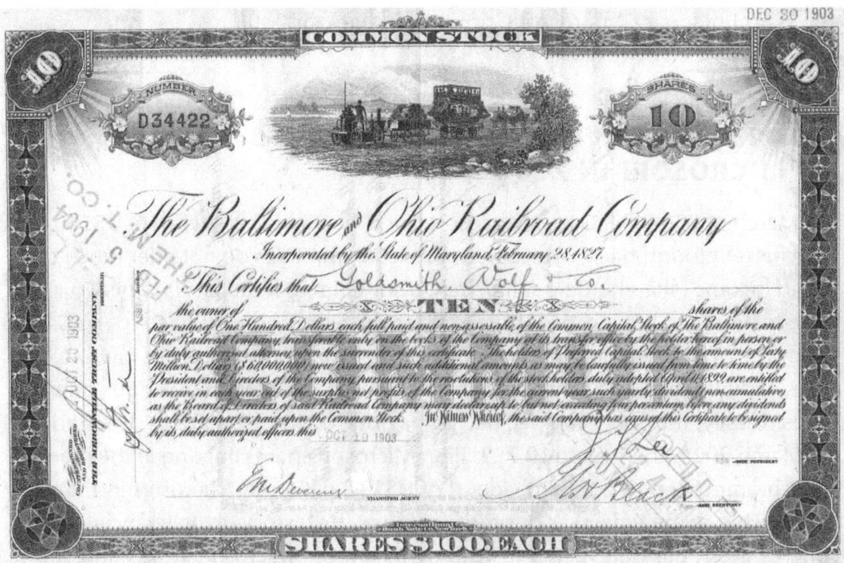

FIGURE 13.2 An Example of a Share Certificate

Figure 13.2 presents a photo copy of a share certificate issued by The Baltimore & Ohio Railroad Company in the United States issued way back in 1903. It shows the share buyer's name, number of shares owned by her/him (10), and the original share price ($100). In recent decades with computers and internet, physical share certificates are virtually non-existent. Shares ownership exists digitally and is traded in the medium of **investment accounts**. In India, such an account is called a **demat account** or a demateralised account. It looks like a saving account statement, which keeps track of which securities are bought or sold, their quantity and their purchase and sale prices. A demat account is mandatory for trading Indian securities. In order to open a demat account, one has to approach a **depository participant (DP)**, which can be a bank, a brokerage firm, or an agent of depository. A list of DPs is provided in the websites of Central Depository Services Ltd. (CDSL) and National Securities Depository Ltd. (NSDL).

If you own 2,000 shares of a company and the company's total number of shares is 200,000, then you have 1% (= 2,000/2,00,000) ownership in the company. If, in a year, the company earns a profit of say $4 million and all of it is paid back to the shareholders, you will receive 1% it, i.e., a deposit of $40,000 in your designated bank account as **dividend** income. If, instead, the management of the company decides that $2 million is to be ploughed back to the company's operations and the remaining $2 million is distributed to the shareholders, your dividend income will be $20,000. In general, *dividend payments constitute the yield to holding a stock.*

See Box 13.1 for an account of a massive, unprecedented dividend payment scheme to the shareholders of Microsoft Corporation back in 2004.

BOX 13.1 MASSIVE DIVIDEND PAYMENTS BY MICROSOFT IN 2004

By March of 2004, Bill Gate's Microsoft Corp. had amassed a cash of US$60 billion—after plough-back. Typically, high-tech companies do not offer much dividend income (shareholders still benefit from holding its stock via capital gains), unless there are prospects of hostile takeover bids. There was a lot of pressure from the Wall Street to use this money other than earning just a low interest rate. Various groups of investors in Microsoft's stock offered various alternatives. Finally, the company decided to pay out US$3 per share as dividend. As of March 2004, there were 10.79 billion Microsoft shares floating in the market, which amounted to a total dividend of US$32 billion by Microsoft in the year 2004. This, at the time, was unprecedented in the history of the financial world. Interestingly, Bill Gates himself, who owns a lot of Microsoft stocks and stood to get US$3.3 billion, announced that this entire amount would go towards his "Bill Gate's foundation." Bill Gate's Foundation operates in India, which has provided massive assistance towards the containment of AIDS in India.

What happens if the company makes a loss? Shareholders get nothing. They are not personally liable for outstanding debts of a public limited company.

The risk of holding a share lies in capital losses, since the shares are heavily traded in the market and their prices can fluctuate a great deal over time. A dip in the share price compared to the price at which a share is bought involves a potential loss. At the same time, price fluctuations also provide the opportunity of making large gains (or a "killing" so to speak) and indeed this is sometimes the motivation behind holding stocks.

Bonds: These are certificates of indebtedness by a firm (includes almost all big corporations in a country), a financial organisation (central banks, commercial banks, etc.), or the government. Bonds offer a guaranteed interest rate, which is typically higher than that offered in a savings account. Like stocks, bonds are traded in the market, and bond prices can vary over time.[9]

A bond is issued with a face value, i.e., the principle (e.g., ₹10,000), a coupon (e.g., ₹1,000), and a redemption or maturity date. A coupon promises the amount that the firm will pay you periodically till the date of maturity. When the bond matures the amount of the face value is returned to the bond owner. The face value and the coupon value define the interest rate. In this example, the interest rate is equal to (1,000/10,000) × 100 = 10%).[10] Physically, like a stock, a bond is also a piece of paper, stating the company's or the bank's name, your name as an owner of the bond, the face value, the coupon value, and the maturity date. Again, in the modern era, like shares, bonds are held in terms of digital records. A physical certificate is not necessary.

BOX 13.2 RISK IN HOLDING PRIVATE BONDS

In principle, bonds carry no or little risk. But, in reality, it is not that simple. There is a **default risk**. The ability to honour bonds would depend on the firm's prevailing financial situation and its past history of paying out to its bond-holders in time. Not just any firm can issue bonds and expect the public to buy its bonds. Even among bonds from those firms that do sell them in the market, the risk varies. There are international companies like Standard & Poor's, Moody's Investors Service, and Fitch Investors Service, who "rates" bonds issued by publicly traded companies based on market surveys. Moody's Investors Service classifies bonds into "A-type," "B-type" and "C-type," among which the first are the safest. Even among the A-type bonds, those rated as "Aaa" are the best, followed by "Aa1," "Aa2," and "Aa3." For example, in 2003, two Indian companies, Tata Power and Indian Oil Corporation, were rated "Ba1" by the Moody's Investors Group. As a company's performance and record changes over time, its bond rating may also change.

Bonds whose rating exceeds a certain threshold are called Investment Grade bonds. (Bonds offered by the two Indian companies cited above belong to this category.) Those whose credit rating is less than the threshold are the so-called *junk bonds*.

Bond prices fluctuate over time. It you hold a bond and want to sell it (before its expiration date), its market price may not be the same as the face value at which it was bought originally. Thus, apart from default risk there is a risk in terms of bond price variation.

The overall point here is that bonds are not risk free.

Compared to stocks, bonds are less risky. Some bonds have virtually zero risk, such as those issued by the government. Bonds issued by private firms may not be totally risk-less, although the firms are supposed to honour bonds whenever the payment is due.[11] *There is a critical difference between a stock and a bond issued by a firm; that is, unlike a stock, a bond doesn't offer any ownership to the company.* As Box 13.2 narrates, bonds carry a default risk and a risk from its own price fluctuation over time.[12]

Stocks and bonds are both referred to by the term: **securities**.

Mutual Funds: A mutual fund is essentially an investment company or trust, which pools funds from small investors and invests the total sum in various individual stocks and bonds. The fund is therefore an intermediary, who invests the funds of small investors in large number of securities. This is indeed quite convenient for a small investor, who doesn't have the time or resources to research on the merits of different securities available in the market. The fund's management does this for the investors. The key thing is that the fund's own investment is highly diversified, so that investing in a mutual fund is not as risky as investing in a limited number of individual securities.

The objective of a mutual fund is pre-specified: which sectors or kinds of securities it holds and whether it targets relatively high-risk, high-return securities or low-risk, low-return securities. You can read it from its prospectus or website. A mutual fund company, also called **Asset Management Company**, typically floats several mutual funds of different categories.[13] Technically, an investor in a mutual fund becomes one of its shareholders. The price of a share is simply calculated as the fund's assets minus liabilities divided by the number of shares. Hence if the fund's investments are doing well, it gets reflected positively in the fund's assets, which translates into a higher price of the fund's share. Also, incomes generated from investments by the funds are also passed on to the shareholders (which is like dividend payments to shareholder of a particular company).

13.4 Optimal Portfolio

From an individual investor's perspective, the central question is, which assets and how much of an asset she/he should hold? A **portfolio** refers to the distribution of asset holdings by an entity. As a simple example, you may be holding 30% of your investments in bank accounts, 60% in real estate, and 10% in stocks, whereas I may be holding 50% of my investment in bank account and 50% in stocks. The question posed above can be framed as, what is the best or optimal portfolio for an individual?

The answer is that *there is no unique portfolio that is the best for everyone. It depends on the individual's liquidity needs and risk preference.* A full analysis of this problem, analogous to the demand for goods in the consumer theory, is beyond thescope of this book. However, there are some general observations.

To "generally" protect ("hedge") against too much of risk, an investor must hold a **diversified portfolio**, meaning a portfolio having assets with varying degrees of returns and risks.

If a person is relatively poor or has urgent needs for immediate consumption, she should invest most of her savings in relatively liquid and less risky assets. Otherwise, she can invest in more illiquid and riskier assets.

Now consider assets that are equally liquid. How much should one invest in relatively high-risk-high-return assets and in relatively low-risk-low-return assets? That depends on an individual's attitude towards risk, particularly how risk-averse he is. In Chapter 12, we studied attitude towards risk and risk-aversion. Mukesh and Prem may be two billionaires, having equal amount of funds to invest. However, Mukesh, by nature, may be more averse to risk that Prem. Then, Mukesh would invest relatively more in low-risk-low-return assets compared to

Prem. The attitude towards risk may not only vary across individuals but also over time for the same individual. If you are in your early forties for example, you can afford to take chances and park a large portion of your savings in high-risk-high-return assets. But as you approach your retirement age you would like to keep your investments in low-risk-low return assets.

ACTIVITY 13.1 BUNTY'S BONANZA

Bunty, your childhood buddy, dropped out of school to join his father's farming occupation in your village near Hoshiarpur (Punjab, India), while you went ahead to complete your graduation in Hoshiarpur, after which you are now doing masters in management. News came of the death of Bunty's ageing uncle who was living in Vancouver, Canada. Soon after, news came that he has left a very decent amount of money for his favourite nephew, none other than Bunty. Converted into Indian rupees, the inheritance amounted to ₹12 million. Soon after, the bonanza was deposited in Bunty's bank account, he was on cloud nine! He threw lavish parties for his friends and relatives, purchased a lot of luxury times for himself and his parents. In all this bonhomie he spent ₹2 million. One day, in your presence Bunty's parents advised him not to spend this money recklessly and keep it for the future. Bunty was receptive to the advice, but he didn't want to buy additional land or jewellery. The only other option known to Bunty and his parents was keeping this money in a saving account or a fixed deposit (certificate of deposit) in a bank. Bunty holds you in high esteem and seek your advice.

As a student of business management, who plans to do take finance as major specialisation next year, tell Bunty the other options where he can keep his ₹10 million. If Bunty leaves the final decision to you, how will you allocate his money in various assets and why? Will you follow the "whole hog" approach or "Don't keep all your eggs in one basket" principle?

We encourage you to try Activity 13.1.

Facts and Insights

- Apart from gifts, a person's (or a family's) assets are built by his (family's) past and current savings.
- An asset has three characteristics: liquidity, return, and risk.
- Rate of return of an asset equals the sum of yield to cost ratio and capital gains/losses to cost ratio.

- Variability of return associated with an asset indicates the risk in holding it.
- Present value analysis compares the profitability of holding an asset vis-à-vis holding a risk-free loan as an asset. It is also used to compare profitability across two assets (without considering risk).
- Future earnings and costs are measured in terms of the current period by means of discounting.
- The market offers real assets like real estate, machines, etc. and financial assets like stocks, bonds, mutual funds, etc.
- Cash and current and saving accounts are very liquid assets.
- A stockholder is personally responsible for the liabilities facing the company to the extent of his sharing-holding (i.e., ownership) in the company.
- Many companies list their shares in a stock exchange.
- The return from holding a stock carries risk, depending on the performance and profitability of the firm which issues the stock.
- Dividend payments constitute the yield from a stock.
- Stock price fluctuations imply risk and an opportunity to make large gains.
- Holding a bond is less risky than holding a stock in the sense that the company is legally obligated to pay interest and principal to its bond-holders irrespective of whether the company is making profits or incurring losses.
- Riskiness of holding bonds arises from the possibility of default and bond price fluctuations.
- Investing in a mutual fund is less risky than investing in an individual stock, because, from the funds it receives from investors, the mutual fund invests in a large number of securities, i.e., its portfolio is highly diversified.
- To generally protect against too much of risk, an individual must hold a diversified portfolio.
- There is no such thing as a portfolio that is the best for everyone. Each one's best portfolio depends on her needs for liquidity and preference towards risk.

Exercises

Descriptive/Analytical

13.1. "The determinants of demand for assets are similar to those of demand for goods and services." Defend or refute.

13.2. In your own words, describe present value analysis.

13.3. "One should invest one's money where the expected returns are highest." Defend or refute.

Short Answer (word limit = 500 approx)

13.4. Which information do we need to have in order to calculate the rate of return of an asset?

13.5. "In general, bonds are riskier than stocks." Comment.

13.6. "In general, individual shares are riskier than investment in a mutual fund." Comment.

13.7. What is the difference between yield and capital gains of an asset?

Quizzes/Numerical

13.8. In Example 13.2, is there any capital gain or loss involved? If so, how much is it?

13.9. Mahesh is looking into buy one stock out of two, A and B. Stock A yields a return of 5% with probability of 60% and 9% with a probability of 40%. Stock B offers a return of 4% with probability of 30% and 10% with a probability of 70%. What is the expected return of each of these stocks?

13.10. Mitchell Burns invested \$2,000 in gold bullion, which he bought at \$520 per ounce. Two years hence, he sold them all at \$566 per ounce. What is his annual rate of return from this investment in two years?

13.11. This year your job is paying \$95,000 per year. Over the next year you expect an increase in salary by \$5,000. If the interest rate is 7%, what is the discounted value of the next year's expected salary?

13.12. An investment in a project gives a yield of \$4,000 for four years starting the next year. (At the end of the project period there is no return of the principle or any sale value of the investment made.) At 10% rate of interest, what is the PDV of this investment?

Appendix 13.A Stock Exchanges in India

As of 2023, there are six stock exchanges in India: Bangalore Stock Exchange, Bombay Stock Exchange (BSE), Calcutta Stock Exchange, Delhi Stock Exchange, Madras Stock Exchange, and National Stock Exchange. The Bombay Stock Exchange and the National Stock Exchange (NSE) are both located in Mumbai. Among these the Bombay Stock Exchange is the oldest (started in 1875), the largest, and the most cited in the media. The National Stock Exchange is the newest, which started in 1993. BSE has over 400 branches across different cities and towns in India. Around 3,500 companies and 6,000 stocks are listed with BSE. (A large company may have different companies producing different products, with each issuing its own shares.) In terms of transactions, it is among the top five stock exchanges in the world. SENSEX is an index, based on changes in the stock prices of 30 well-established and financially sound companies listed with BSE. Movement of SENSEX reflects the general trend of stock prices over time. (BSE also constructs other indices and other stock exchanges have their indices too.)

In order to be listed in a stock exchange, a company must pay an initial fee and annual fees, and signs a contract with the Exchange to abide by its rules. Most rules pertain to transparency. For example, a listed company must disclose its share-holding pattern and profits on a regular basis. In return, the company's performance is seen nationwide, which can attract funds from numerous potential investors. The company also obtains various market-related analyses, because of its membership, it can use for its benefit.

All stock exchanges are regulated by Securities and Exchange Board of India (SEBI), which is mandated to see that the stock exchanges operate orderly and with transparency and fairness to traders.

The price of a particular share can change from one hour to the next depending on market expectations and how much of it transacted. Financial columns of newspapers quote the highest, the lowest, and the closing (at the end of the day) price of shares on the previous working day and its average over a given number of past months.

Notes

1 In many instances, banks pay interest on a quarterly basis.
2 This answer assumes that €60 is taken out for consumption every year, so that the principal remains the same. Otherwise, the interest earnings will be added to the principal (i.e., will be compounded) and the yield will keep increasing over time even if the interest rate is fixed at 6%.
3 In our example, it is positive, hence a capital gain.
4 As you will realise, such a calculation of rate of return is intimately related to discounting and present value analysis to be introduced later.
5 This is same as saying that at 10% interest rate, the future, 2026 value of $100,000 in 2024 is $121,000.
6 It is because if there are two assets, one of which offers a higher expected return combined with a lower risk compared to the other, no one would demand the latter and hence it wouldn't exist in the market in the first place.
7 It is assumed implicitly that the price levels remained unchanged over time. Otherwise, if a positive inflation rate is expected, the real return from holding cash will be negative.
8 The presence of ATM machines narrows the difference between cash and current account.
9 There is an inverse relationship between the interest rate and the price of bonds, which we do not study here.
10 In some cases, the interest rate is explicitly written on the bond in place of the coupon value.
11 Bonds issues by small companies carry a major default risk.
12 As said earlier, bonds are debt instruments. There are other debt instruments such as debentures, commercial paper, certificate of deposits, treasury bills, etc., depending on who issues them, how secure they are supposed to be, and the maturity date (short term or long term).
13 AMCs in India include, among others, SBI Mutual, ICICI Prudential Mutual Fund, Aditya Birla Sun Life Mutual Fund, and Tata Mutual Fund.

14

MARKETS FOR FACTORS OF PRODUCTION

In all chapters thus far, except Chapters 12 and 13, product markets were our focus: which good or service will be produced and consumed, and, if so, how much and at what price. In other words, we dealt with the central problem of "what" facing an economy. Households are the demanders and firms are the suppliers in product markets.

In this chapter we probe factor or input markets, e.g., markets for different types of labour or skill, capital (i.e., machinery and equipment), land, etc. In terms of the link between factors and output discussed in Chapter 7, we ask: What is the level of employment of an input by a firm? How are inputs/factors priced? In factor markets, the roles of firms and households are reversed: firms are the demanders and households the suppliers.

There are dissimilarities and similarities between product and factor markets. Dissimilarities stem from the demanders, and the suppliers in a factor market being opposite of who they are in product markets. Instead of the economy's central problem of "what," the factor market analysis sheds light on the "for whom" problem. In the labour market for example, the price of the labour service is the wage rate. How are wages of different types of labour determined in a market economy? In general, wage incomes across individuals, incomes from land, incomes from money lent, etc. determine income distribution in an economy, which, in turn, determines the differences in the purchasing power over goods and services among individuals or households. This is how the factor market implications are linked to the central problem of "for whom."

The similarity between factor and product markets is that there is a demand side and there is a supply side of a factor. The equality between demand and supply of a factor determines the respective factor price.

DOI: 10.4324/9781003452195-14

14.1 Factor Demand

At a given point of time, a firm faces different prices issues due to various factors. For example, think of a private management institute in India. It employs instructors, and assumes that the average salary of an instructor is ₹40,000 per month. The institute may be situated in a rental property. It must decide on how many rooms or floors in a high-rise building it should rent. The market rent may be ₹90,000 per month per 1,000 square feet area.

Individual inputs vary from the production of one product or service to another. When a carpentry shop makes a chair out of a log of wood, the employment of demand for all those men, women, tools like a saw, hammer, and material such as nails, paint, etc. who participate in the process of turning a log into a chair is decided by the shop owner. A restaurant must decide on how many cooks, helpers, waiters, and waitresses to hire and how much of raw material per month in terms of meat, fish, vegetables, fruits, nuts, spices to buy, and so on.

The question is, given factor prices, how much of different factors should a profit-maximising firm hire?

On the one hand, hiring more of factors will produce more output, generating more revenues (as long as the marginal revenue is positive). On the other hand, hiring more factors will cost more. There is a trade-off. As we shall see, the profit-maximising principle is a marginal condition.

14.1.1 One Variable Factor

Suppose that the employment levels of all factors, except one, are fixed, i.e., there is only one variable input. Let this variable factor be called labour, measured in hours of work. (If all workers must work a given number of hours per day, we can measure labour as the number of workers hired.) In other words, we are not differentiating between different types of workers now. The question is, how many labour hours (denoted by L) should a firm employ?

The total cost of fixed factors is fixed by definition. The total cost of the variable factor is easy to compute. Suppose that the wage rate is £50 per hour. If the firm hires 4 hours of labour, the total cost of labour is $£50 \times 4 = £200$. If 6 hours of labour are hired, the total cost of labour or the total wage bill is $£50 \times 6 = £300$, and so on.

Suppose that, in general, the factor L costs W per unit, i.e., the hourly wage rate is £W. Figure 14.1 draws the **factor price line** or the "wage line" in this case. It is horizontal since the wage rate is unaffected by how many labour hours our small firm hires in the market. (The horizontal factor price line is the counterpart of the horizontal price line for a competitive firm in the product market, studied in Chapter 8.) The *total factor cost or payment to the factor is equal to the area under the factor price line.* For instance, if the firm hires L_1 labour hours, the total wage bill is the area $0WCL_1$.

In the revenue side, the way the firm's total revenue changes with different levels of employment of a factor is the following: (a) a change in the employment

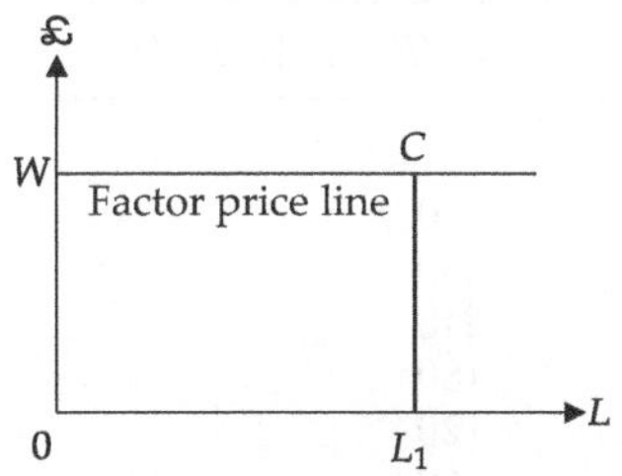

FIGURE 14.1 Factor Price Line

of a factor affects output and (b) a change in the output affects the total revenue. We have *already* studied (a) and (b) in Chapter 7. What remains to be done is to combine or link them. For now, assume that it is a perfectly competitive firm *in the product and factor markets*. That is, the firm under consideration is small in the product market as well. It thus has no market power, and hence a price taker in the product and factor markets.

From Chapter 7, recall the definitions of total physical product (*TPP*) and the marginal physical product (*MPP*). The former refers to different levels of total output at different levels of employment of a factor, keeping the employment of other factors unchanged. The latter, *MPP*, is the increase in total output per unit increase in the employment of a factor when the employment of all other factors is held constant. We also know the shapes of the *TPP* and *MPP* curves. The inverse U-shape of the *MPP* curve follows from the law of diminishing returns.

We develop two more concepts here. The first is the **total value product (TVP)**, defined as $P \times TPP$, where P is the product price. This is indeed the same as total revenue. The second is the **value of the marginal product** (denoted by *VMP*), defined as $P \times MPP$. Equivalently, *VMP* is equal to the increase in *TVP* per unit increase in the employment of the factor. It is because an extra unit employed of a factor generates extra output equal to *MPP*, which will fetch extra revenues equal to the value of this extra output.

An example of a *TPP* schedule is given in the second column of Table 14.1. The associated *MPP* schedule is the third column. To calculate the *TVP* and the *VMP*, we need to know the product price. Suppose that $P = £10$. Table 14.1 lists the corresponding *TVP* and *VMP* schedules in the last two columns.

Particularly relevant for us will be the *VMP* schedule and its properties.

(a) The *VMP* schedule is proportional to the *MPP* schedule—as it is obtained by multiplying the *MPP* schedule by price, which is constant. This implies that the law of diminishing returns also determines the nature of the *VMP* schedule; *VMP* initially increases with factor employment and then diminishes.
(b) The *TVP* of a particular level of factor employment is the sum of *MVP*s up to that level of employment. This follows from the relationship between a "total" and a "marginal."

TABLE 14.1 *TPP, MPP, TVP,* and *VMP* Schedules

Labour Hours (L)	*TPP*	*MPP*	*TVP = P.TPP (£)*	*VMP = P.MPP (£)*
0	0	—	0	—
1	20	20	200	200
2	43	23	430	230
3	64	21	640	210
4	82	18	820	180
5	94	12	940	120
6	100	6	1000	60
7	100	0	1000	0
8	96	−4	960	−40
9	89	−7	890	−70
Product Price = £10				

Property (a) implies that the *VMP* curve, the graphical representation of a *VMP* schedule, will be inverse U-shaped, just as the *MPP* curve. Figure 14.2(a) presents the graph of the *VMP* curve based on the last column of Table 14.1. Property (b) implies that, if we draw a smooth *VMP* curve, the area under it will be equal to the *TVP* (i.e., the total revenue). A general, smooth *VMP* curve is shown in panel (b). For instance, at $L = L_1$, the *TVP* = the shaded area $0ABL_1$.

We are ready to derive the principle that governs how many labour hours a profit-maximising firm should hire. Turn to Figure 14.3 that combines Figure 14.1 and Figure 14.2(b). Let the factor price facing the firm (wage rate) be W_0. The answer is that the firm should hire up to that level, where the factor price line intersects the *VMP* curve; i.e., it should hire L_0 labour hours. In other words, the general, profit-maximising principle of hiring a factor is that:

$$VMP \text{ of a Factor} = \text{Its Price}. \tag{14.1}$$

This condition is parallel to the profit-maximising condition for selecting output, namely, $P = MC$. Indeed, the two conditions are two sides of the same coin. The rationale behind equation (14.1) is analogous to that behind $P = MC$ derived back in Chapter 8. At the level of employment L_0, *TVP* or total revenue = the area $0ACL_0$. The total factor cost = the area $0W_0CL_0$. Thus the gross profit, the difference between *TVP* and the total factor cost, is equal to the area W_0AC.[1] Consider any employment level less (such as L_A) or more (such as L_B) than L_0. We can compute that the profit is less than W_0AC. For instance, at $L = L_A$, it is equal to $W_0AFD = W_0AC - CDF$. At $L = L_B$, it is equal to $W_0AC - CEG$. This proves that profit is maximised at $L = L_0$.

The law of diminishing returns is the key behind equation (14.1). Starting from where the *VMP* of a factor = its price and the *MPP* is diminishing, if the firm hires one extra unit of the factor, the *VMP* will be less than the factor price, i.e., the additional revenue generated is less than the additional cost incurred. This implies

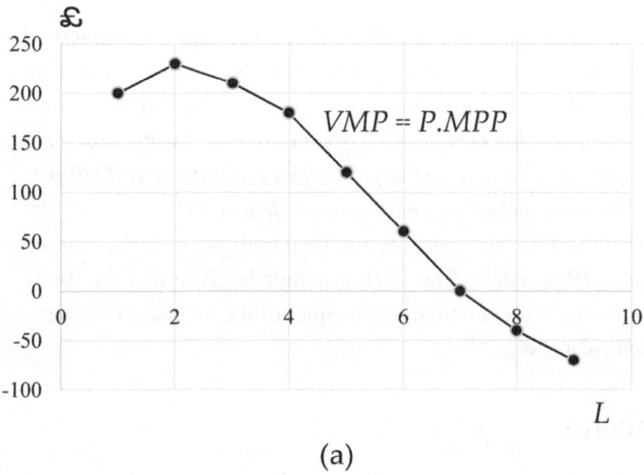

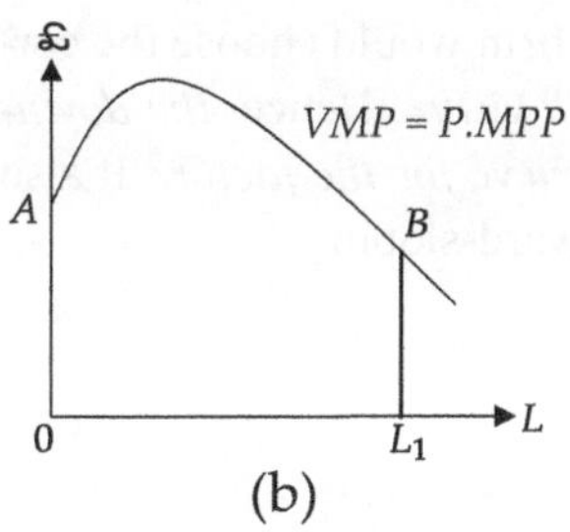

FIGURE 14.2 *VMP* Curve

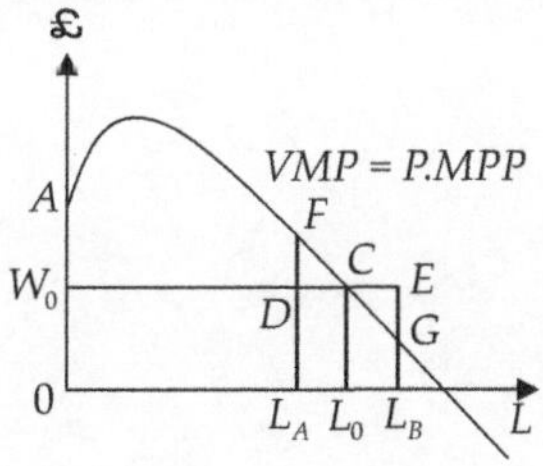

FIGURE 14.3 Factor Employment Decision

less profit than before. Similarly, if the firm hires one less unit than where *VMP* is equal to the factor price, the *VMP* will be higher than the factor price, i.e., the revenue sacrificed by hiring one unit less will be more than the savings on the total factor cost (equal to the factor price). Thus, profit will be less. This proves why profit is maximised when equation (14.1) is met.

Example 14.1

A small garbage-collect company named Clean-City collects garbage from homes in a city in India at ₹20 per home per day. The total physical product (TPP) schedule of labour per day employed by the company is given in Table 14.2. The TPP is defined in terms of the number of households served. All workers are equally efficient, and they all work the same number of hours per day. The price of labour is ₹140 per worker per day. How many workers will be employed by Clean-City?

Answer: We first derive the *MPP* the schedule and then multiply with the market price, ₹20, to obtain the *VMP* schedule. The *VMP* schedule is given in Table 14.3. Equation (14.1) is met when the level of employment equal to six. Hence six workers will be employed by Clean-City. ■

14.1.2 Factor Demand Curve

Note from Figure 14.3 that at $W = W_0$, the firm chooses the corresponding point on the *VMP* curve. Similarly, at any other input price, the firm would choose the corresponding point on the downward portion of the *VMP* curve. Hence, *the downward portion of the VMP curve is the firm's demand curve for the factor.*[2] It also means that a firm's demand curve for a factor is downward-sloping.

TABLE 14.2 TPP

Number of Workers	*TPP*
0	0
1	15
2	31
3	45
4	56
5	65
6	72
7	77

TABLE 14.3 VMP

Number of Workers	*MPP*	*VMP* (₹)
0	-	
1	15	300
2	16	320
3	14	280
4	11	220
5	9	180
6	7	140
7	5	100

14.2 Factor Demand Curve Shifts

Since the factor demand curve is a part of the *VMP* curve, anything that shifts the *VMP* curve shifts the factor demand curve. We consider the following sources of change.

14.2.1 A Change in Product Price

As $VMP = P.MPP$, an increase in *P* increases the *VMP* at any given level of factor employment. Therefore, the factor demand curve shifts to the right. This is illustrated in Figure 14.4. In general, *an increase (a decrease) in the product price shifts the factor demand curve to the right (left).*

This implication underscores an intimate link between product and factor markets. For instance, consider the industry of a particular handicraft, whose product has a worldwide market. On the supply side, there are artisans, who, with the help of raw materials and equipment, make the handicraft. Suppose that in an international exhibition this handicraft attracts a lot of attention. Many people and organisations around the world come to know about it, like it, and place a purchase order for it. Consequently, there is an increase in demand for this handicraft. From the demand–supply analysis in Chapter 2 we know the effect: the price of this handicraft increases.

Now consider the (factor) market for artisans. The increase in the price of the handicraft will shift their *VMP* curve and hence the demand curve for artisans to the right.

The general point is that factor demand is derived from product demand. This is why *factor demand is considered what is called a* **derived demand**.

14.2.2 Technological Change

A technology change can alter the *MPP* of a factor and thereby its demand curve, even when the product price is unchanged. If it is such that the *MPP* of a factor

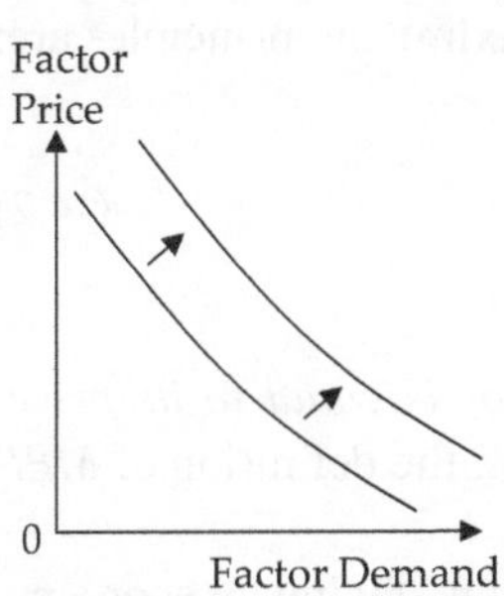

FIGURE 14.4 Product Price Increase and Factor Demand

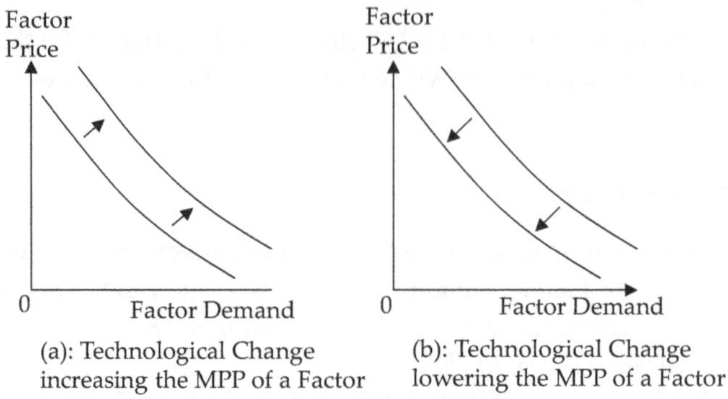

FIGURE 14.5 Technological Change and Factor Demand

increases, then the demand curve for that factor shifts to the right. Figure 14.5(a) shows this effect. Otherwise, if the *MPP* of a factor decreases due to a technological change, then its demand curve shifts to the left. Figure 14.5(b) illustrates this.

For example, it is widely believed by economists that, *in recent three/four decades, the whole world economy has experienced technological progress that has increased the MPP of skilled labour, while its impact on the MPP of unskilled labour is not clear.*[3]

14.3 Many Factors and the Marginal Productivity Theory of Distribution

We have assumed that the firm employs only one variable factor of production. In reality, firms employ many factors, e.g., different types of labour, raw materials, power, various kinds of machines, land, etc. What are the (profit-maximising) principles that govern the *simultaneous* demand/employment of more than one factor?

They are simply the extensions of equation (14.1). If, for example, there are two factors, say X and Y, their respective prices are W_X and W_Y, and their respective marginal products are MPP_X and MPP_Y,then the profit-maximising principles are:

$$\begin{aligned} VMP_X &= P.MPP_X = W_X, \\ VMP_Y &= P.MPP_Y = W_Y. \end{aligned} \tag{14.2}$$

That is, *profit is maximised when the VMP of each factor is equal to its price.* Note that even when there is more than one variable factor, the definition of *MPP* remains valid however.[4]

Recall, from Chapter 1, the central problem of "for whom" facing an economy, which concerns who earns how much. Equation (14.2) implies a theory of this, i.e., *each factor earns the value of its marginal physical product.* It is called the **marginal productivity theory of distribution.**

Of course, we have not yet discussed the supply side of a factor and hence our analysis has not "determined" a factor price; we have only examined how much of a factor a firm would demand at a pre-determined factor price. Yet, at the equilibrium quantity supplied, the *VMP* of a factor must be equal to its equilibrium price. In this sense the marginal productivity theory holds even when the supply side is taken into consideration.

14.4 Monopoly in the Product Market

We have derived the rule for hiring a factor, (14.1) or (14.2), under the assumption that the hiring firm is perfectly competitive in the product market. What is the rule if the firm is imperfectly competitive? There is a minor difference. Remember that a non-competitive firm (e.g., a monopoly) is not a price taker. Hence, the extra revenue generated by selling one additional unit is the marginal revenue (*MR*), not equal to the price. Thus, the extra revenue by hiring an additional unit of an input is equal to the *MRP* of that input × *MR*, defined as the **marginal revenue product (MRP)**. Accordingly, the hiring or the profit-maximising principle with respect to a particular input is that

$$MRP = MPP \times MR = \text{Input Price.} \qquad (14.3)$$

This is a more general condition than (14.1), stating that an *input is paid its marginal revenue product.* (As a special case, if the firm is competitive, then *MR* = Price and thus the *MRP* reduces to the *VMP* of an input.) We can draw an *MRP* curve, similar to the *VMP* curve. Remember that the marginal revenue decreases with output. Thus, as long as *MPP* falls with the employment of an input (due to diminishing returns), *MRP* will also fall, imply that is the *MRP* curve will be downward-sloping. Just as the downward portion of the *VMP* curve is the demand curve of an input for a competitive firm, *the downward portion of the MRP curve is the demand curve of an input for a non-competitive firm in the product market.*

Note that an increase in the demand for the product would shift the *MR* curve to the right. This would shift the *MRP* curve and the demand curve of an input to the right. Thus, the notion of derived demand is the same whether the firm under consideration is perfectly competitive or non-competitive in the product market.

14.5 Labour

So are we have looked at the demand side of any arbitrary input. Remember from Chapter 7 that there are three primary factors of production: namely, labour, capital, and land. There are typical features associated with each one of them. Hence, let us consider these primary factors individually including their supply side and equilibrium in the respective market.

14.5.1 Special Features of the Labour Market

Among the three primary factors of production, labour is human and hence deserves special treatment. Human beings have emotions. They laugh, they cry, shout, and think. Capital and land do not have these emotions (unless a robot is created to laugh or cry). With exactly the same skill set, the productivity of one worker will differ from that of another, because we are human beings, not machines. Unlike human, two identical machines are likely to produce almost identical outcomes. Workers may shirk work; machine can't. Between the two equally paid employees, if one shirks and the other doesn't, the former will get a surplus. Can supervision solve the problem of worker shirking? Not fully. The director or dean of a college can check whether a professor goes to a class in time. He/she can ensure that the professor stays in the classroom for the entire duration. But it is very hard for the director to judge the quality of his lecture. Even spy cameras in the classroom cannot prevent a professor from shirking partially. To be hired, some potential workers may mispresent themselves and overstate their qualifications and skills. This issue is different from shirking.

Unlike non-human inputs, workers can organise and act in unison. ***Trade unionism*** and ***collective bargaining*** are unique features of labour market.

Yet another unique feature is that the labour market relates to performance and reward. Traditional wisdom tells us that the wage rate is determined by labour productivity. The higher the productivity of a worker, the more the reward (wages) he will get and vice versa. However, it has been observed that this functional relationship is not necessarily one-way. The opposite is found in many empirical studies: pay a worker more, he will become more productive/efficient. Productivity becomes a function of reward. Human beings can vary the intensity of and devotion to work. There is a well-known joke in north India. In a village school, a teacher was in the habit of mispronouncing the word "girl" as "geeral." One day, an inspector of schools happened to pass by and heard this mispronunciation. He started reprimanding the teacher. The teacher simply said, "Sir, with a paltry monthly salary of ₹1000, I will pronounce 'geeral.' You raise my salary and I assure you that I'll pronounce correctly as 'girl'."[5]

It has been globally observed that labour market is also subject to ***discrimination***. Empirical evidence across the globe has established two types of discrimination:

- Racial, ethnic, caste discrimination.
- Gender discrimination.

It has been found that in the United States a black worker gets 60% of what a white worker gets even if both workers are equally qualified, competent, and identical in all other aspects except the colour of skin (Wilson & Rodgers, 2016). Similarly, it has been observed that for the same qualification and competence a female worker gets about 65 cents, whereas her male counterpart gets $1 (Gould et al., 2016). In this situation you can well imagine the average wage level of a black woman (some who is black and a woman)!

Discrimination in labour market is an enigma for the economic thinkers. Why does a profit-maximising employer not employ more blacks/women? This will reduce his wage bill without affecting his productivity: a win–win situation. However, this does not seem to be happening over the decades.

In India, discrimination in the labour market manifests in a different dimension, namely, in terms of caste. The daily wages of menial workers belonging to Scheduled Castes and Scheduled Tribes are almost half of what upper caste workers get in agriculture and the manufacturing sectors. In the service sector, this gap is a bit narrow. There is an urban–rural wage gap as well (see Kumar & Hashmi, 2020).

In a democratic set-up, workers constitute a dominant portion of voters. The government enacts a lot of laws regulating their wages and providing them security of service. As a welfare state, governments make various provisions for their welfare.

In what follows, we'll discuss some of the special issues in the labour market outlined above. A reader may consult a textbook on labour economics to learn more about them.

14.5.2 A Basic Model of Labour Market and Wage Determination

There are several kinds of labour. For qualitative analysis however, we can classify them into two broad categories: skilled labour and unskilled labour. Typically, those who are in the labour market and haven't gone to college or any professional school are termed as unskilled labour, while the rest are called skilled labour. Within skilled labour there are various types. One is a chemical engineer, someone else is a professional dress designer, and so on.

In principle, if we horizontally add up the demand curve of a particular kind of labour by various firms in the economy, we obtain the total demand curve of that kind of labour. In Figure 14.6 it is shown as the downward-sloping line *DD*. (ignore the dashed line for now in the figure.)

An increase in the wage rate of a particular skill would increase the number of individuals acquiring that skill. (For example, in the 1990s the lucrative salary of IT professionals has led to a huge increase in the number of students specialising in IT-related subjects.) Thus, the supply curve of a particular skill is upward-sloping as shown by the *SS* curve Figure 14.6.

The intersection of the *DD* and the *SS* curves defines the equilibrium with W_0 as the equilibrium wage and N_0 as the equilibrium level of employment.

We can now determine how an increase in the product demand or product price affects the wage rate and employment. An increase in the product price would increase the derived demand for labour. It would shift the *DD* curve to the right.

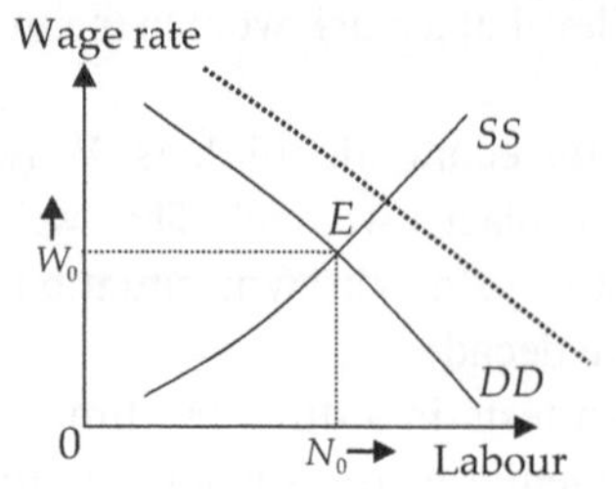

FIGURE 14.6 Demand, Supply, and Market Equilibrium for a Particular Skill

The dash downward-sloping line in Figure 16.6 represents the new demand curve. As a result, both the wage rate and the employment level increase.

In reality, over time the demand for the same kind of skill may very well change, causing a change in its reward. For instance, in the 1990s there was an incredible increase in the demand for computer software personnel. Consequently, the wages in this sector saw a phenomenal increase. More recently however, the demand for software professionals has somewhat slackened, which has depressed wages and employment for such personnel.

The demand–supply approach can also be used to understand why, at a given point of time, one type of occupation or skill commands a higher wage than some other type of skill. For instance, we can understand why skilled labour earns more than unskilled labour. First of all, skilled labour is able to perform relatively important tasks in the production process that unskilled labour cannot. Thus, the *MPP* of skilled labour is relatively higher that of unskilled labour, i.e., the derived demand curve of skilled labour will lie to the right of that of unskilled labour. Second, in a populous country like India, it is likely that a relatively smaller fraction of population gets college or professional education, i.e., the supply of skilled workers is less than that of unskilled workers. Both these factors imply that skilled labour earns a higher wage.

14.5.3 Trade Unions and Unemployment

We have noted the special issues relating to labour as a factor of production. Here, we discuss one distinctive feature of the labour market, namely, trade unions or labour unions.

There are workers' organisations in various sectors of the economy. They voice grievances of workers in a collective way. Sometimes they organise strikes and boycott work for days and weeks. They also try to bargain for higher wages than the employers are willing to offer. The last aspect can be interpreted as wage-fixing or wage-setting by labour unions above the equilibrium (market) rate.

What effect does such wage-setting by trade unions have on the labour market? Turn to Figure 14.7, where L_S denotes the total number of workers. Assuming for

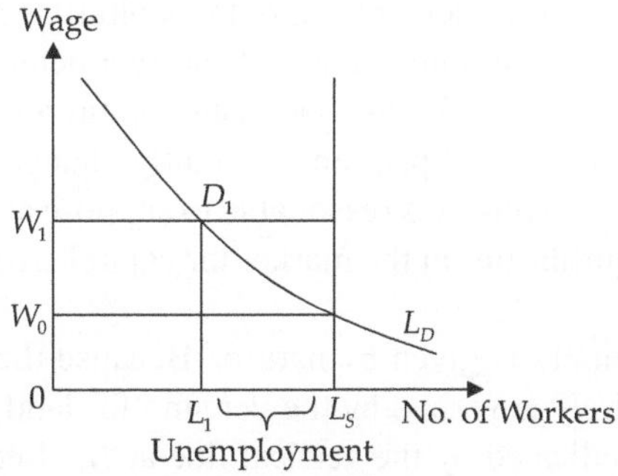

FIGURE 14.7 Labour Unions and Unemployment

simplicity that L_S is given, the vertical line at L_S is the supply curve of labour. The demand curve for labour is denoted by L_D. If there were no wage-setting by trade unions, the intersection of the labour supply and labour demand curves would have determined the market-clearing wage at W_0.

Instead, suppose that the trade union bargains the wage at W_1, higher than the market wage W_0. As a result, the firms will demand less labour. This is indicated at the point D_1 on the labour demand curve, or equivalently, at the point L_1 on the horizontal axis. We see now that there is *unemployment* of labour; L_1L_S measures the number of workers who are unemployed.

Thus, the wage-setting by the trade unions, on its own, contributes to the incidence of unemployment in an economy.[6] See Appendix 14.B for a brief introduction to trade unionism in India.

14.6 Capital and Land

A basic distinction between a factor like labour and other non-human factors like capital and land is that the latter have a use value and an asset value.

Use value refers to the rental earning of a piece of equipment or land. It is the reward for the service rendered. If you own a truck and are renting it for \$50 an hour (for local use), this is the rental income or the use value of the truck. On the other hand, the buying/selling price of truck is its asset price. If you own a trucking company and buy a second-hand truck at \$20,000, then this is the asset price. As another example, a 1,500 square feet flat can be rented out in a central city location for say \$,3000 a month. Then this is its rental income or use value. If the buying/selling price of that flat is \$400,000, then that is its asset value.

In general, the **asset value of capital** or **land** refers to the buying/selling price of capital or land as an asset. As we noted in Chapter 13, an asset essentially generates a stream of income over time, which in the present context is the use value over time. The asset value is the same as the present discounted value discussed in Chapter 13.

How is the use value or rent of capital/land determined? The answer is that it is similar to that of wage in a labour market. There is a demand curve for capital/land along its *VMP* curve; there is a supply curve. The intersection of the two determines the equilibrium rent. There is however a difference between capital and land. Capital is *reproducible* in the sense that its supply can constantly change. (Trucks are manufactured just as TVs or toys.) Thus, it is reasonable to suppose an upward-sloping supply curve of capital. Equilibrium in the market for capital will then look like Figure 14.6.

But this is not the case with land. Its supply is given by nature.[7] Because the supply of land is fixed, the land rent is entirely governed by the demand for land. In Figure 14.8 the fixed supply of land is indicated by the vertical line at N_0. Let DD_0 denote the original demand curve for the use of land in production. The equilibrium rent is R_0. Suppose there is an increase in the demand for the use of land to DD_1. The new equilibrium rent is now R_1. The point to note is that there is no adjustment in payment to land because of any supply changes.

In closing we note that the word "rent" derives from a more general term, **economic rent**, defined as the excess of payment to a factor over the minimum amount, necessary to induce its supply. Put differently, *economic rent is the difference between the payment to a factor and its opportunity cost.* In the case of land, the supply is unchanged irrespective of whether the demand for land is high or low. Thus, *the entire reward to land (except for the expenses required for the maintenance of it) is normally considered as its economic rent.* In Figure 14.8 if the demand curve is given by DD_0, the whole area $0R_0AN_0$ is the economic rent. Similarly, if the demand curve is DD_1, the economic rent is equal to the area $0R_1BN_0$.

It may be remarked that especially when land is able to command a huge rent it attracts a negative attention. It is thought that, unlike labour or capital, no effort or sacrifices are made to create its supply and yet someone is earning a lot because he or she happens to possess some land.[8]

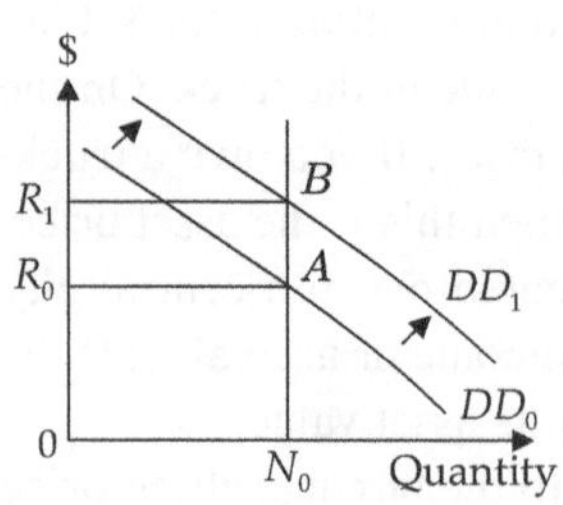

FIGURE 14.8 Land Rent

14.7 Asymmetric Information Problems Facing Firms or Employers

The main insight obtained from the marginal productivity theory is that a factor is paid the value of its *marginal product*. A hospital deciding whether to hire an additional general-practice doctor must think how much *additional* revenue that one more hire would bring to the hospital, not revenues per a general-practice doctor.

While the marginal productivity theory is important, it does not address other potential problems that a manager may face vis-*à*-vis workers. Appendix 14.C addresses two such problems, **adverse selection** (already introduced in Chapter 9) and **moral hazard**. Both issues arise because of asymmetric information, and in addition, informational disadvantage facing a firm or an employer.

Economic Facts and Insights

- Contribution of one particular input towards production is captured by concepts, total physical product (TPP), marginal physical product (MPP), and average physical product (APP).
- Profit maximisation implies that inputs or factors are paid their marginal revenue product. If the firms are competitive, then the inputs are paid the value of their marginal product (since marginal revenue equals price).
- Because product market conditions affect the demand for factors, factor demand is called derived demand.
- An increase in the product price shifts a factor/input demand curve to the right.
- A technology change may shift the demand curve of a factor to the right or left, depending on the type of technology change.
- The demand curve for a factor is downward-sloping because of diminishing marginal returns.
- A firm may be small (competitive) or large (e.g., a monopoly) in the product market but small in an input market as a buyer.
- Empirical evidence shows discrimination in the labour market on the basis of race, ethnicity, caste, and gender.
- Compared to unskilled labour, skilled labour is generally paid more because its marginal productivity is greater (and, in a populous and relatively poor country like India the supply of skilled labour is less than that of unskilled labour).
- In the last two/three decades, the whole world economy has experienced technological progress that has increased the marginal product of skilled labour, while its impact on that of unskilled labour is not clear.

- Wage-setting behaviour of labour unions contributes to the unemployment problem.
- Non-human factors like capital and land have asset value and user value (rent).
- Generally, capital is reproducible, while land is not. Land therefore earns pure economic rent.

Exercises

Descriptive/Analytical

14.1. What are the dissimilarities between product and factor markets?
14.2. Why is the demand for a factor called "derived demand"?
14.3. What is the marginal productivity theory of distribution?
14.4. In the modern age, unfortunately, some kinds of labour are bought and sold as capital and land. Think of bonded labour or illegal trade in human beings, including children. What is the nature of user value in this context? Suppose the government takes active steps to curb such activity. How would it affect the user value and asset value of such labour?
14.5. "In most economies, high wage setting by the labour unions is the main cause of unemployment." Defend or refute.

Short Answer (word limit = 500 approx.)

14.6. Why is the *VMP* curve inverse U-shaped?
14.7. For a competitive firm in the product market, what is the profit-maximising rule for hiring an input? Give economic reasons.
14.8. What is the relationship between the *VMP* curve and the factor demand curve? What is the underlying reason?
14.9. "A change in the factor price and a change in technology both shift a factor demand curve." Defend or refute.
14.10. How will a technology change that enhances the *MPP* of an input shift its demand curve?
14.11. What is marginal revenue product?
14.12. How do the rules for hiring an input differ between a monopoly firm and a perfectly competitive firm in the product market?
14.13. Why are skilled workers paid more than unskilled workers?
14.14. What do trade unions do?
14.15. What is meant by user value of a factor like capital and land? What is meant by their asset value? What is the difference between the two?
14.16. What does economic rent mean?

Quizzes/Numerical

14.17. The *TPP* schedule of a factor is given in the following table.

Factor Employment (hours)	*TPP (units)*
0	0
1	8
2	18
3	26
4	35
5	41
6	45
7	48
8	50

Derive the *MPP* schedule.

14.18. Refer to the previous question. (a) If the product price is \$10, what is the *VMP* when employment is increased from 5 units to 6 units? (b) Given that the firm is perfectly competitive, and the product price is \$10, if the wage rate is \$30/hour, how many hours of the factor will be hired by the firm?

Appendix 14.A Profit-Maximising Conditions with Respect to Hiring Factors of Production

Suppose there are n factors, 1, 2, 3,..., n, the quantities hired of which are $x_1, x_2, x_3, \cdots, x_n$ and whose prices are $w_1, w_2, w_3, \cdots, w_n$. Let $y = f(x_1, x_2, x_3, \cdots, x_n)$ be the production function and let P denote the product price. By definition, the *VMP* of input 1 = $P.\partial f / \partial x_1$. Similarly, the *VMP* of input 2 = $P.\partial f / \partial x_2$, and so on.

We have total revenue = $Py = P.f(x_1, x_2, x_3, \cdots, x_n)$ Similarly, the total cost of n inputs = $w_1x_1 + w_2x_2 + \cdots + w_nx_n$. Thus, profits equal:

$$\pi(x_1, x_2, x_3, \cdots, x_n) = Pf(x_1, x_2, x_3, \cdots, x_n) - w_1x_1 - w_2x_2 - w_3x_3 - \cdots - w_nx_n.$$

This is maximised with respect to $x_1, x_2, x_3, \cdots, x_n$. The first-order conditions are:

$$\frac{\partial \pi}{\partial x_1} = P\frac{\partial f}{\partial x_1} - w_1 = 0; \quad \frac{\partial \pi}{\partial x_2} = P\frac{\partial f}{\partial x_2} - w_2 = 0$$

$$\frac{\partial \pi}{\partial x_n} = P\frac{\partial f}{\partial x_n} - w_n = 0.$$

These conditions are generalisations of equation (14.2). Each first-order condition states that the respective input is paid its *VMP*.

Appendix 14.B Trade Unionism in India

India's first labour union was started when workers of Buckingham and Carnatic Mills formed the Madras Labour Union in 1918. According to the International Labour Organisation's website visited on May 29, there are 12 state- and national-level worker's unions representing both formal and informal sectors of production in India.

Bharatiya Mazdoor Sangh (BMS)	Indian National Trade Union Congress (INTUC)
All India Trade Union Congress (AITUC)	Hind Mazdoor Sabha (HMS)
Centre of India Trade Unions (CITU)	All India United Trade Union Centre (AIUTUC) formerly UTUC (LS)
Trade Union Co-ordination Centre (TUCC)	Self Employed Women's Association (SEWA)
All India Central Council of Trade Unions (AICCTU)	Labour Progressive Federation (LPF)
United Trade Union Congress (UTUC)	National Front of Indian Trade Unions – Dhanbad (NFITU-DHN)

Trade unionism in India faces a challenging road ahead, as India has recently (in 2020) reformed very old labour laws. Three key bills were passed, one of which is Industrial Relations Code. According to it, firms employing up to 300 do not have to seek the government's permission to lay off or close plants. Previously, a company which had more than 100 workers had to seek permission from the government before laying off or closing plants. The Code also makes it more difficult than before to form a recognised trade union, requiring at least 10% of workers as members. Furthermore, workers cannot organise a strike without prior notice or during a reconciliation process.

Appendix 14.C Adverse Selection and Moral Hazard

These are two asymmetric information problems that face a manager vis-à-vis a potential employee or an existing employee.

14.1C Adverse Selection in the Labour Market

Suppose a firm needs a good accountant. Many apply with at least a bachelor's degree (B.A.) in accounting, the minimum required qualification. Not all with a B.A. in accounting are equally skilled. In this situation, there is a problem of finding the applicant with good skills if the firm does not have resources to screen all applicants effectively.

Let's articulate a situation to define this problem more precisely. Assume that there are only two types of applicants: good-hire (good-type) and bad-hire (bad-type). A good-hire's value of marginal productivity is €3,000/month and that of a bad-type is €1,200/month. But the firm doesn't know if any particular applicant is a good- or a bad-hire. Suppose that among the potential applicants from the region, one-third are the good type and two-thirds are the bad type. All the numbers introduced above are common knowledge to firms and applicants. The problem is that *the applicant knows his type, but the firm or the hiring manager does not*, a situation of asymmetric information. What would the firm do? It would calculate the expected value of the marginal product of a hire. This is equal to $(1/3)\times 3{,}000+(2/3)\times 1{,}200=€1{,}800$. Without having the benefit of knowing which applicant is of which type, a competitive firm will be willing to offer a monthly salary of €1,800. Given this salary, consider which type will apply for this job? The answer is: only the bad-type, because the good-type knows they are worth more and look elsewhere. Most people want to further their self-interest. To get the job, a bad-type will not tell the truth: she/he will tell or pretend that she/he is a good-type. Remember that we are assuming a situation where the firm does not have resources to effectively screen out who is good and who is bad. As a result, the firm is likely to get applications from a relatively large number of "lemons." This is the problem of adverse selection.

It is like the market for used cars. Some used cars are good, while others are lemons (i.e., bad). If you are in the market to buy a used car, but cannot distinguish between good cars and lemons, you are not going to pay a price that a good used car should command. As a result, only a few good used cars will come to the market in the first place. Put dramatically, bad used cars will drive good used cars from the market.

As already defined in Chapter 9, an adverse selection arises in the presence of asymmetric information when a better-informed individual uses the information to take advantage of another who does not have this information. An adverse participation in the market is the outcome.

14.2C Moral Hazard

Suppose someone is already hired. How would a manager ensure that a hired employee or a subordinate will work in the total interest of the company? For instance, using the cell phone or surfing the internet during work is not exactly in the interest of the company. A company may have a rule against using internet at work for personal use. However, an (unmarried) employee can always go to a bathroom every now and then to chat with a boyfriend or a girlfriend without being detected. It is impossible to supervise someone all the time. You, as the manager, may think of installing a hidden video camera in bathrooms to prevent this. But this may invite its own unwanted consequences like a lawsuit or police complaint against you for intrusion of privacy.

As another example, suppose you live in Paris and own an apartment complex in Lisbon. You hire a local manager in Lisbon to look after the property and collect rent. The manager can very well take liberty with respect to his own effort and provide excuses that are not verifiable. This is a problem of asymmetric information. The property manager's own effort is private information to him, which is not available to the owner. The result is a net income for you from the property that is much less than expected. This is a problem of moral hazard, where the "**agent**'s" (the property manager's) objective is not aligned with that of the "**principal**" (you as the owner). This is a classic **principal–agent problem** of moral hazard. The phrase "moral hazard" comes from the insurance industry when someone who is insured tends to be insincere. In this example, the property manager gets his salary from you so that he is insured in a way. This results in a behaviour that is not consistent with your objective as the principal.

In both examples, the common elements are asymmetric information and delegation. In the first, an employee in a firm is someone to whom some work is delegated. In the second example, property management is delegated to an individual. Within a corporation, the shareholders delegate the operation of a firm to the CEO. In turn, the CEO delegates activities to managers in different divisions. The shareholders want the CEO to work in their interest. Likewise, the CEO wants the managers under her to work in the interest of the company, and so on. The problem of moral hazard is endemic to almost any organisation. It is irrelevant to ask whether moral hazard problem is present or not. It is a matter of degree.

In sum, adverse selection and moral hazard issues arise in situations of asymmetric information. They are relevant from a managerial perspective in terms of hiring the right people for the right job and motivating people to work. How would a principal mitigate these problems?

14.3C Addressing Adverse Selection

An obvious solution to the adverse selection issue is screening via exams and interviews, a common practice you all know of. Another solution is probation wages: keep an employee on probation or a short-term contract, before offering a regular, long-term contract or a "permanent" position. This way you get to know how good the employee is.

There are other ways in which the adverse selection problems are mitigated, which is more subtle and worth analysing.

Offering Warrantee

Screening can be a costly affair. It is imperfect in any way. In the used car example considered in Chapter 9 and referred to above, you can employ a mechanic to check out a used car, but you would have to pay to the mechanic. Since adverse selection arises when the employer cannot distinguish the good type from the bad type (i.e., separate out wheat from chaff), the good candidate can take an additional step to credibly signal that she/he is good. In the same example, if there is no availability of a mechanic to verify a car's quality, the owner of a good-quality used car can distinguish herself from the owner of a lemon, by offering say a one- or two-year guarantee on transmission or engine failure—something that the owner of lemon will not find economical to replicate, since the probability of failure of a lemon is high and the owner knows it. Offering a guarantee against major problems with a used car is thus a signal.

Requiring an Educational Credential

Likewise, in the job market, a good candidate can signal that he/she is good. How? By education. What do we mean? Let the employer require a higher education degree or diploma for the job. Let's take into consideration that acquiring a higher education is more costly for the bad-type than for the good-type including the effort cost of successfully completing the degree requirements. Therefore, landing the job by not telling the truth (that he is a bad-type) is more costly for the bad-type. It opens the possibility that the higher education cost is high enough such that for the bad-type the net benefit from landing the job is negative, while for the good-type, it is positive. What is the implication? The good-type will apply for the job and the bad-type wouldn't. The problem is solved.

Note importantly that in this scenario, education (a high education requirement) is *not* a "merit good," something that enhances productivity. It simply serves as a means of separating out who is suitable and who is not. It does not deny that higher education adds intrinsic knowledge or merit for the job. It does. The point is that *education has two values: a merit or productivity value and a signal value.* It is the signal value that is relevant here. For the sake of argument, the higher education requirement may not be related to the job at all. But going through the drill and disciple of receiving education acts as a credential or signal for greater ability and aptitude to learn and perform a high-productivity task. Requiring an education credential thus serves to mitigate the adverse selection problem.

Charging an Initial Club Membership Fee

Suppose you want to be an entrepreneur and open a private club in a 10-acre property with facilities like tennis and badminton courts, swimming pools, gym, bars, restaurants, discussion halls, etc. You are creating a value for club members, not just for the facilities provided but also a quality *social interaction.* Many busy-with-work folks and wealthy retirees look for company, political discussions, seminars, and social interaction. The quality of interaction depends on the dedication of its members. In fact, bars and restaurants are omnipresent in various markets in a city. But having a glass of wine or a plate of chicken tikka masala in a club is special because of the social interaction. You may get to sit next to and chat with a high official or some other VIP, find someone who has similar hobbies like yours, and so on. This is not generally possible outside. As said earlier, social interaction, in turn, depends on the participation and dedication of its members: how much time they want to spend in the club for social interaction.

Suppose there are two types of potential members: high-participation (H) and low-participation (L) types. By joining the club, the H-type derive utility U_H and the L-types' utility is U_L. Let utilities be expressed in terms of dollars or money. Assume:

$$U_H > U_L,$$

that is, the H-type participate and enjoy more. As a concrete example, let $U_H =$ \$5,000 and $U_L =$ \$1,000.

Given the information, your objective as the owner-manager of the club is to screen out the L-type and attract the H-type individuals only, who are highly motivated and who enjoy more from what the club would offer. However, there is an adverse selection problem in that some L-types may get a membership and dilute the quality of what the club provides. How should he overcome or mitigate this?

To achieve the goal of offering membership only to the H-type, you have the option of interviewing each applicant or candidate. But this is time- and effort-consuming. But there is another option which does not cost you time or effort—and generates revenue for you. That is: charge an initial membership fee of a "little" over \$1,000, say \$1,100. Guess, who is going to join? Only the H-types, because they will obtain a surplus = 5,000 – 1,100 = \$3,900, while it will be a negative surplus (= –\$100) for the L-type. The joining fee leads to self-selection and solves the adverse selection problem.

Note that the main purpose of the fee is not raising revenue but to screen out whom you do not want. In reality, you see private clubs charge a hefty initial fee for membership. The economic rationale behind this is twofold: (a) raising revenue and (b) mitigating an adverse selection problem. From the point of view of H-types, paying the initiation fee is *a signal* through which they distinguish themselves from the L-types. This is like higher education being a signal of high potential to a prospective employer.

14.4C Addressing the Moral Hazard Problem

How to motivate a worker or a subordinate to perform his duties in a manner that aligns with your (the principal's) interests or objectives? One option is control-cum-supervision and firing in case of laxity or worse. But supervision can be very costly for an employer and firing has its own cost, because replacement is not always easy. You can offer her/him comforts, a gym for workout, etc. Personal touches like listening to, appreciation, and recognition go a long way.

An impersonal, economic solution to the moral hazard problem is to make an agent a stakeholder or a partner in terms of sharing profits; that is, to offer an employee a performance-based pay or what is called an **incentive pay**. A year-end bonus based on profits and offering of stock-options are examples. See Box 14.1 on differences between salaries and bonuses.

BOX 14.1 SALARY VERSUS BONUS

Salaries are contractual payments typically paid on a monthly basis. Mukesh Ambani's salary from the Reliance Industries Ltd. (RIL) has remained around ₹150 million per year. Bonuses are discretionary, typically paid as a lump sum at the year-end. It could be cash and/or stock-and-option rewards and may vary considerably from one year to the next. Bonuses are a very common practice in the private sector. For instance, in early 2021, RIL offered bonuses to its 2,00,000 employees after the announcement that the company's profits were 35% higher in the financial year 2020–2021 than in the previous financial year. In many instances, bonuses are way higher than the annual salary. In some countries (like the United States) bonuses are generally taxed more heavily than salaries.

While (permanent) employees may obtain some bonus, "executive bonus" is sometimes jaw-dropping, compared to their salaries. Melin and Sam (2020) report that, in 2019, Tim Cook, the CEO of Apple, earned over $133 million, most of which was in the form of stock rewards. Sundar Pichai, the CEO of Alphabet Inc. and Satya Nadella, the CEO of Microsoft earned over $86 million and $77 million, respectively, in 2019 and at least 80% of their total compensations were in stock rewards.

Incentive pay cannot however be the only form of compensation realistically since employees may be averse to fluctuations to profits or sales that can be large. They would have families to take care of and save for their children for which a stable income is needed. Hence a combination of fixed income and variable income or incentive pay is the solution.

Notes

1 The adjective "gross" is attached, since fixed costs are not deducted. By definition, profit = gross profit – fixed cost. However, since the fixed costs are given, gross profit is maximised when profit is maximised and vice versa.

2 This is parallel to the supply curve of a firm being the same as the upward-sloping portion of the marginal cost curve (Chapter 8). For simplicity we ignore the "shut-down" possibility here.

3 Another possible source of a shift in the factor demand curve that we have not discussed and which is something to be done in a more rigorous course in microeconomics is the change in the employment of other factors.
4 Appendix 14.A outlines a mathematical treatment of how equations like (14.2) follow from profit maximisation where the number of inputs can be any whole number from 1 upward.
5 There is a famous quote from the former Prime Minister of Singapore Goh Chok Tong back in 1993: "If you pay peanuts, you will get monkeys [for your ministers]."
6 The European economy is a prominent example of this.
7 Of course, the supply of land for residential and business purposes in urban areas grows as rural and farmlands are gradually converted to these purposes. In some countries (like Hong Kong and Japan), some land has been "reclaimed" from the sea. But these processes are rather slow. Unless we are talking about what happens over a fairly long period of time, the supply of land can be treated as fixed.
8 In the late 19th century, Henry George almost won the election for the mayor of New York on the platform that the government should be financed by a single tax—namely tax on landlords only.

Bibliography

Bloomfeld, M. J., Gipper, B., Kepler, J. D., & Tsui, D. (2021). Cost shielding in executive bonus plans. *Journal of Accounting & Economics*, 72 (2–3), 1–24

Gould, E., Schieder, J., & Geier, K. (2016, October 20). *What is the gender pay gap and is it real?* (Report). Economic Policy Institute.

Guay, W. R., Kepler, J. D., & Tsui, D. (2019). The role of executive cash bonuses in providing individual and team incentives. *Journal of Financial Economics*, *133*(2), 441–471.

Kumar, A., & Hashmi, N. I. (2020). Labour market discrimination in India. *Indian Journal of Labour Economics*, *63*, 177–188.

Melin, A., & Sam, C. (2020, July 10). Wall street gets the flak, but tech CEOs get paid all the money. https://www.bloomberg.com/graphics/2020-highest-paid-ceos/

Wilson, V., & Rodgers, W. L. (2016, September 20). Black- white wage gaps expand with rising wage inequality (Report). Economic Policy Institute.

15

GOING GLOBAL

From the discussions in the previous chapters, it must be clear to you by now that exchange of goods and services among economic agents is mutually beneficial to all, with neither side obliging the other. Interpersonal trade enhances society's welfare. This argument extends itself further. Interregional trade does the same. In India, Assam produces plenty of tea; Jharkhand has plenty of coal; hence, it is mutually beneficial to exchange. In the United States, about two-third of nuts is produced in California, whereas the major corn producers are the mid-western states like Iowa, Illinois, and Nebraska. Interregional trade in nuts and corn in the United States is a good thing.

What if we stretch this argument further—beyond interpersonal or interregional to *international* trade? Some of us may feel a bit uncomfortable. The spontaneity with which we agreed to move from interpersonal trade to interregional trade is waned. For some, being *dependent* on other countries hurts the feeling of national pride. In the developed countries, outsourcing to and imports of goods from relatively less developed economies are blamed in terms of "domestic jobs and businesses going outside."

In a developing country and a former colony like India, self-reliance and *Atmnirbhara* Bharat (self-reliant India) are still buzz words. "Let us produce everything that we need without depending on any other country" may sound like a melody to some ears. Looking at it from a historical perspective, it is often said that *flag follows trade.* For example, in case of India, the East India Company entered at first as a trader, which eventually led to British rule. "That cannot be repeated by international trade and investment"; the colonial past gets revived.

Do such fears make sense? We argue that these are mostly misplaced. Economic interest has brought together countries that were once sworn enemies. In 2019,

DOI: 10.4324/9781003452195-15

Vietnam acted as a felicitator to bring together the United States and North Korea to the negotiating table on its soil. The same Vietnam was carpet-bombed several times by the United States in the 1960s. Those who oppose the idea of turning global sometimes cite two reasons, often claimed to be economic.

Importing Is Anti-National: It runs like this. In turning global, we shall be allowing for imports and exports. When we import, we contribute to the generation of income and employment in the foreign country at the cost of denying income and employment to some of our own brethren. It is anti-national. On the contrary, exporters are looked upon as angels. They manage to sell to outsiders and hence contribute to the income and employment of the nation. Hence, we must stress exports and avoid imports. This view is a manifestation of unwarranted national ego and xenophobia. The argument is not new. In the 16th century, *Mercantilists* in England vehemently opposed the East India Company on the grounds that it bought textiles and spices from India and South-East Asia in exchange for gold, thus denting the wealth of "our" (British) nation.

There are serious problems with this argument. First, suppose we grant this argument momentarily and agree that exports are good, but imports are bad. Then, if all countries hold the same view and want to export only, who will they trade with? Moon? Mars? Second, promoting exports and discouraging imports amount to a surplus in the trade balance, which are parts of a nation's savings. If we keep on saving, don't we deprive ourselves from consuming and improving the (material) quality of our lives? This is like someone who wants to save and save and accumulate wealth without much propensity towards spending and enjoying life. Of course, a nation or an economy ought to avoid living beyond its means, i.e., importing more than exporting and running a consistent trade deficit, which would make a country a net debtor to the rest of the world. Hence, balanced trade should be a country's long-term goal, not undue restriction of imports.

Importing May Be Risky: If we are dependent on other countries for essential goods and services, we expose ourselves to the vagaries of supply conditions in other countries and the policy whims of foreign governments. For instance, if South Africa depends too much on the Middle East for oil, then a war in that region or a hostile policy of Arab states or Iran against South Africa (this is completely hypothetical), can land South Africa in the soup. If South Africa is not be able to import oil and cannot achieve sufficient increase in the domestic production of oil, the oil price in South Africa will skyrocket, affecting the daily lives of millions. During the Covid-19 years, we have seen how the world economy was affected by global supply chain issues.

This argument has some validity, but not a whole lot. First, we may not have the natural resources or the technology to produce all essential goods at reasonable costs. Second, even if a country may have the technology, its endowments of primary resources like labour and capital may be such that it is not cost-effective to produce a good domestically vis-à-vis importing it. As an example, the technology of producing TVs very much exists in a technologically advanced country like the United States, but there is virtually no manufacturing of TV in the country. Almost all components for producing TV are made outside of the United States. However, if there is any disruption of supply from abroad, the United States has the technology to produce it at home, although it may take some time to revive a domestic industry in such, rather infrequent, events. The same argument applies to any other nation. Retaining the technology of producing a good is a good idea, even if a country cannot efficiently produce it. Third, there are safeguards against unreasonable hostile trade policy by individual countries under the World Trade Organization (WTO) system, in which 159 countries are members as of 2022.

The overall point is that import dependence carries some risk, but it is infrequent and temporary. It does not justify an inward-looking international trade strategy and an avoidance of imports. This would be somewhat like shunning the use of cars or air travels because of the risk of a fatal accident. Locking ourselves from international economic community in the name of self-sufficiency or exploitation by foreign countries only serves to deny us a better standard of living. Restricting trade may be justifiable but only selectively and temporarily. Provocatively put, *economic self-sufficiency in terms of unduly restricting international exchange is not a virtue.*

In the following analysis it will be made abundantly clear that international trade is mutually beneficial.

15.1 International Trade in Goods and Services

We first discuss how world trade has progressed since the beginning of the 20th century.

15.1.1 World Trade Over Time

The world economy witnessed the first "rising wave" or the **first golden age of international trade** in the early 20th century when trains, motor vehicles, and ships became common modes of domestic and international transport. However, international trading declined substantially during the interwar years and World War II because of wars, the Great Depression, and inward-looking restrictive policies of advanced economies in the wake of massive unemployment during the Great Depression. Things changed dramatically after World War II. International trade started growing and the trend continues till today. The post-World War II period may be called the **second golden age of international trade.**

There are two factors behind the second golden age of trade. First, there was an emphatic realisation by the advanced countries like the United States, United Kingdom, France, etc. that restrictive trade policies hamper economic growth. "Trade is an engine of growth" became the norm among the developed nations. Numerous bilateral and multilateral trade liberalisation schemes were negotiated among them and across a broader group of countries. This includes General Agreement on Tariffs and Trade (GATT) signed in 1947. In the 1990s, it evolved into the **World Trade Organization** or WTO; see Box 15.1.[1]

BOX 15.1 A BRIEF INTRODUCTION TO WTO

Like the United Nations, there are member countries (159 as of 2022) belonging to WTO. However, WTO has more "bite" compared to the United Nations. No member country of WTO has any veto power, and its rulings are binding. Headquartered in Geneva, Switzerland, it oversees the implementation of about 60 agreements reached by the member countries. Major agreements include, among others,

- General Agreement on Trade in Goods.
- General Agreement on Trade in Services (GATS).
- Agreement on Trade-Related Aspects of Intellectual Property Rights (TRIPS).
- Agreement on Trade-Related Investment Measures (TRIMs).
- Trade Policy Review Mechanism (TPRM).

WTO champions freer international trade among member countries by adhering to a large set of rules agreed upon by the members. Importantly, it is a platform for negotiating trade agreements. There is a dispute settlement body within the WTO, which accepts complaints by member countries against possible violations or discriminations in international trade by other member countries, and, delivers a ruling in a time-bound manner. It is hard to argue that it is biased–or at least overly favourable–towards advanced economies.

Among many functions, it prepares country reports on trade policy practised by the respective members and is a source of a lot of information on international trade including data. We strongly advise you to visit its website: https://www.wto.org

The second factor is the discovery of container shipping in the 1950s which substantially reduced the cost of shipping by creating standardisation, economisation of space, and saving labour-intensive tasks. Before the advent of shipping containers, goods were first packed inside bags, barrels, crates, etc. and then loaded into ships and other carriers—a very labour-intensive and relatively inefficient method. Container shipping was designed by Malcolm McLean from North Carolina, USA, a relatively unknown figure among the great discoverers.

International trade entered a different phase in the 1990s when trade in services began to expand dramatically—thanks to information-technology revolution,

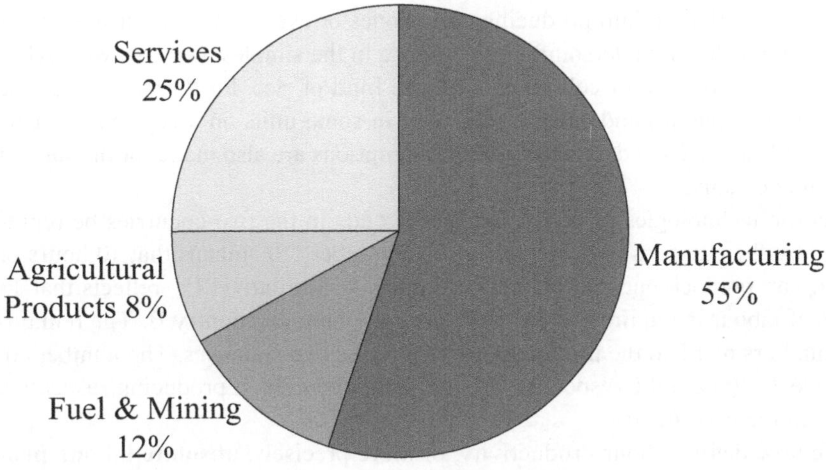

FIGURE 15.1 Share of Broad Groups in World Exports, 2019

particularly the internet. Legal advice from a law firm in New York can be transmitted to a client in Malaysia. With required test results available, a doctor sitting in Mumbai can consult a patient lying in a hospital in Sydney. A teaching or tutoring service can be provided from a different country via Skype or Zoom. There are many other examples. We can surely call it the **third golden age of international trade**. Trade in services now constitutes about 25% to 45% of the total world trade, depending on the feasibility of measuring some forms of trade in services. A break-down of world trade across broad product groups in the year 2019 is shown in Figure 15.1.

15.1.2 Which Types of Goods Would a Country Export?

Why are Brazil and Vietnam major exporters of coffee? Why does the United States export commercial aircrafts to other nations? What is the basis of trade? How does a country benefit from trade? There are several theories or models of international trade.

The Ricardian Theory of Comparative Advantage and Trade

This is the oldest, yet has relevance even today. Developed originally the early 19th century by David Ricardo, a successful businessman in England and one of the best-known classical economists, his theory of trade revolves around the concept of comparative advantage, which is fundamental to international trade.

Imagine that the world consists of two countries only: country A and country B. Both can produce only two goods, say cell phones and rice, with the help of one-factor production, labour. Of course, we all know that many inputs or factors of production go into producing cell phones or even rice. But our one-factor assumption helps in understanding the theory in the simplest possible way. Also, let there be only kind of cell phone and one kind of rice. Furthermore, suppose that both cell phones and rice be measured in some units on a continuous scale allowing fractions and decimals. These assumptions are also made for the sake of convenience only.

Let the technologies of producing these goods in the two countries be represented by the numbers in Table 15.1(a). The number "10" means that 10 hours of labour can produce one cell phone in country A. Similarly, "15" reflects that 15 hours of labour is required to produce one cell phone in country B. The remaining numbers relate to the production of rice in the two countries. The numbers in in Table 15.1(a) are the respective **labour requirements** in producing respective goods in the two countries.

We now define labour productivity, or more precisely, **absolute labour productivity**, as the inverse of labour requirement, that is, units of output produced by one unit of labour. Thus, higher labour requirement means lower absolute labour productivity and vice versa. The absolute labour productivity numbers corresponding to in Table 15.1(a) are given in Table 15.1(b). The latter is also a statement of technologies. The numbers in Table 15.1(a) are constructed (on purpose) such that country A is more efficient in producing both goods, that is, labour productivity in producing either good is higher in country A than in country B. For instance, one unit of labour produces more cell phones (= 1/10) in country A than in country B (= 1/15). The same holds for rice (1/20 vis-à-vis 1/45).

Between countries A and B, when absolute labour productivity in producing a good is greater in one country, we say that that country has **absolute advantage** in producing that good. In our (numerical) model, country A has absolute advantage and country B has absolute disadvantage in producing both goods.

We next define **relative labour productivity** as the ratio of absolute labour productivities, which, as we will see, will be critical. For example, the relative labour productivity in producing cell phone in country A vis-à-vis rice is (1/10) ÷ (1/20) = 2, or equivalently, the relative labour productivity in producing rice vis-à-vis cell phone is (1/20) ÷ (1/10) = 1/2. Likewise, the respective relative labour productivities in country B are 3 and 1/3.

TABLE 15.1 Technologies in Countries A and B

	A	*B*		*A*	*B*
Cell phones	10	15	Cell phones	1/10	1/15
Rice	20	45	Rice	1/20	1/45
(a) Labour Coefficients			(b) Absolute Labour Productivities		

Let's now explore how these two goods will be priced in the two countries in the absence of trade (called **autarky**) and in the presence of trade. This will lead us to determine which countries would export what and why international trade is beneficial. Assume that both goods are produced in perfectly competitive markets whether the countries are in autarky or engaged in free international trade.

Autarky

Let's begin with country A. Recall from Chapter 8 that in the long run, price = average or unit cost in a perfectly competitive market. Thus, the cell phone and rice prices (measured in some units) will be equal to:

$P_c = 10 \times$ hourly wage in country A; $P_r = 20 \times$ hourly wage in country A.

The subscripts "c" and "r" refer to cell phone and rice. The right-hand side is the unit cost of producing the respective good and this is equal to the product's price. If we divide the prices, the relative price of cell phone is:

$$\left(P_c / P_r\right)_{\mathrm{A}}^{n} = 10 \div 20 = 1/2 \text{ kg of rice,} \tag{15.1}$$

where the superscript "n" refers to autarky or no trade. Notice that this is the inverse of the relative labour productivity in producing cell phone. The relative price of a cell phone being equal to 1/2 kg of rice means that if one produces one cell phone, sells it in the market and uses the money for rice, it will fetch 1/2 kg of rice. Inversely, if you have 1 kg of rice, you can exchange that in the market for two cell phones. *Thus, in country A, the relative price of cell phone is ½ kg of rice, and, equivalently, the relative price of rice in terms of cell phone is 2.*

Let's now move to country B in autarky. Similar calculations as earlier yield the relative price of cell phone in terms of rice in country B equal to:

$$\left(P_c / P_r\right)_{\mathrm{B}}^{n} = 1/3 \text{ kg,} \tag{15.2}$$

and the relative price of rice is three cell phones.

Notice importantly that in real terms one cell phone fetches more rice in country A (1/2 kg) than in country B (1/3 kg), and 1 kg of rice gets more cell phones in country B (3) than in country A (2). These statements are two sides of the same coin. In terms of the terminology used in international economics, we say that *Country A has* ***comparative*** *or* ***relative advantage*** *in producing rice and Country B has* ***comparative advantage*** *in producing cell phones.* Simply put, comparative advantage means *the ability to produce and sell a product* **relatively cheaper** *compared to some other product or products.* By definition, in our two-country, two-good scenario, one country *cannot* have comparative advantage in both goods.

Note that country A has absolute advantage in both goods, but relatively speaking, the advantage is greater for rice. This is why country A has comparative advantage in rice. Country B has absolute disadvantage in producing both goods, but less so for cell phone. Hence, it is said to have comparative advantage in producing cell phone.

You can connect comparative advantage with relative labour productivity. In country A, the relative labour productivity is greater in producing rice and in country B it is greater in the cell phone sector. Therefore, *in the Ricardian model, a country has comparative advantage in the good in the production of which the relative labour productivity is greater.* Notice that the comparative-advantage good is relatively cheaper in autarky in the respective country—rice in country A and cell phone in country B.

Free Trade

Starting from the autarky (no trade) situation, suppose the two countries decide to open their borders for free trade. Assume for simplicity that international transport costs of goods are not very high. We will argue now that each country will export the product in which it has comparative advantage. That is, in our model, country A will export rice to country B and country B will export cell phone to country A.

Realise that international trade essentially integrates the national markets of each traded good: cell phone and rice. The implication is that in free trade the same price for the same product will prevail in both countries (barring transport and transaction costs). In other words, free trade leads to the **law of one price**.

The reason is this. If, for instance, rice (cell phone) sells at a lower (higher) price in country A than in country B, one can buy rice (sell cell phone) in country A and sell rice (buy cell phone) in country B and make a profit. This is called **arbitrage**, meaning a simultaneous purchase and sale of the same item to make a profit. If many traders do the same, the relative price of rice will increase in country A and decrease in Country B. In equilibrium, the relative price of rice will be equalised across the two countries. The same holds for cell phone. This is the law of one price—an outcome of the possibility of free arbitrage.

The next question is: Where will the common international price lie vis-à-vis the different autarky prices? The answer is that it will settle somewhere in-between the autarky prices. We can understand this via this analogy. Imagine two water tanks lying next to each other separately, one having water up to 3 feet and the other up to 5 feet. If we now connect them at the bottom through a pipe (which is like free flow of goods between two countries), a common water level will be set at somewhere between 3 feet and 5 feet. The common water level may not be exactly at 4 feet, the average, unless the two containers are identical.

Returning to our model, international trade will lead to an international price of cell phone in terms of rice in-between the autarky prices 1/2 kg and 1/3 kg, say 3/8 kg. That is,

$$\left(P_c / P_r\right)_{\text{International}} = 3/8 \text{ kg}. \tag{15.3}$$

We will not discuss how exactly the international price is determined—something that is covered in a specialised course in international trade. But consider how the trading countries are positioned in free trade in terms of which goods they export and import, and how they are better off compared to no trade. From the standpoint of country A, if it does not trade, it is able to provide two cell phones to its own residents by sacrificing 1 kg of rice, whereas in the international market it can fetch 8/3 (which is greater than 2) cell phones for selling 1 kg of rice.[2] Thus country A benefits from exporting rice in producing which it has comparative advantage. Likewise, country B will gain by exporting cell phone, which is its comparative-advantage good. This is the Ricardian theory of comparative advantage. It illustrates that each country will export the product it has comparative advantage in, and this will benefit each trading country.

General Highlights of the Ricardian Model

Based on its implications we just derived, the general highlights of the Ricardian model are the following:

a. *Comparative advantage is about exploiting sources of dissimilarities for mutual benefit.* At a personal level, imagine that if you have brought a big chicken sandwich from home for lunch and your friend has brought potato chips and your favourite drink, you can both increase your enjoyment from lunch by sharing/trading your differences or dissimilarities. The same applies to trading nations.

b. The Ricardian model teaches us something deeper. That is, even if a country (country A) is more efficient in producing all goods compared to another (country B), it would still benefit from engaging in international trade.[3]

   The following example should help you in further understanding this insight. Suppose you are single and a top-notch consultant, earning €500 per hour. Plus, you have natural culinary skills to cook your desired food. Would you prefer to work as a consultant *and* cook at the same time, which takes time away your time for consultancy? Assume that you can obtain the same food by hiring a cook for €20 an hour. The rational choice is no. While you may be superior in terms of both work and cooking, your *relative* advantage lies in being a consultant as it rewards you €500 per hour, much higher than paying €20 an hour to the cook. Hence, you should trade (export) your skill to the market to maximise your personal gain or surplus. The same applies to a nation.

c. By emphasising labour as a factor of production, the Ricardian model highlights that *labour productivity is an important source of comparative advantage.* What is more subtle is that absolute productivity differences across countries do not, *by itself,* imply lower prices and higher exportability, because higher productivity translates itself to higher rewards for labour and possibly other inputs. (Realise that a skilled worker is more productive compared to an unskilled worker and this is why a skilled worker commands a higher wage.) Indeed, there is considerable international evidence showing that productivity and wages are positively correlated. For international evidence, see Figure 15.2.[4]

Appendix 15.A shows evidence of positive relation between productivity and wage in Indian manufacturing.

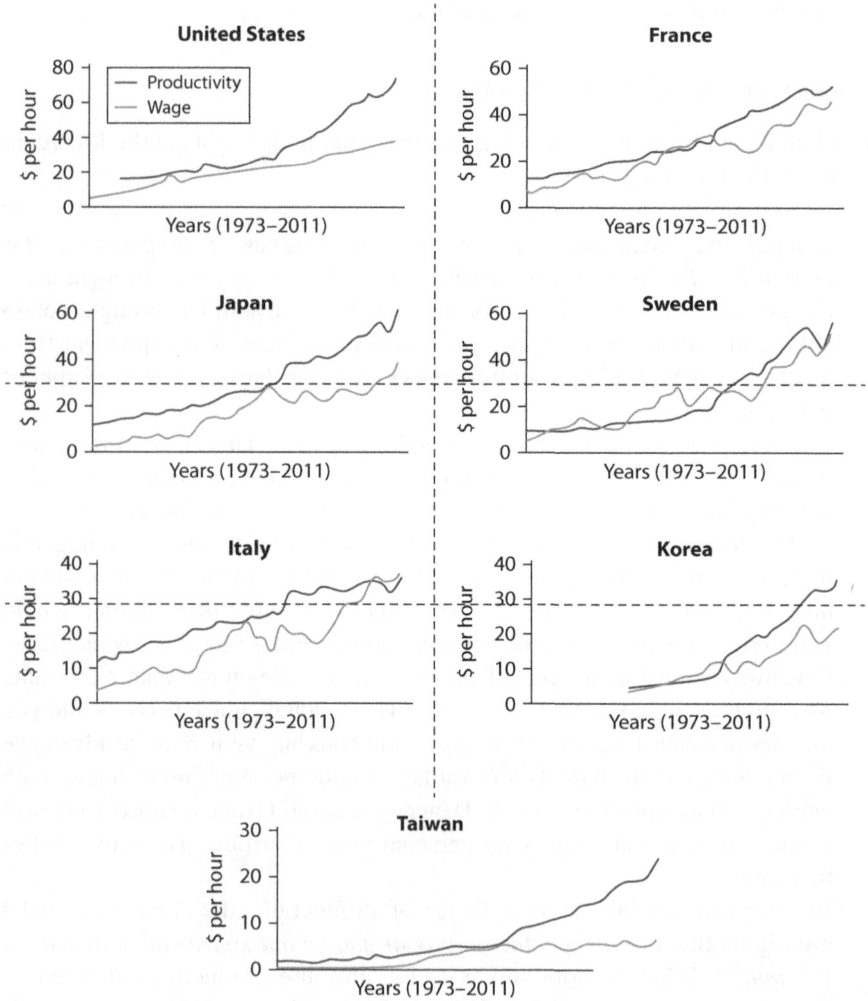

FIGURE 15.2 International Evidence of Productivity and Real Wages, 1970–2010

TABLE 15.2 Bangladesh versus China, 2011

	Bangladeshi Output per Worker as % of China	*Bangladeshi Exports as % of China*
All Industries	28.5	1.0
Apparel	77.0	15.5

Source: (Krugman et al., 2015)

For our purpose, the implication is that higher absolute productivity per se does not necessarily imply lower relative cost or lower relative price at a macro level. It is *relative*, not absolute productivity, which is critical for the export potential of a product. Table 15.2 shows the evidence of *relative* productivity or comparative advantage and exportability relates to Bangladesh vis-à-vis China.[5] Bangladesh is a country with relatively poor infrastructure and equipment compared to China—so labour productivity is likely to be lower across sectors, compared to China. However, in the early 2010s it was much less pronounced in the apparel sector compared to all industries together: relative to China, the Bangladeshi output per worker in the apparel sector was 77% whereas it was 28.5% for all industries combined. Correspondingly, Bangladeshi exports of apparel was 15.5% of Chinese exports of the same, while it was only 1% for all industrial products. The point is that Bangladesh was "gaining on China" in the exports of apparel, where its comparative disadvantage in terms of productivity vis-à-vis China was less.

Other Sources of Comparative Advantage

Relative productivity differences are *not* the only source of comparative advantage, meaning the capability to produce and sell a product at a lower price in the international market. It can stem from differences in the relative supply of factors.

Let us characterise an economy in terms of two factors of production, say, labour and capital, instead of one, and suppress technology differences across the two countries. Assume that both country A and country B can produce two goods, cell phones and rice, which are respectively more intensive in the use of capital and labour in both economies. That is, cell phones and rice are, respectively (relatively), capital-intensive and labour-intensive goods in production. The production possibility curves of the two economies will be shaped differently, as shown in Figure 15.3. That of the relatively labour-abundant country will bulge towards the axis measuring the relatively labour-intensive good, rice, and that of the relatively capital-abundant country will bulge towards cell phones, the relatively capital-intensive good.

It is then intuitive that if, compared to country B, country A is relatively more labour abundant, it would have comparative advantage in producing the relatively more labour-intensive good, that is, rice. Hence, it will be a net exporter of rice and

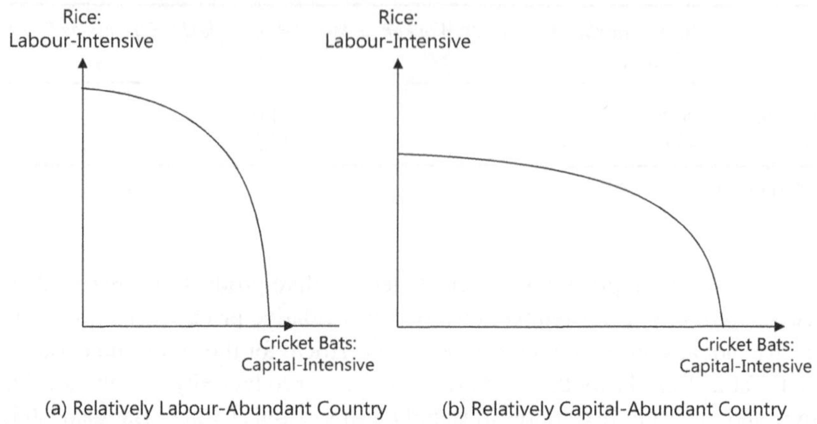

FIGURE 15.3 Production Possibility Curves of Countries

net importer of cell phones. The opposite will hold for country B. This is called the **relative factor abundance model/theory** or **Heckscher–Ohlin model/theory** of international trade. In this view of the world, *a country will have comparative advantage in and be a net exporter of the product which uses its abundant factor more intensively.* In contrast to the Ricardian model, this theory is built on differences in relative factor endowments, not in technology.

A numerical example on the factor abundance theory of trade is in order.

Example 15.1

Consider a world economy having two countries M and N. Each can produce two goods: cars (C) and garments (G). The production of C is more capital-intensive than that of G in both countries. Country M's endowments of labour and capital are 100 and 150. Those of country N are 120 and 300, respectively. In free trade, which country will export which good?

Answer: The ratio of capital to labour endowment in country M is 1.5, whereas the same ratio is 2.5 in country N. Thus, country A is relatively labour abundant and country N is relatively capital abundant. Thus, country M has comparative advantage in the relatively labour-intensive good, which is G, and country N's comparative advantage lies in producing the relatively capital-intensive good, C. Hence, in free trade, country M will export G to country N and country N will export C to country M. ■

In the process, country A will benefit from trade by exporting the good it has comparative advantage in, that is, rice, and importing cell phones. Country B will benefit from trade by exporting cell phones, in the production of which it has comparative advantage.

There is an additional question of importance. Since there are two factors of production, you may ask who benefits from trade? The answer is that *if free trade is allowed, labour will benefit and capital will lose in the relatively labour-abundant country and just the opposite happens in the relatively capital-abundant country.*[6] This is intuitive to see. International trade expands the production of the good which is intensive in the use of a country's abundant factor and thus increases the demand for the abundant factor. As a result, the abundant factor's price or reward increases and it gains. The opposite holds for the relatively scarce factor.

Asymmetric distributional implications imply that the group that would benefit from trade will support a free-trade policy and the group that is likely to lose will oppose free trade. This is something that is observed in developed economies including the United States. In the past, the United States has opened international trade with relatively labour-abundant countries like Mexico, China, and other Asian countries. According to the theory, this would hurt the low-wage workers in the United States and they would oppose. Indeed, low-wage workers in the United States have objected to free international trade with low-wage countries.

What about the aggregative gains for a trading country? Though one group gains while the other loses due to international trade, if we aggregate the gains and losses, a trading country as a whole is a net gainer whether it is relatively labour- or capital-abundant. This was noted earlier.

15.1.3 Other Bases of and Sources from Gains in International Trade

We now cover some material that is not usually taught in a basic course in international trade. But they are as important as what we have covered so far. That is, even if there may be no dissimilarities between countries, i.e., two or more countries may be identical to one another, none having comparative advantage in any product, they can still benefit from international trade.

There are at least three sources of such *non-comparative-advantage gains* from international trade.

Product Differentiation

Assume that countries A and B are identical in terms of resources, technologies, and tastes, and they produce only one product, say cars. Imagine that country A produces three brands of cars, C, D, and E while country B produces brands F, G, and H. Assume, critically, that each brand is different from others, that is, they are basically the same product with the same quality, but there are some differences, say in appearance, colour, etc. This is similar to the difference between say Chinese food, Italian food, and Indian food. Quality and calorie-wise they may be the same, but they affect our taste buds differently. The presence of such varieties in the market is called **horizontal product differentiation**, as opposed to **vertical product differentiation** which refers to intrinsic quality differences.

Realise that in this scenario there is no comparative advantage in producing any brand for either country since the two countries are identical. However, if they open trade, each country now consumes six varieties with half quantity compared to no trade, instead of three. As long as the residents of each country value varieties, this is a source of gain. To understand this further, suppose that you are a family of six in country A, and each has a different taste with respect to cars. If there is no trade between country A and country B, six people will have to consume among brands C, D, and E, whereas if there is international trade, the family can potentially consume all six varieties available now (C to H), one for each person.

Thus, if more varieties are preferred to less, (horizontal) product differentiation or availability of greater number of varieties of a product is a basis of mutually gainful international trade.

Internal Scale Economies

Now assume no product differentiation, and suppose that country A and country B can produce two goods, X and Y, with the help of labour only. Technologies are the same across countries and across X and Y. Each country's labour endowment is 10 (say in crores). Further, let tastes be such that each country's residents consume X and Y in 1:1 proportion. The product possibilities are given in Table 15.3. For instance, 6 units of labour in either country A or country B can produce 3 units of X or (not and) 3 units of Y.

Imagine how much of each good country A and country B produce and consume in autarky. Because of the symmetry in technology and tastes, half of the labour force (5) will be employed in sector X and the other half (5) in section Y, producing 2 units of X and 2 units. Therefore, in the absence of international trade each country will consume whatever is produced, i.e., 2 units of X and 2 units of Y. In this example also, there are no dissimilarities between the two countries, hence there is no source of comparative advantage for either country.

TABLE 15.3 Internal Scale Economies and Gains from Trade

To Produce Amount (X or Y)	*Requires Labour Hours*
0	3
1	4
2	5
3	6
4	7
5	8
6	9
7	10

Now suppose the finance ministers of the two countries allow free trade, along with country A specialising in X (i.e., producing X only) and country B specialising in Y. (We could as well assume country A specialising in Y and country B specialising in X without any change in the conclusion). If so, in view of the last row in Table 15.3, country A would produce 7 units of X and country B would produce 7 units of Y. The two countries can now divide the total output of each good equally between them. How much will now the two nations be able to consume? The answer is 3.5 units of X and 3.5 units of Y, instead of 2 units of each good in autarky. Each country is better off with international trade and specialisation.

How is this possible? As you can guess, the "secret" lies in the pattern of numbers presented in Table 15.3. Notice that the production function or technology of each good is subject to **increasing returns to scale** or **scale economies** (introduced in Chapter 7), meaning that a *proportionate* increase in all inputs leads to a more than proportionate increase in the output. In this example, there are indeed scale economies. Here all inputs mean only one, that is, labour, and observe that an increase in labour input from any level to a higher level always entails more than proportionate increase in input. For instance, if labour input increases from 4 to 5, i.e., there is a 25% increase in labour, the output increases from 1 to 2, a 100% increase. If labour increases from 5 to 8 (a 60% increase), the output rises from 2 to 5 (250% increase). Because there are scale economies, the total world output of each good increases when the two countries specialise in producing one good each. The benefits of scale economies are exploited by specialisation and exchange through international trade, which would not have been possible in the absence of trade.

How do we know if an industry or sector's technology satisfies increasing returns to scale or scale economies? Typically, anything that is produced by **assembly-line technology** entails scale economies. The very rationale behind assembly-line technology is to lower unit cost by producing in mass scale.[7]

Less Monopoly or Oligopoly Market Power

Imagine the market of one product in country A and country B, say, a single variety of TV. That is, only one and the same type of TV can be produced in both countries. Let the demand curve and supply conditions facing the TV market be exactly the same between the two countries. Thus, there is no scope of any comparative advantage.

Further, suppose that there is one producer of TV in country A and one in country B. In this scenario, if the countries do not allow international trade in TV, there will be a monopoly market for TV in each country. Recall the monopoly market studied in Chapter 10. In its goal for maximising profits each monopoly will produce some quantity and charge a monopoly price. We know that, compared to perfect competition, a monopolist produces less and charges a higher price. Now suppose the two countries open up free trade in TV between them, imagine what would happen. The market facing each of the two firms will double, as they have the option of selling in two markets instead of one. However, there is now duopoly competition between the two firms, which did not exist previously in autarky. Thus, *international trade leads to more oligopoly competition and thus less monopoly/oligopoly market power.* In the duopoly equilibrium (studied in Chapter 11), each TV producer will now produce more, which will lower the market price of TV. Consequently, there will be a higher *global* production of TV, which is precisely a result of international trade, which is competition-enhancing. The two countries being identical, each country will be able to consume or buy more TV and benefit. In sum, *international trade effects more competition or a decline in market power, which is a source of gain to consumers worldwide wherever the product is sold.*

15.1.4 Dynamic Gains from Trade

The gains from international trade discussed above are called the **static gains from trade**, referring to a nation's gain in purchasing power due to resource allocation and greater consumption possibilities. In addition to this, there are **dynamic gains from trade** in terms of trade in important intermediate products and in terms of knowledge and exposure gained with respect to technology, marketing, etc., as a result of being a part of the international network of exchange. These gains contribute to the growth of economies and thus are termed as "dynamic." Sometimes it is said that "trade is the engine of growth." These gains are, however, much harder to measure compared to static gains from trade, but they can be very substantive indeed.

15.1.5 Trade Protectionism

Despite the enormous potential for gains from international trade, countries have resorted to **trade protectionism** particularly when there are severe macro issues facing a country or negative sentiments towards foreign countries. For instance, when a country faces a major unemployment problem for business-cyclic reasons, a politically convenient scapegoat is free trade. There is a clamour for protecting domestic industries from foreign competition in order to protect or generate domestic employment. It is always easy to blame others, and protection against international trade has a (false) ring of patriotism. Trade protection takes the form of **tariffs** (taxes on imports as they enter the border of a country), **quotas** and other forms of discrimination against foreign goods. Existing evidence however points towards the contrary. If country A is going to put high tariffs and/or other trade restrictions against country B, country B is not going to take it lying down. It would do the same, leading to a **trade war**. The most famous example of trade war happened nearly 100 hundred years ago during the time of the Great Depression: 1929–1933. The-then advanced countries began to slap tariffs against one another and in no time, so to speak, the world economy was in the middle of a severe depression. What brought countries out of the Great Depression was not trade protection, but expansionary fiscal policy advocated by John Maynard Keynes.

In Chapter 9 we studied market failure and first- and second-best policy intervention. If it is a macro problem of unemployment, a macro intervention, not international trade intervention, is a first-best policy measure. Solving a macro problem by trade policy is at best the second-best.

We import something *because* domestic production is not efficient enough to supply us a product at a lower cost than imports. Thus, if we protect relatively inefficient industries which use our resources inefficiently, the cost of doing so in terms of foregoing our own hard-earned money is actually higher than the cost of importing. This is something not very easy to see, since the benefit of imports is spread over the entire consuming population.

Nationalistic sentiments against a foreign country sometimes erupt because of military engagements or conflicts, spilling into the realm of international trade calling or trade protection and boycott in different ways. See Box 15.2 for a perspective of what happened in India in 2020.

BOX 15.2 BOYCOTT CHINA IN 2020

During and after the border clash with China in the Galwan valley in the Himalayas in the mid-2020, anti-China sentiment in India scaled new heights. It included boycotting Chinese goods. Some people thought it is the only way to punish China. The Indian government didn't explicitly announce a boycott of Chinese goods and businesses in India, but Indian companies were reportedly pressured not to renew expiring contracts or sign new contracts with Chinese companies.

Does this make economic sense for India? The answer is no. Overall, China is India's second-largest trade partner after the United States. As Figure 15.4 shows, in 2019, China is India's top trading partner in terms of imports

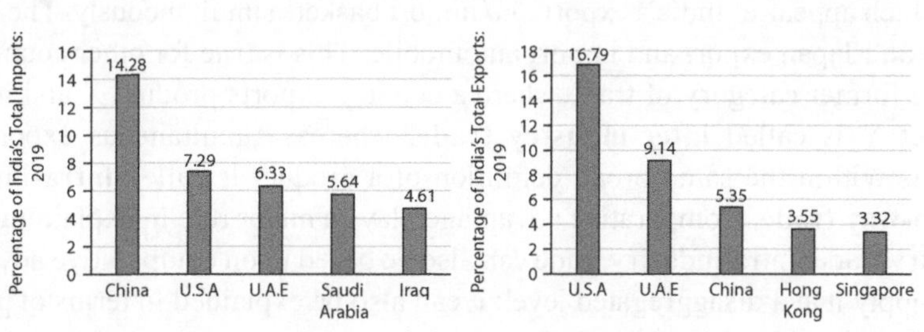

FIGURE 15.4 India's Top Trading Partners, 2019

(14.28%). It is not just finished products that India imports from China. Many intermediate products in some important sectors are imported from China too. For instance, "at least 70% of India's drug intermediary needs are fulfilled by China" (Inamdar, 2020). Figure 15.4 shows also that China ranks No. 3 in terms of India's exports (5.35%) in 2019.

How bad will China be hurt economically because of India's boycott of Chinese goods and businesses? Not much. The simple reason is that whereas China is our second-largest trade partner, India is the 11th largest trade partner of China, according to Wikipedia accessed on May 30, 2021. Furthermore, India runs a deficit with China, that is, Chinese imports from India are less than Indian imports from China.

In sum, "Boycott China" is more beggar-thyself than beggar-thy-neighbour.

There are many other examples of boycotts of foreign goods and services. After the Mohammad comic crisis in 2005/2006, Muslim countries boycotted goods from Denmark. Following Senkaku/Diaoyu Island conflict in 2012, China boycotted Japanese goods for some time.

15.1.6 Inter-Industry Trade versus Intra-Industry Trade

A country exports some products and imports some other products. For instance, as of 2022, major export items of Japan consist of electrical and non-electrical machinery and transport equipment. Among its major imports are petroleum, broadcasting equipment, and computers. India's biggest export product groups are mineral fuels including oil, and gems and precious metal. India imports iron and steel and electrical machinery and equipment, among others.

What is also true and somewhat less obvious is that a nation exports and imports within the same product category. For instance, India also exports iron and steel and electrical machinery and equipment. There are other product groups too, which appear in India's export *and* import baskets simultaneously. The United States and Japan export and import automobile. This is true for other countries.

The former category of trade where a country exports product X and imports product Y is called **inter-industry trade**, whereas simultaneous exports and imports within the same broad definition of a product is called **intra-industry** or **two-way trade**. Comparative advantage plays a major role in explaining *inter*-industry trade. Intra-industry trade can also be based upon comparative advantage if we apply it at a disaggregated level; it can also be explained in terms of product differentiation.

Generally speaking, in any product category, unless very narrowly defined, there are both inter-industry trade and intra-industry trade. For several product groups and for many countries, the volume of intra-industry trade is substantial. As an example, over the period 2001 to 2005, India's share of intra-industry trade in total trade in chemicals with Germany was 45%; see Aggarwal and Chakraborty (2022). For advanced nations, the share of intra-industry trade is more than 50% in many product categories.

15.1.7 International Trade in Services

Our focus thus far has been on international trade in goods. Over the last few decades, especially since 1990s, trade in services has grown more rapidly than trade in goods. As shown in Figure 15.5, during 2005–2017 the annual and cumulative growth rates of services trade far exceed those of manufacturing goods.

It is easy to visualise international trade in goods. You can easily imagine tonnes and tonnes of iron and steel products being loaded at the Mumbai port to be shipped abroad. Most of the cargo ships in the ocean haul goods from one destination to another. What do we mean by trade in services? Services refer to economic transactions that involve the movement of something intangibles from one entity to another. For instance, shipping or transport is a service. If goods from France are being shipped by a foreign ocean-liner, the payment by the French entity to the shipping company for transport is counted as trade in services. Similarly, if you fly from New Delhi to Toronto by Air Canada, the payment for the flight is a service export from Canada to India. A hotel bill paid by an Argentinian tourist in Bangkok is a trade in services. If John Smith sitting in his home in Los Angles is learning Indian music over Zoom from a master in Hyderabad, and, paying the master through money transfer via banks or through credit card, it constitutes international trade in services.

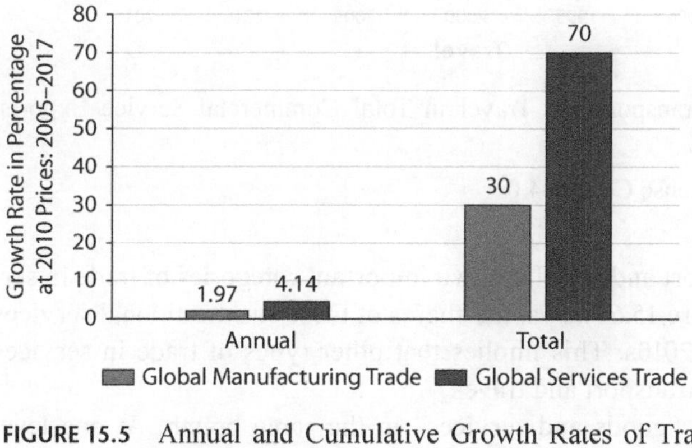

FIGURE 15.5 Annual and Cumulative Growth Rates of Trade in Manufacturing and Trade in Services

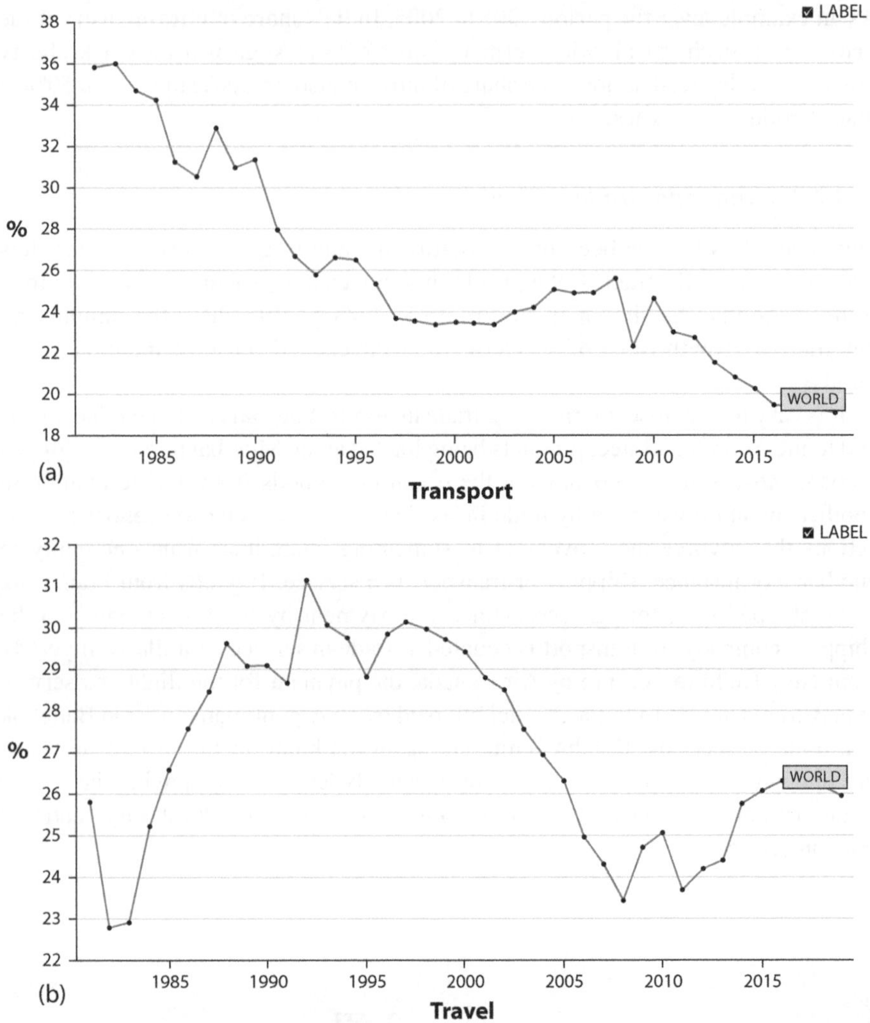

FIGURE 15.6 Share of Transport and Travel in Total Commercial Service Exports, 1982–2019.

Source: World Bank, License CC BY-4.0

Traditionally, transport and travel are two important categories of trade in services. However, as Figure 15.6 shows, the shares of these two traditional services declined in 2000s and 2010s. This implies that other types of trade in services have grown faster than transport and travel.

Economists mention "goods and services" in the same breath. At one level they are similar: they are demanded or consumed, depending on their own prices,

prices of substitutes or complements, income, tastes, etc. Own price along with technology and input prices govern the supply of goods or services. However, services are different from goods by nature. First, unlike durable goods (like TV or a car), there are no "durable services" in the sense that services cannot be stored. This implies that supply and consumption of services must occur at the same time: unlike goods, there cannot be an inventory of services; it does not make sense. Second, the provision of many services requires proximity between producers and consumers, which need not be the case for goods. Third, the service flow from a service has a jointness between a provider and a consumer. For instance, an insurance service depends on the insurance provider as well as the consumer. How far one can benefit from a health insurance policy issued by say Tata AIG depends on the habits of the insurance holder: e.g., whether he or she is a smoker or a heavy drinker.

Keeping some of these differences in mind, WTO classifies and views international trade in services in terms of four modes, the nomenclature of which was devised in the 1980s by Gary P. Sampson and Richard H. Snape.

Mode 1: Cross-Border: Only the service crosses an international border. There is no movement of people or machinery. Delivery of the service can take place, for example, through telecommunications (telephone, fax, television, internet, etc.), or the sending of documents, disks, tapes, etc. About 35% of trade in services are of this type.

Mode 2: Consumption Abroad: To avail a foreign service, a person must travel abroad. This would include international tourism, receiving medical treatment (also called "medical tourism"), moving to a foreign country for study, etc. This mode covers 10–15% of trade in services.

Mode 3: Commercial Presence: To provide service, the service provider must operate a branch abroad through foreign direct investment or FDI (we will study this later in this chapter). Examples are medical services provided by a foreign-owned hospital, and banking services supplied by a subsidiary of a foreign bank. This constitutes about 45–50% of all service trade.

Mode 4: Movement of Natural Persons: An architect moving abroad to supervise a construction work is an example. A prominent example of this mode of service delivery is Indian IT professionals sent by their parent companies in India to work abroad. About 1–2% of service trade falls into this category.

Which countries are the top exporters of services? These are listed in Figure 15.7 for the year 2019, where * denotes countries for which the reported data are preliminary. It may be a bit surprising to some of you that China figures as the sixth largest exporter of services, ahead of India. However, it is a big importer of services, which outweighs its exports. Thus, China is a net-deficit country in trade in

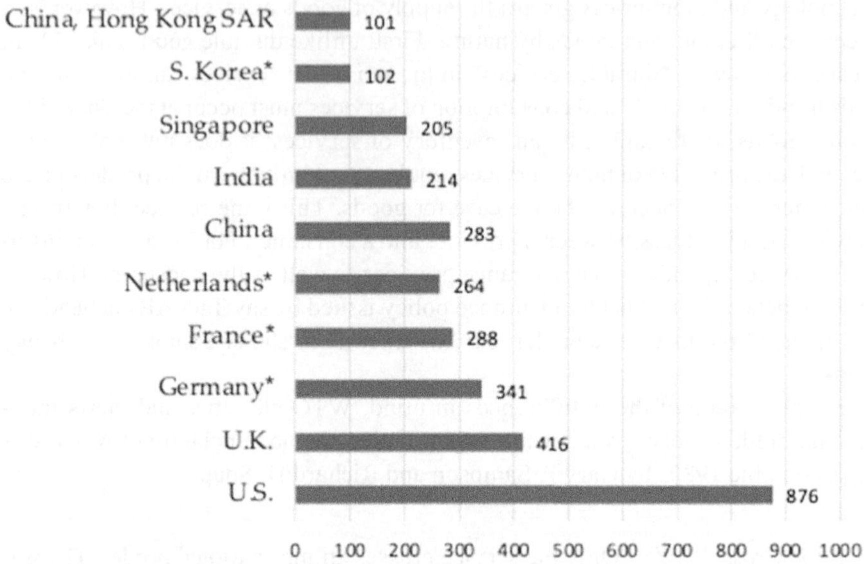

FIGURE 15.7 Top Ten Exporters of Services, 2019, in billions of $.
Source: UNCTAD, *2020 Handbook of Statistics*

services. In 2019, its exports of services minus its imports of service (service trade balance) were nearly a negative 217 billion dollars.[8]

15.2 International Fragmentation and Trade in Intermediates

Dramatic reductions in the cost of international communication have led to what is called **international fragmentation**: different parts of goods or a service are produced at or supplied from different international locations.

Consider iPhone. iPhone batteries are produced in Asia, mostly in China, software is written in India, and designs are made in the United States. Barbie dolls are an excellent example of international fragmentation. The toy design, moulds, and paints are done in the United States. Plastic and hair suppliers are from Taiwan and Japan. Cotton clothing comes from China. Final assembly is done in Indonesia, Malaysia, and China. Cambodians have digitised Harvard school papers (although English is not their first language). Many call centres, an important part of customer assistance for various products and services, are located in India.

Figure 15.8 depicts a concrete example of outsourcing/offshoring involved in the production of Boeing's 787 Dreamliner. Results from a survey reported in (Grant Thornton, 2014), where business leaders were asked: "Do you currently or have any plans to outsource business processes?," indicate that outsourcing is quite popular among business leaders.

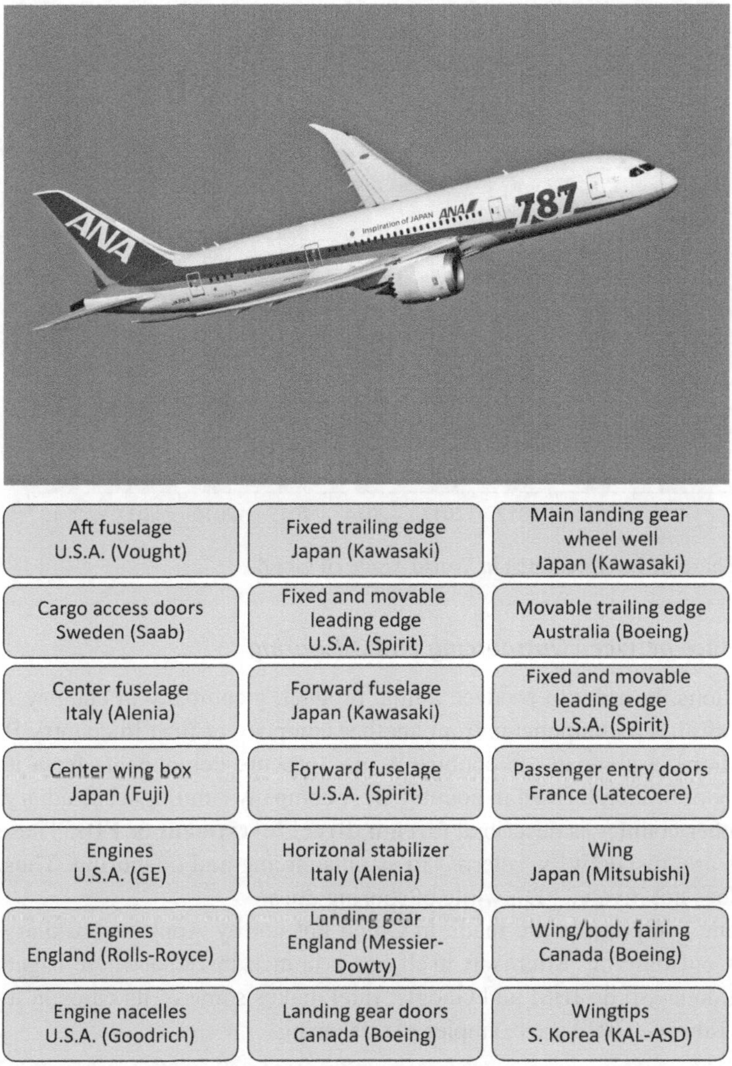

FIGURE 15.8 Production of Boeing 787 Dreamliner

Realise that fragmentation involves trade in intermediates used to produce both goods and services. *Indeed, the volume of trade in intermediates compares with that of final goods and services.* As data from WTO shows, international trade in intermediates constitute more than 40% of the total world trade in goods (see Figure 15.9). If we subtract trade in fuel products, the share of intermediates jumps to more than 50% of world trade in goods.

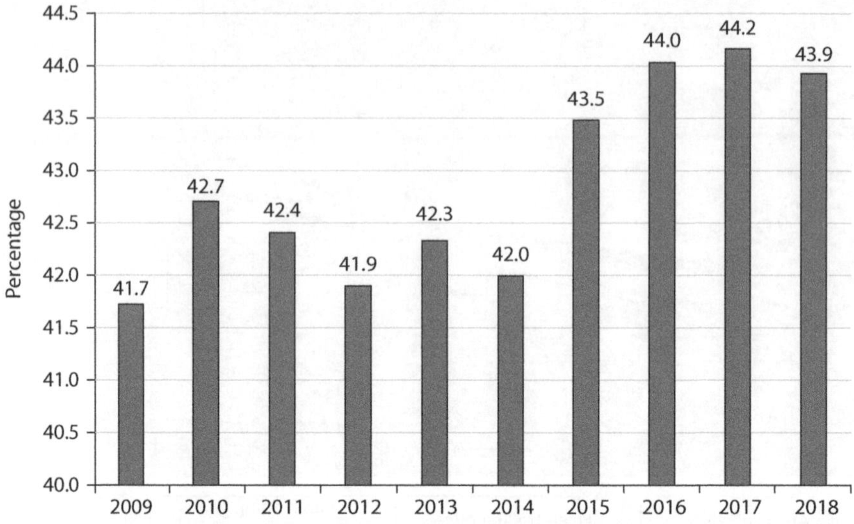

FIGURE 15.9 Share of Intermediates in World Trade of Goods

15.2.1 Difference between Outsourcing and Offshoring

In some situations, in order to produce a final product, a company in country A may import unfinished components from another company or firm in country B. In other situations, a company in country A may procure components from its own subsidiary or branch located in country B. A company running a subsidiary/branch in another country is described **foreign direct investment** or **FDI**. These two situations are, respectively, referred to as outsourcing and offshoring. Thus, outsourcing does not involve FDI, while offshoring does.

Some iPhone components are made in China but not by Apple's subsidiary. Hence, this is outsourcing. Microsoft itself has a branch in India where it gets programming done. So do IBM and Google. Intel makes some of its chips in its subsidiary in Taiwan. These are examples of offshoring.

15.2.2 Value Chain: Essential to Understand Outsourcing and Offshoring

A value chain refers to how the idea of a product first surfaces, how it is operationalised, and finally how it is ultimately sold in the market. A rudimentary value chain in an international context is presented in Figure 15.10. It begins with the concept and design of a product in the R&D stage. The next stage is the production of various components, which is followed by assembly. In a more elaborate value chain, packaging may be added after assembly. Next, the product is transported to various distribution centres or warehouses. Marketing and sales strategies are

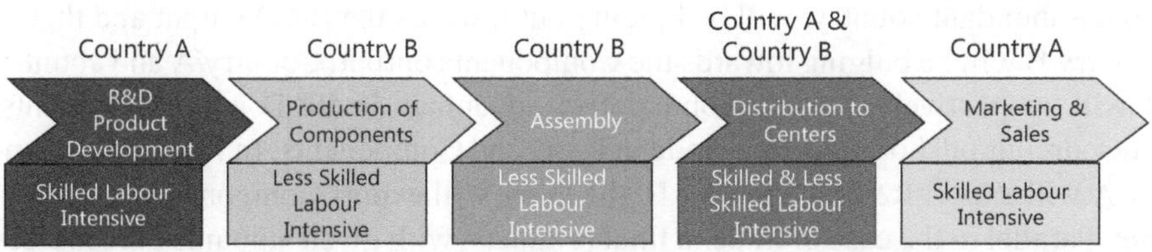

FIGURE 15.10 International Value Chain

then formulated. Retailing is the last stage, where the product reaches the consumers. One can add another task after sales, that is, after-sales services like online help or customer care services.

Which task is done where depends on cost consideration or comparative advantage. We can think in terms of the relative factor abundance theory and technology of different tasks. Suppose that in our two-country world economy model, country A and country B produce two intermediate activities, namely, R&D and Components, with the help of two factors of production, namely, high-skill labour and low-skill labour. Suppose that country A and country B, respectively, are relatively high-skill-labour-abundant and relatively low-skill-labour-abundant. Moreover, R&D is a high-skill-labour-intensive task, whereas Components is a low-skill-labour-intensive task. Assume that once both these intermediate goods are produced, they are combined without cost to produce one final good for consumption.

In the framework of the factor-endowment theory, we can think of the production possibility curve (PPC) of a country for the production of the two tasks: R&D and Components. They would look like the PPCs drawn in Figure 15.11,

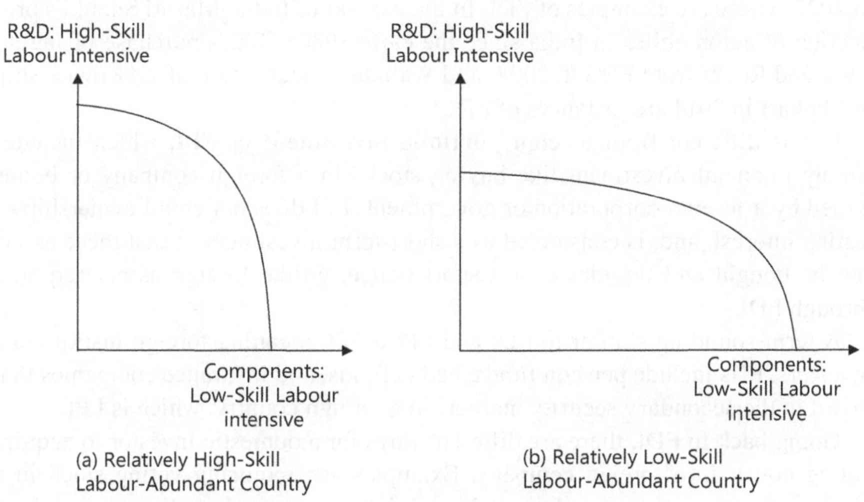

FIGURE 15.11 Comparative Advantages in Production Stages

which is similar to Figure 15.3. The PPC of country A, the relatively high-skill-labour-abundant country, will be bulging out towards the R&D output and that of country B will be bulging towards the Components output. Country A and country B will, respectively, possess comparative advantage in R&D and Components. Outsourcing/offshoring means trade in R&D and Components. In free trade, country A will export R&D to country B, the latter will export Components to the former. Parallel to the case of trade in final products, with given amounts of resources available, each country as a whole is able to "consume" the two tasks in its production so as to produce more of the final good, obtain greater utility, and be better off.

Equivalently, for both countries, the cost of producing the final good falls with trade in the tasks. Hence, *outsourcing/offshoring slices the value chain towards greater efficiency.*

15.3 Foreign Direct Investment (FDI)

A manager may have to be involved in not just exporting or importing products but also managing business abroad. Production of goods and services on a foreign soil comes under the rubric, **foreign direct investment** or **FDI**. FDI means *an investment by an individual or a company in a business located in another country, which involves ownership, control or "lasting interest."* A working definition of lasting interest is an ownership of at least 10% of voting in a business located abroad. This is not a hard definition, however.

Samsung of South Korea has foreign subsidiaries in the United States, United Kingdom, and other countries. Microsoft of the United States has subsidiary in Ontario, Canada, since 1985. Tesla, the leading electric car manufacturer in the United States started to build a plant in Germany 2019 and it was officially opened in 2022. These are examples of FDI. In the context of India, Maruti Suzuki's production of automobiles in India since the early 1980s, Tata's purchase of Jaguar and Land Rover from Ford in 2008, and Walmart's acquisition of 77% ownership of Flipkart in 2018 are instances of FDI.[9]

FDI is different from **foreign portfolio investment** or **FPI**, which includes simply financial investment like buying stocks in a foreign company or bonds issued by a foreign corporation or government. FPI does not entail ownership or lasting interest, and, is considered as a short-term investment in that these assets can be bought and liquidated in a short notice, unlike foreign assets acquired through FDI.

A term sounding similar to FDI and FPI is FII, meaning foreign institutional investors. FIIs include pension funds, hedge funds, and insurance companies that invest in the secondary security markets in a foreign country, which is FPI.

Going back to FDI, there are different ways for a domestic investor to acquire voting power in a foreign company. Examples are acquiring voting stock in a foreign company, merger and acquisition, joint venture, and starting a subsidiary.

FDI is the vehicle by which real capital, meaning machinery, plant, and technology (in a general sense), moves from one country to another.

15.3.1 Three Types of FDI

In relation to a foreign investor's main existing line of business, FDI can be classified into three types.

Horizontal FDI: Investing abroad in the same industry falls under horizontal FDI. Honda of Japan building a plant in the United Kingdom is an example.
Vertical FDI: This is where a party invests abroad in a product in a supply chain. As an example, Microsoft of the United States has a subsidiary in Hyderabad, India, since 1998, called Microsoft India Development Center, for conducting R&D.[10]
Conglomerate FDI: Conglomerate FDI is where an investment is made in a completely different industry. Virgin Group owned by Richard Branson of the United Kingdom went into clothing business in the late 1980s. It opened clothing stores in France, named Virgin clothing. This is an example of conglomerate FDI.[11]

Among the three categories, horizontal FDI is the most common.

15.3.2 Trends and Patterns

Not only international trade in goods, FDI in the world economy has grown over the decades up until the 2010s. FDI is a flow concept: how much of investment is "flowing" into a country or outside from a country within, say, a year. Typically, FDI is measured by "net inflow" or "net outflow." **FDI net inflows** include funds from abroad (i.e., foreign residents or companies) to build plants, hire people, etc., and to own domestic shares with a "lasting interest" plus reinvestment of earning from the past FDI minus repatriation of capital or profits from the venture and repayment of long-term loans. **FDI net outflow** is just the opposite: flow of funds from a source country to a foreign country to build machinery, etc. net of repatriation and loan repayments from abroad. Although highly unusual, FDI net inflow or net outflow can be negative. For example, the FDI net inflow into India was negative during the years 1975–1977. Figure 15.12 graphs the time-series of FDI net inflow for the global economy. We see that FDI has grown much more rapidly in the first two decades of the 21st century than in the late decades of the 20th century.

Table 15.4 records the top ten countries in terms of FDI inflow and outflow in 2021. Notice that the United States tops the list in both categories. It means that it is the most favourite destination for FDI and it is also the top-source country for FDI. For most nations, there is both outflow and inflow of FDI.

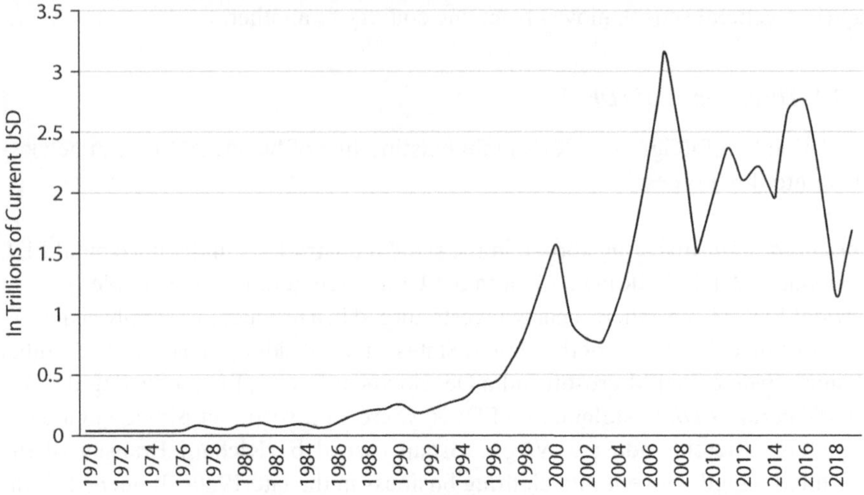

FIGURE 15.12 FDI Net Inflow: World, 1970–2019

TABLE 15.4 FDI Inflow and Outflow, Top 10 Countries, 2021 (Measured in US Dollars)

Rank	*FDI Inflow*	*FDI Outflow*
1	United States	United States
2	China (Mainland)	Germany
3	Hong Kong (China)	Japan
4	Singapore	China (Mainland)
5	Canada	U.K.
6	Brazil	Canada
7	India	Hong Kong (China)
8	South Africa	Russian Federation
9	Russian Federation	Ireland
10	Mexico	S. Korea

Source: World Investment Report 2022, World Bank

Just as two-way international trade, there are two-way FDIs in that FDI may flow into a sector in a country, say Germany, while FDI from Germany into a foreign country may occur in the same sector and even into the same country from where investment occurs in Germany. As an example, in the automobile sector, India's Tata owns Jaguar and Land Rover in the United States and the Ford Motor Company has a subsidiary in India, called Ford India, which produces and markets different models.

15.3.3 Is FDI Inflow Good or Bad for an Economy?

FDI—or for that matter international trade in products—is considered by some as a zero-sum game: if one party wins the other must lose. That is, foreign companies making profits, say in Nigeria must imply a loss for Nigeria. This is an inward-looking mindset and wrong. International trade and FDI are generally a positive-sum game. Both parties—the foreign firm or the multinational corporation (MNC) and the host country—gain, although the distribution of gains may be unequal.

Figure 15.13 depicts a "macro" situation where foreign capital competes with domestic capital in a perfectly competitive market. Let K denote the volume of domestic capital as a homogeneous factor of production for the national output and let MP_K denote its marginal physical product curve, drawn as a straight line for simplicity. Since the sum of the marginal product equals the total product (see Chapter 7), the national output (real GDP) is shown by the area under the MP_K line, equal to the trapezoid $0ABK$. Domestic capital stock being equal to 0K, the marginal product of capital is r_0; hence the total earnings to capital are equal to the rectangular area $0r_0$BK. This is the amount of the national output accruing to the domestic capital owners. The rest of the national output, equal to the triangle r_0AB goes to other factors of production like labour who work with capital to produce the national output. National output is same as the national income. Consider this as the initial situation.

Now suppose that the country allows FDI, i.e., foreign capital equal to KF. Assume that domestic and foreign capital are exactly alike, i.e., perfect substitutes,

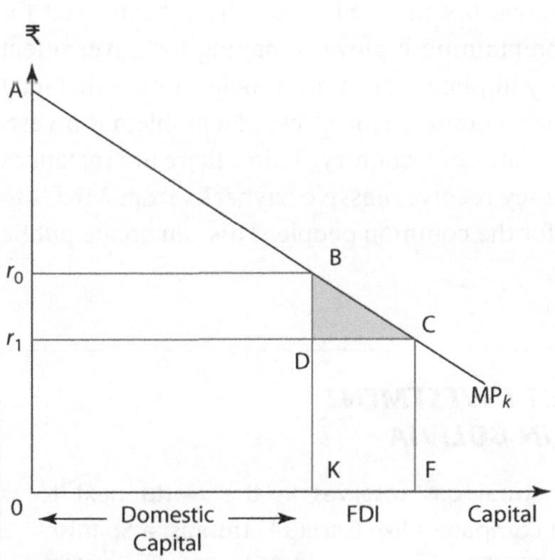

FIGURE 15.13 Gains from FDI

so that there is no quality or performance difference. With domestic and foreign capital working side by side the national output expands to the larger trapezoid 0ACF. Because there is more capital in the aggregate, the value of the capital's marginal product falls to r_1 by virtue of the law of diminishing returns. Both domestic and foreign capital get r_1 per unit of capital. However, foreign capital (= KF) is not owned by the residents of the host country. Therefore, their total earnings amounting to the rectangle KDCF must be subtracted from the total output to arrive at the national income. The host nation's national income is equal to 0ACF − KDCF = 0ACDK. Comparing this with the original level of national income, 0ABK, we see that there is a net national income gain from FDI, measured by the triangle BCD. This is called a **deadweight gain**, accruing to the host country. This gain arises because of diminishing returns to capital: the fall in the real reward to capital (from r_0 to r_1) is equivalent to a fall in the price of imports. FDI inflow is like the import of capital.

Appendix 15.B shows that there are gains from FDI inflow when the foreign firm has monopoly power.

Consider alternative environments. Suppose the product produced by the MNC is not sold in the host country. Then consumer surplus for the host country is zero and there is zero gain for the host country, *not* negative. Even when the product is sold in countries outside of the host country, as long as the MNC hires some of the domestic factors that were previously unemployed or employed at very low wages, their earnings from employment in the MNC minus their opportunity costs constitute gain to the host country in terms of "gainful employment."

However, nothing in the world is perfect. We do not claim that things are always hunky-dory with FDI inflow. First, to attract foreign investment, foreign companies are sometimes lured with tax breaks (**called tax holidays**) for a few years by the host governments. The foregone tax proceeds could have been used for other purposes like building and maintaining highways, paying for government employees, etc. Second, an MNC may implicitly promote a social culture that may be at odds with social norms of the host country. This is less of a problem if investments come from non-resident expatriates of a country. Third, there are instances where political leaders and bureaucracy receive massive paybacks from MNCs to the extent that there is little benefit for the common people. This can create public discontent. See Box 15.3.

BOX 15.3 FOREIGN DIRECT INVESTMENT AND PUBLIC DISCONTENT IN BOLIVIA

Bolivia has the second-largest natural gas reserves in the world next to Venezuela. In early 2000s, foreign companies like Brazil's Petrobras, a Spanish-Argentine company named Respol YPF along with British Petroleum, US's Exxon, and France's Total were the extractors. While investment and extraction in the natural gas and export earnings from this sector increased dramatically, the gains didn't trickle down to the common mass.

While Bolivia's export earnings from the hydrocarbon sector, which consists mostly of natural gas, was growing rapidly in the early 2000s, the same period witnessed an increase in the poverty rate from 63% in 1999 to 68% in 2003 (O'Hare & Rivas, 2007). This had severe political repercussions. Four presidents traded the office in a span of five years, culminating with Evo Morales elected as the President in 2005, who took drastic steps of increasing the share of the State in the extractive industries and moved to a left-oriented policy regime.

Evo Morales remained in power till 2019, when he stepped down under severe protests against his grip on power while undermining democracy. After remaining in exile in Mexico for about a year, he returned to Bolivia in 2020 as his left-wing party got elected. But he is not the president.

However, FDI inflow is generally beneficial to the host country. Advanced economies have no inhibitions against MNCs. In smaller or less advanced economies, if MNCs are welcomed and provided conducive business opportunities without much interference, both legal and illegal, by the country's political system and bureaucracy and they are sensitised on local culture, enormous benefits can be harnessed. Just as international trade, FDI inflow can strongly contribute to an economy's growth.

Facts and Insights

- Opposition to free international exchange of goods and service, especially importing of goods and services, stems from two arguments: importing is anti-national and risky.
- Economic self-sufficiency in terms of unduly restricting international exchange is not a virtue.
- The world economy witnessed the first "rising wave" or the first golden age of international trade in the early 20th century when trains, motor vehicles, and ships became common modes of domestic and international transport.
- The period after 1950 may be called the second golden age of international trade. There are two factors behind the second golden age of trade: (a) realisation by the advanced countries like the United States, United Kingdom, France, etc. that restrictive trade policies hamper economic growth and (b) invention of container shipping.
- The third golden age of international trade started in the 1990s when international trade in services began to expand dramatically—thanks to information-technology revolution, particularly the internet.

- World Trade Organization is a powerful multilateral governing body on international trade, which oversees the implementation of about 60 agreements reached by member countries that cover trade in goods, trade in services, intellectual property rights, trade-related investment measures, and a whole lot more. It also has a time-bound dispute settlement process, which accepts complaints by member countries against possible violations or discriminations in international trade by other member countries. Unlike the United Nations, no country possesses any veto power.
- International trade allows more exchange possibilities—and this is the source of gains from trade for each trading country.
- Comparative advantage, not absolute advantage, is a powerful predictor of which types of goods are exported by which countries. It means the ability to produce and sell a product relatively cheaper compared to some other product or products.
- Comparative-advantage basis of international trade implies that a country would export a product, in whose production it has comparative advantage vis-à-vis its trading partner.
- Comparative advantage highlights exploiting sources of dissimilarities for mutual benefit.
- In the Ricardian model, a country has comparative advantage in the good in the production of which the relative labour productivity is greater.
- Each country exports the product in which it has comparative advantage.
- Ricardo's theory of comparative advantage and trade emphasises labour productivity as an important source of comparative advantage and exportability of a product.
- In many countries, productivity and real wages are positively correlated.
- Free international trade tends to integrate national markets and equalise prices of same products across countries by virtue of arbitrage.
- Beside labour productivity or more generally technology differences, comparative advantage stems of differences in relative factor endowments of trading countries. This is called the relative factor abundance model/theory or Heckscher–Ohlin model/theory of international trade. In this view of the world, a country will have comparative advantage in and be a net exporter of the product which uses its abundant factor more intensively.
- According to the Heckscher–Ohlin theory, if free trade is allowed by a relatively labour-abundant country and a relatively capital-abundant country, the former will export labour-intensive goods and the latter will export capital-intensive goods. Furthermore, labour will be benefit and capital will lose in the relatively labour-abundant country and just the opposite will happen in the relatively capital-abundant country.
- There are two types of product differentiation: horizontal and vertical. Horizontal product differentiation refers to the same basic product with the same quality but with differences in style, colour, design, etc. Vertical product differentiation relates to quality differences.

- There are non-comparative-advantage bases of mutually beneficial international trade. That is, trading countries can benefit from trade even if neither has any comparative advantage in producing a good. Such gains are due to accessing more differentiated products available in the international market, exploiting internal scale economies and higher oligopoly competition in the presence of market access by foreign firms.
- In addition to static gains from trade, referring to a nation's gain in purchasing power due to resource allocation and greater consumption possibilities, there are dynamic gains from trade in terms of trade in important intermediate products and in terms of knowledge and exposure gained with respect to technology, marketing, etc. because of being a part of the international network of exchange. These gains contribute to the growth of economies.
- Inter-industry trade refers to a country exporting and importing different goods, whereas intra-industry trade refers to exporting and importing of same goods. Both types of trade coexist side by side.
- Since the 1990s, international trade in services has grown more rapidly than that in goods.
- The share of transport and travel in total commercial trade in services has decreased over the recent decades.
- WTO classifies and views trade in services in terms of four modes of international movement of services, the nomenclature of which was devised in the 1980s by Gary P. Sampson and Richard H. Snape. These are (i) Mode 1: cross-border, (ii) Mode 2: consumption abroad, (iii) Mode 3: commercial presence; and (iv) Mode 4: movement of natural persons.
- Nearly half of all trade in services occurs through Mode 3.
- The United States and United Kingdom are the top exporters of services in terms of their valuation. Although China is a major exporter or services, it is a *net* importer of services, i.e., its import of services exceeds its export of services.
- Dramatic reductions in the cost of international communication have led to international fragmentation: different parts of goods or a service are produced at or supplied from different international locations.
- International fragmentation involves trade in intermediate goods. Indeed, the volume of trade in intermediates compares with that of final goods and services.
- International fragmentation occurs through outsourcing and offshoring, where the former refers to trade in intermediates with outside parties and does not involve foreign ownership or direct foreign investment (FDI), while the latter involves FDI and trade with own subsidiaries or foreign branches.
- The pattern of outsourcing/offshoring can be viewed in terms of value chain and comparative advantage. Outsourcing/offshoring slices the value chain towards greater efficiency.
- FDI is an investment by an individual or a company in a business located in another country, which involves ownership, control, or lasting interest. A

working definition of lasting interest is an ownership of at least 10% of voting in a business located abroad.

- FDI is different from foreign portfolio investment or FPI, which includes simply financial investment such as buying stocks in a foreign company or bonds issued by a foreign corporation or government. FPI does not entail ownership or lasting interest. It is considered as short-term investment in that these assets can be bought and liquidated in a short notice, unlike foreign assets acquired by FDI.
- The term FII stands for foreign institutional investors. FIIs include pension funds, hedge funds, and insurance companies that invest in the secondary security markets in a foreign country, which is FPI.
- There are three types of FDI: horizontal, vertical, and conglomerate. Horizonal FDI is the most common of the three.
- FDI has grown much more rapidly in the first two decades of the 21st century than in the late decades of the 20th century.
- Many countries experience both FDI inflow and FDI outflow at the same time.
- Countries like the United States and China rank high in terms of FDI inflow and FDI outflow.
- Typically, FDI is mutually beneficial to the source and the host country, i.e., it is positive-sum game, although the distribution of gains may be unequal.
- To attract FDI, host countries offer tax holidays in some instances.
- The presence of FDI may lead to cultural conflicts. If corruption and kickbacks are associated with foreign companies on a country's soil, it can create resentment.
- The negative outcomes of FDI are not necessary, however.
- Just as international trade, FDI can be growth-enhancing.

Exercises

Descriptive/Analytical

15.1 What are the fears that we normally espouse against foreign trade in general and imports in particular? How far can these be justified based on principles of economics?

15.2 Identify those hurdles which arise in the smooth conduct of international trade which are normally absent in interregional and interpersonal trade.

15.3 "If two countries are identical, there are no gains from international trade between them." Defend or refute.

15.4 After nearly four decades of growing co-operation in international trade, why are so many countries looking "inwards" and putting barriers to free trade in recent years?

15.5 Imagine a world without any barriers to the free movement of products, services, capital, and labour. Give a panoramic view of such a world.

15.6 "Foreign outsourcing of services from the United States to India is good for India and bad for the United States." Defend or refute with reasons.

Short Answer (word limit = 500 approx.)

15.7 Distinguish between absolute and comparative advantage with suitable examples.

15.8 Identify five labour-abundant countries and five labour-intensive commodities. State the basis on which you identified these countries and commodities.

15.9 Give ten (hypothetical) examples of trade in services, which are outside of the text.

15.10 Write a short note on four modes in which international movement of services takes place with suitable examples (out of the text).

15.11 What is outsourcing? Comment on its growing use in manufacturing with suitable examples.

15.12 Distinguish between foreign direct investment (FDI) and foreign portfolio investment (FPI) with suitable examples.

15.13 Give two actual examples of conglomerate FDI in the global economy outside of the text.

Quizzes/Numerical

15.14 Using World Bank's Comtrade data available for free, list the top five trading partners of Germany and India for the year 2020.

15.15 As a student of management, you must be aware of 5-point, 7-point, and 10-point scale. On a 10-point scale (10 means most efficient/skilful), the medical skills and culinary skills (cooking) of Dr. Das and her maid, Geeta, are given in the side table.

	Dr. Das	Geeta
Medical Skills	9	1
Culinary Skills	5	4

Clearly Dr. Das is a better medical person and a better cook than Geeta. Does it mean that Dr. Das should do both the medical practice and cooking and Geeta should do "nothing" in their 8-hour work schedule every day?

15.16 Suppose labour hours (L) is the only input required to produce two goods, grapes and bananas, and the quality of labour hours is uniform. Given below is the number of L required to produce one tonne grapes and one tonne bananas of identical quality in two countries, Brazil and Peru. Answer the following questions.

	Grapes	Bananas
Brazil	80	40
Peru	120	50

a) Which country has absolute advantage in the production of which commodity over the other?

b) Which country has comparative advantage over the other in which commodity?

c) How can trade be mutually beneficial between Brazil and Peru, assuming there are no transport costs and trade barriers?

d) What, if due to some technological improvements, the labour hours (L) required to produce one tonne of grapes in Peru reduce from 120 to 100 labour hours, *ceteris paribus*?

15.17 Like most others in your peer group, you invariably use products of international brands like Adidas (Germany), Nike (US) and Levis (US). Go to nearby multi-brand showroom or mall and check the products of these brands for the countries where they were made like "Made in Germany," "Made in US," "Made in Italy," etc.) Describe your experience.

15.18 Country X produces two goods: C (computers) and S (shoes). The labour coefficients are 4 and 2, respectively, for sector C and sector S. Starting from autarky, suppose this economy engages itself in free trade with the rest of the world and the international relative price of good C in terms of good S is $P_C / P_S = 3$. Which good will X export and why?

	India	Foreign
Labour	80	40
Capital	120	50

15.19 Consider the Heckscher–Ohlin theory of international trade. Suppose there are two countries, India and a Foreign country. Each country can produce two goods: C (computers) and S (shoes). The technologies are the same between the two countries for either of the two products, and the production of shoes is relatively more labour-intensive, compared to that of computers. The respective factor endowments are given in the side table. Which country will export which goods and why?

15.20 Construct a numerical example of your own to show that in the presence of increasing returns to scale, international trade and specialisation can lead to increase in consumption, even if there is no basis of comparative advantage for any trading country.

15.21 (This is hypothetical.) Tests show that Richard Stokes, who lives in the United States, needs two stents for his partly clogged arteries to the heart. He does not have any insurance and the procedure including hospital stay will cost him $30,000 in the United States. He finds out that the Apollo Hospital in New Delhi will do the same for him along with an additional stay in the hospital for a week after the procedure for recuperation and a free trip to Taj Mahal (prior to the medical procedure), all for $10,000. He pays this amount to Apollo in advance through his credit card. Searching over Yatra.com, he books an onward ticket with Air India (Chicago to New Delhi, direct) for $800 and a return ticket with United Airlines (New Delhi to Chicago, direct) for $850. While in India, he spends $2,000 on food, buys $8,000 worth of jewellery for his fiancé, and buys and ships a Kashmiri carpet costing $6,000 to his home in Chicago. There are altogether six transactions. Which ones of these transactions count towards international trade in services and why?

Appendix 15.A Real Wage and Productivity Growth in India

Jain (2019) studies the wage and productivity in Indian manufacturing during the period 2000–2001 to 2015. The positive relationship between wage and productivity holds in terms of their respective growth rates (see Figure 15.14).

Appendix 15.B Gains from FDI Inflow When the Foreign Firm Has Monopoly Power

To see this, we employ the "monopoly picture" from Chapter 10. Figure 15.15 depicts the equilibrium. The foreign monopoly produces output y_m where $MR = MC$ and charges the price p_m. Assume, for now, that the product is sold

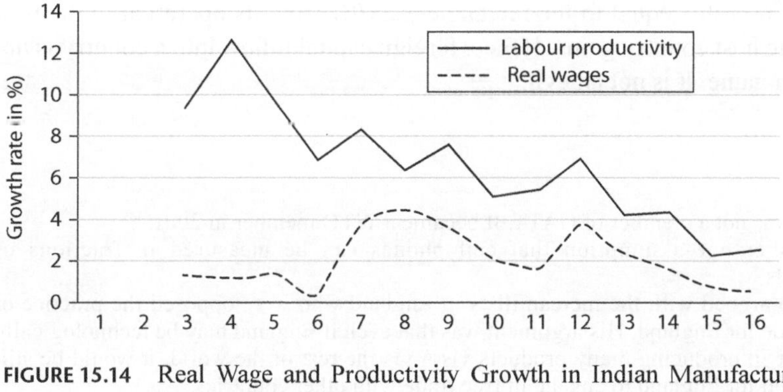

FIGURE 15.14 Real Wage and Productivity Growth in Indian Manufacturing, 2000–2001 to 2015–2016.

Adopted from Figure 2 of Jain (2019), these are 3-year moving average of growth rates. The horizonal axis measures the years from 2003–2004 to 2015–2016. Originally published in *Margin: The Journal of Applied Economic Research*, Vol. 13 Issue 1. Copyright National Council of Applied Economic Research, New Delhi © 2019. All rights reserved. Reproduced with the permission of the copyright holders and the publishers, SAGE Publications India Pvt. Ltd, New Delhi.

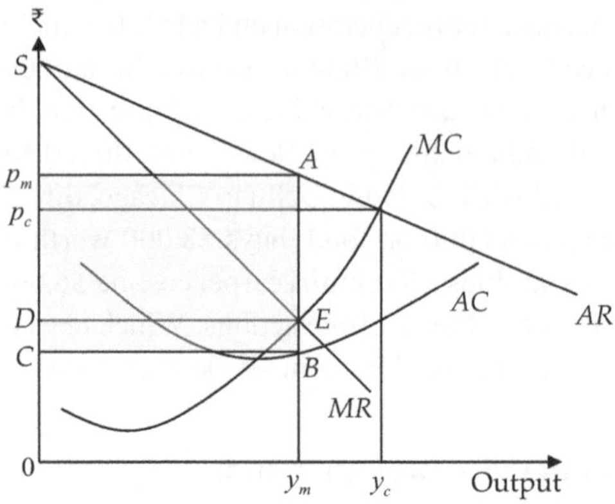

FIGURE 15.15 Foreign Monopoly

entirely in the host country and all factors of production also belong to the host country, which are fully employed so that the *MC* measures their competitive opportunity cost.

The measure of social welfare developed in Chapter 9—equal to the sum of consumer surplus and producer surplus—is applicable here, except that profits do *not* belong to the host country. Hence, the host country's social welfare is simply equal to the consumer surplus. In Figure 15.15, the consumer surplus equals the triangle above the price line p_mA, i.e., p_mSA. This is the gain to the host country from foreign investment. The point is that even though the foreign firm obtains its abnormal profits equal to the rectangle p_mABC from its operation in the host country, the host country gains. Hence, foreign capital inflow into a country is *not* a zero-sum game. It is not an evil.

Notes

1 China was not a member of GATT. It became a WTO member in 2001.
2 Remember our assumption that cell phones can be measured in fractions or decimals.
3 Ricardo argued with the mercantilists in England who were opposed the practice of free trade for England. His argument was that even if England may be technologically superior in producing many products vis-à-vis the rest of the world, it would be still beneficial for England to engage in free trade with other countries.
4 There are no later publications of such charts by the US Bureau of Labor Statistics.
5 This is adopted from McKinsey and Comany (2012) and Krugman et al. (2015).
6 This is known as the Stolper–Samuelson theorem, discovered around the time of World War II.
7 As some of you might know, the assembly-line production started in the early 20th century at the Ford Motor Company, USA.
8 Let us not forget that China is the top country in terms of being an exporter of goods.

9 Reinvesting profits from overseas operations, as well as intra-company loans to foreign subsidiaries are also considered foreign direct investments.
10 Microsoft's main R&D centre is in Redmond in the state of Washington in the United States.
11 In 2013 it filed for bankruptcy in France.

Bibliography

Aggarwal, S., & Chakraborty, D. (2022). Which factors influence India's intra-industry trade? Empirical findings for selected sectors. *Global Business Review*, 23(3), 729–755. https://doi.org/10.1177/0972150919868343

Grant Thornton. (2014). Outsourcing: Driving efficiency and growth (International Business Report 2014). Grant Thornton International Ltd.

Inamdar, N. (2020, June 25). Can India afford to boycott Chinese products? *BBC News*. Retrieved May 30, 2021, from https://www.bbc.com/news/world-asia-india-53150898

Jain, H. (2019). Wage–productivity relationship in Indian manufacturing industries: Evidences from state-level panel data. *Margin – The Journal of Applied Economic Research*, *33*(3), 277–305.

Krugman, P. R., Obstfeld, M., & Melitz, M. (2015). *International trade: Theory and policy* (10th ed.). Pearson.

McKinsey and Company. (2012). *Bangladesh's ready-made garments industry: The challenge of growth* (U. No. Monthly Bulletin of Statistics). McKinsey and Company.

Michaels, D., & Sanders, P. (2009, October 8). Dreamliner production gets closer monitoring. *Wall Street Journal*.

O'Hare, G., & Rivas, S. (2007). Changing poverty distribution in Bolivia: The role of rural–urban migration and urban services. *GeoJournal*, *68*, 307–326.

Sachitanand, R., & Goyal, M. (2016, October 30). Why the threat of a boycott of Chinese products is more bark than bite. *The Economic Times*.

U.S. Bureau of Labor Statistics. (2012, September). *Edition: Charting international labor comparisons*. U.S. Department of Labor.

GENERAL APPENDIX

In economics we consider a consumer, who wants to maximise her satisfaction or utility, subject to her budget constraint. We also consider a producer who wants to minimise the total cost of producing a given amount and maximise profits. Mathematically, these examples refer to maximising or minimising a mathematical function.

A.1 Single-Variable Case

Consider the simplest case of y being a continuous and twice-differentiable function of a single variable x, i.e., $y = f(x)$, where f is a continuous function and the derivatives f' and f'' exist. Suppose that x can vary between two real numbers, a and b. Figure A.1(a) illustrates the case where a function f is maximised in the interval $[a, b]$. Notice that, (i) at the point where $f(x)$ is maximised, i.e., at x_0, the slope of the function is zero and (ii) around x_0, the slope declines gradually (from being positive to zero and from zero to negative), as x increases. Thus, the conditions for the maximisation of $f(x)$ are that:

$$f'(x) = 0 \tag{A.1}$$

$$f''(x) < 0. \tag{A.2}$$

Figure A.1(b) illustrates the case where a function $f(x)$ is minimised at x_1. Notice that at this point the slope of the function is zero, and, around x_1, the slope

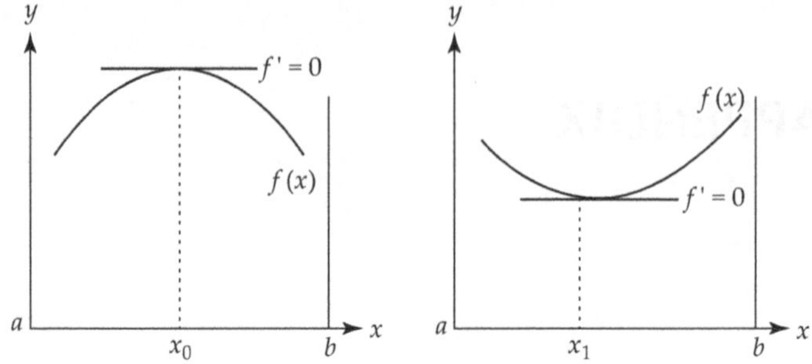

(a) Maximisation

(b) Minimisation

FIGURE A.1 Maximisation and Minimisation of a Function

increases (from being negative to zero and from zero to positive), as x increases. Thus, the minimisation conditions are that:

$$f'(x) = 0 \tag{A.3}$$

$$f''(x) > 0. \tag{A.4}$$

Equations such as (A.1) and (A.3) are called the **first-order condition**. Thus, we see that the first-order condition of maximisation or minimisation of a function is the same, namely, $f'(x) = 0$. Inequalities like (A.2) and (A.4) are called the **second-order conditions**, which, of course, differ between maximisation and minimisation of a function.

A.2 Many-Variables Case

We consider here the first-order condition only. Suppose y is a function of many variables: $x_1, x_2, x_3, \ldots. x_n$. It is maximised with respect to all n variables and the maximum occurs in the interior of the intervals to which $x_1, x_2, x_3, \ldots$ and x_n, respectively, belong. Then the first-order conditions are generalizations of (A.1), i.e., each partial is equal to zero:

$$\frac{\partial f}{\partial x_1} = 0, \quad \frac{\partial f}{\partial x_2} = 0, \quad \ldots\ldots.., \quad \frac{\partial f}{\partial x_n} = 0 \tag{A.5}$$

These are also the first-order conditions of a minimisation problem, i.e., if the function $y = f(x_1, \ldots. x_n)$ is minimised with respect to $x_1, x_2, x_3, \ldots$ and x_n.

A.3 Constrained Optimisation

In microeconomics, we consider situations where a function $y = f(x_1,....x_n)$is maximised or minimised, subject to a constraint: $g(x_1,....x_n) = 0$. What are the first-order conditions? We introduce a function called the Lagrangean, defined as

$$L = f\left(x_1, x_2, \ldots, x_n\right) + l \cdot g\left(x_1, x_2, \ldots, x_n\right),$$

where l is an "extra" variable, called the Lagrangean multiplier. We have $L = L\left(x_1, x_2, \ldots, x_n, l\right)$. Assuming interior solution once again, the first-order conditions are:

$$\frac{\partial L}{\partial x_1} = \frac{\partial f}{\partial x_1} + \lambda \frac{\partial g}{\partial x_1} = 0, \text{ or } \frac{\partial f / \partial x_1}{\partial g / \partial x_1} = \lambda \tag{A.6}$$

....

$$\frac{\partial L}{\partial x_n} = \frac{\partial f}{\partial x_n} + \lambda \frac{\partial g}{\partial x_n} = 0, \text{ or } \frac{\partial f / \partial x_n}{\partial g / \partial x_n} = \lambda \tag{A.7}$$

$$\frac{\partial L}{\partial \lambda} = g(x_1, x_2, ..., x_n) = 0. \tag{A.8}$$

We can eliminate λ from the above equations and obtain,

$$\frac{\partial f / \partial x_1}{\partial g / \partial x_1} = \frac{\partial f / \partial x_2}{\partial g / \partial x_2} ...... = \frac{\partial f / \partial x_n}{\partial g / \partial x_n}, \tag{A.9}$$

which are the first-order conditions of constrained optimisation.

Equations (A.9) are the first-order conditions without the Lagrangian multiplier yet equivalent to (A.6) to (A.8).

PARTIAL ANSWERS TO SELECT QUESTIONS

Chapter 1

1.2 (Hint) New PPC will start from the same point on the axis on which you have taken wheat and end up to the right of the original PPC on the axis on which you have taken computers. You need to argue why such a shift occurs.

1.8 It is a "positive" question—because it is not concerned with whether associating with WTO is good or bad for the agricultural sector.

1.10 Refute.

1.11 It will shift out to the right.

1.12 Bribe giving: benefit—time and trouble saved; cost—amount of bribe.

1.15 Providing more jobs increases the salary burden of the government for which it has to either increase taxes and/or to reduce its expenditure on health, education defence, building infrastructure, etc. These are constraints.

1.18 c)

1.19 Maximum number of plates of *chaat* = 100. If 100 plates of *chaat* are offered, then *gol gappas* serving = 0. Maximum number of *gol gappas* serving = 300. If 300 *gol gappas* are served, the *chaat* plates served = 0. You have two extreme points of the axes. Make a few combinations and then draw *PPC*.

1.20 Inverse relationship; as x increases, y decreases.

1.21 Direct or increasing relationship.

1.22 (A) horizontal straight line, (B) vertical straight line.

1.23 Recall your understanding of linear and quadratic functions.

1.24 In reality, no country is purely socialist or purely capitalist. These are extreme/theoretical situations. All countries will fall within these extremes. You can place countries like the United States and the United Kingdom somewhere near purely capitalist which means that economic management in these countries is largely left to market forces. Similarly, you can put a country like China on the left-hand side of the scale and interpret accordingly.

Chapter 2

2.4 Market demand and market supply curves are based on different factors, although they work in unison to determine the market price. Hence, we refute. The market demand curve depends on the number of demanders, their preferences, income, prices of related goods in consumption, while the market supply curve depends on prices of related goods in production, technology, business taxes, etc.

2.7 Equilibrium price may increase, decrease, or remain the same, while the equilibrium quantity transacted will increase.

2.9 Your demand for petrol will increase today. It is because it will save you some money compared to if you decide to fill in your tank later.

2.10 There will be an expectation that land price will increase in the near future. This will increase or shift out the current demand curve for land.

2.14 This will shift in the supply curve since an increase in tax increases the cost of compliance with laws. The new equilibrium price will be higher, and less quantity will be sold.

2.16 This will shift the aggregate supply curve to the right. Equilibrium price will decline. As long as the individual domestic firms are small, their supply curves will not be affected. But, since the equilibrium price is less, they will have to come down on their supply curves and be able to sell less.

2.18 Both goods are not normal. Seeing movies is a normal good, while eating-out in MacDoland's is an inferior good.

2.21 No; the opposite is true.

2.22 His supply curve will be a vertical straight line.

2.23 Defend.

2.24. (a) Price = 30, Quantity = 40; (b) Quantity demanded will be zero. No quantity will be sold.

2.26 In the first case (reducing price) it will be a movement along the same demand curve while in the other case (additional advertisement) it will be the outward shift of the demand curve.

Chapter 3

3.4 Gupta's family's demand for petrol is elastic (i.e., the price elasticity is greater than one).

3.11 In a market segment, where elasticity of demand of your service/product is high, you should keep the price low and sell more; where in case of low elasticity of demand, keep the price high, and sales volume low.

3.12 Hint: look at the nature of commodities.

3.13 In short run, due to highly inelastic demand, such an artist can manage to get very high fee, but in medium and long term, he runs the risk of pricing himself out as alternatives/substitutes emerge in due course.

3.14 6/14.

3.15 Price elasticity of demand is greater than one (Recall that when price and total revenue move in opposite direction, the elasticity of demand is greater than one and vice versa).

3.16 Inelastic.

3.17 3%.

3.18 1/3 or 33.33%.

3.19 (a) (i) 40, (ii) 20, (iii) 0; (b) (i) between 20 and 40 (ii) between 20 and 40.

Chapter 4

4.3 Inferior good is one for which the income effect is negative, i.e., all else the same, the higher the income the less is the quantity demanded. Giffen goods are that subset of inferior goods for which this perverse income is so strong that it outweighs the substitution effect, so that for such goods an increase in price leads to a higher quantity demanded, i.e., the law of demand does not hold.

4.6 It refers to the price ratio between two products. If a movie ticket is for $10 and a chicken sandwich sells for $6, the relative price of movie ticket vis-à-vis chicken sandwich is 5/4 and the relative price of chicken sandwich in terms of movie ticket is 4/5.

4.13 Disagree. The marginal utility theory assumes that the marginal utility of money (a unit of currency) is given. Hence there is no income effect. It only considers the substitution effect of a change in price.

4.14 The marginal utility schedule in terms of dollar or money is the following.

Minutes of call	MU in dollars
0	–
1	50/96 = 0.52
2	45/96 = 0.47
3	40/96 = 0.42
4	35/96 = 0.36
5	30/96 = 0.31
6	25/96 = 0.26
7	20/96 = 0.21
8	15/96 = 0.16

Since the price is $0.25, the answer is 6 minutes.

4.15 This family should consume more carrot halwa, because the marginal utility (from consuming 3.5 kg of this good) in terms of rupees = 100/2 = ₹50, which is greater than the price (₹40).

4.16 5 chicken rolls and 4 ice creams. You have to work out the details.

4.17 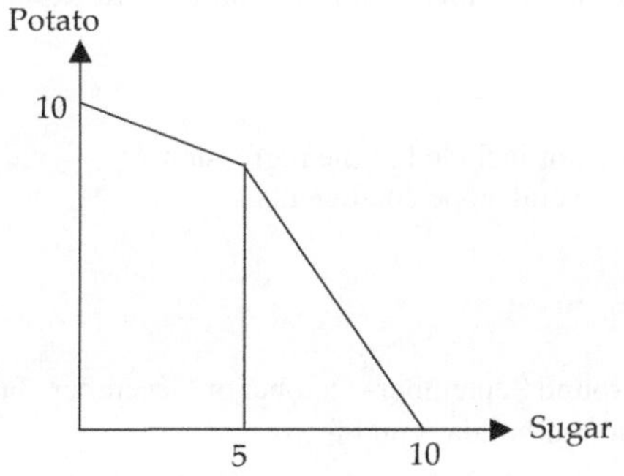

Chapter 5

5.4 She should prefer cash (according to the theory).

5.5 Both lead to parallel shifts, but the former shifts the budget line to the right, whereas the latter shifts it to the left.

5.9 At a private level, a gift in cash may be felt as impersonal. Many subsidy programmes for the poor are in kind, because a cash subsidy may be "misused" in terms of buying goods that are not essential, spending on hard drinks, illegal drugs, etc.

5.12

$$\left(\frac{224}{200}-1\right)\times 100 = 12$$

5.21 The consumer will prefer the indirect tax programme.

5.22 It will look as follows. The slope = 1.1.

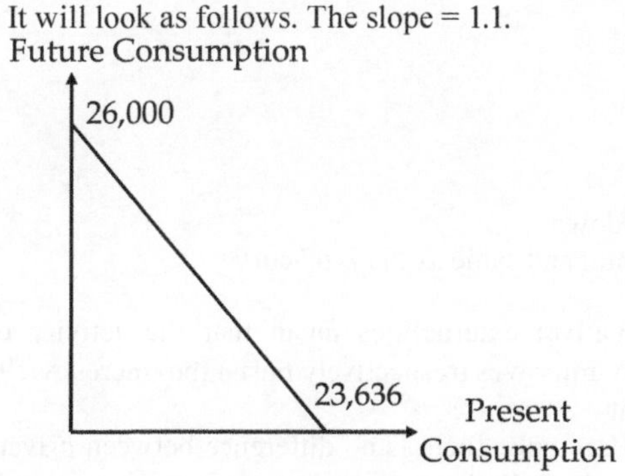

5.25 (a) No change in current demand, (b) Reduce.

Chapter 6

6.3 Refute. It is because the equation can still be linear in the coefficients, e.g., a log-linear equation. Try to find another example. You have to expand this answer.

6.10 The slope coefficient.

6.11 No, it can be a Giffen good.

6.13 It is the effect of (other) factors not included in the regression.

6.15 One intercept coefficient and several slope coefficients.

6.16 A positive sign.

6.21 It will be negatively sloped.

6.23
$$-0.3\times 5+1.5\times 6=7.5\%$$

6.24 In every year the sales peak around September–October or December–January because of the concentration of holidays and festivals.

Chapter 7

7.5 It is increasing, constant, or decreasing returns to scale according as $\alpha+\beta>1$, $\alpha+\beta=1$, or $\alpha+\beta<1$.

7.7 It is because of diminishing marginal returns.

7.17 Disagree. In the private sector, if a firm incurs losses consistently, it either goes out of business, or it must massively restructure itself on an urgent basis. Neither holds for a public sector firm.

7.21 Diminishing marginal returns.

7.23 The marginal product is positive.

7.38 *TFC* = 10. The *MC* schedule is as follows:

Output	*MC* ($)
0	–
1	15
2	10
3	8
4	11
5	15
6	22
7	30
8	40

7.39 It shifts these curves up.

7.40 It shifts these cost curves down.

7.43 The *LMC* curve is horizontal and same as the *LAC* curve.

7.45 Defend.

7.46 Positive (respectively negative) externalities mean that the activity of one economic agent directly improves (respectively hurts) the interest/welfare of another economic agent.

7.47 If we think of India's welfare only, there is no difference between private cost and social cost, because the pollution being caused affects Ghana, not India.

7.49 Issuing bonds is riskier, because the firm must pay to the bondholders (who are the creditors) even when it is making losses. But, on the other hand, if the business is good and there are profits, the servicing bonds are less costly. There is no pressure to raise funds by equity (stocks) which amounts to stockholders taking additional risk.

7.50 As output increases, the price falls along the demand curve that faces a monopoly firm. Thus, total revenue increases but not linearly with output. The marginal revenue decreases, which makes the total revenue curve concave.

7.52 Defend.

7.53 Diminishing returns to scale.

7.54 (a) and (b) increasing returns to scale; (c) and (d) constant returns to scale; (e) decreasing returns to scale.

7.55 The firm should hire more of capital and less of labour.

7.56 Refute.

7.57 Refute.

7.58 Total variable cost.

7.59 Less. Recall that AFC falls continuously. Hence at the level of output where AVC is minimised, a further small increase in output increases the AVC by a marginal amount, which is less than the decrease in AFC. Hence ATC falls. Therefore, the output at which ATC is minimum is higher than the output where the AVC attains its minimum.

7.60 TFC.

7.63 We know that Price/MR = $e_p/(e_p - 1)$. Given $e_p = 3$, the right-hand side is equal to 3. In the left-hand side, price = \$12. Thus, MR = \$4.

Chapter 8

8.7 (i) There are large number of firms and (ii) the product is homogeneous.

8.8 It is a straight line through the origin, because the market price is the same, irrespective of how much a firm produces and sells in the market. Put differently, it is a straight line because the firm is a price taker.

8.9 Because the firm is a price taker.

8.11 Because a marginal increase in output from the point where $p = MC$ holds and MC is decreasing in output would fetch higher profit.

8.18 Revenues = ₹10 lakh.
Accounting costs = 2 + 3 + 4 = ₹9 lakh.
Accounting profit = 10 – 9 = ₹1 lakh.
Implicit cost = ₹2 lakh.
Economic profit = 10 – 9 – 2 = – ₹1 lakh, i.e., it is a loss of ₹1 lakh.

8.19 Refute.

8.20 \$4 since this is the minimum of the average variable costs.

8.21 Refute.

8.23 Market period is that short period during which no inputs can be changed. Hence, supply cannot be changed, and the price elasticity of supply is zero.

8.24 In the long run each firm produces 20 units and the market price = min LAC = 50. From the demand schedule, at this price the quantity demanded = 1,000 units. Thus 1,000 units are sold at the price €50. Since each firm produces 20 units, the number of firms must equal 1,000/20 = 50.

8.25 noindent
The total cost function $y^2 - 10y + 28$ implies the marginal cost function:

$$MC = \frac{d}{dy}\left(y^2 - 10y + 28\right) = 2y - 10.$$

If the market price is 20, then $p = MC$ condition is: $20 = 2y - 10 \Rightarrow y = 15$.

Chapter 9

9.4 It refers to the situation where a particular type and magnitude of government policy serves society the best, but either the government chooses a less efficient policy or the correct type of policy with a too less or too high degree of intervention.

9.6 $p = MC$.

9.7 Defend. There are however conditions like no externalities or public goods.

9.8 Agree. You have to write the reasons.

9.13 Non-rivalry and non-excludability.

9.18 Second-best policies refer to those, which achieve their intended objectives but at a higher social cost compared to some other policy that also achieves the same objective. You must provide an example.

9.19 Less.

9.20 Disagree. You must give reasons.

9.21 (a) first-best, (b) second-best, (c) second-best, (d) second-best.

9.22 (a) private, (b) private, (c) public, (d) local public goods, (e) private (you may not be able to exclude others from enjoying the fragrance, but others cannot use your perfume bottle), (f) private (similar to (e)), (g) public, (h) local public goods.

Chapter 10

10.1 Monopoly, monopolistic competition, and oligopoly. The above list is sufficient, but to be exact, there are others too, like duopoly, duopsony, and oligopsony.

10.5 Compared to market equilibrium in perfect competition, in a monopoly market the price is higher and the quantity sold is less.

10.7 Price discrimination means that consumers in different markets are being charged different prices for the same good. The condition is that there is no scope for the consumers in the low-price market to resale the product in the high-price market.

10.10 A firm whose long-run average cost curve is downward sloping (relative to demand).

10.11 Refute.

10.12 As long as $MC > 0$, the condition $MR = MC$ implies that $MR > 0$. That is, at the monopoly equilibrium, an increase in the quantity sold brings more total revenues. From the consumers' perspective, this is the same as saying that lowering price (and buying more) implies a higher total expenditure. From the relationship between price change and total expenditure discussed in Chapter 3, this can happen if and only if the price elasticity of demand is greater than one.

10.13 Defend.

10.16 The greater the price elasticity in a market, the less is the price.

10.18 If it is natural monopoly, we have the average cost curve falling with output. This implies $MC < AC$. Hence, if the regulated price, p, is equal to MC, we have $p < AC$. This implies that the firm would incur a loss (at such a regulated price).

10.19 Yes, it will happen if the average cost increases with output. In this case, we have MC > AC. Hence, if p = MC, then p > AC; this means abnormal profit.

10.24 Refute.

10.26 Refute.

10.27 Smaller.

10.29 Less; higher.

10.30 Bilateral monopoly.

Chapter 11

11.2 No. There are many oligopoly models depending on how many sellers (or buyers) in the market, nature of competition, nature of the product, etc. Cournot and Bertrand models are some examples. You have to expand on this.

11.8 Both will switch on their booster pumps.

11.9

		You	
		Head	Tail
Yusuf	Head	(−1, 1)	(1, −1)
	Tail	(1, −1)	(−1, 1)

11.13 Quantity sold by the firm from Andhra Pradesh will decrease and that by the local firm will increase.

11.14 The best response function of the CNG-run taxi stand will shift to the left. The amount produced by this taxi-stand will decrease and that by the other taxi-stand will increase.

11.16 Zero-sum game. (a_2, b_2).

11.17 (Movie, Movie); (Dance, Dance).

11.19 Yes. You must identify them.

11.20 Less, 4 units.

11.21 Refute.

11.22 Refute.

11.23 15

11.24 No. New firms will enter.

11.25 Market price = ₹7.50 and quantity sold 10,000 − 250 × 7.50 = ₹8, 125.

Chapter 12

12.3 Under uncertainty, for each choice available, an agent faces a probability distribution of payoffs. Suppose a monopolist has three output choices available: $q = 2, 5,$ and 9 units and for each quantity produced and sold, the market price is uncertain. That is, the market demand curve is uncertain. There is no uncertainty about the cost of production. Suppose that if 2 units are sold, the market price will be \$30 and \$40 with probabilities 0.7 and 0.3. If 5 units are sold, the market price will be \$26 and \$35 with probabilities 0.65 and 0.35. If the monopolist produces and sells 9 units, the probability distribution of the market price is (\$20, \$29; 0.8, 0.2). Based on this and information on costs of production, for each output choice there will be two profit outcomes and a probability distribution associated with it. The expected utility hypothesis says that we can define a utility function of payoffs (profits in this example) and the overall value or valuation of a choice is indicated by the expected value of the utility from the payoffs associated with the choice. A rational agent will make that choice (in the example, choose that q) for which the expected utility is the maximum.

12.6 It is the amount that a risk-averse individual would like to forgo or pay, relative to a risk-neutral person, in order to avoid the risk. Suppose an individual faces an uncertain bundle which pays €100 and €150 with probabilities 0.4 and 0.6. The expected payoff is $100 \times 0.4 + 150 \times 0.6 =$ €130. By definition, the risk-averse individual will prefer €130 with certainty to the uncertain bundle, while a risk-neutral person will be indifferent between €130 with certainty and the uncertain bundle. The latter will be willing to pay zero to avoid risk. What is the amount with certainty that the risk-averse individual would like to have so that he is indifferent between this and the uncertain bundle? It is something less than €130. Suppose it is €110. Then, the risk-premium is the difference between what a risk-neutral person would like to have instead of the uncertain bundle and what a risk-averse person would like to have instead of the uncertain bundle. The former is €130 and the latter is €110. Hence, the risk premium = 130 − 110 = €20.

12.7 Refute. The mean and the variance of Lottery A are 37 and 1701. Those of Lottery B are 38.5 and 1851.75. Lottery B has a higher variance *and* a higher mean. Thus, we cannot say that Lottery B is more uncertain.

12.11 The expected payoff is $0.3 \times 25 + 0.5 \times 36 + 0.2 \backslash time\ 64 = 38.3$. The associated utilities are $25^{0.2} = 1.90$, $36^{0.2} = 2.05$, and $64^{0.2} = 2.30$. The expected utility $0.3 \times 1.90 + 0.5 \times 2.05$ and $0.2 \times 2.30 = 2.05$. The certainty equivalent of utility $2.05 = 2.05^5 = 36.60$. Hence, the risk-premium $= 38.3 - 36.60 = 1.7$.

12.13 We first check whether (12.6) holds. We have $U' = 0.2X^{-0.8}$.
Hence $U'(W) = U'(50000) = 0.2 \times (50000)^{-0.8} = 0.0000348$
and $U'(W - L) = U'(35000) = 0.2 \times (35000)^{-0.8} = 0.0000463$.
The l.h.s. of (12.6) $= (1-q)/q = 7.33$ and the r.h.s. of (15.6) $=$
$[(1-b)/b] \times U'(W)/U'(W-L) = 9 \times 0.0000348 / 0.0000463 = 6.764$.
Hence, the equation (12.6) is met, implying that the person will buy some insurance. But we see that the equation (12.7) is not met since $q > b$.
Therefore, the person will not buy full insurance.

Chapter 13

13.4 (i) Initial (cost of) investment, (ii) its yields, and (iii) future sale value of the asset.

13.5 Bonds are not generally riskier than stocks. If a bond is bought and held till the date of maturity, there is no risk if there is no default. But there is a default risk unless the bonds are issued by major governments. If you want to sell a bond before maturity, there is a risk in terms of capital gains and losses since bond prices vary over time.

13.9 The expected return on Stock A = 0.05 × 0.6 + 0.09 × 0.4 = 0.03 + 0.036 = 0.066, i.e., 6.6%. The expected return on Stock B = 0.04 × 0.3 + 0.10 × 0.7 = 0.012 + 0.07 = 0.082, i.e. 8.2%.

13.10 The figure $2,000 is immaterial since prices are given to us. There are only capital gains, no yield. We apply the discounting method and treat the rate of return, say R, like an interest rate. We set up the equation: $520(1+R)^2 = 566$. Solving this, $R = 0.043$, i.e., 4.3%.

13.12 We have

$$PDV = \frac{4}{1.1} + \frac{4}{(1.1)^2} + \frac{4}{(1.1)^3} + \frac{4}{(1.1)^4}$$

$$= 3.636 + 3.305 + 3.005 + 2.732 = 12.678,$$

i.e., $12,678.

Chapter 14

14.2 It is because the demand for a factor depends on the demand for the product which the factor (among other factors) helps to produce.

14.4 User value in this context is the value of labour services obtained. Suppose bonded labour is used for household work. Then, it is the value of these services. If instead, it is used in a factory or some other production activity, then the user value is the VMP or the marginal revenue product. If the government cracks down on such activity at the purchase-sale points and where such labour is used, the demand for such illegal labour will fall and hence the asset value and user value will both decrease.

14.6 It is because of diminishing marginal returns.

14.9 No; you refute.

14.10 It will shift to the right.

14.13 It is because the marginal product of skilled workers is higher.

14.16 User value is simply the rental value. Asset value refers to the purchase or sale value of capital or land.

14.18 (a) $40, (b) 6 or 7, both generate the same maximum profits.

Chapter 15

15.3 Refute. If there is production differentiation, scale economies, or oligopoly competition, countries will gain from trade even if they are identical. You have to elaborate these points.

15.6 You refute. It is good for the United States as well (under certain assumptions).

15.7 Absolute advantage is where the productivity of one sector in one country is higher than that in the same sector in another. Comparative advantage is where the relative productivity of one sector vis-à-vis another is greater.

15.15 (Hint: Check the comparative advantage.) Dr. Das should devote her entire time of 8 hours to the medical profession, while Geeta should concentrate on cooking.

15.16 (a) Brazil has absolute advantage in producing both grapes and bananas. (b) Brazil (Peru) has relative advantage in producing grapes (bananas). (c) Brazil would export grapes to Peru and import bananas from Peru. (d) No country has comparative advantage over the other in producing either good.

15.18 In autarky (meaning absence of trade), the relative price of C in country X is $4/2 = 2$, while, in the international market, the relative price of C is 3. Hence, country X has comparative advantage in and exports C.

15.19 The labour/capital endowment ratio is $80/120 = 2/3$ in India and $40/50 = 4/5$ in a Foreign country. Hence, India (Foreign) is relatively a capital (labour)-abundant country. According to the Heckscher–Ohlin theory, India and a foreign country would have comparatively an advantage in producing computers and shoes as these are, respectively, more capital- and more labour-intensive in production. India (Foreign) would be the net exporter of computers (shoes).

15.21 (i) Credit card payment to Apollo of $10,000 counts towards service exports since medical treatment is a service. (ii) Payment to Air India is also trade in services (international transport). (iii) Payment to United Airlines does not count towards international trade since Stokes is a US resident and United Airlines is an US carrier. (iv) His spending on food in India is counted in international trade in services. Jewellery and carpets are commodities. Thus (v) and (vi) are entered in the category of international trade in goods, not international trade in services.

INDEX